Irby, Wirral
Excavations on a Late Prehistoric, Romano-British and Medieval Site, 1987-96

Robert A. Philpott and Mark H. Adams

with contributions by

Alex Bayliss, Simon Bean, H. E. M. Cool, Ron Cowell,
David Dungworth, Julie Edwards, Jennifer Foster, Laura Griffin,
Jacqui Huntley, J. B. Innes, Elaine Morris, Cynthia Poole,
Jeff Speakman, Sue Stallibrass, Margaret Ward,
David F. Williams and Ann Woodward

2010

Published by National Museums Liverpool

British Library Cataloguing in Publication Data
Irby, Wirral: Excavations on a Late Prehistoric, Romano-British and Medieval Site, 1987-96

Authors: Robert A. Philpott and Mark H. Adams
© Trustees of National Museums Liverpool

Printed in Great Britain, 2010
ISBN 978-1-902700-41-0

Contents

Figures

iv

Plates

Contributors

Dr Mark Adams, Senior Project Officer, Field Archaeology Unit, National Museums Liverpool

Dr Alex Bayliss, Scientific Dating Team, English Heritage

Dr Simon Bean, former Curator of Antiquities, National Museums Liverpool

Dr H. E. M. Cool, Barbican Research Associates, Nottingham

Ron Cowell, Curator of Prehistoric Archaeology, National Museums Liverpool

Julie Edwards, Archaeologist (post-Roman finds), Cheshire West and Chester Council

Laura Griffin, Senior Finds Archaeologist, Worcestershire Historic Environment and Archaeology Service, Worcester

Jacqui Huntley, English Heritage North East Regional Science Advisor, Newcastle-upon-Tyne

Dr Jim Innes, Experimental Officer, Department of Geography, University of Durham

Dr Elaine Morris, Director, Centre for Applied Archaeological Analyses, School of Humanities (Archaeology), University of Southampton

Dr Robert Philpott, Head of Archaeology, National Museums Liverpool

Cynthia Poole, independent researcher

Jeff Speakman, Assistant Curator of Archaeology, National Museums Liverpool

Dr Sue Stallibrass, English Heritage Archaeological Science Adviser for North West England, Department of Archaeology, University of Liverpool

Margaret Ward, freelance consultant

Dr David F. Williams, English Heritage Ceramic and Lithic Petrology Project, Department of Archaeology, University of Southampton

Dr Ann Woodward, 17 Great Western Road, Dorchester, Dorset DT1 1UF

Acknowledgements

In 1987 the first salvage recording of a Romano-British ditch exposed in a back garden at Irby was carried out by Robert Philpott, following notification by the owner's son, Mr John Rogers, that pottery had been observed in the side of a construction trench. This was followed in 1991 by small-scale excavations, funded by Liverpool Museum. In 1992, the Field Archaeology Unit of Liverpool Museum began the research excavation at Irby which was run jointly with the University of Liverpool as a teaching exercise for undergraduates and Continuing Education students, an arrangement which continued until the close of the excavation in April 1996. From 1987 to Easter 1995, the excavation was funded from the Purchase Fund of the National Museums and Galleries on Merseyside (now National Museums Liverpool) and contributions from the University of Liverpool from 1992-6. From June 1995 to April 1996 the excavation and the subsequent post-excavation analysis were funded by English Heritage.

The Irby excavations were a complex logistical exercise which required the input of many individuals. The successful outcome depended on the goodwill and generosity of a number of people, and in particular the landowners, Mrs Margaret Rogers, Mr J. H. Billington, Mr John Price, Mr R. and H. Ormsby, Mr and Mrs John Kay, Mr and Mrs F. Colquitt, and Mr and Mrs C. M. Allchurch, who suffered patiently the disturbance to their lawns and flowerbeds over several seasons.

The English Heritage monitors provided a great deal of support and encouragement through the life of the project. Grateful thanks are due to Clare de Rouffignac, Jan Summerfield, John Humble, Kath Buxton and Gareth Watkins, as well as to the former English Heritage inspector for the North West, Gerry Friell, for their encouragement for the project.

The finds reports represent a valuable contribution from a number of specialists: Dr Simon Bean (Roman coins), Ron Cowell (lithics), Dr H. E. M. Cool (metal, glass and amber objects), Julie Edwards (medieval pottery), Jacqui Huntley (plant remains), Laura Griffin (Roman coarse pottery), Dr Elaine Morris (briquetage), Ian Panter (finds conservation and X-radiography of most of the ironwork), Cynthia Poole (fired clay), Dr Sue Stallibrass (animal bone), Margaret Ward (samian), Dr David F. Williams of Southampton University (petrological analysis of the refractory material and prehistoric ceramics), and Dr Ann Woodward (prehistoric pottery). Alan Bowden of the Department of Earth Sciences at Liverpool Museum kindly advised on the metal ores. Dr Jeremy Evans provided valuable assistance to Laura Griffin on the Roman pottery identification and dating; Quita Mould gave advice on the shale/jet objects, while Geoff Egan confirmed the identification of the medieval key. Dr Jennifer Foster contributed a most useful comment on the bull's head mount from Crewe. In addition, Dr Cool wishes to express her thanks to Professor William Manning for his advice on the padlock while Ann Woodward would like to thank Carol Allen for allowing her to read her report on the Bronze Age pottery from Oversley Farm, Manchester Airport prior to publication. Most of the specialist finds reports were prepared in 1998 with minor revisions in 2009-10.

Thanks are due to the staff of National Museums Liverpool's Conservation Division, notably Suzanne Kitto, formerly of the Department of Metals Conservation, who took X-rays of some of the ironwork, and for the initial assessments of finds to Gill Dunn of Chester Archaeology (Roman pottery) and Michael Nevell of the University of Manchester Archaeological Unit (prehistoric pottery). Dr Alex Bayliss (Ancients Monuments Laboratory) not only contributed the critical series of radiocarbon dates on the Irby site but also kindly re-calibrated earlier radiocarbon dates from other sites for greater consistency throughout the report.

The staff of the University of Liverpool played an important role in the development and running of the teaching excavation. Thanks are due in particular to Dr Peter Davey and Dr Jennifer Lewis of the Centre of Continuing Education, and those who facilitated the teaching excavation, Dr Roger White, Jennifer Mirdamadi, Prof. E. Slater, Dr Phil Freeman and Dr Joan Taylor all from the School of Archaeology, Classics and Oriental Studies.

The site supervisors, Janice Grove (1992), Dr Mark Adams (1993-96), and Dr Roger White (1992-94), bore the greatest responsibility for the excavation, recording and supervision on the site, and the results bear testimony to their professionalism and skill. In addition, the Liverpool University undergraduates, Continuing Education students and volunteers who undertook most of the recording as well as the physical work are owed a debt of gratitude.

Grateful thanks are due to those current and former colleagues in National Museums Liverpool who assisted in the preparation of the report: Jeff Speakman for assistance at all stages of the project, on the finds database, his thorough work in preparing the material for the specialists and for pasting up the drawings, Susan Nicholson kindly discussed the medieval documents and boundaries, Ron Cowell contributed not only the Early Prehistoric and Bronze Age discussion sections but as ever gave generously of his time and scholarship in numerous discussions on aspects of the site. Clare Ahmad digitised the parish and township base maps.

The finds drawings were the work of Mark Faulkner, Rob Reid (prehistoric pottery), John Swogger and Susie White. Clara Paillard undertook the French translation and Dot Boughton the German. Sue Vaughan created the index.

Mrs Jenny Whalley is also to be thanked for reporting the discovery of pottery in 1987 to the then Archaeological Survey of Liverpool Museum which began the whole programme and for bringing to our attention the pottery vessel found during the Second World War.

Sadly both Mrs Margaret Rogers and Mr Harry Billington died before this report saw the light of day. The report is dedicated to them for their great kindness and friendship as well as their enormous contribution to the success of the project. Without their continued interest and active encouragement, this important site would never have been recognised and investigated.

The site archive and finds are deposited at National Museums Liverpool, UK (accession number 1995.105).

Summary

This report presents the results of archaeological excavations of a multi-period site in north-west England, undertaken by National Museums and Galleries on Merseyside (NMGM) between 1987 and 1996, and largely funded by English Heritage. The discovery of Roman pottery during building work at Mill Hill Road, Irby, Wirral, in 1987 led to small-scale excavations by NMGM to investigate the context. These identified a Roman ditch and other features. At that time, few Romano-British rural sites were known in lowland north-west England and fewer had been examined archaeologically. Accordingly, a programme of extensive excavations was developed, which examined over 40 trenches across a series of suburban gardens, as a teaching excavation with the University of Liverpool, and later as a research project with funding from English Heritage. The project aims were to investigate the chronology, economy and physical organisation of the sequence of settlements, to characterise the agricultural and craft activities practised there and to examine the environmental context within which these occurred.

Although initially interpreted as Roman in date due to the dominant material culture, the extensive deposits proved to belong to a complex multi-period site. The report presents the key structural elements identified within the complex and difficult stratification. Poorly defined activity in the Mesolithic and Neolithic periods was followed by occupation dated to the mid Bronze Age by radiocarbon dating, when two roundhouses were accompanied by structured deposits of a previously unknown pottery type. An Iron Age phase produced a substantial assemblage of Cheshire VCP, as well as features with mid Iron Age radiocarbon dates, but contemporary structures were difficult to identify. Romano-British occupation followed from the late 1st or early 2nd century through to the late 4th century and probably beyond. A palisaded enclosure was succeeded by a ditched enclosure, to which a second ditched enclosure was then appended. The earliest structures were roundhouses, but in the later Roman period rectilinear and subrectangular buildings were constructed within the interior. The intensity of occupation, which resulted in a dense mass of post-holes, rendered the identification and dating of individual structures problematic.

Probably in the early medieval period, the enclosure ditches were deliberately filled in and several buildings with gullies or stone wall foundations were constructed. Detailed analysis of the stratigraphy, the presence of a distinctive bow-sided building form and a Saxo-Norman cresset lamp in a foundation trench, suggested this represented Anglo-Scandinavian activity. The settlement may be the original '-by' or farm of the Norse township-name 'Irby', associated with the documented phase of Norse settlement from Ireland in the early 10th century AD. Subsequently, the site was occupied by a group of later medieval buildings, using a combination of earth-fast posts and rubble foundations. This probably represents a farmstead in use during the 13th-15th centuries and forms the latest occupation on the site.

The material culture was dominated by Roman finds, which form a regionally important rural assemblage of pottery, glass beads, metalwork and other finds, providing a baseline for comparison with other regional assemblages. Other significant finds include Mesolithic and Bronze Age lithics, mid Bronze Age pottery and metal-working waste, including mould fragments, a unique Iron Age carved steatite spindle whorl, a VCP assemblage and an Iron Age brooch. The Saxo-Norman lamp and the small later medieval pottery assemblage are also discussed.

Environmental sampling by English Heritage provided valuable evidence for the changing nature of cereal consumption. Naked barley and emmer were dominant in the mid Bronze Age, a pattern which persisted into the Roman period, before changing to bread wheat, barley and oats in the early medieval period.

The final section sets the structures, finds and environmental evidence in a wider geographical and chronological context. The site has produced important new regional evidence for rural settlement extending over three millennia. The Bronze Age, Romano-British and early medieval settlement evidence is of a type so far very little known in the region. Finally, the site shows a pattern of repeated occupation which is becoming common in the region, perhaps a feature of stable and conservative land-holdings over long periods of time.

Résumé

Ce rapport présente les résultats de fouilles archéologiques sur un site du le Nord de l'Angleterre couvrant plusieurs périodes historiques. Effectuées par les *National Museums and Galleries on Merseyside*[1] (NMGM) entre 1987 et 1996, elles furent principalement financées par English Heritage, l'agence patrimoniale britannique. C'est la découverte de poteries romaines en 1987, durant des travaux sur Mill Hill Road à Irby dans la province du Wirral, qui conduit à des fouilles de petite envergure par NMGM afin d'en découvrir l'origine. Ces fouilles permirent d'identifier un fossé romain et de nombreuses trouvailles archéologiques. A cette époque, peu de sites ruraux romano-britanniques étaient connus dans le bas Nord-Ouest de l'Angleterre et très peu de ces sites avaient fait l'objet de fouilles archéologiques. Par

---

[1] Musées et Galleries Nationaux du Merseyside, aujourd'hui appelés National Museums Liverpool

conséquent, un programme de fouilles intensif fut mis en place donnant lieu à plus de 40 tranchées au cœur de nombreux jardins de banlieue. Ces fouilles débutèrent d'abord par une excavation pédagogique en collaboration avec l'Université de Liverpool, puis donnèrent lieu à un projet de recherche financé par English Heritage. Les buts de ce projet étaient d'étudier l'organisation chronologique, économique et physique d'une succession d'établissements humains, de caractériser les activités manuelles et agraires caractéristiques du site et d'en examiner le contexte environnemental.

Bien que d'abord daté de la période romaine au cause de la culture matérielle dominante, ces vastes dépôts s'avérèrent appartenir à un site beaucoup plus complexe, dénotant d'une occupation millénaire. Ce rapport présente les éléments structurels principaux identifiés dans cette stratification difficile et complexe. Des activités peu définies datant des époques Mésolithique et Néolithique furent suivies par une occupation datée au Carbone 14 du milieu de l'Age de Bronze grâce à la présence de deux rotondes et de dépôts hiérarchiques contenant des types de poterie inconnus auparavant. L'époque de l'Age du Fer produisit un amas considérable de briquetage de Cheshire ainsi que des éléments datés au Carbone 14 du milieu de l'Age du Fer, les structures contemporaines étant difficiles à identifier. L'occupation romano-britannique suivit du premier siècle ou début du 2ème siècle jusqu'à la fin du 4ème siècle et probablement au-delà. Un mur palissade fut remplacée par une enceinte entourée de fossés, à laquelle une seconde enceinte entourée de fossés fut ensuite apposée. Les structures les plus anciennes sont des rotondes, mais durant la période romaine postérieure, des bâtiments rectilignes et structures rectangulaires furent construits à l'intérieur. Cette occupation intense qui résulta en une masse dense de troux de poteaux rendit l'identification et la datation des structures individuelles problématique.

Probablement durant la première moitié du Moyen-âge, les fossés clôturés furent délibérément remplis et de nombreux bâtiments avec caniveaux ou fondations en pierre furent construits. L'analyse détaillée de la stratigraphie, la présence d'un bâtiment aux parois archées et d'une lampe saxon-normand dans un fossé suggèrent la présence d'une activité anglo-scandinave. Cette colonie est peut-être la ferme originale qui donna le nom de la bourgade Norse d'Irby, souvent associée à une phase documenté d'établissement Norse venant d'Irlande au début du 10ème siècle. Par la suite le site fut occupé par un groupe de bâtiments médiévaux plus récents, utilisant une combinaison de poteaux de fond et de fondations de gravas. Cela représente probablement une ferme et ses dépendances habités durant les 13ème et 15ème siècles et constitue l'occupation la plus tardive du site.

La culture matérielle fut dominée par des trouvailles de l'époque romaine qui forment un important ensemble clos de poterie rurales, perles de verre et ferronnerie entre autres et procure un point de comparaison avec d'autres collections régionales. D'autres trouvailles significatives incluent des pierres taillées de l'époque mésolithique et de l'Age du Bronze, des poteries datant de l'Age du Bronze et des déchets de ferronnerie dont des fragments de moule, une fusaïole en stéatite, exceptionnelle découverte datant de l'Age de Fer, un ensemble de briquetage et une broche datant de l'Age du Fer. La lampe Saxo-Normande et l'ensemble clos de poterie médiévale plus récente sont aussi analysés dans ce rapport.

Un échantillonnage de l'environnement effectué par English Heritage procure des preuves précieuses sur la nature changeante de la consommation de céréales. La consommation d'orge nu et de Triticum dicoccon dominait au milieu de l'Age de Bronze, une pratique qui persista jusqu'à la période romaine avant d'évoluer au profit de l'utilisation du froment panifiable, de l'orge et de l'avoine au début du Moyen-âge.

La section finale replace ces structures, trouvailles et évidences environnementales dans un contexte géographique et chronologique plus large. Le site a produit de nouvelles preuves régionales importantes de la présence d'établissements ruraux se prolongeant durant plus de trois millénaires. Des évidences d'habitations datant de l'Age de Bronze et des périodes romano-britannique puis médiévale sont un type peu connu dans la région pour l'instant. En définitive, ce site démontre un modèle d'occupation qui devient commun dans la région, peut-être caractéristique d'une possession des terres stable et traditionnelle durant de longues périodes.

Zusammenfassung

Die hier vorliegende Abhandlung stellt die Ergebnisse der archäologischen Ausgrabung eines mehrphasigen Siedlungsplatzes im Nordwesten England zusammen. Die Ausgrabung der Siedlung bei Irby wurde von den National Museums and Galleries on Merseyside (NMGM) zwischen 1987-96 durchgeführt und zum größten Teil finanziell von English Heritage getragen.

Im Jahre 1987 führte die Entdeckung von römischer Keramik während der Bauarbeiten an der Mill Hill Road, Irby (Wirral) zu einer klein angelegten Grabung des NMGM um die Befunde genauer zu untersuchen. Diese Rettungsgrabung führte jedoch zu der Entdeckung eines römischen Grabens und anderen Befunden aus der romano-britischen Zeit.

Da in den späten 80er Jahren nur wenige romano-britische Fundstellen in den Tiefebenen Nordwestenglands bekannt und noch weniger archäologisch untersucht worden waren, wurde diesen

Befunden große Bedeutung beigemessen. Dieser anfangs nur klein angelegten Rettungsgrabung folgte deshalb eine Serie von wesentlich umfangreicheren Ausgrabungen. Ein großer Teil dieser Grabung waren die über 40 Schnitte, die in den Gärten der Vorstadt angelegt wurden und zu erst als Lehrgrabung der Uni Liverpool und dann als Forschungsgrabung weitergeführt wurden. Die finanziellen Mittel für die Forschungsgrabung stellte English Heritage bereit. Die Hauptziele dieser Grabungen waren das Studium der Chronologie und der Wirtschaft der einzelnen Siedlungen und die Erkundung der einzelnen Lagepläne der jeweiligen Siedlungen. Desweiteren sollten die Grabungen sowohl eine Beschreibung der landwirtschaftlichen und handwerklichen Aktivitäten als auch eine genaue Untersuchung der damaligen Umwelt und Umwelteinflüssen liefern.

Obwohl man zu erst vermutete, daß es sich um eine ausschließlich römische Fundstelle handelte (die römischen Funde überwogen beträchtlich), handelte es sich aber tatsächlich um einen mehrphasigen Siedlungsplatz. Der hier vorliegende Bericht stellt sowohl die wichtigsten Funde der Siedlung(en) als auch seine sehr komplexe und nicht immer einfache Stratigraphie vor. Obwohl Funde aus der Mittel- und Neusteinzeit kaum vorliegen, konnten jedoch C14-Daten für zwei Rundhäuser aus der mittleren Bronzezeit ermittelt werden. In zeitgleichen Gruben wurde Keramik von einem bisher unbekanntem Typ gefunden. In der eisenzeitlichen Schicht wurde eine große Anzahl Keramikscherben vom Typ "Cheshire VCP" (Very Coarse Pottery) entdeckt, ebenso wie Befunde, die C14 Daten in die mittlere Eisenzeit datieren. Einzelne eisenzeitliche Gebäude waren jedoch schwer auszumachen.

Im ersten nachchristlichen Jahrhundert begann dann eine längere Besiedlungszeit: von der romano-britischen Era (Ende 1.-2. Jh.) bin hin in das späte 4. Jh und darüberhinaus. Einer älteren Palisadenumzäunung folgte eine neuere Grabenanlage, zu der später eine weitere Grabenanlage hinzugefügt wurde. Die frühesten Gebäude waren die bronzezeitlichen Rundhäuser und in der späteren Römerzeit wurden rechteckige Gebäude im Innern der Grabenanlage errichtet. Die große Dichte der mehrphasigen Keramik in den jeweiligen Befunden machte eine genaue Identifizierung und Datierung der einzelnen Strukturen jedoch schwierig.

Die Grabenanlagen wurden wahrscheinlich im Frühmittelalter verfüllt. Zur gleichen Zeit wurden mehrere Gebäude mit Abwasserrinnen und Steinfundamenten errichtet. Eine detaillierte Analyse

der Stratigraphie, die Entdeckung einer konkaven (d.h. schiffsförmigen) Gebäudeform und einer normanno-sächsische Wandlampe (cresset) in einem der Fundamentgräben läßt auf eine anglo-skandinavische Besiedlung schliessen. In jener frühmittelalterlichen Siedlung mag der skandinavische Name der Fundstelle 'Irby' ihren Ursprung gehabt haben. Diese Besiedlung der aus Irland stammenden Skandinavier läßt sich mit Dokumenten aus dem 10. Jh. belegen. Nach der anglo-skandinavischen Besiedlung wurde an dieser Stelle eine Gruppe spätmittelalterlicher Gebäude errichtet, die in das 13.-15. Jh datieren und sehr wahrscheinlich die letzte Bebauung des Fundplatzes darstellen.

Wie oben schon erwähnt datieren die Funde von Irby hauptsächlich in die römische Zeit. Vom regionalen Standpunkt aus liegt mit dem Fundplatz Irby eine sehr wichtige Sammlung von ländlicher Keramik, Glassperlen, Metallarbeiten und anderen Funden vor, die eine ideale Basis zum Vergleich mit Funden anderer Regionen bieten. Weitere sehr wichtige Fundgruppen sind die Silexfunde aus der Mittelsteinzeit und Bronzezeit, die mittelbronzezeitliche Keramik und die Überreste der lokalen Metallverarbeitung. Als wichtigste Funde sind unter anderem zu nennen: Gußformenfragmente, ein einzigartiger Spinnwirtel aus Speckstein, die oben genannte VCP Keramik und eine eisenzeitliche Fibel. Die normanno-sächsische Lampe und die spätmittelalterliche Keramik werden auch im Einzelnen behandelt.

English Heritage übernahm die Entnahme von Bodenproben, welche zeigten, daß sich der Getreidekonsum mit der Zeit sehr veränderte. Von der Mittelbronzezeit bis in die römische Zeit waren 'hüllenlose' Gerste (*Hordeum vulgare* L. var. *nudum Hook.* f.) und Emmer dominant, während im Mittelalter Brotweizen, Gerste und Hafer bevorzugt wurden.

Im abschließenden Teil des Berichtes werden die Gebäude, Funde und die Ergebnisse der Bodenproben in einen grösseren geographischen und zeitlichen Kontext gesetzt. Irby hat neue und wichtige regionale Funde für eine ländliche Siedlung erbracht, die sich über drei Jahrtausende erstreckt. Die Bronzezeit, die romano-britische Phase und die frühmittelalterliche Besiedlung waren bisher nahezu unbekannt in dieser Region. Abschließend ist es jedoch wichtig zu bemerken, dass mehrphasige Fundplätze wie Irby in dieser Region nicht die Ausnahme sind. Diese langanhaltende, mehrphasigen Besiedlung einzelner Siedlungsplätze könnte auf eine stabile, konservative und effektive Wirtschaft über einen längeren Zeitraum hindeuten.

1: Introduction

Robert Philpott and Mark Adams

Discovery of the Site

The existence of an early archaeological site at Mill Hill Road, Irby, Wirral came to light when a near-complete Roman pot was shown to Liverpool Museum staff in the early 1980s. The vessel had been found by Mr Jim Rogers in his garden during the 'Dig for Victory' campaign in the Second World War and had been kept in a powdered milk tin in the pantry for 40 years before being shown to museum curators. It was identified as an imitation samian Dr. 38 flanged bowl (SF9999). In 1987 the construction of a kitchen extension in the same garden revealed further pottery sherds which were reported by Mr John Rogers, the son of the site owner, to a local amateur archaeologist, Mrs Jenny Whalley, who in turn contacted Robert Philpott at Liverpool Museum. As a result, a section of Romano-British ditch was observed and recorded in the sides of the construction trench (Philpott 1993; 1994). Subsequently, the site owner, Mrs Margaret Rogers, invited the Museum's Field Archaeology Section to excavate further in the garden to place the ditch in a wider context.

Previous Work and Archaeological Background

Small-scale excavations were undertaken in 1989 and 1991 by Robert Philpott to assess the extent and survival of Romano-British deposits within the same modern garden. These confirmed the alignment of the original ditch and revealed traces of occupation deposits on its presumed interior. Together with the presence of the pottery, this suggested a settlement of some kind. However, while some very limited information had been recovered for the chronology of occupation, nothing was known of the character of the settlement or its extent. No structural evidence other than the ditch had been encountered and nothing was known of surviving structures which might lie within the site. The state of preservation of any surviving occupation deposits in the vicinity, particularly in view of the location of the site within a 1920s housing estate, was also unknown.

The opportunity to resolve some of these questions was presented when Mr J. H. (Harry) Billington who owned not only the adjacent orchard but also the neighbouring house, both of which fronted onto Thorstone Drive, generously offered to allow the Museum to carry out larger-scale excavations there. Subsequently, the owners of further neighbouring plots also offered their gardens for investigation.

The investigation of the site should be seen in the context of the low level of research into Romano-British rural settlement in the lowland north west of England

in the early 1990s. The site at Irby was considered to have excellent potential to contribute towards an understanding of the subject and was selected for excavation as part of a long-term research programme which was being undertaken by the Field Archaeology Unit at Liverpool Museum. The large-scale excavation began in 1992 and continued each Easter and summer until April 1996. The post-excavation work was conducted by Liverpool Museum, with a series of specialist consultants and funded by English Heritage. At the time the programme began, the only datable material from the site was Romano-British. During the excavation it became clear that the site also had prehistoric and post-Roman phases of activity, but the full complexity of the phasing only emerged during post-excavation once the radiocarbon and finds reports were received.

The Irby area had previously produced some evidence of Romano-British activity. A number of brooches and coins had been found by metal-detector users in Irby and neighbouring townships. In the field immediately to the north of the site, fieldwalking had produced several sherds of Romano-British oxidised ware and a 4th-century coin had been found on the west boundary hedge of the same field (J. Whalley pers. comm.). Three more Roman sherds were found in fieldwalking in November 1988, dispersed across the field. The thin scatter of pottery is likely to represent dispersal through manuring of arable fields, although it is possible that the extension the settlement originally extended further to the north. A group of about ten 4th-century Roman coins was recovered from a spot about 330 m to the north of the site in grubbing out a hedge boundary. In 1989 a rim sherd of Roman pottery was found by Mrs Whalley in the garden of the neighbouring house (117 Mill Hill Road). A service trench in the front garden of 113 Mill Hill Road also produced a further sherd of Romano-British pottery. A dolphin brooch was recorded from a field about 350 m north-west of the site in 1983. In the regional context of north-west England, this constitutes a significant concentration of Roman material.

Topography, Geology and Soils

The excavated site lies about 1 km north of the modern village centre of Irby, centred at NGR SJ 253 832 (Fig. 1.1, Pl. I). It lies in an area of former fields which were developed for housing in two phases during the 1920s and the 1960s, and is now covered by several houses and gardens. Immediately to the north of the site the land remains as arable fields. The situation is on a fairly level area at a little over 60 m AOD, just below the crest of one of a series of prominent parallel Permo-Triassic sandstone ridges which run along the Wirral peninsula. The present ridge runs north-south and culminates in Irby Hill 300 m to the north. The ground slopes gently

Fig. 1.1: Location of the excavated site at Irby (built-up areas shaded)

Plate I: Aerial photograph of the excavation site in its landscape setting, from SE in June 1992, by R. Philpott

down from west to east. Local watercourses consist of Greasby Brook running north-south about 300 m to the west, while Arrowe Brook arises less than 1 km to the east, although the original course of this is difficult to determine due to changes in the land drainage pattern associated with post-medieval and earlier enclosure of the land.

The site lies on the junction of the waterstone and basement beds of the Triassic Keuper sandstone series (Geological Survey Sheet 96). Close by to the east and west, deposits of boulder clay lap up the lower slopes of the hill, though the site is underlain by well-drained brown earth soil of the Rivington series, a brown earth described as a slightly stony, well-drained permeable non-calcareous sandy loam. The soil is easily cultivable, the main limitation being a tendency to drought for grass and, to a lesser extent, other crops (Beard *et al.* 1987, 31-2). In the wider area there are less well drained typical stagnogley soils of the Clifton series which have formed on the boulder clay slopes *c.* 100 m to the east; and humo-ferric podzols of the Delamere series on the crest of the hill *c.* 100 m to the north. The latter are permeable and well drained sands or loams. The stagnogleys are currently used for a mix of arable and grassland, while podzols are easily worked and capable of growing a wide range of crops, though many areas on the Wirral are rocky and support a heathland vegetation (Beard *et al.* 1987, 18-22).

The underlying geological deposits across much of the site consisted of Triassic sandstone bedrock, thin deposits of sandstone brash or sands derived from weathering of the bedrock. The sands which underlay much of the south and west of the site were soft, unconsolidated and pale reddish or yellowish brown in colour. The sandstone brash overlay the top of the bedrock and consisted of a 20-100 mm thick deposit of tabular and angular sandstone fragments 20-60 mm across in a mid-reddish brown sandy loam or a coarse, pinkish red sand. Many of the tabular fragments in this deposit were aligned with the bedding planes in the underlying bedrock and it was clear that this deposit was derived from chemical and physical weathering of bedrock (i.e. the C horizon). In the easternmost part of the site, investigated by two linked trenches (XIIA, XIIB), the subsoil consisted of dark reddish brown boulder clay with occasional rounded cobbles.

In areas underlain by soft sands there was often a considerable degree of ambiguity as to where the junction between anthropogenic and geological deposits actually lay. In some cases features were only clearly defined when two or three shallow spits of apparently natural sand had been removed. This has given rise to the apparent anomaly in the stratigraphic matrices of some post-holes being sealed by natural sands. Wherever possible these features have been re-assigned to the correct point in the matrix. In addition, occasional fragments of pottery appear to have intruded into these deposits; most are small fragments, less than 5 g in weight, which can be attributed to the effects of trampling, root action and animal disturbance. Occasional larger fragments and one or two clusters may be due to the presence of cut features which were not detected.

Research Aims

The investigation of the Romano-British site at Irby in the late 1980s and early 1990s was undertaken against a background of the most rudimentary understanding of Iron Age and Romano-British rural settlement in the lowland north west of England at the time. The state of knowledge of Roman Cheshire was considered in detail in the Victoria County History (Petch 1987). The lavish detail of the treatment of Chester, and to a lesser extent the industrial and military sites of Cheshire, re-inforced by stark contrast the poverty of the prevailing understanding of the Romano-British countryside, which could be dealt with in only three pages. Few Romano-British rural sites were known in the region before the programmes of aerial reconnaissance of the 1980s and 1990s and even fewer had been investigated archaeo-logically. A Roman villa had been excavated in 1980-2 at Eaton-by-Tarporley, Cheshire (Mason 1983; 1984; Petch 1987, 211), and minor interventions had taken place on a Romano-British enclosure at Halton Brow, near Runcorn, Cheshire (Brown *et al.* 1975; Newstead and Droop 1937) while stone foundations had been found at Saltney, near Chester (Newstead 1935; Thompson 1965, 16). Within Merseyside, when work began at Irby, the situation was even worse. The Irby excavation was only the second archaeological investigation of a Roman settlement within the post-1974 county bounda-ries. The first had taken place as long ago as 1926, when Professor Robert Newstead had recovered 23 sherds of Roman pottery of 2nd-4th-century date, a post-hole and traces of occupation deposits on Hilbre Island (News-tead 1927). Within the Wirral peninsula, the only certain settlement of Roman date was the coastal site at Meols, known only from chance finds recovered along the erod-ing shore during the 19th century but the same erosion had probably removed any surviving physical settlement component (Hume 1863; Watkin 1886, 274-85; Chitty and Warhurst 1977; Griffiths *et al.* 2007). In the Mersey-Dee region as a whole, most of the sparse evidence for Roman activity in the countryside consisted of chance finds of artefacts with no associated structures (cf. Petch 1987, 212-5). This included small clusters of coins and other finds which pointed to rural sites in Wirral. The growth of metal detecting from the late 1970s onwards has produced a thin scatter of further finds, for the most part coins and brooches. In some cases these coalesced into small concentrations in places like Ness, Thurstas-ton and West Kirby, where they probably indicated the location of discrete rural settlements (Philpott 1991, 62, fig. 1). At a number of other locations widely distributed in Cheshire, Merseyside and south Lancashire, further clusters of finds undoubtedly point to rural settlement sites, a situation enhanced by the success of the Port-

able Antiquities Scheme from 1997 in encouraging the reporting of finds.

In the 1980s concerted efforts began to redress the balance towards investigation of the rural scene. Aerial reconnaissance by Dr Nick Higham and Rhys Williams in Cheshire, and Gill Chitty in Merseyside produced a small number of enclosure sites which were undated but were presumed to be late prehistoric or Romano-British. The presence of at least one site in Wirral was indicated by a then undated oval enclosure with three circular structures in the interior at Telegraph Road, Irby, about 1 km from the Mill Hill Road site (Pl. I). The only comparable site in the region to have received any substantial investigation was a late Iron Age site at Great Woolden Hall Farm in Salford in 1989 which also produced Romano-British pottery but no associated features (Nevell 1999b).

The original research aims of the excavation were defined in the light of this poverty of comparative data for late prehistoric and Romano-British rural settlement in the lowland north west. The aims were as follows:

1. To recover evidence for the morphology of the settlement at Irby during the Iron Age and Romano-British periods, and of the use and organisation of space within the core area of the settlement.

2. To recover evidence to determine the continuity or otherwise of the Iron Age to Romano-British occupation, and to determine the physical relationship between the two settlements.

3. To recover detailed overall plans of structures within the settlement and to examine chronological developments in building plan and construction methods through analysis of datable artefacts in association with the stratigraphic sequence.

4. To recover environmental evidence to assist with reconstructing the agricultural practices (the species and types of crops grown, crop processing methods, the presence of weeds, and other diagnostic plants), to reconstruct the vegetational and faunal environment of the site, and to determine the use of natural food and other resources.

5. To recover evidence for the market and trading connections of the site, its economic and social status, and the economic basis of the settlement (e.g. minor industrial activities, such as iron smelting and smithing) through the recovery of a suitable sample of artefacts.

6. To identify zones of different activity or use of the site, and to determine the functions of buildings, pits and other features, by recording appropriate spatial data from artefacts.

Period	Phase	Structure no	Description
I	P1		Mesolithic
		-	Mesolithic activity represented by lithics, no features
	P2		Late Neolithic/Early Bronze Age
		-	Neolithic activity represented by lithics, no features
II	P3		Middle Bronze Age (*c.* 1500-1100 BC)
		S27A / S27B	Mid Bronze Age structure(s)
		S28	Mid Bronze Age structure
	P3/4	F7	Prehistoric pit of uncertain function
II			Middle Iron Age (c. 400-200 BC)
	P4	-	Iron Age activity; uncertain structural features and VCP
		S32	Possible Iron Age structure; arc of post-holes
		S33	Possible Iron Age structure; arc of post-holes
III			Early Roman (late 1st-early 2nd century)
		-	Small amount of pottery but no certain features,
IV			Roman (early/mid 2nd-4th century AD)
	R1	S2	Fence line
	R2	S4	Palisaded enclosure
		S25	Palisade slot
	R3	D1	Eastern ditched enclosure
	R4	D3 / D1	Western enlarged ditched enclosure
		S26	Gateway
		S5	Palisade Trench
		S30	Stake-hole alignment on N edge of Ditch 3
		S1	?Circular building
		S12	Roundhouse
	R5	S13	Polygonal building
		S14	Enclosure or subsquare structure
		S17	Wall gully
		F4	Pit
		F9	Pit or hearth (6139), associated with F14
		F2	Kiln/oven
	R6	S10	Elliptical Building
		S11	Four-post structure (uncertain)
		S15	?Elliptical Building
	R7	S9	Rectangular building
		D1, D3	Infilling of Ditches 1 and 3
		F1	?Oven/Kiln
	R8	D4	Shallow east-west ditch
V			Late Roman-Early Medieval (4th-10th/12thcentury)
	EM1	S29	Foundation trench, rectilinear building
	EM2	S3	Curvilinear/bow-sided building
		S6	Curvilinear/bow-sided building
		S7	Curvilinear/bow-sided building
		S24	Saxo-Norman structure
	EM3	S16	Curvilinear/bow-sided building
	EM4	S8a/S8b	Elements of two separate rectilinear buildings
		F3	Pit
VI			Later Medieval (13th-14th/15th century)
	M1	S18	Rectilinear building
		S19	Rectilinear building
		S23	Rectilinear structure
		S20	Rectilinear structure
	M2	S21	Rectilinear structure
		F8	Clay-lined pit (6126)
	M3	F6	Medieval pit/oven
	M4	D5	Possible medieval ditch
VII			Post-Medieval and modern deposits
		-	Post-medieval ploughsoil
		-	Horticultural pits and trenches since 1950s

Table 1.1: Summary of Periods, Phases and Key Structures

Plate II: Aerial view of excavations across gardens in June 1992, from south

Inevitably as the excavation progressed these aims were modified and developed. The original aim of the excavation had been to investigate the Romano-British site. It was considered that the archaeological deposits were sufficiently extensive and well preserved to have considerable potential to produce data on the nature and chronology of Romano-British settlement in the region, and to contribute significant information on the environmental, economic and social conditions in a region which had seen very little investigation of Romano-British rural sites. As small-scale trenching progressed, prehistoric lithics and pottery, notably Cheshire Stony VCP (Very Coarse Pottery, see Chapter 4), were discovered, raising a further set of questions over the duration of occupation of the site, and in particular of the potential for continuous occupation from the Iron Age to the Romano-British period. The research aims were widened therefore to examine the chronology of the site and the physical relationship between the late prehistoric and Romano-British occupation. Consequently, the sequence and character of structures, as well as the nature of activities practised on the site, were of some importance. An examination of the economy of the settlement was also required, investigating the agricultural basis of the settlement, the activities practised there, and the evidence for exchange and trade through the artefact assemblage.

It was only during post-excavation analysis that the radiocarbon determinations revealed that the later prehistoric activity belonged to two distinct phases, the mid Bronze Age and the Iron Age. In addition, analysis of the stratigraphy and finds indicated that an important part of stratified deposits and associated structures was post-Roman in date, and activity of at least two phases in the early and later medieval periods was also present.

Excavation and Recording Strategies

The constraints of modern buildings, boundaries, orchard trees and gardens meant that excavation was piecemeal and the opening of large areas impossible. By the close of fieldwork no fewer than 46 trenches had been excavated. Trenches ranged in area from 3 m² to 140 m², though many of the smaller trenches were later subsumed within larger areas. The total excavated area measured approximately 2500 m² spread over eight separate gardens (Fig. 2.1, Pl. II). Five of these were in Mill Hill Road (nos 115 and 117 Mill Hill Road and the former garden of no. 113, and nos 105 and 107) with a further trench in no. 93 Mill Hill Road). Two more lay in the rear gardens of nos 2A and 4 Thorstone Drive. The largest area available was the then vacant orchard plot which is now occupied by a house, no. 2 Thorstone Drive (NGR SJ 253 852). A further small area to the rear of 111 Mill Hill Road was monitored as a watching brief in 2004.

The layout and shape of trenches was determined by the existence of modern structures, fence lines, hedges or trees rather than any archaeological considerations. The confined space meant that trenches had to be small

Plate III: View of Trench XXI during excavation, from east

enough to allow for the storage of spoil. This required that even large plots had to be excavated in a series of small, overlapping trenches.

Many of the excavated features at Irby are most easily interpreted as post-holes. Nearly all of them were filled with material similar or identical to the material through which they were cut. In most cases it was impossible to identify the edges of cut features until the surrounding deposits had been excavated almost to the natural subsoil. This situation was often exaggerated during dry weather when desiccation of the soil and bright sunlight bleached out any contrast which might have been observed, a problem encountered frequently as much of the excavation took place in June and July. A number of strategies were adopted to overcome these problems. During dry spells the site was frequently hosed down and water allowed to soak into the site. Special care was taken after wet weather to look for any contrasts in soil colour or texture which might be revealed.

The most effective method was found to be to excavate the site as a series of thin spits, re-planning the trench after the removal of each. This allowed the sandstone blocks which filled many of the cut features to be identified long before the cut itself became visible and also made it possible to attempt to identify retrospectively the level from which the feature was cut. An identical strategy was adopted on the Breiddin and Beeston Castle excavations which had encountered exactly the same difficulties of poor definition of vertical

stratigraphy (Musson 1991; Ellis 1993, 35).

One disadvantage of this approach is that it only identifies the lowest point from which a feature was cut and assumes that the packing material did not protrude above the contemporary ground surface. In many cases it is possible, or even likely, that the feature was in fact cut from a stratigraphically higher position which could not be identified. In addition it is also likely that large numbers of intrusive features were present but did not either contain sandstone packing in their fill or penetrate deep enough to disturb natural deposits. These features may have been missed in the prevailing soil conditions. A further complication is that post-holes or gullies with packing stones that originally protruded above the original ground surface would be assumed to be cut from too high in the sequence. This has had serious consequences for our understanding of the stratigraphy.

Many of the structures discussed in Chapter 2 overlap one another and although the precise sequence is not always clear, it is obvious that few can be contemporary. The finds associated with these buildings are in most cases sparse and not well dated, so the absolute chronology of the sequence is poorly defined. The layers associated with these features are probably best regarded as 'transformed occupation deposits' as defined in (Needham 1996, 21) and were broadly similar to the dark earth deposits recognised, for example, at Runneymede (Needham 1996, 22). However, the processes involved in the formation of

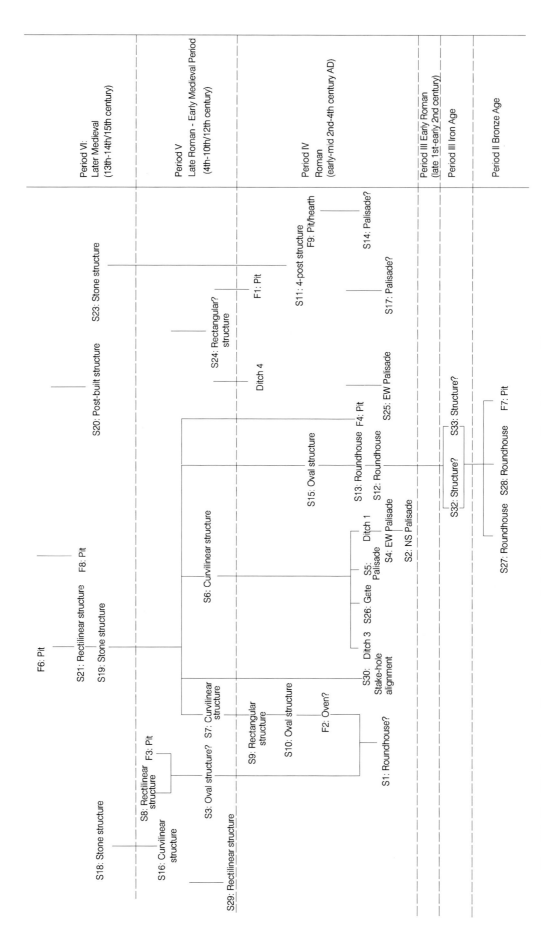

Fig. 1.2: Simplified stratigraphic matrix to show relationship of main structures (S) and features (F)

these deposits remain poorly understood (Goldberg and Macphail 2006, 271). At Irby, the layers appear to have suffered extensive trampling and reworking, both during deposition and subsequently, resulting in the contamination of earlier deposits and obscuring the relationships between features and layers (cf. Matthews 1993). With this in mind there may be an artificially late date assigned to certain buildings on the basis of a very few sherds of later intrusive material in layers through which the buildings apparently cut. The dating for individual structures has therefore depended more on the internal evidence of finds in the fills of features than on finds in layers through which they were cut. In many instances though, even the relative date of buildings cannot be determined with certainty. Most were constructed using individual post-holes, consequently even where building plans overlap the chances of cross-cutting relationships occurring is low. Other buildings were constructed using shallow gullies or foundation trenches. Although these occasionally exhibit cross-cutting relationships, in most cases the fills were so similar as to be indistinguishable. In addition the gullies rarely contained packing material and consequently most were not identified until the surrounding deposits, which were also very similar, had been excavated to natural sands or bedrock. This will have had the additional effect of further contaminating the layers through which they were cut with later finds.

Layout and Format of Report

Description of the Phases

Over 30 structures (including ditches, palisade slots and buildings) and another ten or so significant features have been identified on the site. In most cases it has proved difficult to establish the chronological sequence and the evidence for the preferred position is presented. The phasing is often based on poorly defined cuts, with a large degree of uncertainty about the level from which they were originally cut. A large number of post-holes could not be assigned to specific phases or structures and a substantial number of buildings probably existed on the site which cannot now be recognised. The variety in building plan, with circular, bow-sided and rectangular structures, also increases the number and variety of potential alignments and also the difficulty of identifying alignments within the mass of features.

The discussion below is divided by broad chronological Period and by Phase. Phases are seen as representing major alterations to the layout of the settlement, such as the erection of a new building or laying out of new boundary ditches. In some cases a structure may have been in use for more than one phase and considerable overlapping of the lives of settlement elements must have occurred. The term Period is used to represent the broader chronological division of the stratigraphy and generally it is only at this level that an attempt has been made to give absolute dates. Some structures are not well established in the sequence and are phased tentatively (see Fig. 1.2), with the proviso that they may in some cases be earlier or later than the assigned phase.

Numbering Sequences

Trenches were allocated a sequence of Roman numerals (see Fig. 2.1 for overall trench plan); any gaps in the sequence on Fig. 2.1 are a result of the amalgamation of trenches. Context numbers and finds numbers take a simple numeric sequence, the latter being preceded by SF. Phases are labelled in sequence. Structures (S1 onwards), ditches (D1-D5) and other significant features such as pits and ovens (F1-F9) are referred to by numerical sequences which were allocated in the early stages of post-excavation analysis before significant dating evidence discussed in the text became available. The original numbers have been retained to avoid re-numbering throughout the archive so these are not in chronological sequence. Furthermore, some putative structures were rejected in post-excavation analysis so the numerical sequence is incomplete (see Fig. 1.2).

9

Fig. 2.1: Plan of trenches excavated at Mill Hill Road and Thorstone Drive, Irby, 1987-2004

10

2: Structures and Stratigraphy

Robert Philpott and Mark Adams

Introduction

This section provides a detailed analysis of the chronological and structural development of the site. Figure 2.1 shows all of the excavated cut features on a single plan. Table 1.1 and Figure 1.3 present the overall phasing and a simplified stratigraphic matrix of the main structures and features respectively.

Period I: Early Prehistoric Period

Phase P1: Mesolithic

Mesolithic activity is represented by up to about 45 pieces of struck flint and chert (see Chapter 4, *Lithics*) but its usefulness for interpreting activity of this date on the site is limited by the fact that it occurs as residual material in later contexts. No features can be positively assigned to this phase. The Mesolithic finds tend to occur over the sandy subsoil which underlies the eastern half of the site but it is unclear whether this accurately reflects the original distribution of these artefacts.

Phase P2: Late Neolithic/Early Bronze Age

There is also some evidence of late Neolithic and/or early Bronze Age activity in the form of struck flint but this is similarly of limited value as it too is residual (Chapter 4, *Lithics*). Because of difficulties in closely dating small assemblages of flintwork on typological grounds alone it is currently unknown to what extent material of this date continued to be used in the middle Bronze Age when it would overlap with the earliest phase of structural evidence on the site, which is of that period (see Period II, below). Only one context without pottery contained struck flint; a flint scraper (SF8227, Fig 4.2, 22) from context 9777. The fills of this feature were very similar to those containing later prehistoric finds but a single typologically indistinct implement cannot either be used to date the feature nor automatically be assumed to belong to the middle Bronze Age and must be regarded as being residual. Like the Mesolithic material, it is probable that activity at this date resulted in flint being deposited on the former ground surface and subsequent occupation has reworked these deposits, leading to the incorporation of the flint in later features and layers.

Period II: Later Prehistoric Period

The earliest coherent features were sealed by the major Romano-British occupation deposits. In some cases, the features also contain prehistoric pottery or flint, or both. Two main phases of later prehistoric activity

have been identified but these cannot be distinguished through stratigraphy alone because the great majority of the features belonging to this period were truncated to natural subsoil by later activity. Eight radiocarbon dates from four contexts indicate two distinct prehistoric phases (see Table 2.1). These centre on two episodes, the mid Bronze Age with six separate dates from three features, and the mid Iron Age, based on two identical dates from the same feature. In most cases separation into two phases can also be made on the basis of ceramic finds in the fills. Analysis of the prehistoric ceramics indicates there are two distinct groups, the first associated with mid Bronze Age radiocarbon dates, the second marked by the presence of Cheshire Stony VCP salt containers and probably of middle Iron Age date.

The presence of at least one building, as well as mid Bronze Age pottery of a type not so far recorded elsewhere in the region, suggests domestic occupation. Clay 'weights', oven furniture and mould fragments for the manufacture of copper-alloy objects indicate not only cooking but also metalworking. The Iron Age deposits also contain Cheshire Salt Containers (VCP), and some industrial waste which strongly suggests that these deposits are the result of domestic occupation rather than other activities, such as ritual or funerary activity.

It is impossible to be certain whether features without finds belong to a chronologically distinct aceramic period, such as the later Iron Age, or whether they simply reflect the relatively low level of material culture present in the main datable phases. Such an 'aceramic' phase may in fact be represented by the relatively large quantities of VCP on the site (479 sherds). A similar situation was encountered within an Iron Age and Romano-British enclosure site at Bryn Eryr, Anglesey where the only Iron Age ceramics consisted of VCP, which consistently occurs in deposits which pre-date the Romano-British or are occasionally contemporary with them (Longley *et al.* 1998, 192).

Unless stated otherwise, all of the features in this phase contained dark greyish brown sandy loam with 2-5% charcoal flecks. Most contained occasional fragments of heat-cracked stone. Some of the post-holes in this phase contained large sandstone packing stones. Some seem to represent post-holes from which the post was removed on demolition of the structure, though some of the smaller examples may actually have been stake-holes. Others were settings for vertical timber posts which decayed *in situ*.

Radiocarbon Dates, *by Alex Bayliss*

The radiocarbon samples were processed and dated by the Oxford Radiocarbon Accelerator Unit (Hedges *et al.* 1989; Bronk Ramsey and Hedges 1997). The

Fig. 2.2: Plan of main trenches showing main cut features of all pre-modern phases

Laboratory No.	Sample No.	Radio-carbon Age (BP)	δ¹³C (‰)	Context	Finds	Dated material	Calibrated date range (95% confidence)
Period II: Later prehistoric							
OxA-9558	2415(a)	3075 ± 60	−22.2	8236 (post-hole 8224)	SF7303: clay weight; SF7304: undiagnostic fired clay; SF7305: fired clay oven plate/cover, SF9114: charcoal	emmer grain	cal BC 1500-1120
OxA-8487	2415(b)	3085 ± 40	−23.3			*Triticum* sp.	cal BC 1440-1210
OxA-8587	2369(a)	3005 ± 65	−23.7	8171 (post-hole 8197)	SF10601 and SF10602: prehistoric pot; SF10566 and SF10580 lithics	*Triticum* sp.	cal BC 1420-1010
OxA-8484	2369(b)	3155 ± 45	−23.0			*Triticum* sp.	cal BC 1520-1310
OxA-8485	2409(a)	2275 ± 40	−22.1	8227 (cut 8228)	SF7302: La Tène II/III brooch	*Triticum* sp.	cal BC 410-200
OxA-8486	2409(b)	2270 ± 40	−24.5			hazelnut shell	cal BC 410-200
OxA-8518	2116(a)	3045 ± 40	−26.8	3337 (gully 3338)	SF5540, SF5541: prehistoric pottery	charcoal, *Corylus/Alnus* sp.	cal BC 1410-1130
OxA-8519	2116(b)	3000 ±35	−25.9			charcoal, *Prunus* sp.	cal BC 1380-1120
Period V and later: Early medieval and later medieval							
OxA-9533	1038(a)	106.5 ± 0.5 PMC	−25.6	3087 (fill of large posthole 3093)	SF9624: Industrial waste; SF9354: S Gaulish samian base dated AD 70-110; SF9353, 10785, 10784: 3 oxidised ware sherds; SF9355 BB1 sherd with girth groove	charcoal, roundwood	after AD 1950
OxA-9534	1038(b)	1649 ± 31	−25.1			charcoal, roundwood	260-530 cal AD
OxA-9557	2677(a)	1705 ± 50	−20.4	9603 (fill of gully 9579: Structure 29)	SF7991: Coin of AD 337-40; SF7995 Grey ware rim; SF10735 industrial waste residue; SF8005, 7994: 2 bone fragments; SF8006 fired clay	barley	350-600 cal AD
OxA-9668	2677(b)	1595 ± 45	−22.6			barley	230-440 cal AD

Table 2.1: Radiocarbon dates by the Oxford Radiocarbon Accelerator Unit

results are conventional radiocarbon ages (Stuiver and Polach 1977), except for OxA-9533 which is quoted as a percentage of modern carbon (Mook and van der Plicht 1999).

All results have been calibrated using OxCal v3.5 (Bronk Ramsey 1995) and the data of Stuiver *et al.* (1998). Date ranges (Table 2.1, Fig. 2.3) have been calculated using the maximum intercept method (Stuiver and Reimer 1986) and are quoted at 95% confidence unless otherwise specified.

Phase P3: Middle Bronze Age (*c.* 1500-1100 BC)

This is the first phase to which stratified deposits can be positively assigned. One well defined building plan and elements of at least one other structure have been recognised. There are also groups of features which may belong together and in a few cases these associations are reinforced by the presence of sherds from the same vessel. There is no evidence within the excavated area of an enclosure palisade or ditch surrounding the settlement remains in this phase. Either the settlement was unenclosed at the time or any boundary lay outside the excavated area, although shallow ditches could have been truncated by later features.

Layers of later prehistoric date

Surviving later prehistoric layers fell into two main categories. The first was the base of the occupation

deposits where they graded into underlying soft sands. Often these deposits appeared at first to be undisturbed sands but exposure to weathering and trowelling revealed occasional sherds of prehistoric pottery and other artefacts. It appears that the artefacts infiltrated through worm, animal or root action into the soft underlying material. Finds in these layers were usually prehistoric, reflecting the greater proportion of early material in the lowest cultural deposits which was available for incorporation. Similarly the interface between the sandstone brash (B/C horizon) and those above was not always well defined and the deposits often contained small numbers of artefacts which once again have infiltrated through worm action (cf. Cornwall 1958, 51-4). These deposits occurred over much of the solid bedrock but in some places this zone was missing, and soil occupation deposits directly overlay competent bedrock, suggesting the weathered deposits had either been exposed during the life of the settlement or they had been removed through later activity. Related to the last was the presence of fissures and irregularities in the upper surface of bedrock which had become filled with soil, occasionally containing artefacts. It was not always easy to distinguish these from anthropogenic features (cf. 3404, Structure 27). A number of what were tentatively interpreted during excavation as 'early' linear features were likely in fact to be natural fissures in the surface of bedrock.

The second major category consisted of Bronze Age occupation deposits reworked through subsequent Iron

13

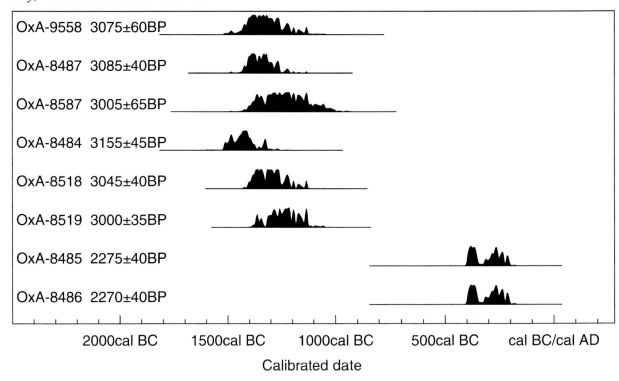

OxA-9558 3075±60BP

OxA-8487 3085±40BP

OxA-8587 3005±65BP

OxA-8484 3155±45BP

OxA-8518 3045±40BP

OxA-8519 3000±35BP

OxA-8485 2275±40BP

OxA-8486 2270±40BP

2000cal BC   1500cal BC   1000cal BC   500cal BC   cal BC/cal AD

Calibrated date

Fig. 2.3: Probability distributions of calibrated radiocarbon dates from prehistoric samples

Age activity and more notably through the intensive Romano-British activity. This released much of the later prehistoric pottery and other artefacts to be incorporated as residual material in the later, Romano-British, layers, leaving only pockets of early deposits surviving intact at the base of the soil profile. The lack of clearly defined interfaces between deposits meant discrimination of these during excavation was not easy. Excavation of layers in spits was undertaken to attempt to isolate during post-excavation areas of early soil layers which could not be detected visually during excavation. The majority of the layers in this category were restricted in extent and limited in depth. Undulations in their upper surface, minor intrusive features or animal burrows may have remained undetected, resulting in the presence of some intrusive later material in otherwise later prehistoric deposits.

The principal prehistoric deposits survived in Area VIII. One layer (contexts 3341, 3349 and 3350) contained only two mid Bronze Age sherds (SF5612, SF5313). As it was cut by a prehistoric gully 3338 which yielded mid Bronze Age radiocarbon dates, it represented a relatively well preserved remnant of a prehistoric occupation layer. Another later prehistoric layer, 6188 in Trench XXXVI, contained VCP, daub and industrial waste.

The deepest stratigraphy on site was found in Area XLI where the earliest layers were 9757 and 9776. The latter lacked finds but closely resembled layer 9757, which had some Bronze Age pottery (SF8199), VCP (SF8200), a rubbing stone (SF8202) and a hammer stone (SF8205), suggesting that it was an Iron Age layer which had reworked earlier, Bronze Age, deposits, despite the presence of two small (<1.5 g), probably intrusive,

Black-Burnished ware (BB1) fragments (SF8211).

The structural evidence for this phase consists of a number of post-holes and several short sections of structural gullies or slots (Figs. 2.4 and 2.7). There are two possible reconstructions of the evidence which are discussed below. In one case some of these elements can be combined to form a single structure, S27; in the second case, these elements form two overlapping structures (S27A and S27B), probably one directly succeeding the other.

The two reconstructions both include two pairs of features linked by pottery. In one case sherds from the same large vessel occur in two features. Sherd SF5757 in post-hole 3365 (fill 3364) is the same vessel as that in the elliptical post-hole 3404 (fill 3403). Context 3365 was originally taken to be part of Romano-British gully 1154, but it contained only prehistoric pottery so is more likely to be a separate post-hole or short gully which was cut by the Romano-British feature. Two features both in S27B are linked by the presence of mid Bronze Age pottery. A sherd (SF5541) in fill 3337 of gully 3338 is probably part of the same vessel as SF7998. The latter comprises a group of ten large decorated rim and wall sherds (Fig. 4.8, no 88) with fresh unabraded surfaces, in a stone-packed post-hole, context 8353 (fill 8351).

Structure 27

This group of features can be reconstructed in two ways. The first results in a circular building (S27) about 14 m in diameter which consists of a short section of curving gully (3338, 3346, 6333) and a number of stratigraphically early post-holes (Fig. 2.5). A second

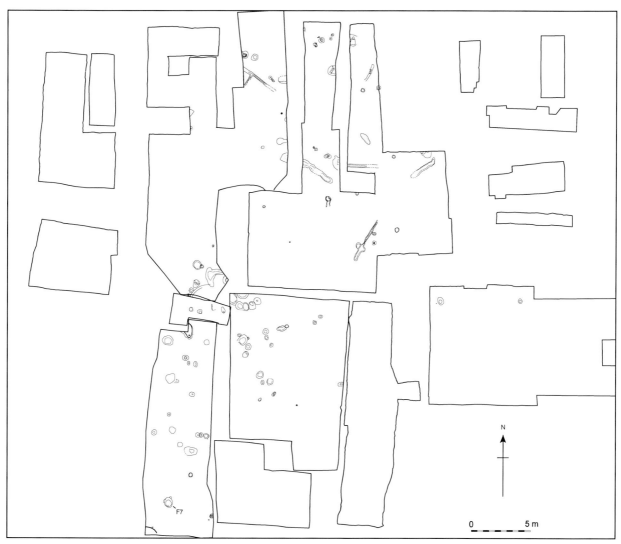

Fig. 2.4: Plan of all Period II features

ring of post-holes, less well defined, may form an outer circle 15 m in diameter. A concentration of large post-holes, with some recutting, in the south-west of the circuit may represent the entrance. Comparative evidence from other sites suggests that the entrances were particularly prone to requiring frequent repair or replacement of posts, and are sometimes elaborated with a porch (see Chapter 5). The Irby building differs from the majority of these house plans in having a

Plate IV: Post-hole 8353 showing packing stones (8352) and large Bronze Age pottery sherd (SF7998) in fill 8351

short section of continuous foundation trench in the interior ring, opposite the putative entrance. This reconstruction of S27 results in a very large structure of a type which has not previously been found in mid Bronze Age contexts in this region. The integrity of this reconstruction is supported by similar radiocarbon dates from two features at opposite sides of the circuit of S27B, the gully (3338) and a post-hole in the southern part of the arc (8197). Gully 3338 (fill 3337) with its associated gully 3346 (fill 3344) contained a large quantity of burnt material which produced two radiocarbon dates of cal BC 1410-1130 (OxA-8518) and cal BC 1380-1120 (OxA-8519). The post-hole 8197 contained fill 8171 which was rich in cereal remains, including emmer, hulled barley, naked barley and a few hazelnut fragments. Remains of *Triticum* sp. from this deposit were radiocarbon-dated to cal BC 1420-1010 (OxA-8587) and cal BC 1520-1310 (OxA-8484).

Instead of arranging the available post-holes into one double-ring structure, an alternative reconstruction would see the component elements of S27 rather as two successive and overlapping circular structures, S27A and S27B (Fig. 2.6). This has the merit of producing

Fig. 2.5: Phase P3. Mid Bronze Age structure S27, possible reconstruction

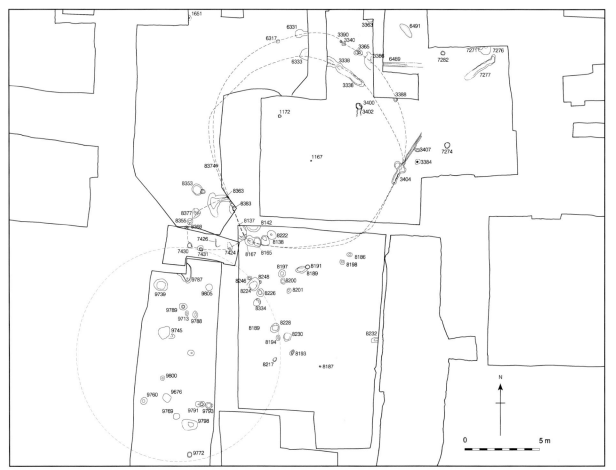

Fig. 2.6: Phase P3. Mid Bronze Age, alternative reconstruction of structures S27A and S27B, and S28

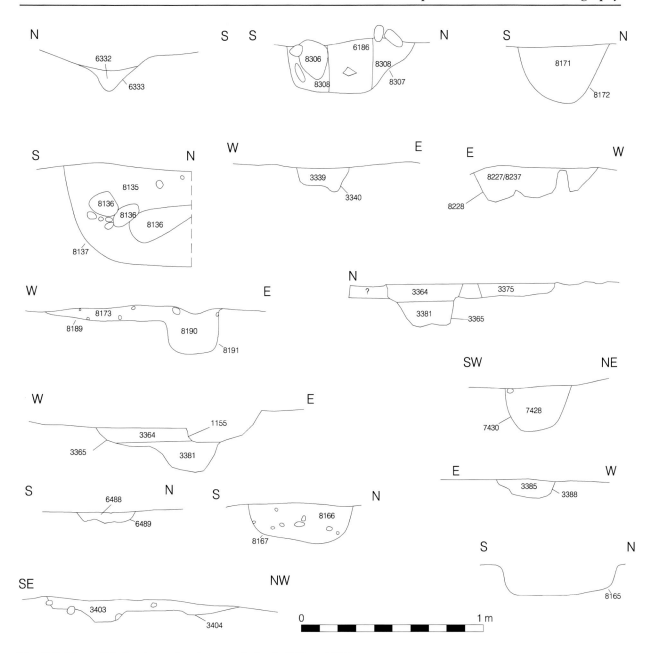

Fig. 2.7: Phase P3. Sections of major post-holes in S27 and S28

two building plans of slightly smaller diameter, each measuring a little under 14 m with a maximum offset of 1.5 m between the two.

Another deliberate deposit of a pottery vessel in post-hole 3404 suggests that this also belonged to the circuit of this structure. On excavation, 3404 was interpreted as a narrow gully, 0.2 m wide on average, which had been refilled with sandstone brash, the same material into which the feature was cut, with a prominent elliptical-shaped 'swelling' up to 0.88 m wide near the southern end. A group of 22 large sherds of lightly abraded mid Bronze Age pottery was found deposited in the dark reddish brown fill of the elliptical feature. The difference between the soil fill and the dense sandstone brash of the 'gully', as well as the character of this narrow feature, makes it highly likely that the 'gully' was in fact a natural fissure in the upper surface of bedrock which

had been cut by the elliptical post-hole. The deliberate incorporation of the larger part of a pottery vessel in the post-hole was indicated by the presence of many joining sherds of the same vessel. The alignment of the southern end of the 'gully' coincides fairly closely with the projected alignment of S27A, and it could be tentatively suggested that the brash-filled gully here represented a part of the earlier building alignment, while the post-hole element of 3404 might be part of a slightly later structure, S27B.

A further heavily truncated gully, (6489, Figs. 2.5 and 2.7), lying close to the wall of this structure at the southern end of Trench XXXVII and running westwards towards one of the substantial posts of the external wall, may be a drain to prevent surface run-off entering the structure. The fill 6488 lacked finds.

Fig. 2.8: Distribution of Bronze Age pottery across site

Environmental remains from several of the constituent post-holes of S27 were consistent in their components. Four of the eight features sampled had large quantities of burnt grain (contexts fill 7422, cut 7424; fill 7423, cut 7426; fills 8144/8135, cut 8137; and fill 8171, cut 8197), one had modest quantities (fill 8173, cut 8189), while the three others had very few remains. The four rich samples were markedly similar in their suite of cereals, each with relatively low levels of hulled barley and indeterminate barley, much higher proportions of naked barley, and in three of the four a higher level of emmer grains, in addition to emmer glume bases, and spikelet forks, as well as one complete spikelet in context 7422. Three also contained hazelnut shells, which were present in S28 samples but almost completely absent from other prehistoric samples. Jacqui Huntley (see Chapter 3, *Charred Plant Remains*) suggests that the presence of large amounts of burnt cereals, including emmer grains surviving as spikelets, indicates either this building or one nearby was associated with the storage, or possibly processing, of cereals. The similarity of the component elements strongly suggests that these were contemporary deposits within a single phase.

Structure 28

A further mid Bronze Age structure may be indicated by stratigraphically early features to the south of S27 (Fig. 2.6). These contain few finds so the dating cannot be confirmed on artefactual grounds. One post-hole fill (8236) produced two closely similar radiocarbon dates in the mid Bronze Age; this feature had a padstone on the base and the lower fill contained much unfired clay and daub. Another post-hole (7424) which may belong to this alignment contains mid Bronze Age pottery but it lies close to the alignment of S27 and is more likely to belong to that structure.

The environmental remains from this group of post-holes (fills 8215, cut 8217; fills 8225 and 8240, cut 8226) conform to the same narrow suite of cereal types as those in S27. Of the two fills of post-hole 8226, context 8225 is rich in cereals, including large amounts of naked barley grains, along with emmer grains and other fragments, including spikelets; there is some hulled barley and a few hazelnut fragments, while context 8240 contains grains of hulled barley, naked barley, and emmer. There are also some emmer glume bases and spikelet forks, as well as one spelt glume.

18

Other Mid Bronze Age Evidence: Feature 7

A single small pit (F7, cut 9778), 0.81 m in diameter and 0.17 m deep, was excavated at the south end of Trench XLI, 16 m to the south of the main concentration of Bronze Age features (Fig 2.4). The fill, 9777, was a very dark brown loamy sand containing large amounts of charcoal and burnt bone. Laid against the base of the pit were three large pieces of carbonised wood about 0.20 m long and 0.10 m wide but these fragments did not form a coherent structural setting. Environmental assessment revealed no seeds but quantities of iron-stained charcoal. The pit contained a flint scraper of uncertain prehistoric date (SF8227). Both the date and the function of the pit are uncertain, and the flint artefact could be residual rather than necessarily indicating a Bronze Age date.

Discussion

The evidence belonging to the earliest stratigraphical phase has produced a rare example for the region of what appears to be a middle Bronze Age farm, with evidence of cereal cultivation and consumption, metal-working and possibly textile production. The structural evidence consists of a gully and series of post-holes which indicate earth-fast posts for buildings, probably of roundhouse type, possibly of double-ring form, with traces of other structure(s) of uncertain form nearby.

Together the environmental and artefactual evidence from the site indicates the use of a distinctive type of locally-made pottery, in association with cereal remains and clay oven fragments and furniture. The cereal grains indicate cultivation of emmer and naked barley. There is also evidence of bronze-working on site, on the basis of four mould fragments in a quartz-tempered fine fabric, although this may represent no more than a single episode of manufacture, using a two-valve mould, though it was not possible to determine what kind of bronze object was being cast in the mould. Initially this was thought to be late Bronze Age bronze-working by analogy with material from the Breidden (see Chapter 4, *Refractory Material*), but radiocarbon determination dates this phase of activity to the middle Bronze Age.

The small group of pottery which is radiocarbon-dated to the middle Bronze Age is unique in character. The spatial distribution of prehistoric pottery other than VCP is centred on the north central area of the excavation (Fig 2.8). It is probably no coincidence that it lies in the vicinity of the probable circular building and near the features with radiocarbon dates in the Bronze Age and is, perhaps significantly, also absent from the trenches in the west and north-east of the excavated area. Other finds from mid Bronze Age contexts include both of the Type 1 spherical clay weights recovered from the site (see Chapter 4, *Structural Daub and Fired Clay*). The first, SF7303 in context 8236 (cut 8224), was dated by a radiocarbon determination (Table 2.1), and the same

context had a perforated oven plate or cover (SF7305). The second Type 1 weight (SF8797) was in context 7422 (cut 7424) in association with mid Bronze Age pottery, a feature which formed part of S27.

While the chronology of the various activities and artefact types is not closely dated, the radiocarbon dates provide the most objective chronological information, though not wholly without problems of interpretation. It is uncertain whether what appears to be a long sequence of activity within the Bronze Age should be compressed into one or more shorter episodes. Certainly the consistency of the six radiocarbon measurements from three separate features, which are statistically indistinguishable (T'=8.7; T'(5%)=11.1; df=5; Ward and Wilson 1978), suggests that the middle Bronze Age activity on the site was of short duration (Alex Bayliss pers. comm.). The uncertainty of the typological dating suggests that some of the struck flint could belong to the late Neolithic/early Bronze Age but there are no regional parallels to identify middle Bronze Age flint assemblages as typological dating of regional assemblages is far less secure than radiocarbon determinations, yet even so this material cannot be shown to be dated to the mid Bronze Age and thus contemporary with the structural activity (see Chapter 4, *Lithics*). The possibility of residuality cannot be discounted as, for example, fill 8362 (cut 8363) which lies within the wall circuit of Structure 27 contained three flint objects and prehistoric pottery.

Phase P4: Middle Iron Age (*c.* 400-200 BC)

Structural Evidence

Only a few features can be assigned to the Iron Age with any degree of certainty. There are a number of post-holes and short sections of gullies which are stratigraphically early, being sealed by Romano-British deposits, but where finds or radiocarbon dates are absent it is not possible to distinguish between the Bronze Age and Iron Age phases and they are included with the Bronze Age features on Figure 2.4. A small number of post-holes contain VCP but lack later, Roman, pottery, and of these a few are likely to be Iron Age in date on stratigraphical grounds. These are very widely scattered across the site, apart from a small concentration in the centre of Trench XLI. In addition, some features assigned to the Iron Age coincide with the gullies of later, Roman, roundhouses and may be minor repairs to those structures, the VCP being residual. However, the presence of post-holes indicates at a minimum that the occupation included post-built structures. Two arcs of post-holes can be reconstructed which incorporate some probable Iron Age features (S32, S33). The remainder of the post-holes make little in the way of coherent structural plans but may form part of a considerably more intensive occupation than is implied by the two putative reconstructions below. Other stratigraphically

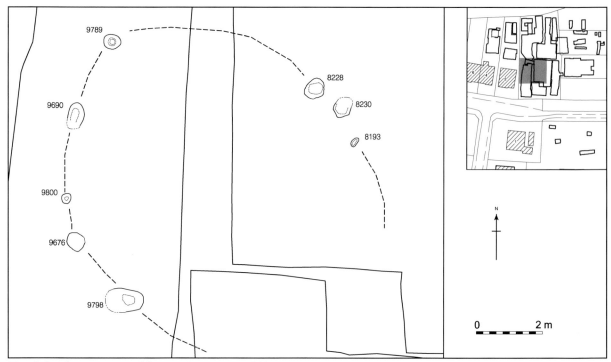

Fig. 2.9: Phase P4. Possible Iron Age stucture S32

early features without finds may also be of this phase but are impossible to date.

Structure 32: Arc of Post-holes

Amongst the stratigraphically early post-holes in Trenches XLI and XIX is an arc (Figs. 2.9 and 2.11), which represents nearly three-quarters of a sub-circular structure, with a diameter of about 7.5 m. This contains only one feature of certain Iron Age date, post-hole 8228, with Iron Age radiocarbon dates (Table 2.1) and a La Tène II/III brooch (SF7302) in the fill. The other post-holes lack finds but are stratigraphically early, although some may in fact be part of Structure 28.

Structure 33: Arc of Post-holes

A somewhat less convincing arc of post-holes occurs in Trench XLI, including one feature containing VCP (9588). This may form part of a circular structure (Fig. 2.10 and 2.11), though it has not been possible to establish its exact form or dimensions.

Other Iron Age Evidence

The mid to late Iron Age is represented in both the artefactual and radiocarbon record. Two radiocarbon dates from a hazelnut shell and charred *Triticum* sp. seeds were obtained from post-hole 8228 (fill 8227), at 95% confidence, of 410-200 cal BC (OxA-8485-6). The same post-hole fill (8227) also contained a La Tène II/III type brooch (SF7302) but no other finds. Typologically the brooch cannot be dated more closely within the later Iron Age, though these dates are consistent with the 3rd-century BC date on stylistic grounds for the steatite

spindle whorl (SF2931) found in a secondary context in Structure 18.

A further class of evidence is a small group of ten sherds which were initially classified as Roman BB1 but which were suggested by Jeremy Evans as possibly belonging to the late Iron Age or early Roman period (see Chapter 4, *Roman Pottery*). They are dark-grey to black in colour from handmade vessels, with sandy or in the case of one group calcareous fabrics. They lack diagnostic typological characteristics and the contexts in many cases are mixed with later Roman and sometimes later finds. In the circumstances it is difficult to assess the evidential value of these although comparison with future finds may help to resolve the dating issue.

However, there is no clear evidence for the nature or duration of the Iron Age activity. It may have been relatively short, within the period of the radiocarbon date and spindle whorl, but a longer period cannot be ruled out. The close spatial match between the distribution of the VCP (Fig 2.12) and the later, Romano-British occupation could be used to suggest continuity into the Roman period, but other than a group of ten sherds of undiagnostic handmade pottery mentioned above, there is nothing that need date to the later Iron Age period to bridge the gap of two hundred years or so between the activity attested by the radiocarbon date and the beginning of the Roman occupation. However, the presence of a mid Bronze Age phase on precisely the same spot with no suggestion of continuous occupation from then to the Iron Age suggests that external factors, which are archaeologically invisible, may have determined the repeated use of the same site for all the main settlement phases here.

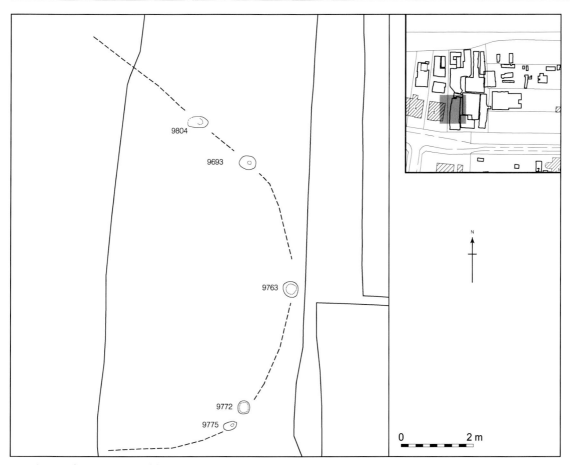

Fig. 2.10: Phase P4. Possible Iron Age structure S33

The only environmental evidence which could be positively associated with this phase was from context 8227 and was low in quantity and poor in quality, consisting of hulled barley and a few Triticum sp. grain. Perhaps significantly it lacked the strong emphasis on emmer and naked barley which were evident in features associated with mid Bronze Age activity though the quantities involved were too low for this to be conclusive.

The decorated steatite spindle whorl has been dated on stylistic grounds to the 3rd century BC (Chapter 4, *Steatite Spindle Whorl*; Plate XIX; Fig. 4.4). It was found securely stratified within the wall of Structure 18 (context 4001), a later medieval structure. The object

could have arrived on the site soon after its manufacture, or at any time within the intervening centuries until its deposition in the wall. It is impossible to determine whether it was an heirloom or a 'found' object which had been deliberately inserted in the later wall, although the other evidence for Iron Age activity makes it likely to have been an importation during the Iron Age.

The third Iron Age element of the artefact assemblage is Cheshire Stony VCP (Morris 1985). The rims probably indicate a minimum of five vessels amongst the total of 479 sherds (see Chapter 4, *Cheshire Salt Containers*). The great majority of sherds occur alongside Roman material with relatively few found stratified in earlier features. As discussed earlier there is virtually no over-

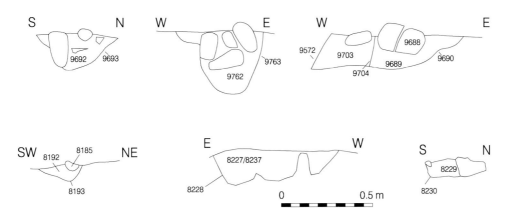

Fig. 2.11: Phase P4. Sections across post-holes in S32 and S33

Fig. 2.12: Distribution of Iron Age VCP across the site

lap with the mid Bronze Age pottery, other than where the latter is very likely to be residual in later features or layers. In itself the VCP is not closely diagnostic of date and at other sites it has been dated from *c*. 400 BC to the early Roman period, with the possibility of a slightly earlier date at Brook House Farm, Halewood where VCP was excavated from contexts dated by radiocarbon to 830-420 cal BC (Beta-118138; 2560 ± 60BP) and 360-40 cal BC (Beta-117712; 2140 ± 40BP) (Cowell and Philpott 2000, 45).

The possibility should be considered that some of the VCP at Irby dates to the early Roman period. At Collfryn, Powys and Bryn Eryr, Gwynedd VCP may have continued in use into the early Roman period (Britnell 1989; Longley *et al.* 1998, 192). The earliest closely datable Roman pottery at the site consists of a small amount of samian of the period AD 70-110 but much of this is clearly residual in later contexts such as ditch fills alongside later material or is very battered and abraded and so far from new when deposited. The freshness of some sherds of VCP could indicate that some material belonged to the Roman period, but equally it may simply mean that the material was derived from disturbed Iron Age deposits and was rapidly reincorporated into sealed Roman deposits or features without a long period of trampling.

Occurrence of VCP with mid Bronze Age Pottery

Both VCP and mid Bronze Age pottery are present together in several types of context. Examination of the contexts does not support the interpretation that the Bronze Age pottery and VCP were in contemporary use. The first group consists of the great majority of contexts; in addition to either VCP or mid Bronze Age pottery, or both together, they also contain Roman pottery. Here the prehistoric material of both types is likely to be residual in later deposits.

The second category consists of four layers (6954, 8334, 9560 and 9757) which have both VCP and mid Bronze Age pottery but which lack later material. These are poorly defined layers which lay at the interface of natural sands and the earliest occupation deposits; they cannot be considered as securely stratified deposits. It is probable that some material from overlying deposits (for example, VCP) has sunk into the soft sands through worm or animal action.

The third category comprises three cut features which contain both types of early ceramics. Two of these consist of a tiny scrap of material identified as VCP along with larger mid Bronze Age sherds. The fill of a foundation gully in Structure 27, 3337, produced six sherds of mid Bronze Age pottery and two mid Bronze

Age radiocarbon dates (Table 2.1) as well as a tiny sherd of VCP weighing 0.3 g, found in a sieved sample. The feature had been cut by a later, Romano-British one, raising the possibility of some contamination near the junction between the features. The next context is a post-hole fill, 3401, possibly part of a structural gully (3400) with a sherd identified as VCP weighing only 0.1 g (SF5970) along with a larger prehistoric sherd. In both cases, the VCP sherds are too small to erect the hypothesis of contemporary use of the two types and it is a strong possibility that these minute sherds are intrusive.

The final feature is fill 3403 (part of Structure 27). This was at first interpreted as a narrow gully (3404) containing 22 sherds of mid Bronze Age pottery, some of them large fresh and unabraded, packed in a close concentration at a point where the gully widened. Review of the evidence suggests this was in fact an elliptical post-hole which had cut through a long natural fissure in bedrock. Most if not all the sherds came from the same vessel (Fig. 4.8, no 89) and the material has the appearance of a 'foundation deposit', which had been set deliberately in the post-hole. The presence of five medium-sized sherds of VCP alongside a mid Bronze Age pottery vessel in the same deposit is difficult to account for, although another post-hole (3323) which cut 3403 from a higher level provides a potential source of contamination which might have introduced later material.

In conclusion, other than two tiny and possibly intrusive sherds of VCP in two separate features, there is only one feature where VCP and a mid Bronze Age pottery vessel appear together (3404, fill 3403), which is itself cut by an intrusive feature. With this one exception, there is a marked distinction therefore between features with mid Bronze Age pottery and VCP, suggesting a genuine chronological difference between the two.

There is little difference between the distributions of the non-VCP prehistoric pottery and the VCP (Figs 2.8 and 2.12). Both were thinly but extensively scattered across the site, largely in later occupation deposits or soil horizons, though non-VCP pottery was more common at the northern end of the site. However, to what extent this reflects the lack of depth of deposits is uncertain. This suggests that the material has been incorporated into Roman or later occupation deposits through extensive trampling or reworking of the deposits. Later disturbance is likely to be a major factor in the difficulty in identifying Iron Age features. If the VCP does represent a phase of Iron Age occupation, as seems very likely, then it appears to have been extensive and to have covered broadly the same area as the Romano-British settlement which followed it. While this might appear to be potentially an argument for continuity between the two phases of settlement, it should be noted that the same spot has been used repeatedly in the past for settlement and factors other than continuity of

occupation may be involved.

Other Undated Prehistoric Features

There were a number of short sections of stratigraphically early gully, especially in the northern part of the site, which may have formed parts of prehistoric buildings or palisade lines. Although they are likely to indicate prehistoric activity and the presence of structural remains, the absence of any coherent pattern to these features means that they cannot be linked to specific buildings. The same is true of a scatter of post-holes, which despite displaying some concentrations (such as the northern part of Trench VI), do not form clear spatial patterns. Some features may represent fragments of buildings, the full plans of which were neither visible nor retrievable. The lack of finds means that they cannot be dated more closely than to the later prehistoric period.

Other than individual post-holes, the main potential structural elements consist of three features (Fig. 2.5). The first is a short section of curving gully, 7277 in Trench XLIII (the fill, 7276, lacked finds), which measured 1.9 m long but was cut at the southern end by a later feature. Another short gully to the north (Trench XXXVII) also lacked finds (cut 6526; fill 6525) and a small T-shaped slot (6324 Trench XXXVI) could also form part of a similar structure, possibly a palisade, though they are more likely to be natural fissures in the upper surface of bedrock into which soil and artefacts have infiltrated from overlying occupation deposits.

Prehistoric finds of uncertain date

Several categories of find may belong to the prehistoric period but cannot be closely dated. They consist of worked stone objects, such as hammer stones, rubbing stones and saddle querns, fired clay objects, and heat-shattered stone. The two certain saddle querns and the one probable example are a type generally found in prehistoric contexts rather than later (SF8009, SF8620; SF7007) (cf. Longley 1998, 248) while the white granite rubbing stone (SF8210), which probably represented the opportunistic use of a glacial erratic, was in a prehistoric context. A beehive quern was re-used as a packing stone in a post-Roman context (SF8268), although the object may belong to the late Iron Age or earlier Roman period. In the north east of England this type of quern was already in production in the 2nd century BC and continued throughout the Roman period (Buckley and Major 1998, 241-3). In the north west of England there is insufficient evidence to date the full range of their production but two examples occur in a Roman military context at Ribchester (Howard-Davis 2000, 297-300) while at Prestatyn, across the Dee estuary from Irby, a Hunsbury-type beehive quern was found in a Romano-British context dated to AD 70-160 (Blockley 1989, 124-5).

The small amount of industrial waste from iron smithing which occurred in prehistoric deposits is likely to be intrusive. There is nothing specifically diagnostic of prehistoric ironworking.

Heat-shattered stones were present in considerable quantities on the site although they were neither collected systematically nor their volume or weight measured. Their presence on the site is consistent with a prehistoric date in the lowland north west. Such stones occurred at Great Woolden Hall, Dutton's Farm, Lathom, Brook House Farm, Bruen Stapleford and Brunt Boggart, Tarbock which all had later prehistoric phases of activity but they were conspicuous by their absence on two excavated sites which saw no occupation before the Roman period (Court Farm, Halewood and Ochre Brook, Tarbock). There appears on current evidence to be a consistent correlation with later prehistoric occupation and the presence of these indestructible finds in Roman phases at Irby and elsewhere suggests residuality from earlier activity (see Chapter 5).

Discussion of the Iron Age Evidence

In view of the difficulty of defining the Iron Age occupation at Irby, drawing parallels with other sites is neither easy nor necessarily productive. The presence of one probable and one possible circular structure brings the site into the regional pattern of Iron Age settlements with circular structures. Such features can be seen at recently excavated settlements at Bruen Stapleford (Fairburn 2002a), Sharpstones Site E (Gaffney and White 2007, 93-5), Mellor (Noble and Thompson 2005), and Lathom (Cowell 2005a), and at Great Woolden Hall (Nevell 1999a). It is uncertain whether the settlement at Irby was enclosed during the Iron Age as all of the excavated ditches and palisades contained later material.

In one respect Irby appears to share similar problems of the survival of deposits which is found at other Iron Age sites in the area. Deposits consist of heavily truncated gullies and post-holes, some of which appear to form circular buildings (S32, S33), though these have been severely disturbed by later activity. The absence of any further evidence for structures could be due to the relatively restricted area excavated. Some or all of the post-holes may be the remains of four- or six-post structures though it is impossible to be certain about the details of any of these arrangements.

Stratification at the hillfort at Beeston Castle (Ellis 1993) also was also marked by extensive truncation of the prehistoric phases making it equally difficult to identify individual structures. Gullies and stone-packed post-holes similar to those excavated at Irby were present (e.g. Ellis 1993, 21, fig. 8, Period 2A). These were interpreted as a palisade marking the limits of the settlement. Stone-packed post-holes in the interior

were interpreted as the remains of roundhouses (Ellis 1993, fig. 23). However, these deposits suffered from similar problems of truncation and the small trench sizes do not aid interpretation. In fact reference is also made to similar problems in correctly identifying the stratigraphic position of features. Although several possible structures are identified, Ellis recognises that these were not very well defined (1993, 35-6). Comparison with the Iron Age hillfort at the Breiddin suggests that the post-holes could be reconstructed to form four-post or even six-post structures though the excavator had to acknowledge the tenuous nature of many of the reconstructions (Musson 1991, 79).

Sharpstones Hill Site A in Shropshire also suffered from extensive truncation by later activity (Barker *et al.* 1991). An apparently similar pattern of gullies to that seen at Irby was present. These features were interpreted as field boundaries and were associated with a diffuse scatter of post-holes analogous to those seen at Irby. In fact, several of the fills of features at Irby appear to be very similar to those at Sharpstones Hill, e.g. F71/1 (Barker *et al.* 1991, 23) containing charred soil, charcoal, burnt stone, small fragments of burnt bone and pottery. This is very similar to the contents of the features at the junction of Trenches XXXVI, XIX and XLIV which suggests that they had a similar function, even if exactly what that function was remains unclear.

Period III: Early Roman (late 1st-early 2nd century AD)

One of the main research aims of the excavation was to determine whether occupation was continuous from the late Iron Age into the Romano-British period. It was hoped that this could be achieved by analysis of the stratigraphic sequence, allied with a tightly dated chronological sequence derived from artefacts and/or radiocarbon dates. These hopes were not realised due to the nature of the site and the sparse artefact assemblage. The stratigraphic sequence was not sufficiently well defined to enable distinct phases of occupation to be isolated within the later prehistoric to Romano-British period. Ironically, it is the very density of later activity and settlement which has denied us the chance to discern a sequence of building plans amid the mass of post-holes which may have shed light on the transition from the late Iron Age to the Romano-British period.

The early Roman phase, like the Iron Age phase, has proved difficult to distinguish archaeologically and no features or deposits could be conclusively dated to this phase, despite the presence of finds dating to the late 1st to early 2nd century. One possibility is that any structural evidence for the early Roman period was obliterated by later activity. This does not seem likely given that prehistoric features survive on this part of the settlement, although the prehistoric deposits tend to survive as cut features into the natural sand or rock, and the associated occupation deposits have largely been reworked (see above), a process which may also have obliterated any ephemeral early Roman deposits.

A further consideration is that the nature of the deposits on the site militates against too rigid an interpretation of the dating of the overall occupation deposits on the site. The major occupation deposits were not clearly identifiable as discrete stratigraphic units and the interfaces between layers were not well defined. This suggests that the presence of small quantities of intrusive later Roman pottery in overall layers might be responsible for indicating an artificially late date. The possibility of intrusive material infiltrating into earlier deposits through burrowing animals, root action or through the more substantial reworking or trampling of deposits also needs to be considered. This may mean that some features which were observed as cutting through particular occupation deposits have been dated too late by the rigid treatment of the integrity of the layers. If this is the case, as seems likely given the amount of late 1st and particularly 2nd-century pottery in the main area, then the sequence should begin in the late 1st century. It is likely that the material within the negative features is more reliably associated with the feature, despite all the usual problems of residuality, than material in layers through which the feature was thought to cut at the time of excavation.

The artefacts provide nothing positive in the way of evidence to span the gap of over two centuries between the mid Iron Age and the early Roman period. The fragmentary La Tène II/III brooch (SF7302) is not closely datable (see Chapter 4, *The Metal Objects*) and though it could fall in the period between the 3rd century BC (the date of the steatite spindle whorl, SF2931), and the late 1st century AD, when the earliest diagnostic Roman pottery appears on the site, it is perhaps more likely to conform to the two radiocarbon dates from the same feature which were consistent at 410-200 cal BC (Table 2.1). The site also produced a substantial group of VCP (479 sherds), a vessel form and fabric which is generally characteristic of the mid to late Iron Age but the material is not in itself closely datable.

It would be unwise to assume, however, that the absence of suitable datable artefacts on what is essentially an aceramic site (with the exception of VCP), and one very poor in durable material culture as a whole, remained unoccupied during the late pre-Roman Iron Age. It could be argued that the very existence of an Iron Age settlement with a small number of unambiguous mid Iron Age dates on the same site as a native settlement where the introduction of the pottery occurs in the late 1st century AD might be a strong candidate for continuous occupation. The absence of corroborative evidence, whilst frustrating, is not surprising, given the sparse nature and poor dating of the material culture of the later Iron Age in the region.

The earliest datable Roman artefacts consist of six sherds of South Gaulish samian from the period AD 70-110, representing 14% of the total samian sherds. However, there is little coarse pottery that needs to belong to the later 1st century other than a small group of undiagnostic handmade pottery sherds which were initially classified as Roman Black-burnished ware (BB1) but which have been suggested by Jeremy Evans as late Iron Age or early Romano-British (J. Evans pers. comm.). The grey wares, though rarely diagnostic of form, tend to fall into the late 1st-early 2nd century AD, to be replaced largely by oxidised wares in the 2nd century (J. Evans pers. comm.) but some grey ware is certainly of 3rd-century form (e.g. the pulley rim form Fig. 4.9, 125-126). The volume of grey wares is not great but comprises 8% by weight and 9% by sherd count of the pottery assemblage. To take a minimalist interpretation, the samian could have been manufactured in the latter part of the production range and might conceivably have arrived on the site no earlier than the first decade of the 2nd century AD. If the small quantity of samian represented the adoption of high-status wares before the use of domestic coarse pottery became established at this rural site, a date in the late 1st century is possible.

By the 2nd century pottery becomes more common (see Chapter 4, *Roman Pottery*), although it is noticeable that the volume of black-burnished ware, which is the predominant ware type in use during the 2nd century, is much lower in the period AD 120-200 than for the 3rd-mid 4th century. Little of the early pottery appears to be associated with recognisable structures and a large proportion is residual in later contexts.

On the face of it, the small volume of late 1st-century pottery suggests that the settlement saw only a low level of activity during that period. However, it could also result from the relatively slow adoption of pottery in the rural communities of the north west in the early Roman period. There is not necessarily a direct relationship between volume of pottery recovered and the duration or intensity of activity. An example may be Brook House Farm, Halewood where the Iron Age enclosure sees early Roman occupation, possibly after an interruption, but only a tiny Roman pottery assemblage was recovered from the site (Cowell and Philpott 2000, 45-6). A similar pattern of material culture can be seen in Wales and elsewhere in the north of England during the early Roman period. At Collfryn, for example, pottery use was low in the early Roman period and increased in the 3rd and 4th centuries AD (Britnell 1989). Thus, in a period when little pottery was used, the probability is high that early Romano-British features will lack diagnostic Roman pottery.

A second possibility is that the principal focus of activity at this period lay outside the excavated area. This is the more likely explanation as some late 1st and 2nd-century pottery is present on the site as a whole and a substantial area to the east, which was almost certainly enclosed within the settlement, remains unexcavated. The arrangement of the palisades and ditched enclosures suggests that the initial enclosure during the Romano-British period lay to the east of the major excavated area, and was only extended later to the area of the principal excavation.

The presence of some archaeological features in the eastern enclosure is strongly suggested by the presence of Roman pottery and large stone blocks which had been dumped in the enclosure Ditch 1 (including the original evaluation excavation for the kitchen extension in 115 Mill Hill Road). The quantity of stone in the ditch suggests buildings were present in the vicinity, possibly from wall footings or removed from post-hole packing, while the presence of pottery and other finds in the relatively short sections of ditch which were excavated suggest some occupation debris, perhaps from activity within this part of the enclosure. A Roman pottery handle in a white micaceous fabric with a grey core was found in the front garden of 113 Mill Hill Road when a service pipe was excavated in November 1987. In addition, in the area which lay to the east of the main north-south ditch in Trench XXV/XXVI there are structural remains and Romano-British pottery including five sherds of samian, but only one of these is southern Gaulish. This small concentration could indicate that earlier activity lay to the south-east of the main excavated area. However, the absence of extensive excavation there makes this somewhat speculative. If correct, however, there is a further implication in terms of settlement shift. The density of VCP in the main

garden plot suggests that the focus of activity lay there during the Iron Age; the lack of VCP from trenches to the east may suggest that the focus of the site shifted eastwards in the early Roman period, before expanding back westwards over the disused Iron Age area with the construction of the enclosure formed by S25 (palisade slot) and its possible successor Ditch 3.

In conclusion, the stratigraphic sequence and artefact assemblage are not sufficiently strong either to support or refute the hypothesis that the site saw continuous occupation from the late Iron Age into the early Roman period.

Period IV: Roman (early-mid 2nd-4th century AD)

By the 2nd century AD, the first substantial elements of Romano-British structures can be recognised on the site within what later developed into a complex sequence of buildings marked by large stone-packed post-holes and gullies. During the 2nd to 4th century the settlement saw not only construction and reorganisation of the buildings on the site but also changes in the way in which the settlement was enclosed.

The following narrative attempts to make the most coherent sequence out of the stratigraphical and artefactual evidence, with the proviso that in many cases it has proved difficult to identify the relationship between buildings and enclosures in anything other than the most general terms (see discussion in Chapter 1).

Fig. 2.13: Phase R1. Palisade slot S2

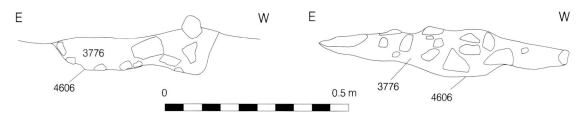

Fig. 2.14: Phase R1. Sections across palisade slot S2

The Enclosure Sequence

The presence of palisade slots and ditches indicates that the settlement at Irby was enclosed at certain stages during its occupation. However, the overall sequence of development of the enclosure is not clear and the stratigraphic relationships with buildings were either missing or were not sufficiently clear to enable all the critical elements of the sequence to be determined with certainty. The following discussion considers the main alternatives and attempts to reach a coherent sequence, taking into account the location and layout of structures inside the enclosure, evidence of the finds, and the limited stratigraphical information.

Phase R1: Enclosure palisade

Stratigraphically, the earliest potential enclosure feature is a palisade slot, S2. It was located in Trench XXI but was not observed in trenches to the north. It presumably either stopped or turned before reaching the neighbouring trench, or, as so often at Irby, it did not cut the bedrock to the north so left no surviving archaeological trace.

Palisade slots are linear features which have been used in the sense defined by Cunliffe (1987, 97) as a narrow trench measuring 0.2-0.6 m wide, varying in depth within the same range, and with vertical sides; they are mostly straight or nearly so. They represent the bedding trenches for fences or palisades, which if dug from the contemporary ground surface would have supported a fence of upright timbers.

Structure 2: Palisade slot

A narrow gully (4606, 4647) ran north-south across the full length of Trench XXI (Fig 2.13). It measured 0.35-0.40 m wide and 0.15-0.24 m deep with a U-shaped profile (Fig 2.14). The fill (3776) was a dark reddish brown sandy loam containing very frequent sandstone pebbles. A distinct widening of the gully at one point (4647) may mark the position of a substantial post.

The gully is likely to have been a palisade slot forming a fence line, probably part of an enclosure of unknown extent. This interpretation is supported by the high proportion of sandstone in the fill, suggesting rapid backfilling with freshly excavated bedrock, and also by the presence in this area of another, but later, palisade

slot, S5 (3707) in Phase R3, close by and on virtually the same alignment, which appeared to replace S2.

S2 was cut by the foundation gully of the later curvilinear building, S3 of Phase EM 2, which probably dated to the early medieval period (see below). Some oxidised ware, industrial waste, fired clay and charcoal were present in the fill. A sherd from a constricted neck jar (SF5285) is dated to the mid 2nd-3rd century and joins with a sherd found in layer 3616 (SF3021). The gully was interpreted as cutting two layers, 4605 and 4612, the latter of which contained a small calcite-gritted sherd (SF5672) and a late 3rd-4th-century Oxfordshire colour-coated sherd (SF5363). On the face of it these indicate a *tpq* of the 4th century AD for the gully but the likelihood of intrusive material appearing in poorly defined occupation layers makes the dating far from secure. Stratigraphically an earlier date is preferred.

Phase R2: Palisaded enclosure

There is good evidence that the palisade line of Phase R1 was succeeded by a palisaded enclosure. A long stretch of palisade (S4, Fig 2.15) can be traced running eastwards for at least 20 m parallel to the east-west section of Ditch 1 (Phase R3). At the point where S4 turns southwards at its western end, it was cut through by the north-south section of Ditch 1. Thus Ditch 1 and cut S4 were not in contemporary use but represented successive phases of enclosure. Given its considerable length, the palisade presumably formed a substantial boundary fence.

A further palisade slot S25, aligned east-west, ran close to the southern edge of Ditch 3 in the western enclosure but there is no direct stratigraphic information to determine whether the ditch or the palisade was the earlier feature, although the palisade was stratigraphically early. In view of the replacement to the east of a palisade (S4) by a ditch (D1), it is possible that the same sequence was followed here in the western enclosure. An alternative is that both palisade S25 and Ditch 3 were in contemporary use. This is discussed below.

Structure 4: Palisade slot

Structure 4 was a palisade slot (cuts 116, 813, 2808) which ran for about 20 m east-west and appears to have

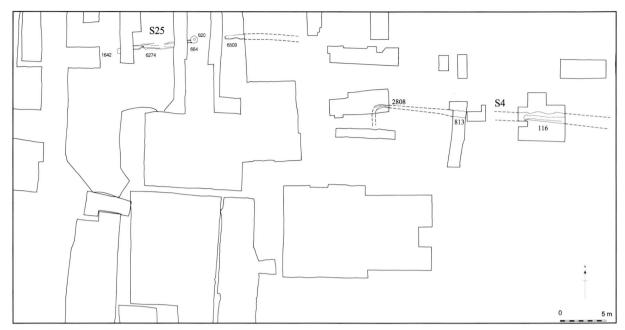

Fig. 2.15: Phase R2. Palisade slots S4 and S25

defined a palisaded enclosure (Figs 2.15 and 2.16). The slot measured between 0.26-1.00 m wide and 0.10-0.20 m deep with a flat base. For most of its excavated extent it was truncated to bedrock. The presence of quantities of crushed sandstone in the fill of this feature suggests that the freshly dug bedrock was replaced as packing for the palisade.

The slot certainly pre-dated Ditch 1 and its associated ditched enclosure (Fig. 2.15). Ditch 1 cut through this feature at the point where it began to turn south, at its western end in Trench XVII. As the slot fails to reappear in other trenches further south, either it stopped soon after the turn, or it followed the same line as the later ditch which then removed it.

The only finds recovered from S4 were small quantities of undiagnostic oxidised ware (six sherds in 119) and two undiagnostic sherds of BB1 (SF8375 in 119, SF1309 in 2807). The latter provide a *tpq* of AD 120. One piece of industrial waste in 119 indicates some iron working prior to or contemporary with its construction; there is also a piece of possible shaped fired clay.

An enclosure formed by a palisade, S4, could have been contemporary with the possible palisaded enclosure to the west suggested by the slot S25, though the truncation of deposits has removed any direct stratigraphic relationships which might have confirmed this. The area enclosed by S4 contains no datable features, nor any that

make coherent structures, although only a small area was excavated and this was largely truncated by later activity to bedrock.

Structure 25: Palisade slot

Structure 25 represents several sections of a palisade slot which ran close to the southern edge of Ditch 3 (Figs. 2.15 and 2.17). It consists of slot/gully 6509, 664, 6274 and a post-hole, 1642. Post-hole 620 may have been for a post set at the terminus of gully 664 or a later feature but the relationship between the two features was ambiguous. Although the slot was not recognised until it cut weathered bedrock at two points, it was seen at a higher level in other sections. The apparent disparity is not surprising as the difficult ground conditions made it hard to see many features unless they were packed with stones. The consistent alignment and occurrence of the slot in several trenches suggest these elements formed part of a single continuous palisade slot. Despite their close proximity, there was no direct stratigraphic relationship between S25 and Ditch 3 to determine whether or not they were in contemporary use.

The slot is very shallow in both cases where it cut the bedrock (Fig. 2.17), no more than 80 mm deep in context 6274 and only 50 mm deep in context 6509. To the east in Trench XXXVII the gully may have ceased as a linear feature and become a series of discrete post-holes.

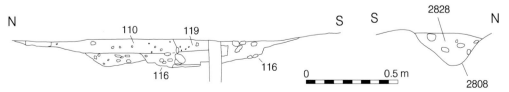

Fig. 2.16: Phase R2. Sections across palisade S4

Plate V: Phase R3. Ditch 1 (1214), cut into sandstone bedrock in Trench IX

The only datable find in the fill is a sherd of Bronze Age pottery (SF711 in context 1625) though this is considered likely to be residual. In Area XXXVI the palisade slot S25 cut through 6276, a layer with one sherd of samian (dated AD 140/160-200) and other Roman pottery including BB1, greyware and undiagnostic oxidised ware. This suggests a date of the mid 2nd century at the earliest.

One possibility is that both the palisade and ditch were in use at the same time. This would preclude the presence of a bank, unless the palisade was set within the bank in a slot which penetrated through the contemporary ground surface. This would have the effect of allowing an extended duration of the life of the enclosure represented by S25 and D3 together.

The alternative view that the palisade preceded the ditch appears more convincing. The slot occupied a position immediately south of the ditch which an internal bank would be expected to take. If there were a bank, it is difficult to see the ditch and palisade existing at the same time. Certainly, there is a precedent for this sequence of events in the eastern enclosure where the palisade line was clearly replaced by a ditch. If the same sequence occurred here, it has the merit of indicating an early palisaded enclosure to the west and disposes of the difficulty of the close proximity of the slot (6274) and Ditch 3 by assigning them to different phases.

Furthermore, as Ditch 3 appears to have been filled in by the mid-late 4th century, there is ample time for the palisade to be replaced by the ditch, within a period of two centuries or more.

There is an interesting parallel with the palisade slot to the east (S4) which was cut by the north-south ditch (D1). The absence of the gully (S4) from Trench XIV to the south of the junction suggests the ditch followed roughly the same line as the palisade and therefore may have replaced it. Palisade S25 appears to have been replaced by a ditch (D3) on a similar alignment, but set just slightly to the north. In both cases it implies that it was necessary to retain the line and position of the boundary, presumably because it respected existing structures in the interior of the enclosure.

There are parallels for enclosures formed by discontinuous gullies in the Iron Age, for example at Normanton le Heath, Leics., at Gamston, Notts. (Thorpe *et al.* 1994, 11) and in at least two of the conjoined enclosures at Dalton Parlours, West Yorks. where Enclosures I and III were replaced by ditches in the Iron Age (Wrathmell and Nicholson 1990, 12, 17, figs 9 and 15). The discontinuous nature of the gullies may be a result of truncation by later disturbance which has removed the shallowest sections of the features. Irregularities in the contemporary ground surface may have resulted in an inconsistent depth of cut into the subsoil.

Phase R3: The eastern ditched enclosure

At some stage in the Roman period the probable enclosure palisade S4 was replaced by Ditch 1 (Fig 2.18), which was dug into bedrock and sandstone brash. It is not clear whether S25 remained in use or not. The full extent of the ditch was not revealed by excavation but its size and extent make it likely to have formed an enclosure. It ran for at least 58 m east-west, then turned at the north-west corner to run southward for at least a further 65 m. If originally symmetrical in form, the single, excavated corner and parts of the north and west sides suggest the enclosure was subrectangular in plan, with a slight angle in the middle of the northern arm. The subrectangular form is common amongst Romano-British enclosures not only in the north west but also in neighbouring regions, though less regular forms have been noted and the overall shape of this example in plan is uncertain.

The eastern enclosure: Ditch 1

Ditch 1 (Figs. 2.18 and 2.19, Plate V) measured approximately 0.70 m wide and was 0.40-0.50 m deep. The cut was truncated to bedrock along much of its length.

This ditch was traced eastwards for at least 28.5 m

Fig. 2.17: Phase R2. Sections across palisade slot S25

from a sharp turn in the north-west as far as the original kitchen extension of 115 Mill Hill Road where rescue recording in 1987 first brought the existence of the site to light. Trench XII further east, in the front garden of the same house, also located a ditch cutting boulder clay which is almost certainly the extension of the same feature, indicating a minimum length of 58 m. From the turn at the north-west corner, the ditch ran southwards for at least 23 m into Trench XXI. A further trench to the south (XLV) also revealed what is very likely to be the same feature, giving a total north-south length of at least 65 m.

There is no clear indication of the extent of the enclosure to the east or south, although a trench excavated in the rear of no. 95 Mill Hill Road, about 140 m south of the angle of the ditch, revealed no archaeological deposits, suggesting the occupation site did not extend this far. A watching brief conducted during construction of a small extension to the rear of 111 Mill Hill Road found no *in situ* deposits, though fragments of slag and Roman pottery suggested that this area lay within the enclosure.

The sparse finds from the primary fill of Ditch 1 suggest that it was not finally filled in before the mid-late 4th century. Most of the finds appear to be residual but they include a few sherds with date ranges extending into the 4th century. The dating evidence is discussed in detail below.

The only point at which the ditch had any relationship to the surrounding deposits was along its western edge in Trench XXI. Even here the adjacent deposit (3616) was so thin that it was difficult to be certain of its relationship with the ditch.

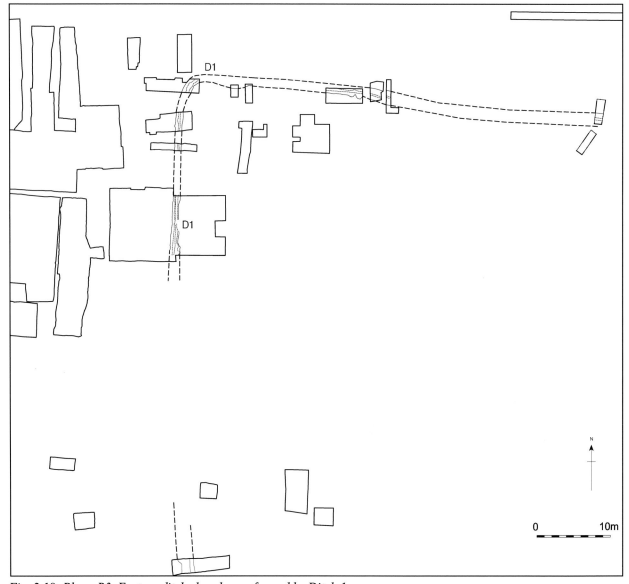

Fig. 2.18: Phase R3. Eastern ditched enclosure formed by Ditch 1

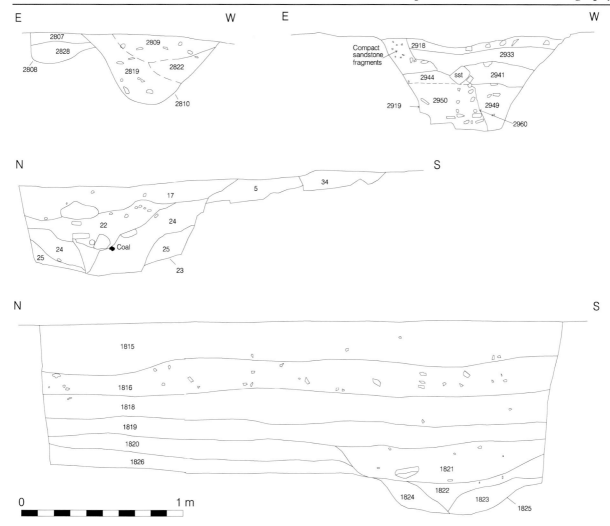

Fig. 2.19: Phase R3. Sections across Ditch 1

Several pits in Trench XLV may be associated with this phase, although because all deposits in this area were truncated to natural and no datable finds were recovered, it is impossible to be sure if they were contemporary with the ditch or were part of other phases.

Phase R4: The western ditched enclosure

Abutting against the ditched enclosure of Phase R3 was another ditched enclosure to the west. This was formed by the east-west Ditch 3 on the north side, and the gateway, S26 (Fig. 2.20). The other sides of the western enclosure were not located within the excavation. Given the spatial relationship of the ditches where the western enclosure abutted the rounded north-west corner of Ditch 1, the eastern enclosure was either earlier than, or contemporary with, that to the west.

A gateway (S26), marked by substantial post-holes, controlled access to the new ditched enclosure at the junction of Ditch 1 with Ditch 3. Ditch 3 may have replaced an enclosure defined by a palisade (S25), although an alternative interpretation, which allows Ditch 3 and S25 to co-exist, is also possible.

Associated with the north-south stretch of Ditch 1 was a palisade slot S5. The slot ran parallel to Ditch 1 but stopped at its northern end precisely at the post-holes of the gateway, S26, suggesting the gate and palisade form elements of a contemporary arrangement. The palisade in this position would have provided an additional barrier to the ditch within the settlement.

The western enclosure: Ditches 1 and 3

Ditch 1 may have been re-cut along part of its length (the recut was originally designated Ditch 2) and this activity may relate to the creation of the new enclosure. Ditch 3 was similar to Ditch 1 but shows slightly more variation in its profile. In the sections where it was cut into the brash it had a shallower, more rounded profile, probably as a result of weathering of the sides whilst the ditch was open (Fig. 2.21).

Unlike the overall layers in which much trampling and infiltration of intrusive finds may be expected, the primary fills of the ditch were securely sealed so in general one can place greater confidence in the dating evidence of finds in these contexts than in the overall

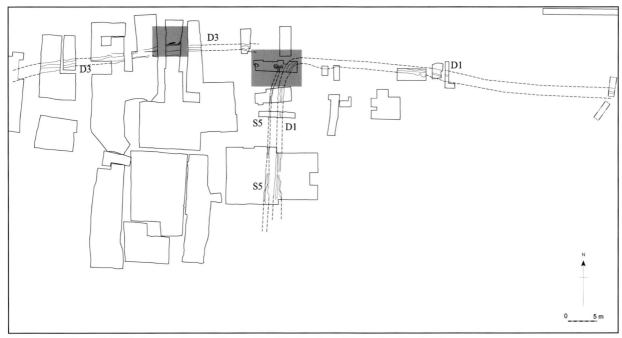

Fig. 2.20: Phase R4. Ditched enclosures formed by Ditches 1 and 3, and palisade S5

soil horizons. There is little diagnostic pottery in Ditch 3 but the infilling, probably deliberately, does not appear to have taken place before the mid-late 4th century. The dating evidence is considered below.

The newly dug western ditch (Ditch 3) lay a little to the north of palisade line S25 (Fig. 2.15). As discussed above, the ditch may have replaced the line of the palisade or it may have been contemporary with it. If the former, the ditch respected the existing boundary alignment and presumably also avoided the structures within the existing enclosure.

The full extent of the western enclosure is uncertain. Ditch 3 was traced for a distance of 36.5 m from Trench XXXV in the east, close to the gateway, westwards as far as Trench XXXVIII. Its presence in Trench XXIII could not be determined because of a requirement to preserve the structures there *in situ*. However, there are grounds for believing that the ditch did not extend much further west. First, the ground slopes down fairly steeply a few metres to the west of the westernmost trench (XXIII), so on topographical grounds the enclosure ditch is likely to have turned southwards within or very close to this trench. Secondly, the location of buildings (S12, S13) within the enclosure (together with a dense mass of post-holes which could not be resolved but clearly belong to further structures there) demonstrates a strong preference for a position which would be exactly midway across the enclosure east-west, if the ditch did curve at this point. Though the evidence is circumstantial, together these factors suggest a westernmost extent of about 50 m for this ditch. As regards the extent of the ditch to the south there is even less to go on, but assuming the enclosure contained the Roman deposits noted in the gardens to

the south of the main excavation, and if it were broadly parallel to the extended Ditch 1, it suggests an extent of at least 65 m.

Structure 26: Gateway to western enclosure

Immediately to the west of the angle of Ditch 1 was a group of three post-holes, two to the east and one to the west, separated by a gap of 2.7 m (Fig. 2.22 and 2.23, Plate IX). Their position suggest the post-holes formed a gateway into the western enclosure. The precise arrangement cannot be determined as the excavation was limited in this area, but the western ditch (Ditch 3) was noted in Trench XXXV only 2.5 m away to the north-west while a further trench on what would have been its extended line failed to find the ditch, suggesting it stopped just outside Trench XXXV and that the resulting gap formed an entrance.

Plate VI: Phase R3. Ditch 1 part-excavated (2810), with palisade slot S5 (2812) to left

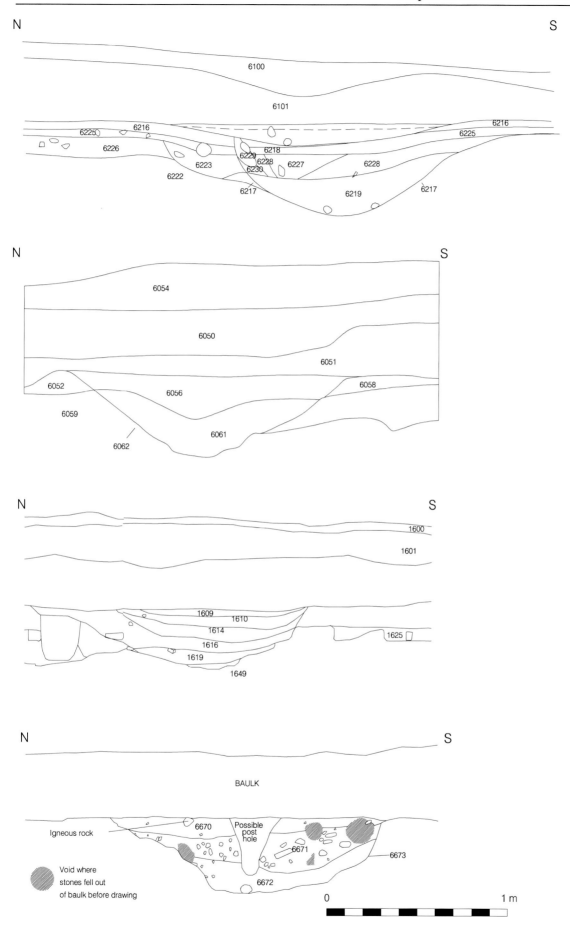

Fig. 2.21: Phase R4 Sections across Ditch 3

Plate VII: Ditch 3 (6673), Trench XXXVIII from the east

The post-holes for the gateway were substantial. Two adjacent post-holes to the east of the entrance had contained large vertical posts. The cut for one (2917) was sub-rectangular, measuring 0.36 by 0.51 m with the long axis aligned north-south, and 0.28 m deep; the other (2915) was elliptical, measuring 0.73 by 0.63 m with its long axis aligned east-west and *c.* 0.30 m deep. Post-hole 2917 had an unusual, step-shaped profile (Fig. 2.23), shallow to the east (20 mm deep), and vertical-sided to the west, with traces of a post-pipe. Both contained sandstone cobbles up to 0.20 m across; those in 2915 were more obviously arranged around a post-pipe (2928) which measured at least 0.30 m across. One substantial post-hole (2935) was located to the west of the entrance. This was an elliptical cut measuring at least 0.65 by 0.42 m and 0.14 m deep. Two other hollows in the upper surface of bedrock were interpreted as natural irregularities.

Dating evidence was slight. The construction of the entrance had a *tpq* of AD 120 from one undiagnostic sherd of BB1 (SF1353) in the fill of post-hole 2935.

Plate VIII: Ditch 3, detail of section (context 6673) in Trench XXXVIII, from the east

It is likely that the large post-holes served to support substantial gate-posts but without complete excavation of the entrance area it is uncertain whether there are different phases or a more complex tower structure, as has been recorded elsewhere (see Chapter 5). The evidence as excavated within a limited area is consistent with a simple gate (either single or double-leaved) hung on sizeable posts, linked to a short section of fence, represented by adjacent post-holes, to the bank to the west and to the palisade line to the east.

Structure 5: Palisade line

A linear gully (cuts 3707, 3730, 2210, 2812) aligned parallel to the line of Ditch 1 ran north-south across Trenches XIV, XVII and XXI (Fig. 2.20, Plate VI). It measured 0.30-0.44 m wide and 0.04-0.16 m deep with steep sides running to a pointed base in the north, while to the south the flat base followed bedding planes in the bedrock (Fig. 2.24). Pick-marks made with a sharp, pointed metal tool were observed along the sides. The gully had been cut by a large pit (F3, 3724) in Trench XXI.

Plate IX: Phase R4. NW angle of Ditch 1 and post-holes for gate S26, from east

The palisade line terminated to the north exactly midway between the two eastern post-holes of the gateway and there is little doubt that the palisade ran up to this side of the gate. This is an important relationship as it provides strong support for the view that the palisade was contemporary with Ditch 1, to which it ran exactly parallel.

The palisade may have served to reinforce the boundary formed by the dividing ditch. The presence of BB1 gives a *tpq* of AD 120 for the fill of the palisade slot. Although not closely datable, this accords in general terms with the post-120 date for one of the gateway post-holes.

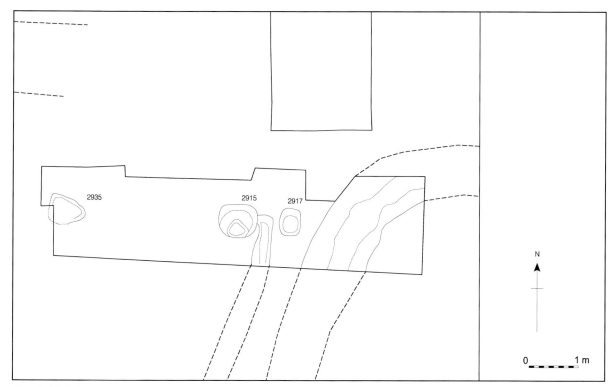

Fig. 2.22: Phase R4. Detail of S26 gateway (for location see Fig. 2.20)

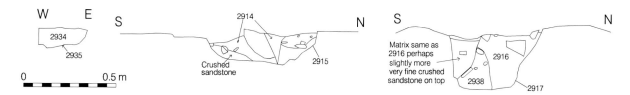

Fig. 2.23: Phase R4. Sections across features in S26

Structure 30: Possible stake-hole alignment

A row of six possible stake-holes (S30, Fig. 2.25) was set close to the northern edge of Ditch 3 (cuts 731, 732, 733, 734, 735, 736); none of the fills had any finds. Unsurprisingly, they were not recognised until the lowest soil layer was removed but their position appears to be deliberate and they may have formed a stake-built palisade along the outer edge of the ditch. They were visible only in Trench VI and no such features were recognised elsewhere along the ditch edges and it is possible that these were not genuine features but animal disturbance.

The internal structures: Structures 1 and 12

Two Romano-British buildings within the main excavated area are stratigraphically early and, apart from palisades or ditches, may be the first identifiable Roman structures (Fig. 2.26). The first building, S1, was formed by a curving foundation gully and though its complete plan did not survive, it was probably either circular or curvilinear in form. The second was a circular building, S12, which lay to the west of S1, and was composed of a circular gully and post-holes. There is no certainty that they were contemporary but both are stratigraphically early in their respective areas. The sparse finds information suggests a date of after *c.* AD 120 for S12 but for S1 the only evidence suggests an early Roman date, although a late Iron Age date cannot be entirely ruled out. As the spacing may have been deliberate to allow both to co-exist, they have been placed in the same phase.

It is uncertain whether the settlement was enclosed at this point. It is argued above that the palisade line S25 on the north side of the enclosure probably has a *tpq* of AD 140/160, and may have been replaced by a ditched enclosure represented by Ditch 3, although the palisade and ditch may have co-existed. Whichever was

Fig. 2.24: Phase R4. Sections across palisade S5

Area	Cuts	Fills	Finds
		East-West Ditch 1	
1987		Salvage recording	SF8273 BB1 rim and shoulder sherd, 240-270
I	20	Later fills 21, 26, 29, 30;	**30**: SF8387 oxidised ware (undated); SF8384, 8382 BB1 (undated); SF8383 slipped oxidised ware sherd (undated); SF8385 copper-alloy fragment; also small bone and daub fragments **29**: daub only **26**: SF8357 orange ware (undated); SF8381 BB1 bowl (not closely datable) **21**: SFs 8348, 9709 BB1; SFs 8441, 8439, 8421 oxidised ware; large daub and tiny bone fragment.
I	20	Early fills 24, 28, 32, 25, 31, 33	**31**: SF8386 2 hobnails; SF9766 bone; SF9787 large daub fragment **25**: SFs 8403, 8374 oxidised ware (undated); SF9784 daub **24**: SF8432, SF8440 oxidised ware; SF8372 BB1; 1 daub and 1 bone fragment **28, 32, 33**: no finds
I	23	Later fills 22 and 27;	**22**: some later material including a pre-decimalisation penny but also much pottery; SF8393 medieval sherd **27**: SF8431 2 joining rim sherds oxidised ware (3rd-4th century)
V	404	403, 405	**403, 405**: no finds
XLVI	9905	Upper fill 9900= Site I87 01	**9900**: no finds
XLVI	9905	9901= Site I87 02	**9901**: no finds
XLVI	9905	Primary weathered fill 9902= Site I87 03	**9902**: no finds
XLVI	9905	9903 = Site I87 06	**9903**: no finds
		North-South Ditch 1	
IX	1235	1226=1236: primary fill of ditch	**1226**: SF844 oxidised ware (undated); **1236**: no finds
XIV	2204	2205, 2206, 2211	**2205**: SF592 iron nail; **2206**: 5 fragments of industrial waste; **2211**: no finds
XVII	2810	2809, 2819, 2829;	**2819**: SF1327 BB1 sherd (undated); SF1300 greyware sherd with rivet (undated); SF1301 Central Gaulish samian AD 120-200; also 6 fragments of industrial waste **2809, 2829**: no finds
XVII	2823	2822	**2822**: SF1329 and SF1332 oxidised ware (neither dated); also 3 fragments of industrial waste
XVIII	2919	2933, 2941, 2949, 2950	**2933**: SF1335 BB1; SF1334 Central Gaulish samian AD 120-200 **2949**: SF10801 oxidised ware; industrial waste fragment. **2941, 2950**: no finds
XVIII	2919	Primary fill 2944	**2944**: SF1345, SF1347, SF1348 3 sherds BB1 (all undated)
XXI	1214	Upper fill of 1214	**3705**: SF4023 Nene valley colour-coated ware (mid 2nd-late 4th); SF4058 Central Gaulish samian AD 160-200; SF4057, SF4049, SF8863 3 sherds oxidised ware (undated); 8 fragments industrial waste
XXI	1214	Fill of 1214	**3755**: SF5244 BB1 sherd everted jar rim of probable 3rd-4th-century date, SF5331 BB1 sherd (120-350+); SF5325 2 oxidised ware sherds (undated); SF5273, SF5328, SF5241 oxidised ware sherds; SF8272 East Gaulish ware samian AD 160-240; 13 fragments industrial waste and some fired clay.
XXI	1214	Primary fill of 1214	**3756**: no finds
XXI	4621	4620 fill of internal ditch	**4620**: no finds
XLV	7611	7603	**7603**: SF8811 oxidised mortarium sherd undated; SF8682 haematite fragment; SF10812 lithic
XLV	7611	7602 Ditch cut, 7602 Upper fill of N-S ditch	**7602**: SF8615 Mesolithic core
XLV	7635	filled by 7622, recut by 7611	**7622**: no finds

Table 2.2: Fills of Ditch 1 with finds and dating evidence

Area	Cut	Fill	Finds
XXXVI	6217	Primary fill: 6219	SF6758 BB1 dated 200-350; SF6763 colour-coated ware; SF6759 2nd century oxidised ware
		Secondary fills: 6230, 6229, 6228, 6227	No finds
VI	689	Primary fills: 680, 684, 703, 702, 703, 710, 711	**680**: SF1018 late 4th-century jar rim; SF1089 VCP; **702**: SF1116 mid 2nd-late 4th-century Nene Valley colour-coated ware
	689	Secondary fill 700	SF1062 Rilled shell-tempered body sherd, perhaps late 4th century SF1068: BB1 jar rim, C3-C4
	689	Secondary fill 660	SF996 BBW ware; SF952 oxidised ware; SF1043 grey ware
XI	1612	Primary fills 1619, 1649	**1619**: Fired clay only; **1649**: no finds
	1612	Secondary fills: 1616, 1617	**1616**: SF332, SF329, SF348, SF349: 4 undiagnostic sherds of BB1; **1617**: no finds
XIII	2012	Primary 2016	**2016**: No finds
XXXVII	6476	Primary 6475	**6475**: SF7103 2nd century or later East Gaulish samian
		Secondary fills 6468	**6468**: SF10608 medieval sherd; 3 Romano-British sherds incl. SF10547 undiagnostic BB1
XXXVIII	6673	Primary 6672	**6672**: SF7760 and SF7762 undiagnostic oxidised ware

Table 2.3: Fills of Ditch 3 with finds and dating evidence

the case, the creation of a defined enclosure suggests that they existed around some structural component, particularly as the overall pottery assemblage shows some occupation on the site by the 2nd century. On stratigraphical grounds, three separate palisade lines could have existed with S1. The eastern side of the enclosure therefore could have been formed by palisade S2 (see above) or possibly by S4.

The spacing of the two buildings suggests, without proving the case, that they respected the ditched enclosure. The most economical interpretation is that an enclosure (either palisaded, or ditched) was created at the same time as the earliest Roman buildings within it, but the quality and distribution of datable finds does not permit certainty on this.

Structure 1: Romano-British roundhouse; 2nd century AD or later

Structure 1 consisted of a shallow curving gully, cut 4607 (fill 3789), which ran in an arc from the north-western corner of Area XXI into the west-facing baulk (Fig. 2.26). As excavated it measured 5.20 m long, 0.40

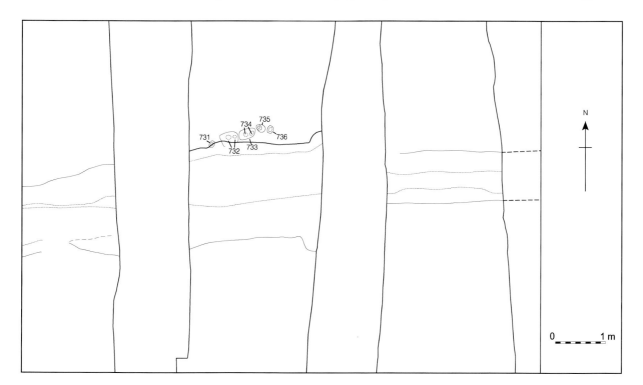

Fig. 2.25: Phase R4. Detail of S30 (for location, see Fig. 2.22)

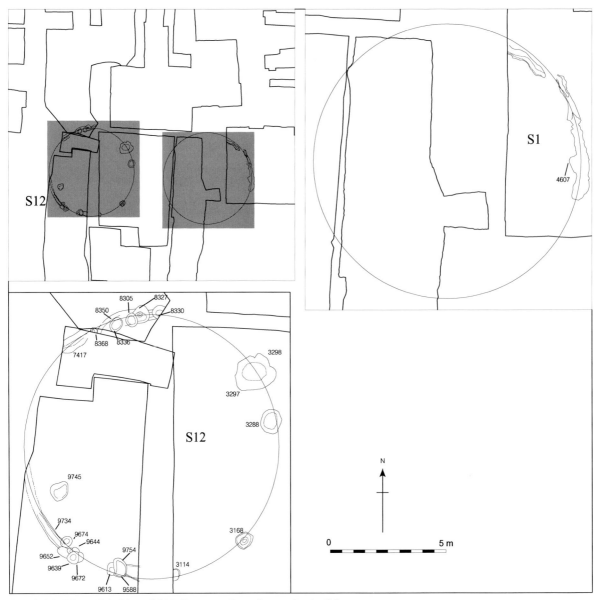

Fig. 2.26: Phase R4. S1 and S12, Romano-British circular buildings

m wide and 0.20 m deep, with gently sloping sides to a dished base. In places the cut was difficult to detect because the fill, which was a dark reddish brown sandy silt loam containing occasional sandstone inclusions, was very similar to the surrounding material (Fig. 2.27).

The finds in the fill of the gully did not include any certain Roman material, although there is some industrial waste, and an undiagnostic fired clay object (SF5369). This indicates that some iron smithing had taken place before or during the construction of the building.

The only portion of this structure to survive was located in Trench XXI and it appears that it was truncated by later activity to the west. Consequently it is difficult to be certain of its exact shape in plan although a circular building is the most likely option. Projecting the arc of the gully in a circle gives a diameter of about 13-14 m. This is slightly larger than the other roundhouses at

Irby which measure about 11 m in diameter. There is a possibility that this is a section of a building with a curvilinear plan similar to those discussed below, such as Structures 3 and 7 in Phase EM2. A slight deviation in alignment approximately 1.0 m from the northern end suggests that this might be the case. There is insufficient evidence to prove this either way but the probable post-Roman date of the curvilinear buildings makes it more likely that S1 is a roundhouse

The feature cut a loam and sandstone brash deposit, 3783, which contained a little industrial waste, a piece of fired clay, prehistoric pottery (SF5171) but only one sherd of undiagnostic Roman oxidised ware (SF5023).

Fig. 2.27: Phase R4. Section across S1

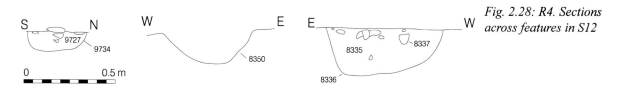

Fig. 2.28: R4. Sections across features in S12

The gully is likely to be structural, i.e. a 'ring-groove' as it is termed by Harding (1974, 41) or at Fisherwick (Smith 1979), rather than a gully for drainage of a roundhouse. Despite the absence of obvious post settings in the gully, the free-draining nature of the soil suggests that a separate drainage gully would not have been required.

Structure 12: Circular building

Structure 12 was recognised as a series of short sections of gully and truncated post-holes forming a circular building about 11 m in diameter (Fig. 2.26). At its best preserved, in Trench XLI, the gully measured 0.38 m wide and 0.13 m deep with a shallow, flat-bottomed profile (9734, Fig. 2.28). The same structure showed as short sections of gully in Trenches XLIV and XXXVI (7417, 8350; Fig. 2.26). A projection of the circle formed by these features crosses a series of post-holes which were stratigraphically contemporary with the gullies.

Many of the post-holes were heavily truncated and were excavated as discrete entities, but some appeared during excavation as a complex of intercutting features. The difficulty in recognising features which lacked quantities of packing stones makes it likely that in fact some of these complexes were observations of the same gully at different stages in the excavation. The resulting pattern of contiguous post-holes or of dense intercutting complexes can be resolved into a coherent structure.

One such example in Trench XLI was apparently cut by a complex group of inter-cutting pits (9674, 9644, 9652, 9339, 9672), which were probably post-settings or repairs to the wall of this structure. This dense mass of post-holes in the south-south-west part of the structure could be associated with an entrance with recut post-holes, though there is no obvious pattern to their arrangement and this interpretation is uncertain. In Trench XXXVI a short section of gully 8350 excavated low in the sequence, was interpreted as having been cut by a series of stone-packed post-holes which fall exactly on the line of the gully (8336, 8305, 8327, 8330). The gully fill 8349 has no finds.

S12 was disturbed for some of its length by the construction of Structure 13 (discussed below) which overlapped it and was offset by a maximum of about 2.2 m to the north-west. With the probable exception of the post-holes mentioned above, no packing material was found in the gully but it is likely to have been constructed in the same way as S13.

A number of the component features for S12 contain only VCP (e.g. fills 3110, 3166; 9664) suggesting that it cut through layers rich in VCP and the material is residual. It is rather less likely that the VCP is Roman for reasons discussed below. The only direct evidence from structural elements of the building which suggest a Romano-British date are an oxidised ware sherd in post-hole fill 8335 (SF7923) and another oxidised sherd (SF8707), which can be dated no more precisely than to the 2nd to mid 3rd century, in 7416, the fill of the construction gully. However, post-hole 8336 cut through 6189, a layer which contained black-burnished ware, oxidised ware and some VCP. The foundation gully 9734 (in Trench XLI) was sealed by layer 9560 which contained much prehistoric material and only one possible Roman sherd, along with a fragment of lead. The layers cut by elements of Structure 12 do include Roman pottery in small quantities, although the relatively large amount of VCP suggests the features were cut through earlier, Iron Age, layers and rapidly back-filled. The dating evidence then suggests construction in the mid 2nd century or later, after the introduction of BB1 to the site (cf. post-hole 8336 above).

Some components of the structure contain industrial waste, including a smithing hearth bottom in context 6145 (SF7692), indicating that prior to or during the life of the structure iron smithing was taking place on the site. A fragment of a rotary quern in post-hole fill 8335 (SF7917) also indicates grain-processing in the immediate vicinity and confirms the Romano-British date of the feature. The fills of post-holes in S13 (see below) also contain fragments of quern and oven superstructure. It is suggested that this may have been derived from demolition of S12, and relate to the activity of this structure, and were incorporated in the post-hole fills of its successor, S13. However, there is some evidence that an extended period of time elapsed between the demise of S12 and the construction of S13. This is discussed further below.

Phase R5: S13, and other possibly contemporary structures, S14, S17

Structure 12 went out of use, or more likely was dismantled, and was replaced by another building, Structure 13 (Figs 2.29 and 2.30). Although the close spatial overlap between S12 and S13 might be taken to suggest that S13 replaced S12 after a very short interval, in fact the stratigraphy suggests that S13 was cut from higher up, after the accumulation of a deposit which contained 4th-century pottery. The dense concentration of post-holes in this area strongly suggests that other buildings were constructed in this part of the site and some possible curvilinear alignments were noted but their stratigraphical position was too uncertain for them to be confirmed. Another structure (S14) may have been constructed at this time, to the north of the roundhouse, though this may have been present alongside S12. The dating evidence suggests that the settlement was enclosed by Ditch 3 in this phase.

Structure 13

Structure 13 was constructed within a polygonal gully measuring *c.*12.9 m across externally and 11.7 m internally (Fig. 2.30). As excavated, the gully measured 0.23-0.36 m wide and 0.14-0.35 m deep (Fig. 2.31). The actual depth of the cut was probably significantly deeper (up to 0.45 m) because it was not excavated from its correct stratigraphic position, but from the point at which the packing material could be identified since the remainder of the fill was identical to the surrounding material. It was one of the easiest excavated buildings to identify at Irby because it had a well-defined foundation and most of the plan was exposed.

Three substantial stretches of the foundation gully were identified. The best preserved section was excavated in Trench XXXVI. Context 6153 was a curvilinear cut across the southern end of the trench extending for 4.30 m, and measuring 0.30-0.35 m wide and 0.30-0.35 m deep. It had very steep sides and a dished base with a sharply concave break of slope. On closer inspection this part of the gully was seen to consist in plan of a number of short straight segments approximately 1.20 m long rather than a smooth arc, giving strictly a polygonal rather than a circular building. The short lengths presumably represent the intervals between the vertical posts and therefore of panels set between them.

The fill was dominated by a large number of sub-angular and tabular red sandstone cobbles measuring up to 0.30 m across with an average size of 0.15 by 0.20 by 0.15 m. Approximately 60% of these were tabular, many of which were set on edge against the sides of the cut, others were apparently slumped into it. Voids with a diameter of 0.09 m occurred at an average spacing of 0.30 m. The matrix surrounding the stones was a dark brown to very dark greyish brown sandy loam containing shattered igneous rock, sandstone pebbles and charcoal flecks.

No direct continuation of the foundation gully was located in Trench XIX. However, a line of inter-cutting post-holes represents its last remains (contexts 8213, 8203, 8207, 8219, 8146, 8103). The north-eastern segment of this structure was represented by linear 'dumb-bell' feature, 3202, in Trench XIX. It consisted of a straight U-shaped cut measuring 4.2 m long, and

0.25 m wide at its narrowest, with two large post-pits at the terminals with a maximum diameter of 1.10 m. It was shallowest in the narrow, central portion with a depth of 0.14 m. The terminals were 0.40 m deep with bowl-shaped profiles. The fill was dominated by a large number of red sandstone cobbles and blocks. These were smallest in the central section, where they ranged in size from 0.15-0.20 m long; most were tabular and set on edge, and smaller cobbles had been used to pack spaces. This deposit graded into the terminals which were filled with larger sandstone cobbles up to 0.35 m across. The southernmost contained a block set on bedrock at the base of the cut, while the other cobbles appeared to have been tipped randomly into the cut. The northern terminal contained larger cobbles, two of these were tabular and set on edge with their long axes parallel to the orientation of the feature, they sloped towards the west. The fill around these cobbles was a dark reddish brown sandy loam with flecks of charcoal and daub. Trench VIII just clipped the north-eastern corner of this structure and contained a short section of the foundation gully (1160).

The central portion of this feature contained packing for seven or eight small vertical posts, measuring *c.* 80 mm in diameter positioned at intervals of 0.25 m, which had almost certainly decayed *in situ*. The northern terminus probably contained a much larger post, though because the packing has slumped following its decay, it is difficult to be certain of its size. Although the southern terminus was excavated with this deposit it is more difficult to be certain that it was contemporary, the character of the packing was different, suggesting that the post had been deliberately removed and it was slightly off the main axis of this feature. However, the character of the fill was identical and the relationship of the packing stones between it and the central portion gave no clue as to a stratigraphic relationship. Similar structures have been excavated on other sites, notably at Old Oswestry hillfort (Hughes 1996).

Finds from the structural gully and the post-holes which comprise S13 are few and are not closely datable. Eight sherds of VCP were recovered alongside a few sherds of Roman pottery, worked stone and fired clay. The only pottery which provides any chronological information are two sherds of BB1, giving a broad *tpq* of AD 120 (SF6799, BB1 in context 6130; SF7909, BB1 in context 9571). Context 9609 contained SF8013, a sherd of abraded oxidised ware and SF8008, a clay weight of sub-rectangular form, while SF7163 was a sherd of grey ware in context 8148. If the BB1 conforms to the date of the great majority of this material on the site, then it is likely to belong to the period *c.* AD 200-350, though an earlier date is not precluded on these grounds.

Fired clay was found in a number of features. A post-hole or pit 8146 in the south-east quadrant of the structure contained a large quantity of well-preserved

Fig. 2.29: Phase R5. Structures S13, S14 and S17

structural daub with wattle impressions (fill 8143). These included 58 horizontal or rod impressions, as well as the only evidence from the site of vertical sails in the form of two split poles. These are interpreted as oven walls (Chapter 4, *Structural Daub and Fired Clay*). The good preservation of these friable fragments suggests that the oven was demolished and the remains rapidly dumped in the fill of the pit. The same fill (8143) also contained two fragments of a flat rotary quern (SF7168, SF7169), and a rubbing stone (SF7141). The coincidence of all three elements suggests that grain processing and food preparation was carried out in the immediate area shortly before S13 was constructed. Given that S13 was a replacement of one or more earlier roundhouses, including S12, it is conceivable that the post-hole fills for S13 contains demolition superstructure and a discarded quern from such activity practised within or immediately outside these buildings.

Although the finds from the fill of this structure indicate a *tpq* of AD 120 they do not enable the chronology to be refined much beyond that. A more useful indication is given by datable finds in layers cut by and sealing the structure. The pottery from layers which were cut by the building includes some 4th-century material. Context 3062 has a 4th-century Nene Valley colour-coated sherd (SF3303), as well as two sherds of late 4th-century calcite-gritted ware (SF3204, SF4487), but also a little probably intrusive medieval pottery (e.g. SF3197). Layer 3096 contains one sherd of late 4th-century calcite-gritted ware (SF5501). Layer 3150 also contains two sherds of shell-tempered ware, probably of

late 4th-century date (SF6177, SF6160). There is also a considerable amount of earlier Roman pottery. Of the layers sealing the building, 6121 has a few datable finds: two 3rd-mid 4th-century BB1 sherds (SF6649, SF6700), a 4th-century Nene Valley colour-coated ware dish base (SF6665); there are four other BB1 sherds (SF6596 has one Gillam type 11, late 3rd to early 4th century), one oxidised ware sherd, and several VCP sherds. Layer 3102 which seals 3202 (the 'dumb-bell' feature of S13) contains much Roman pottery including seven sherds of undated oxidised ware, a 4th-century Nene Valley sherd, and eight fragments of BB1/greyware.

There is environmental evidence from a number of contexts within this structure. A sample from context 6149 (fill of 6153) contained just four cereal grains, probably residual, since one was *Triticum dicoccon*, another of naked barley and one Hordeum indet., 1 *Triticum* sp. One context, 6130, contained a large number of charred seeds, including one fragment of *Pisum sativum*, pea, and a range of cereals including oats, hulled barley, naked barley, rye, hexaploid Triticum, bread wheat and spelt wheat; another sample from 6138 contained high level of oats, hulled barley and bread wheat.

The polygonal ground plan of this building suggests rather than vertical planks set on edge of the type which are attested in at least three late prehistoric roundhouses at Hengistbury Head (Cunliffe 1987, 86), it is more likely to have been constructed using short sections of wattle and daub panel attached to posts set in the gully.

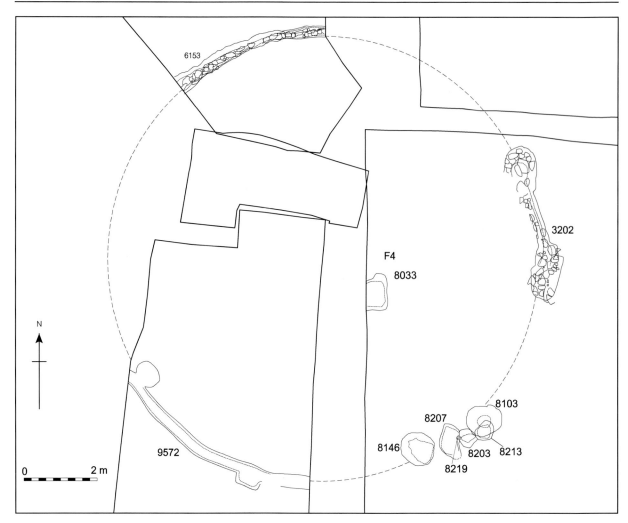

Fig. 2.30: Phase R5. Circular structure S13 with F4

The only major post-holes within the gully alignment of this structure were the two at the terminals of the 'dumb-bell' structure, although occasional gaps in the packing material in other sections may have represented the location of posts.

The few datable finds suggest that this was probably a 4th-century roundhouse which cut layers containing numerous prehistoric finds and some Roman material, including 4th-century pottery, as well as being sealed by layers containing some late 3rd-4th century material. The dating is discussed further below.

Implications of the dating evidence for S13

The preceding identifiable structure S12 had a *tpq* of AD 120. Experimental archaeology has shown that

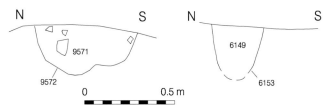

Fig. 2.31: Phase R5. Sections across S13

roundhouses could have had a long life if carefully maintained. A minimum lifespan of the building is likely to have been at least 20 years (cf. Harding *et al.* 1993) but the maximum would potentially be much longer, depending on the type of timber and the care with which the building was maintained. The Pimperne House, built in 1976, was demolished in 1990 when it was found to be in good structural condition, apart from the porch, the posts of which had already been replaced after eight years (Reynolds 1993). A long-running experiment at Lejre, Denmark has found that wattle and daub structures can be maintained for 25-30 years by the continual replacement of posts but it was considered that beyond 50 years it was considered more worthwhile to build a new house. Depending on the quality of the material used, a straw thatched roof could last between 25 and 50 years (M. Nicolajsen pers. comm.).

The implications of the dating of building S13 require detailed consideration. There are two main alternative interpretations of the evidence. The first accepts the stratigraphy and finds evidence as it stands. On the face of it, the stratigraphic relationships combined with datable pottery within layers indicate that the construction of S13 did not take place before the mid or late 4th century at the earliest. There appear to be too many 4th-century sherds within the various layers cut by S13 to dismiss them all as intrusive. The packing stones within the gully of S13 showed up high in the sequence of soil deposits as an unusually well defined feature for this site. If the integrity of the surrounding layers is accepted then the gully cuts through several deposits recorded separately in different trenches which contain 3rd and 4th-century pottery, including calcite-gritted ware. This provides a *tpq* of the late 4th century for the building.

The second interpretation questions the integrity of the deposits containing the 4th-century material and argues that the formation of the deposits was more complex than the above would suggest. In particular the apparent cut of the building through occupation deposits is in some way misleading and the layers through which S13 appear to be cut may have been reworked following its demolition, thereby incorporating later material in the matrix. Following this argument, S13 may date to earlier in the Roman period, probably in the late 2nd or 3rd century. This interpretation is derived from reservations over the understanding of the processes which led to the formation of the deposits present on site. The gully and post-holes for S13, as many other buildings on the site, were recognised through the identification of packing stones in the fill of the features protruding above the excavated surface. The cuts for the features were not in most cases well defined. The assumption was made that the packing stones were either buried below the ground surface or protruded only a short distance above the contemporary ground surface, although during the life of the building the surrounding ground surface may have been eroded or accumulated against and over the packing stones. There appear to be two principal ways in which the later material may have become incorporated in the soil deposits around the structure. The first involves the reworking of the occupation deposits immediately around the building through human and animal activity whilst the remains of the disused gully itself were protected from extensive reworking and intrusion of later material by the packing

Plate XI: Structure 13 (context 9571) from the east

stones. In poorly differentiated soils like those at Irby such a process would give the appearance on excavation that the gully was cut through the reworked deposit. The second involves the assumption that the packing stones of the house gully actually protruded above the ground surface during the life of the building. After the demolition of the building, later soil deposits accumulated against the packing stones, which remained *in situ*. The packing stones were the chief indicator by which most structural cut features were recognised during excavation. By contrast, the soil fills of features were often not distinguishable at the same level as the packing stones and were only clearly distinguishable when lighter coloured soils were encountered close to the natural subsoil.

One important consequence follows from the latter interpretation. The succession of at least two circular structures on this part of the site, and probably more, which are implied by the large numbers of post-holes despite the lack of clear alignments, would span the period from the mid 2nd to before the mid 4th century rather than extending as late as the late 4th century. Otherwise there is what might be considered an unacceptably long period between the two identifiable roundhouses, even allowing for the existence of others,

Plate X: Structure 13 (stones 3158, 3193) from the south-east

S

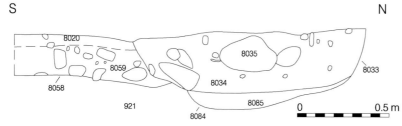

8020
8059
8058
8035
8034
8033
921
8085
8084

N

Fig. 2.32: Phase R5. Section across pit F4

0   0.5 m

poorly defined examples, in the sequence. This would allow the curvilinear post-built structures (S10, S15) to fall into the period before the rectangular building, S9, which is the sequence suggested by the stratigraphy in Trench XL. The second interpretation also suggests that the ditched enclosure remained in use through the life of the roundhouses.

overlapping their predecessors. It may be that some of the post-holes belong to other circular buildings in a succession of rebuilt structures, though none are securely linked. Although the stratigraphic sequence as excavated suggests that the constituent post-holes belonged to a variety of phases, the difficulty of determining the level at which features were cut may obscure genuine associations between post-hole alignments.

Feature 4

A very large post-hole or pit in Trench XIX (Fig. 2.30) appeared to be contemporary with Structure 13. Cut 8033 measured at least 1.30 m in diameter and 0.30 m in depth, running into the western section. It was filled by a dark reddish brown sandy silt loam with sandstone pebbles, shattered cobbles of igneous rock including granite, charcoal, daub and one fragment of coal (fills 8034, 8035, Fig. 2.32). Associated with this fill were a number of very large sub-rounded sandstone blocks up to 0.35 m across. These apparently formed a partly collapsed rectangular setting, probably for a very large timber post which appears to have decayed *in situ*. This feature bears a number of similarities to the large post-hole in Structure 12.

Other potential structures

A dense concentration of post-holes in the area of the two roundhouses, S12 and S13, indicates that at least one, and probably several, other buildings stood at this location. Many Iron Age and Romano-British rural sites display a tendency to rebuild circular buildings

Structure 14: ?Subrectangular structure

Structure 14 consists of a well-defined steep-sided gully

Plate XII: Structure 14 during excavation, showing packing stones, from the south

(6178, 6172 and 6175) in Trench XXXVI, forming two sides of a rectangular structure or enclosure (Fig. 2.33). The gully was aligned roughly south-west by north-east to a rounded corner and then turned to run towards the south-east. The cut was 0.60-0.78 m wide and 0.09-0.36 m deep and was at its shallowest just to the west of the corner. The profile was uniform along the entire length of the cut, steep-sided with a sharp break of slope down to a flat base (Fig. 2.34). The lower fill was a dark reddish brown sandy loam up to 0.14 m thick containing shattered crushed sandstone. Overlying it was a very dark greyish brown sandy loam containing shattered igneous rock, sandstone pebbles, crushed sandstone, flecks of reddish brown clay and charcoal flecks. Occasional lenses containing up to 10% charcoal were also present. Within this fill was a concentration of sandstone cobbles and shattered igneous cobbles approximately 0.20 m wide and 0.10 m deep in the upper part of the fill. The edges of this deposit were never very well defined though it tended to be present towards the southern edge of the cut, while at the corner it occurred in the centre. Larger sub-angular sandstone blocks (up to 0.30 m across) were associated with the cobbles, particularly at the western end of the feature.

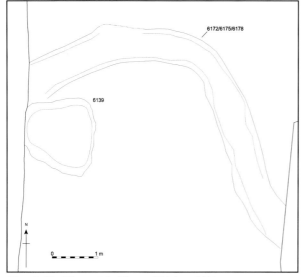

6172/6175/6178

6139

N

0   1 m

Fig. 2.33: Phase R5. Plan of S14 and F4

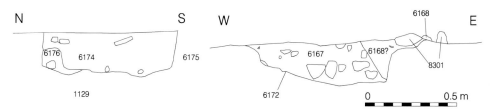

Fig. 2.34: Phase R5. Sections across S14

functioned to demarcate a fenced plot attached to the successive roundhouses, although the association with these structures is uncertain. If correctly interpreted, it would provide useful evidence of subdivision and internal zoning within the enclosure.

With one possible exception, this feature was quite unlike any others on the site. The nearest parallel lay in Trench XXIX where a feature of broadly similar shape and dimensions (S17) appeared to be overlain by Structure 18, the latter interpreted as medieval in date. S14 is too narrow and shallow and the sides are too steep for it to be an enclosure ditch, and in any case it does not continue into Trenches VIII or XIX. The alternative is that it had a structural function. The cobbles may represent packing against a wall constructed of timber panels, boards or posts. Part of the problem in interpreting this is that its full extent is unknown. It would appear that its south-west corner lies somewhere in the unexcavated area between this trench and Trench XXXIX.

Interpretation of this structure is made difficult by partial survival and the incomplete plan. There are two main possibilities. The first is that it is a roofed building of sub-square or sub-rectangular form. The two missing walls to south and west were either not recognised amid the dense mass of features in Trenches XIX and XLI, terminated within the baulks, or did not survive due to shallow foundations. Similar sub-square structures are known from Whitton, Glamorgan and in recent excavations on a Romano-British site at Birch Heath near Tarporley, Cheshire, where the complete plan of one building of regular sub-square appearance was revealed (Fairburn 2002b, 62-4, ill. III.4). The flared entrance is very similar to the Whitton structure (Jarrett and Wrathmell 1981, fig. 37.2) which dates to the 1st-2nd century and the details of the construction using pebbles as packing material are very similar.

The second possibility is that it is a palisade gully for a fence. Where it was observed, the feature was comparatively well defined and substantial; there is a slight but distinct curve outwards of the eastern side, which would have resulted in a concave wall. The balance of probability is that it was not a building but a subdividing fence. Its position may indicate that it

The majority of the finds are prehistoric or are undiagnostic, with much VCP, daub and industrial waste in 6167 and only a small number of Romano-British finds in 6174. Context 6167 has a variety of material including mostly single examples of oats, hulled barley, *Triticum* (hexaploid), *Triticum dicoccon*, *Triticum spelta* glume, an assemblage which on this site is probably later than the prehistoric period (see Chapter 3, *Charred Plant Remains*).

F9: Pit/hearth

A shallow pit, possibly a hearth, lay close to the gully of S14 in Trench XXXVI (Figs 2.33 and 2.35), and may have been associated with that structure. The stratigraphic relationship between the two was ambiguous and it is possible that this feature was actually significantly later than S14. Context 6130 (fill of 6139) was rich in cereal and other remains. The cereals include oats, cf. *Secale cereale*, hulled barley, naked barley, hexaploid Triticum, *Triticum aestivum*, spelt wheat, pea, and others including a glume of spelt, and a rachis node of *Triticum aestivum*; in addition there were also sedge and Bromus grain and two legume fragments per 10 litres. This is an important context containing much bread wheat but the presence of some spatter indicates smithing.

Structure 17

Structure 17 consisted of a curving gully (cut 5368) running from the western side of Trench XXIX and turning gradually south to leave the trench in the south-west corner (Fig. 2.36). It measured 0.50-0.87 m across with near-vertical sides and a flat base (Fig. 2.37). Only a 0.50 m section was excavated due to the limited time available and the constraints placed upon the excavation. The cut appeared to have a slight shelf on the northern (outer) side. The fill (5367) was a uniform dark reddish brown sandy loam containing sandstone pebbles, glacial erratics and charcoal flecks.

There were no finds either in the fill or in the layer through which it was cut, 5363. However, the building was

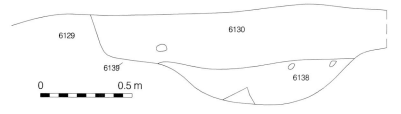

Fig. 2.35: Phase R5. Section across F9

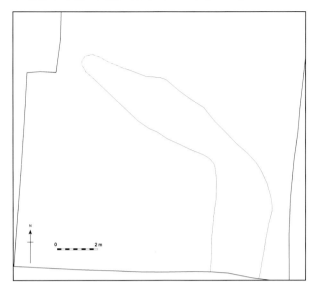

Fig. 2.36: Phase R5. Plan of S17

sealed by a layer, 5345, which contained, alongside several residual sherds of VCP, a radiate coin of Tetricus I, dated AD 271-4 (SF8255).

This structure was similar in form to Structure 14 and may have been of similar date. However, Structure 17 itself contained no datable material and can only be dated by reference to Structure 18 which sealed it. It is included here for convenience in the absence of clearer dating evidence.

Feature 2: Possible Oven

This feature was heavily disturbed by later activity so its exact shape is uncertain. The cut 9096 (Fig. 2.38) was probably originally keyhole-shaped in plan with a bulbous eastern end which narrowed to a linear portion in the west. The maximum width at the east end was approximately 1.0 m, narrowing to *c.* 0.75 m wide at the west end. The total length was 2.40 m and the feature was 0.27 m deep. The sides of the cut were nearly vertical, running sharply to a flat base which sloped slightly to the south. The lowest fill was a firm yellow clay 9094, up to 90 mm thick containing shattered igneous cobbles and charcoal flecks. This was overlain at the eastern, bulbous end by a layer of yellowish red sandy loam containing frequent sandstone pebbles and charcoal 9093. This was in turn sealed by another thick layer of clay 9033 *c.* 0.10 m deep (Fig. 2.39).

The plan of the feature suggests some function such as an oven. It is possible that this structure collapsed during

use or construction which may explain the apparent lack of fired clay.

The environmental evidence for this feature included a number of burnt glume fragments which may indicate chaff as a starter fuel within this feature (see Chapter 3, *Charred Plant Remains*). A sample from the flue of a pottery kiln at Catterick produced large numbers of charred glume bases, and heather, suggesting this material was used as fuel (Huntley and Stallibrass 1995, 52).

As excavated the feature is located just within the southern wall gully of S9. It is uncertain whether this position was deliberate and the oven was an internal structure within building S9 in Phase R7 (see Fig. 2.38).

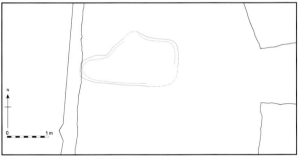

Fig. 2.38: Phase R5. Plan of F2

It is conceivable that it related to a later building on this spot, S7 in Phase EM2, or was independent of both structures. Other than two joining BB1 sherds (SF7996, SF7997), indicating a date after AD 120, the finds are undiagnostic.

Phase R6: Structures of uncertain date (possible Roman): S10, S15, S11

S10 and S15 (Fig. 2.40) are sub-rectangular or oval structures markedly different in plan to the roundhouses. S11 was a small four- or six-post structure to the south of S10. Dating evidence for S10 is slight; two sherds of late 2nd-mid 3rd-century date are presumably residual but there is no direct stratigraphical relationship between S10 and S9 in Phase R7 which appeared in the same trench, even though the post-holes of S10 were observed low in the sequence. Although possibly Roman, a later date is also feasible and it is placed in this phase for convenience.

The fact that they may form rectilinear or curvilinear structures rather than circular suggests they do not

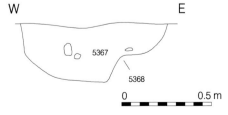

Fig. 2.37: Phase R5. Section across S17

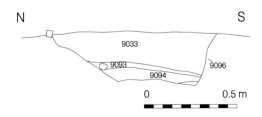

Fig. 2.39: Phase R6. Section across F2

belong to the same Romano-British phase as the roundhouses. Their position is also incompatible with their being in the same phase as other curvilinear buildings. Thus S10 overlaps S7 and S9, as well as what are interpreted as medieval buildings such as S19. S15 cuts across the area of Romano-British structures S12 and S13, which it probably post-dates. The phasing of these structures is difficult, and they fit into the Roman period only if the dating evidence for S13 is revised in accordance with the discussion above.

Structure 10

Structure 10 consists of an alignment of post-settings spaced at intervals of 1.0-2.6 m apart (average *c*. 1.50 m) in Trench XL (Fig. 2.40). The structure consisted of a post-hole alignment which can be interpreted as forming either a curvilinear structure or alternatively part of a rectilinear building, constructed using individual posts rather than foundation trenches (Fig.

2.41). The exact stratigraphic position of this structure is uncertain, as most of the features comprising it were located in areas truncated to bedrock and had no relationship to the surrounding deposits. Very few of the features composing this structure contained packing material which made them very difficult to identify so it is possible that they were cut from higher in the stratigraphic sequence. Stratigraphically it was observed lower in the sequence than Structure 9, though no direct relationships were observed between the two.

The curvilinear alignment forms an arc running roughly north-south across the centre of the trench. There is some uncertainty about the line at its northern and southern ends where there are at least two possible alternative lines depending upon which features are accepted as part of this structure. There is a possibility that some of these represent repairs to the wall at that point. Alternatively they may be part of an entrance extending into the eastern edge of the trench or one

Fig. 2.40: Phase R6. Plan of structures S10 and S15

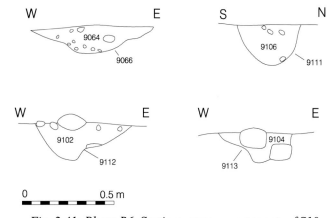

Fig. 2.41: Phase R6. Sections across components of S10

of them (cut 9146) could be part of an arrangement of internal roof supports (as seen, for example, at Court Farm, Halewood: Adams and Philpott in prep.). Whichever line is used, there is insufficient evidence to extrapolate to the dimensions of the whole building.

Like S15, S10 lies in an area where post-holes are not densely concentrated so, unlike other areas of the site, it is possible to identify potential structural alignments. However, the limited nature of the excavation means alternative reconstructions are plausible for both. If it is a curvilinear building, it might be assumed to be broadly contemporary with the other curvilinear buildings. It is not clear whether or not the ditches were still open whilst this structure was in use.

Only four of the post-hole fills contained finds. Two Nene Valley colour-coated sherds in 9103 (SF8053 and SF8054) give a *tpq* for this structure of the late 2nd-mid 3rd century or later.

The position of S10 overlaps with S7, though it is not clear which was earlier. The finds in the fill may be significant although the high degree of residuality in the later phases makes arguments based on a few sherds very unreliable. The fact that S10 was observed only as a series of cuts low down in the soil deposits suggests it might be earlier than S7, S3 and S6. This latter observation gains some weight from the interpretation of the curvilinear buildings as post-Roman in date, as buildings like S10 could be earlier than S7.

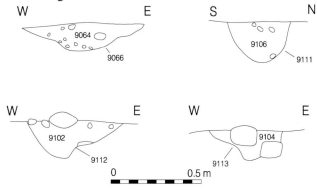

Fig. 2.42: Phase R6. Sections across S15

Structure 15

There are two main possibilities for the form of Structure 15 using the features within Trench XLI (Fig. 2.40). The exact shape of this structure is unclear although the section of it which lies in Trench XLI suggests a curvilinear or sub-rectangular building 5.50-6.50 m wide but of unknown length. It appears to have been constructed using individual posts set at 1.5-2.0 m intervals. This is similar in form, size and orientation to Structure 10.

Structure 11

At the southern end of Trench XL (Fig. 2.40) is a group of post-holes which could be interpreted as a small rectangular structure, measuring 1.2-1.5 m east-west by 1.6-1.8 m. The post-holes were composed of heavily truncated circular, polygonal and elliptical cuts cut into bedrock (Fig. 2.43). They were 0.17-0.22 m in diameter and 0.04-0.07 m deep with vertical sides and flat bases.

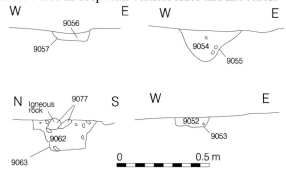

Fig. 2.43: Phase R6. Sections across S11

The larger elliptical cut was 0.41 x 0.29 m and 0.20 m deep, 9051 tapered to a point. The fills were dark greyish brown to dark reddish brown sandy loams containing red sandstone chips and charcoal.

Composed of five posts laid out in a rectangle, this structure is very similar in form to the four-post structures commonly seen on Iron Age and Romano-British rural settlements. Cuts 9063 and 9049 may also form part of this structure. The post on the north-eastern edge may be part of another structure. No finds were recovered from the fills and this part of the site was truncated to bedrock, so the date of this structure is unknown. It has been placed in this phase purely for convenience. The great number of post-holes on the site may obscure the presence of other similar structures.

The interpretation above is only one possibility for these post-holes; alternatively, they could form part of one or more structures of which post-holes are evident in neighbouring trenches to the west (XIX and XLII).

Four-post structures are common features on Iron Age sites, and have been found on other Romano-British sites in the region, including Court Farm, Halewood

(Adams and Philpott in prep.). Two four-post structures have been excavated at Lathom, West Lancashire; one pre-dates a roundhouse of the 2nd-1st century BC while the other is undated but probably late prehistoric (Cowell 2002, 3). At Brook House Farm, Halewood a four-post structure was found, in a probable association with a gully which contained Cheshire Stony VCP and produced a radiocarbon date of 830-410 cal BC (2560 ± 60 BP; Beta-118138) (Cowell and Philpott 2000b, 36-7).

Other late 3rd-4th-century features

One context, 9702, which did not obviously form part of any defined structure but lay north of S15, contained a near-complete BB1 flanged bowl dated 270-350 (SF8078). The vessel had been deliberately deposited within what may have been a post-hole, potentially cut from much higher up than the point at which it was recognised.

Phase R7: Mid-late 4th-century or later buildings: S9 and the infill of Ditches 1 and 3

Three elements of the site are attributed to the same phase, as all are associated with mid-late 4th-century finds. These comprise a building marked by foundation gullies, F1 which is a feature of uncertain function and the deliberate infilling of the enclosure ditches (Fig. 2.44). The diagnostic finds are very limited, and it is conceivable that the individual sherds in question are intrusive or, perhaps more pertinently, that they are residual late Roman material in post-Roman features.

At some point perhaps in the mid-late 4th century a rectilinear building, Structure 9, was constructed. Its relationship with S7, which overlaps this building, is

unclear, there being no unambiguous stratigraphical relationship between the two structures. However, it is considered that S7 is probably later since the post-holes of the latter structure were observed higher in the stratigraphical sequence. The scarcity of packing materials in the gullies of S9 means these were probably not identifiable at their original level.

The enclosure ditches (D1, D3) may have been infilled by this phase, as the primary fills contain pottery suggesting infilling no earlier than the mid-late 4th century. The poorly dated Ditch 4 to the north-west could have been in use at this phase or may be a later feature.

Another structure which could belong to this phase is S29. However, the radiocarbon dates provide slightly stronger, if still equivocal, evidence for a post-Roman date and accordingly it has been phased separately.

Structure 9

Structure 9 was a rectilinear building, aligned east-west, measuring internally 6.3-6.6 m wide (externally about 7.8 m wide). Only the north and south walls are clearly defined, by a series of short gullies, measuring on average 0.50 m wide but varying considerably in depth (Figs. 2.44 and 2.45). The full extent of the building was not determined but it was at least 11.5 m long and may have been at least 15 m long if two ends were formed by the post-hole alignments suggested below.

The southern wall of this structure consisted of two stretches of the same gully, located in adjacent trenches. In both trenches the gully (cuts 9116 and 8012) measured c. 0.50 m wide and c. 0.30 m deep and ran east-west across the trenches.

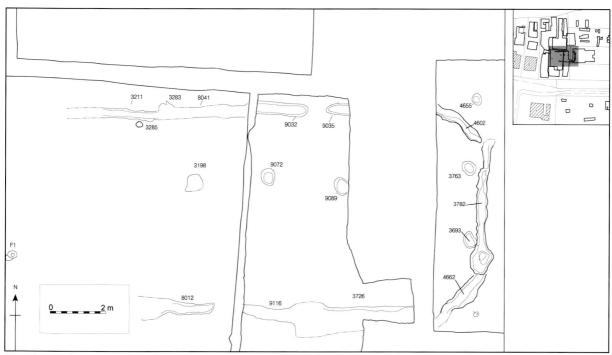

Fig. 2.44: Phase R7. Plan of Structure S9

The northern wall was composed of a linear gully very similar to that which made up the southern wall. This took the form of two linear cuts (8041, 3211) in Trench XIX. Contexts 3285, 3283 may represent repairs or alterations to this structure. In Trench XL the same wall continued as two further cuts, 9032 and 9035 apparently separated by a gap of 0.6 m, potentially marking an entrance. Three large sandstone blocks within the fill of 9032 were probably packing stones, as was a concentration of sandstone cobbles in the eastern part of the fill of 9035, while a tabular sandstone lump rested against the edge of the cut for 9022. These may mark the position of the main vertical timbers.

On the northern side a narrower foundation slot (3211) projected further to the west than the southern slot. Both the eastern and western walls appear to have consisted of post-holes rather than foundation trenches, although two possible candidates for the eastern wall need to be considered first. A possible contender for the eastern wall is a foundation gully with curving edges (3782) which could be interpreted as part of S7 (see below). The loss of the foundation gully at the west end of the south wall, however, suggests it was not always a prominent feature and it may have been so shallow as to be completely truncated in places. Alternatively, the eastern wall may have been formed by a north-south row of four post-holes in XXI spaced at regular intervals of just over 2.5 m centre to centre, which are probably the best candidates for the east wall of this building. The finds are not diagnostic of date but include industrial waste and in two cases abraded Romano-British pottery. The most convincing alignment is shown in Figure 2.44. However, this is far from certain and the same post-holes could form part of S21 (see below).

The fill of gully 4662 (4660) contained a sherd of undiagnostic BB1, another of oxidised ware and a sherd of undated but possible colour-coated ware sherd, SF6200. If a Wilderspool fabric, as is possible, it is likely to date to AD 90-230.

As for the western end of the building, it was difficult to isolate likely post-holes amongst the mass of features in the area around S12 and S13, and it appears to have been obscured or truncated by dense pitting.

Several of the features inside this structure may be internal supports for the roof but it has been impossible to determine their stratigraphic relationship with the gullies and they may form part of other structures. The most likely possibilities for the northern half are shown on Figure 2.44; other features in the area are not stratigraphically contemporary or unsuitably placed. Several possible candidates exist for the southern half, though all are most likely later than this structure.

A series of post-holes and smaller cuts were stratigraphically contemporary with this structure in Trenches XIX and XL. Some of these may represent internal arrangements such as roof supports. Alternatively they may have belonged to another undefined structure.

Relationship between S9 and S13

Two stratigraphic relationships were crucial to the broad phasing of the site and of the structural sequence. First, the fact that the southern foundation gully of S9 was overlain by the cobble wall of a later stone building, S19, provides clear stratigraphic evidence that this building pre-dates the later medieval occupation.

The second key element of the stratigraphy concerns the relationship between the roundhouse S13 and the rectangular structure S9. The relationship depends on two observations. First, it was considered during excavation that the northern wall slot of S9, 3211, ran up as far as the 'dumb-bell'-shaped stone-packed trench for S13 (cut 3202), which was later taken to mean the gully cut the stone-filled feature. Secondly, the two structures were recognised at different levels during excavation, elements of S9 being recognised lower in the stratigraphic sequence than S13. The gully for S9 (3209) was recognised after removal of layer 3118 although it had shown as a dark stain during the cleaning of 3118; the dumb-bell-shaped element of S13, with its fill 3117 and its packing stones showed up in the surface of 3118 and 3119, so this feature (cut 3202) certainly cut those layers.

At face value, these two considerations taken together should indicate that the roundhouse S13 was later than building S9. However, there are two important grounds for believing that this is unlikely. First, the sequence of a late Roman rectangular building succeeded by a circular one would run counter to the general rule that circular buildings of Roman date are superseded by rectangular ones. Secondly, the sequence suggested by the diagnostic finds would be overturned. In view of the importance of this relationship, the stratigraphy was re-examined and an alternative sequence proposed.

First, the possibility should be considered that the foundation slot 3211 was in fact dug across the stone-packed trench 3202 but failed to show up because of the massive stone filling in the latter feature. As a relatively shallow feature at its western end it would not be inconceivable for the foundation trench 3211 to have been carried over the stone packing in 3202 rather than removing it, the stones of the underlying feature providing a solid foundation for the posts and panels of the rectangular one. However, as the gully itself was not recognised until somewhat later in the excavation than the stone-packed feature (3202), the two features were not exposed together so the relationship could not be examined during excavation.

The second consideration is that the foundation gully was very difficult to see in the prevailing soil conditions. Not only were strong reservations expressed at the time of excavation over the precise level from which the southern gully 8012 was cut, but also another structural element of S9 (8041) did not show up until lower down in the sequence, and was moved up the matrix during post-excavation analysis to match 3211 with which it was interpreted as being associated.

The southern gully of S9, 8012 (fill 8011), was observed after removal of 3204 and 3227 (spits) but the feature had been observed previously in the sides of two post-holes and it was noted that it only showed up against sandstone brash, but was suspected to have been cut from higher up as conditions at the time of excavation were hot and dry, making it impossible to detect slight soil differences.

One further piece of evidence is that of finds in the fills of the structures and in the layers through which the features cut. One of the stretches of gully in S9 (9032 in Trench XL) contained a mid-late 4th-century sherd of shell-tempered ware (SF7823), while the south wall has a sherd of central Gaulish samian and a BB1 rim (SF7033), dated broadly to AD 200-350 (J. Evans pers. comm.) in context 8011 which filled 8012. None of the finds in the fills of the roundhouse S13 need date to any later than the 2nd century. However, the layers cut by S13 include 4th-century finds, though few are closely diagnostic. The single shell-tempered sherd in S9 could of course be intrusive, even though it was well stratified. However, the weight of finds evidence does argue for both the roundhouse S13 and S9 being relatively late in the Roman period. Although the dating evidence for both S13 and S9 indicates that both may belong to the late 4th century or later, the sequence of the two buildings makes it more likely if both are Romano-British that a circular building was replaced by a rectangular one. Unfortunately the evidence is not particularly strong for either case.

The apparent stratigraphical problem may be another product of the difficult circumstances of excavation. In the very dry conditions the relatively stone-free foundation gully of S9 failed to show up at a high level in the sequence as there was insufficient contrast between the fill and the surrounding soil deposit. By contrast, the relevant section of S13 was heavily packed with sandstone and was therefore recognised as soon as the top of the packing stones became visible.

Infilling of Enclosure Ditches 1 and 3

This phase saw the infilling of the enclosure ditches, Ditch 1 and Ditch 3, although there is not a great deal of datable material in Ditch 3 to determine the date of its disuse and infilling. Several sherds occurred in primary fills but had wide date ranges which could, with one

exception, allow a mid 3rd-century date for the infilling of the ditch without invoking a substantial degree of residuality. Thus an abraded mid-late 4th-century shell-tempered ware jar rim in the primary fill of Ditch 3 (context 680; SF1018) could conceivably be intrusive as it occurred in an area of animal burrowing. However, the late date is supported by other datable material contained in primary fills, a BB1 sherd dated 200-350 (context 6219) and a mid 2nd-late 4th-century Nene valley sherd (context 702). If the long-lived types were manufactured towards the end of their date ranges, the infilling could have occurred in the mid-late 4th century, allowing the shell-tempered ware sherd to be contemporary with the fill rather than intrusive. The late 4th-century date for the infilling is supported by a shell-tempered ware sherd from a secondary fill, 700 (SF1062). The medieval sherd in the later fill 6468 (SF10608) may result from either an unrecognised cut feature or from settlement of medieval layers into the compressed Roman ditch fills.

Finds in Ditch 1 included, alongside a few undiagnostic BB1 and oxidised ware sherds, one BB1 sherd dated 240-270 and another of 3rd-4th-century date, as well as one Nene valley colour-coated sherd of mid 2nd-late 4th in an upper fill (see also Tables 2.2, 2.3). Although the evidence is slight, the balance of probability comes down on the side of the enclosure ditches being filled in during the 4th century or later.

Within the eastern enclosure, the fills of Ditch 1 included large sandstone blocks along with a few relatively large unabraded fragments of pottery and a broken sandstone rotary quern (SF8373). The nature of the deposits suggests the ditch was rapidly and deliberately infilled, in part with discarded building material, in a purposeful act to level off the area, and perhaps create a larger area unencumbered by ditches. Ditch 3 also appears to have been deliberately backfilled after an initial silting. A deposit of sand and broken sandstone (660, 700) above the primary fill appeared to be bank material derived from upcast of the rock-cut ditch pushed back in.

It is conceivable that another ditch (D4) was created at this time to the north of Ditch 3 to expand the internal area and erase the internal partition whilst retaining the enclosure itself. However, the lack of good dating evidence in Ditch 4 and the poor stratigraphic information makes this uncertain. What does seem clear is that the enclosure ditches were infilled before the construction of two curvilinear buildings (S3, S6) for which the dating is discussed below.

Feature 1

Feature 1 consisted of a shallow circular cut (8154), measuring 0.34 m in diameter and 0.10 m deep (Fig. 2.44). It was filled by a very dark brown sandy loam (8083) with frequent, occasionally quite large, charcoal inclusions. Yellow clay was also present at the southern

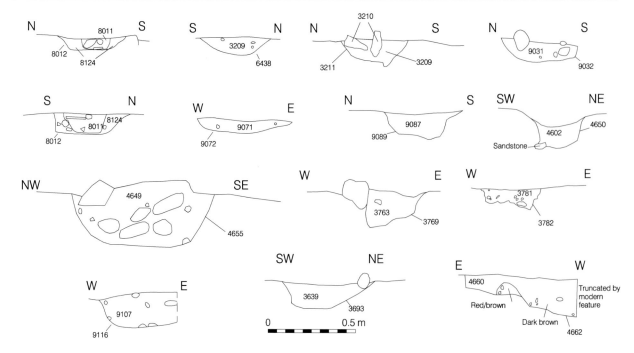

Fig. 2.45: Phase R7. Sections across features in S9

end. Burnt animal bone was present within the fill and three sandstone cobbles up to 0.95 m across. The presence of calcined bone may indicate a rubbish pit which included disposal of burnt food remains. The fill contained a single six-rowed barley rachis internode, a hulled barley grain and a single emmer grain which, if this is a Roman feature, ought to be residual material. There were no other finds from the fill 8083.

Phase R8: Late Roman or later ditches

Ditch 4

A further ditch, Ditch 4, was observed running parallel to Ditch 3 on its northern side. Ditch 4 was represented by a linear cut 6285 measuring 0.48-0.55 m wide and *c.* 0.20 m deep, which ran east-west across the northern end of Trench XXXVI (Fig. 2.46). The sides sloped gently at about 30° to a slightly dished base. This feature was not located in the trenches to the east or west, though an area of heavily disturbed ground at the eastern end of Trench XXVII may represent the last vestiges of this feature. At its eastern end in Trench XXXVI it was truncated by a large modern pit and it is possible that any continuation to the east lay just outside the northern end of Trench VI.

There was only a small amount of cultural material in the fill, including a small BB1 sherd (SF10571) and small fragments of greyware (SF6971). The small size of the fragments suggests they may have been residual occupation material rather than freshly deposited rubbish contemporary with its infilling.

It is uncertain whether Ditch 4 belongs to the Roman period and formed an extension to the area of the

enclosure. It ran closely parallel to Ditch 3 and may therefore respect its alignment. It could therefore represent the second enclosure ditch of a bivallate enclosure. Alternatively, as suggested above, it might instead represent the expansion of the enclosed area by moving the boundary line northwards. However, the virtually complete lack of finds within the ditch and its rather different appearance, with a shallower profile, very sandy fill and poorly defined cut, make it likely to belong to a different phase.

It may be significant that the field boundary immediately to the north of Ditch 4 follows almost exactly the same alignment. The boundary is shown on the earliest surviving map of Irby dated 1824. However, it is likely to be of considerably greater antiquity as it forms the boundary between the parishes of Woodchurch and Thurstaston within the township of Irby (see Chapter 5).

Period V: Late Roman - Early Medieval Period (4th-10th/12th century)

The existence of structures of late Roman or post-Roman date, in the broadest sense, is indicated by the presence of several structures which form up to eight phases of construction. Although the direct dating evidence is poor, the identification of a sequence of activity together with the use of distinctive building plans and sparse finds make a strong case for a sequence of occupation extending from the early to late medieval period.

The infilling of the enclosure ditches and the erection of buildings very close to their former line, or in one case across the infilled ditch, suggest that the enclosure formed by Ditches 1 and 3 was no longer functioning. The possibility that the enclosure was enlarged to the north by Ditch 4 is discussed above.

There is only a single artefact, a near-complete spike lamp (discussed below), which supports an early medieval date for these structures. It is considered that the Roman pottery from the fills of the foundation gullies of the curvilinear buildings (S3, S6, S7) is residual. However, the early medieval period was virtually aceramic in the north west, with the exception of the largely urban phenomenon of Chester Ware (Rutter 1985), and the scarcity of metalwork and other diagnostic finds is equally notorious (see Chapter 5 for discussion of this point). The possibility of an early medieval date is enhanced by the radiocarbon dates for S29 which extend to the mid 5th and the end of the 6th century. The radiocarbon dates from the feature, combined with a coin which has a *tpq* of *c.* AD 340, may indicate that the site did not cease to be occupied with the end of Roman administration in Britain.

Stratigraphically, the curvilinear buildings appear to post-date the circular buildings and must therefore belong to the very end of the Roman period or later. These are not closely paralleled elsewhere as Romano-British buildings and their form in plan is more reminiscent of post-Roman structures observed elsewhere in Britain. These buildings are discussed in more detail below.

Phase EM1: Late Roman-Early Medieval (late 4th century – 6th century AD)

One structure, S29, may belong to the very late Roman or early medieval period. The arguments for this dating are considered below. It should be noted, however, that this structure may belong in the same phase as S9, Phase R7.

Structure 29

Structure 29 consists of a foundation gully or trench (cut 9579) at the extreme south end of Trench XLI (Fig. 2.47), which measured at least 3.40 m long, 1.10 m wide and 0.08-0.40 m deep. The sides sloped gently at about 45° to a flat base (Fig. 2.48), while at the eastern end there was a distinct step towards the base about 0.05 m deep. The fill sat around two groups of angular, sub-angular and rounded sandstone cobbles up to 0.43 m across though most were *c.* 0.20 by 0.20 m. No order could be seen to the packing of these blocks which appeared to have been tipped in with the fill. The gully appeared to be the foundation trench for a rectilinear building, the stones perhaps forming packing material which was disturbed on demolition of the structure. It lies on the southern edge of the main excavated area and presumably belongs to a largely unexcavated structure, of unknown dimensions, further to the south.

The fill of the foundation gully contained a small amount of Romano-British pottery. Two sherds are diagnostic: SF7995 in context 9603 is a mid 2nd-century grey ware jar rim, while SF7988 in 9567 is BB1 with obtuse lattice decoration dated to AD 200-350. Rather more closely datable is a *Constantinopolis* coin, issued AD 337-340 (SF7991), in context 9603. The same context produced two radiocarbon dates, both from barley, of 350-600 cal AD and 230-440 cal AD (OxA-9557 and OxA-9668; Table 2.1). The finds and radiocarbon dating make it impossible to distinguish between a late Roman feature, of the second half of the 4th century, and one which dates to the 5th or 6th century but contains residual Romano-British material.

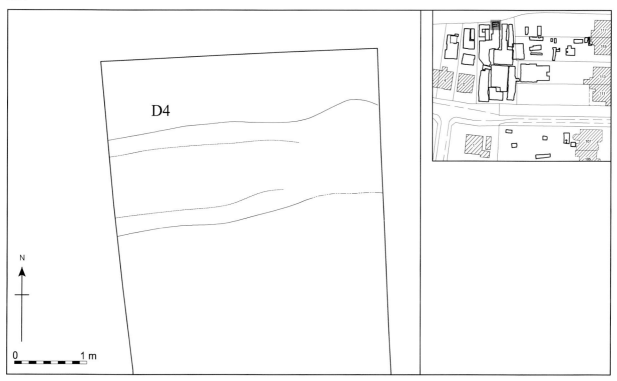

Fig. 2.46: Phase R8. Plan of Ditch 4

As excavated, the gully was interpreted as sealed by layer 9505 but in post-excavation analysis it was considered possible that the gully cut through 9505, on the grounds that packing stones were visible higher up. In that case, the gully was sealed by 9503, an occupation deposit at the base of ploughsoil. Context 9505 contained some Romano-British pottery; alongside two earlier, residual BB1 sherds (AD 120-200) are SF7778, a BB1 jar sherd dated 160-200 and also SF7645, a BB1 flanged bowl dated possibly 270-350.

Phase EM2: Structures S3, S6, S7, S24: Anglo-Scandinavian to Norman period, 10th-12th century

The next major phase of construction consists of two distinct groups of contexts, representing four structures. The first group comprises several stretches of flat-bottomed curvilinear gullies. In no case was the full extent of the gullies recovered but their form and the presence of concentrations of packing stones along their length suggest they are foundation gullies for buildings rather than palisade slots for fences. They have been interpreted as forming three curvilinear buildings, S3, S6 and S7 (Fig. 2.49 and 2.52). The stratigraphic relationships between these buildings and the roundhouses, S12 and S13, were not well defined and their dating to this phase is largely by analogy with other sites (see Chapter 5).

The second group of contexts consists of a well-defined building with a stone foundation, S16, which has been assigned to this phase on the grounds that it appears to post-date the Roman occupation and the ditched enclosure, whilst being sealed by the clay floor of a probable medieval building, S18. The curvilinear nature of the wall may denote a cultural association with the other structures of this form. However, the details of its construction were very different from S3, S6 and S7 so it has been assigned to a phase in its own right (EM3). The full argument for the dating is discussed in Chapter 5.

The construction of three curvilinear buildings represents a substantial reorganisation of the settlement. Their position suggests that the enclosure ditches could not have remained open at the same time. One appears to cut an enclosure ditch, another lies over the ditch alignment and the third lies so close to the ditch that it would intrude on any internal bank. Thus, if the curvilinear buildings formed part of a single phase of construction, the enclosure ditches must already have been filled in. The disuse and infilling of the enclosure ditches appears to have taken place in the mid-late 4th century from the sparse datable finds (Tables 2.2, 2.3), although a later date for the infilling is conceivable if residual Roman material were incorporated in the fills. The curvilinear structures by themselves are not well dated. They post-date the Roman period on stratigraphical grounds so the relatively small quantity of finds within the fills, which in most cases consists of Romano-British pottery or undiagnostic clay or industrial waste, is residual.

The fourth structure, S24, is situated to the south (Fig. 2.52). It is significantly different from the other structures in this phase, as it is rectilinear and constructed using individual posts. However, it is dated to this phase by finds evidence from within the fill of one of the post settings.

Stratigraphic Relationships for Phase EM2

The direct stratigraphic evidence for the dating of these structures is poor and in some respects contradictory and they are dated largely by analogy with other sites.

The most crucial relationship was in the south-western corner of Trench VIII, where structures S12, S13 and S7 all converge. The existence of the first two of these buildings had not been recognised when this trench was excavated. In addition, the alignment of the three structures was later seen to have just cut across the corner of the trench with very little of the features visible. The packing stone fill of S13 is clearly visible as context 1160 but its southern portion where the gully 1113 (of S7) would have met has been removed by a large stone-filled pit (1081), destroying any evidence of the relationship between the two structures.

The second important stratigraphic relationship concerns the foundation gully for S3 and the north-south enclosure ditch (D1). The rock-cut foundation gully for S3 cut the north-south palisade slot, S2, but was disturbed by the digging of a later pit (F3) close to Ditch 1. A narrow section of intact rock between the edge of the pit and the lip of the ditch had been cut by a slot (3773) which continued the projected line of gully (3787) of S3. During the excavation it was considered that the foundation gully of S3 was cut by the ditch, as there was no sign of the gully running across the top of the ditch, nor did the gully reappear in the bedrock to the east of the ditch. However, given the tendency for the upper fills of ditches to settle and consolidate, it would be far from easy to recognise a shallow feature which lacked stone packing running across the infilled ditch. It is therefore conceivable that the ditch had actually been filled in before the gully for S3 was dug. Consequently there is no direct evidence for the relative date of this building and the ditch. Although the fill of S3 contained two sherds broadly dated up to the early 3rd century, these could be residual.

A third stratigraphic relationship involves the relative sequence of S1 and S7. There is some evidence that the eastern end of S7 (assuming this to be formed by 3782, discussed below) also cut the circular or curvilinear S1 of Phase R4, though this merely proves that S7 post-dates the early-mid 2nd-4th century AD.

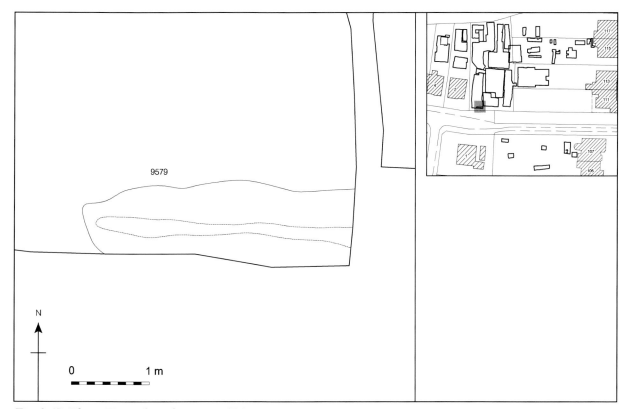

Fig. 2.47: Phase EM1. Plan of structure S29

One important stratigraphical relationship is that the gully of S3 (3786, 3787) was clearly cut by the foundation gully 3684, which was seen as part of a building of uncertain form, S8b (see Phase EM4 below).

Structure 3

Structure 3 is represented by a stretch of curving gully in the north of Trench XXI (Fig. 2.49). The gully measured 6.3 m long (3786, 3787), with a gap and a further slot (3773) representing a continuation with a total length of 8.0 m. The gully was *c*. 0.50 m wide but only 0.10 m deep (Fig. 2.50). There was a continuation of the line of the gully to the east, which survives as a shallow cut (3773) in an upstanding section of bedrock between the cut of Ditch 1 to the east and a rock cut pit 3724 to the west. There was no sign of a continuation of the gully in Trench IX to the east of the ditch but the bedrock was very high on that part of the site and the occupation deposits in that area had also been completely removed down to the bedrock. It is possible that such a shallow feature, if it did not cut the bedrock, would have been truncated at that point. The total dimensions of this structure are uncertain, there is little of the total plan available and it remains a possibility that the gully is

a palisade slot for a fence rather than an enclosed and roofed building.

There is a slight hint of a change in alignment at the western end as if it makes a small turn and there is also a large stone-packed post-hole at this point. The gully of S7 in Trench VIII also had post-holes along its alignment; perhaps they were excavated as discrete features simply because the packing stones showed up well before the rock-cut gully itself.

Residual Roman finds in the foundation gully (fill 3766) include only two datable sherds. One of these, SF4960, is a mid 2nd-early 3rd-century white-slipped orange ware sherd, the other, SF4962, is in a Wilderspool fabric so probably dates to AD 90-230. There is also industrial waste in two sections of gully, indicating metalworking prior to the construction of the building.

Structure 6

Structure 6 consists of a curving stretch of foundation gully (Figs. 2.49 and 2.51) 0.50-0.60 m wide in Trench VIII (cut 1155, fill 1154; cut 1083, fills 1082, 1084). It was filled with a dark sandy loam containing large amounts of charcoal, especially in the lowest fill, and some lumps of yellow clay measuring up to 100 mm across, the latter possibly representing structural daub but no coherent form was evident. In addition there was a slightly raised concentration of small

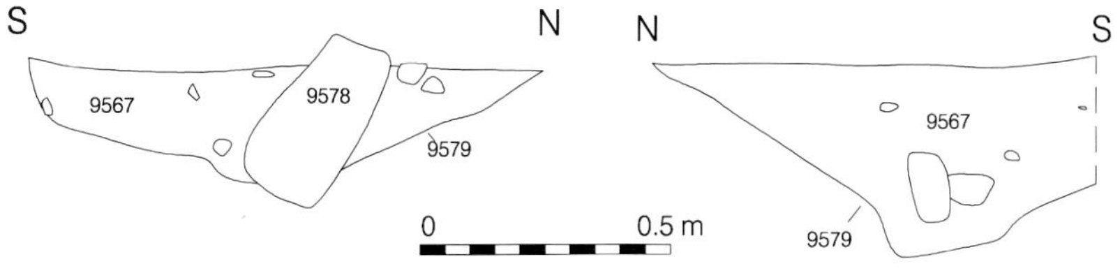

Fig. 2.48: Phase EM1, section across features in S29

55

stones against the sides of the cut. Clusters of small, rounded sandstone cobbles occurred at intervals of approximately 0.50 m but no obvious structure could be seen to these groups. The gully was at its deepest to the east but towards the baulk was becoming increasingly shallow, suggesting that it may not have survived to the west where it would have to have been cut into bedrock and the western part of this structure could not be traced in the adjacent trench to the west, Trench XXXVI.

The western part of the structure may have been constructed using individual posts rather than a continuous trench but there are few post-holes which fit a coherent pattern and as a consequence the overall plan of the structure is difficult to determine. However, the excavated portion forming the eastern end suggests a curvilinear building. The southern wall of this structure is presumed to lie in the unexcavated area between Trenches VIII and XXXVI. The eastern end of the building was found to have a gently bowed form, with slight but distinct angles from which the curving sides ran, as distinct from the more angular form of S7. The maximum observed width was about 5.50 m but in the absence of structural evidence for the western portion the overall length of the building could not be determined.

One post-hole (cut 1176: fill 1175) had been cut in the base of the gully (1155) near the north-east corner of the structure (Fig 2.49). Two further post-holes (1053 and 1126) were set on the precise line of the gully and may have been part of the structure, though 1053 may equally be part of Structure 21, Phase EM2. Post-hole 1126 contained six large tabular and sub-rounded sandstone cobbles used as packing for a post. Tabular blocks were set against the northern and western edges of the cut, while other rounded blocks surrounded a central void *c.* 0.15 m across. These stones sat in a matrix of dark brown sandy loam containing shattered igneous rock, sandstone pebbles, lumps of yellow clay up to 100 mm across and charcoal flecks. A very large lump of clay sealed the central void. The gully (1155) widened significantly at its south-eastern end to 0.77 m and was also slightly deeper at this point and it is possible that this too accommodated a post.

One post-hole, 1049, which occupies a central location at the east end of the building, may be an internal roof support.

Dating evidence for this structure is sparse. Finds within the gully fill include white ware, amphora sherds and two fragments of BB1 jar with obtuse lattice, dated AD 200-350. In the gully (fill 1154) and in the vicinity there are also several joining sherds of Dressel 20 amphora, dated to the 1st-3rd century AD. This form was originally used for the transport of olive oil but is likely in this rural context to be reused (Tyers 1996, 87). The finds are almost certainly residual.

It was difficult to determine the precise level from which the gully 1155 was cut. During excavation, it was recognised cutting through layers 3336, 3343, 3345, and 1110. In post-excavation analysis it was reinterpreted as having been cut from a higher level, at least through layer 1104 and possibly also through 1038 on the grounds that a linear band of clay was visible in 1104 at the same point. This area of clay, though, may relate to later buildings and there appears to be no sign of it on the plan at that higher level. Layer 1104 contains one calcite-gritted ware sherd (SF4082, so late 4th century) and a BB1 sherd (SF4083, dated 240-350), suggesting a late Roman date. A limited environmental assemblage included a few grains of hulled barley, a Triticum floret base and a fragment of hazelnut shell and a Bromus sp. grain. Layer 1038 contains some Roman pottery and an early 4th-century coin (SF3997). If 1155 did cut 1038, then the coin in 1038 gives the building a *tpq* of AD 318/320. If it is post-320 then it would post-date the ditch immediately to the north.

Furthermore, if S6 cut 1038, then it is most unlikely to be contemporary with the enclosure ditch which is very close by to the north (1.7 m between the southern edge of the ditch and the edge of the gully), since it overlaps with the position of any bank inside the ditch. They are unlikely to have co-existed unless there was no internal bank at this point. Thus, taking account of the uncertainties discussed above, this indicates a *tpq* for the building of AD 320 based on the presence of the coin and of the late 4th century if the calcite-gritted ware is not intrusive, but reservations over the integrity of the layers make this uncertain. Crucially, the infilling of the ditch in the 4th century provides a *tpq* for S6.

Structure 7

Structure 7 is represented by an 8.5 m length of shallow east-west gully (1113) with a distinct curve in Trench VIII (Fig 2.52, Plate XIV). The gully had a flat base and steep or vertical sides, and was cut largely into sandstone (Fig. 2.53). Set along the line of the gully were a number of stone-packed post-holes which were observed before the cut of the gully itself became visible but their position within the gully suggests they formed part of the structure, supporting the main vertical timbers.

Tracing the rest of the structure is difficult amid the numerous post-holes to the south, west and east. A possible eastern end is to be found in Trench XXI as a length of straight gully (3782) with curving returns at either end (cut 4662 to the south; 4602 to the north) although, as discussed above, this could also be part of Structure 9 in Phase R7 (see Fig. 2.44). The northern return (4602) may connect with the gully of S7. The picture is confused by a short straight slot (3737) which has the same alignment but was seen at a higher level and is very likely to belong to a separate structure (see Structure 8a, Phase EM4).

Fig. 2.49: Phase EM2, Plan of structures S3 and S6

If the building is assumed to be symmetrical, it would have had dimensions in the order of approximately 18 x 13 m. Given the large size of this reconstructed structure, an alternative interpretation is that the eastern end of S7 fell within the unexcavated area between Trenches XL and XXI. In that case, the gully 3782 may form the eastern end of S9 (see above).

The western end may be marked by post-holes rather than a gully but there is no clear evidence of this. The

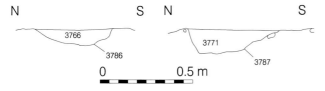

Fig. 2.50: Phase EM2. Section of features in structure S3

area where the western wall is likely to have been positioned contains a dense mass of post-holes from a succession of buildings and recognising discrete alignments is very difficult. In addition, a building of such a width must have had internal posts to bridge the roof span. There are a few post-holes which may fit this role but identification of suitable candidates is complicated by the presence of S9 (see above), which may have had aisle posts in similar positions to those expected in S7.

The fill of the main gully 1113 (1112) contains four sherds of Romano-British pottery, none of which is closely datable. Three sherds are of oxidised ware and one is BB1, the latter at least providing a *tpq* of AD 120. There is also a quantity of fired clay which includes SF4514, part of an oven plate or cover, and a piece of ceramic roof-tile (SF4513). There is only a very small quantity of highly fragmentary and abraded roof-tile at the site, and certainly far too little to roof even a small structure (see Chapter 4, *Roman Tile*). It is likely to have been brought into the site in small quantities for purposes which cannot now be determined. However, the material in the fill is highly likely to be residual.

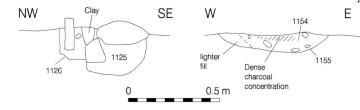

Fig. 2.51: Phase EM2. Sections across S6

During excavation, gully 1113, was observed as cutting layer1109 and being sealed by 1085, but in post-excavation analysis the gully was reinterpreted as also cutting 1039. Layer 1039 contains much Roman pottery, as well as residual VCP, and an occasional intrusive post-medieval sherd. The component post-hole cuts (1090, 1092, 1097 and 1070) were considered on excavation to cut 1085. Layer 1085 has a few BB1 sherds and other undiagnostic Roman pottery alongside some residual prehistoric pottery. Other post-holes (1087, 1091 and 1117) were excavated as part of the gully.

Some confidence in ascribing this plan to a structure as opposed to a palisade gully, for example, is lent by other buildings here. S6 (see above) has a slightly curving end wall and flaring side walls, even though the remainder of the structure could not be traced. Similarly S3 has a curving gully with a hint of an angle and a return to the gully. Thus at Irby there is no complete plan for a structure of this type but only fragments of three buildings of curvilinear type. In plan, the bow-sided walls of S7 and possibly S3 are reminiscent of an aisled building about 20 m long at Roystone Grange, Derbyshire, which was demolished about AD 250-300 (Hodges 1991, 76, fig. 55). The platform for the structure at Roystone also has straight ends, providing a parallel for the curving stretch of gully to the north east of S7. There are also some similarities with curvilinear buildings excavated at Court Farm Halewood which have been dated to the 3rd to 4th century (Adams and Philpott in prep.) though these have more rounded ends than the Irby examples. However, the stratigraphy

Plate XIII: Structure S6 (cut 1155), from the east

at Irby suggests this is an early medieval building, consistent with the majority of parallels for bow-sided structures (see Chapter 5).

Structure 24: Probable Rectilinear Building, 10th-12th century

A small fragment of a building was formed by a group of post-pits in Trench XXV/XXVI (Figs 2.52 and 2.54, Plate XV). The main element was a T-shaped cut (5043) into bedrock, with a large post-pit beyond the end of each arm of the 'T' (5055, 5063), which measured at least 1 m across. The total dimensions of 5043 were 1.60 m east-west by 1.91 m, the two arms measured 0.75 m wide and the cut was 0.30 m deep. A smaller post-hole (5030) to the north of the junction may also have belonged to the same structure.

Plate XIV: Gully of Structure S7 (1113) from the east

The lowest fill of 5043 was a dark reddish brown silty sand containing charcoal flecks and small fragments of stone. This material only occurred on the eastern side of the cut and appeared to represent a weathered deposit. Sealing this were dumps of yellowish brown clay spread across the base of the cut; this was in turn sealed by large sandstone blocks up to 0.22 m across. Mixed in with this material were pieces of industrial waste, clay fragments and the cresset or spike lamp (SF4888). This was in turn sealed by a thin layer of mid reddish brown silty sand.

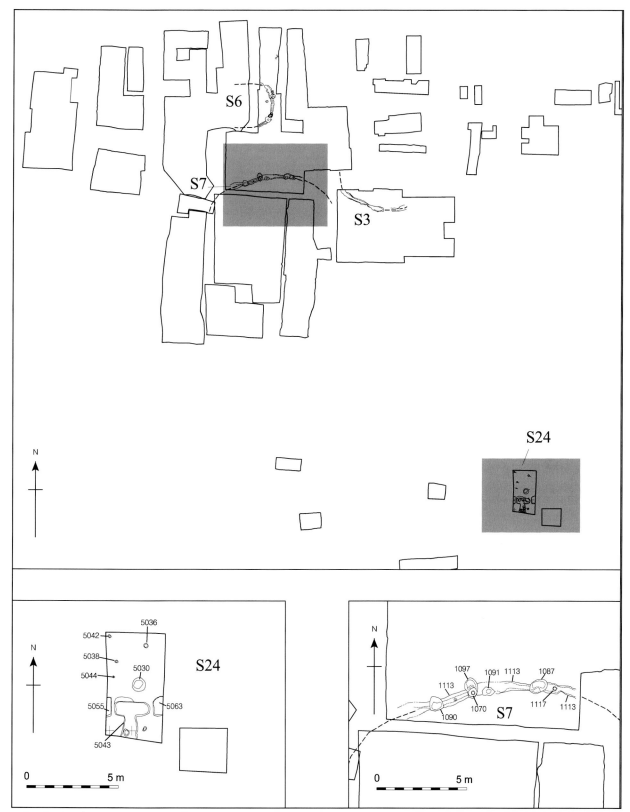

Fig. 2.52: Phase EM2. Plans of structures S24 and S7

The large post-pit to the west, context 5055, contained a dark reddish brown silty sand with occasional small sandstone fragments and charcoal flecks. It was about 0.14 m deep and measured about 1.0 m north-south but the western part lay under the baulk. The eastern post-pit, context 5063, had a similar fill and dimensions.

Post-hole (5030), lay to the north of the T-shaped cut,

5043. The lowest fill of cut 5030 was a thin layer of mid-brown fine silty sand 30-40 mm thick (5029). This was sealed by a substantial tabular sandstone block laid flat on the base of the cut which the excavator interpreted as a post-pad. This is almost certainly incorrect as the pit was cut into very stable bedrock and a pad stone would be unnecessary. The upper part was filled by a mid reddish brown silty sand containing clay

59

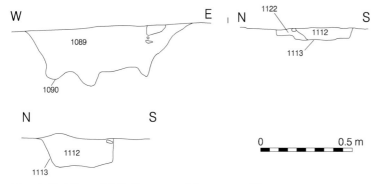

Fig. 2.53: Phase EM2. Sections of features in S7

nodules, charcoal flecks and sandstone pebbles. This fill also contained a substantial fragment of a sandstone bee-hive quern (SF8268, Fig. 4.6, no 59; see Chapter 4, *Other stone objects*). The quern (also recorded as context 5045) probably represents packing material re-deposited in the cut after the removal of the post.

The fills of 5043 (5034, 5048, 5052, 5057, 5058 and 5061) contained a single sherd of VCP, a considerable quantity of Romano-British pottery, and the Saxo-Norman spike lamp. The prehistoric and Romano-British pottery is therefore residual in a 10th-12th-century feature. The fills of the adjacent post-pits 5055 and 5063 are also relatively rich in Romano-British pottery, but if they are correctly seen as part of S24 with 5043 then the material is all residual. There is a predominance of greyware, at least one sherd of which appears to be a BB1 copy of 3rd or 4th-century date, but also a little oxidised ware and an amphora sherd are present. The fill of 5030 also has three sherds of Romano-British grey ware alongside two fragments of industrial waste.

A group of four smaller post-holes (5036, 5042, 5038 5044) may be associated with the structure, whether structurally or as an external fence or similar element, or they might form part of an earlier post-built structure. They are placed in this phase for convenience.

In view of the large size of the post-holes and their packing stones, Structure 24 appears to be part of a substantial timber post-built structure. The row of

three elements 5055, 5043 and 5063 may indicate a principal wall while the T-shaped cut suggests the junction of an internal partition with the main wall. The limited evidence is reminiscent of the large post-pits in Saxo-Norman buildings at the early medieval manor at Goltho, Lincs. (Beresford 1987), Mellor, Greater Manchester (Newman C. 2006, 119, fig. 5.4; Mellor Archaeological Trust 2006) and at Forden Gaer, Montgomeryshire, the latter measured *c.* 40 by 15 m with aisle posts 8.5 m apart (Blockley 1990). However, the limited extent of the structure recovered precludes further comment on the dimensions and overall plan of the structure. A set of similarly sized post-holes in Trench XLV to the south west may be related (Plate XV) to this structure, though the area exposed was insufficient to confirm this.

The relatively high concentration of Romano-British pottery in the fills of the component post-holes suggests that this part of the site saw considerable activity in the Roman period. It indicates that the settlement and occupation extended at least this far south during that period.

Discussion of the phase

Both spatially and stratigraphically all three curvilinear buildings formed by gullies (S3, S6, S7) and the stone foundation S16 (in Phase EM3) could have co-existed together on the site, although S3 and S7 are rather close together, with a gap of only 0.8 m. This narrow gap might suggest the buildings developed sequentially, perhaps over some decades, rather than all being in contemporary use.

S7 lies well within the western ditched enclosure, and may have replaced S13, the latest of the sequence of circular/polygonal buildings. Of the other three curvilinear buildings, S3 appears to overlie the infilled ditch (Ditch 1), so construction of S3 requires the enclosure to have gone out of use. Both S6 and S16 lie

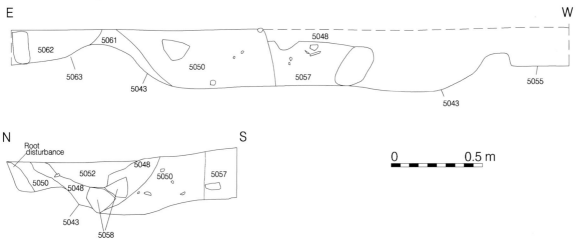

Fig. 2.54: Phase EM2. Sections across features in structure S24

Plate XV: Structure S24 from the south

uncomfortably close to the northern enclosure ditch (D3) and are unlikely to have been constructed so close to an open feature. Although S3 and S7 need not have been contemporary, it is uncertain which was the earlier. A plausible scenario is that all four buildings post-date the infilled enclosure ditches and represent a phase of the site when the Romano-British ditched enclosure has been obliterated. The buildings pay no heed to the existence of the infilled ditches and may represent the establishment of a farmstead on a site where signs of earlier habitation were evident but not sufficient to influence in detail the layout of the new settlement. It is conceivable that the ditches survived as visible hollows and were finally fully infilled in order to lay out the new settlement. Both Ditches 1 and 3 appear to have been deliberately infilled, using some of the bank material and disposing of stone blocks and a broken quern in the fill. The infilling may have taken place during the 4th century but the possibility that this occurred even some centuries later cannot be wholly discounted. The absence of diagnostic early medieval cultural material from the ditches does not automatically rule out the possibility, since the region as a whole has produced few datable finds for the whole early medieval period. Alternatively the site could have remained in occupation from the late Roman continuously through the early medieval period, though in the absence of material culture or unequivocal radiocarbon dates this too is incapable of proof. The radiocarbon dates from S29 open the possibility of an early post-Roman date, while the stratigraphic sequence, however uncertain in matters of detail, requires some activity between the late Roman period and the 13th century.

The existence on the site of at least two phases which post-dated the Roman period but pre-dated the high medieval is supported by two categories of finds. In an isolated trench (XXV/XXVI) in the southern part of the site a Saxo-Norman lamp was found in a building foundation trench. The near-complete spike lamp (SF4888: Fig. 4.14, no 208) of probable 10th to 12th-century AD date within the fill of the foundation gully

5043 of Structure 24 confirms that at least one of these features was Saxo-Norman in date. The function of this group of features is undoubtedly structural, and most can be easily accommodated in a single building. All of the features in Trench XXV were truncated to the natural subsoil. Although only a relatively small area was excavated the relative high density of Romano-British pottery suggests flourishing occupation during that period in this part of the site. The Roman pottery therefore must be residual. The existence of this one datable find provides a rare anchor point in the otherwise floating chronology of the later deposits at Irby, and gives unambiguous confirmation of 10th-12th-century activity on the site. Significantly, it opens up the possibility that other structures also dated to this period.

The second find is less certainly indicative of activity of this period. Fragments of amber (SF692), probably from a bead, were found in context 610, a layer stratigraphically just below the interface between the top of deposits rich in Romano-British material and the post-medieval ploughsoil. Amber beads are known in prehistoric and Roman Britain but were considerably more common in the Norse period. Given the stratigraphic position and the well documented Viking settlement in north Wirral from the beginning of the 10th century, a Norse date for the find is more likely.

The stratigraphic sequence and the sparse dating evidence which shows activity in the 10th-12th century provide a context within which to consider the building forms. The most consistent parallels for bow-sided structures within the early medieval period are Viking in origin. Building forms in Norse rural settlements within the Irish Sea and Atlantic regions as well as Hiberno-Norse urban centres, notably Dublin, developed a series of bow-sided building forms which at least in outline match closely the Irby structures. However, the internal details which might confirm this identification have not survived. The detailed argument is presented in Chapter 5. The credibility of the curvilinear structures is enhanced by the presence of the stone foundation S16, possibly of similar plan though perhaps of a slightly later date in view of the construction technique, since not a great deal of the plans of any of the buildings can be recognised.

Phase EM3: Building with stone foundation, 11th/12th century?

Structure 16

Although somewhat different in construction technique from other buildings, Structure 16 appears, from the short section excavated, to share the same curvilinear outer walls. S16 was located at the northern end of Trench XXIX/XXIII (Fig 2.55, Pl. XVI). It consisted of a group of sandstone foundations *c.* 0.70 m across and one to two cobbles deep. The cobbles were sub-rounded and sub-angular *c.* 0.15 m across up to 0.40 m and ap-peared to be laid randomly. The east-west wall (contexts 5364, 4060; interstices 4074) ran across the northern half of the trench and began to curve gently northwards approximately 2.0 m from the western edge of the trench. A north-south wall (context 4068; interstices 4069) joined the north side of the first wall at the point where it began to curve. Both walls were constructed at the same time. No cut was observed for any of these fea-tures, the soil matrix around them appearing identical to the material in the surrounding layers.

These walls clearly represent the foundations of a building. The plan of the excavated portion suggests a broadly rectilinear plan but the slight curvature of the east-west wall may indicate a curvilinear or sub-rectangular structure although this could be an accident of preservation. Only a very limited area was excavated so the overall dimensions and plan of the building are unknown. However, the wall is narrow and probably supported a timber superstructure on a sill beam, though an upper wall of cob or turf is a possibility. The foundations, using a shallow line of cobbles, are similar to those of the overlying building S18, as well as S19 to the south-east, though the walls of S16 are narrower.

The relationship between S16 and S18 is tenuous, in part due to the difficulty in identifying cuts and also due to the fact that the critical junction coincided with the point where Trenches XXIII and XXIX met. In addition, there was no datable material associated with S16 although it was sealed by clay floors associated with S18 so it clearly pre-dated that structure. However, the records do show that S18 stopped immediately to the south of and in a line with the south wall of S16; this is not easy to explain unless either S18 respected S16, indicating they were in contemporary existence, or S16 cut the wall S18. There were no finds in the interstices of the wall of S16.

The two walls of S16, contexts 4060 and 4068, were considered on excavation to have been overlain by 4064, a layer which lacked finds. However, this relationship was not clear and during post-excavation analysis this was re-interpreted on the evidence of the plans so that the wall cut through layer 4058 and was sealed by 4003. Although a few stones of 4060 do protrude into 4058, the vast majority are sealed under it. Context 4058 also lacked datable finds, containing only fragments of fired clay, coal and charcoal.

Other than fragments of fired clay and one very abraded white ware sherd of Roman date (SF3501), finds in context 4003 included a large sherd of a Hartshill-Mancetter mortarium (SF2900) and an intrusive post-

medieval black-glazed sherd. There was also a small amount of industrial waste, two crucible fragments (SF3488, SF3500) and a piece of lead melt.

Two contexts which were sealed by S16 had Romano-British pottery. Context 4066 contained a possible colour-coated sherd (SF3518), while context 5359, which underlay the wall 5364, produced a sherd of shell-tempered ware (SF8235) dated to the mid-late 4th century, along with an iron nail shank. This ought to give a *tpq* for the structure, although the usual reservations over placing undue reliance on one datable sherd apply here.

Discussion

The attribution of S16 to a separate phase from the Phase EM2 buildings (S3, S6, S7 and S24) is based on the different form of construction using a stone foundation. The stratigraphic and finds evidence indicate a *tpq* of the mid-late 4th-century sherd for the wall of S16. The location of the building just north of the projected line of Ditch 3 in a position which would intrude on the ditch indicates that the latter had ceased to exist. An abraded mid-late 4th-century sherd was found in the primary fill of Ditch 3, suggesting the ditch did not go out of use before the 4th century. Together these imply a post-Roman date for the building, presumably after the former line of the ditch was no longer visible. The fact that the clay floor of S18 overlay S16 provides another important stratigraphic relationship. S18 was tentatively dated to the medieval period. The slight curvature of the stone wall of S16 is not by itself diagnostic of date but in the light of the presence of bow-sided structures elsewhere on the site (S3, S6, S7), it is most appropriate to assign this to the same general building type. It is suggested that these structures are Norse in origin. Despite the difference in construction, Viking-Age Scandinavian buildings recorded in mainland Scotland and the Scottish Isles, as well as in the northern Atlantic such as the Faroes, Iceland and Greenland, took a remarkably similar form, using stone foundations or wooden construction (e.g. Larsen and Stummann Hansen 2001, 116-7, fig. 3). Such a difference may in part have a chronological basis, since the introduction of sill beam construction using low stone walls was a later development than earth-fast timbers. However, Scandinavian buildings were adapted to a variety of construction techniques, dependent on available raw materials, including post-hole structures, albeit ill-defined, at Cottam, stone walls in the Western Isles and wattle and daub in urban contexts in Viking Dublin. The cultural affinities are discussed in more detail in Chapter 5.

Phase EM4: Structures 8a/8b

Two structural gullies for one or more rectilinear buildings in Trench XXI, S8a and S8b are tentatively assigned to this phase. The latter post-dates the large curvilinear building, S3. Both lack either definitive stratigraphical or finds evidence for the attribution, and neither is represented by a complete plan being no more than a single linear slot aligned north-south (Figure 2.56) lying parallel to one another in Trench XXI. Both were sealed by 3616, one of the upper layers of occupation deposit in Trench XXII. Spatially, they overlap other buildings so are not contemporary with them. This phase may represent a distinct phase of activity but it is by no means certain that these two structures were in contemporary use and they are placed here for convenience.

Structure 8a

The first gully, 3737, was 1.15 m long, 0.30 m wide and 0.18 m deep, with vertical sides and a flat base. The fills were dark reddish brown loamy sands containing occasional red sandstone pebbles and glacial erratics; 3768, a tabular sandstone block laid on bedrock was provisionally identified as part of the fill of 3737 during post-excavation analysis. There are no diagnostic finds in the fills of 3737 other than an undated oxidised ware sherd (SF3957) in 3735.

Structure 8b

The second slot or gully, 3684, was 4.35 m long, 0.93 m wide and 0.35 m deep. Its profile was slightly more irregular with convex sides and a dished base. The feature has a slight curve to the east in plan. One important stratigraphic relationship was that it cut the curvilinear foundation trench of S3. The fill was similar material to that in 3737 and contained a single datable sherd (SF3598) of Central Gaulish samian dated AD

140-200, along with a Roman hobnail (SF5822), as well as large amounts of industrial waste, slag and possible crucible slag. Environmental sample includes cf. *Secale cereale,* hazelnut shell, Triticum sp. grain, hulled barley and Hordeum indet., all in small quantities.

The two gullies terminate at different points and as probable foundation trenches they may well form components of two separate structures, most of which may have lain outside the excavated area. They do serve to indicate the presence of probable rectilinear structures in this phase even though their full plan was not recovered. Extensive truncation of deposits to the east of these gullies may account for the loss of their other elements.

Feature 3

Cut 3724 was a large, elliptical, rock-cut pit aligned north-south in Trench XXI (Figs. 2.56 and 2.57, Plate XVI). It measured 2.85 m long and 1.25 m wide and *c.* 0.50 m deep. The sides were neatly cut into bedrock at an angle of *c.* 75° and were slightly stepped where the rock had been split off along bedding planes. The southern edge sloped at a lesser angle, *c.* 45°. The base of the cut was very flat, following bedding planes in the rock.

This feature contained a number of fills. The lowest fill was a very dark grey to black sandy silt (3715) containing frequent fragments of charcoal up to 20 mm across and occasional sandstone pebbles. The other fills, (3679, 3728, 3706, 3703) were very similar, varying only slightly in the percentage of sand, silt or charcoal. Fills 3712, 3711 and 3710 were even richer in charcoal and when first identified were interpreted as

Fig. 2.55: Phase EM3. Plan of Structure 16

Plate XVI: Structures S16 (foreground) and S18 of Phase M1, from the north (see Fig. 2.55)

posts which had burnt *in situ*. Later excavation revealed that they were in fact lenses of the same deposit. The charcoal from 3715 was described as 'remarkably clean and reasonably well preserved', and included not only many cereal grains of bread wheat, oats, barley and rye, but also a wide variety of other seeds including many *Polygonum lapathifolium/persicaria*, some radish pod fragments, small grasses, brome grass, other Polygonum species and docks as well as Sieglingia (Huntley, Appendix Table 3).

The function of the pit is uncertain. The infilling of the feature with distinct layers of fresh and unabraded charcoal-rich material may simply represent disposal of rubbish in a convenient open pit. However, the fills may be connected with the use of the feature and there is a high proportion of industrial waste in the feature which indicates ironworking in the vicinity prior to the infilling of the pit. Against this is the fact that there were no signs of heating on the sides of the cut and it serves no obvious metallurgical function.

The fills included carbonised seeds which further suggest no direct link with metallurgy but there is little pottery and it may be residual. The large number of sandstone blocks (3630, 3631) within the fills of this feature looked very much like packing stones of a post-hole set into the soft fill of the pit; there was also a cut in the base which lay under this, so the post-hole was probably later than the fill of the pit.

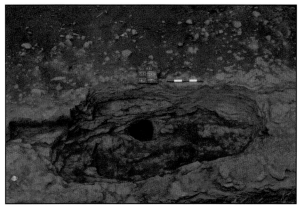

Plate XVII: Pit F3 (cut 3724) from the east

The pit cut through the palisade (S5) which had fallen into disuse, though it is uncertain whether the ditch had also become disused. Although the pit was far enough away not to intrude on the ditch which lay immediately to the east (and parallel to S5) and both ditch and pit could have co-existed, the finds in the fills of the two features suggest the pit was not dug until after the ditch had been filled in.

The few finds may indicate a 4th-century or later date for this feature, though there is little datable material. The presence of bread wheat is consistent with a post-Roman date, though the assemblage is quite similar to that from 6130, a post-hole in S13, interpreted as Romano-British in date (see Chapter 3, *Charred Plant Remains*).

Period VI: Later Medieval (13th-14th/15th century)

Late in the stratigraphic sequence is a series of structures with rather different methods of construction from the preceding buildings. They consist of S21, S23, S18, S19, and S20 (Fig. 2.58). Spatially several of these buildings overlap so not all of them could have co-existed and at least two distinct phases are present. There is some indication that a long period of occupation may be involved, potentially continuous from the early medieval period. Few finds are associated directly with these buildings and it is probable that much of the material in the fills of post-holes or gullies is residual, the buildings having been constructed through Romano-British deposits containing 4th-century and earlier material.

Phase M1: Later Medieval Period: 13th-14/15th century

A later medieval phase on the site probably dating to the 13th-14th or 15th century is suggested by a series of finds and buildings which appear at the top of the stratigraphic sequence, immediately underlying the post-medieval ploughsoil but cutting through layers containing significant quantities of Roman pottery. A limited amount of medieval pottery was also recovered from the ploughsoil itself. In view of the scarcity of finds and dating evidence, the medieval pottery will be discussed first to present the evidence for a medieval phase of activity. The structures which are most likely to be associated with that activity are then considered.

Medieval Finds

A total of 30 certain or probable later medieval sherds were recovered from the site. Julie Edwards has concluded that a small number of Red/Grey wares are 13th-14th century in date; other sherds are later in date (see Chapter 4, *Later Medieval and Early Post-Medieval Pottery*). In addition, there is a single diagnostically

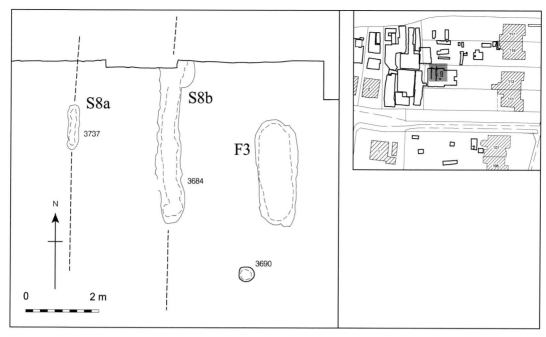

Fig. 2.56: Phase EM4. Plan of structures S8a and S8b, and pit F3

medieval metal find, a sheet metal key (SF284, no. 437, Fig. 4.19).

The position of the medieval sherds is significant. Nearly half of the probable or certain sherds occur in layers which lay immediately below the post-medieval ploughsoil and at the top of sealed occupation deposits or in deposits just below those (usually excavated as spits of the upper surface) (SF972: context 629, contexts 5320, 5321, probably 9002, 9958, 1003). Three sherds and the medieval key (SF284) in post-medieval ploughsoil (contexts 3001 (2 sherds), 5123, 1007 - key) were probably derived from reworking of medieval deposits over the site. Ten sherds occurred in occupation deposits (context 607 (5 sherds); 3062; 1039 (2 sherds); 3102 (make-up or trample below cobbled surface 3107 in XIX); 6204 - occupation layer sealing ditch 6217; 7200).

Significantly, a few sherds also occurred in stratified features. A green-glazed pottery sherd (SF3661) was securely stratified in a stone-lined post-hole (context 1078) which is interpreted as forming part of S21, a possible medieval sherd was found in another post-hole of S21 (SF986; context 655), while other medieval glazed sherds in the fills of separate post-holes (3022, fill 3023, SF9349) and (6666, fill of 6665, SF6363), though the latter was very poorly defined, probably indicate a medieval structure in the north-western part of the site.

In addition, three sherds were found in the fills of enclosure ditches. Two medieval sherds (SF8393, SF9792), probably from the same vessel, were found in context 22, the uppermost fill of Ditch 1 in Area I. One was a large base sherd of a bottle (SF8393) with a wire-trimmed base of gritty ware, dated to the 14th-15th century (J. Axworthy pers. comm.). This may have an implication for the date of the coal which was found in the same context in the ditch. There was some residual material within context 22, but the position of the sherds suggests that either some medieval material was

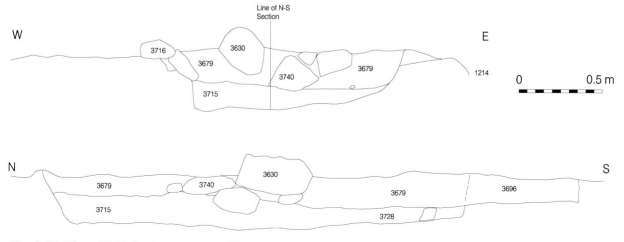

Fig. 2.57: Phase EM4. Section across pit F3

deposited in a slight hollow left by the consolidation of the Roman ditch fills or a small medieval pit or post-hole which cut through the upper ditch fills went unrecognised. The other (SF10608, context 6468, fill of ditch 6476 in XXXVII;) may have resulted from medieval occupation layers slumping into the ditch through compression of the fills.

The quantity and stratigraphical position of the material indicates that there was a phase of medieval occupation on the site. The sherds are too numerous and varied, deriving from several different vessels, to be attributed to manuring or casual loss. A few sherds are stratified within features. The condition of the medieval pottery supports the view that the medieval occupation was more than casual or short-lived. Many sherds are very small and abraded, and by itself the fragmentation and abrasion of the material requires a period of occupation in which the pottery was crushed and trampled rather than casual loss or a dispersed manuring scatter. The medieval activity also seems to have disturbed and reworked the upper part of the Romano-British occupation deposits.

Structure 18

The deposits comprising this structure were only partly excavated so their interpretation is provisional. It is conceivable that they do not relate to a structure but are in fact rubble deposited as the upper fill of enclosure Ditch 3 (Phase R4), the projected line of which passes through this point. The principal cause for uncertainty is the great width of the rubble foundations (Figs 2.58 and 59) which are up to 3 m across. Whilst this may be partly attributed by dispersal as a result of collapse and ploughing, it is significantly greater than other structures at Irby. However, some of the details discussed below suggest a structural function. Its full plan and relationship to the other parts of the site were unclear as the excavated area was limited. It appears unlikely that the site was enclosed by ditches unless Ditch 5, the late ditch under the modern field boundary to the north of the plot (see Phase M4 below), was present at this period.

S18 consists of two separate sections of wall (5302, 5344) divided by a gap, in which was found the remains of a heavily damaged clay floor (5330). The northern section was composed of a massive linear arrangement of sandstone cobbles and lumps, which measured up to 0.45 m across (average *c.* 0.20 m), set in a matrix very similar to the surrounding layers. The feature ran north-south in the extreme north-eastern corner of the trench.

The gap between the walls appeared to define a passageway or entrance to the structure. This was aligned east-west at an angle of approximately 120° to the wall line. A patchy layer of yellow clay *c.* 50 mm thick (4004, 5331, 5330) occupied the space. The clay had been heavily disrupted by modern ploughing

but consisted of patches of flat compressed clay *in situ*, which probably represented the clay floor to this passageway, overlying a dump of material as its make-up. This deposit represented the only identifiable floor surface at Irby.

Approximately 1.8-1.9 m to the south was the other section of the rubble foundation of this structure (5302). The rubble foundations were composed of a band of unmortared sub-angular and rounded sandstone blocks ranging in size from 30 mm to 0.30 m and averaging *c.* 0.20 m. The total exposed length was 7.16 m and it was 2.90 m wide. Detailed examination of the plans shows that there was a grading of the stones, those to the east being distinctly smaller than those to the west. In addition there appears to be a slight curve to the east on the southern half of this structure.

Wall 5302 terminated abruptly to the north with a squared end within Trench XXIII. The details of construction at this end appear complex though this may be at least in part due to its excavation in isolation from the bulk of this feature. A single squarish slab of red sandstone (4079) was laid flat at the extreme north-eastern corner of the sandstone deposit 4002 and measured 0.40 by 0.40 by 0.12 m. Its position adjacent to the probable entrance suggested a padstone for a door post. A little to the west of the padstone, set within the wall, was a group of larger sandstone cobbles up to 0.37 m across (4049) set on edge in a rough circle *c.* 1.00 m across. These were almost certainly a post-setting for a vertical timber within the wall itself.

The northern portion (context 5344) of this structure contained within it a number of voids *c.* 0.20-0.40 m across and 0.15 m deep, filled with the same material that made up the matrix. These had the appearance of spaces in which vertical timber posts had been set. No similar features were noted in the southern section.

A series of layers recorded separately with context numbers 5324, 5346, 4050 and 4051 were probably components of a single cobbled surface which possibly formed an entrance or threshold to the building. Contexts 5334, 5325, 5360 and 5361 may originally have formed a contiguous surface with this to create an external yard to the east of this structure. It was composed of two layers of rounded sandstone cobbles and glacial erratics, *c.* 30-60 mm across, set in a matrix of dark brown sandy loam containing charcoal flecks.

The clay floor sealed the stone foundation of S16. As the latter sealed a deposit containing a sherd of mid-late 4th-century shell-tempered ware, the construction of S18 has a *tpq* of the late Roman period, and is far more likely to represent a medieval structure than anything earlier.

The wall alignments of S18 could be reconstructed as one end of a subrectangular structure, but too little was

Fig. 2.58: Phase M1. Medieval buildings S18, S19, S20 and S23

excavated to make this at all certain. Even a modest dispersal or movement of the edge of the sandstone lump deposit comprising the wall would produce a very different outline configuration.

Apart from one find, there is no datable material from the wall foundation or the post-holes associated with it. The exception is a remarkable find discovered firmly embedded in the upper part of the foundation of wall 4001, a 3rd-century BC steatite spindle whorl (SF2931). This may have been found on the site as a relic from the Iron Age occupation and placed within the foundation wall during construction in the medieval period. It may have been considered to hold some talismanic significance.

Environmental samples contribute little to the discussion. Context 5321 has one Triticum grain, while layer 5341 has one *Triticum aestivum*, one hazelnut and one sedge fragment; the latter layer also contained SF8218, a BB1 sherd dated AD 270-350; and a fragment of bronze-working mould, probably of Romano-British date (see Chapter 4, *Refractory Material*).

Structure 19

Structure 19 was a rectilinear building of uncertain width but at least 29 m long (Figs. 2.58 and 2.60). It is possible that it actually formed a single structure with S23, though at *c*. 12-13 m across this would be more than twice the usual width of medieval buildings of this type.

It was originally noted as a well-defined linear band of red sandstone cobbles (3056) running east-south-east to west-north-west across Trenches XXI and XIX. The section in Trench XIX (3056) measured 0.8-1.0 m wide, but was never more than three cobbles, or 0.20 m thick (Fig. 2.61). The cut for this feature was never very well defined and was little more than a shallow scoop into the underlying deposits. The cobbles measured up to 0.25 m across, with an average size of about 0.13 m, and were mostly sub-rounded to sub-angular. Their size and density of distribution decreased to the west to the point so that within 1 m of the western baulk of Trench XIX the feature was scarcely perceptible. The cobbles sat in a matrix of dark reddish brown sandy loam which was identical to the surrounding deposits. The point where this feature began to fade out coincided with 3095, 3097 and 3098, a wall identical to the above, and suggested a return aligned north-north-east by south-south-west; this petered out after 1.5 m. Although from some distance away clear edges could be seen to the deposit, on closer inspection it appeared to grade into the surrounding deposits which also contained a high proportion of sandstone cobbles and it is possible that the ill-defined edges were created by plough disturbance.

Three post-holes (3126, 3123 and 3153) were sealed by this wall in Trench XIX and may belong to an earlier structure but are included within this phase because the packing material they contained protruded into 3056 and appeared to be integrated with it. They probably represent internal post settings within the wall.

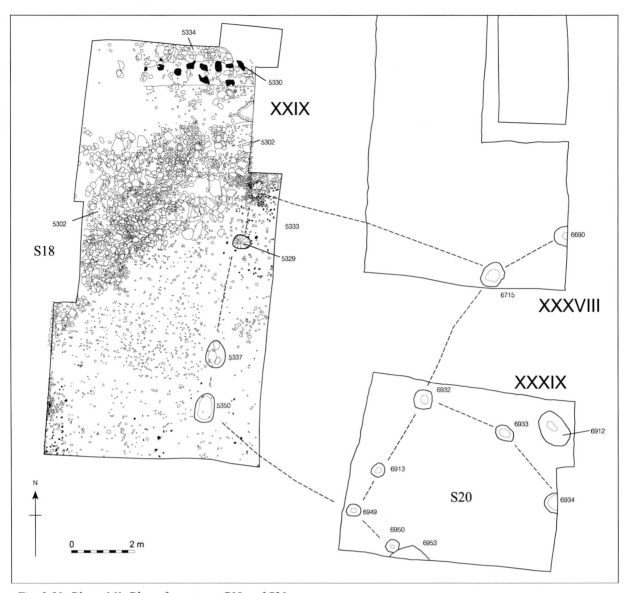

Fig. 2.59: Phase M1. Plan of structures S18 and S20

The same wall was also prcscnt in Trcnchcs XXI (3617), XL (9005) and XLI (9510). These sections were largely identical to that excavated in Trench XIX, though the section in Trench XLI was much less well defined and was only one to two cobbles deep. Several of the larger stones in Trenches XIX, XL and XXI had deep scratches in their upper surface which were probably created by plough damage.

The western wall of the building was not positively identified in the excavated area. However, it may have been constructed using a different technique. The reason for the absence of the north wall is not clear; there was no obvious alignment of post settings within the features in that area. One possibility is that it was totally destroyed by ploughing. However, there was a slight slope from north to south and it is perhaps more likely that wall 3056 was intended to even this out by providing a dwarf wall for timbers, perhaps a sill beam. If this is the case, the absence of the north wall may indicate the use of cruck construction for this structure. Many surviving cruck structures in the region (Addyman

1981) use padstones to support the cruck blades. These will leave minimal subsurface evidence.

The interstices of the wall contained several datable finds. In Trench XIX 3056 contained a securely stratified coin of 'Falling Horseman' type (SF5237), and a small amount of late BB1 (e.g. SF5431, dated 270-350). In Trench XXI 3617 they consist largely of Roman pottery (17 sherds), including a sherd of shell-tempered ware of mid-late 4th-century date (SF4110), and a considerable quantity of industrial waste. However, one small medieval sherd (SF5026 in 3617), together with the stratigraphical observation that the wall seals the infilled internal enclosure ditch (Ditch 1), indicates that this earlier material is residual. A single post-medieval sherd is assumed to be intrusive.

The construction using rounded sandstone blocks and lumps, without bonding material such as clay or mortar, suggests that the northern foundation was a low dwarf wall on which a timber superstructure was erected to keep the timber raised off the ground and dry. There are

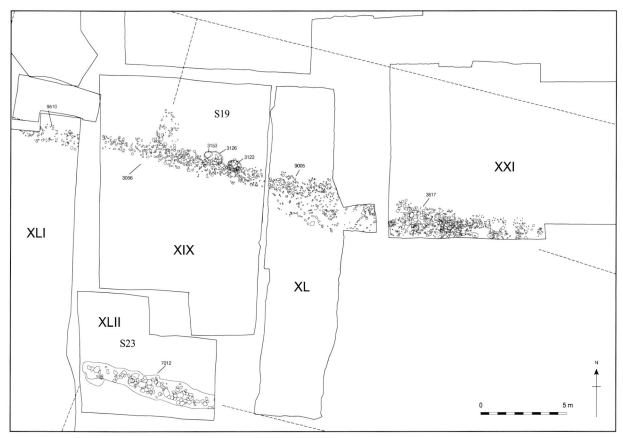

Fig. 2.60: Phase M1. Detailed plan of S19 and S23

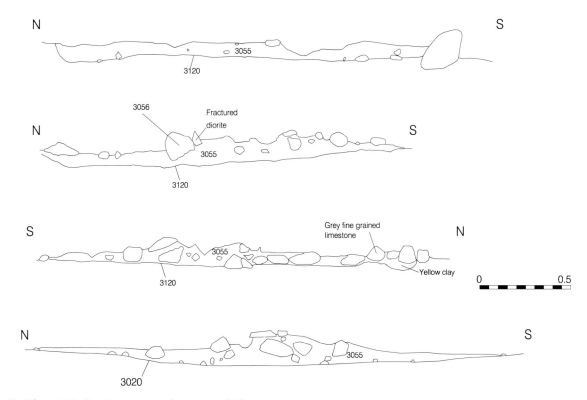

Fig. 2.61: Phase M1. Sections across features in S19

suggestions that a few vertical timbers were set in the ground through the wall but principally the wall served to support horizontal timbers as sill beams onto which the uprights were jointed.

Structure 23

This feature ran parallel to and may in fact be the southern wall of S19 though it was very different in construction from 3056. It was constructed in a linear

69

cut 7012 running east-south-east by west-north-west across the trench from just short of the east-facing baulk of Trench XLII into the west-facing baulk (Fig. 2.61). In profile it had near-vertical sides (Fig. 2.62) and a slightly irregular, almost flat base. Its width was variable but was generally 1.20 m, the depth increased from 0.18 m in the west to 0.24 m in the east.

When first identified it was unclear whether this was a single feature or a group of related post-holes. As excavation progressed by reducing the surrounding deposits in spits, it became apparent that this was in fact a single feature. Although most of the stone blocks appeared to have been tipped randomly into the cut, several voids were present which suggested that structural timbers were present. The voids were *c.* 0.20 m across and spaced at approximately 1.00-1.50 m intervals in a slightly zigzag pattern.

The fill (7013) contained thirteen sherds of Roman pottery including BB1, oxidised wares and a sherd of calcite-gritted ware (SF8532). Stone objects included two quern fragments (SF8555, SF8556) in 7009.

Discussion

Structures S18, S19 and 23 may be contemporary, as they are similar in construction method, consisting of a deposit of sandstone cobbles and stratigraphically, all are high in the sequence. S18 appears to seal S16 while S19 also seals several Roman and early-medieval buildings (S1, S12, S13, S7 and probably S9). Both appear to seal the infilled enclosure Ditches 1 and 3, although Trench XXIX was not fully excavated due to constraints on excavation in that area. However, the ditch alignment clearly ran towards the building and it is likely that the building sealed the infilled ditch, though the sides of Trench XXIII (which was excavated to the top of the natural subsoil) showed no ditch at that point. In Trench XXI building S19 clearly sealed the internal ditch, Ditch 1; the building alignment also diverges from that of the enclosure suggesting the ditch was no longer a significant feature at the time. There is no stratigraphic difficulty with the two stone buildings co-existing, and the pottery evidence is consistent with both buildings having been cut through Roman deposits.

Harder to explain is why the S18 wall stops just before reaching S16, with a narrow but clear gap separating the two. The presence of the padstone and post-setting in the wall of S18 argues for this being a coincidental juxtaposition, rather than the wall of S16 being inserted through or being respected by the wall of S18.

The use of a similar construction technique for two substantial buildings, possibly both sealing the infilled enclosure ditch, is consistent with a phase later than the main Romano-British settlement. Certainly the enclosure ditch (and also its internal bank in the northern area

of the excavation) has gone out of use by this time, suggesting that some time elapsed between the disuse of the enclosure and the construction of these buildings.

Structure 20

Structure 20 is composed of a series of post-holes in Trenches XXIX, XXXVIII and XXXIX, forming a roughly rectilinear arrangement which may have represented a post-built structure aligned roughly north-north-east by south-south-west (Figs 2.58 and 2.59). The walls in each case run into unexcavated areas so the full plan cannot be confirmed. The structure appeared to have been demolished and the post-holes backfilled with packing material upon removal of the posts. Cuts 6715 and 6690 in Trench XXIX may also form part of this structure. A thin layer of yellowish red clay (6915) containing flecks of charcoal, 0.40 m in diameter and 40 mm thick, may have been a fragment of surviving floor surface, or debris from construction; it was interpreted on excavation as a hearth as both charcoal and industrial waste were present, though there was no evidence that any of the burning had occurred *in situ.*

It is not clear whether the large pit 6912 was part of this structure, although the presence of a yellowish brown clay suggests it was associated in some way with it. There is similar doubt over cuts 6690 and 6715 in Trench XXXVIII, although they are stratigraphically contemporary with S20, they lie off the main line of the structure, especially if the features in Trench XXIX are accepted as part of it. These comprise a line of four post settings (5350, 5337, 5333 and 5329) which may form the western end of the building. However, although stratigraphically contemporary they are on a slightly different alignment to the rest of the structure.

Dating evidence is poor for this structure. There are no datable finds in the main constituent post-holes of Structure 20. The layer 6904, through which several of the post-holes are cut (post-holes 6932, 6933, 6934, 6913 and 6949), contains only two Romano-British oxidised ware sherds, neither of which is diagnostic of date.

Two layers seal the post-holes of the structure. The upper layer 6902 contains a single Romano-British sherd of oxidised ware. The lower layer 6903 contains BB1, oxidised ware, a Nene valley sherd and white ware. Other than the Nene valley sherd, which is dated only broadly to the mid 2nd-late 4th century, there is nothing closely diagnostic and the material is in any case residual. If 5348 (the fill of pit/post-hole 5350) is included, this has a little environmental evidence and a lead spindle whorl (SF6591).

Phase M2: Later Medieval Building (14th century?)

The main components of this phase are a series of large

rock-cut post-holes measuring up to 2 m across (Figure 2.63) which in most cases were revealed immediately below the post-medieval ploughsoil where packing stones were visible. Many of them were curvilinear in plan, others were dug to a carefully laid out square plan. Although it might be assumed that these lie parallel to the main axis of the building, this need not be the case. Richmond has shown, for instance, in some Roman military timber buildings that the post-pits may not be neatly aligned with either one another or with the main axis of the structure; often the post is rammed hard up against one side of the post-hole to benefit from the stability of the undisturbed ground (Richmond 1961, 18, fig. 1.2). At Irby all of the post-holes contained large sandstone blocks which had been used to pack the post into position. In many cases the post appeared to have rotted *in situ*, though in others the stone had either collapsed after the post had rotted or as the post was removed when the structure was abandoned.

There is some indication from the stratigraphic sequence that S19 was earlier than S21; layer 3101 was interpreted as sealing the stone wall foundation of S19 (3055) but was cut by post-holes within S21.

Structure 21

Structure 21 was a large building with large timber posts set in well founded post-holes with substantial packing stones. It was rectangular in plan with a series of post-holes in a north-south alignment in Trench VIII and a parallel linear gully in Trench XLIII, which formed the west and east walls (Figs. 2.63 and 2.64). Although less well defined than Structure 19, this building shared one common feature in that the long sides were constructed using different techniques. It was also a similar size measuring at least *c.* 19 x 7.5 m. The south end appeared to be fairly well established but no clear alignment was visible for the northern end.

The west wall of the building was noted first, appearing as a distinct north-south linear alignment of post-holes in Trench VIII immediately under the post-medieval ploughsoil. The most obvious components of this wall were a series of large stone-packed post-holes 1058, 1076, 1079 and 1101 and two adjacent shallow pits with pad-stones (1056, 1057). This alignment of post-holes was unusually clearly defined for Irby (although the spacing is a little irregular) and was continued in Trench XIX by cuts 3105, 3132, and 3084.

The most obvious candidate for the eastern wall of this structure was a north-south gully 7251 measuring at least 3.6 m long in Trench XLIII. The northern end had been destroyed by two later features cutting through it. The first was a probable oven or kiln (F6) in the same alignment (discussed below), though there was considerable difficulty in determining the relationship between the two, the sequence of fills being very similar.

The coincidence of the alignments with the structural gully suggests the kiln or oven was deliberately situated over the demolished wall line. Perhaps a linear hollow remained visible on the surface which was used as an indicator of softer ground for construction of the feature. The continuation of this feature was not readily identifiable in Trench XXI but may be represented by a series of small cuts (3731, 3739, 3693, 3764, 3769, 3741, 3763, 3752, 3798, 4615).

A well defined alignment for the south wall was represented by two evenly spaced, large post-holes with stone packing (cuts 9082; 9025) which would make this building at least 27 m long. The northern wall was less well defined. A band of post-holes running just south of the ditch in Trench XXXVII (cuts 6493, 6485, 6449 and 6446) may be part of the northern wall, particularly if cut 676 (which contained a medieval sherd in its fill) is accepted as the north-western corner. However, this group was not identified until relatively low in the stratigraphic sequence, though this may be because of the absence of packing material. Cut 6435 is a possible alternative but is more likely to be a hearth or similar feature as it showed extensive evidence of burning.

As regards the interior, a clay area (1028) may be a small survival of part of the floor. Other post-holes in the interior of similar character to the west and south

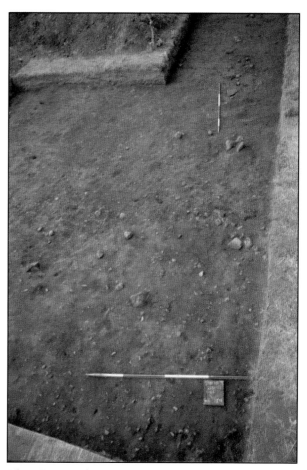

Plate XVIII: Phase M2. Pre-excavation view of packing stones of post-holes of W side of S21 in Trench VIII, from S

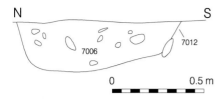

N   S

7006   7012

0   0.5 m

Fig. 2.62: Phase M1. Section across S23

walls may mark a partition. Cuts 3214 and 3080 were associated with a short section of east-west aligned gully which may be part of an internal partition, though the possibility that it was part of another structure cannot be eliminated. Cuts 9030, 9009 and 9115 could be part of the internal arrangements of this structure but may also be part of another structure.

In the absence of surviving internal features, its function is uncertain and it may have been an ancillary building of the type recorded in late medieval documents rather than a house. Its considerable size would argue for a barn over the other structures such as a bake-house, kiln, or stable which in general tended to be smaller than barns on the same holdings (cf. Wrathmell 1989, 9).

There is little directly datable material associated with the components of this structure. In fact the finds from the fills bear some resemblance to those encountered in the fills of the earlier phases, i.e. occasional fragments of oxidised ware, VCP and industrial waste, and there was also a single fragment of samian ware. However, this feature cut through layers containing Hartshill-Mancetter mortaria and BB1 which dated these features to the 3rd century AD or later. The posts in Trench VIII were set at irregular intervals and were also associated with very little datable material. However, there are two pieces of artefactual evidence that support a much later date. First, context 655 (fill of 676) contained an eroded and burnt sherd (SF986) which may be medieval rather than Roman in date (J. Evans pers. comm.). Secondly, a small sherd of green-glazed pottery (SF3661) recovered from the lower fill (1078) of post-hole 1079 is probably a fragment of a 13th-century mid-Cheshire jug (J. Axworthy pers. comm.; see Chapter 4, *Later Medieval and Early Post-Medieval Pottery)*.

Other large post-holes (cuts 3093, 3233, 7017) in Trench XIX containing large stone blocks used as packing around a post were apparently contemporary with this structure but could not be directly related to it. These were likely to relate to a substantial structure, the form of which could not be determined.

Feature 8: Clay-lined pit (6126)

Cut 6126 (Fig 2.63) was an unusual clay-lined pit of uncertain function. It had a circular cut, lined with a layer of dark yellowish brown clay containing occasional flecks of charcoal, very fine pebbles of sandstone, igneous rock and possible flint. The lining

was *c.* 40 mm thick and extended up the sides of the cut. It was sealed by a brown gritty sandy loam containing shattered igneous rock, sandstone pebbles and charcoal flecks. Two larger sandstone cobbles up to 0.23 m across were also present. It was possibly a hearth although no burning was present.

Phase M3: Medieval Feature (14th-15th century?)

This phase consists of Feature 6, which cut through the foundations of Structure 21.

Feature 6: Pit

This substantial pit, 7216, apparently cut 7213, a linear feature to its south though they were probably part of the same feature (Figs. 2.65 and 2.66). The relationship between these features was ambiguous because of the near-identical nature of the fills. In fact the only reason for assuming that 7216 was later was the presence of a very few pebbles and a couple of larger cobbles tipping towards the centre of its fills 7216/7245. Not only were the fills similar but they were deposited in a similar sequence, i.e. washed-in material, followed by clay/fired clay from the west and south, then very charcoal-rich material, finally by dumped material containing large stones.

The cut was probably elliptical in plan with an excavated north-south length of 1.38 m indicating a minimum 'real' length of approximately 2.50 m. It was 1.87 m wide and 0.54 m deep, with an asymmetrical east-west profile.

The excavation of both features was hampered by a series of problems, chiefly that as the fills had settled the overlying deposits had also settled into the resultant void. This meant that their full extent was not apparent at first, and there was some confusion as to their edges and which feature cut which. This was further compounded by the dry conditions at the time of excavation and the similar nature of the fills of 7216 and 7213.

If cuts 7216 and 7213 were a single feature the result would be a linear feature broadening significantly to the north. This may be due to the fact the northern end was cut into sandstone brash. If this feature was allowed to weather before being back-filled, the widening could be caused by differential weathering of the sandstone brash. However the distinction between the two has been retained because of the evidence for a stratigraphic relationship between them.

The function of this feature remains unclear. There was clear evidence for burning within the fill, though this may be material derived from processes taking place elsewhere and dumped in a convenient hole in the ground; none of the sides of the cut were obviously

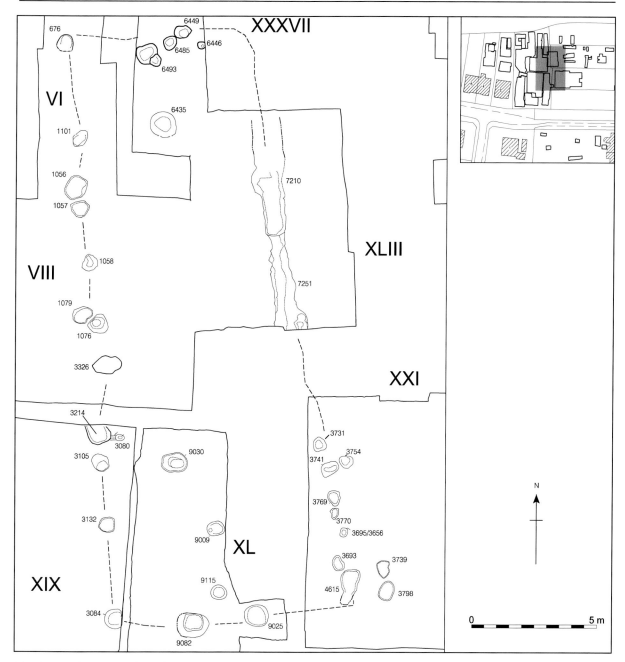

Fig. 2.63: Phase M2. Plan of S21 and pit F8

burnt. The presence of the yellow clay might suggest that this feature was broadly contemporary with similar features in Trenches XXV and XL.

The structural gully which was interpreted as part of S21 was cut by this feature. There was minimal artefactual evidence for a medieval date for S21, based on an abraded 13th-century green-glazed sherd in a component post-hole. Allowing for the wear on the sherd, F6 is likely to be no earlier than the 14th century in date.

Phase M4: Possible Medieval Phase

Ditch 5

Under the line of the hedge which forms the modern northern limit of the site a section of ditch (cut 7455)

was excavated. It was exposed in a trench only 1 m wide and was very shallow, measuring less than 1 m deep. This feature was probably the precursor of the hedge which lies along the parish boundary. As the parish boundary appears to have been of late Saxon origin it is possible that the ditch was of some antiquity. However, no datable material was recovered and the loose sandy fills suggested to the excavator a relatively recent date for the infilling.

Layout and Function of the Medieval Site

There appear to be at least two phases of medieval occupation at Irby. However, the absence of a secure and well-defined stratigraphic sequence allied with the scarcity of associated artefacts which might assist with the dating of the structures makes it very difficult to

73

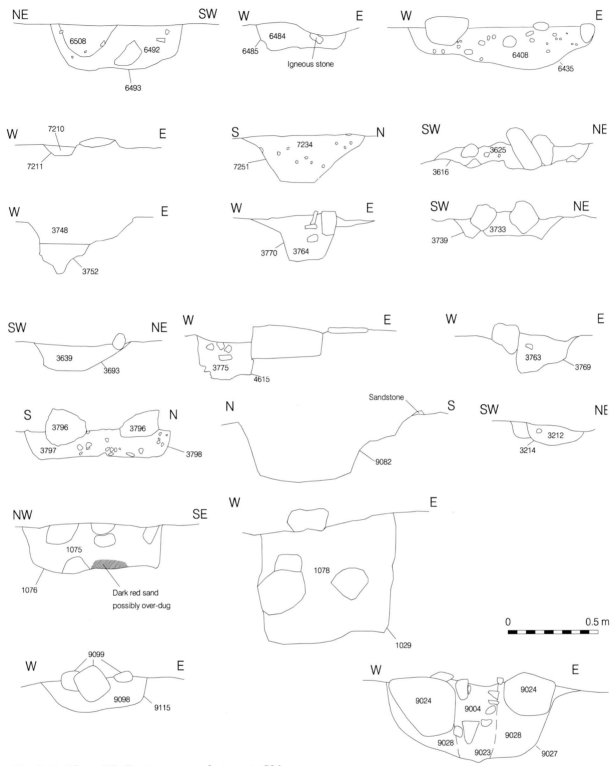

Fig. 2.64: Phase M2. Sections across features in S21

identify aceramic phases or structures.

The layout of the later medieval structures at Irby had the appearance of a farmstead with buildings set out in an L-shape on two sides of an open yard. The surface of the yard was possibly consolidated with stone, though trampling by animals may explain to some extent why the stratigraphy in Trench VIII was thinner and more hollowed out than elsewhere on the site. The only floor surface which survived within a structure was a damaged clay floor of Structure 18 and possibly a

small section in S21, so there was no information of the function of the buildings. On the evidence of the plans alone one building could be interpreted as a house (S19), while the building with massive timber posts and padstones (S21) resembled an open-fronted barn.

The major post-hole buildings of the latest phase of medieval occupation point to a substantial timber-built constructions, using well founded and large timbers. Whether such a construction was appropriate for a peasant house or was a higher status construction is uncer-

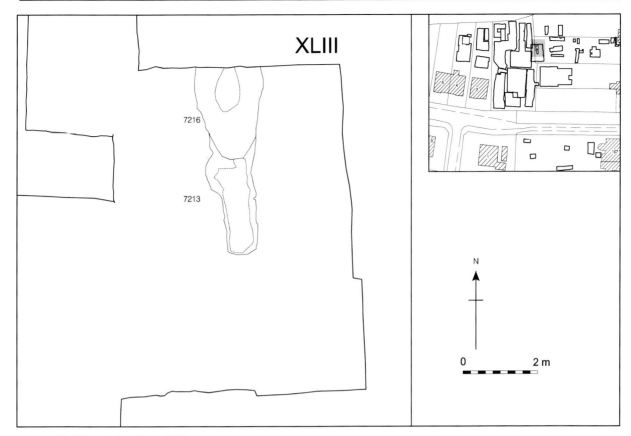

Fig. 2.65: Phase M3. Plan of F6

tain. Christopher Dyer has demonstrated in the West Midlands that peasant houses in the medieval period were built by specialist craftsmen. They were not necessarily short-lived and flimsy constructions (Dyer 1986). The finds assemblage at Irby might argue for a modest – indeed materially almost invisible – status for the occupants. However, subsequent excavations at contemporary sites of manorial status such as Ince Manor, Scholes Hall in Eccleston, St Helens, Bromborough Court and Newton Hall, Newton-le-Willows (Adams and Speakman 2001; Ahmad and Adams 2004; Adams 2009; Adams and Pevely 2006) have shown that even relatively high-status sites in the area need not be associated with large quantities of durable material culture, and it may reflect as much the differential survival of organic and inorganic artefacts as differences in status.

Period VII: Post-Medieval and Modern

The whole site was covered by an extensive deposit of ginger sandy loam which represented a post-medieval ploughsoil. Finds within the ploughsoil included a relatively small quantity of Romano-British pottery, a few sherds of medieval pottery and a larger quantity of post-medieval material, indicating that material continued to be incorporated into the matrix as late as the 20th century. Some post-medieval material also seems to have intruded into earlier deposits through plant and animal action. The post-medieval pottery suggested the spreading of farm and domestic middens, perhaps from the associated farm or from the village itself, to manure the land.

The ploughsoil had been cut by a range of garden features, cultivation trenches and planting pits, which post-dated the construction of the houses along Mill Hill Road in the 1920s and those in Thorstone Drive in the 1960s. These deposits are not described in detail here though a full listing is provided in the excavation archive. The large plot which was an orchard at the time of the excavation (no 2 Thorstone Drive) was last ploughed in the 1950s and subsequently planted with fruit trees (J. H. Billington pers. comm.). This activity and associated gardening led to the development of a dark humic cultivated soil over the ploughsoil.

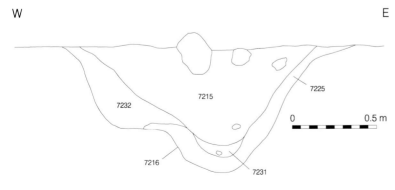

Fig. 2.66: Phase M3. Section of F6

3: Environmental Evidence

The Animal Bone

S. Stallibrass

Introduction

Three of the main aims of the project concern: evidence for the environment of the site and the exploitation of natural food resources; evidence for trade, economy and social status; and the identification of any spatial patterning in building functions and past human activities at the site. Animal bones can often contribute to studies of all three of these aims. Usually, they are less directly relevant to the other three main aims, which relate to structural and chronological aspects of the settlements.

The animal bones: their preservation and recovery; methods of analysis and initial results

Hand-recovered material

Animal bones were recovered routinely by hand during excavation, but the shallow deposits and free-draining sediments were not conducive to the preservation of vertebrate material except for burnt (nearly always calcined) bones and, occasionally, teeth.

Only 358 fragments were recovered, from approximately 143 contexts. The fragments tend to be small: typically 10-20 mm in maximum length, reflecting diligent collection by the excavators.

These have been scanned for the presence of any potentially identifiable fragments. A list of contexts producing animal bones was provided by the excavator. This has been annotated using a code for the type of preservation (calcined, charred, unburnt) and any identifications or notes, and is included in the site archive. None of the burnt fragments can be identified with certainty, although many of them appear to derive from sheep-sized animals rather than cattle-sized animals.

A few fragments were not burnt. These include some teeth and some post-cranial bones. Many of these derive from contexts described as ploughsoil, modern disturbance etc., including a very large, slightly immature turkey sternum, with a fine knife cut indicative of meat removal (context 5510) and a mature lumbar vertebra of a small dog of cairn terrier size (context 5123).

Other unburnt material derives from contexts that may relate more directly to much earlier activities at the site; in particular: some cattle teeth (a possible 'set' of three upper molars plus one lower molar) from a ?votive

deposit (context 5323) in pit 5333, Trench XXIX. These could be the remains of a complete head. A cattle molar tooth was also recovered from context 5348 (a fill of a pit (5350) of uncertain function) and another cattle tooth was recovered from context 5358. These items probably survived due to being buried in some of the deeper deposits on the site. Even here, unburnt bone has disappeared, leaving only teeth (which have a much higher proportion of mineral:organic content than bone, and which are, therefore, more resistant to diagenetic agencies). They may also be relatively late in the archaeological sequence. Pits 5333 and 5350 cut through layers containing 4th-century material, and context 5358 may relate to a similar pit. The deposits could relate to any time between the 4th - 15th/16th centuries. All three contexts are in the same area of the site: Trench XXIX.

Parts of a very young kitten skeleton were recovered from a cobbled layer 1229 that was stratified between 1205 (an upper fill of a probable enclosure ditch 1214) and 1221. This type of bone is highly susceptible to degradation and is likely to have survived only if protected by deep deposits or if inserted rather recently. Since the layer lies close to the top of the stratigraphic sequence, it seems most likely that a small corpse was inserted into the layer and that the cut or scrape was not detected during excavation.

One small and delicate fragment of a marine bivalve, possibly a tellin, was recovered from context 9691. This is an interface layer between occupation levels and natural sands, and may derive directly from the latter. It is not clear whether this shell is modern or 'fossil'.

No substantial deposits of marine shells were excavated (R. Philpott pers. comm.). It is possible that the 'aggressive' burial conditions tended to decompose shells as well as unburnt bone. Oyster shells, in particular, are frequently found on Romano-British sites, particularly those close to suitable coastlines, and their scarcity at Irby may be due to taphonomic factors rather than to any genuine absence in the past.

Material from sieved bulk sediment samples

Bulk sediment samples of at least 10 litres each were taken from every excavated context. A selection of these was processed by flotation using 500 μ mesh for both the flots and the residues. Samples were selected in order to represent a range of context types from all chronological periods, and to investigate contexts of particular interest.

At first, bulk sediment samples were processed by the Liverpool Museum Field Archaeology Unit, and small quantities of finely comminuted calcined bone were extracted from sorted residues of forty-three of these.

The fragments were almost all less than 10 mm in maximum length. Apart from two fragments of ungulate tooth enamel, all of the fragments consist of fully calcined bone. Some are so small that they probably formed part of the sediment matrix, and their rounded edges suggest that they may have been reworked from earlier deposits.

A scan of all of the material reveals that none of the fragments is identifiable to species (or element), but there appears to be a bias towards animals of sheep-size rather than cattle-size. There is no indication of the presence of any human bone.

A further 142 samples have been processed at the Durham University Environmental Archaeology Laboratory. The residues from these samples have not been sorted for animal bone since the results from samples already processed do not appear to justify the time required.

Discussion

Calcined bone tends to survive in sedimentary conditions where even tooth enamel decays beyond detection or recovery. This is because (although the organic component is virtually eliminated) the inorganic material is recrystallised into a very stable form. In order to become fully calcined, the bone requires heating to a high temperature. This can occur by accident, but can also occur when bone is deliberately burnt as a method of disposal (in 'bonefires', now spelt 'bonfires') or as part of an industrial process.

Clearly, the calcined animal bone recovered from Irby is not suitable for analyses of environmental, trade or social aspects of the archaeological settlements, but the distributions through time and space might be relevant to considerations of industrial functions and to the question of whether or not there were hiatuses between periods of occupation. That is, if a site was still partially occupied by structures and refuse, these might be cleared by fire prior to reorganisation and rebuilding. In contrast, if a site had been abandoned for several decades, piles of previously noxious waste (such as middens containing animal bones) might have decayed beyond notice.

A plot of the spatial distribution of the bone revealed no significant concentrations.

An alternative hypothesis: that the small fragments of calcined bone are the remains of midden material spread onto the fields during post-medieval times, and have become reworked into underlying deposits, is unlikely,

since the majority of the hand-recovered fragments do not appear to have been reworked to any major extent.

General discussion and summary

Vertebrate remains from this part of Britain are extremely scarce (Stallibrass 1995) and studies of Iron Age and Romano-British rural settlements, in particular, are hindered by this paucity of material. Unfortunately, the poor preservation conditions at Irby perpetuate this problem. Nothing can be said relating to the economy of the site in terms of animals and their products, other than to note that cattle and, almost certainly, sheep, were represented in the few fragments recovered.

The fact that the small calcined fragments appear to be sheep-sized more often than cattle-sized should not be taken to indicate a dominance of sheep remains at the site. Recent excavations of two Early Iron Age to post-Roman settlements at Port Seton, East Lothian (Haselgrove and McCullagh 2000) have revealed that sheep bones were more likely than cattle bones to become calcined (Hambleton and Stallibrass 2000). Indeed, at the Port Seton West site, only calcined bone survived (McCullagh pers. comm.), in sandy conditions that are probably not unlike those obtaining at Irby. Patterns of disposal often appear to have been different for sheep and cattle bones (pers. obs.). Whilst sheep/goat bones tend to dominate collections of unburnt animal bones from sites in southern Britain (in areas where better preservation conditions are less likely to have biased species representations), this pattern should not be presumed to have been the case in areas further north. Urban and military Roman sites in northern England (where greater depths of stratigraphy have often permitted better bone preservation than that obtaining at shallow rural sites) tend to contain significantly greater proportions of cattle bones than do similar sites in southern England. It is of particular research interest to investigate whether this difference is a development from earlier, Iron Age patterns, but the Irby material is not suitable for investigating this question.

The main item to note is that bones certainly were present at the site, probably throughout all of the main periods of occupation, and that some of these were subject to very high temperatures. This could have been caused by various activities, including the accidental or casual incorporation of bones into fires, the deliberate use of bones as fuel, or the deliberate cleaning-up of noxious debris.

A full catalogue is retained as part of the site archive.

Charred plant remains

J. P. Huntley

Introduction

Bulk samples were taken from a wide range and number of contexts for examination of charred plant remains and other material in order to investigate crop husbandry practices and landscape use. An assessment of a selection of these bulk samples was carried out (Huntley 1996), which demonstrated the presence of cereal grain and chaff in some. No patterns with respect to feature type, trench or provisional date, however, were found. Given the abundance of remains in some contexts the site had clear potential to address questions relating to crop husbandry and further samples were analysed. Contexts to analyse were chosen by a combination of random sampling by the excavator and targeting those areas initially assessed as being rich.

Radiocarbon dates were obtained on short-lived plant remains from some contexts although these were chosen on archaeological grounds alone.

Methodology

Samples were processed in the Durham laboratory by flotation with both flot and residue retained upon 500μ mesh after earlier experiments undertaking the work at Liverpool proved unreliable due to inadequate water supplies and drainage. The residues were checked for biological material, pottery or artefacts whilst the flots were examined under a stereomicroscope at magnifications of up to x50. For the flots, notes were made of the matrix components and seeds were identified and counted. Identification was by comparison with modern reference material held in the Department of Archaeology at the University of Durham. Although non-charred plant remains were present in many samples they are assumed to be modern or at least unrepresentative of the contemporary death assemblage and, hence, have been ignored. The free-draining soils suggest that it is unlikely that non-charred material has survived for long though. In many instances several bags of flot had been produced due to processing individual tubs of sediment over some years. Data were amalgamated to the context level for final analysis. Data were entered onto a computer using PHYTOPAK (Huntley *et al.* 1981) for ease of table manipulation and application of multivariate analyses. The full matrix data produced from this suite of programmes were also transferred to a Microsoft Access database in order to link to the archaeological information. The data were then standardised to seeds per 10 litres processed in order to enable valid comparisons between contexts to be made. Discussion relates to these standardised data unless otherwise stated. Nomenclature follows Clapham *et al.* (1962) with Tutin *et al.* (1964-80) volume 5 for cereals. For simplicity, all propagules are referred to as 'seeds' although strictly some are fruits or other fruiting parts.

For investigations of spatial patterns the site plan was scanned and then imported to ArcView with the sample grids attached as tables and, again, plotted in ArcView 3 for the PC.

Cereal grains were counted if they were estimated to be more than half complete, otherwise they were noted as being common and fragmentary in the technical report.

Figures are presented in the text with the main data tables collected together in Appendix 1.

Results and Discussion

Of the 144 contexts analysed, only 105 contained any plant remains (Appendix 1). Many of the flots produced were small (<50ml) although a few reached some litres of material. Modern vegetation – roots (coarse and fine), bark fragments and leaves – were present in many of the samples and are considered simply to reflect the shallow stratigraphy of the site. Clearly leaves were from the contexts near or at the surface but fine roots, in particular, were present throughout. They are not considered to represent a problem regarding contamination of the samples principally because they were very fine and would not have produced a cavity in the soil wide enough for the ingress of charred seeds. Technical descriptions by sample form part of the site archive; this also includes samples which were only assessed.

The matrix components

Not surprisingly charcoal formed the bulk of the flots. This was not rigorously identified although general notes were made about its form. Oak was not dominant other than in some contexts, detailed below, mixed species were common and heather-type wood was present in many samples. This latter may represent the burning of peat but could also reflect roofing material either deliberately or accidentally burnt during activity on the site. Some of the contexts contained coal although only ever in small amounts. Cinder/clinker was also recorded which could be the result of burning wood or coal. The charcoal was a mixture of well preserved material ranging from some with all diagnostic characters clearly visible through to rather glassy or tarry looking material which presumably had been burnt at higher temperatures. This would allow sulphurs etc. to melt and congeal with any surviving organics. Whilst they may indicate high temperatures, these could have been attained in a vigorous domestic fire and do not necessarily mean industrial processes. However, vitrified spatter and hammerscale and spatter are present in some samples and at least smithing is assumed to have been taking place at times on the site. Bone was rare and

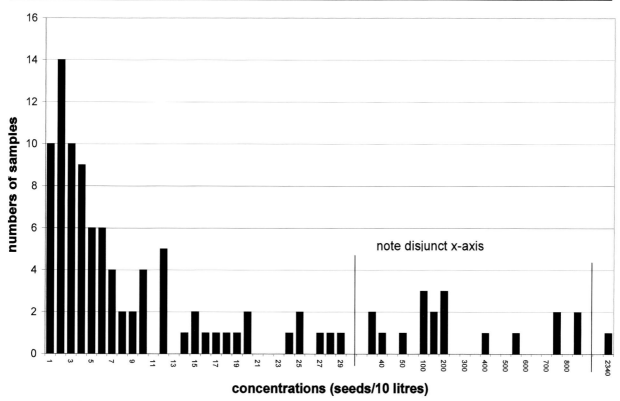

Fig. 3.1: Seed concentrations frequency plot

only preserved as fragmentary calcined pieces – again suggesting a high temperature (of the order of at least 800° C or so). At such temperatures the charcoal is likely to have become tarry as would any charred cereal grains present, thus there may be some biased assemblages present. Burnt material consisting of bases of grasses or sedges – so-called monocotyledonous rootstock – may well represent the burning of peat as a fuel or remains of a destroyed roofing material.

Plant concentrations

Charred plant remains survived in many contexts although only at high concentrations in rather few (Figure 3.1). The figure shows a skewed distribution typical of almost any prehistoric site in northern England. Most samples contain fewer than 5 seeds/10 litres and only 39 (~25%) containing more than 10 seeds/10 litres. However, the highest concentration is 2340 seeds/10 litres. Many of the cereal grains were coated in a mineral deposit which sometimes flaked off cleanly although, more often than not, fragmented the whole grain when this coating was eased off. It is therefore likely that grain remained in the residues to some degree but time did not allow for their systematic examination under the microscope. For some reason, perhaps related to their relatively large size, the wheat grains seemed particularly prone to these concretions.

Distribution of samples

Given the nature and duration of the excavations numerous trenches were excavated over several

gardens and this has proved immensely complex for archaeological interpretation. Samples have been analysed from 13 of these trenches and from four of the five phased groups plus an unphased group ('blank' below), although samples within this group are believed to have stratigraphical integrity. The latter are contexts which are associated with each other in spatial groups but cannot be tied to the overall dated stratigraphy of the site. Their being undated therefore reflects site logistics not site integrity.

Table 3.2 below provides a breakdown of all samples by period and broad context types sampled.

Middle Bronze Age to Iron Age samples are well represented (Table 3.2) as is 2nd-4th-century material and then 12th-15th century material. The other periods either have no samples (Period III late 1st-early 2nd century) or few (Period V 5th-12th centuries). Unphased, but stratified, material is common.

In terms of seed presence, only Period II has less than 20% barren samples with generally about a third of the samples in the other periods producing no seeds. Clearly this is disappointing but not unusual.

Regarding context types, the majority are fills of post-hole or pits with gully fills the next most common – these were a mixture of roundhouse gullies and other such linear features as distinct from ditch fills. Low numbers of any other one feature type make it unreasonable to try to investigate contents of specific feature types. Thus all are treated as equal.

	II	III	IV	V	VI	VII	Unphased	Total
Beamslot fill	1		2	1				4
Clay					2			2
Fill construction trench			2					2
Fill ditch			2				1	3
Fill gully/linear	6		8	1				15
Fill hearth/furnace/oven			2		5			7
Fill pit	1		2	4	5			12
Fill post-hole	24		7	1	16		11	59
Layer			1		1		11	13
Misc fill	3		1		2		1	7
Modern					1	1	2	4
Ploughsoil							1	1
Soil					3			3
Unknown	1		2				9	12
Total	36	0	29	7	35	1	36	144

Table 3.2a: Samples by period and context type

	II	III	IV	V	VI	VII	Unphased	Total
Beamslot fill	1							1
Fill construction trench			1					1
Fill ditch			2				1	3
Fill gully/linear	2		3					5
Fill pit	1			2				3
Fill post-hole	1		4		8		7	20
Layer					1		4	5
Misc fill	1							1
Modern						1	2	3
Soil					3			3
Unknown							4	4
Total	6	0	10	2	12	1	18	49
Percent barren samples	17%		34%	29%	34%	100%	50%	

Table 3.2b: Samples barren of seeds by period and context type

The plant remains

Due to the nature of the soils only charred remains are considered to be contemporary with activity on the site. Uncharred blackberry and elderberry seeds were present in several and abundant in a few contexts. Whilst they may represent contemporary material as they are woody and thus somewhat resistant to decay they are more likely to represent modern intrusive material. A few contexts contained the typical chickweed, fool's parsley and fat hen which almost certainly reflect modern material. All of these have been ignored with respect to any discussion.

Ecological habitats

For initial discussion purposes each taxon was assigned to a single category – either a specific ecological habitat or, in the case of cereals, as grain or chaff/straw categories. The ecological categories are over-simplified given that many taxa occur in several places but they

have been kept broad and give a general impression of the data (Fig. 3.3).

Cereal grains dominate the site assemblage reaching nearly 80% of the remains identified. Cereal chaff is next, followed by the broad group of weedy taxa (includes strict arable weeds, ruderals, grassland and, although arguable, heathland taxa such as *Sieglingia decumbens*). Even so they only constitute about 6% of the assemblage. Woodland and scrub taxa, including hazelnut shell fragments, reach just over 1% and other economic taxa (just flax and peas for this site) a meagre 0.03%. The broad conclusion therefore is that the assemblage consists mostly of cleaned grain but whether this reflects the activity of the site itself or, at least in part, the conditions of preservation will be discussed below.

More information, relating for example to local soil conditions, can be gained by looking at the individual taxa within these groups.

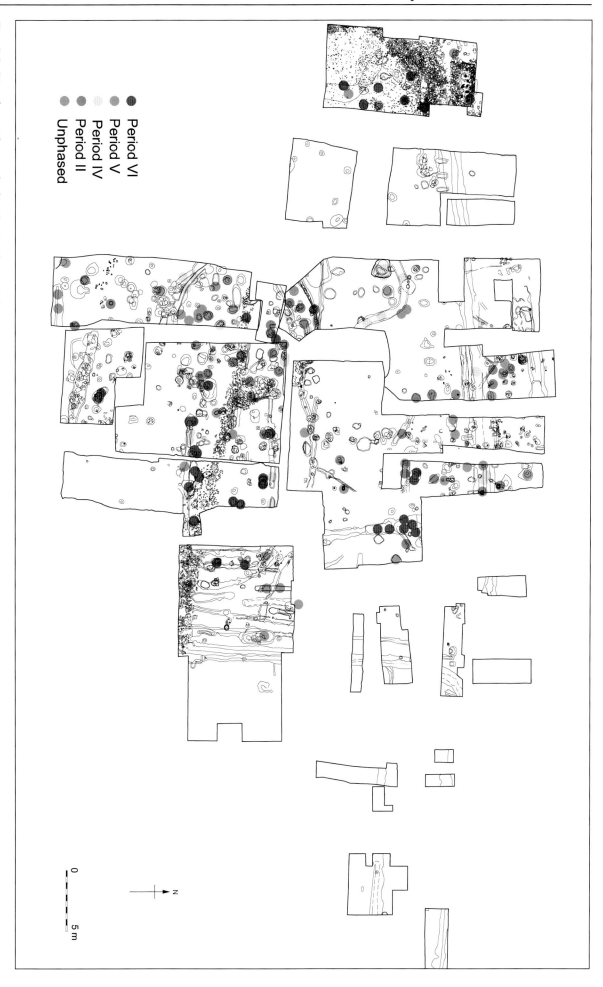

Fig. 3.2: Site plan with sample distribution by period

Period VI
Period V
Period IV
Period II
Unphased

0   5 m

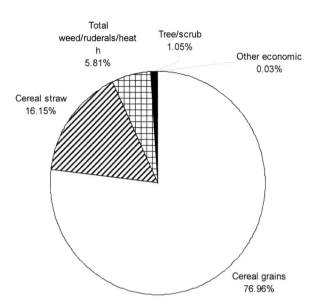

Fig. 3.3: Proportions of ecological habitats (all samples)

Economic taxa other than cereals

Only two taxa are involved – *Linum usitatissimum* (flax) and *Pisum sativum* (pea). The former occurs once and the latter twice; a further >4mm legume fragment was present and probably either another pea or *Vicia faba* (Celtic bean). As none of these species requires heat for drying prior to storage they have a relatively low chance of being burnt and hence preserved; thus they are almost always at low concentrations in charred assemblages. They can simply be interpreted as being used by the people at Irby but with no inference as to their importance in the economy.

Arable weeds, heath and more ruderal taxa (Table 3.3)

What may be considered strict arable weeds (category 'a') today are all characteristic of nutrient-enriched and somewhat heavier, damp soils which is somewhat of a surprise given the apparently sand-derived soils in the vicinity of Irby, though less well drained Stagnogley soils are present on the Boulder Clay slopes *c.* 100 m to the east. They may, of course, simply indicate well manured soils and thus even relatively intense agriculture. Although the classical arable weeds such as cornflower and corn cockle are very rare before the medieval period, taxa such as corn spurrey and corn marigold have a somewhat older history and could just have been expected in this assemblage especially as at least the latter two are also characteristic of lighter sandy soils. Their absence might therefore lend weight to the interpretation that the soils probably were being well manured during site occupation.

Sieglingia, today, is most common at the edges of heather moorland although its regular occurrence

amongst prehistoric and medieval charred cereal assemblages has lead to it being considered an arable weed of the past (Hillman in Kelly 1982). This is a possibility here although burnt heather twigs and wood are a regular, if not abundant, feature of the assemblage as well. Thus the *Sieglingia* with heather fragments may have arrived in grassy heath turves being used as either fuel or building material. *Sieglingia* is the most frequently occurring taxon, the only one represented by seeds, of this broad group.

		% occur-rence	# sam-ples	sum
a	Anthemis cotula - stinking mayweed	1.9	2	2
a	Chenopodium album - fat hen	4.8	5	5
a	Fallopia convolvulus - black bindweed	14.4	15	46
a	Galeopsis tetrahit - hemp nettle	1.0	1	1
a	Galium aparine - cleavers	6.7	7	22
a	Polygonum aviculare - knotgrass	4.8	5	5
a	Polygonum lapathifolium	1.0	1	3
a	Polygonum lapth./persicaria	9.6	10	125
a	Polygonum periscaria - pale persicaria	11.5	12	100
a	Veronica hederifolia	1.9	2	2
a/h	Sieglingia decumbens - heath grass	14.4	15	96
g	Plantago lanceolata - ribwort plantain	3.8	4	5
g	Rumex acetosella - sheep's sorrel	1.0	1	1
h	Pteridium aquilinum frond fragment - bracken	1.0	1	2
r	Brassica sp(p).	2.9	3	3
r	Cirsium sp(p). - thistles	1.0	1	1
r	Hyoscyamus niger - henbane	1.9	2	6
r	Raphanus raphanistrum pod frag. - radish	6.7	7	67
r	Rumex obtusifolius-type - docken	6.7	7	9

Table 3.3: Arable weeds, heath and more ruderal taxa

The more ruderal taxa (r) are principally non-annual species and thus presence of their seeds suggests longer term growth, certainly they would not seed during a single cereal cycle. Over time, some of their seeds may build up in the soil of fields only cultivated every few years but it is difficult to see how they would then become charred along with the cereals. It seems more likely that they represent plants growing around the settlement itself which may have had periodic clearing events or simply seeds being blown onto bonfires or into drying hearths etc. Thus their presence may be chance rather than anything else although clearly reflects the nature of the vegetation around the site to some degree. Of the taxa recorded radish pod fragments are the most common. These may reflect a crop being grown for

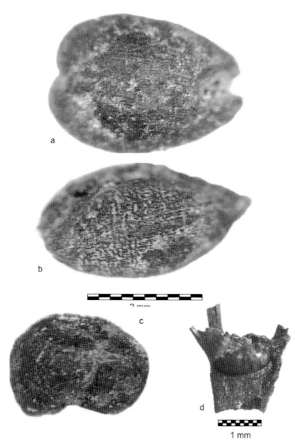

Fig. 3.4: Hordeum *remains. a: dorsal view of grain of naked barley; b: lateral view of naked barley grain showing clear wrinkles; c: end on view of naked barley grain showing rounded profile; d: 6-row rachis node of* Hordeum

its peppery oil – well loved by the Romans according to classical literature – or may reflect our native wild species simply opportunistically growing around the farm yards or even as an arable weed.

Wet ground (Table 3.4)

	% occurrence	# samples	sum
Carex (lenticular) - sedges	1.0	1	4
Carex (trigonous) - sedges	8.7	9	14
Eleocharis palustris - spike rush	1.9	2	2
Juncus - rush	1.0	1	1
Scirpus lacustris	1.0	1	1

Table 3.4: Wet ground species

These, too, are a rarely occurring group and all of them could easily have grown at the edges of wetter fields amongst cereal crops or arrived on-site via animal dung which was subsequently burnt. Their relative paucity certainly implies that the majority of the fields represented in this assemblage were well drained.

Broad/unclassified taxa (Table 3.5)

As with the majority of the other taxa, these could mostly have been found amongst crops in somewhat weedy fields. The relatively high numbers of brome grass caryopses probably reflect the fact that they are similar in size to cereal grains and thus are difficult to separate from them. Vetches/tares could have been in grassland but the almost absence of true grassland taxa suggests that this habitat is poorly represented in this assemblage and that the tares were from species which typically twine their way through cereal crops.

	% occurrence	# samples	sum
Bromus sp(p). grain - brome grass	19.2	20	66
Compositae undiff.	1.0	1	1
Gramineae <2mm - small grasses	5.8	6	9
Legume <4mm - vetches/tares	13.5	14	42
Legume pod fragment	1.0	1	1
Polygonaceae undiff.	2.9	3	4
Ranunculus repens-type - buttercups	1.0	1	1
Viola sp(p).	1.0	1	4

Table 3.5: Broad/unclassified taxa

Trees/scrub (Table 3.6)

This category is represented mostly by the remains of edible fruits and thus may well have been deliberately brought to the site as food. Equally the plants could

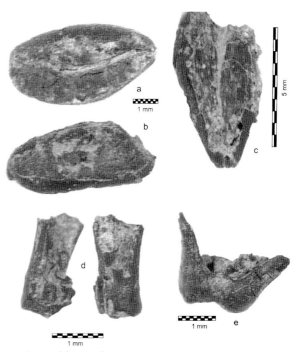

Fig. 3.5: Triticum dicoccon *remains. a: ventral surface of grain showing twisted groove; b: lateral view, emphasising twist; c: spikelet of two grains; d: glume base; e: spikelet fork*

have been growing or been planted around the site. Nothing is particularly outstanding and clearly the remains are relatively low in numbers. Only charred seeds of elderberry and blackberry have been included here; their uncharred remains were abundant in a few contexts where they are not necessarily considered to be contemporary with site activity.

	% occurrence	# samples	sum
Corylus avellana nut frag. - hazel	20.2	21	70
Ilex - holly	1.0	1	1
Malus/Pyrus - apple/pear	4.8	5	40
Rosa thorn	2.9	3	3
Rubus fruticosus - blackberry	1.0	1	1
Sambucus nigra - elderberry	3.8	4	5

Table 3.6: Trees/scrub

Cereals (Table 3.7)

This is the most important group of the assemblage. A variety of species is present and these reflect periods of occupation as discussed later below. Both naked and hulled barley grains were present. Hulled grains have an angular cross section and a longitudinal 'stripy' effect where the glumes are tightly pressed to the caryopsis. There are often parallel tramlines along the ventral groove (somewhat S-shaped or twisted in lateral grains of the 6-row variety), again reflecting remains of the glumes. The broadest point on the grain was mostly about the middle. They were generally well filled grains but some clearly were immature – no measurements were taken since the preservation was rarely 'excellent' and any such data would have been inaccurate.

The naked grains were smaller and more triangular in dorsal view with broadest point definitely near the non-embryo end; they were typically plump and rounded in cross section. Their surface was more crinkled with clear transverse wrinkles (Fig. 3.4). Many were at least partly obscured by sand grains and concretions thus precluding measurements being taken. When this material was eased off, the surface of the grain often came away too. Likewise it was not often possible to determine whether embryos were straight or set at an oblique angle in either the naked or the hulled grains. Whilst this gives suggestions as to whether the 6-row or the 2-row varieties were present, the chaff gives a much better indication – although clearly it does not itself determine whether the naked or the hulled were the 2- or 6-row. Chaff determined that at least 6-row barley was present since the positions of three, as opposed to one, grains on individual rachis internode sections were obvious.

Naked barley grains were the more abundant but hulled grains occurred in more samples.

	% occurrence	# samples	sum
Avena grain - oats	16.3	17	198
Cerealia undiff.	48.1	50	1559
Hordeum naked - barley	17.3	18	2506
Hordeum hulled - barley	52.9	55	659
Hordeum indet.	29.8	31	493
Secale cereale grain - rye	3.8	4	13
cf. Secale cereale	1.9	2	4
Triticum dicoccon - emmer wheat	25.0	26	2737
Triticum aestivo-compactum type grain - bread wheat	11.5	12	274
Triticum sp(p). grain	31.7	33	237
Triticum (hexaploid)	7.7	8	89
Triticum spelta - spelt wheat	3.8	4	5
Triticum cf. spelta	1.0	1	1
Avena awn	2.9	3	8
Culm nodes - cereal straw	1.0	1	1
Hordeum rachis internode	6.7	7	59
Hordeum 6-row rachis internode	1.9	2	8
Hordeum basal internode	2.9	3	6
Secale rachis internode	1.0	1	1
Triticum dicoccon glume base	22.1	23	1256
Triticum dicoccon spikelet fork	13.5	14	359
Triticum dicoccon spikelet - complete	1.0	1	1
Triticum glume	13.5	14	42
Triticum spelta glume	24.0	25	74
Triticum spelta spikelet fork	2.9	3	3
Triticum spikelet fork	1.0	1	2
Triticum brittle rachis internode	12.5	13	18
Triticum aestivum rachis node	2.9	3	3

Table 3.7: Cereal taxa

Wheats were abundant too. Although it is not reliable to identify grains to species (Hillman *et al.* 1995 for 1996) there were clear groups which are considered to best represent species and thus some categorisation was undertaken using the following criteria. Grains were determined as emmer from their slightly tapering to bluntly triangular dorsal view with a high dorsal ridge and steeply angled embryo (Figure 3.5). Many showed impressions of the glumes. Spelt grains were more parallel-sided, had rounded ends and were much flatter with a less steeply inclined embryo. Again glume impressions were obvious in many. Bread wheat as such only included rather rounded and dumpy grains but with a steep embryo leaving the somewhat parallel-sided grains but with broadest area above half way plus rounded embryos as either 'hexaploid' class (i.e. spelt or bread wheat) or even just 'wheat'.

Chaff is far more reliable for specific identification and does, in fact, confirm the presence of the three main wheat species. Emmer glumes are generally thick and chunky with both the primary and secondary keels well

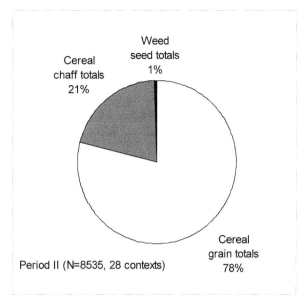

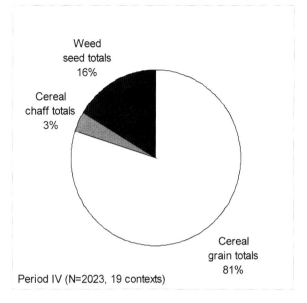

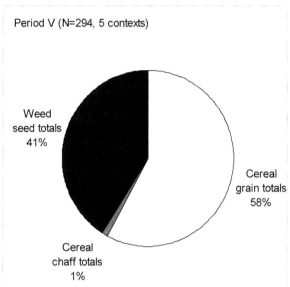

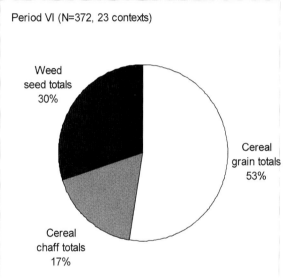

Fig. 3.6: Proportions of cereal grains, cereal chaff and weeds

defined but tertiary venation is minimal (Fig. 3.5). The angle at the primary keel is less than 90°. Spelt glumes have a reasonably well defined primary keel but then secondary and tertiary veins are almost equally distinct giving a clear stripy effect to the glumes. The angle at the primary keel is more than 90° giving a smooth rounded appearance to the inside of the glume. Bread wheat chaff takes the form of either the rachis internodes with a characteristic shield shape and vague blunt patches of tissue where the glumes had been inserted or, more commonly, of the glume bases themselves attached to a small plate of tissue. Even when highly degraded these have an obvious and characteristic shape. Brittle rachis internodes in the tables could refer to those of either emmer or spelt – they have obvious clean breaks at their ends compared with the more jagged appearance (and different shape) of those of bread wheat.

Oat grains and chaff were recorded. The grains are typically longer and narrower than any other cereal and have a V-shaped embryo occasionally with remains

of hairs still visible. The grains themselves cannot be identified as coming from wild or cultivated species. The only chaff recorded were fragments of the twisted awns. However, these are also present on other wild grasses and therefore cannot be conclusively identified as coming from oats. From the relatively low numbers recorded it is possible that we only have the wild species or a contaminant and that oats are not a crop in their own right.

Rye grains and chaff were identified too. Rye grains are especially similar to those of immature wheat but have a blunt and flat distal end, a very pointed embryo end (often asymmetric) and high dorsal ridge. They are often exceptionally shiny in appearance when charred. Their rachis internodes are similar to those of immature barley but have a much less well defined basal node, less flared at the upper end and are generally slimmer and more parallel sided. The rye is sufficiently uncommon to suggest that it was a contaminant of, probably, wheat crops rather than being a crop in its own right.

Overall the assemblage is dominated by a mixture of emmer wheat and naked plus hulled barley but bread wheat, spelt and possibly oats are also likely to have been grown as specific crops but the rye may well have been just a contaminant.

Crop husbandry: processing stages

Cereals have to be taken through various defined stages before they can end up in the cooking pot. These are well worked out using ethnographic models (see, for example, Hillman 1981) and widely used for interpreting charred seed assemblages. By looking at the proportions of the grains to chaff, and indeed weed seeds, as well as at the quality (size, aerodynamics etc.) of the weed seeds it is possible to investigate the stages of crop processing represented or not in an assemblage. However, this is best done for discrete periods or places of activity, or even at the individual sample level, rather than for the site as a whole.

First, evidence for harvesting and threshing of whole crops can be provided by the presence of culm nodes which represent the straw itself although cannot be determined to any species. Their very low presence (a single node!) at Irby suggests that straw was not a commodity discarded in these contexts. Thus it may be concluded that primary processing debris is not present in this assemblage although may well have been elsewhere on the site.

Figure 3.6 presents the proportions of cereal grain to chaff to weed seeds for those periods with more than 100 seeds counted in total. "n" refers to the totals of seeds with number of contexts analysed also presented. The weed seeds category includes those taxa which have been noted as possibles in the ecological discussion above but discount tree/scrub taxa and the perennials of

the ruderal class. It does therefore include annuals from the ruderal group, grassland and *Sieglingia* as well as the "typical" arable weeds. Cereal grain dominates all periods but there are striking differences between the proportions of weeds and chaff. In Period II weeds are more or less absent with chaff reaching 21%, by Period IV weeds are gaining importance at 16% with chaff decreasing drastically to 3%, whilst Period V has almost no chaff but over 41% weed seeds. Period VI sees chaff increasing again to 17% with weeds reducing to 30%. Overall, therefore, there is a shift from more chaff to more weeds through time. Can, or even should, this be related to presence of different processing stages?

Ratios grain:chaff:weeds

Three ratios have been calculated in order to determine stages of crop processing represented. These are: 1) glume to grain ratios for the glume wheats, 2) chaff to grain ratios for barley and 3) total cereal grains to weed seeds. Table 3.8 presents the data for each sample with more than 50 items for any ratio calculated. All fragments of definitive glume wheats have been included thus *Triticum* (hexaploid) has been omitted since it may represent bread wheat, a free-threshing species. Data for spikelets and spikelet forks have been multiplied by two as each comprises two glumes. Brittle rachis internodes have been omitted. All barley remains are included irrespective of being hulled or naked. The "weed seeds" category excludes trees/scrub, perennials and economic taxa as described above. The method used for calculating these ratios thus differs from that of van der Veen (1992) in that indeterminate cereal grains are excluded whereas she apportioned them to wheat or barley in proportion to the identified material. In the case of Irby this was not felt acceptable since free-threshing wheat was demonstrably present and could bias wheat grain totals.

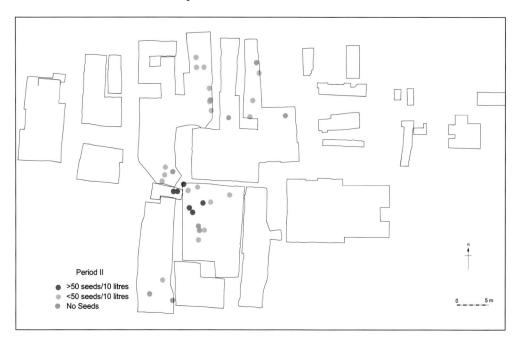

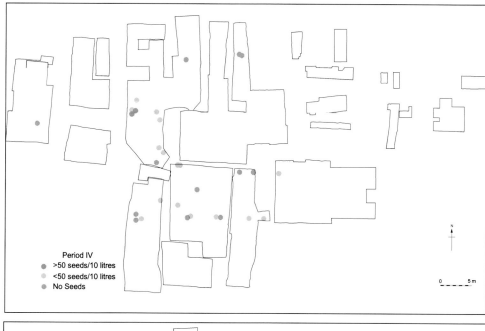

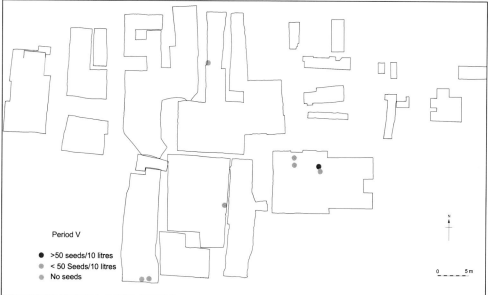

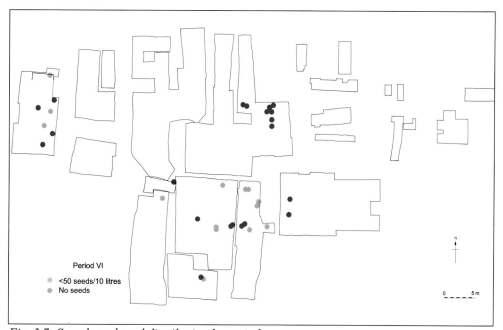

Fig. 3.7: Sample and seed distribution by period

Period	II	II	II	II	II	II	II	II	II	IV	IV	IV	V	VI
Phase	P3	P3	P3	P3	P3	P3	P3	P4	P3	R5	R5		EM4	M3
Context number	8236	8223	8171	7422	7423	8135	8240	9764	8225	6130	6138	8040	3715	7244
Structure			S27	S27	S27	S27	S28	S32	S28	S13	F9		F3 pit	F6
Total barley chaff		28	10	26				43	2					1
Total barley grain	221	1049	690	493	97	82	286	10	53	365	102	26	45	1
Chaff:grain ratio		0.03	0.01	0.05				4.3	0.04					
Total glume wheat chaff	105	732	650	202	14	149	64	21	42	1		4		11
Total glume wheat grain	208	645	990	174	59	272	266		70	1				
Glume:grain ratio	0.5	1.13	0.66	1.16	0.24	0.548	0.24		0.6					
Total weeds				14	2	1	21	4	5	293	15		120	33
Total cereal grain	429	1694	2360	677	171	604	552	11	123	1026	427	65	158	30
Weed to grain ratio				0.02	0.01	0.002	0.04	0.364	0.04	0.29	0.04		0.76	1.1

Table 3.8: Grain/chaff/weed data for contexts with more than 50 items in any ratio

Ears of emmer and spelt consist of spikelets and some of emmer were complete in one or two samples. Each spikelet generally contains two glumes and two grains thus a ratio of 1 will reflect complete spikelets. If the ratio is much more than 1 (more glume bases than grain) then Hillman's (1981) fine-sieving residue is probably represented. If much less than 1 (more grain than glume) then cleaned products are implied.

The 2-row barley only appears for certain during the medieval period in northern England and thus it is assumed that the barley present in Periods II to V is 6-row; that in Period VI, 13th-15th centuries, could be either. For barley ears, making the assumption of it all being 6-row, there are three spikelets, each with a single grain, per node thus leading to a ratio of 0.3 for complete ears. A ratio of much greater than 0.3 suggests more chaff thus winnowing/coarse sieving residues whilst a ratio of much less than 0.3 suggests fully processed grain.

If there are many more weed seeds than grain (a ratio of much greater than 1) this probably reflects cleaning by-products.

Although there are relatively few contexts reaching the calculation criteria there are nonetheless differences in processing by-products represented. Again, these show a trend through time since the contexts are arranged in temporal order. Period II samples suggest that some contexts are producing complete emmer spikelets with their almost 1:1 ratio but that others are representing cleaned grain with values of 0.2 or so. None suggests that fine sieving debris is present. It is often argued that the glume wheats were stored in the spikelet which would be more resistant to attack by grain weevils, the glumes being extremely tough, and that the final parching and cleaning stages were carried out immediately prior to us-

age. Certainly this could have been the case in some of the contexts here. The problem is that glume bases often burn away in advance of the grain as evidenced in modern experiments (Boardman and Jones 1990) thus their absence might simply be a taphonomic effect. These samples likewise contain minimal weed seeds as would be expected in a cleaned/stored product but they, too, are likely to burn away prior to the grain. Absence of these items therefore cannot necessarily reflect original absence of the material.

For many contexts the barley story is the same – low ratios, if chaff is even present, suggest that the barley is basically a cleaned product. However, one context (9764) of Period II Iron Age date has a very high chaff:grain ratio and almost certainly represents debris from the early stages of processing a barley crop. Interestingly, it contains minimal evidence for wheat although there is a very high proportion of indeterminate cereal grains. If these were all assumed to be barley then the ratio would have been 0.34 (125 grain:43 barley chaff) making the material whole ears. Thus considerable caution is needed in interpreting any of these ratios!

As noted above, weed seeds become more common through time up to Period V and the ratio of weeds to grain certainly increases throughout. However, it rarely goes above one, and then with quite small numbers overall, thus more often there are more grains than weeds. Fine sieving or other by-products are therefore not dominant in any context.

The weed seeds can be categorised by their size and aerodynamics which can also provide evidence for particular processing stages as demonstrated by (Jones 1984). Most of those present in the Irby assemblage are classified as small, free and heavy representing the by-product from the fine sieving stage.

Thus apart from taphonomic considerations, which are not quantifiable, it can be argued that the earlier contexts contain more or less completely processed cereals whilst the later material includes some of the fine sieving waste. As already commented however, other stages of processing may be occurring elsewhere on the site. In addition, clearly there is less emmer as time progresses with bread wheat values increasing and the nature of bread wheat, being a free-threshing wheat, means that its chaff remains are not as likely to be as prominent as those of emmer. The bread wheat rachis will remain more or less intact after threshing and be used as straw.

Period-level discussion

Tables, individually numbered, are presented as Appendix 1. For the sake of comparisons the data are presented as seeds/10 litres sediment processed throughout these tables.

Looking at a more archaeological discussion, there are considerable variations between contexts within periods thus specific contexts may offer particular interpretations. For more detail at the context level, the technical report in the site archive should be consulted. Here the broader discussion and conclusions are made.

Samples associated with groups but not dated to specific periods are generally rather sparse in their plant remains and no individual context offers a reliable interpretation. The most common and abundant remain is just about indeterminate cereal grains suggesting that preservation is rather poor in these contexts or that material was moved around prior to burial, more so than in many other contexts.

Period II contexts (Appendix Table 1) represent later prehistoric times and fall into two distinct groups. The first is mid Bronze Age, the second middle Iron Age, though only one context (8227) can be positively dated to the latter and most of the samples probably belong to the Bronze Age. They contain the richest samples for the site with eight of the 27 samples containing charred plant remains at concentrations of greater than 100 items per 10 litres. There is a clear preponderance of naked barley grain and emmer grain and glume bases. Hulled barley is moderately abundant occurring in 18 of the 28 contexts but spelt wheat rare (in six of 28), and then only as glume bases. Two of the rich samples have moderate numbers of indeterminate cereal grains suggesting poorer preservation (contexts 8135 and 8171) although each has either as many, or twice as many, identifiable grains as indeterminate cereals. Context 8171 is the fill of a truncated post-hole within Structure 27 and has 833 items per 10 litres. This would suggest that the associated building, or one very nearby, was concerned with

cereal storage or possibly processing. The assemblage suggests that storage is more likely particularly as several of the emmer grains remained as spikelets. The same applies to 8223, the richest sample on the site with 2340 items per 10 litres. It too was a post-hole fill. Context 8173, an oval feature, contained some moderate numbers of calcined animal bone fragments. Other samples from Trench XIX, mostly post-hole fills, were varied although with a few rich contexts (8236 and 8223). Context 9764 – another post-hole fill – contained moderate numbers of 6-row barley chaff. The single seed of flax and the few fragments of apple/pear were restricted to this period too – the latter perhaps reflecting use of wild native food resources and which are characteristic of earlier prehistoric periods elsewhere. Flax would have been used for its fibre and possible oil but a single seed hardly lends itself to interpretation.

In summary then, Period II samples are dominated by naked barley grain and emmer grain and/or chaff with few weeds or other cereal taxa. There are no strongly contrasting contexts in terms of taxa although concentrations do vary widely. There are no apparent statistical trends, suggesting that the period was relatively stable in terms of cereal usage even if there was an apparent cultural change from Bronze Age to Iron Age as demonstrated by the radiocarbon samples. Arguably, apples were used, though this is based upon a small number of seeds.

Comparative and dated sites in the north west are absent and thus it is difficult to see how, or indeed if, Irby fits a regional pattern. In the north east, emmer is the dominant wheat throughout the Bronze Age and early Iron Age but has generally been superseded by spelt wheat by the later Iron Age (Huntley and Stallibrass 1995; van der Veen 1992). As van der Veen notes though, emmer was retained for longer north of the Tyne and she argues for a cultural or social reason rather than an environmental one. More recent work contradicts this, however, with spelt frequently occurring in lowland sites north of the Tyne (University 2008), although emmer clearly was retained in upland sites. Southern Scotland tends to retain emmer for longer too (Huntley 2000a). Naked barley is rare in the north east but generally reflects earlier sites again; sites however are few and far between and most such sites are, in fact, in northern Scotland or the Islands. On the face of it then, the Irby samples might represent the earlier part of this period but equally the north-west regional pattern may not follow that for the north east and Scotland. Until further sites are excavated and dated, and have well sampled deposits, Irby will stand as the 'type site'. The radiocarbon dates suggest that Period II, or at least part of it, is earlier than at first thought. The latest dates obtained were on cereal grains from context 8227 and calibrate to 410-200 BC (OxA 8485: 2275±40 and OxA 8486: 2270±40). Other dates were clearly earlier and centred around 1400-1100 calibrated BC (Table 2.1).

	II	III	IV	V	VI	VII
Avena grain - oats	1		33	17	5	1
Cerealia undiff.	370		121	20	17	1
cf. Secale cereale			1	2		
Hordeum hulled - barley	179		68	7	13	1
Hordeum indet.	261		27	20	5	1
Hordeum naked	2160		13	0	1	1
Secale cereale grain			1	5		
Triticum (hexaploid)			4	5	17	1
Triticum aestivum grain	2		32	12	2	1
Triticum cf. spelta				0	1	1
Triticum dicoccon	2186		7	0	4	1
Triticum sp(p). grain	15	2	64	3	25	1
Triticum spelta			4	0	4	1
Anthemis cotula - stinking mayweed			1	1		
Bromus sp(p). grain			6	4	38	2
Carex (lenticular) - sedges			1			
Carex (trigonous) - sedges	1		2	0	4	1
Chenopodium album - fat hen	5		2	0	2	1
Cirsium sp(p). - thistles						1
Compositae undiff.						
Eleocharis palustris - spike rush			1			
Fallopia convolvulus - black bindweed	12		4	2	3	1
Galeopsis tetrahit - hemp nettle						1
Galium aparine - cleavers	16		1		5	1
Gramineae <2mm - small grasses	3	1	2			
Juncus - rush						1
Hyoscyamus niger - henbane	2				4	1
Plantago lanceolata - ribwort plantain			1			
Polygonum aviculare	2		1	1		
Polygonum lapathifolium			1			
Polygonum lapth./persicaria	2		2	44	4	1
Polygonum periscaria	1		7	1	7	1
Polygonaceae undiff.	5		2			
Pteridium aquilinum frond fragment						
Ranunculus repens-type						
Raphanus raphanistrum pod frag.			10	5		
Rubus fruticosus						1
Rumex acetosella					1	
Rumex obtusifolius-type	1		3	1		1
Sambucus nigra				0	5	1
Scirpus lacustris						1
Sieglingia decumbens	2		4	2	9	1
Veronica hederifolia			1			
Viola sp(p).						
Avena awn			2			
Culm nodes - cereal straw					1	1
Hordeum 6-row rachis internode	23					
Hordeum basal internode	6				1	1
Hordeum rachis internode	71				2	1
Secale rachis internode	1					
Triticum aestivum rachis node			1		1	1

Triticum brittle rachis internode	3		10	1	5	1
Triticum dicoccon glume base	1018		15		2	1
Triticum dicoccon spikelet - complete	1					
Triticum dicoccon spikelet fork	276		2	1	2	1
Triticum glume	4		11		15	1
Triticum spelta glume	28		9	1	23	1
Triticum spelta spikelet fork					2	1
Triticum spikelet fork				0	2	1
Brassica sp(p).			3	1		
Corylus avellana nut frag. - hazel	32		1		6	1
Ilex - holly				1		
Legume <4mm	8		2		6	1
Legume >4mm						
Legume pod fragment						
Linum usitatissimum - flax	1					
Malus/Pyrus - apple/pear	36					
Pisum sativum - pea			1			
Rosa thorn		1			2	1
Total	6734	4	484	157	246	42

Table 3.9: Period summary data (seeds/10 litres)

Thus the botanical interpretation of the Irby assemblage representing the earlier Bronze Age based upon other northern sites does seem to fit.

Period IV contexts (Appendix Table 2) are mostly associated with the mid-2nd- to late 4th-century during which the roundhouses and rectangular buildings were constructed. The samples are from a range of context types – beam slots, linear gullies, ditch fills and various pits and post-holes. The 19 contexts are all relatively clean but six have concentrations of about 20 items/10 litres and two considerably more – 6130 with 128 items/10 litres and 6138 with 177 items/10 litres. About one-third of the cereal grains are indeterminate and this again would suggest poorer preservation or movement of items prior to burial. Naked barley only occurs in three contexts although emmer grains and/or chaff are more abundant, being recorded in 10 contexts – all in low concentrations only though. Hulled barley is scattered through ten of the nineteen contexts with two contexts having moderate concentrations, namely in 6138 (41/10 ltres) and 6130 (24/10 litres). Spelt remains are sparse, occurring in only three contexts. Samples from later Roman activity in northern England nearly always are dominated by hulled barley and spelt wheat with bread wheat, oats and rye present although not abundant. Emmer and naked barley are hardly ever recorded. The most likely argument relating to these Irby samples is that the contexts were kept relatively clean but that earlier material was being mixed in with contemporary deposits which would certainly be possible with the relative shallow stratigraphy. However, with few comparative sites again, it could be that emmer retains popularity for longer in the west.

Only five contexts were sampled from Period V (late Roman to early medieval, 5th-12th centuries), and only one of these (3715) contained any concentrations of seeds (Appendix Table 3). It was dominated by oats, indeterminate barley grain, bread wheat grains and periscaria seeds. The bread wheat in particular strongly suggests a later date than Roman. The other contexts had sufficiently low concentrations as to be of no interpretative value.

The 23 Period VI contexts sampled (Appendix Table 4) have now been dated as medieval, though dates are generally uncertain. A single radiocarbon date on cereal grains from 3087 of 260-530 cal AD (Table 2.1) is of the later Roman or early post-Roman period and suggests the presence of residual material. Plant remains are relatively sparse throughout the samples thus offering no conclusive interpretations. Spelt wheat and hulled barley are just about the most common items and naked barley and emmer are rare. Bread wheat is very rare and there are only a few scattered fragments of oats. If the dates of this period were not known at all, the plant assemblage would fit as a species-poor fairly typical Roman suite but this does not fit in with it being later than Period IV. It is probably fair to say that the data are too few to offer an interpretation. The one context (5324) from later medieval Period VI (Structure 18) contains a single sheep's sorrel seed.

Table 3.9 presents the summary data at the period level – again standardised to seeds/10 litres. It emphasises the relative richness of the Period II samples with naked barley, emmer grain and chaff. The other dated periods clearly have a range of species but nothing is dominant. The group of non-assigned samples clearly has much more in common, in general, to Period II samples.

General discussion and summary

Irby has produced a contemporary charred assemblage dating from the mid Bronze Age through to medieval. Coal and cinders were present in many of the flots although they were dominated by wood charcoal. Charcoal species were varied and clearly heather wood was a well used commodity – whether specifically as fuel or the remains of burnt roofing etc. is unclear. However, the presence of burnt monocot culm bases suggests that poorly humified peat was being used as well, though whether as fuel or roofing is again unclear. The seed assemblage is dominated by charred cereal grains although a few contexts do have sufficient cereal chaff or weed seeds to suggest that fine sieving by-products are present. These together imply that the occupants of the site were probably both processing and growing their own cereals although the fine sieving debris by itself might suggest processing of spikelets brought in from elsewhere. Many of the samples, however, clearly reflect the background activity of the site and cannot be used to interpret specific activities in specific contexts. Other, non-sampled contexts, may of course have produced different evidence and any interpretations offered refer only to the specific contexts analysed here.

Weed seeds suggest in the main that soils were nutrient-enriched and somewhat heavy with very few denizens of acidic sandy soils represented. This is a little at odds with the local soils today which tends towards sandy, looking at the nature of the soil samples; however, manure was probably widely available and no doubt used and less well drained, Stagnogley soils are present *c.* 100 m to the east.

Naked barley and emmer wheat dominate the Bronze Age contexts which parallels the evidence from the north east of England. Whilst chaff of emmer is quite common, weed seeds are relatively rare. This may reflect a stored product, emmer either as grain or in spikelets, but it could reflect preservational or taphonomic conditions. The high levels of mineral concretions on many grains might indicate that more delicate material has probably been lost.

It is disappointing that no samples derive from the early Roman period (Period III) as this is the one period with comparative material from the north west at Carlisle. The majority of the contexts analysed from Period IV, the 2nd-4th centuries AD, have produced limited results in general although a few richer contexts were analysed. They are considered to contain at least some residual material but there is, nonetheless, a dearth of spelt grain or chaff which would have been expected for deposits of this date. Whilst the published evidence indicates that Roman military material from the north west (for example Huntley 2000b) is similar to that from further north and east it may be that the native farmers around Irby retained their preferences for emmer and naked barley and that these continued as the staple crops for some considerably longer period in the north west. Of Period V little may be said as the few contexts sampled had very low concentrations of seeds. However, the few rich samples have a bread wheat, barley and, possibly, oat suite more suggestive of post-Roman times, if the site had been in the north east again, and would thus fit with the general dating of the period. Spelt may have been used during this period but the evidence is very limited. Other native sites of this period in the north west await to be investigated. The medieval material of Period VI is likewise generally low in seed concentrations. It does not, however, reflect a typical medieval assemblage of bread wheat but equally the naked barley and emmer of the earlier prehistoric periods is missing. Spelt is recorded in very low concentrations.

Thus, in summary, Irby has, as many sites still do, asked more questions than it has answered. On the face of it, its assemblage suggests that local farmers retained emmer and naked barley cultivation for longer than elsewhere in the north but then apparently made the transition straight to bread wheat and oats with spelt remaining rather poorly represented. Clearly, further material from similarly dated native sites urgently needs acquiring.

Pollen analyses from the Romano-British enclosure ditch (D1)

J. B. Innes

Introduction

Pollen analysis was conducted upon four sediment samples from primary contexts of the Romano-British enclosure ditch (D1). Standard pollen preparation techniques were used (Moore and Webb 1978), involving the disaggregation and removal of organic material by alkali digestion using a 10% solution of sodium hydroxide, followed by acetylation. The samples were highly mineral in nature and so required the use of hot hydrofluoric acid to remove silicates. In all samples pollen preservation was generally poor, and so those pollen grains most affected by corrosion were not recovered in any quantity, and the pollen counts are perhaps slightly biased towards types which are more resistant. Pollen concentrations were, however, quite high so that total land pollen counts (excluding fern and moss spores) of over 300 grains were achieved in each case. This provides statistically valid counts which may be expressed in percentage form, and so the results from Irby are shown in Table 3.10 as percentages of total land pollen. Although not included in the pollen sum, fern and moss spore counts are shown as percentages of it. Plant nomenclature follows Clapham *et al.* (1962).

Context 10					
Pinus	<1	Corylus/Myrica	<1	Calluna	2
Betula	2	Gramineae	6	Pteridium	3
Alnus	8	Cereal-type	<1	Sphagnum	<1
Quercus	<1	Cyperaceae	3		
Tilia	<1	Taraxacum	65		
Salix	6	Plantago lanceolata	2		
Context 17					
Betula	4	Calluna	2	Plantago lanceolata	4
Alnus	5	Gramineae	6	Senecio	<1
Ulmus	<1	Cyperaceae	2	Pteridium	<1
Salix	2	Rosaceae	2	Sphagnum	<1
Corylus/Myrica	2	Taraxacum	59	Chenopodiaceae	<1
Context 19					
Pinus	1	Gramineae	21	Taraxacum	40
Betula	4	Cereal-type	6	Cruciferae	<1
Alnus	8	Cyperaceae	4	Rosaceae	<1
Salix	<1	Chenopodiaceae	<1	Senecio	1
Corylus/Myrica	3	Centaurea cyanus	1	Matricaria	<1
Hedera	<1	Plantago lanceolata	1	Pteridium	3
Lonicera	<1	Polygonum aviculare	<1	Filicales	<1
Calluna	1	Spergula arvensis	<1	Sphagnum	<1
Context 25					
Betula	6	Gramineae	15	Pteridium	2
Alnus	8	Cyperaceae	6	Sphagnum	<1
Salix	1	Rosaceae	1	Taraxacum	55
Corylus/Myrica	2	Calluna	1	Plantago lanceolata	2
Lonicera	1				

Table 3.10: Pollen percentages from the enclosure ditch D1 (Period IV)

Results

Although differences in detail occur, the four Irby samples are sufficiently similar to be discussed together. All samples are characterised by relatively low percentages of tree and shrub pollen, being 17% of total land pollen in each case, except that of the sample from context 17, in which they rise to 23%. Shrub types tend to be more important than forest trees. The counts therefore reflect generally open vegetation conditions dominated by herbaceous plants, with perhaps a little scrub woodland nearby. Gramineae (Grasses) are well represented, but the most abundant single herb recorded is Taraxacum (Dandelion) type which achieves between 40% and 65% of total land pollen. High totals of Taraxacum type pollen (Liguliflorae) have been commonly reported from sediments recovered from archaeological contexts, however, and particularly from mineral soil deposits in such situations. These are due mainly to differential preservation factors (Bottema 1975; Dimbleby 1985) since these pollen grains are highly resistant to corrosive processes.

The rest of the pollen counts contain a highly diverse assemblage of pollen types in which a wide range of trees, shrubs and herbs occur in low percentages. Betula (Birch) and Alnus (Alder) are the most common woody taxa and probably represent local shrub vegetation. Forest trees such as Quercus (Oak), Tilia (Lime), Ulmus (Elm), and Pinus (Pine) are present only as one or two grains in the entire analysis. Grassland herbs which support the Gramineae and Taraxacum counts are Plantago lanceolata (Ribwort Plantain) and Cyperaceae (Sedges), while low but consistent values from Pteridium (Bracken) also suggest open conditions. More herb types, however, are evidence of arable cultivation and Cereal-type pollen grains are found in samples from contexts 10 and 19. These grains could have originated in non-cultivated grass taxa such as Agropyron (Couch-grass) but they resemble closely grains of Triticum (Wheat) and Hordeum (Barley) type as defined by Andersen (1979) and almost certainly represent local farming activity. Cereal-type pollen reaches 6% in the sample from context 19, which is a considerable proportion of total land pollen given the low production and dispersal properties of cereal grains. This high frequency is accompanied by other herbs which may signify arable farming, including *Centaurea cyanus* (Cornflower), *Spergula arvensis* (Corn Spurrey) and *Polygonum aviculare* (Knotgrass). Less secure indicators such as Chenopodiaceae (Goosefoot family), Senecio (Groundsel) type, Cruciferae (Cabbage family and Matricaria (Mayweed) type also occur. There are few indications that a significant amount of heathland existed nearby, the values for Pteridium and Calluna (Heather) being very low indeed.

Discussion

The pollen evidence from the Irby ditch samples therefore records a landscape of mixed vegetation, but one in which woodland was considerably less important that grassland or cultivated ground. There is no reason to suppose that this area of the Wirral would naturally have been other than forested, and so the generally open landscape may be assumed to be a legacy of earlier deforestation, presumably for the mixed farming which

is represented clearly in the pollen assemblages. There are no indications in the pollen assemblages themselves as to the chronology of the sediments from which they were recovered, but the close similarity suggests that the four contexts sampled are probably closely comparable in age, there being no discernable change in the vegetation cover between their deposition. The clear evidence of cereal farming and a deforested landscape show them to be more recent, and probably considerably so, than the Elm Decline of 5000bp which occurred in the early Neolithic period. This pollen evidence would be quite consistent with a Roman-period date, a time during which much clearance of woodland, often with the presence of cereal cultivation, is shown by the pollen record to have occurred in the Merseyside region (Howard-Davis *et al.* 1988; Innes and Tomlinson unpub.)

4: The Finds

Lithics

R. W. Cowell

Introduction

The lithic assemblage from Mill Hill Road, Irby comprises 205 pieces of struck flint and chert and 21 pieces of natural flint. Nearly all of this was found redeposited in later contexts. This lack of stratigraphic control means that the assemblage is of limited value as it can only be dated through its typological and technological characteristics. In the north west, however, stratified independently dated sites are rare so that even dating the assemblage through typological analogy involves much uncertainty. Therefore, national trends mainly have to be used to identify the chronology of stylistic and technological changes in the characteristics of local assemblages. As these need not be exactly applicable to this region such analogies could be misleading.

A second feature of local assemblages is that they are often comparatively small. This makes the statistical trends within them less viable than would be the case for larger assemblages, where such trends can be more confidently taken as representative of the original structure of the assemblage. Thus small assemblages do not generally receive detailed analysis. In the lowlands of this region, however, it seems likely that only rarely will large lithic assemblages be forthcoming that could overcome this difficulty (Middleton 1993). But, as lithics are the most common form of evidence relating to the nature of prehistoric landuse and settlement in the region, less than ideal data has to form the basis for interpretation if progress is to be made in providing explanations for the archaeological material that is representative of this region. It may be possible eventually to gauge the validity of the conclusions reached from this type of data once a large enough database of individual assemblages exists (Cowell 2000a; 2005b).

A slightly less than standard approach is also taken here to the classification and analysis of the assemblage. This is partly due to the nature of the raw material available locally in prehistory and the technology by which it was worked, which differs from many areas where raw material choice is more plentiful. Local assemblages may therefore have their own distinctive characteristics that could be hidden or overlooked in standard approaches. Other regional analyses have also found it necessary to structure lithic analysis reports in a non-standard way (Healey 1987).

The Context

The stratigraphic evidence for the prehistoric elements of the site consists of occupation deposits, principally in Areas VIII and XLI and the features associated with the middle Bronze Age Structure 27, along with a few miscellaneous features that on stratigraphic grounds appear potentially prehistoric (see Chapter 2).

The occupation layers could not be clearly defined during excavation and were dominated by the existence of Romano-British finds and features. Hence, only restricted pockets of prehistoric layers, of limited depth, have been identified. In some cases these were associated with middle Bronze Age pottery, while in others middle Iron Age finds associated with Bronze Age pottery suggest reworking of the earlier deposits in the first millennium BC. The struck lithics that occur in the occupation layers show potential mixing of material over a long period with activity of Mesolithic and later date being represented (see Chapter 5). Those finds from prehistoric layers are shown in Table 4.1, but they provide little indication of the date of such deposits from the lithics alone.

The features associated with Structure 27 are the most coherently identified prehistoric contexts, with good middle Bronze Age and reasonably convincing structural associations. Only one of these features (8197, fill 8171), however, produced struck lithics, which are Mesolithic in date (SF10566, microlith; SF10580, north Wales chert debitage). The fact that they occurred in a post-hole with prehistoric pottery and cereals, which produced two middle Bronze Age dates, means that they are residual.

Context	SF	Artefact	Period
6165	7315	Retouched flake	PU
6165	7316	Flake	PU
6165	7615	Flake	PU
6165	7626	Bipolar flake	PU
6165	7616	Debitage chip	PU
8339	8339	Debitage chunk	PU
8322	7854	Debitage chunk	PU
6198	7798	Microlith	M

Key: M - Mesolithic, PU - Prehistoric uncertain

Table 4.1: Struck lithics from basal occupation layers

There are several miscellaneous features, post-hole 9745 (fill 9744), a small pit (9778; fill 9777) and a beam-slot (8363; fill 8362), which included struck lithics (Table 4.2). This material is difficult to date on its own and so can neither suggest a date for the features nor can the lithics themselves be confidently dated by association. One piece (SF8178) occurred with two sherds of middle Bronze Age pottery, but the artefact sample is so small that it is not clear whether the finds are associated or whether one or both categories are residual, although stratigraphically there are grounds for believing that the features themselves may be prehistoric.

Context	SF	Artefact	Period
9744	8158	Retouched blade fragment	EP
9744	8178	Bipolar blade	EP?
8362	8069	Debitage chunk	PU
8362	8070	Blade-like flake	PU
9777	8227	Scraper	PU
8070	8362	Blade	EP

Key: EP - Early prehistoric (i.e. Mesolithic/early Neolithic),
PU - Prehistoric uncertain

Table 4.2: Struck lithics from miscellaneous features, potentially prehistoric in date

The Assemblage

The components of the assemblage are presented in Table 4.3, divided into the major groups deriving from the lithic reduction process. A glossary of terms associated with this process is included at the end of this volume.

Raw Material	Chert	Flint	Indet.	Total
Cores	1	14		15
Removals	13	38		51
Debitage	16	75	6	97
Implements	4	36	2	42
Total	34	163	8	205

Table 4.3: Breakdown of raw materials by artefact group

The two main raw materials used on the site are flint (80%) and chert (17%), with the rest being of indeterminate type. Small flint pebbles provide the bulk of the raw material, with all flint cores being discarded at less than 40 mm long while some were originally only *c*. 20 mm long. Seventy per cent of the flint is in the colour range of shades of grey to brownish grey and reddish or yellow-brown, with lustrous and opaque types, ranging in quality from fairly good to poor. Natural nodules of this kind have been recorded widely across the boulder clay areas of the county during fieldwalking (Cowell 1991a) and in prehistory would have been potentially available in inland areas where soil was disturbed, in stream banks and on the beach.

Of those pieces from Irby with appreciable cortex there are nine reasonable contenders for a beach origin and a further 16 with a water-smoothed cortex that has presumably originated either in rivers or at the coast, assuming it did not occur during the transport of the pebbles within the glacially derived boulder clay. Sixty-three pieces have a rough cortex that suggests a boulder clay origin unaffected by water. The rest of the flint comprises miscellaneous colours, most of which is probably from the boulder clay, and a small amount of indeterminate source, often because the material is too small to be clearly identifiable.

Of the chert, 19 (56%) of the 34 struck pieces are from the same source as is used on two nearby sites, at Greasby Copse *c*. 1 km to the north-east, and Thurstaston Dungeon *c*. 1.5 km to the south-west of Irby, where this material was found almost exclusively and has been dated to the early Mesolithic period on typological grounds (Cowell 1992). Most of these types of chert can be ascribed a source in north Wales (Longworth 2000). They consist of colours ranging from black to grey-brown, to purplish-blue to white. Most is of reasonably good, lustrous quality with a proportion of poorer, granular grey-brown material.

The rest of the chert from Irby is more difficult to source purely from macroscopic inspection. Other than pieces too small to identify, they consist of various dark or light grey cherts about which little can be said. It is likely that virtually all chert was brought to the site by human agency. If it were not all from north Wales, then the next nearest potential source would be the Pennines. Two small pieces of pebble chert represent the only examples that could have been collected locally from the boulder clay.

Cores

Type of core	Bipolar	Platform/ bipolar	Platform	Indet.
Blade	1	3	1	
Flake	4	2		2
Split pebble	2			
Total	7	5	1	2

Table 4.4: Technology of the cores

Apart from one chert example, all the cores are flint. There are six platform cores in the assemblage. Only one seems to have been solely reduced through hand held percussion (Fig. 4.1, no. 1). Five others, which have produced either small blades or narrow flakes, have been at least partially reduced in a bipolar fashion, which is indicated by the crushing, irregular fractures and prominent impact bulbs opposite the striking platforms (Fig. 4.1, nos 2-5; SF9802, not illustrated). This was evidently done to allow the removal of usable flakes as the original pebble became difficult to handle. All the cores of this kind are less than 13 g in weight.

In the core debitage category, associated with a platform technique, are three flint core rejuvenation flakes, two of which (nos 10-11) have horizontally removed the striking platform. The latter is of prepared form similar to three of the cores (nos 3-5).

Numerically, there are more cores that are associated primarily with reduction through the bipolar method. The two largest of this type have been used to produce either blade-like flakes or large flakes (nos 6-7). The former of these is a dark grey chert, which is not obviously one of the north Wales types, the other is boulder clay flint. All the remaining cores are very small, being less than 10g. Only on one (no. 8) has there been an attempt to produce small blades. Others have resulted from the removal of small, less regular flakes or are little more than split pebbles (no. 9). Two flint bipolar cores have been used subsequently as the blanks for retouched artefacts (Fig. 4.3, nos 45, 47). Additionally, there are two flint pebbles, weighing 13 g and 29 g respectively, that have been tested with the removal of a few irregular flake scars.

Removals

As with the cores, there are two contrasting technological characteristics within this category, although clear-cut trends are obscured somewhat by the low numbers involved.

	Blades	Blade-like flakes	Flakes
Bipolar			
Flint	1		18
Chert			1
Standard			
Flint	3		9
Chert	1	2	1
Total	5	2	29

Table 4.5: Technology of complete removals by material

Of the complete removals, fewer have been produced by a standard knapping technique than by the bipolar method. However, if a further 10 incomplete but still reasonably classifiable pieces (not represented in Table 4.5) are included, seven of chert and three of flint, the number for standard blades is increased so that the standard class slightly outnumbers the bipolar one. There may, however, be an unrecognised bipolar element within the standard removal category, as experimental work has shown that such removals do not always need to exhibit classic bipolar characteristics (Healey 1987).

The main characteristics of the bipolar flakes, which are mainly flint, are a degree of scaling and bashing on one end, often both, which might represent rebound fractures from the anvil or possibly scarring from trying to remove other flakes from the pebbles. In contrast, the chert removals, particularly if seven *largely* complete examples not shown in Table 4.5 are included, appear to have been produced mainly by a standard knapping technique.

There may also be a relationship between the different stages of the reduction sequence present in the assemblage and the two kinds of technology used. Incomplete but *essentially* whole removals are included here to give a sample of 48 in total.

The presence of primary flakes implies that complete flint pebbles were brought to the site for working down. This is the smallest category of a small sample, only eight pieces (16%), making firm conclusions difficult, but superficially it might suggest that the initial opening up of pebbles was not carried out on this part of the site to any great degree. However, against this should be seen the bipolar core category, which does suggest the on-site working of pebbles, and most of the few primary removals present have also resulted from bipolar reduction (Table 4.6).

This might be further emphasised by the category of secondary removals in the assemblage. The bipolar method is a less controlled form of reduction and so the initial opening up of a pebble this way could result in fewer flakes with a completely cortical dorsal side through pebbles shattering more irregularly. The number of secondary bipolar removals might thus be used to strengthen evidence for the practice of bringing complete small pebbles, mainly flint, to the site and reducing them there on a stone surface.

The nature of the cortex on these pieces suggests that the flint came from each of the potential source categories mentioned above i.e. the drift deposits, the beach and river/beach.

	Primary	Secondary	Tertiary
Bipolar			
Flint	6	11	4
Chert			1
Standard			
Flint	2	4	9
Chert		1	10
Total	8	16	24

Table 4.6: Removals by reduction stage

Chert does not have a cortex as such but imported chert at the other excavated Wirral sites mentioned above does have regular, natural angular edges, which reflect its original deposition in long thin beds in limestone. Occasionally the more lustrous bedded chert at these sites has a thin band of very coarse, opaque gritty material either within it, or sometimes forming an outer 'skin' to it. Primary flakes exhibiting neither of these characteristics are found in the Irby chert assemblage. The chert appears to have been treated in a different way from some of the flint, although here again conclusions must be cautious because of the small sample. The virtual absence of chert cores on site and the fact that most chert removals belong to the tertiary class suggests that selection and initial preparation of this material took place elsewhere. The chert pieces also appear to have resulted largely from standard knapping techniques.

	Blades	Blade-like flakes	Flakes
Flint			
Bipolar	2		19
Standard	7		9
Indet.		1	
Chert			
Bipolar			2
Standard	8	2	1
Total	17	3	31

Table 4.7: Form of all removals (including largely complete examples)

Both complete and largely complete examples have again been used as the sample to analyse the form of the removals (Table 4.7). Here the trend is towards the production of flakes at the expense of blades. This is substantially accounted for by the presence of the bipolar technique on site, which has been responsible for 21 out of the 31 flakes. The smaller, blade group is about equally divided between flint and chert, with the majority being standard removals.

Debitage

	Flint	Chert	Indet.	Total
Chips	38	8	2	48
Small flakes	4		2	6
Chunks	24	6	1	31
Core debitage	2	1		3
Implement re-sharpening flakes	6		1	7
Microburins	1	1		2
Total	75	16	6	97

Table 4.8: Debitage categories

In the debitage class, the chip category particularly is probably under-represented in the assemblage, relating no doubt to the finds retrieval methods, which did not utilise wet sieving. Experience of other local assemblages suggests that the debitage figure ought to be nearer 80%, rather than the 48% represented here (Cowell 2000a).

Retouched artefacts

In the small number of local assemblages so far studied, formal tool categories only represent a small proportion of the total implement types, while pieces characterised by miscellaneous retouch are comparatively more common. On the wider regional scale it has been suggested that the emphasis on formal tool types, notably microliths, in Mesolithic assemblage analyses may result in biased interpretations of site function (Spikins 1999, 115). Equal weight is given here to all types of retouched artefacts.

Blank Form	Standard	Bipolar	Debitage	Indet.
Microliths	4			
Truncated blades	1			
Scrapers	3	3	1	5
Piercers	6	1	1	
Retouched blades	4			
Retouched flakes	2	5		
Retouched waste		1		1
Composite tools	1	2		1
Total	21	12	2	7

Table 4.9: Retouched artefacts

This category represents 21% of the total assemblage, although the potentially reduced numbers for small debitage, mentioned above, will act to artificially inflate the implement percentage. There are indications from other sites in the North, that certain kinds of small prehistoric sites may be marked by a relatively high percentage of implements, rather than the feature being purely a statistical factor (Healey 1987).

Microliths
In this category are four abruptly retouched bladelets, three of flint and one of brown quartzite. Of the bladelets, two, both broken, have abrupt retouch along either one or both straight edges (nos 12-13), the former being burnt. The other two have fine points with microlithic retouch, but both have evidence of smoothing wear at the tip (nos 14-15) which suggests they are not projectile points. In the debitage category there are two microburins, one of chert and one of flint (nos 17-18). A flint blade with oblique retouch may also be of this period (Fig. 4.2, no. 16).

Scrapers
Ten of the twelve scrapers are flint and two of chert and they fall into two rough typological groups. Two flint scrapers (Fig. 4.2, nos 19, 23) are made on standard thick flakes, both broken across the butt. The thumbnail

type (no. 19) has fairly abrupt parallel retouch, while the second (no. 23) has a broad almost denticulated edge. Others use reasonably large chunky mainly bipolar flakes or split pebbles as blanks, two of which (nos 21, 26) are thermally fractured. Apart from the scale flaking of no. 20 they tend towards almost denticulated edges (nos 21-25). No. 24 has a scraping edge along its left hand side, with a retouched, heavily worn, edge meeting it at a sharp angle; the point thus formed has been slightly worn. Two composite pieces each include a hollow scraper element (nos 25-26). The second sub-group comprises scrapers on much smaller flake blanks, generally with semi-abrupt retouch around the end and partly down each side (Fig. 4.3, nos 27-28). No. 29 is made on a brown chert standard flake blank. One scraper is made on a piece of debitage (no. 30),

Piercers
Most of the examples included in this category do not fall into a traditional typological classification of pierc-ers, where retouch is used to shape a point, although one (no. 31) has been interpreted as a broken version of this type. However, there are consistent traits within the Irby assemblage that suggest less formal versions were utilised on site. In some cases there are traces of wear, or damage potentially caused by use around the tip, sug-gesting use without prior retouch on a suitably shaped part of a flake (nos 32, 34-36), while others have very fine retouch (nos 33, 37). No. 34 is made on a flake of north Wales chert, the others are made from flint. Only two of the pieces, both flint, use a bipolar blank (e.g. no. 37), the others use standard flakes.

There are two pieces (not illustrated) that have a fine spur along a modified edge, rather than a point. One of these (SF292) is formed on the tip of a slightly irregular blade fragment, the other (SF2979) on the distal end of a chip, *c*. 8 mm long. There is evidence of smoothing around the tip of the latter example, which probably reflects use.

Miscellaneous retouched pieces
There are 12 pieces in this category, all in flint. Four are standard blades with short lengths of informal retouch along an edge (not illustrated). One larger broken blade (no. 38) has semi-invasive scale flaking along one edge and may subsequently have been used as a piercer. Of the seven retouched flakes, one is probably a standard flake (no. 39) while six use a bipolar blank (nos 40-44, 46). Three of these have semi-invasive retouch (nos 43, 44, 46). The other retouched pieces use debitage as blanks, including a core (no. 45) and a waste chunk (no. 47).

Discussion

In the north west, potential analogies for the kind of characteristics outlined above are rare due to the almost complete lack of stratified, dated, stone tool assemblages from the region. The main exception to this comes from the site at Oversley Farm, Manchester Airport, which has produced the most meaningful regional evidence for a radiometrically dated, stratified lithic assemblage of Neolithic and Bronze Age date (Garner 2007). The site lies on glacial sands and gravels in the Bollin valley (NGR SJ 815838), which would provide a regular sup-ply of flint pebbles as raw material for stone tool manu-facture. This is a somewhat different topographic setting and raw material source to that at Irby, so analogies between the lithic technology used at the two sites has to allow for potential idiosyncratic features resulting from different local conditions but in the regional context the Airport site is the best evidence there is currently by which to judge unstratified lithic assemblages.

The mixed, residual nature of the assemblage must again be emphasised, making interpretation difficult. However, there are some typologically distinctive elements within the assemblage that suggest there are several chrono-logical phases represented. On form, the straight-backed bladelets and the points on bladelets (Fig. 4.2, nos 12-15) fall within the micro-triangle complex of the later Mesolithic (*c*. 7800-4000 BC). The obliquely blunted blade (no. 16) may also be Mesolithic. The microburins (nos 17-18) show that microliths were also being manu-factured on site. The blades and single platform blade cores (Fig. 4.1, nos 1-5) also imply a Mesolithic date, although typologically they are also found in the early Neolithic period. The core rejuvenation flakes (nos 10-11), which appear to have been associated with blade cores, would also seem to best fit this phase.

Most of this Mesolithic material uses flint and appears to be mainly derived from a standard flaking technology, although a bipolar technique may have been used, perhaps late in the reduction sequence as raw material became less easy to handle.

Although there are no forms typical of the early Me-solithic (*c*. 8500-7800 BC) on the site, the presence of imported north Wales chert suggests that such a phase of activity did exist at Irby. Outside Wales, the use of this raw material is only recorded on the Wirral, where it is associated with obliquely blunted microlith assemblag-es, which nationally are generally of this date (Jacobi 1978; pers. comm. on seeing the Greasby material).

Without radiocarbon dates for the Greasby assemblage it is not clear to what extent this raw material use continued into the later period in Wirral, although there is one late microlith form in north Welsh chert from Thurstaston. Chert is used in Neolithic and Bronze Age contexts at the Manchester Airport site but here it is characterised as being of local pebble origin, which appears not to be the case at Irby. On the basis of the current evidence in the region, the presence of this chert type in undated contexts on Wirral sites is ascribed as being most likely of early Mesolithic date.

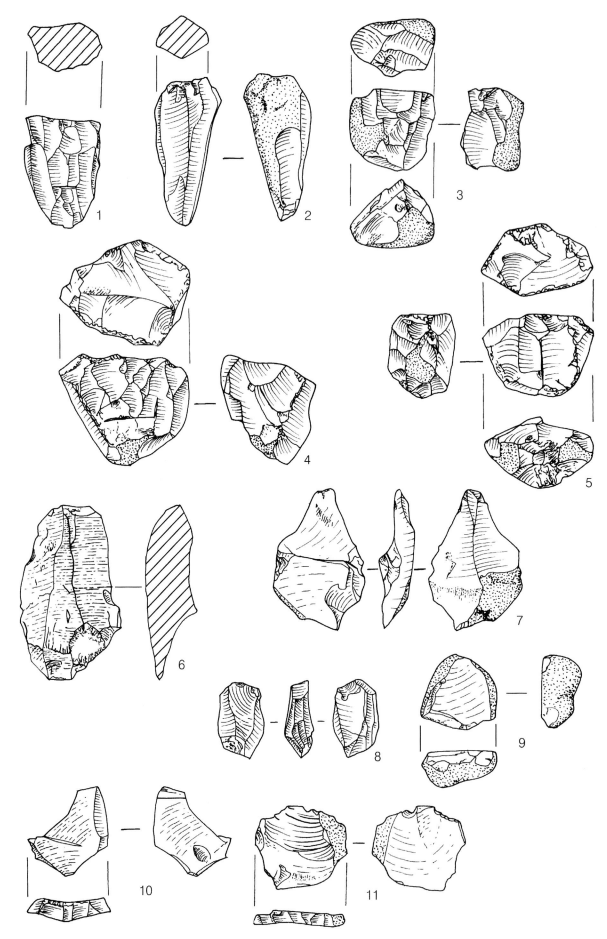

Fig. 4.1: 1-11. Lithics. Scale 1:1

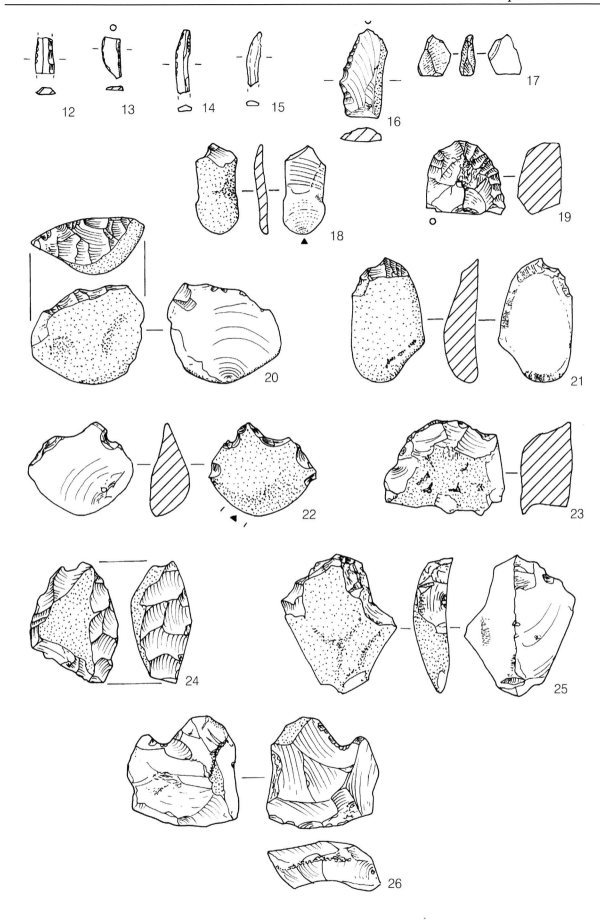

Fig. 4.2: 12-26. Lithics. Scale 1:1

A group of material represented by a number of flint scrapers (Figs 4.2, 4.3, nos 19-30) may include at least some that belong to the later prehistoric period, although it is not always possible to date scrapers confidently by morphology alone as some forms are found throughout prehistory (Healey n.d). One scraper (no. 21) was found in a pit with Bronze Age pottery and could belong to that period although the general lack of further such associations on the site makes this unproven. Some of the Irby types such as the denticulate and hollow scrapers (nos 22-26) can be associated with early Bronze Age assemblages in other parts of the country (Pryor 1980). There are also some similarities with scrapers such as nos 20-22 to those from a coastal site about 50 km to the north at Lytham St Anne's, Lancashire, which has been assigned to this general period (Middleton *et al.* 1995, 90). However, a number of Mesolithic coastal sites in Scotland contain similar scrapers on split pebbles. These include in south-west Scotland, Low Clone (Cormack and Coles 1968, fig. 8) and Barsalloch (Cormack 1970, figs 7, 8), although relevant examples are from topsoil contexts. On the east coast at Morton this type occurs in good Mesolithic contexts (Coles 1971, figs 20, 22, 25, 27). Surface sites in south Wales also produce denticulates and large convex type scrapers on split pebble flakes alongside numerous late Mesolithic microliths (David 2007). There are two examples (Fig. 4.3, nos 27-28) of small, tablet-like scrapers that have good parallels in the assemblage from the chambered tomb of Trefignath on Anglesey. Here their stratigraphic association is not totally clear but on balance they appear to date to the late Neolithic period (Healey 1987). The occasional example is also found in early Bronze Age levels at the Manchester Airport site (Wenban-Smith 2007, fig. 92, no. xvii). However, outside the region such scrapers are also found on late Mesolithic sites, such as at Howick in Northumberland (Waddington 2007). The dating of many of these types, therefore, is ambiguous.

The technology associated with the scraper group from Irby is mixed. Some use standard flake blanks (nos 19 and 23), while nos 20-22 and 25 are formed on split pebbles, some using a bipolar method. The two composite tools use possible bipolar blanks (nos 24, 26). This latter group introduces the question of the dating of the bipolar technology, sometimes referred to as scalar (David 2007, 128), on the site in general. In the Irby assemblage, the technique forms the basis for approximately 30% of the cores (not including the platform ones) and removals and for 25% of the implements.

Only 3% of the bipolar material is chert, the rest being flint. If the argument outlined above for the limited chronological use of chert on Wirral is valid, then it would seem unlikely that the bipolar technique was a feature of the early Mesolithic.

There are indications from a number of flint platform

cores in the assemblage that the technique may have been used to produce blades and small flakes, but probably only as a minor component and probably late in the reduction sequence. These could, on form, potentially belong to the later Mesolithic or early Neolithic period. The other material typologically associated with these cores suggests that it is more likely to have been during the former rather than the latter period, but the separation between the two in this region is seldom clear on the basis of stone tool assemblages alone.

The bulk of the bipolar material at Irby, however, appears to be of uncertain or later prehistoric date. There are a number of parallels between some flakes, cores and retouched pieces at the Manchester Airport site (e.g. Wenban-Smith 2007, fig. 93, nos iv, v, vii, ix) and Irby to suspect that some of the bipolar pieces at Irby may be early Bronze Age in date. The scrapers on bipolar flakes (Fig. 4.2, nos 25-26) also have been suggested above as potentially being early Bronze Age.

In the implement class at Irby the informally retouched flakes are also mainly associated with a bipolar technology. These, however, are impossible to date without some stratigraphic association, although many pieces in Figure 4.3 would not look out of place in early Bronze Age levels at the Manchester Airport site (e.g. Wenban-Smith 2007, fig. 92, xvi, fig. 93, iv). The other chronologically ubiquitous class of implement in the assemblage, the informal piercers (nos 33-39), are also of *ad hoc* type, with little attempt generally having been made to shape the working edge. However, standard removals appear to have been used for most of these. This could mean that either, there was a phase of occupation that included the *ad hoc* manufacture and use of tools based on both standard and bipolar techniques, or that the different technologies represent similar *ad hoc* activities taking place in chronologically separate occupations. However, neither of these options can be satisfactorily assigned to any particular period.

The bipolar technology is generally encountered in coastal areas of western Britain where the main raw material comprises beach pebbles. Bipolar technology is generally thought to be of post-Mesolithic date, although there are no well-dated assemblages that show this incontrovertibly. Jacobi (1980) suggests such industries in south Wales may lie possibly at the very end of the Mesolithic, by analogy with Scottish coastal Mesolithic sites that continue into the period when Neolithic technologies were current in Britain. However, on the balance of evidence he favours a Neolithic or early Bronze Age date, while Norman (1977) using evidence from coastal Cornish sites also suggests a post-Mesolithic date is likelier for the technology. David (2007, 129) outlines a few examples from Wales and Cumbria with typological or radiocarbon dated associations that also suggest an early Bronze Age date. Given the unstratified nature of the Irby assemblage

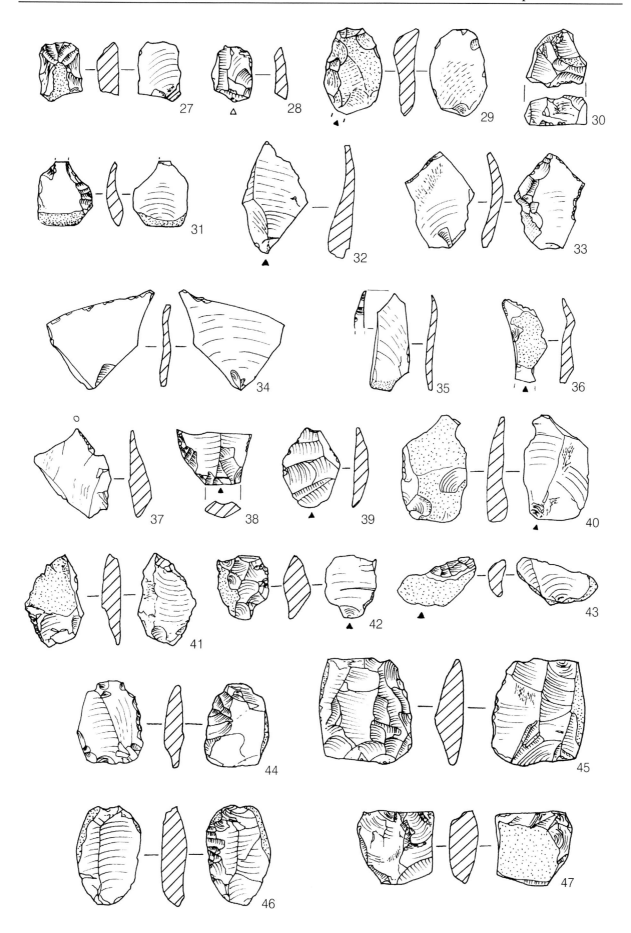

Fig. 4.3: 27-47. Lithics. Scale 1:1

such potential chronological associations make confident attribution of much of it difficult. On balance, although some of these implements may be associated with the Mesolithic occupation there are grounds for thinking that, based on a few typological traits and the presence of the bipolar technology, there may also be a post-Mesolithic element, perhaps most likely Bronze Age included within the lithic assemblage. If some of these date to the early Bronze Age period, there is no regional evidence to suggest whether or not these types continued to be used into the period during which the Irby structure was in use. Middle and late Bronze Age contexts at Oversley Farm, Manchester Airport produced only a few struck lithics, with little indication that they were contemporary with the limited structural evidence of that date (Wenban-Smith 2007, 109).

Catalogue of illustrated lithics

Fig. 4.1. Cores and core debitage: flint, nos 1-5, 7-11; chert, no. 6

1. Platform core. SF8615, context 7602.
2. Platform core, possible opposed bipolar blow. SF7046, context 6214.
3. Platform core, crushing damage opposite striking platform. SF7865, context 8334.
4. Platform core, irregular flaking damage on edge opposite striking platform. SF007, context 100.
5. Platform core, crushing damage opposite striking platform. SF4381, context 5103.
6. Core, bipolar. SF6602, context 6204.
7. Core, bipolar, flakes struck from two directions. SF4139, context 3753.
8. Core, bipolar. SF5880, context 3102.
9. Bipolar split pebble. SF10526, context 8020.
10. Core rejuvenation flake, platform removed. SF5775, context 5511.
11. Core rejuvenation flake, platform removed. SF9566, context US.

Fig. 4.2. Implements; flint, nos 12-14, 18-26; chert, no. 17; quartzite, no. 15.

12. Microlith, rod. SF1401, context 3000.
13. Microlith, rod. SF1027, context 690.
14. Microlith. SF7798, context 6198.
15. Microlith, worn sides and tip. SF10566, context 8171.
16. Obliquely blunted blade, reddish yellow flint. SF7832, context 6187.
17. Microburin. SF10749, context 8164.
18. Microburin. SF2512, context 3090.
19. Scraper, convex on thick flake blank. SF9654, context US.
20. Scraper, convex on split pebble. SF3684, context 1039.
21. Scraper, convex on split pebble, possible natural fracture origin. SF8227, context 9777.
22. Denticulate, split pebble blank, probably bipolar. SF8839, context US.
23. Scraper, convex on thick flake blank. SF3271, context 3062.
24. Scraper, side on possible bipolar flake. SF7364, context 6167.
25. Scraper, convex with utilised adjacent hollow, bipolar flake. SF6449, context 6103.
26. Scraper, hollow with crushing on opposite edge, probable natural flake. SF92, context 1003.

Fig. 4.3. Various implements; flint, nos 27-28, 30-33, 35-47; chert, nos 29,34

27. Scraper, tablet. SF2169, context 3312.
28. Scraper, tablet, burnt. SF9496, context US.
29. Scraper, end and side. SF04, context 3.
30. Scraper, end on waste blank. SF10139, context 2073.
31. Piercer, tip broken. SF6055, context 3150.
32. Piercer, worn natural point. SF4476, context 5100.
33. Piercer, fine retouch from alternate sides to produce point. SF6916, context 8020.
34. Piercer, fine retouch/utilisation around natural point. SF6517, context 6119.
35. Piercer, minimal retouch/damage to one side of natural point. SF8264, context US.
36. Piercer, minimal retouch/damage to one side of natural point. SF71, context 1003.
37. Piercer, fine retouch to one side of natural point. SF292, context 200.
38. Retouched blade segment, possibly broken edge used as a piercer. SF9050, context US.
39. Retouched flake. SF02, context 1.
40. Retouched bipolar flake. SF8198, context 9757.
41. Retouched bipolar flake. SF375, context 2201.
42. Retouched bipolar flake. SF8265, context US.
43. Retouched bipolar flake. SF8021, context 9560.
44. Retouched bipolar flake. SF42, context 1002.
45. Retouched bipolar core. SF5565, context 5105.
46. Retouched bipolar flake. SF3774, context 1039.
47. Retouched bipolar chunk. SF7315, context 6165.

Steatite Spindle Whorl

Jennifer Foster

48. Spindle whorl, carved from a darkish green soapstone/ steatite (also known as talc); approx. Munsell colour 5G/1 to 5G/2, a lighter green where it has been recently scratched. D 46 mm, D of hole 13.5 mm, max T 15.5 mm, wt 47.2 g. SF2931, context 4001, wall of Structure S18. Fig. 4.4, Plate XIX.

The whorl is deeply carved. There are four opposing knobs, each decorated with two circles; these were originally engraved, but all are worn, making the original design difficult to see. However, the designs appear to be different on each, for example a puffy spiral on knob *d* at the top (as drawn), a half-moon shape at the bottom. Knob *c* on the other hand has a half-moon shape at the top. Between each knob and joining them are raised diagonal lobes.

Although in a few places (e.g. in the undercut under the lobes and circles) the carving marks can still be seen, most of these would have been polished away in the manufacture. The object had certainly been used, as the raised parts of the decoration are rubbed and shiny. However, the central hole has not been subjected to wear; on the edge can still be seen a few shaping marks where the hole was rounded. It was not drilled, but cut from both sides. A tiny ridge between the top and bottom was left on the inner surface: any larger and the hole would have had a classic hour-glass shape.

The lack of wear in the hole gives a clue as to how this object was used. It does not seem to have been hung loose from the central hole, as the softness of the stone and the weight would definitely have worn the hole through. It is too large for a bead. Although there are stone beads from the Iron Age most are half this size and have much smaller holes. It could have been a weight, but any tied strap would have obscured the decoration. So the other alternative is that it was mounted on a central rod. It could have been a sceptre top, in which case the wear would be due to handling. But, close examination shows that the greatest wear is mainly on the top side and on one side of the raised areas. This is consistent with gentle brushing (e.g. against clothing) while being spun horizontally, and always in the same direction (Fig. 4.4), typical of course of spinning and indicating that this is a spindle whorl. The design would indeed look spectacular as it span.

The weight is also consistent with its use as a spindle whorl. Iron Age spindle whorls are generally of this shape and size: four of the larger stone examples from the Breiddin weigh between 60 and 110 g and have diameters of 50-60 mm (Musson 1991, 156-8) and there are similar examples from Dinorben (Savory 1971,

55-6). In the west spindle whorls are generally of stone rather than pottery.

At first sight it seems unusual to have made any functional object from such a soft stone as talc, but there is a balance here between ease of carving and use. In fact in Scotland, where there is a greater deposit of talc (Highley 1974), soapstone/steatite was used for cup-shaped lamps and spindle whorls (Close-Brooks 1972, 296). Some are decorated but only with linear whorl patterns. This whorl has been very carefully kept and may have been used only for special occasions, or fabrics; there are no ancient scratches, though a very deep modern scratch. Were it used very consistently, the carving would probably have completely worn down; however, I have traced no experiments on soapstone objects, so it is difficult to be sure.

Dating of an object like this, found in a later context, can only come from the decoration. The design is quite simple: circles joined by diagonal lobes, but is typical of numerous pieces of Celtic art, particularly in the relief Plastic style of the 4th and 3rd centuries BC, e.g. as part of a much more complicated design on a bronze armlet from the river Tarn (Piggott 1970, no 126). On a Bavarian neck-ring of the 4th century BC (Megaw and Megaw 1989, 121) a lobe ends in a puffy spiral just like the upper design on the *d* knob on the Irby whorl. These are early parallels, and, though the motif continues later, for example on the Wandsworth shield boss and the Battersea shield, on later pieces the lobes are stretched thin, unlike the fat Irby lobe. Also, the Irby circles are not symmetrical or a mirror image, the voids are unimportant in the design, and there are no trumpet scrolls, which appears to rule out a date in the 1st century or beyond. On balance a 3rd-century BC date seems most likely.

Decorated stone objects are rare in Britain as a whole. A few objects from Wales bear some similarity to the Irby whorl. There is a simple serpentine ring with incised spiralling imitating a glass bead from Coygan Camp (Wainwright 1967, fig. 21, 3), and a similar ring from Dinorben (Savory 1971, fig. 1, 3). A small bronze bead from Coygan Camp (Wainwright 1967, fig. 23, 7) has two opposed lobes, though the rest of the design is far more complex. Also there are parallels in Irish art: the same diagonal lobe ending in two circles appears on

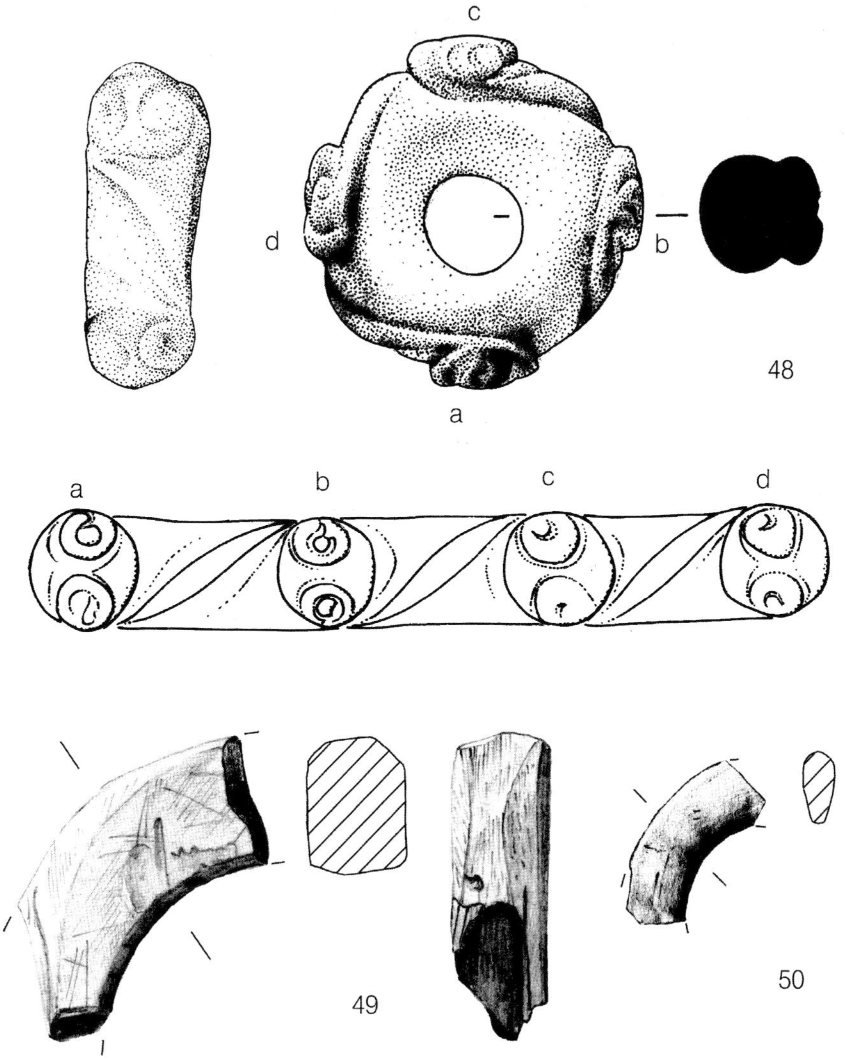

Fig. 4.4: 48. Steatite spindle whorl; 49-50. Shale or cannel coal objects. Scale 1:1

Plate XIX: 48. Steatite spindle whorl (SF2931)

either side of the Clonmacnois torc (Raftery 1983, fig. 143) and on a ring-headed pin from Co Sligo (Raftery 1983, no 408). There are few decorated portable stone objects from Ireland, except quern stones incised with linear Celtic spirals, e.g. that from Co. Galway (Raftery 1983, figs 183-4). But perhaps the closest parallel for the puffy spiral design was carved on an Iron Age beehive quern stone from Blochty, Anglesey (Wheeler 1925, 203, fig. 83).

So the affinities of this spindle whorl are with Ireland and Wales rather than further east. The talc from which it was made probably came from the nearby source at Anglesey (Highley 1974, 6), but there is no reason why it should not have been made on or near the site. The only doubt as to its provenance is that it was found deliberately buried in a later context and could, of course, have come from another site. However there is a brown deposit, probably of boulder clay, on parts of the surface of the whorl; this deposit must have occurred before it was placed in black humic soil in the wall. Boulder clay occurs on the eastern side of the site, so it was probably found there in the medieval period.

Shale or Cannel Coal Objects

Robert Philpott

49. Fragment of a cannel coal or jet armlet; an unfinished piece, with flat upper and lower sides exhibiting saw marks and a roughly faceted exterior surface. SF3070, context 3914, base of Romano-British occupation layer. Max. W of ring 17 mm, T 11 mm.
50. Fragment of undecorated shale or jet bracelet of flattened oval section. The fragment is too small to determine whether the original shape was circular or oval. SF7455, context 6905; occupation deposit with late 3rd-early 4th-century pottery. Max. W 7 mm; max. T 3 mm.

It is difficult to distinguish between jet, shale or cannel coal without analysis (Allason-Jones and Miket 1984, 302; Crummy 1983, 36). The material of these two pieces has not been analysed.

Stratigraphically, no. 50 is probably late Roman in date, associated with a Hartshill-Mancetter reeded mortarium sherd. No. 49 occurs in an occupation deposit containing late prehistoric pottery and industrial waste; while the latter suggests a Roman date, it could be a residual find of either Bronze Age or Iron Age date. The unfinished piece indicates working of the objects on the site, whether through importation of the part-finished item or working from the raw material.

Shale bracelets have been found on Romano-British sites of differing status in north Wales and north-west England. Excavations in Handbridge across the Dee from Chester have produced shale and jet working waste dating to the Roman and possibly early medieval periods (Archibald and Archibald 2005, 38, fig. I.28). In Wales they occur at Dinorben (probably of Roman date: Gardner and Savory 1964, 185-6), Prestatyn (Blockley 1989, 131, nos 18, 19) and Pentre Farm, Flint (Webster 1989, 86, no. 1). Three shale bracelet fragments were recovered from deposits dated to the last quarter of the 1st century AD at Ribchester (Howard-Davis 2000, 295, fig. 86, nos 1-3). Romano-British rural sites include Court Farm, Halewood, where 11 fragments from five bracelets were recovered (Adams and Philpott in prep.), while one fragment was recovered from Oversley Farm, Styal (Garner 2007, 118-9, fig. 124). The suggestion that their distribution suggests a military connection reflects the past emphasis of archaeological excavation in the region rather than the original distribution, as they are now appearing in small but significant numbers on rural sites.

Cannel coal was available in the Carboniferous coal measures of south-west Lancashire. Camden (1695, 802) records that deposits of cannel coal were exploited at Haigh near Wigan. It had the unusual properties of burning with a clear smokeless flame and was easily being worked, taking a black marble-like appearance when polished. In the 17th century candlesticks, spoons and other ornaments were made from cannel.

Other Stone Objects

Mark H. Adams

Introduction

The assemblage of stone objects from Irby consists of 67 items, in a range of types, including carved stone objects, rotary querns, saddle querns, whetstones and 'rubbing stones'. Most of the stones used were either locally quarried red sandstone or glacial erratics from nearby deposits of boulder clay.

Description of stone objects

The full catalogue of stone objects is held separately as part of the excavation archive. This report only contains descriptions of significant objects.

Most of the stone objects from the assemblage appear to be rubbing stones. These could have served a wide range of functions though the uniaxial direction of the striations on most suggest a backwards and forwards rubbing motion rather than a rotary grinding motion or use as a roller.

Miscellaneous Stone Objects

Large stone objects are dealt with first, smaller objects and those with limited evidence for utilisation are catalogued summarily in tabular form.

Large Stone Objects

51. A trough carved from a single block of medium-grained red sandstone. About one quarter is broken off across the corner. A flattened rim 50-80 mm wide surrounds the central flat-bottomed basin. The base is very crudely worked and was probably not intended to be seen. Although the basin and upper surface have been finely worked, only very indistinct punch marks survive. This indicates that these surfaces were exposed to weathering and/or wear for some time prior to burial. Overall dimensions *c.* 500 x 400 x 150 mm, trough is 60 mm deep. SF7784, context 9024, packing of Phase VI post-hole.

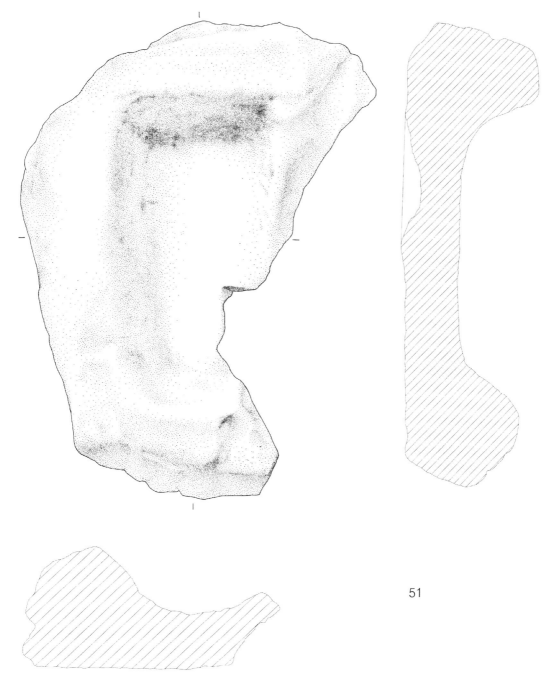

51

Fig. 4.5: 51. Stone trough. Scale 1:4

The function of this object remains uncertain. Because the sandstone it is carved from is very porous, it cannot have been intended to hold liquid unless it was lined with a material such as pitch or lead. Such a lining would substantially reduce the amount of liquid it could hold; in addition it would have protected the surface from wear or weathering. The roughly dressed lower surface suggests that it was set flush with a surface, possibly the ground. One possible use is as a socket for a timber post.

52. A finely dressed block of fine-grained red sandstone, with three flat dressed faces, finished using a punch. Three faces are rough and have been broken the other three faces were dressed. All of the corners are slightly rounded. Possibly an architectural fragment. Dimensions 350 x 300 x 200 mm. SF7803, context 9535, packing of un-phased but probably early or later medieval post-hole.

53. A roughly prismatic block of fine-grained red sandstone with a 'hog's back' profile in section. One of the faces appears to be slightly polished by wear or abrasion. This may be part of a broken saddle quern or a heavily worn architectural fragment such as a step. Dimensions 350 x 240 x 90 mm. SF8188, context 9752. Packing of un-phased but probably early or later medieval post-hole.

54. A large sub-rounded block of fine-grained red sandstone, probably from field clearance. Two hemi-spherical depressions are present on roughly opposite sides; tool marks suggest they were produced using a punch. The function of these is unclear, although it is possible that this block may have served as a setting for a door post. Dimensions *c.* 250 x 250 x 200 mm. SF8619, context 7025. Period VI? Post-hole.

Querns

Saddle querns

55. One half of a saddle quern, in fine-grained red sandstone, broken across its mid-point. A polygonal slab, with two broad faces very smooth and polished with a slight depression (1-2 mm) towards the centre, and one polished facet on the edge. The other unbroken surfaces are roughly dressed and squared off. Dimensions 220 x 170 x 80 mm. SF8620, context 7025, Period VI? post-hole.

56. Fragment of saddle quern, in white granite, broken across the middle. The surviving portion of the dished working surface measures 220 x 220 mm and is 30 mm deep from the rim. The other surfaces are all unworked. Probably a glacial erratic rather than an imported stone. SF8009, context 9614, post-hole in Structure 15 Period IV.

57. A probable saddle quern, in fine-grained red sandstone. The lower surface and sides are crudely dressed and squared off. On the upper surface is a depression measuring 120 x 110 mm and *c.* 15 mm deep. Dimensions 220 x 200 x 85 mm. SF7007, context 8046, Structure 13, Period IV.

58. A rubbing stone in white granite, possibly for use with a saddle quern, from an unaltered rounded cobble. Dimensions 150 x 100 x 100 mm, broken across the middle. SF8210, context 9738, Period II post-hole.

Beehive quern

59. About a quarter of the upper stone of a beehive quern, carved from coarse-grained red sandstone. The outer surface is coarsely dressed and the presence of a number of broad (100-120 mm) facets suggests the use of a bolster to produce this surface. The upper surface is broadly flat though heavily pitted where softer minerals (feldspar?)

have weathered out. All of the other surfaces are rough and broken. No trace of the handle socket is present in this portion. The heavy wear on the inner surface and the absence of tool marks suggests that this quern was broken after a long period of use. 490 x 290 mm. The curvature of the sides suggests an original total dimension of *c.* 700-900 mm and height of 290 mm. SF8268, context 5029, fill of post-hole in Structure 24, Period V.

Rotary querns

60. Lower half of a rotary quern in coarse-grained red sandstone. The lower surface has been roughly dressed into a low dome, and the sides are nearly vertical and quite straight. Neither side has any tool marks. The upper surface has been neatly dressed into a slightly domed but irregular surface. The socket in the centre of the quern is of square section, 32 x 32 mm at the top, narrowing gradually to a point at the base. It is 70 mm deep. The profile of this feature suggests that it was finished, if not produced, using a chisel rather than a drill. The upper surface is covered with voids from weathering out of softer inclusions within the rock. Total D 380 mm, minimum T at edge 80 mm, maximum T at centre 130 mm. SF8373, context 24, Ditch 1, Period IV.

61. Two joining fragments forming about half of the lower stone of a rotary quern in fine-grained red sandstone. The outer face has been roughly dressed into a low dome shape using a punch tool. The sides have been more carefully worked using a narrow bladed chisel or punch. A small area of punch tool work survives in one corner; this matches up with similar tool marks on SF5234. The inner surface is smooth with a slightly rippled texture suggestive of final finishing with a bolster or axe. There are traces of a sub-square central hole. The survival of tool marks on the working surface suggests that it broke either during or soon after manufacture. Original D *c.* 380 mm, max. T *c.* 110 mm, thinning to 40-60 mm at the edges. SF3282, context 3063 and SF5234, context 3055, walls of Structure 19, Period VI.

62. Broken fragment of a rotary quern in medium-grained red sandstone. The upper surface is worn smooth and no tool markings can be seen. Oval central socket, measuring 25 x 30 mm and tapering to the base. The dimensions at the base were *c.* 25 x 25 mm. Dimensions 170 x 95 x 68 mm. SF7108, context 8013, post-hole in Structure 9, Period IV.

63. A slab of fine-grained red sandstone. The two large faces are very flat and smooth with irregularly spaced dimples *c.* 5-10 mm in diameter and 1-3 mm deep. Both of these faces appear to have been dressed flat with a punch and then ground flat. The other faces are all broken. Probably a fragment of a broken rotary quern. Dimensions 155 x 120 x 70 mm. SF7134, context 8014, post-hole in Structure 9, Period IV.

64. A fragment of rotary quern. A slab of fine-grained red sandstone. Only the upper surface and a small fragment of the side survive. Both have been finely dressed, probably using a punch tool. A small fragment of the central socket survives. This appears to have been oval with one side at least 30 mm long. Dimensions 140 x 115 x 42 mm. SF7169, context 8143, Structure 13, Period IV.

65. Small fragment of quern stone. A small portion of the central perforation survives which may have been oval, similar to SF6544. Part of the working surface also survives. Both surfaces appear to have been finely dressed using a punch tool, the survival of tool marks suggests that it broke during or soon after manufacture. Dimensions 110

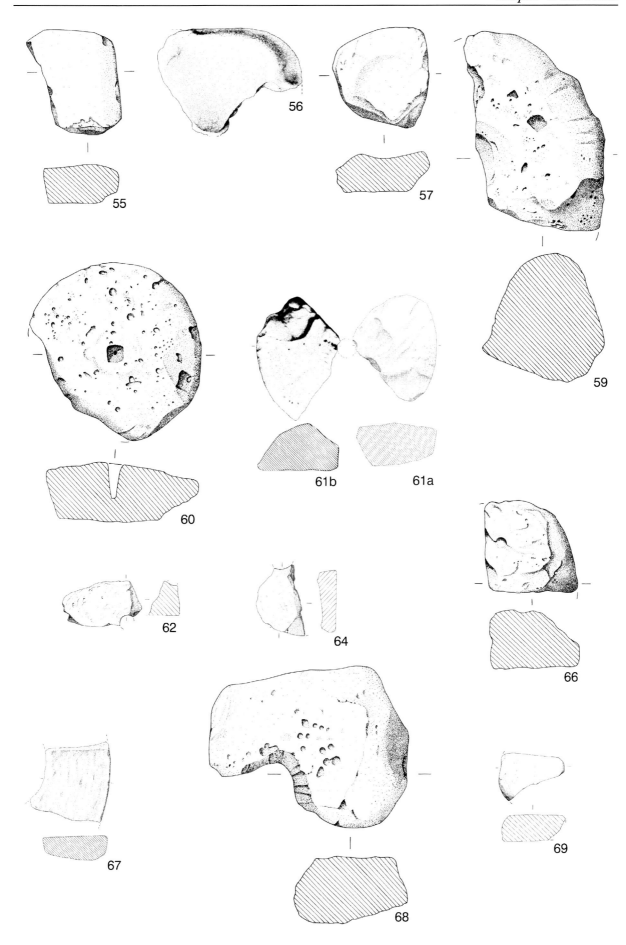

Fig. 4.6: 55-69. Stone objects. Scale 1:8

x 70 x 40 mm. SF7168, context 8143, Structure 13, Period IV.

66. About one quarter of a broken quern stone in very coarse-grained red sandstone. No tool marks survive on any face and it is only the general size and shape which suggest that it may be a rotary quern which broke during manufacture. The shape could be caused by fortuitous fracture along joint and bedding planes. Dimensions 200 x 190 x 110 mm. SF7801, context 8044, un-phased post-hole.

67. Fragment of an upper stone. A finely worked slab of fine-grained red sandstone, originally part of a much larger, probably circular object. The inner surface curves unevenly, projection of the line of this curve indicates that the central hole was oval, measuring *c.* 0.15 x 0.10 m. All of the unbroken surfaces are very finely worked with a punch tool. Dimensions 175 x 160 x 60 mm, but original diameter 400-500 mm. SF6544, context 3219, Period VI? post-hole.

68. One-half of an upper quern stone, broken in the early stages of manufacture. Part of a roughly squared off block. Approximately one-third has broken off across one corner, through the central perforation. The central perforation appears to have been intended to be oval, measuring *c.* 120 x 130 mm at the top. The inner surface has been coarsely dressed with a punch tool, working from both sides of the block to give a biconical perforation. The other unbroken surfaces have been very roughly worked, apart from one which is smooth and rounded, possibly as a result of weathering. Some of the broken surfaces may have been produced with a bolster or axe though at least one may be due to accidental damage during excavation. Original dimensions *c.* 420 x 350 x 160 mm. SF6611, context 3213, Structure 21, Period VI.

69. Small fragment of lower(?) quern stone in fine-grained red sandstone. A small segment of the outer surface survives. This has been neatly dressed with a punch tool, its curvature suggests that the original diameter was *c.* 0.40 m. One of the other surfaces is very highly polished suggesting that this quern broke during use. Dimensions 140 x 90 x 55 mm. SF7053, context 6204, Period IV occupation debris.

70. Small fragment of a lava quern stone. Only a small part of the original surface survives and it is impossible to identify as an upper or lower stone. Dimensions 100 x 30 x 30 mm. SF8124, context 5321, Period VI? occupation deposit.

Other Small Stone Objects

This group includes six main categories: rubbing stones, whetstones, tiles, hammer stones, other utilised stones and a possible mould. Rubbing stones are distinguished from whetstones primarily on the basis of shape and their larger size, and less obvious preparation for use. Whetstones are defined as being altered in some way, such as by squaring off at least one edge and are usually produced in finer grained and harder stone than the rubbing stones. This group also includes some possible stone tiles and hammer stones. The largest category is utilised stones, which have slight evidence for use, normally consisting of randomly orientated striations, although in many cases these may actually be the result of natural processes such as scratches or grooving through glacial movement. One object may be a stone mould for the casting of a pin.

Hammer Stones

Two hammer stones were found, both in a hard, dense quartzite.

71. Waterworn cobble in which a depression *c.* 30 mm in diameter and 3 mm deep has been produced by hammering on each of the broadest faces. Abrasions and small peck marks on each of the other surfaces may also result from its use as a hammer. Note the similarity to 8022. Dimensions 110 x 75 x 55 mm. SF9562, unstratified.

72. Rounded cobble with one highly polished face over an area *c.* 45 x 50 mm. A depression 20 mm in diameter and *c.* 2 mm deep in the centre of the polished area may have been caused by hammering with a sharp point. It is in a similar quartzite to SF9562. Dimensions 85 x 75 x 48 mm. SF8022, context 9631, fill of a post-hole in Structure 15, Period IV.

?Mould

73. A slab of fine-grained stone (unidentified type). One face is very flat and almost polished; the sides are rough and slightly rounded. The other face is also rough and heavily pitted. A groove with a U-shaped profile runs across the centre of this face and is 5-10 mm deep, narrowing to 4 mm; the break of slope at the top is indistinct. At 35 mm from the other end it starts to widen significantly until it is 20 mm wide and flat-bottomed. There is a possibility that it terminates in a point. The function of this object is unclear though it may be a (unfinished?) mould for casting a pin. Dimensions 122 x 111 x 40 mm. SF3183, context 3062, unphased but relatively late in sequence (late 4th century or later?).

Rubbing Stones

Thirteen stones appear to have been used as rubbing stones. They are not described individually here, though a catalogue is included in the archive. Hard, fine-grained waterworn cobbles, probably glacial erratics from nearby deposits of boulder clay, seem to have been preferred (11 out of 13), though one was in a soft marl, another in red sandstone. The average size was 95 x 72 x 42 mm and all had parallel striations and/or polish on at least one face. They occurred in a variety of contexts including ploughsoil, as packing in the foundations of a roundhouse (S13) but most are from unphased contexts, such as occupation deposits.

Tiles

Two small sub-rectangular slabs of sandstone were identified as possible stone tiles.

74. A slab of fine-grained micaceous sandstone, not native to the area. It has been cleaved along the bedding plane and appears to have been burnt. Dimensions 110 x 95 x 6 mm. SF8752, context 7043, a layer at the interface between natural and occupation deposits.

75. A tabular fragment of red sandstone, lower face is formed by cleavage along a bedding plane, the upper surface by abrasion. The corner at the junction between the upper face

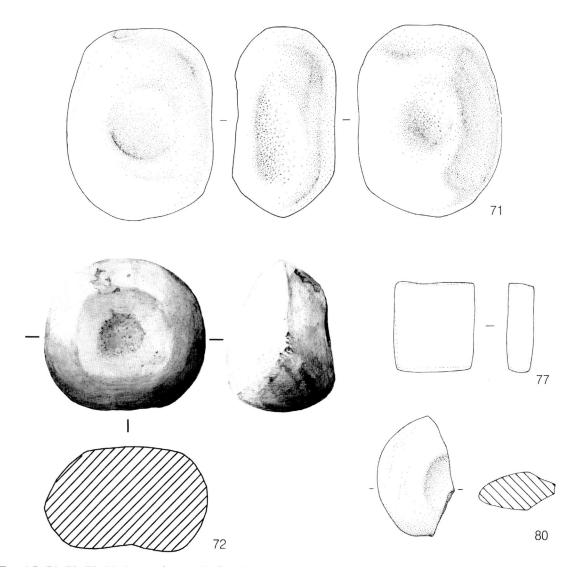

Fig. 4.7: 71, 72, 77, 80. Stone objects. Scale 1:2

and two of the sides are rounded and abraded. Dimensions 80 x 65 x 25 mm. SF6993, context 8061, Structure 13 Period IV.

Whetstones

Four possible whetstones were identified. All were in hard grey sandstone apart from no. 79 which was in Keuper sandstone.

76. A V-shaped stone with a notch 10 mm across worn 2-3 mm deep in the centre of the 'V'. Dimensions *c.* 88 x 40 x 15 mm. SF7759, context 6671, fill of Ditch 3, Period IV.
77. A squared-off and flattened cobble, with all faces polished with crisp, slightly rounded corners, three of which are slightly faceted, giving the object an 'aerofoil' shape in cross-section. Broken. Dimensions 47 x 45 x 9 mm. SF7467, context 9502, base of ploughsoil.
78. An elongated cobble with a roughly lozenge shaped profile. All of the faces are slightly polished, but one exhibits light pitting and short, shallow striations aligned with the long axis of the stone. Dimensions 172 x 72 x 32 mm. SF7779, context 9505, base of ploughsoil.
79. A sub-rectangular slab of stone. One surface has a linear

depression *c.* 10 mm deep and *c.* 60 mm wide with a very shallow, dished profile. The sides slope evenly to the edge of the slab. The absence of any tool marks suggests that this surface was created by cleavage along ripple bedding. Dimensions 160 x 120 x 55 mm. SF8262, unstratified.

Other modified stone

80. A water-worn cobble with a lenticular profile. An attempt has been made to produce a hole through the centre but the object appears to have broken in the process. On each of the broad faces there is a shallow, dish-shaped depression *c.* 30 mm in diameter and 8 mm deep produced by a pecking tool. Both of the main surfaces are covered in small, randomly oriented scratches, indicating that the shape of the cobble was modified slightly by abrasion. 65 x 45 x 23 mm. SF4267, context 3063.

Discussion

The worked stone from Irby consists of the following objects:

Type	Total	% of Total	% of Objects
Hammer stone	2	1.4	3.0
Querns	16	11.1	23.9
Moulds?	1	0.7	1.5
Rubbing stone	12	8.3	17.9
Rubbing stone?	1	0.7	1.5
Tile?	2	1.4	3.0
Utilised stone	14	9.8	20.9
Utilised stone?	12	8.3	17.9
Whetstone?	3	2.1	4.5
Others	4	2.8	6.0
Total Objects	*67*	*46.6*	*100*

Table 4.10: Summary of worked stone from Irby

Utilised stones formed the largest group (26 objects, 38.8%). In most cases these were glacial erratics or field clearance stones which appeared to have been altered by rubbing or grinding, though these cannot be associated with any particular process and may have served a range of functions. They are also in themselves undatable and occur in a wide range of contexts from some of the earliest through to ploughsoil. Some of the stones in this group appear to have been worked with tools in an attempt to produce a dressed surface and may therefore have served a structural function.

In one case (SF4267) an attempt has been made to pierce the cobble.

The commonest types of worked stone artefact for which a function can be presumed are rubbing stones and whetstones (total of 16 objects, 33.9%). These could have been used for a wide variety of tasks including sharpening of metal tools. A range of stone types was used with no particular type being favoured. These are also undatable and appear throughout the stratigraphic sequence. The presence of SF7467 in context 9502 at the base of ploughsoil provides potentially a late date based on the stratigraphic location; an early medieval date would not be out of the question. All of these objects were either otherwise unaltered, water-worn cobbles locally available from the boulder clay or small fragments of locally outcropping Keuper sandstone. Most show striations aligned with the long axis of the cobble (where this exists) suggesting that they were used with a backwards and forwards rubbing motion.

Four large sandstone blocks appear to be derived from a structure or structures, which were at least partly built of stone. They were all roughly dressed blocks, possibly quarried, one (SF8619) may have been used as a setting for a door post. All of them had been reused as packing material in late post-holes, though apart from the stone trough only SF8619 could be confidently assigned to any particular phase (Period VI). However, it is likely that all were relatively late, and may therefore relate to medieval structures.

The function of the stone trough (SF7784) is not clear and few parallels could be found. It would have held very little liquid, and would probably have been porous unless lined with lead or bitumen. Its inner surface shows little sign of wear, which suggests it was not used for grinding or pounding, though it is possible that it broke during manufacture. It was re-used as packing in one of the latest, probably early medieval, post-holes on the site and therefore can only be dated to before the 11th century AD. The closest parallel is a similarly sized and shaped trough from the villa site at Dalton Parlours (Buckley and Major 1990). This was also broken and deposited in a secondary context (the fill of a well). However, one side retained traces of a shallow overflow channel on one side and it is possible that a similar feature may have been present on the missing section of the Irby trough. The association of the Dalton find with a larger trough suggested that it may have formed part of the drainage system to the villa and it is possible that the Irby example could have performed a similar function. Its presence at Irby may suggest that a substantial building or buildings was located nearby. A rectangular trough, a little smaller than the Irby example, measuring 0.28 x 0.22 x 0.12 m deep in red sandstone was found in Castle Street, Carlisle in Period 9, of late 2nd to mid 3rd-century date (Padley 1991, 162, no 609. fig. 148). Alternatively it may have served as a setting for a timber post although the presence of numerous rock-cut post-holes and bedrock lying close to the present surface, this seems unlikely.

The occurrence of this material in secondary contexts shows that whatever structure, or structures, they belonged to were demolished prior to the construction of the post-built structure for which these stones were used as packing material.

Two tabular fragments of sandstone could have been used as either floor or roof tile, though these could equally be the chance result of cleavage along bedding planes. It is possible that they were contemporary with the building material discussed above. Alternatively, similar objects have been interpreted as 'mats' for hot cooking pots (Addyman and Priestley 1977, 139) though in the present context this would seem unlikely.

The presence of what is probably stone building material suggests that a substantial building was located nearby. However, this evidence should be considered in the light of the almost complete absence of ceramic building material such as roof tile. Roof tiles are known from similar sites in the region (Ochre Brook, Court Farm and Lathom), although up to the present these are all associated with buildings constructed according to a native tradition. The material at Ochre Brook was clearly derived from the manufacture of roofing tile for the 20th Legion at Chester. That at Court Farm was heavily broken and appeared to represent secondary reuse of material derived from outside the site. The context of the Lathom material is not presently clear. Whatever, and wherever, this structure was it appears to have had an organic (thatch or turf) roof and must therefore have been influenced at least in part by native building traditions, though the suggestion of the provision of a drainage system indicates that it was also a relatively sophisticated structure.

The possible fragment of stone mould should be treated with the other evidence for metalworking on site. Its occurrence in a relatively late context could argue against this interpretation, open moulds of this type are generally believed to have gone out of use by the end of the Bronze Age. However it is difficult to envisage any other function for the strange, and apparently intentionally produced hollow, and it is very possible that this object is also in a secondary context.

The partly-made and broken fragments of rotary quern strongly suggest that these objects were also being manufactured on site using locally quarried stone. These can be used to reconstruct the stages in the production of rotary querns. Most seem to show that a suitably sized block was selected and roughly cut to size, the central perforation or socket was produced using a punch. The block then seems to have been worked up using a punch. The use of axes/bolsters appears to have been restricted to final finishing. Apart from the single fragment of lava quern, all of the Irby quern stones could have been manufactured locally. SF6544 compares most closely with Curwen's flat-topped, early Romano-British type (1937, 143, figs 15-17). All of the quern stones occur in secondary contexts, usually reused as building material and therefore provide no information on the location of milling activities. There is a roughly equal number of upper and lower stones present.

The other quern stones themselves are not closely datable. In the north east, where the chronology of late prehistoric settlements and associated artefacts is far more refined than in the north west, beehive querns began in production in the 2nd century BC and continue throughout the Roman period (Buckley and Major 1998). Although generally considered to be a native type, they occur at both rural and military sites during the Roman period, occurring at Castleford, West Yorks. and Ribchester, Lancs. (Buckley and Major 1998; Howard-Davis 2000, 297-300). Closer to Wirral, a Hunsbury type beehive quern from Prestatyn was found in a Period II context, dated *c.* AD 70s-160 (Blockley 1989, 124-5). However, the Irby example discussed above had been redeposited in an early medieval context. Flat rotary querns are generally dated to between the 1st and 4th centuries AD.

It would appear that most of the Irby querns are present in secondary contexts: seven of the 17 fragments occur in post-Roman contexts, eight occur in 3rd-century or later contexts and two occur in unphased but probably 3rd-century or later deposits. Only the white granite rubbing stone (SF8210) occurred in a prehistoric context.

At the time of the production of the initial assessment report, there was little to which this assemblage of material could be directly compared. Eleven quern stones were excavated from the Romano-British contexts at the Breiddin hillfort (Musson 1991), though only one was a rotary quern, the remainder all being saddle querns. Otherwise, there seems to have been a similar pattern of usage, all of the materials could be found locally and a wide variety of stones were used as rubbers, pounders, whetstones and grinders. The stone finds from Beeston Castle (Henson and Hurcombe 1993) show a very similar pattern of exploitation of local resources for quern stones and opportunistic use of glacial erratics for a wide range of functions. Saddle querns are recorded in some quantity from Iron Age hillforts at Dinorben and Moel y Gaer in Clwyd but only one from Moel Hiraddug (Guilbert 1982, 51, n. 104).

Recent excavations along the line of the A5300 in Tarbock, north of the Mersey (Cowell and Philpott 2000) produced very few finds of this type. Two possible rubbing stones were recovered from the site at Brook House Farm, a fragment of imported lava almost certainly from a quern at Ochre Brook, and only two possible rubbing stones were recovered from Brunt Boggart.

The best parallel is the settlement at Court Farm, Halewood, also located north of the Mersey (Adams and Philpott in prep.). This produced a much larger assemblage, analogous to that from Irby. However, there are some significant differences. For example, the Court Farm assemblage contains a significant proportion of quern stones manufactured in millstone grit and therefore imported from the Pennines to the east. In addition Court Farm also had exotic objects such as cosmetic palettes in a stone possibly imported from north Wales. This contrasts with the rather more insular nature of the assemblage at Irby which at first sight suggests that the external contacts of the Irby settlement were more limited. However, this evidence directly contradicts the evidence from the pottery and therefore it is more likely that this difference is due to the availability of raw materials. Irby is located on a sandstone ridge and consequently close to ready supplies of stone. The sites north of the Mersey were all located on boulder clay and hence had little direct access to available stone, though outcrops of red sandstone are located within a few kilometres. The quern stones at Court Farm were produced in a mix of red sandstone and millstone grit. Grit-stone is significantly harder and gives a much better grinding surface. Perhaps the differences in these assemblages are indicating that if suitable stone was available on site or within a short distance then that was used exclusively. However, if the source of stone was further away then the suitability of the material for its purpose was regarded at least equally to the cost/effort of transportation.

A further contrast with sites north of the Mersey is provided by the presence of the single fragment of Mayen lava quern at Irby. These are normally associated with military sites (e.g. Welfare 1985) although they occur in limited quantities on civilian sites (e.g. Buckley and Major 1990). They were standard items of military equipment and were imported into the north west with the Roman army from the AD 70s. Peacock, however, considered that the trade in lava querns declined by the 3rd century and most examples on dated sites occur in the 1st or 2nd centuries (Peacock 1980). They are currently unknown from civilian sites north of the Mersey, with the exception of Ochre Brook, a special category of site with its evidence of tile manufacture for the 20th Legion. It is most likely that the presence of this fragment at Irby is a consequence of its relative proximity to Chester rather than necessarily any direct contact with the military. Lava querns are not closely datable and the present example is too small to retain any diagnostic features.

The contrasts between these assemblages may reflect other differences between these sites. The lack of worked stone from the A5300 sites may be a consequence of the limited area excavated though it could also be due to the short duration of settlement at Ochre Brook and its possible status as a depot for the manufacture of tile.

The worked stone from Irby to some extent corroborates the information derived from studies of other aspects of the material culture. The inhabitants seem to have been engaged, at least on a 'part time' basis in the manufacture of goods (i.e. quern stones) possibly for export/trade with other settlements. The lack of items such as fine palettes, which occur on other sites in Merseyside (e.g. Court Farm, Halewood: Adams and Philpott in prep.) could be connected with the relatively low status of the occupants. However the presence of possible building stone suggests that to view Irby as a low status settlement would be over simplistic.

Heat-Shattered Stones

Heat-shattered stones are common in the overall layers at Irby and were observed for instance in the eastern section of Ditch 1. They are glacial or river pebbles often fist-sized or smaller, which exhibit surface reddening and interior grey reduction, occasional crazing of the surface and angular breaks.

Heat-shattered stones have been discovered at sites from the Bronze Age and Iron Age both within the region and outside it (Philpott 2000b, 159-60). They have been noted in early Bronze Age contexts at Brunt

Boggart, Tarbock (Philpott 2000b, 120), and at three sites occupied in both the Iron Age and Romano-British period at Lathom, West Lancashire, at Great Woolden Hall, Salford and Mellor, Stockport (Cowell 2002; Nevell 1999b; Mellor Archaeological Trust 2002; Noble and Thompson 2005, 23). The Iron Age site at Bruen Stapleford, Cheshire also produced quantities of heat-shattered stone (Fairburn 2002a, 51). In neighbouring regions they have been found at the Iron Age enclosure at Fisherwick, Staffs (Smith 1979), and Sharpstones Hill, Shropshire (Barker *et al.* 1991). Further afield, fire-cracked pebbles were found in two pits at an Iron Age enclosure at Wanlip, Leics., one of which produced an early Iron Age radiocarbon date (760-250 cal BC; Q-3277; 2355 $\pm$ 55 BP), as well as in a variety of other features at this site (Beamish 1998, 17). They have been observed in fieldwalking at undated enclosure sites at Sinderland House Farm, Warburton and Winwick (Hall *et al.* 1995, 161-2) and in small quantity in a field which had previously produced a concentration of Romano-British finds at Duckington, Cheshire by Liverpool Museum Field Archaeology Unit in 2001.

The function of heat-shattered stones has been the subject of some debate (e.g. Hodder and Barfield 1991). An alternative name 'pot-boilers', by which they are sometimes known, reveals one of the most consistently held views on their use for cooking, although it is something of a misnomer in certain contexts, where the use of heated stones appears to coincide with aceramic phases of settlement. The general view of their use, supported by early Irish texts, is that the stones, which had been heated over wood fires, were placed in water-filled pits until the water boiled. Meat wrapped in straw could be boiled in this fashion (Gillespie 1991). Other uses have been proposed, based on archaeological evidence or ethnographic practice, ranging from beer making, drying meat or fish, butter production, leather preparation and fulling (Barfield 1991, 62). Barfield in addition notes the use of heated stones to evaporate brine during salt production at Droitwich, and creation of steam to bend timber (1991, 62-4).

Heat-shattered stones and charcoal comprising burnt mounds in Wales have been suggested as cooking places, at intervals from the early Bronze Age possibly into historic times. Other activities would not be precluded, such as fulling cloth, preparing timber or as a sauna or sweat-lodge (Kelly 1992, 93; Barfield 1991). Burnt mounds represent the accumulation of charcoal, possibly ash (though this does not always survive) and stones which were used until they shattered. They often have associated with them trenches or pits and usually indicate repeated activity over some time at the one location. Heat-shattered stones are also found in settlements, where they may represent the same activity undertaken within a domestic settled context, where the stone does not accumulate but is dumped or dispersed around the settlement.

Heat-shattered stones were found in great abundance, including 1917 litres from the enclosure ditch alone, at an Iron Age site at Bromfield, Shropshire (Stanford 1995, 105-7). Stanford considers that they were used in conjunction with clay-lined pits for boiling meat (1995, 107). He observes a discrepancy between the occurrence of burnt 'boiling stones' in lowland settlements in Shropshire and Herefordshire in the Iron Age and their absence from hillforts such as the Wrekin, Croft Ambrey, Midsummer Hill and Credenhill (1995, 129). He suggests this may reflect differences in cooking methods between upland and lowland sites, depending on the availability of gravel for the stone, or a functional difference between lowland farms which specialised in slaughtering animals, curing skins and boiling the meat, possibly as a seasonal activity.

There appears to be a distinct chronological distinction in the region between late prehistoric sites which tend to produce heat-shattered stones, and Romano-British sites which do not. In the lowland north west Romano-British sites which were not preceded by Iron Age occupation, such as Ochre Brook, Tarbock (Philpott 2000c) or Court Farm, Halewood, have not so far produced heat-shattered stones. This may indicate that the techniques which resulted in the creation of heat-shattered stone were no longer current in the Romano-British period, although it is uncertain whether there is a simple chronological distinction or a difference in function between the sites. Heated stones may have been used in leather or wooden vessels to boil water or to cook food without damaging the organic container (Fowler 1983, 197). The decline in their use may be related to the introduction of ceramic cooking vessels which could be stood over a fire without shattering. Many of the black-burnished sherds from Irby were sooted on the exterior indicating they had been used for this purpose. In this respect it may be significant that heat-shattered stones were found in the aceramic post-Roman site at Whithorn, Dumfries and Galloway (Hill 1997, 473-4), indicating that these processes re-appear once ceramic cooking vessels were no longer available.

Minerals

Analysis of Coal Samples

Mark H. Adams (based on reports from P. D. Hopper and P. E. Harrison)

Introduction

Coal was observed in a number of contexts at Irby, notably in the fill of the enclosure ditches and within some of the post-holes, and is therefore of Roman to medieval date. Samples of coal from slag heaps from the nearest colliery at Neston, Wirral were submitted for analysis at TES Bretby by D. Hopper. These were compared with analyses of coal from a stratified context (context 22 in enclosure Ditch 1, Area I) at Irby which were performed by P. E. Harrison of British Coal (TSRE).

Analyses

Petrographic Analysis- Rank determination by Vitrine Reflectance

The mean maximum reflectance value of the coal was:

| Neston | 0.73% ± 0.03% |
| Irby | 0.64% ± 0.04% |

The Irby sample was noted to be weathered and showed traces of heat alteration.

Palynological Analysis

The stratigraphically significant species present in the spore assemblages showed that both samples were of Carboniferous Age and derived from the Lower Coal Measures.

Conclusion

The coal from the slag heap at Neston was not considered to be from the same seam as that from Irby, though the two coals are likely to be have derived from the same locality with the Neston coal being from deeper workings (generally rank increases with depth).

Haematite

Robert Philpott

Haematite is a relatively pure iron ore (Ferric oxide), low in phosphorus. In the north west of England the main sources are western Cumbria and Furness (Tylecote 1986, 124-6). Eighteen fragments of haematite were recorded on the site, ranging in size from tiny flecks weighing 0.1 g to larger lumps up to 91.4 g in weight; only three pieces weigh over 20 g. In six cases the pieces have been polished. Of these, one was at the base of ploughsoil while the others are derived from layers or features of probable Romano-British date.

Catalogue (none illustrated)

81. Nodule with two worn and polished surfaces. Wt 9.5 g. SF3890. context 1039 (unphased, occupation deposit).
82. Broken nodule with two polished surfaces. Wt 16 g. SF3032, context 3072 (unphased layer)
83. Pointed flat fragment, one curved and faceted, polished side, and one straight side. Wt 3.4 g. SF4276, context 3672 (unphased layer).
84. Broken nodule, smoothed on both breaks with striations on one side from polishing narrow hard items? Wt 12.5 g. SF8682, context 7603, fill of Ditch 1, Period IV (cut 7611).
85. Small irregular nodule with one polished surface. Wt 7.7 g. SF9427, context 3000, Base of modern ploughsoil.

86. Large nodule, polished flat on one side with groove from polishing ?objects; outer face polished and faceted. Wt 75.6 g. SF8792, context 7043, unphased interface layer with sandy subsoil.

A number of pieces of haematite from Irby occurred in contexts which were rich in industrial waste from iron working, notably in pit 3724 (two fragments from two different contexts); they also came from the enclosure ditch (D1) and from overall layers such as 1039 and 3062 which contained considerable quantities of industrial waste. There is no evidence at Irby of iron smelting though smithing waste is common in the Roman period (see Chapter 4, *Industrial Waste*). It is likely that the haematite was found as small nodules present in the boulder clay.

However, the fact that some pieces had been deliberately utilised argues for a different function for some of the material. The smoothed or polished surfaces on six pieces are consistent with their use either as a colouring, burnishing or polishing agent. This function is supported to some extent by the presence of other metalworking debris, including bronze moulds and crucibles, probably of Roman date (see below), and is supported by evidence from other sites.

Discussion

On Roman and later sites three principal uses have been identified for haematite. The first exploits the mineral's high iron content as an ore for smelting. Haematite for this purpose occurred in ditch fills at Lousher's Lane, Wilderspool in both massive and reddle form, the latter being powdered haematite. The source was thought likely to be Cumbria or north Wales in the region of Roman lead mines around Caerwys (Hinchliffe and Williams 1992, 113, 165). In the post-Roman period at Whithorn, Dumfries and Galloway, haematite was associated with a spread of iron ore and some had been heated, suggesting roasting before smelting (Chadburn and Hill 1997, 471). In both cases, an industrial function was assumed for the ores, haematite being one of the richest iron ores. At Irby, some of the material occurs in a rough unworked form but it is unlikely that the haematite represented ore for smelting although the site produced evidence of iron smithing.

The second use of haematite exploits its bright reddish-brown colour. Haematite is soft and can be easily rubbed onto a surface as a pigment. An oyster found in a well at a Roman villa at Gorhambury, Herts. contained haematite which had probably been used as a pigment for wall painting (Neal *et al.* 1990, 73).

The presence of haematite on the site at Irby in another form, deliberately smoothed or polished, accords with a third use of the mineral for polishing metalwork. One of the Irby pebbles has linear streaks and worn grooves on the surface, indicating a hard object had

been rubbed against the stone. Occurrences of polished lumps of haematite have been noted elsewhere in the region. On the north Wirral coast at Meols haematite was found which had derived from eroding occupation deposits from settlements of prehistoric, Roman and later date (Ecroyd Smith 1866, 212; 1867, 185; 1872, 150). Smith noted that the lumps of material from Meols were sometimes pierced and invariably had one rubbed surface, often being worn to a triangular profile. Four pieces survive in the Grosvenor Museum, Chester. Ecroyd Smith considered that the pierced lumps were amuletic in function. He identified a source for the mineral on the Dee coast at Dawpool near Thurstaston in west Wirral, less than 3 km from the Irby site (1867, 106-7). While the unstratified nature of the Meols assemblage makes accurate dating impossible, the material was consistently listed in the Roman section of the finds reports, suggesting it had been found on that part of the shore which produced Roman finds. However, a medieval date there is quite possible, in view of other evidence for metalworking on the site (Egan 2007, 181). On another Merseyside site, the Romano-British rural site at Court Farm, Halewood, there were not only several deliberately smoothed nodules of haematite but also crucibles of Romano-British date which were used for manufacturing copper-alloy objects of some kind. Fieldwalking at a Romano-British enclosure site in Southworth, near Winwick, Cheshire, produced a smoothed pyramidal lump of haematite. At Castleford, West Yorkshire a highly polished lump of haematite from Egremont in Cumbria had been probably used for burnishing (Clarke 1998, 254, 256, no 38). At Whithorn, a second group comprised 21 lumps of botryoidal haematite, of which 18 had been artificially smoothed. These were present in phases dating from the mid 8th to 13th century AD, with a group of polishers associated with late 12th-century metalworking on the site. Here they were interpreted as use for polishing fine metalwork (Chadburn and Hill 1997, 240, 471). A similar function was proposed for haematite found in medieval London (Egan 2007, 181).

Galena

Robert Philpott

87. A large lump of galena (lead ore) with cubic crystals. SF2185, wt 155.8 g, context 3307, a probable Romano-British occupation layer.

Galena is not native to Wirral but lead deposits occur in Carboniferous limestone at Halkyn Mountain across the Dee estuary in Flintshire in north Wales which were extensively exploited during the Roman period (O'Leary *et al.* 1989, 2). A number of lead items were found at Irby but there is no evidence for smelting at Irby. This single piece may have been brought over as a curiosity for its unusual weight and obvious crystalline structure.

In an interesting echo of the Irby site, a single piece

of galena was also recovered at Lousher's Lane, Wilderspool, which was probably derived from north Wales or the Bakewell area of the Peak District (Hinchliffe and Williams 1992, 165).

Prehistoric Pottery

Ann Woodward

At Irby, a total of 146 sherds of prehistoric pottery, weighing 1936 g, were found. The form and fabric of the diagnostic sherds immediately suggested that the pottery dated from early in the 1st millennium BC. Thus the assemblage was deemed to be of significant regional and national importance. Only a relatively small proportion of the sherds (35%) definitely derived from *in situ* stratified contexts, but these accounted for much of the total assemblage by weight. The stratified material was found in the fillings of five structural gullies or slots and six post-holes belonging to the earliest structural phase detected on the site: Phase P3 of Period II. Rim fragments were fairly common, at 14% of the assemblage but, interestingly, base angles were totally absent. Decorated items and shoulder fragments both occurred at the level of 3%.

Fabric

Eleven fabrics identified by macroscopic examination and use of a hand-lens were subsequently studied petrologically by David Williams (see below, *Thin-section petrology of late prehistoric pottery and fired clay*). The fabric types may be described in brief and grouped as follows:

Sandstone and igneous inclusions. Fabrics 1, 2, 4, 5, 7 (Williams 1 to 5). Fine micaceous clay matrix with sparse quartz and inclusions of sandstone, plus variable inclusion of fragments of rhyolite, gabbro, dolerite or lava.

Sandstone and igneous inclusions plus sand. Fabrics 3, 6, 9 (Williams 6 to 8). Variable inclusions, as for the first group, but the fabrics are in general slightly more sandy.

The individual fabric types within these two groups clearly related in some cases to groups of sherds from single vessels.

Vesicular. Fabrics 8, 10 and 11 (Williams 9 to 11). These fabrics were characterised by variable densities of voids, both angular and rounded in shape. The original inclusions in Fabrics 8 and 10 appear to have been pieces of carbonised wood. Fabric 8 also contained clay pellets.

All the pottery could have been made locally according to the petrological evidence. The igneous inclusions are angular and were deliberately crushed and added

as temper. As noted by Williams, the range of rocks employed reflects those used in the manufacture of rubbing stones found on the site. The fine-grained micaceous clay seen in most of the sherds was also identified in one of the fired clay samples examined by Williams and may derive from local marine deposits.

	Sandstone and igneous	Sandstone, igneous and sand	Vesicular	Totals
Period II	45 (88%)	5 (10%)	1 (2%)	51
Other	35 (37%)	54 (57%)	6 (6%)	95
Total	80 (55%)	59 (40%)	7 (5%)	146

Table 4.11: Prehistoric pottery by phase and fabric group

Table 4.11 shows that fabrics of the first group with sandstone and igneous inclusions were most common in the *in situ* deposits of Period II. In the later (Roman) contexts the more sandy fabrics and the vesicular sherds were more often represented. This may suggest that some of the material from post-Period II contexts was later than the Period II vessels, and could have been residual from a post-Period II Iron Age horizon which has been totally disturbed by later activity. However, so few vessels were represented in the Period II levels that such a comparison may not be significant. Also, there was no petrological evidence to support the idea that some of the post-Period II sherds might have belonged to later stages of the Iron Age.

Form and decoration

As very few vessels are represented, all are illustrated and they are described individually.

Illustrated sherds (Fig. 4.8)

Period II
88. Rim and upper wall of a straight-sided vessel with simple, slightly internally bevelled rim. The exterior surface is decorated with rough diagonal rows of very faint pointed oval impressions, made with a blunt instrument possibly of wood or bone. SF7998, fabric 2, context 8351. Part of S27, Phase P3 (see Plate IV for sherd *in situ*).
89. Two joining rim and upper wall fragments from a vessel of slightly convex profile, the rim with a distinct internal bevel. SF6014 and SF6039, fabric 1, context 3403. Part of S27, Phase 3.
90. Joining shoulder sherds from a vessel with a very slightly angled, thickened shoulder. SF6020 and SF6036, fabric 1, context 3403. This shoulder might belong to the same vessel as the rim fragments, no. 89, above.
91. Expanded, internally bevelled rim sherds from a thinner-walled and slightly necked vessel. The exterior surface carries faint vertical finger smearing and some uneven short rows of faint oval and rectangular impressions, similar to those on no. 88 above. SF5612 and SF5760, fabric 3, context 3350.
92. Rim sherd from an open vessel with internally bevelled rim. Faint thumb or finger smearing and impressions are

visible on the exterior surface and below the interior bevel. SF8068, fabric 3, context 8362.

93. Rim sherd with internal bevel. SF5540, fabric 3, context 3337. Part of S27, Phase 3.

Post-Period II

94. Rim sherd with external expansion and internal bevel. Along the top of the rim there is a row of very faint oval impressions. SF2351, fabric 2, context 3307.

95. Everted rim with internal bevel. SF9031, fabric 3, context 8332.

96. Rim with internal bevel. SF5505, fabric 5, context 3336.

97. Rim with internal bevel. SF8259, fabric 1, context 6216.

98. Sharp shoulder fragment with traces of faint oval impression ornament. SF1035, fabric 2, context 658.

99. Small wall sherd decorated with random fingernail impressions. SF5656, fabric 3, context 3352.

100. Wall sherd decorated with faint oval impressions. SF9650, fabric 3, unstratified.

Plate XX: 91. Bronze Age sherd (SF5760), showing surface detail

A minimum of ten vessels are represented by the diagnostic sherds and, of these, a minimum of four were decorated. Fabrics not represented amongst the diagnostic sherds are 6 and 9 of the sandstone, igneous and sand group and the three vesicular fabrics (Fabrics 8, 10 and 11). Therefore, the total minimum number of vessels represented is 15. It is likely however that there were rather more than this.

Taphonomy

Most of the prehistoric pottery from the site was abraded. In Period II a significant proportion of sherds, 33%, were fresh and unabraded, but 47% were very abraded. In the post-Period II Roman or later contexts much of the residual prehistoric pottery (48%) was slightly abraded, but 21% of the sherds were fresh and unabraded. The fresh sherds from these later contexts included examples from all three major fabric groups, so, again, no clear suggestion of a destroyed Iron Age horizon could be sustained.

Within the *in situ* Period II deposits usually only small segments of rims were represented. However, in context 8351 (no. 88 above) 26% of the vessel rim survived. As the overall weight statistics showed, sherds from Period II contexts were much larger than those from later contexts. Their average sherd weight was 32 g, compared with a general average sherd weight of 14 g for the whole assemblage.

Vessel size and function

No patterns of sooting or visible residues were observed on the pottery. Only four rim diameters could be measured and these conformed to a fairly tight size range (200 to 260 mm) which denotes vessels of a medium size. Sherd thickness (which is recorded in the archive) is remarkably uniform, and no cups or very large storage vessels appear to have been represented in the assemblage. The fabrics, as far as diagnostic

sherds are concerned, are also fairly uniform, whilst the vesicular fabrics are not particularly fine or thinner-walled and, represented only by plain wall sherds, cannot be linked to specific vessel types.

Discussion

The prehistoric pottery assemblage appears to represent a single phase of site activity. The occurrence of fabrics amongst the Period II and post-Period II contexts is slightly different, but the similarity of the rim forms throughout and the lack of any clear dating indications from petrological analysis means that it is not possible to promote a distinct phase of post-Period II prehistoric pottery use on the site. The Period II assemblage is unique in character and is dated by radiocarbon to the middle Bronze Age (see Chapter 2, *Radiocarbon Dates*). The post-Period II items (26% of the total assemblage by weight) are thought to be residual, but there is a slight possibility that some of the vesicular and more sandy wares may belong to the middle or late Iron Age. However, it seems more likely that the Iron Age period at Irby was mainly aceramic, as at Beeston Castle, Cheshire (Royle and Woodward 1993, 74) and in other neighbouring areas.

Most rim types at Irby are internally bevelled and/or externally expanded, and vessel profiles are mainly straight-walled, although examples of a sharp shoulder (no. 98) and a slightly thickened rounded shoulder (no. 90) are present. Prior to the availability of the results of the radiocarbon dating programme, it was concluded that these characteristics indicated a possible late Bronze Age or early Iron Age date for the Period II assemblage. However, these formal features are not well matched in the major assemblages of late Bronze Age date from the region: Mam Tor, Derbyshire (Coombs and Thompson 1979), Beeston Castle (Royle and Woodward 1993) and The Breiddin (Musson 1991). In these cases the main vessel type is the round-shouldered necked jar, and rims tend to be flat, or simple and everted. The same applies to Assemblage I from Willington, Derbyshire (Elsdon 1979), which may be of slightly later date.

The Period II material is the first major assemblage of middle Bronze Age date to have been identified in the region. The only other pottery of this date known in the North-West is a small group from Oversley Farm, Manchester Airport (Allen 2007). Otherwise, the material can be compared with urns belonging to the Cordoned and Biconical Series, or their derivatives, from the Pennines and the Midlands region. The generally straight-sided profiles, or slightly bipartite forms indicated by the sharp and rounded shoulder fragments, can be matched amongst Cordoned Urns, and related types, from sites such as Eaglestone Flat, Derbyshire (Barnatt 1994, fig. 12, 3; fig. 13, 5, 5A and 6; fig. 14, 7 and 9), Willington, Derbyshire (Manby in Wheeler 1979, fig. 64, 108) or Eye Kettleby, Leicestershire (Woodward and Marsden forthcoming: eight vessels). Although most of these urns are decorated with geometric motifs in cord or incised technique, a few are plain (e.g. Barnatt 1994, fig. 14.9, which also displays a very straight-sided profile).

Most of the urns from these sites also have internally bevelled rims, and this stylistic feature is also found very commonly amongst the urn assemblage from Bromfield in Shropshire (Stanford 1982, figs 16-18). This long-lived and unusual urnfield includes many vessels of bipartite form which appear to derive from the Biconical Urn Series of the later early Bronze Age. The urns carry various decorative schemes including incised geometric motifs, rows of fingertip or fingernail impressions or horseshoe handles, and it is amongst this assemblage that the only clear parallel for the oval impressions found at Irby can be identified (Stanford 1982, fig. 17, P7). The middle Bronze Age sherds from Oversley Farm, Manchester Airport are rather different from the Irby material. The five rims represented are all of rounded or simple type, not bevelled, and there is one example of a low fingertip-impressed cordon (Allen 2007, ills. 111 to 115 and 132). The only feature in common with the Irby sherds is one instance of random fingernail decoration.

The group of six middle Bronze Age radiocarbon dates from Irby are statistically indistinguishable, suggesting that the activity dated was of short duration, some time

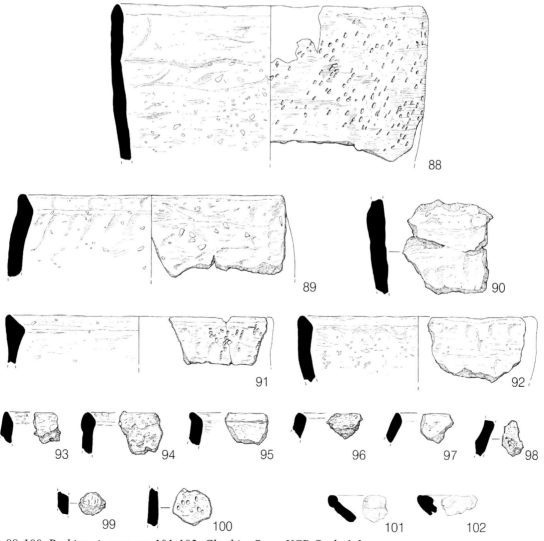

Fig. 4.8: 88-100. Prehistoric pottery; 101-102. Cheshire Stony VCP. Scale 1:3

in the second half of the second millennium cal BC (see Chapter 2). The middle Bronze Age pottery from Oversley Farm was associated with Early Bronze Age ceramics in a midden context and was dated rather earlier to 1985-1660 cal BC (Allen 2007). The Cordoned Urns at Eye Kettleby were associated with dates of the later early Bronze Age period (1690-1554 and 1686-1554 cal BC), while a vessel with fingertip decoration only carried a middle Bronze Age date of 1412-1299 cal BC (Woodward and Marsden forthcoming). The long ceramic sequence represented at Bromfield probably spanned the whole millennium from *c.* 2000 to *c.* 1000 cal BC (Stanford 1982, 316).

Most urns belonging to these series of the later early Bronze Age and middle Bronze Age periods in middle and northern England are characterised by distinctive igneous inclusions. The various igneous inclusions identified at Irby, including rhyolite, gabbro and dolerite, could have been derived from local drift deposits (see *Thin-section petrology* below). Such fabrics can be compared with those of the Bromfield urns, containing fragments of the local Clee Hills dolerite (Stanford 1982), and the fabrics of the Eye Kettleby vessels which often contained pieces of granite or granodiorite, probably from the Charnwood region nearby (Williams in Woodward forthcoming). The occurrence of carbonised wood inclusions in some of the vesicular fabrics at Irby is of particular note, and can be matched at Oversley Farm, where some of the Early Bronze Age (Collared Urn) sherds contained charcoal and burnt wood, possibly derived from inclusions of dung (Allen 2007).

The Irby assemblage is the first major group of middle Bronze Age ceramics to have been excavated in the north-west. Parallels have been drawn with urns from the midland counties and the Pennines, but these are all derived from sepulchral round barrow or urnfield sites. The domestic material from Irby is therefore of considerable interest. The small amount of domestic pottery recovered from the midden deposit at Oversley Farm, Manchester was rather dissimilar in style. The Irby pots are all of medium size, whilst the urnfield assemblages display more varied repertoires, with small, medium and larger vessels represented. The comparative rim diameter ranges are 126-290 mm at Eaglestone Flat, 200-280 mm at Eye Kettleby and 80-270 mm at Bromfield. This data might suggest that the domestic wares were limited to a single size range, but the ceramic group from Irby is very small, and it may be too soon for such a conclusion to be advanced.

Thin-section petrology of late prehistoric pottery and fired clay

D. F. Williams

Introduction

A small programme of petrological analysis was undertaken on a representative selection of late prehistoric pottery and fired clay from the 1987-1996 excavations. Before thin sectioning, the sherds and clay samples were initially studied with the aid of a compound microscope (x20) and reference is made to Munsell Color Charts in the descriptions. Irby is situated in an area of Triassic formations, mostly Bunter Sandstone and Keuper Marl, covered by deposits of Boulder Clay (Geological Survey 1 inch Map of England Sheet No. 96).

Petrology and Fabric

1. Rim sherd. SF6010, Context 3403, Trench VIII.
2. Decorated wall-sherd. SF5541, Context 3337, Trench VIII.
3. Plain wall-sherd. SF1125, Context 0706, Trench VI.
4. Plain wall-sherd SF5505, Context 3336, Trench VIII.
5. Plain wall-sherd. SF5758, Context 3364, Trench VIII.

The five sherds in this group share a number of common fabric characteristics. The most noticeable feature in the hand-specimen is the presence of a number of light and dark coloured rock fragments set in a fairly fine-texture somewhat micaceous clay matrix. The sherds are normally light brownish-grey to dark grey in colour (10YR 5/2 - 4/1). In thin section all of the sherds can be seen to have a fairly fine-textured mica-rich clay matrix, in which the mica is composed predominantly of small shreds of muscovite. Scattered throughout the clay matrix are fragments of a range of igneous and sedimentary rocks, easily seen in the hand-specimen. In some cases these reach over 3mm across but the majority are normally well below this in size. The sedimentary rock is a fine-grained to medium-grained sandstone and is present in all of the sherds. The igneous rocks are more varied and include rhyolite, gabbro, dolerite, a weathered felspar-rich rock and lava. The quartz content tends to be sparse and mainly silt-sized or just above.

Sherds nos 6-8 also contain igneous inclusions, although in this case the fabrics are slightly more sandy than the first five sherds described above.

6. SF2553 Context 1039 Tr. VIII
Plain wall-sherd
Soft, sandy fabric with visible scattered rock fragments, reddish-brown surfaces (5YR 5/3) and dark grey inner core (5YR 4/1). Thin sectioning shows moderately

frequent grains of quartz, together with small pieces of sandstone, discrete grains of felspar, several fragments of a weathered igneous rock, possibly a rhyolite, and a piece of dolerite.

7. SF7264 Context 6276 Tr. XXXVI
Plain wall-sherd

Soft, sandy fabric with noticeable inclusions of rock fragments, light red surfaces (2.5YR 6/6) and dark grey core (N4/). In thin section, frequent subangular grains of quartz ranging up to 0.60mm in size are set in a micaceous clay matrix. Also present are several fragments of an olivine-gabbro (some over 3mm in size) together with discrete grains of plagioclase felspar and some clinopyroxene.

8. SF1122 Context 0725 Tr. VI
Plain wall-sherd

Soft, sandy fabric, reddish-grey in colour (2.5YR - 5YR 5/2). Thin sectioning shows that the clay matrix is dominated by frequent ill-sorted subangular quartz grains ranging up to 0.70mm in size, set in a somewhat micaceous clay matrix. Also present is a little chert, a few small discrete grains of plagioclase felspar, one or two very thin elongated voids containing a little carbonized material, iron oxide and a fragment of granitic rock.

9. SF7300 Context 8221 Tr. XIX
Plain wall-sherd

This is a soft, sandy and somewhat vesicular fabric, reddish-yellow in colour throughout (5YR 7/6 - 6/6). Thin sectioning shows moderately frequent subangular grains of quartz, mostly under 0.40mm in size but with a few slightly larger grains. Also present are flecks of mica and some fine-grained argillaceous material. The latter are probably clay pellets rather than deliberately added "grog". In the hand-specimen this sherd is somewhat vesicular with some large irregular-shaped holes in the surfaces, often quite deep. There seems to be no evidence that this represents calcareous material that has burnt or leached out or large fragments of stone like the material above. A few small pieces of carbonized ?wood were noted in the hand-specimen (x40), so it is perhaps possible they could represent even larger fragments. Alternatively, they could instead be the result of insufficiently wedged clay.

10. SF9352 Context 3062 Tr. XIX
Plain wall-sherd

Soft, friable fabric containing frequent elongate voids, dark grey outer surface and part core (2.5YR N4/), buff inner surface and part core (7.5YR 7/4). Thin sectioning shows a fine-textured clay matrix which is dominated by frequent voids, mostly small and elongate. Also present are sparse silt-sized quartz grains, some flecks of mica and a little iron oxide. The shape and frequency of the voids suggest that they represent an added temper of chopped grass or chaff which was subsequently burnt out during the firing of the vessel.

11. SF5789 Context 3345 Tr. VIII
Plain wall-sherd

A fairly soft fabric, also characterized by frequent voids, light brown outer surface (7.5YR 6/4) and greyish-brown inner surface and core (10YR 5/3). Many of the voids are small and elongate as described for no. 10, but a number are larger and more angular in shape. Under the compound microscope (x40) one or two carbonized pieces of ?wood can be made out, and so it seems likely that it is this material that is responsible for the larger more angular voids. Thin sectioning reflects the hand-specimen study, showing many voids occurring throughout the clay matrix, both small and elongate and larger and more angular. Also present are sparse quartz grains, generally silt-sized, flecks of mica and some iron oxide. The clay matrix appears to be slightly more micaceous than for no. 10.

12 SF8138 Context 9637 Tr. XLI
Fired clay

Thin sectioning shows a fairly fine-textured micaceous clay matrix (mostly flakes of muscovite), containing a scatter of silt-sized quartz grains with a few slightly larger grains. Also present are a few small pieces of siltstone, some clay pellets, a little iron oxide and a few elongate voids, some of them still containing carbonized vegetation. The sparseness of the latter suggest that they almost certainly occur naturally in the clay and probably represent small pieces of root material.

13. SF6045 Context 1109 Tr. VIII
Fired clay

Soft, crumbly sandy fabric, greyish-brown in colour throughout (10YR 5/2). One or two carbonized pieces of ?wood were noted under the compound microscope (x40). Thin sectioning shows a clay matrix packed with ill-sorted subangular grains of quartz that are over 1mm across on occasion but with the majority below 0.40mm in size. Also present are some flecks of mica, a few discrete grains of felspar, chert and a little iron oxide.

Comments

The fabric similarities of the first five sherds suggest that they may well have been made in the same production region, despite the varied range of rock types present. This may also be true for sherds nos 6-8 as well. Given the wide range of igneous glacial erratics found in the local Boulder Clays of the region (Wedd *et al.* 1923), it is possible that the source for this pottery may have been fairly local.

It seems significant, for example, that the range of igneous rock fragments present in this pottery can mostly be paralleled from the catalogue of rubbing stones found at the site and attributed to glacial erratics recovered from the local boulder clays (see above, *Other Stone Objects*). Moreover, despite the variability of igneous rocks between some of the sherds, six of the eight sherds (including the first five) also contain pieces of sandstone, a sedimentary rock commonly found in the area (Wedd *et al.* 1923). The fine-grained micaceous clay seen in the majority of the sherds has also been noted in one of the fired clay samples, no. 12 and may represent the fine and silty clay previously noted by Poole at Irby and thought to derive from local marine deposits (see below, *Structural Daub and Fired Clay*). Many of the igneous fragments in the pottery are angular in shape and may have been crushed and added as temper by the potter. Prehistoric pottery with a similar range of crushed glacial drift material is known from Beeston Castle, where a local source was considered for the majority of the material (Royle and Woodward 1993). The same may well be true for the later prehistoric pottery from Irby. It is worth noting, however, that the general fabric groupings described by Morris for Stony VCP, from the Middlewich/Nantwich area of Cheshire also include some similar rock types to those found in the Irby material, though the fabric of VCP tends to be somewhat coarser in texture than for most pottery (1985, 357-366).

Sherd nos 9-11 are more difficult to source as they contain fairly common non-plastic inclusions, though the organic tempered sherd no. 10 is reminiscent of a vesicular sherd from Irby previously looked at by the writer (ITS SF8195 Context 5341, see below), while it is assumed that the fired clay samples nos 12 and 13 are most likely locally derived.

Cheshire Salt Containers

Elaine L. Morris

Introduction

A total of 479 sherds (2005 g) of very distinctive ceramic material known as Cheshire salt containers or VCP (Very Coarse Pottery; cf. Gelling and Stanford 1965) was identified. This material has been studied in detail and shown to have derived from vessels used to dry and transport salt from brine springs in central Cheshire to settlements in the wider region during the second half of the first millennium BC (Morris 1985), and also into the early Roman period (Britnell 1989).

Description

The sherds are highly fragmented with a mean weight of only 4 g, and a spread of weights between less than 1 g and 56 g per sherd. Subtle and distinct variations in wall thickness, firing conditions, colour and surface finish indicate that several vessels are represented within the collection. Six rim sherds, probably from five different vessels, one fragment from a base, and 472 body sherds and flakes were identified. The rims, two of which are illustrated (Fig. 4.8, 101-102), are typical of this ceramic

material with both rounded and folded-over examples known (Morris 1985, fig. 7-8; Britnell 1989, fig. 26). Some body sherds display the concave profile of these flaring, open forms and others the very distinctive handmade manufacturing technique which appears to be based on the addition of collars or coils of clay upon another to build up the vessel walls. The joins of these clay collars/coils are then roughly smoothed together on the exterior creating a weak point for breakage but with little surface treatment on the interior where pronounced folds can be seen. The angled joint is clearly visible on two sherds and the interior folds on four sherds in the Irby collection, while collar-to-collar joins are visible on two examples.

A complete salt container vessel is expected to measure from approximately 220 to 260 mm high (no complete vessels have been recovered), with rim diameters ranging from 180-230 mm and much smaller bases from 120 to 160 mm across (Morris 1985, 235; Britnell 1989, fig. 26). Sherd walls measure from a thin 5 mm up to 21 mm thick, with the majority ranging between 7-14 mm thick. This is a highly variable range of wall thicknesses for a single type of pottery which suggests that there was no expected or required close standard of wall thickness for these coarse, industrial ceramic containers.

The majority of sherds are pink, orange or reddish-orange in colour from oxidised firing; occasional examples display unoxidised, pale grey wall cores. Twelve sherds also bear the very distinctive white colouring which is indicative of salt water in contact with a slightly calcareous clay matrix in a heating environment (Morris 1985, 345-6, 353).

The coarse fabric of Cheshire salt containers is characterised by the presence of ill-sorted, frequent, angular fragments of fine-grained acid igneous rocks (rhyolites) and less frequent pieces of microgranite/ granophyres and micaceous siltstone/fine sandstone in a sandy clay matrix (Morris 1985, 357-64, tables 2-4). Four pieces of this material from Irby were selected for petrological comparison to this fabric description. All four pieces correspond to this description (Ancient Monuments Laboratory Report No. 111/97).

Interpretation

The range of inclusions found in the fabric is consistent with an interpretation that the source for this particular combination of angular inclusions and clay matrix is the glacial drift of the central Cheshire Plain. The white colouring on the exterior of these open profile, vase-shaped vessels, their oxidised condition in contrast to the traditional pottery found associated with these sherds which tends to be black, grey, brown and reddish-brown in colour, and the wide distribution of the vessels originally up to 140 km from central Cheshire (Morris 1985, 364-70, figs 9-10, table 5; 1994, fig. 4A) have all tended to support the theory that this material was used to dry and transport salt throughout the region. It is hoped in the future that a later prehistoric salt production site will be found and excavated in the area of the Nantwich, Middlewich or Northwich brine springs in order to confirm this interpretation. At present only Roman and medieval salt production have been recorded in Cheshire (Harris and Thacker 1987).

The inclusions in the salt container fabric are also very different from the major later prehistoric pottery fabrics which are dominated by local sandstone inclusions (see below, *A note on the petrology of some prehistoric ceramic material*) rather than central Cheshire rhyolites. This supports the conclusion that these containers were not of local origin.

Dating

Period II is the earliest phase where sherds of Cheshire salt containers were recovered at Mill Hill Road. However, these 14 sherds were recovered from Period II securely in association with middle Bronze Age pottery in Phase P3 (see above, *Prehistoric Pottery*; see also Chapter 2 above). Prior to this association on the Wirral peninsula, the earliest stratified occurrences had been from ceramic and aceramic Iron Age deposits dated to *c.* 400 bc and later (Stanford 1984, 83-7; Morris 1985, 367-70) or from about 800-250 cal BC (Ellis 1993, 85-6, table 33). These examples placed the earliest known use and deposition of Cheshire salt containers into the middle third of the first millennium BC and confined to the Cheshire-Shropshire Plain (Morris 1985, fig. 9). The late Bronze Age occupation phases from two sites, the Breiddin hillfort in Powys (Musson 1991, 130-2) and Beeston Castle (Royle and Woodward 1993, 74), did not have sherds of Cheshire salt containers, despite the presence of this material in the Iron Age phases at these sites. Therefore, it appears that salt production did not take place at the brine springs of central Cheshire until the middle of the first millennium BC, i.e. the early Iron Age. Therefore, the presence in Period II deposits of 14 salt container sherds in association with middle Bronze Age pottery is most likely to indicate that this pottery was redeposited in an Iron Age phase rather than actually being in contemporary use with the salt container material. However, evidence for middle Bronze Age coastal salt production has been found in Britain, at Brean Down in Somerset (Foster 1990, 165-73) and at Welland Bank Quarry in Lincolnshire (T. Lane, pers. comm.), and, therefore, the future prospect of discovering Bronze Age salt production in the Cheshire Plain cannot be fully dismissed at the present time.

Elsewhere, the majority of Cheshire salt container sherds have been found in otherwise aceramic contexts of the pre-Roman Iron Age, as at Bryn Eryr on Anglesey (Longley 1998, 248), Collfryn in Powys (Britnell 1989, 124-5) and Beeston Castle (Royle and Woodward 1993,

74) and also in pottery-bearing contexts within the region, most notably at the Breidden (Musson 1991, 130), and outside the immediate region (Morris 1985, table 5, fig. 10). Therefore, the presence of a relatively large quantity of Cheshire salt container material at the Mill Hill Road site strongly suggests that there is an aceramic phase of Iron Age occupation but that this phase of activity had first of all disturbed middle Bronze Age occupation deposits (Phase P3) incorporating pottery of that date into its artefact evidence and then subsequently had been disturbed by Roman occupation.

At Irby, 467 sherds were found in association with late Roman pottery in Periods IV-V and are considered to have been redeposited in these phases or horizons, or in unphased contexts. The few small and abraded sherds of early Roman samian in these deposits are interpreted as redeposited pottery (see Chapter 2 above). There are as yet no securely dated and stratified contexts elsewhere in the region which have produced Cheshire salt container material from contexts later than the 2nd century AD in date (Britnell 1989), and which are also without late Iron Age deposits containing this distinctive material that could allow for redeposition activity taking place.

The presence of this material on middle-late Iron Age sites as far east as Nottinghamshire (Trent Valley) (Knight 1992) and Leicestershire (Elsdon 1991; 1992; 1994) and as far south as Croft Ambrey (Stanford 1974, 210-4, fig.100, 6), Midsummer Hill (Morris 1981; Stanford 1981, 149, fig. 68) and Conderton Camp (Dane's Camp) in Hereford and Worcester (Morris 1985, fig. 10, tables 3 and 5) indicates that Cheshire salt was in some demand during the later part of the first millennium BC well beyond its original zone of distribution (Morris 1985, figs. 9-10) despite the presence of at least one other inland brine source in the area, Droitwich (Hereford and Worcester) (Morris 1985, 338-52, figs. 3-6, table 1; Rees 1986; Woodiwiss 1992).

Conclusion

This sizeable collection of Cheshire salt container material provides an extremely useful addition to the growing number of Iron Age sites where the trade of Cheshire salt can be demonstrated. The greater part of the Irby collection was redeposited in later Roman contexts, as was much of the prehistoric pottery, but the presence of an aceramic Iron Age phase at the site was likely to have been real and is fully supported by the presence of radiocarbon dates within cal BC 410-200 from post-hole 8228 which also contained the La Tène II/III brooch. The limited dating evidence may not encompass the full range of Iron Age occupation for the site at Mill Hill Road, but suggests that the material was in use during the middle Iron Age at Irby.

This collection is important as the first group of later prehistoric Cheshire salt container material to have been published in detail from the Wirral peninsula. Nearby in the Manchester area, over 40 sherds of this material were recovered at Great Woolden Hall Farm (Nevell 1989; 1999a) and these were indicated as the most northerly examples of the material, a statement which still holds true some ten years later. At that site, two sherds, probably from the same vessel, were recovered from the trench of a circular structure (Nevell 1989, fig. 5, 3A/3B). The salt container sherds were not directly associated with domestic pottery but were stratified earlier than a sherd of probably later prehistoric, or native type, and then disturbed by Romano-British ploughing (Nevell 1989, 42-43). This building at Great Woolden Hall, Circular Structure 1, may well represent the same 'aceramic' phase argued for at Mill Hill Road, Irby.

List of illustrated Cheshire Salt Containers (Fig. 4.8)

101. Rim sherd. SF390, context 1012.
102. Rim sherd. SF6669, context 6121.

A note on the petrology of some prehistoric ceramic material

D. F. Williams

Petrology and Fabric

1. ITS 3. SF5321, Context 3055, Trench XIX.
Droitwich briquetage?

Three, very small, irregular fragments of fired clay in a soft, rough, friable, slightly sandy fabric, light reddish-brown throughout (between 5YR 6/4 - 5/4). Thin sectioning shows frequent subrounded to subangular quartz grains, average size below 0.50 mm, shreds of mica, a few clay pellets and a little iron oxide.

Due to the small size of ceramic sample and the commonly encountered range of non-plastic inclusions present, it is difficult to try to allocate a likely source on this evidence alone. There may be similarities between this material and the description of the sandy, marly, Droitwich briquetage Fabric (1) (Morris 1985, 342-3). The fact that no 'marl' or limestone appears in the Irby section does not necessarily rule out this material from belonging to a Droitwich salt-container, since limestone can be rare or absent in some of the latter fabrics, which derive from the local Keuper Marls (Morris 1985, 344-5). However, a sandy fabric containing pieces of 'unwedged' clay has also been found amongst the plentiful fragments of fired clay and daub recovered from Irby, thought to derive from the local clays, which include Keuper Marls as well as boulder clays (see below, *Structural Daub and Fired Clay*). Without further work on the fabrics of the local Irby pottery, it is probably unwise to speculate about the possible origins of these small fragments of fired clay.

Petrologically, the following four sherds can all be accommodated within the general fabric groupings described by Morris for Stony VCP, thought to originate from the Middlewich/Nantwich area of Cheshire (1985, 357-66; Royle and Woodward 1993).

2. ITS 4. SF7563, Context 9503, Trench XLI.
Stony VCP

Fairly soft, rough, sandy fabric containing small angular fragments of igneous and sedimentary rock, reddish-yellow outer surfaces (5YR 7/8) and light grey core (7.5YR N7/). Thin sectioning shows moderately frequent ill-sorted grains of quartz ranging up to 0.70 mm in size, with the majority silt-sized and just above, shreds of mica, a few discrete grains of potash and plagioclase felspar and several fragments of igneous and sedimentary rock. The rock fragments are composed for the most part of porphyritic rhyolite, with a little biotite-granite and a fine-grained micaceous sandstone.

3. ITS 5. SF8151, Context 5321, Trench XXIX.

A somewhat similar fabric to No. ITS4, if slightly coarser in texture.

4. ITS 6. SF7341, Context 6168, Trench XXXVI.

Soft, rough fabric containing large angular fragments of biotite-granite and also a fine-grained igneous rock, light pinkish-white (5YR 8/4) to light reddish-brown (5YR 6/3) throughout. The fabric is particularly distinctive in the hand-specimen as there are large prominent flakes of biotite mica, both in the pieces of granite and as discrete grains. In thin section, large fragments of biotite-granite can be seen together with some porphyritic rhyolite. Also present are discrete grains of quartz, biotite mica, plagioclase and potash felspar and some iron oxide. Unlike Samples Nos ITS4, ITS5 and ITS7, which have a very sandy clay matrix, in this sherd the clay matrix is fairly clean and fine-textured.

5. ITS 7. SF6955, Context 6458, Trench XXXVII.

A similar looking fabric to nos ITS4 and ITS5 but with more visible inclusions of rock. In thin section these seem mostly to be of a granitic composition, with a single piece of porphyritic rhyolite and a little micaceous sandstone.

Roman Pottery

Laura C. Griffin

Introduction

The excavation at Mill Hill Road, Irby produced 2592 sherds of Roman pottery with a combined weight of 14.42 kg. The pottery consisted primarily of body fragments with highly abraded surfaces and a soft matrix. Eleven main ware types were recovered: amphora, Black-burnished ware I (BB1), calcite-gritted ware, colour-coated ware, grey ware, oxidised ware, oxidised mortaria, samian, shell-tempered ware, white-firing mortaria and white ware. A further type, a handmade dark-grey to black ware, originally thought to be BB1 was considered to be possibly late Iron Age or early Romano-British in type.

Both weight and number of sherds have been quantified in order to give a balanced representation of the assemblage which contains a high number of small and abraded sherds. It has not been possible to calculate the Estimated Vessel Equivalent (EVE) or give a realistic minimum vessel count but where feasible, sherds have been cross-joined.

Ware type	Total no of sherds	% total sherds	Total weight (g)	% total wt
Amphorae	23	0.9	586.1	4.1
Black-burnished 1	871	33.6	4551.6	31.6
Colour-coated ware	83	3.2	459.7	3.2
Calcite-gritted ware	31	1.2	96.4	0.7
Grey ware	230	8.9	1160.2	8.1
Oxidised mortaria	16	0.6	274.5	1.9
Oxidised ware	1140	44.0	4929.3	34.2
Samian ware	57	2.2	251.5	1.7
Shell-tempered ware	20	0.8	107.1	0.7
White mortaria	73	2.8	1550.2	10.78
White ware	30	1.1	121.1	0.8
White ware?	17	0.7	295.0	2.1

Table 4.12: Quantification of the Roman pottery

The level of abrasion within the assemblage has prevented comment on surface treatment or the presence of slips to any degree and more sherds than those mentioned may have originally had a different appearance from that which is now seen.

Pottery has been discussed by ware type rather than phase for the reasons outlined in the structural report.

Oxidised Wares

This assemblage consists primarily of local oxidised ware vessels commonly known as Cheshire or Lancashire Plain wares (Webster 1982). These broad terms cover a wide area of many local kilns, the majority unlocated but recognised by different fabric types. These fabrics reflect the local geology of Permo-Triassic sandstone deposits overlaid by glacial drift, which results in inclusions being essentially the same or very similar; in some cases even thin-sectioning has been unsuccessful in separating those from different centres.

Fabric number	Total no of sherds	% total of sherds	Total wt of sherds (g)	% weight of sherds (g)
-	263	20.7	394.1	8.00
54	29	2.54	75.1	1.52
55	2	0.18	4.1	0.08
56	31	2.72	121.2	2.46
57	5	0.44	24.9	0.51
58	19	1.67	102.2	2.07
59	75	6.58	432.3	8.59
60	7	0.61	25.0	0.51
62	34	2.98	222.9	4.52
64	1	0.09	4.1	0.08
66	120	10.53	622.9	12.64
67	17	1.49	73.2	1.48
68	14	1.23	28.9	0.59
69	22	1.93	79.5	1.61
70	55	4.82	296.1	6.01
71	2	0.18	4	0.08
72	1	0.09	2	0.04
73	6	0.53	22.7	0.46
74	47	4.12	223.2	4.53
75	1	0.09	2.1	0.04
76	1	0.09	1.5	0.03
84	1	0.09	1.3	0.03
93	1	0.09	6.1	0.12
105	9	0.79	63.1	1.28
108	6	0.53	25.7	0.52
109	3	0.26	7.5	0.15
110	25	2.19	56.2	1.14
111	70	6.14	482.4	9.79
112	58	5.09	205.6	4.17
113	32	2.81	182.1	3.69
114	10	0.89	76.1	1.54
115	21	1.84	48.3	0.98
116	12	1.05	41.6	0.84
117	23	2.02	147.9	3.00
118	21	1.84	120.7	2.45
119	6	0.53	60.9	1.24
120	5	0.44	13.2	0.27
121	20	1.75	52.0	1.05
122	15	1.32	205.3	4.16
123	3	0.26	24.1	0.49
124	4	0.35	12.2	0.25
125	31	2.72	266.1	5.40
126	2	0.18	2.1	0.04
127	2	0.18	19.2	0.39
128	8	0.70	47.6	0.97

Table 4.13: Romano-British pottery by fabric

The oxidised ware sherds from Mill Hill Road (Fig. 4.15) have been divided into fabric groups using a binocular microscope (x20) and comparison with a reference collection formed from assemblages of local sites within Merseyside. Fabrics have been designated a number from a sequence covering pottery of all periods. Fragments below 0.5 g in weight have not been grouped, as they are too small to give a realistic proportion or range of inclusions. These have been denoted by the symbol '-'.

It is probable that some of these fabrics were produced on the same kiln sites but with different tempers added to the clay. However, due to a lack of kiln sites yet discovered in the Cheshire/Merseyside region these relationships cannot yet be identified and therefore the large number of fabric groups is not supposed to represent individual kiln sites. This is also the same for reduced wares below.

Sherds that can be attributed to a specific kiln site are those of fabric group 56 which have been identified as Wilderspool products based on distinctive beaker sherds from Southworth Hall, Cheshire and mortarium sherds known to be kiln material from the production centre. Other possible fabrics from these kilns include fabric groups 118 and 123. These result from cross-referencing with other fabric reference series from sites in the north west region (J. Evans and S. Rátkai pers. comms).

A small number of sherds were identified as coming from the production site at Ochre Brook, Tarbock (Philpott 2000a). It is known that this site had links with the 20th Legion at Chester through the supply of tile and it is possible that a small number of vessels were traded as an off-shoot of this. The tiles would have been transported via the Mersey and Dee estuaries and it is possible that some pottery vessels may have found their way to Irby through the local markets.

Only 39 different vessels could be identified within the oxidised pottery group. This is almost certainly related to post-depositional survival due to oxidised wares accounting for 44% of the total assemblage. Of those forms that could be identified, the most common was the jar with twenty individual vessels recognised. Due to the low survival rate of diagnostic sherds, it was not possible to look at the relationship between form and fabric.

Grey Wares

Grey wares are thought to have been produced on the same kiln sites as oxidised wares using the same clay sources. The addition of different tempers and firing in a reducing atmosphere resulted in the distinct colour. The same problems exist in the sourcing of these sherds to individual production sites and even less research has been undertaken on these fabrics.

A total of 228 grey ware sherds with a combined weight of 1160.2 g were recognised. Of these, one beaker, one bowl/dish and five jars can be positively identified, two with part of an everted rim surviving (Fig. 4.9).

As with the oxidised wares, a fabric type series has been formed to distinguish between different grey wares. A total of 26 fabric groups have been identified from this site and designated a number from the overall sequence.

Fabric number	Total no of sherds	% total of sherds	Total wt of sherds (g)	% weight of sherds (g)
-	39	17.10	36.30	3.26
72	1	0.44	4.70	0.42
77	9	3.95	16.00	1.44
78	9	3.95	25.70	2.31
79	2	0.88	18.10	1.63
80	6	2.63	31.90	2.87
81	2	0.88	10.40	0.93
83	10	4.39	45.00	4.04
84	17	7.46	89.50	8.05
85	1	0.44	7.90	0.71
89	3	1.32	8.30	0.75
90	6	2.63	20.90	1.88
91	14	6.14	65.90	5.92
92	4	1.75	14.40	1.29
93	6	2.63	73.10	6.57
94	6	2.63	87.40	7.86
95	21	9.21	102.90	9.25
96	8	3.51	70.40	6.33
97	6	2.63	22.80	2.05
98	5	2.19	36.80	3.31
99	3	1.32	15.50	1.39
100	6	2.63	20.55	1.85
101	1	0.44	0.90	0.08
102	24	10.53	138.00	12.41
104	5	2.19	4.40	0.40
105	11	4.82	129.60	11.65
106	3	1.32	15.00	1.35

Table 4.14: Romano-British pottery by fabric

Black-Burnished Ware (BB1)

Black-Burnished Ware category I from production centres in Dorset was commonly transported along the Western seaboard, making it a widely available coarse ware in the north west. The material was produced in a sandy fabric which, as a result of recent work in Dorchester, has been seen to consist of a number of closely related fabrics rather than a single homogeneous type (Seager Smith and Davies 1993, 249). The fabrics have been widely discussed and are not considered in detail here.

A total of 871 sherds weighing 4551.6g were recovered from the site. The majority are undiagnostic and dated from the earliest recorded appearance of the ware in north-western England around AD 120 (Fig. 4.10). The ware continued to be supplied to Irby probably until the mid 4th century (J. Evans pers. comm.). Although the great majority of the material is not closely diagnostic, there is a strong emphasis amongst datable sherds in the period AD 200-350, and relatively few pre-dating

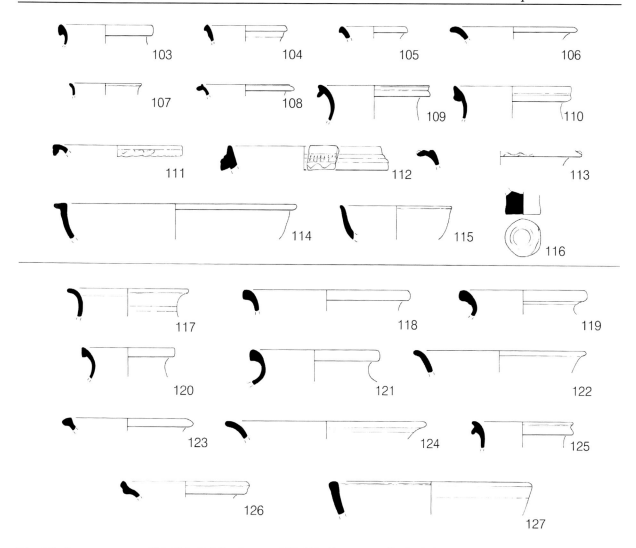

Fig. 4.9: Roman pottery. 103-116. Oxidised ware; 117-127. Grey ware. Scale 1:4

AD 200. Identifiable forms have been assigned a type number and date range from the Wessex Archaeology type series and are prefixed with the initials 'WA' (Seager Smith and Davies 1993). A total of 63 jars, 41 bowls/dishes and two miniature jars/beakers were identified.

The high proportion of Black-Burnished ware jars which display traces of sooting supports the view that these vessels were primarily used as cooking pots. The majority of jars fall into a date range of 3rd-mid 4th century (WA types 2 and 3), coinciding with the decline of the local industries in the Cheshire Plains area. However, there are twelve diagnostic sherds of the 2nd century indicating that these jars were being employed alongside those of local fabrics.

There are a large number of bowls/dishes within this fabric assemblage, far outnumbering those of local manufacture of which there are only fourteen. Sooting on a small number would suggest that some were used over the fire, presumably for food preparation but not in the same quantity as the jars. It would seem, therefore that the majority were used at a different stage of food preparation, possibly in the serving of food as everyday tableware.

White Ware

Of the 47 sherds of white ware recovered, one is diagnostic and can be identified as the handle from a 1st-2nd-century flagon. The handle sherd is of a distinctive micaceous fabric, unlikely to be of local manufacture (J. Evans pers comm.). A near-complete flanged bowl in white ware copies Dr. 38 but the source is uncertain (SF9999). The only other identifiable sherd is that of a roughly formed base, possibly from a bowl or dish. The remaining sherds are very small and abraded with no surface remaining. This coupled with a distinct lack of work previously done on white wares in the north west has resulted in a lack of comparative information for this assemblage.

The most likely origin for the remaining sherds is the Nene Valley region and examination by binocular microscope confirms this to some extent, although size and condition of the fragments prevents absolute certainty.

At least 13 sherds have large surface voids which may have resulted from trituration grits and are therefore possibly mortaria. It is likely that further sherds are also from this class of vessel.

Amphora

All 23 sherds of amphora are undiagnostic body sherds but the fabric is consistent with Dressel 20 form and therefore dating between the early 1st and mid 3rd centuries. Only five of these sherds cross-join, although it is likely that the remaining sherds account for only a small number of vessels as usual for rural sites of this period in the north west.

Colour-Coated Ware

The 82 sherds of colour-coated ware recovered can be attributed to three kiln production sites, Nene Valley, Oxfordshire and Wilderspool (Fig. 4.11).

Wilderspool
Only seven sherds could be attributed to the local production site of Wilderspool; of these four were identified as being from the same vessel, a 2nd-century beaker with a dark brownish grey slip on both surfaces. The remaining three sherds are very small and highly abraded with traces of a brownish red slip on the exterior. One has faint impressed decoration and another a stepped profile.

Oxfordshire
Twenty-eight sherds of Oxfordshire colour-coated ware were identified, accounting for a maximum of seven vessels. Of these, two are flange-rimmed bowls, two are foot-rings from imitation samian vessels and one is a copy of a Dr. 38. Of the remaining sherds, one displays impressed triangular wedges and rouletted vertical lines. The slips are typical of Oxfordshire types with reddish brown displayed on open vessels and dark brown on closed. All diagnostic sherds fall into a date range of between AD 240-400+.

Nene Valley
Sherds from Nene Valley accounted for the largest proportion of colour-coated ware on the site. Of the 47 sherds, the only diagnostic are nine fragments of the 'Hunt Cup' type with typical barbotine scrolls and dots, animal decoration, impressed lines and a pinkish orange/brown slip on both surfaces. These sherds may represent two different beakers, although there are no cross-joins present. They date to between the late 2nd-mid 3rd centuries.

Mortaria

Oxidised mortaria
Sixteen sherds of oxidised mortaria were recovered, of which only six are diagnostic. One rim and its adjoining

sherds can be identified as being Oxfordshire in origin and of Young's type C97, imitating samian form 4 (Young 1977). It has traces of an exterior red slip and can be dated to AD 240-400.

The remaining rim sherds are distinctive in appearance with a hooked rim of the same tradition as those of an early 2nd-century date from Wilderspool (Fig. 4.11). However, only one definite Wilderspool product was identified on the basis of fabric. The remaining sherds have rims which are significantly more hooked and fabric which is less sandy than vessels typical of the above production site and therefore are unlikely to be of that origin (J. Evans pers. comm.). It is probable that like much of the oxidised ware in this assemblage, these vessels are from an unknown production site on the Cheshire Plain.

White-Firing Mortaria

The 73 mortarium sherds of this group can be attributed to two production sites, Oxfordshire and Hartshill-Mancetter (Fig. 4.11).

Oxfordshire
Fifteen sherds of Oxfordshire mortaria were recovered of which four rims of Young's M22 were identified and can be dated between AD 240-400.

Hartshill-Mancetter
Of the 58 sherds identified in this fabric, only eight are diagnostic rims. These have been dated using known sequences and adjusted for the north west by Jeremy Evans. The majority are of hammerhead form and date from the early 3rd to mid 4th century, although the earliest has a hooked rim and dates from AD 130.

Shell-Tempered Ware

The shell-tempered ware from Irby forms an unusual assemblage made up entirely of rim sherds (Fig. 4.11). All are of South Midlands fabric and date to the late 4th century. As in the case of the calcite-gritted ware, there is no evidence of sooting, although the surface of one sherd appears to have been heated. The lack of sooting, however, could be explained by the assemblage consisting exclusively of rim sherds which by their nature display less sooting than body sherds.

Calcite-Gritted Ware

Of the 31 sherds of calcite-gritted ware recovered, none is diagnostic although there is one jar neck present. The fabric is consistent with that of North Yorkshire and therefore dates to the late 4th century (J. Evans pers. comm.). The majority of the sherds are very small and highly abraded with no cross-joins evident. Surprisingly, there is no evidence of sooting, although traces may have been lost during post-excavation processes.

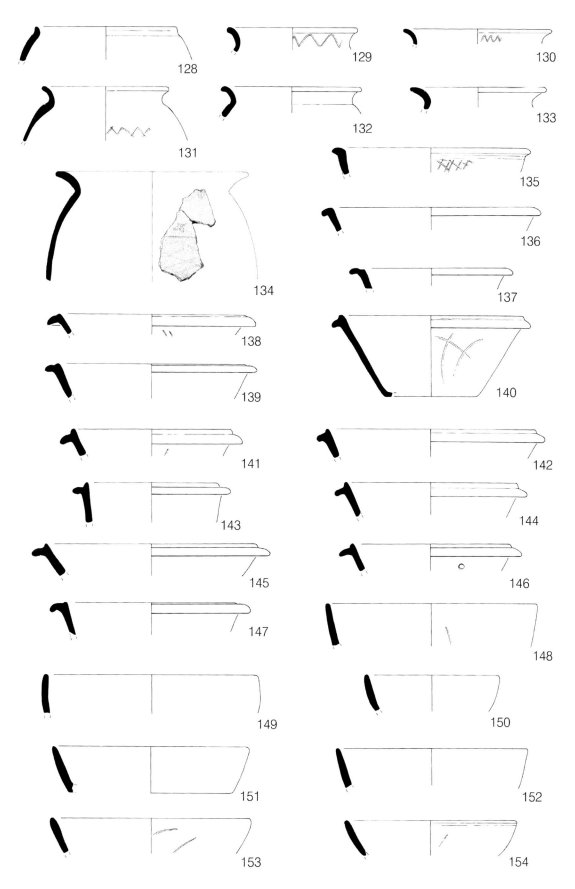

Fig. 4.10: Roman pottery. 128-154. Black-burnished ware. Scale 1:4

Handmade Sherds

Ten undiagnostic handmade sherds in a dark-grey to black fabric were originally identified as BB1 but it has been suggested by Jeremy Evans that they are potentially late Iron Age or early Romano-British in date (not illustrated). Most are in a sandy fabric though four sherds (all listed as SF4834) are calcareous. The contexts provide no useful information on the dating as, with one exception, the sherds all come from soil layers containing later Romano-British pottery as well as residual prehistoric material. The only deposit which could be late prehistoric in date was a spit of a deep undifferentiated layer (3913), which at that level contained VCP, but the presence of copious iron-smithing waste suggests this too was of Roman date.

SF10799; SF747; SF4834 (4 sherds); SF3078; SF3192; SF5531; SF5677.

Catalogue of Illustrated Roman Pottery

Oxidised Ware
103. Constricted-neck jar. Cf. Wilderspool: Webster 1973, no. 10. Late 1st to late 2nd century. SF3259, context 3062.
104. Everted rim jar. Cf. Gillam 107; Manchester: Walker *et al.* 1986, 113, no. 2963. 2nd century. SF7427, context 9503.
105. Everted rim jar/beaker. Cf. Manchester: Walker *et al.* 1986, 113, no. 2963. 2nd century. SF8653, context 7043.
106. Everted rim jar. Cf. Wilderspool: Webster 1992, no. 225. 2nd century. SF285, context 1007.
107. Beaker. Cf. Wilderspool: Webster 1973, no. 42. Late 1st-late 2nd century. SF699, context 1821.
108. Pulley-rim jar. Cf. Wilderspool: Webster 1992, no. 4; Whitchurch: Webster 1968, no. 295. Late 2nd-3rd century. SF3714, context 1039. This form is found in Severn Valley Ware through most of the Roman period, occurring at Wilderspool in the 2nd century and is produced in local wares in the North-West in the 3rd and 4th centuries (Webster 1976; 1992; 1988, 141).
109. Pulley-rim jar. Webster 1976, nos 10 and 11; Webster 1992, no. 679. 3rd-4th century. SF8413, context 14.22.
110. Pulley-rim jar. Webster 1976, no. 9. 3rd-4th century. SF8431, context 14.27.
111. Pulley-rim jar with frilled edge. Cf. Wilderspool: Webster 1973, nos 11-13. 3rd-4th century. SF8439, context 14.21.
112. Drop-flanged, frilled rim, with two bands of series of incised vertical lines on stepped profile; differentially fired sherd with reduced core and partially reduced/cooked surfaces. Possible variant of Young 1977, M22. AD 240-400? SF8048, unstratified.
113. Tazza, rim with frilled decoration. Gillam 347; Cf. Wilderspool: Webster 1992, no 357. 2nd century. SF3769, context 1039
114. Reeded flange-rimmed bowl, two incised lines around top of rim. Cf. Wilderspool: Webster 1992, nos 359, 433, 479. Late 1st-early 2nd century. SF3251, context 3062.
115. Small bowl/dish. Cf. Wilderspool: Webster 1992, no. 311. Mid 2nd century. SF7326, context 6244.
116. Pedestal base of ?beaker. SF781, context 610.

Grey Ware
117. Everted rim jar. Cf. Wilderspool: Webster 1992, no. 128; Manchester: Webster 1974, no.181. Late 1st to 2nd century. SF6228, context 3160.
118. Everted rim jar. Cf. Wilderspool: Webster 1992, nos 214, 557; Northwich: Webster 1971, no. 23; Whitchurch: Webster 1968, no. 246. 2nd century. SF2472, context 3617.
119. Everted rim jar. Sooting around top of rim interior and exterior of neck. Cf. Wilderspool: Webster 1992, no. 114. Mid 2nd century. SF7995, context 9603.
120. Constricted-neck jar, reduced with areas of oxidation on the exterior. Cf. Wilderspool: Webster 1992, no. 493; cf. no. 102 above in oxidised ware. Late 1st-2nd century. SF2130, context 3616.
121. Jar rim. Cf. Wilderspool: Webster 1992, no.557, Northwich: Webster 1971, no. 23; Whitchurch: Webster 1968, no. 246. Mid 2nd-early 3rd century. SF5062, context 3617.
122. Everted rim jar. Cf. WA type 2, no. 209. 3rd century. SF1501, context 3054.
123. Jar, in powdery micaceous fabric. Cf. Manchester: Webster 1974, no. 247. SF4818, context 5024.
124. Everted rim jar. Copy of BB1 jar in grey ware. Cf. WA type 3, no. 350. Date 3rd-4th century. SF4846, context 5041.
125. Pulley-rim jar. Webster 1976, no.11; Wilderspool: Webster 1992, no. 602. See also no. 108 above in oxidised ware. 3rd-4th century. SF8435, context 14.110.
126. Pulley-rim jar or flagon rim only? Cf. Lancaster: Webster 1988, no.174. 4th century? SF9561, context 3703.
127. Straight-sided bowl, thick-walled, two incised lines close to the rim, faint wavy line below. SF7929, context 9073.

Black-Burnished Ware (BB1)
128. Miniature jar/beaker. Gillam 30-32. Date 120-200, SF8762, context 7043.
129. Everted rim jar, cf. WA type 1, no. 105. Date 120-160/180. SF7727, context 9505.
130. Everted rim jar, cf. WA type 1 no. 68. Date 150-230. SF7639, context 9505.
131. Everted rim jar, acute lattice decoration, Gillam 6-7, cf. WA type 2, no. 264. Date 160-?200. SF7778, context 9505.
132. Everted rim jar, cf. WA type 2, no. 209. Date 200-250. SF5908, context 3096.
133. Everted rim jar, sooted interior of rim and cooked interior, cf. Gillam 138, WA type 2 no. 196. Date 250-350. SF1451, context 3303.
134. Everted rim jar, obtuse lattice in unburnished zone delimited by single horizontal line. Abraded surfaces with crazing and obvious exposure to heat. 'X' graffito on shoulder. WA type 2. Date 240-270. SF8273, I87 salvage excavation, unstratified (Fig. 4.12).
135. Flange rim bowl/dish, narrow incised lattice decoration. Date 120-150/170. SF7890, context 9036.
136. Flange rim dish, faint incised intersecting arcs. Date 120-200. SF5484, context 5124.
137. Flange rim bowl/dish. Gillam 227. Date 210-300. SF1545, context 3903.
138. Flange-rimmed bowl. Date 200-270. SF8695, context 7043.
139. Flange rim bowl with flange higher than the mouth with a groove around junction; variant of drop flange? Date 200-350. SF4505, context 3062.
140. Drop-flange-rimmed bowl, near-complete vessel, intersecting arc decoration; exterior sooted. Date 270-350. SF8078, context 9697.

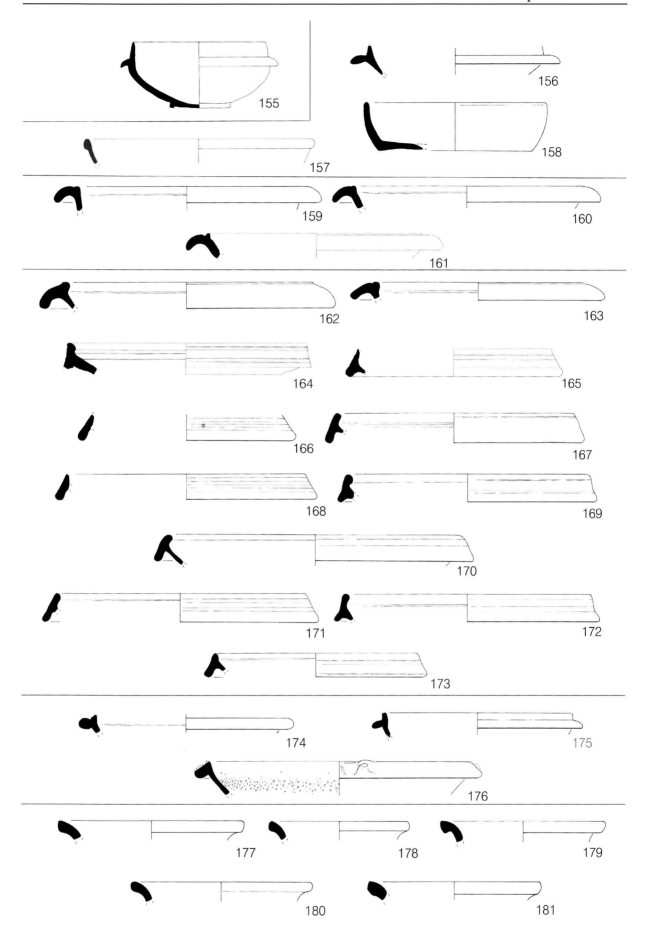

Fig. 4.11: Roman pottery. 155. White ware; 156-158: Colour-coated ware; 159-161. Oxidised mortaria; 162-173. Hartshill-Mancetter mortaria; 174-176. Oxfordshire mortaria; 177-181. South Midlands Shell-Tempered Ware. Scale 1:4

141. Drop-flange-rimmed bowl, abraded. Date 270-350. SF8814, context 7043.
142. Drop-flange-rimmed bowl. Date 270-350. SF1032, context 672.
143. Drop-flange-rimmed bowl. Gillam 228. Date 270-350. SF1658, context 3061.
144. Drop-flanged-rimmed bowl, interior possibly cooked. Date 270-350. SF5823, context 3096.
145. Drop-flange-rimmed bowl, heavily burnt with little surface remaining. Date 270-350. SF6677, context 6213.
146. Drop-flange-rimmed bowl, rim sherd with iron rivet still present in wall. Date 270-350. SF6060, context 3150.
147. Drop-flange-rimmed bowl. Gillam 227. Date 210-300. SF1119, context 1324.
148. Plain-rimmed dish, crazed exterior surface. Date 200-350. SF8534, context 7006.
149. Plain-rimmed dish. Cf. Gillam 327, 329, WA 20. Date 200-350. SF908, context 1230.
150. Plain-rimmed dish, with cooked interior. Date 200-350. SF2068, context 3307.
151. Plain-rimmed dish. Date 200-350. SF8628, context 7031.
152. Plain-rimmed dish. Date 200-350. SF8639, context 7031.
153. Plain-rimmed dish, intersecting arcs. Date 200-350. SF6492, context 3237.
154. Groove-rimmed dish. Date 200-350. SF8059, context 9097.

White Ware

155. Flanged bowl, creamy white fabric with numerous quartz sand inclusions and clay pellets, copy of Dr. 38. Possibly Wilderspool but a close parallel is recorded at Ribchester where it is suggested that various although unknown sources may be involved in the production of this fabric (Dickinson *et al.* 2000, 165, fig. 25 no 51). SF9999, unstratified; found in WW2 in 115 Mill Hill Road garden.

Colour-Coated Ware

156. Oxfordshire colour-coated ware bowl, Dr. 38 copy. Cf. Young 1977, no. C51. Mid 3rd to late 4th century. SF5825, context 3096.
157. Oxfordshire colour-coated ware bowl with rolled rim, red slip coating. Cf. Young 1977, C46. Date 340-400+. SF1108, context 640.
158. Nene Valley colour-coated ware bowl. Possible rivet hole. Howe *et al.* 1980, no. 87. 4th century. SF8640, context 7041.

Oxidised Mortaria

159. Flange rim mortarium. One incised line around rim and another around top of wall. Similar form to Wilderspool but different fabric. Early 2nd century. SF3322, context 3612.
160. Flange rim mortarium. Early 2nd century. SF5732, context 5311.
161. Flange rim mortarium. Form similar to Wilderspool type, Webster 1992, no 436, but fabric different. Early 2nd century. SF753, context 1031.

Hartshill-Mancetter Mortaria

162. Beaded, flange rimmed mortarium. Date 130/140-170. SF6690, context 6215.
163. Beaded, flange rimmed mortarium, 1 faint, incised line around bottom of flange. Lead rivet through flange. Date 160/170-200. SF7465, context 9502.
164. Reeded hammerhead rim mortarium, 5 incised lines on rim, small black iron ore triturarion grits. Date 220-350. SF575, context 1611.
165. Hammerhead reeded rim mortarium, 4 incised lines on rim. Date 220-350. SF620, context 1221.
166. Reeded hammerhead rim, 5 incised narrow lines on reeded rim. SF7505, context 6905.
167. Hammerhead rim mortarium. Date 220-350. SF7942, unstratified.
168. Hammerhead rim mortarium, 5 incised lines on the reeded rim. SF8040, context 5301.
169. Hammerhead rim, slightly concave. Segontium 30, Gillam 280. Date 210/230-340. SF8450, context 7005.
170. Reeded hammerhead, 2 faint incised lines of reeded rim. Segontium 23, Roman Lancaster 252. Date 210-340. SF8542, context 7013.
171. Reeded hammerhead, 3 incised lines on reeded rim Gillam 280, Webster 1992, no. 539. Date 210-350. SF9554, context 3001.
172. Hammerhead mortarium rim, 3 incised lines on rim, concave. Mid 3rd-mid 4th century. Segontium 29, 35, Webster 1992, no. 428. SF7646, context 9505.
173. Reeded, hammerhead rim mortarium, 4 faint incised lines on rim. Date 260-350. SF9610, unstratified.

Oxfordshire Mortaria

174. Oxfordshire flanged mortarium rim with multicoloured Sub-angular quartz trituration grits. Young 1977, M22. Date 240-400+. SF7771, context 9015.
175. Oxfordshire flanged mortarium rim with a few surviving multicoloured quartz trituration grits. Young 1977, M22. Date 240-400+. SF8041, context 5301.
176. Oxfordshire flanged mortarium rim with multicoloured sub-rounded-sub-angular trituration grits. Young 1977, M22. Date 240-400+. SF8582, context 7024.

South Midlands Shell-Tempered Ware

177. Jar with square-cut rim. Voids where shell inclusions have dissolved out. Sanders 1973, Form 2. Late 4th century. SF582, context 610.
178. Jar with undercut rim. Voids where shell has dissolved out. Sanders 1973, Form 3. SF1073, context 701.
179. Jar with undercut rim. Sanders 1973, Form 3. Late 4th century. SF6226, context 3160.
180. Jar with square-cut rim. Cooked surfaces. Sanders 1973, Form 2. Late 4th century. SF7903, context 9036.
181. Everted rim jar with cooked exterior. Late 4th century. SF6245, context 3165.

Functional analysis of the assemblage

The functional groups of this assemblage have been created from diagnostic sherds present and are classified as follows: amphora, beakers, bowls/dishes, flagons, jars, mortaria and *tazze*. Bowls and dishes have been combined to form a single category, as most sherds are too small to determine the ratio of diameter to height. The figures below do not represent a minimum vessel count but show the relative proportions of diagnostic types recognised within the excavated assemblage.

The dominant vessel type, accounting for nearly 40% of the assemblage is the jar. This is consistent with a rural assemblage where jars were far more widely used than the other major category of bowls/dishes (Evans 2001, 28).

Vessel form	Total no. of vessel forms	% of vessel forms
Amphora	10	3.64
Beaker	5	1.82
Bowl/dish	82	29.82
Jar	104	37.82
Flagon	1	0.36
Miniature jar/beaker	4	1.45
Mortarium	68	24.73
Tazza	1	0.36

Table 4.15: Identifiable Roman pottery forms

Other forms identified include mortaria, amphora and *tazze*, indicating a degree of Romanisation and specialised function, e.g. mortaria were particularly efficient in the preparation of various foodstuffs and *tazze* were used to burn incense. This level of Romanisation is also consistent with the small number of coins recovered, a feature not seen on similar sites in the area, such as Court Farm, Halewood.

The large number of jars and mortaria indicate a close relationship between the pottery assemblage and the preparation and cooking of food. In contrast, a low number of tablewares such as beakers and flagons are in evidence. One possible explanation for this may be that the native community at Irby only adopted Roman forms or vessels that had particular benefits or specific functions, so the use of ceramic jars for cooking and storage had great advantages over products produced of wood or leather, particularly for liquids. Ceramic vessels could be placed directly into a fire and left unattended without risk of being consumed by the flames. The nature of fired clay also means that vessels could conduct and retain heat more efficiently for longer than those of organic materials. This allowed slow cooking of a wide range of foodstuffs improving flavour and digestibility of many vegetables and cereals (McCarthy and Brooks 1988, 123).

In the case of tablewares, the more traditional materials alongside black-burnished ware dishes, bowls and beakers may have served this function well, with only a small number of finewares either for display or prestige.

Sooting

A number of sherds display evidence of sooting (Table 4.16). Evidence of sooting itself can contribute to determining the function of a vessel and as expected, the highest proportion is on external surfaces indicating use for cooking in the majority of cases. By far the most frequent examples of sooting can be seen on vessels of black-burnished ware I, suggesting this ware type to be the primary fabric for cooking wares. This follows suit with the majority of other Romano-British rural

assemblages where soot appears consistently on jars of a heavily tempered fabric derived from Iron Age traditions (Evans 1993). Experiments have shown this to be due to the high level of thermal shock resistance provided by the inclusions within this fabric when heated to high temperatures needed for cooking and in assemblages with high numbers of black-burnished ware sherds, it is possible to show that the proportion of jars, dishes and bowls with sooted surfaces was so great in comparison to the rest of the sherds, that it is unlikely to have occurred accidentally (Evans 1993). Furthermore, the presence of sooting on cooking vessels is higher on rural assemblages than urban and it has been suggested that this may be due to native methods of cooking over an open fire being employed rather than the use of more Romanised clay ovens (V. Bryant pers. comm.).

The sparse evidence of sooting on vessels of oxidised and reduced ware suggests that they were primarily used as storage or table wares and confirms them to have been less efficient as cooking wares on native rural sites.

Ware type	Function	Sooted interior	Sooted exterior	Sooted interior and exterior
BB1	Unknown	4	38	7
BB1	Bowl/dish	2	8	1
BB1	Jar	6	6	5
GRW	Unknown		13	
GRW	Jar			1
OXW	Unknown	2	3	3
WHW	Unknown		1	

Key: BB1 Black-burnished 1; GRW Grey ware; OXW Oxidised ware; WHW White ware

Table 4.16: The occurrence of sooting by ware type

Sherds which display sooting on interior surfaces are fewer in number and may indicate different uses for vessels, especially when seen on jars whose narrow necks would have largely prevented any internal burning from straightforward cooking methods.

Some pots are thought to have been used to cover the hearth at night, as a safeguard against the building catching fire. The upturned pot would have stood over the hearth to cover the flames in much the same way as later medieval curfews. The fire would continue to burn within the vessel, thus causing soot deposits on the interior. A further possibility may have been the use of hot embers placed in one pot to heat the contents of another standing directly above in the process of steaming.

The burning of pottery following discard can also be identified as a cause of both internal and external sooting and often identified by its occurrence along breaks. In the case of vessels from Irby, this is not seen in any significant number and therefore the majority of sooting can be attributed to functional causes.

Repair of vessels

Nineteen vessels show evidence of repair in the form of a rivet hole drilled into the vessel wall (for coarsewares see Table 4.17; the samian is discussed below); two examples retain the corroded rivet *in situ*. Two types of riveting can be seen at Irby: dovetailed holes in three samian vessels and the more common straightforward round holes in the remainder. The surviving rivets are made from iron or lead, the former being more common.

No.	SF	Con-text	Type	Notes
182	720	1205	BB1 jar, body sherd	Iron rivet in slot
183	6387	6903	BB1 jar abraded, body sherd	Iron rivet in hole
184	1558	3306	BB1 jar rim, sooted; 200-350+	Circular lead rivet hole
185	3619	1061	BB1 flange rim bowl; 120-350+	Rivet hole near rim
186	6060	3150	BB1 flange rim bowl; 270-350+	Iron rivet present in circular rivet hole in wall (see no 146)
187	10755	-	BB1 abraded body sherd, 120-350+	Iron rivet.
188	9355	3087	BB1, burnt body sherd; 240-350+	Broken rivet hole.
189	8786	7094	BB1 body sherd from jar under shoulder, 120-350+	Circular rivet hole.
190	5209	3797	Nene Valley colour-coated vessel, mid 2nd-late 4th century	Burnt with rivet hole
191	8640	7041	Colour-coated ware bowl, late 4th century	Possible a rivet hole (see no 158)
192	1300	2819	Greyware body sherd	Iron rivet
193	7465	9502	Hartshill-Mancetter mortarium sherd, 160/170-200	Lead rivet through flange (see no 163).
194	9373	5101	Oxidised ware, body sherd; date uncertain	1 circular rivet hole drilled through
195	8774	7043	Oxidised ware; 2 joining sherds; date uncertain	2 body sherds, one with rivet hole and iron rivet *in situ*
196	8465	7200	Oxidised ware; date uncertain	Uncertain rivet hole
197	8811	7603	Oxidised ware mortarium with possible rivet hole (or missing inclusion)?	1 abraded body sherd with a single white quartz trituration grit

Table 4.17: Riveted coarseware vessels

On sites where pottery was clearly abundant, repair of vessels was usually characteristic of high-status finewares. However, in the case of Irby, in addition

to two samian vessels, evidence of repair can also be identified on coarsewares including black-burnished and oxidised ware vessels and one Hartshill-Mancetter mortarium.

The use of riveting on coarsewares is also found at Court Farm, Halewood and Mellor and seems to be characteristic of rural assemblages in the region (Leary 2005, 47). Similar patterns have also noted on sites in north Wales where access to markets was more restricted (J. Evans pers. comm.; Britnell 1989, 124). However, in the case of Irby with access to a wider variety of pottery types than any other known sites in the vicinity, the reasons must be more complex. A further possibility during the later occupation of Irby may be associated with the collapse of large industries. This would have made it more difficult to obtain many common coarsewares including black-burnished ware and mortaria, therefore once broken these vessels had to be repaired rather than replaced.

Dating

The dating evidence gained from the pottery assemblage has been limited due to poor survival of diagnostic sherds. However, from those forms that have been identified it is possible to identify a pattern emerging which is repeated throughout the north-west but also bears many similarities to that observed at *Segontium* (Webster 1993, 256).

In the 1st and early 2nd centuries, as expected, the local coarsewares are dominant. This trend can be seen partly as continuation of the traditional Iron Age industries and partly due to demand created by the influx of new population. In the north west, kilns on the Cheshire Plains were flourishing at this time. However, from the 2nd century onwards, black-burnished ware was becoming the dominant cooking ware throughout much of western Britain partly due to demand from the legions stationed on Hadrian's Wall and also due to mass production leading to a cheap but efficient cooking ware. This influx of black-burnished ware is traditionally thought to coincide with the decline of the local industries in the late 2nd-early 3rd centuries. However, not only are imitations of Severn Valley ware pulley-rim vessels dated to between the 3rd and 4th centuries found, but high proportions of Cheshire Plains ware are found in later contexts alongside late BB1 sherds. Some of this pottery will be residual but it seems unlikely that such large quantities could have survived over 100 years of daily domestic use before breakage or discard.

The late 2nd-3rd centuries also see an increase in both samian and Nene Valley colour-coated wares (Webster 1982, 20) which although on a small scale at Irby in comparison to larger urban sites is still in significant amounts for a rural site in the region. The seven sherds of Wilderspool colour-coated ware can also be attributed to this period and may indicate the local production centres attempting to compete with the larger industries of the south.

This period also sees the first mortaria from the Hartshill-Mancetter and Oxfordshire kilns, trading connections which continue through to the end of the 4th century. The large number of these sherds in comparison to the earlier oxidised mortaria suggests that these Romanised forms were not being fully utilised until later into the Roman period and that the native population was still employing traditional methods of food preparation in the 1st and 2nd centuries. Those manufactured at Holt in the 1st and 2nd centuries were primarily for use by soldiers in the 20th Legion (Grimes 1930).

The late 3rd century continues to see an influx of non-local wares including BB1 and Oxfordshire colour-coated ware. This colour-coated ware includes a number of samian imitations, the originals of which would have been harder to obtain at this time. Much of the local oxidised ware production does seem to have ceased by this period and the non-local wares dominate the assemblage.

By the mid-late 4th century, the exportation of BB1 ceased and the absence is reflected in the Irby assemblage accordingly. The resulting void is filled by the shell-tempered wares from the South Midlands and calcite-gritted wares from east Yorkshire which dominate the late 4th-century assemblage of the site. This is seen throughout the region, including the latest levels at Lancaster, with these kiln sites becoming the major source of pottery in the area by AD 380 (Webster 1982, 22).

Social and economic implications

The pottery assemblage from Irby is one of the largest from a Romano-British rural site in the region. The assemblage displays far more diversity of form and fabric than other comparable sites within the immediate Merseyside area and is currently one of largest groups excavated from a site in lowland north-west England.

The range of fabrics and amount of pottery coming from a variety of regions such as Oxfordshire, Hartshill-Mancetter and the presence of fabrics from the late periods such as shell-tempered and calcite-gritted ware suggest that the site at Irby was on a more important supply route with better access to markets than those sites to the north of the Mersey and further inland. One suggestion for this may be the nearby port of Meols.

Many coins, brooches and other items have been found at Meols and the port stands out from the rest of the Wirral as an area of importance during the Roman period (Hume 1863; Watkin 1886, 274-85; Philpott

2007c; 2007d). If the transport routes of pottery from the Midlands are plotted, it can be seen that wares such as Oxfordshire are transported by water to the Bristol Channel and then follow the same route as BB1 along the Western seaboard, presumably stopping at Meols en route to Hadrian's Wall (Tyers 1996, *passim*). In contrast, the pottery from the Hartshill-Mancetter and South Midlands kilns appears to have been transported overland following the main Roman routes northwards. This variation in transport routes accounts for the absence of Oxfordshire products and high proportion of Hartshill-Mancetter vessels on sites to the north of the Mersey and the relative wealth of Irby in comparison. In addition, the high proportion of local wares also suggests a high level of interaction with the surrounding hinterland of the Cheshire and Lancashire plains.

Irby is a long-lived site as testified by a continuous supply of pottery from the Iron Age through to the late 4th century if not beyond. During this time, the settlement also significantly expanded in size indicating a stable economy based on successful agriculture which enabled survival for a period of several hundred years. The range of finds and number of buildings suggest that Irby was actually a small hamlet rather than a single farmstead (J. Evans pers. comm.). Although the range of pottery is clearly predominantly domestic, there are sufficient numbers of fine wares to suggest a certain amount of wealth and status. This is reflected in the presence of coins, indicating a degree of commercial exchange and other 'luxury' items including the presence of amber and unusual types of glass beads.

The Contribution of Pottery to Dating

Mark Adams

Although the pottery assemblage from Irby is one of the largest from a rural site in north-west England, only a very small proportion (136 sherds or 5.2%) is usable for dating purposes. Much of the pottery is heavily broken and abraded, the average sherd weight being *c.* 9.5 g. In addition, much of the pottery that can be dated can only be placed within very broad date ranges. Furthermore, few joining sherds are present, which makes it impossible to identify stratigraphically contemporary deposits using that technique. Those joins which can be identified have little relevance for dating purposes because they lie within contexts which can be linked on purely stratigraphic grounds.

These problems are further compounded by the difficult excavation conditions, which mean that it is very likely that many of the excavated layers contain intrusive material belonging to features which were not identified. For example, the layers sealing Period II contain several late 3rd-late 4th-century sherds. However, as many of these weigh less than 10 g it is likely that they are intrusive. If they are omitted, a date in the 2nd century AD is suggested by the larger sherds present. Even so, no structural features can be dated to this period which suggests that at this time the occupation was centred on another part of the site, or that the evidence was destroyed by later activity.

The later phases are subject to similar problems caused by mixing, the difficulty experienced in isolating stratigraphic units, and the broad date ranges of the finds present. It has been impossible to date accurately the phases within this period. In reality the best estimate is that Period III as a whole dates to between the early 3rd to late 4th centuries AD.

The relatively small size of most of the sherds suggests that at some point they have been subjected to a significant degree of crushing and abrasion, possibly as a result of trampling by animals and/or people. Distribution plots were produced of sherd weight using both spatial and chronological criteria. It was hoped that the spatial distribution plots would highlight areas of greater trampling which might be expected to contain a higher proportion of small sherds. Unfortunately no patterning could be distinguished; in fact distribution by weight was remarkably consistent across the site. This suggests that the whole excavated area was at some time subjected to these processes.

Plots of average weight by phase were also produced to test the theory that later deposits would contain a greater proportion of trampled material in comparison to earlier, less disturbed deposits. The earlier deposits might be expected to be protected by the layers which had accumulated above them and therefore to contain larger sherds. This distribution was also remarkably flat, each phase having an average sherd weight of 5-10 g. This suggests that the excavated deposits contained a uniform quantity of fine, trampled material, and that therefore they were thoroughly mixed during the occupation of the site.

In conclusion the pottery contributes little to the dating of individual phases of occupation and is only useable in the very broadest terms. The prehistoric pottery and VCP provide clear evidence of occupation in the

mid Bronze Age and Iron Age (cf. above, *Prehistoric pottery*; also Chapter 2, *Radiocarbon Dates*). Although there is evidence to suggest occupation in the 2nd century AD, this cannot be linked directly to any structures which may have been located elsewhere or have been destroyed by later activity. The later Roman phases can only be dated using the pottery to the 3rd to 4th centuries AD.

The main cause of these ambiguities appears to be the long duration and intensity of occupation at Irby. Trampling by humans and animals, and other activities such as the digging of post-holes, has caused the deposits to become so thoroughly mixed, and the pottery to be so finely comminuted to make any distinctions which may once have been present impossible to differentiate. The contribution of the pottery to dating the latest phases is difficult to assess. Any rural medieval phase is likely to be aceramic until the 12th or 13th century, and the postulated medieval activity here contains significant quantities of residual Romano-British pottery.

Graffiti on Roman Pottery (Fig. 4.12)

Robert Philpott

Two body sherds bore graffiti scratched after firing.

198. Wall sherd of grey ware vessel, probably a jar, date uncertain. LV[with traces of a third stroke on broken portion. SF4889, context 5054.
199. Sherd of BB1 jar with obtuse lattice decoration. 'X' crudely incised on shoulder, AD 240-270 (J. Evans pers. comm.). SF8273, from fill of Ditch 1 in 1987 salvage work.

Both of the above could be personal marks, the X representing an illiterate owner rather than a numeral (Evans 1987, 201). Jeremy Evans has noted the low incidence of graffiti on rural sites in Britain, with a particular scarcity in the north (Evans 1987).

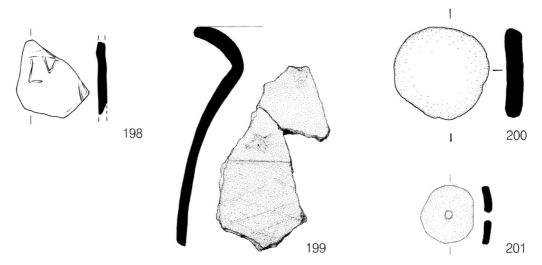

Fig. 4.12: 198-199. Graffiti on Roman pottery; 200-201. Roman ceramic objects. Scale 1:2

Ceramic Objects (Fig. 4.12)

Robert Philpott

200. Disc, base sherd of BB1 dish or bowl, cut and neatly trimmed as a ?gaming counter; probably later Roman (J. Evans pers. comm.). Diam 50 mm. SF9557, context 3001.
201. Spindle whorl, cut out of body sherd of Romano-British oxidised ware vessel, orange sandy fabric with pale grey core. Oval 30 x 26 mm, hour-glass perforation 4 mm in diameter. SF20, context 802.

The Samian

Margaret Ward

The small size of the samian assemblage, which consists of 53 sherds, has been noted already (Philpott 1994, 29). There is a maximum of 47 vessels in this collection, which is summarised here on Figure 4.13 and Table 4.18. The sample is so small and the condition of the sherds was so poor that few conclusions could be drawn. Most of the sherds could be dated only vaguely within the date ranges of *c.* AD 70-110 and *c.* 120-200. Indeed, 51% of the total consisted of indeterminate scraps whose fabric was difficult to attribute to any centre of production. However, it may be noted that a fairly small proportion (15%) was produced in South Gaul (before *c.* AD 110).

Since the condition of the material made it impossible to estimate minimum numbers of vessels represented, only maximum numbers have been calculated. Of the 47 vessels, 36 (77%) originated in Central Gaul, where all but one were produced after *c.* AD 120. The possible exception was a tiny chip from a vessel which may have been produced at Les Martres de Veyre in the Trajanic period. At least 14 of the Central Gaulish sherds were thought to have been manufactured in the later second century, and one (a fragment probably from a mortarium form Dr. 45) appeared to have been produced after AD 170.

Four sherds may have been produced in East Gaul in the Antonine period or later, forming up to 9% of the total. However, this material consisted merely of scraps whose place of manufacture and date of origin was far from clear. Their evidence cannot be relied on and it is impossible even to say how many vessels these four fragments represented. Two scraps were recovered from Trench XXI (3775) and may well have belonged to the same vessel; a decorated sherd, from Trench XXXVII context (6475), is listed below as no. 204; an indeterminate fragment from Trench IX (1205) probably represented a different vessel.

It may be noted that very few of the sherds in this collection were more than soft scraps which had suffered considerable abrasion and erosion in the soil, resulting in the total loss of the surfaces of some sherds. As for

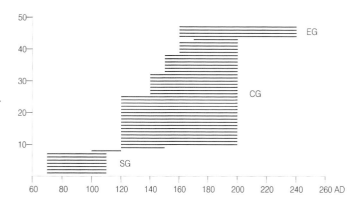

Fig. 4.13: Diagram summarising all samian vessels (maximum numbers) by fabric and date of manufacture

their life in use, the few small fragments of footring and basal sherds which survived were in such poor condition that no evidence of wear from primary use could be recognised.

The most significant feature of the collection was the presence of three sherds displaying rivet holes. This seems to suggest that a large proportion of the samian ware on the site could have seen repair work (see nos 205-207 below). Whether the repairs were successful or not is unclear: the sherds are broken through the rivet holes and only one showed any trace of the rivet, which in that case was probably lead (no. 206). The three vessels appear to have been repaired using the cut, dove-tailed variety of riveting which has been thought the more popular method in the 2nd century (see Marsh 1981, 227; but cf. Ward 1993, 19; also Ward 1989, 154). All three vessels indeed may have been produced in the late 2nd century. All were clearly considered valuable enough for the owner to have their repair attempted. It may be suggested that their repair may have taken place at the time when samian was in ever shorter supply, after *c.* AD 200. It is evident that at this remote site in the far corner of the Roman Empire, such a commodity as this fine tableware was held in enough esteem to make the repair even of the less valued plainware worthy of its attempt.

Only one piece could be identified as having been burnt, and that was a fragment of 2nd-century Central Gaulish ware recovered from Trench XLIII.

Catalogue of the Decorated Samian

A catalogue of the remaining samian is held as part of the excavation archive.

202. A rim sherd from a moulded bowl of form Dr. 37 from Central Gaul, in good condition, with only a fragment of the ovolo surviving. This is possibly Rogers 1974, type B103 which was used at Lezoux by various potters, including Advocisus, in the later 2nd century. Possibly from the same bowl as another piece from the same context. SF5714, context 5321.

	C.15	C.23	18R	18/31R	31	31R	33	35	45	ind.	37	Total
SG			1							6		7
CG	1	2		1	2	3	2	3	1	18	3	36
EG										3	1	4
Total	1	2	1	1	2	3	2	3	1	27	4	47

SG - South Gaulish; CG - Central Gaulish; EG - Eastern Gaulish; C - Curle; ind. - indeterminate:
other headings, Dragendorff forms

Table 4.18. Summary of samian forms and fabrics from all contexts (maximum number of vessels)

203. A battered sherd of CG. bowl form Dr. 37, with a fragment only of the panelled decoration. Inside beaded borders (Rogers 1974, A2) lies an ornament (Q6) used by several potters, including Advocisus, in the later 2nd century. Possibly from the same bowl as the preceding item. SF5749, context 5321.
204. A small, badly eroded and abraded fragment of a bowl of form Dr. 37. The rather orange fabric seems to indicate East Gaulish rather than Central Gaulish production, but the origin of this small scrap is unclear. A fragment only of the moulded decoration remains: probably the back legs of an animal. 2nd century or later, if East Gaulish. SF7103, context 6475.

Repaired samian
205. A badly battered rim of CG dish form Dr. 18/31R or 31R, produced in the range *c.* AD 140-200 and after *c.* AD 160 if the form is 31R. The piece has broken across a dove-tailed rivet hole, in which no signs of the rivet remain. SF6265, context 3165.
206. A sherd from the lower wall/base of a CG dish of form Dr. 31R produced *c.* AD 160-200. The vessel had been repaired: this piece is broken through a dove-tailed rivet hole, which retains traces apparently of lead. SF6716, context 6218.
207. An abraded rim sherd from a CG dish of form Dr. 31R, manufactured *c.* AD 160-200. The vessel has broken through three or more dove-tailed rivet holes, in which no signs of the rivets remain. SF8723, context 7043.

Roman Tile

Jeff Speakman

A very small quantity of tile was recovered from the excavations. Most pieces are abraded fragments with no diagnostic features. Identification and dating has therefore been largely based upon comparison with tiles and tile fabrics found elsewhere in Merseyside (Ochre Brook and Court Farm, Halewood). There are also a number of fragments of fired clay in generally similar fabrics, which may represent undiagnostic tile.

Romano-British Fabrics

The excavation produced no diagnostically identifiable fragments of Romano-British roof-tile, although 25 fragments (weighing 265.8 g) of probable Romano-British fabric are recorded.

There are four fabrics identifiable using a x10 hand-lens.

1. Oxidised orange firing fairly sandy.
2. Fine, smooth fabric; pink in colour
3. Fine, smooth fabric; pink in colour with common haematite/marl inclusions.
4. Fine, smooth fabric; pale pinkish-buff in colour.

Due to the fragmentary nature of the group of material the fabric variations, especially amongst the finer fabrics, may represent only variations in firing and the quantity of inclusions found within one tile rather than true fabric differences.

Discussion

The volume of probable and certain Romano-British tile, numbering 25 fragments with an average weight of little over 10 g, is tiny when seen against the size and weight of an individual tile. The poor preservation of many of the fragments means that many lack any diagnostic characteristics and are little more than amorphous fired clay. Some of the pieces are also quite fine and may be from pottery vessels.

The quantity and quality of identifiable roof-tile fragments is interesting in itself, suggesting that there were no buildings with tiled roofs in a settlement of some size and complexity for the region. Indeed this negative information would seem to provide further evidence to the nature and type of rural settlement patterns in the area. The small quantity of tile is more likely to represent stray material brought from outside for some purpose unconnected with roofing than to hint at the possibility of some as yet unidentified substantial building in the vicinity.

Medieval and Later Pottery

Saxo-Norman Lamp

Robert Philpott

208. Spike or cresset lamp, with shallow bowl surmounting a solid blunted spike, hand made in one piece. Complete profile present. The reduced grey fabric has numerous quartz inclusions and sparse shell fragments (freshwater?), with sooting in the interior. 10th-12th century. SF4888, context 5034, Period V, fill of gully in S24. Fig. 4.14.

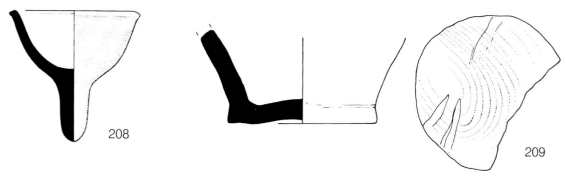

Fig. 4.14: 208. Saxo-Norman spike lamp. 209. Medieval pottery base. Scale 1:2

The ceramic hanging lamp with a spiked base, usually known as a spike or cresset lamp, is characteristic of the Saxo-Norman period in England. The lamp was suspended in a metal loop and held a floating wick fed by a small quantity of oil in the bowl (McCarthy and Brooks 1988, 116-7, fig. 58). Spike lamps were manufactured in the major traded ceramic types such as Thetford ware and Stamford ware in eastern England. The spike lamp is found in Stamford ware from the late 9th-12th century (McCarthy and Brooks 1988, 156, fig. 77, no 128), and in Thetford ware and Thetford-type ware in the 11th-12th century, becoming more frequent in Later Thetford Ware in the 11th century (McCarthy and Brooks 1988, 161, fig. 82, nos 175, 176). Examples can also be cited from Southampton in Saxo-Norman ware dated to the 11th-12th century (McCarthy and Brooks 1988, 188, fig. 100, 399), while a less close parallel in form in Thetford-type ware, dated to the 11th-early 12th century, was found at Great Yarmouth (McCarthy and Brooks 1988, 167, fig. 86 no 249). In well-dated stratified deposits in London, spike lamps occur in Local Grey ware in late 11th/early 12th-century contexts, and although they survive until as late as the 14th century, they are scarcer from the late 12th century onwards when glass hanging lamps become more common (Keys and Pearce 1998, 127). The parallels for the Irby example suggest a 10th-12th-century date.

The fabric of the Irby lamp does not appear to be consistent with Saxo-Norman Chester ware due to the presence of shell fragments (J. Edwards pers. comm.). Cresset lamps are not known in Chester ware fabric from Chester or from Stafford, the town which has revealed the only known production sites (Ford 1999). The provenance of the Irby lamp is unknown but it is likely to be an introduction from south-eastern England

Later Medieval and Early Post-Medieval Pottery

Julie Edwards

Introduction

A total of 36 certain or possible medieval sherds and a further nine non-local post-medieval sherds were examined from Irby. Generally sherd size is small and the pieces are all quite badly abraded with surfaces being partly or totally worn away. In most cases the small size and absence of any distinguishing characteristics of form restricts identification to general fabric types. The fabrics have been identified by the terms employed in the fabric reference collection of Chester Archaeological Service. The sherds have been recorded by count and weight on standardised recording sheets, this report discusses the individual pieces and comments on aspects of the assemblage as a whole. Only one sherd is sufficiently diagnostic of form to merit illustration.

Medieval wares

Red/grey wares

Nine sherds are in red- or grey-firing fabrics with a lead glaze appearing green or brownish yellow (SF947, SF1549, SF6363, SF7547, SF8287, SF8469, SF9321, SF9349, SF10781). The sherds are all abraded but in character the fabrics are all similar to wares known to have been produced in Cheshire in the 13th and 14th centuries. One sherd (SF7547) is part of the thumbed base of a jug, which is also similar to types found in Chester. The boulder clays covering Cheshire and extending into the West Midlands were used to manufacture these wares, therefore potteries may also have existed over the county boundaries.

Three more sherds are possibly of similar red/grey ware, but are too abraded to be certain; these consist of SF5894, SF6324 and SF7325.

Red/grey wares are widely distributed throughout Cheshire and along the North Wales coast and are the most common type of medieval pottery found in Chester in the 13th/14th century.

Pink/white wares

Four sherds occur in pink/white wares. These consist of SF743, SF5483, and SF8281. A further sherd, SF9361 with a slight trace of green glaze, is similar to glazed whitewares found in Chester in the late 13th-14th century, of unknown provenance.

One very small fragment (SF5483), weighing 1g, is in a hard sandy pink fabric with a clear glaze appearing brown. This and an abraded sherd SF8281 are similar to wares produced in the Ewloe area of Clwyd. A coin hoard dated *c.* 1361 (Rutter 1977) was found in a vessel made of this type of ware. This evidence as well as stylistic comparisons suggests production in the 14th and 15th centuries.

Similar Coal Measures clays were used to produce pottery elsewhere in the north west as well as the Midlands. This sherd is so small that, as with the red/grey wares, it is hard to ascribe firmly the ware to any particular production source.

South Lancashire Sandy Wares

209. Base sherd of medieval jug or jar, hard fabric with numerous angular and sub-angular quartz inclusions; reduced core, oxidised surfaces. Curved concentric wire drawing marks on underside of base. SF8393, Site 14 context 22, upper fill of enclosure ditch. Fig. 4.14.

Two sherds from the same context may be from the same vessel (SF8393, SF9792). The fabric is consistent with medieval sandy wares found across the Mersey in South Lancashire and Merseyside (e.g. Speakman 2000), rather than Cheshire fabrics.

Unidentified wares

One medieval sherd with abraded oxidised surfaces and a reduced core is medieval in date, probably of Cheshire manufacture (SF3197).

Several other sherds are so abraded with fabrics that contain mainly quartz grains and lack diagnostic features that it is uncertain whether they are medieval, but they appear sufficiently different from the main Roman fabrics to be distinctive.

One very small sherd has a pale reduced grey fabric with a greenish yellow reduced glaze (SF3661). The sherd is so small that it is hard to date. In the light of the original assumption that the site was Romano-British in date, it was considered possibly Roman in date. The sherd was compared with a piece of Roman Holt glazed ware and the quartz inclusions were much finer in the Irby sherd. Further work is required to try and determine the date of the sherd but even then the size of the sherd may make a firm identification difficult. However, the recognition of a medieval phase suggests it is far more likely to be medieval in date.

Seven other severely abraded but unglazed sherds in sandy fabrics may be medieval. These comprise SF972, SF986, SF3770, SF4385, SF5026, SF5635 and SF10608.

Early Post-Medieval wares

North Devon gravel-tempered wares

Five sherds were found: SF9319, SF9320, SF9322, SF9323 and SF10852. The ware is distinguished by the presence of coarse inclusions including quartz and mica. Where glaze survives it is a reduced green colour, except the dripping pan (SF10852) which has internal yellowish brown glaze. One sherd has traces of soot on the exterior, another has an unglazed smoothed area which may be the scar left by an applied feature such as a handle.

The most diagnostic sherd is SF10852, from the side of a handmade straight-walled dripping pan, with internal yellowish brown glaze and unglazed externally (cf. Grant 1983, fig. 40, no. 13; R. Philpott pers. comm.). It was recovered from upcast in a drainage trench at 113 Mill Hill Road. There is sooting along the top of the rim.

North Devon gravel-tempered wares occur scattered around the Liverpool Bay area and are evidence of 17th-century trade along the west coast of Britain.

This ware and the types of forms in which it was made have been discussed elsewhere in relation to sites where it has been found (e.g. Miles and Saunders 1970; Evans 1979; Allan 1984; 148-50).

Unidentified sherds

Two very abraded sherds were retrieved from context 5101; the sherds are so worn and small that it is impossible to identify them firmly but they appear to be post-medieval in date. One (SF10820) is in a fine soft pink coloured fabric. One side (the underside?) has spots of a clear glaze appearing a golden brown/orange colour; the other is coated in what appears to be a decayed glaze. The piece is so small and abraded it is difficult to identify with any certainty but the fabric does resemble a post-medieval slipware fabric.

The second sherd (SF10821) has a soft, fine fabric with scant remains of a glaze which appears opaque and white and is probably a tin-glaze. The sherd may be part of a tin-glazed ware vessel but of what form or provenance it is not possible to identify.

Continental wares

Two sherds are French in origin and 16th/17th century in date.

Sherd SF10819 has a fine soft pink fabric. On one surface are the scant remains of a fine white slip which has traces of manganese brown/purple and copper green painted decoration. The sherd is a post-medieval Saintonge polychrome ware produced in the 16th and

17th centuries in the south-west of France (see Hurst *et al.* 1986, 83-5 for a description and discussion of these wares). Similar polychrome wares are found in Chester and along the north Wales coast; post-medieval Saintonge wares are also known from Liverpool (Davey 1991, 136) and Meols (Axworthy 2007).

Sherd SF10818 is made of a fine white fabric with a clear glaze, appearing yellow, which is flecked orange and green. The sherd is from the rim flange of a dish. The edge has a fluted 'pie-crust' finish bordered on the interior by two parallel incised lines. The fabric is very similar to Beauvais earthenwares (Hurst *et al.* 1986, 106-16) but the form is not paralleled in published examples of the ware and would seem to be unusual in Britain. However, similar forms have been noted in Beauvais, France and in Chester (J. Axworthy pers. comm.).

As with post-medieval Saintonge wares, small amounts of Beauvais wares occur in Chester and the Liverpool Bay area.

Discussion

This small and rather battered assemblage reflects the types of medieval and post-medieval wares which occur in the area of Wirral, Chester and north Wales. The presence of the decorative French imports is interesting, as generally such wares are associated with ports and 'high status' dwellings, although Irby is close to the outports of Chester. The presence of Cheshire red/grey wares and possible Ewloe wares adds to evidence about the distribution of these wares.

The remaining post-medieval sherds are not discussed here as they are derived from the post-medieval ploughsoil or more recent deposits and they relate to post-medieval agricultural manuring practices on the site rather than occupation.

Structural Daub and Fired Clay

Cynthia Poole

A total of 2306 finds of daub and fired clay was made available for analysis. All those that had been excavated had been plotted two-dimensionally as either individual fragments or small groups of fragments, each being bagged and numbered separately. A small proportion had been recovered by wet sieving, but only a sub-sample of about a hundred were examined for the analysis. All the daub and fired clay had been weighed, producing a total of 12.7 kg. The discussion below uses the number of 'finds', which is closest to being a fragment count, though a small number of 'finds' consisted of more than one fragment. Where the word 'daub' is used below it should be taken to include fired clay.

The daub was found in a wide variety of contexts including discrete features such as post-holes, pits, gullies, ditches, hearths and walls, though the greater part appears to have come from layers – plough soils, occupation, make-up or floor levels. Slightly less than half the daub (44%) could be assigned to dated contexts based on the stratigraphy.

The majority of daub fragments weighed under 5 g and many of these were 1 g or less. This fact alone inevitably meant that the majority of samples would yield little or no information apart from its location at a particular point on the site. It is debatable whether the latter is of any real value in the interpretation of the daub *per se*. The spatial plot of all daub does not throw up any pattern apart from a greater density in the centre of the excavated area.

Fragment size has inevitably limited the amount of information that can be obtained. Elsewhere the analysis of average fragment size (Poole 2000c; 2000d, 115) has shown that fragments under 20 g rarely have diagnostic characteristics. If such pieces were rejected for Irby it would virtually eliminate the whole daub collection. It is also known from other sites such as Maiden Castle, that daub recovered by wet or dry sieving does not produce any additional information. It was decided to scan the whole of the Irby collection: being packed in transparent polythene bags it was possible to select for more detailed study only those fragments which appeared to have some shaping surviving or were larger than average and could provide more detail of the clay fabrics.

The Fabrics

As a result of the nature of the collection, the fabric was not identified for all samples because many were too small. Three fabrics have been identified on the basis of visible constituents sometimes with the aid of a hand lens (x10). The lack of large fragments and samples has produced difficulties in assessing the full range of characteristics of each fabric or judging whether they are merely variants of a heterogeneous clay source. Certain samples appeared to exhibit characteristics grading between two fabric types.

Fabric A: This was a fine silty clay generally streaked or variegated in colour – pink/grey or reddish yellow/light brown, depending on the intensity of baking. It contained no or very few inclusions in the form of rare quartz sand or grit. One sample had a thin lens within it of pure quartz sand.

Fabric B: This was generally well baked or fired covering a wide range of colours and shades of pink, red, brown, yellow and grey, though generally a reddish shade dominated. The clay matrix was mixed with a medium-high density of fine-medium sized sand, mostly rounded and subrounded quartz. Larger inclusions found in low density were grit and rock fragments of quartz, ?haematite/Fe (iron) fragments, sandstone, siltstone and clay globules.

Fabric C: This was a similar well baked or fired clay, occurring in various shades of brown, red, reddish yellow and less commonly grey. It contained a high density of medium and coarse sand, frequently angular or mixed subangular/subrounded. It also contained a variety of grit and rock fragments up to 12 mm size of quartz, ?haematite/slag/Fe fragments, sandstone, siltstone (or a fine grained rock), clay globules or unwedged clay. The rock fragments ranged from very angular broken pieces to small rounded waterworn pebbles.

It is assumed the sources of clay would have been local, either the local boulder clay or estuarine clays. The variations and gradations observed within and between the fabrics probably reflect the mixed nature of the local boulder clays, which was probably the source for all the fabrics. At first it was thought Fabric A might be estuarine in origin, but the presence of sand grains and thin sand lenses within it implies it too is boulder clay. If all the fabrics derive from the boulder clay it is possible they were in reality one fabric, which exhibited the mixed characteristics of the boulder clay. It was therefore considered appropriate to undertake thin-section analysis, the results of which are presented above (see *Thin-section petrology*).

The Forms

The daub and fired clay can be divided broadly into structural material and individual objects, though there may be overlap between the sub-categories of both groups in terms of function and activities. Structural daub and clay covers ovens, hearths and furnaces. Technically it should include genuine daub from house walls, but evidence for such material is extremely rare and on most sites non-existent. For the daub to have a chance of surviving the house would have had to burn down with sufficient intensity to fire or at least bake the daub. Moreover, house daub traditionally has a high organic content (straw, dung, animal hair) and such a fabric is not normally encountered. Irby is no exception to the rule of an absence of house daub.

Individual objects can cover a wide range of items, which may be domestic (spindle whorls, beads weights), industrial (oven furniture, tuyere, moulds, briquetage) or constructional (bricks, tiles).

At Irby 80% of the daub and fired clay samples retained no original surfaces, shaping or characteristics: they were universally small worn, rounded or irregular fragments. The remainder can be divided into 18% structural and 2% individual objects.

Structural Daub

Wall (Not illustrated – SF8143)
There were 29 samples (1.25%) of wall daub, twelve of which occurred in the top of a pit (cut 8146, part of Structure 13, Period IV, Phase R5). This was the only structural category where sufficient diagnostic characteristics survived to designate it with certainty. Though none of the fragments were especially large, most had sufficient number of wattle impressions to discern the interwoven pattern typical of wall daub. A total of 81 horizontal or rod impressions were identified; of these 58 occurred on daub from the pit 8146, which was the only daub to produce evidence of vertical sails, in the form of two split poles. The wattles measured between 4 and 22 mm in diameter with the peak at 14 mm, a range closely comparable with sizes recorded elsewhere (Table 4.19). Where more extensive groups of wall daub have been found such as at Danebury and neighbouring sites (Cunliffe and Poole 1991; Poole 2000) all the evidence indicates that this form of daub derives from ovens, having formed part of the upper walls of the oven dome. There is no reason to interpret the wall daub from Irby any differently.

	Rods			Sails	Planks
	SF8143	All other	Total	SF8143	
4 mm	-	1	1		
5 mm	6	2	8		
6 mm	3	2	5		
7 mm	2	-	2		
8 mm	-	1	1		
9 mm	3	2	5		
10 mm	4	1	5		
11 mm	2	1	3		
12 mm	2	1	3		
13 mm	6	1	7		
14 mm	9	6	15		
15 mm	6	1	7	+ split	
16 mm	4	-	4		
17 mm	1	1	2		
18 mm	3	-	3	1 split	
19 mm	1	-	1		
20 mm	2	2	4		
21 mm	3	1	4		
22 mm	1	-	1		
Total	58	23	81	2	1

Table 4.19: Wattle impressions: numbers and diameters

Oven Plates and Covers (none illustrated)
These are dealt with together here as there are no indisputable examples of either form from Irby. Material from other sites indicate that oven plates took the form of a flat circular disc pierced by a random arrangement of vertical circular or oval perforations *c.* 25-60 mm in diameter with cylindrical, funnel or hour-glass shaped profiles. The underside may be covered in straw, wattle or plank impressions, singly or in combination. Oven covers were flat or gently domed circular plates with a central circular hole 120-150 mm in diameter encircled by smaller circular perforations 15-25 mm in diameter.

Eighteen finds from Irby were assigned to this category on the basis of minimal characteristics – in most cases the partial survival of a small circular perforation or with even less certainty organic impressions or a curving moulded edge. (Both plates and covers could be made as a portable unit and so had a moulded outer rim.) Details of all the samples are summarised in Table 4.20. The presence of a single perforation cannot be regarded as incontrovertible evidence alone, as single perforations in the same size range have occasionally been observed in the side of oven walls, possibly openings allowing a tuyere to be inserted. The surviving thickness of the fragments from 15-50 mm is compatible with oven plate or cover. Twelve of these finds were from occupation deposits, mainly from the upper levels though examples occur through out the stratigraphic sequence, though the evidence for disturbance of these deposits (see Chapter 2) suggests that this cannot be relied upon as evidence of date. Six fragments were from sealed contexts, though these were also spread through the stratigraphic sequence. For example, SF7305 was from the fill of a post-hole (8224) associated with Structure 27, Period II, Phase P3, whilst SF8541 and SF5347 were found in the wall of Structure 19, Period VI, Phase M1.

SF	Perforation size in mm/shape	Impressions	Thickness (mm)
1427	-	Straw/fine stems	-
2102	25 mm; ?2nd present	-	>28
3209	?Rim of central hole of oven cover	-	>12
3781	?Edge of perf. present	-	-
4101	33 mm; hourglass profile	-	18-25
4325	?polygonal	-	-
4514	?65 mm; hourglass profile	-	c.50
5347	50 mm	-	15
6767	Edge of perf. ?40-50 mm	-	?25-26
7156	?Curved outer edge of circular plate		>24
7187	Outer edge circular & angled	Seeds	>25
7305	22 mm, oval, perf. blackened	-	>20
7511	10 mm	-	>15
7513	12 mm	-	>20
7550	15 mm	-	>16
7566	15 mm	-	>12
8531	Curving edge of perf.	-	13-22
8541	32-16 mm; funnel shaped perf.	-	>50

Table 4.20: Oven plate/cover summary of features

General Oven Daub (none illustrated)
This category includes fragments with some shaping, but no genuinely diagnostic characteristics. A small number of samples (18) had at least two or three original conjoining surfaces forming an edge or corner. The edges included both straight and curved examples, with flat or rounded edges. These flat edges might be at right angles or an acute angle to the main surfaces. Such moulded edge could derive from the outer margins of oven plates or covers or from openings in the oven wall for stoking or loading the oven.

The remaining fragments merely retained areas of a plain surface (352 samples in total). Of these ten had a blackened surface, probably a result of burning or smoking of the surface. A further fourteen had some organic impressions on the surface: these comprised fine grass or straw stems, chaff and seeds. The rest exhibited a variety of surfaces from very smooth and even to rough and irregular, which might be flat or curving, both concave and convex.

Evidence of the moulding and shaping of the clay survived as finger ridging and individual finger tip impressions. Ridging occurred as the fingers dragged across the clay surface leaving a series of parallel linear grooves and ridges. Individual finger or thumb tip impressions were circular or oval concave depressions left where the clay had been pressed firmly. Such features are usually found on the interior surface of an oven, rather than the exterior.

Industrial (Fig. 4.15: SF8258, no. 255; SF6448, no. 252)
A small number of samples (seven) may derive from some type of industrial activity (but see *The Industrial Waste* below for further vitrified material). These small fragments had patches of vitrified, vesicular clay and may be fragments of furnace lining. Two other pieces may also relate to industrial activity. One appears to form a simple pinched rounded rim with part of finger tip depression on its edge, from a cylindrical object with external diameter of 35-40 mm (internal 20-25 mm) and the wall 80 mm thick. The rim is glassy and greyed on the lip and outer surface for a distance of 9 mm. The fragment may be part of a tuyere. The second piece might be a fragment of mould: it has a smooth convex outer surface with flattened edges and a shallow hollow interior forming an oval shape with a further shallow, narrow groove running down the length, slightly off-centre.

Individual Objects

A small number of finds are fragments of individual small objects. Possible fragments of brick and tile (5) were identified. Other pieces appeared to be the walls (6-10 mm thick) of small vessels or containers (7), possibly briquetage in some cases. One had a straight cut edge, a feature which commonly occurs on briquetage containers and another small bowl-shaped vessel with a flattened rim may have been a crucible fragment, though no slag adhered to the surface. Some roughly finished, irregular spherical objects no more than 20-30 mm diameter may be purely accidental forms. A small fragment that appeared to be the rounded end of an oblong bar with a flattened circular section 12 x 14 mm may have been the tip of a fire bar (Fig. 4.15, no 251; SF4973). Another possible fire bar of triangular section (SF6829) with converging incised lines may have been deliberately decorated. Fire bars of triangular cross-section were found at Bury Hill, Hampshire (Poole 2000b, 61), although here they had larger dimensions than the Irby fragment. The V-shape pattern is similar to impressed herringbone decoration found on fired clay fragments at Suddern Farm (Poole 2000c, 130, fig. 3.88, Ov. 13 and Ov. 14).

Spindle Whorls/Beads (Fig.4.15, no. 248, SF941): There were three very fragmentary small objects that may have been pieces of spindle whorl or beads. They were generally sub-spherical in shape with diameters *c.* 35-40 mm and heights of 20 mm or more. On only one did sufficient survive to retain the hint of a perforation. None were recovered from contexts to which a date could be assigned.

Weights/Bricks: This category comprises a range of forms, which may represent a number of disparate functions. All dimensions and forms are summarised in Table 4.21.

Type 1: Spherical Weights (Fig. 4.15, no 242, SF7303; no. 247, SF8797)
Two objects were assigned to this category, both very similar in size and form and found in post-holes associated with Structure 27, Phase P3. They were essentially pudding or bun-shaped with one end slightly flattened: this asymmetric shape suggests that they had a top and base. They had diameters of 100 and 110 mm and heights of 58 and 86 mm. The larger, complete one weighed 1100 g, whilst slightly under half of the smaller survived with a weight of 220 g, allowing its total weight to be estimated at about 450-500 g. Both were pierced by a single perforation, which tended to be oval in form and widest at the external surfaces 23-27 mm wide decreasing to about 20 mm in the middle of the objects. There is no evidence of wear on the perforations to suggest that they had been suspended. They both appeared to have been moulded with the fingers rather than being made by an implement such as a stick, which would account for the slightly irregular splayed form of the perforations. The exterior surfaces were fairly even and smooth and both had been partly burnt black or grey – one on the slightly flattened end and one on the more rounded 'top'. It is not clear whether firing and burning of the objects relates to their manufacture or to some secondary use, perhaps as oven bricks. This is probably a mid Bronze Age type.

Type 2: Cylindrical and Subrectangular Weights
There were eight objects allocated to this type, which can be divided into three sub-types. Two finds were very small fragments and their identification as objects in this category is by no means certain.

Type 2a (Fig. 4.15, no 239, SF2772) were more subrectangular in form, the surfaces being flat or slightly bowed, well smoothed and with a rounded top. The two examples are incomplete having only part of the top corner surviving together with the perforation. They measured 60-75 mm wide at right angles to the perforation and 70-80 mm parallel with the perforation. Their lengths were incomplete, but would have been in excess of 50-70 mm. In both examples the perforations were smooth and even, apparently made with a stick and measured 14 and 16 mm diameter. The perforation was nearer to one end than the other, suggesting a top and base and that it was intended to be suspended. However on only one does the top of the perforation survive and though there is a slight discoloration along it which could be interpreted as an incipient groove, there is no indisputable evidence of wear from suspension. Only SF8008 was from a dated context, 9609, the fill of the gully of Structure 13, Phase R5. This type resembles late Bronze Age-early Iron Age forms (cf. Elsdon 1979).

Type 2b (Fig. 4.15, no. 226, SF775) was similar in size to 2a, but was more cylindrical and rounded in form. It was found in unphased occupation deposits and had a circular section 65 mm in diameter and measured 90 mm long. Both top and base were well rounded with a slight hint of flattening on the base; all surfaces were very smooth and well finished. The perforation measured 13-15 mm in diameter, was placed about 20 mm from the top end and appeared to be made with a finger rather than a stick. There was no sign of any wear on the perforation from suspension. It weighs 239 g and is about 65% complete indicating a total weight in the order of 360 g. Three more fragmentary finds have been tentatively identified as this type on the basis of the curved surface indicating a diameter/thickness of 50-75 mm, but none of these pieces had a perforation surviving.

Type 2c is a tentative third category for a larger sized cylindrical weight. The only example represented by a fairly small fragment had a diameter of about 120 mm, a smooth plano-convex surface and was pierced by a perforation 15 mm in diameter.

Type 3: Triangular oven bricks/weights (Fig. 4.15, no. 240, 4205)
There were two finds that could be allocated to this category, neither from a phased context. One was very fragmentary having only a remnant of surface pierced by a perforation 10 mm in diameter at an angle to the surface (in any other forms a perforation would be at right angles to any surface). The other example is fairly small measuring 70 mm along one side by over 28 mm thick. The surfaces were smooth and flat, with curving edges and rounded corners. There was no sign of any perforation surviving on this one, but a shallow groove occurred over the apex of one corner possibly to allow it to be tied around its exterior. The smaller than average size and the lack of any perforations, though uncommon do have parallels elsewhere such as Hengistbury Head (Poole 1987) and Woolbury, Hampshire (Poole 2000a, 61, fig. 1.31, 7.2). Grooves across the corner apices are

known from Danebury, Hampshire (Poole 1984, fig 7.48, no. 7.61; 1991), Dragonby (May 1996, fig. 13.1, 4, 6, 7 and 11), and Thistleton, Cambridgeshire (Poole unpub.).

SF	D/ L	T	W	PD	Type	Shape	Phase
941	30-35	c.20	-	+		Sph/ bicon -	
961	c.35	>20	-	-		Cyl/ barrel	-
5702	40-50	>15	-	-		?Coni- cal	-
7303	110	86	-	20	1	Sph	-
8797	100	58	-	20	1	Sph	P3
2772	>50	60	60 *	14	2a	S-R	
8008	>63	>60	70 *	16	2a	S-R	R5
775	95	65	60	13-15	2b	Cyl	-
1045	-	c.75	-	-	?2b	Cyl	-
5987	-	?50-60	?50-60	-	?2b	Cyl	-
8064	-	55	60	-	?2b	Cyl	-
5349	-	120	120	15	2c	Cyl	EM2
5369	-	-	-	-	?2		R4
2002	-	-	-	10	3	TOB	-
4205	70	>28	-	-	3	TOB	-
7654	>60	>60	>45	None	?4	Block	-
7837	65-80	70	40	None	4	Block	-

* Estimated total dimension. D-diameter; L-length; W-width; PD-perforation diameter
Cyl Cylindrical; S-R Sub-rectangular; TOB Triangular oven brick; Sph Spherical

Table 4.21: Spindle whorls and weights: dimensions (in mm) and types

Although the traditional interpretation of these objects is as loomweights, there is increasing evidence to suggest these are in fact some sort of oven furniture. The arguments in favour of such a theory have been fully discussed elsewhere (Poole 1995).

Type 4: Brick/Weight (Fig. 4.15, no. 244, SF7837; no. 243, SF7654)
The two objects allocated to this type take the form of solid blocks of clay without any perforations and were found in unphased occupation deposits. SF7837 is very evenly shaped in the form of a squared corner, 50 mm thick with a shallow circular depression (from a finger tip probably). However since it is incomplete it could form the corner of a freestanding oven plate or cover rather than a small object. SF7654 is nearly complete and is a trapezoidal clay block measuring 65-80 mm by 70 mm and 40 mm thick with a smooth flat surface on one side, but the other face was damaged. The

side surfaces were very variable in quality with many hollows, grooves and finger depressions from moulding. A narrow groove 3.5 mm wide across one corner may be a stem impression or possibly from a string pressed into it. Its weight was 309 g and it had been fired. This type is probably best interpreted as some form of oven furniture, rather than as weights.

It is already clear that the objects generally categorised as weights may have had a variety of functions. The Type 1 weights could have been used as drill weights, whilst the Type 2 are more likely to have been suspended if used as weights. Types 3 and 4 may have been some sort of oven furniture and it is possible the other types were put to a secondary use in ovens. If not, firing must have been a normal part of the manufacturing process.

Discussion

The daub has been dealt with as a whole in the categories discussed above because of the small quantity of diagnostic material, which was too little to consider by phase. A general observation is that most of the dated structural material is assigned to Period IV, and with the roundhouses in Phase R4 and R5. This pattern is also reflected in the non-diagnostic fragments. The explanation appears to lie in the larger number of structures and features assigned to these phases and so the daub is emphasising a more general pattern of denser occupation and the associated debris thus generated.

The weights/bricks are distributed fairly evenly throughout the length of occupation, though certain types may belong to different periods. The two dated Type 1 weights are assigned a mid Bronze Age date, one from a radiocarbon date, the other from associated mid Bronze Age pottery. The cylindrical and sub-rectangular weights are largely from layers of occupation deposit to which it has not been possible to assign a date, though it is likely that most are associated with the Roman phases. The sample is too small however to have any statistical significance. All other dated small objects are assigned to mid-late Roman phases.

The striking feature of this collection of daub and fired clay is the very low numbers of fragments with any form of shape (20% of samples) or even fewer with any diagnostic features (5%). This is in contrast to Iron Age sites in the south of England: at Danebury and sites of the Danebury Environs Project quantities of unidentified fragments was 4-15% by weight, or by fragment count 15-23%, the latter being a more comparable quantification to Irby. This contrast can be accounted for by a small number of factors in particular the on site policy on recovery and the lack of storage pits at Irby. The recovery of all fragments at Irby, especially in the trenches used for training excavations, ensured many small non-diagnostic fragments would be

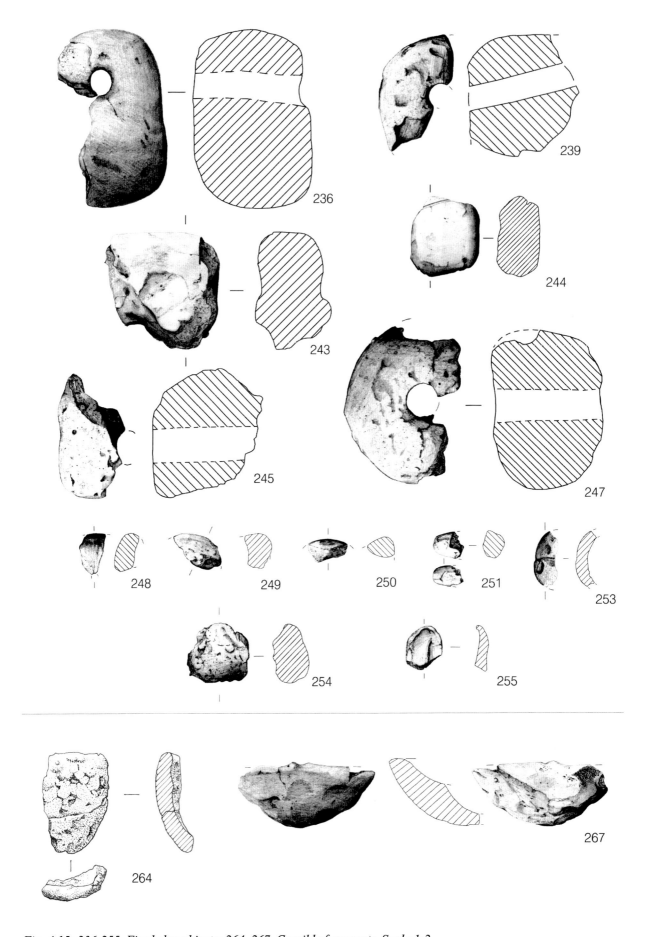

Fig. 4.15: 236-255. Fired clay objects; 264, 267. Crucible fragments. Scale 1:2

retained, whereas at the Danebury Environs sites there was a deliberate policy of sorting and discarding by the specialist on-site.

The second factor mentioned – the lack of storage pits in the north west of England – must be a key reason for the absence of large well preserved groups of oven daub. There was only one group from Irby in a comparable situation, which comprised a small concentration of wall daub in the top of a post-hole or small pit, 8146, part of Structure 13 in Phase R5.

Instead at Irby most of the fired clay and daub was found in layers ranging from plough soils, occupation levels, laid surfaces and floors and other natural or artificial soil accumulations. Essentially the daub fragments were discarded rubbish that became incorporated into contemporary deposits largely by accident rather than design and were subsequently subjected to intensive battering from trampling by animals and humans, ploughing and other activities. When daub or fired clay was continuously subject to such treatment, it would quickly break up and disintegrate with surfaces rapidly worn and damaged. This is the state of most of the daub from Irby and even the diagnostic fragments exhibit various degrees of wear.

Clearly the nature of the site and post-depositional conditions have been important factors in the quality of the dataset. In spite of the limited nature of the material sufficient detail survives to allow some identification of forms and structures present. It appears much of the material derives from ovens, which probably in some cases followed native Iron Age designs of circular domed structures supported on a wattle framework and possibly on occasion incorporating oven plates or oven covers. These are likely to have been used for domestic cooking and baking. There is also a small quantity of material that could point to industrial activities being undertaken.

The bases of a number of ovens and hearths were identified during excavation, including typical Roman designs (keyhole /dumb-bell shaped bases), but none of the daub has been directly linked to any of them.

Catalogue of Small Objects

Weights and Oven Bricks

236. Cylindrical weight - Type 2b: the weight is about two-thirds complete measuring 90 mm long, 60 x 65 mm wide and having a total estimated weight of about 367 g. It was pierced by a single perforation 13-15 mm in diameter placed about 20 mm from the top of the object. The perforation appeared to have been made with the fingers, moulded from either side and so far as it survives there was no sign of wear from suspension. The weight is cylindrical with very smooth surfaces and having a rounded top and the base only slightly flattened. Fabric C; fired. SF775, context 1630, unphased post-hole. Fig. 4.15.

237. Small fragment of object with well smoothed curving surface; most probably part of cylindrical weight. Fabric C; fired. SF1045, context 2021, Unphased layer at base of occupation deposits.

238. Triangular oven brick ('loomweight'): small fragment with smooth flat, but slightly undulating surface pierced at a diagonal to the surface by a perforation 10 mm in diameter. Fabric A; fired. SF2002, context 3061, unphased layer at base of plough soil.

239. Subrectangular? weight - Type 2a: a fragment representing about one fifth of the whole object derives from the top corner. It measured 60 mm wide and >50 mm long and weighed 110 g, with the total weight estimated at 550 g. It was pierced at a distance of 25 mm from the top by a single perforation 14 mm in diameter, which was smooth and even apparently made with a stick. The weight is square in section with flat sides and faces, though the top forms a curving plano-convex surface; the base did not survive. Fabric C; fired. SF2772, context 3071, unphased layer of occupation deposit.Fig. 4.15.

240. Triangular oven brick/weight: fragment of triangular shaped object with smooth flat surface and curving edges. Over the apex of the corner there is a shallow hollow or groove. No perforations observed. Fabric B; fired. SF4205, context 3063, unphased layer of occupation deposit.

241. A small fragment, with no diagnostic features, only two flat smooth surfaces at right angles joined by a rounded edge. SF5369, context 3789, part of Structure 1, Phase R4

242. Spherical weight - Type 1: complete pudding shaped weight, 110 mm diameter, 86 mm high, 1100 g. It has one flattened side, the rest being rounded and convex. The overall shape is slightly uneven and the surface slightly irregular with shallow hollows. The perforation is oval in cross-section apparently moulded with an irregular surface having depressions probably made by the finger tips. The perforation measures 17 x 21 mm at the flat base, 20 x 27 mm in the centre and 22 x 23 mm at the rounded top. Fabric C; fired and burnt/blackened around the top. SF7303, context 8236, Fill of post-hole 8224 associated with Structure 27, Phase P3.

243. Fragment from the corner of a rectangular object measuring >60 mm x >60 mm x >45 mm and weighing 170 g. The corner and angles are well rounded, the surfaces smooth with flat and even sides. The top surface has a large circular depression measuring 25 x 20 mm and 10 mm deep. Fabric B; fired. SF7654, context 9505, base of modern ploughsoil. Fig. 4.15.

244. Weight/brick - Type 4: this object was complete measuring 80 - 65 mm long by 70 mm wide and 40 mm thick; it weighed 309 g. It was sub-trapezoidal in shape with one flat smooth face, but the other damaged and apparently more irregular; the sides were variable in quality and profile with various hollows and grooves from moulding. The corners and angles were all rather rounded. There is a groove across one corner 3.5 mm wide, which may have been a stem impression or resulted from twine pressed into the clay. SF7837, context 9558=9560, unphased layer at base of occupation deposits. Fig. 4.15.

245. Subrectangular weight - Type 2a: corner fragment of the weight, measuring > 63 mm long and with an estimated width of *c.* 70 mm. It was pierced by a perforation 16 mm in diameter with a smooth even surface possibly made with a stick. The weight had smooth even, slightly undulating surfaces; the faces of the weight were slightly bowed and the angles rounded. SF8008, context 9609, fill of gully for Structure 13, Phase R5. Fig. 4.15.

246. ?Cylindrical weight - Type ?2b: small fragment, diameter 60

mm, thickness 55 mm. It had a smooth even curving plano-convex surface: its overall form might be similar to 775 or be more discoidal. SF8064, context 9596, unphased layer at base of occupation deposits.

247. Spherical weight: Nearly half complete fragment, pudding shaped with flattened base, which has smoother finish than irregular rounded surface. The flattened base is blackened with burning continuing round sides and down perforation. The perforation appeared to be moulded with the fingers, rather than made with a stick. 100 mm diameter; 58 mm high; 217.8 g (complete weight estimated at 484 g); perforation 18 x 23 mm at base edge, 20 mm centre. Fabric C; fired and burnt. SF8797, context 7422, fill of post-hole 7424 associated with Structure 27, Phase P3. Fig. 4.15.

Spindle Whorls

248. Small fragment with smooth curving convex surface and hint of a perforation. Spherical/biconical in form. Fabric B; fired. SF941, context 1040, fill of unphased post-hole 1069. Fig. 4.15.

249. Fragment with smooth flat surface and rounded curving edge at right angles. Cylindrical/barrel form. No perforation surviving. Fabric C; fired and burnt. SF961, context 1038, unphased layer of occupation deposit. Fig. 4.15.

250. Small fragment from outer edge of circular, pudding-shaped object with concave base; very smooth even surfaces. Perforation did not survive. Fabric B; fired. SF5702, context 5321, unphased layer of occupation deposit. Fig. 4.15.

Miscellaneous

251. Fragment of clay bar: rounded end of bar with circular cross-section 12 x 14 mm; only 15 mm length surviving. Smooth plano-convex surface, but with shallow groove impressed down one side. Fabric B; fired. SF4973, context 3101, unphased layer of occupation deposit. Fig. 4.15.

252. Tuyere: small fragment from the rim of an object with external diameter of 35-40 mm and internally 20-25 mm. It has a simple rounded rim with the wall thickening to 8 mm. There is a possible fingertip impression flattening one part of the rim, which is glassy and greyed on the lip and outer edge up to 9 mm from the rim edge. Fabric B; fired. SF6448, context 6103, unphased layer of occupation deposit.

253. Ball: a roughly spherical but irregular form with exterior surface even and curved, but with slightly flattened facets. Measures 25 x 28 mm wide. In the interior is a large void 18 x 12 mm, triangular in shape possibly made by a stone around which the clay ball had been moulded. SF6769, context 8085, unphased occupation deposit. Fig. 4.15.

254. Ball: irregular flattened ball, that appears to be deliberately moulded to this shape, rather than accidentally worn or broken; one side was smoother, bulbous and rounded in contrast to the more irregular and flatter side opposite. It measures 34 x 36 x 22 mm and weighs 19.3 g. One or two small stem (?grass) impressions. Fabric C; fired. SF7158, context 6250, fill of unphased post-hole 6251. Fig. 4.15.

255. Mould?: fragment with smooth convex outer surface with flattened facets round edge. The interior forms a smooth oval shape with a shallow depression running down its long axis slightly off-centre. Measures >25 mm long x 22 mm wide x 7 mm thick. Wt 3.1 g. Fabric B; fired. SF8258, context 5347, fill of unphased post-hole 5356. Fig. 4.15.

255a. Fire bar? Fragment of clay bar with triangular cross section 22 x 17 mm; length in excess of 26 mm, broken at both ends. Two flat smooth surfaces set at right angles to each other; the

third surface is smooth and plano-concave. The wider flat surface has two converging lines, 6 and 8 mm long, forming a V shape; this may have been a fragment of decoration. Wt 5 g. Fabric B. SF6829 context 6221.

The Industrial Waste

Mark H. Adams (with a contribution by David Dungworth)

Introduction

A total of 4292 fragments of industrial waste, weighing approximately 39.7 kg, was excavated at Irby. The material was examined under a binocular microscope with artificial illumination. Three broad categories of waste have been identified: slag, vitrified waste products, and mixtures of slag and vitrified materials. Each of these types of material can be further sub-divided on the basis of features such as morphology and density; these groups reflect different aspects of the metallurgy practised at Irby. Virtually all of the material was excavated from Period IV (2nd-4th century AD) contexts. Other than a concentration in Trench XXII, there appeared to be no significant spatial patterning to the distribution and it could not be directly associated with any of the excavated structures. All of the material occurred either in the fills of post-holes or re-deposited in occupation deposits.

Summary identification of industrial waste

A detailed catalogue of the industrial waste is provided as part of the excavation archive.

1. Slag. All of the Irby slag is dark grey in colour with a grey or greyish brown streak. Although it is not possible to be certain (see below) this indicates a fayalitic composition typical of slag of this period. Many of the pieces examined contained small white inclusions about 1 mm across which are probably quartz grains. The following types of slag have been recognised amongst the Irby material.

1.1 Hearth Bottoms. These are small cakes of slag, generally circular in plan with a diameter of about 60 mm ($\pm$ 20 mm) and with a plano-convex cross-section, the thickest part is 15-20 mm thick. In some cases they are sub-rectangular in plan. Although a few complete examples were examined, many are broken. In all cases, fragments of the hearth lining were observed to adhere to the base. This consisted of vitrified material (clay?) and heavily burnt/vitrified sandstone some of this was pitted and had a slightly powdery appearance, probably due to the slightly acidic soil conditions. Where evidence for fuel was present (impressions/inclusions) this consisted exclusively of charcoal fragments 5-10 mm across. Many of these pieces show locally vitrified zones on their upper surface. Varying degrees of porosity were observed in these cakes, presumably reflecting local conditions in the hearth. All of these slags are heavily stained with iron corrosion products, and although without further work (see below) it is not possible to make conclusive statements, the absence of other corrosion products makes it likely that these cakes of slag result from the smithing of iron, such as the manufacture of small tools, weapons, or nails, or alternatively the preparation of blooms of iron for working into artefacts.

1.2 Slag Runners. Eleven runners of slag were examined. These have a 'ropy' texture; none of them is larger than 30 mm long and consequently cannot be used as evidence for tapping of slag from the furnaces. They probably formed as a result of flow within the furnace.

1.3 Slag Droplets. Twenty-three droplets of slag were examined. These are too large to be classified as smithing debris (see below) and could result from a number of metallurgical processes.

1.4 Smithing Debris. A selected group of residues from wet sieving were scanned using a small magnet to recover hammer scale, slag droplets, spatter etc. Almost all of the samples scanned produced droplets of slag and small plates of hammer scale though quantities greater than 5 g per 10 litres were never recovered.

1.5 Slag Fragments. Approximately 180 fragments of slag were examined which were too incomplete to be assigned to the above categories; however, most of these appear to be fragments of hearth bottom or furnace bottom. Some of the broken surfaces show a distinctive variegated metallic lustre of the type commonly associated with the copper sulphide mineral bournite (Cu_2S). However, other minerals can exhibit this lustre and this cannot be used as definite evidence for copper metallurgy at Irby.

2. Vitrified Material. Approximately 1393 (8.93 kg) fragments of vitrified material were examined. This group of material is quite varied in character; it is typified by the presence of a glassy crust which ranges from pale bluish green to dark green to black in colour. In many cases the whole piece consists of this material; however, in others it seals a core of only partly vitrified or of fired clay, other pieces have a highly vesicular structure. The unvitrified clay ranged from mid to dark reddish brown in colour and many fragments had a purplish tinge. It is possible that in some cases chilled slag, or crucible slag, has been included within this group of material. All of the examples examined contain at least some quartz grains; many contain partly fused fragments of sandstone which appear to have been used in the construction of the structures from which much of this material derives. Most of this material is amorphous and cannot be classified further. However,

a few fragments can be identified as belonging to either furnaces or crucibles.

2.1 Hearth Walls. Fragments of hearth wall were identified on the basis of the presence of a thick, heavily vitrified crust over fired, orange clay. These are usually about 30 mm thick, some up to 40 mm; very few pieces larger than 50 mm across are present; however, of those examined all have flat surfaces indicating that the hearth from which they derive was of slab-sided construction rather than with curving walls. One fragment appears to preserve part of a hole in the furnace wall, possibly for the insertion of bellows.

2.2 Crucible Fragments. Twelve fragments of crucible or possible crucible were excavated from a range of contexts though most were found within the occupation deposits which occurred across the site. Although found in association with Romano-British pottery it is possible that some at least are either residual finds from earlier contexts or intrusive material from later phases. One fragment (Fig. 4.15, no 264, SF7360) was found within the fill of a post-hole, though this could not be related to any structures and contained no datable material.

Four of the fragments identified as crucible were non-diagnostic fragments of wall recognized purely on the basis of their fabric, which was similar to those of more complete vessels. All of the fragments were in a fine-grained fabric, some with occasional inclusions of grit, which in some areas has fired to a distinctive pale grey or purplish grey colour. Three of the fragments were sections of rim which exhibited a distinctive cherry red vitrification.

Five of the fragments were of sufficient size to allow an identification of the form. SF2945 Context 3088 is a fragment of conical crucible base (e.g. Tylecote 1986, fig. 50, 5, 9), whilst SF8110, SF8120 and SF8121 are likely to be fragments from the same shallow, bowl-shaped crucible. All of the rims from this vessel exhibited the same cherry red vitrification seen elsewhere and in addition SF8121 retained traces of metallic copper alloy. SF7360 is a large fragment of deep crucible with triangular mouth (e.g. Tylecote 1986, fig. 50, 9) in a fine-grained purplish grey fabric, in this case with small (*c.* 0.5 mm) inclusions of charcoal and some red stained vitrification around the rim.

In general where the form of the crucible is identifiable it is consistent with a date in the later Iron Age, Romano-British or post-Roman periods. Context 5321 was a late Roman/early medieval layer sealed by a cobbled floor, context 6279 an unphased post-hole (estimated date of 2nd to 4th century AD), 6672 was the primary fill of a 3rd to 4th century enclosure ditch, 3088 was a 2nd-3rd-century AD layer of occupation debris. All appear to have been in secondary contexts.

The crucible fragments were analysed using energy-dispersive X-ray fluorescence (EDXRF) by David Dungworth at the Ancient Monuments Laboratory. Copper, zinc, lead and tin were detected on all of them, confirming that they were used to melt copper alloys. Gold, silver and mercury were not detected.

It is not possible to offer any firm suggestions about the composition of the alloys being melted in the crucibles for a number of different reasons. The different elements present in copper alloys oxidise at different rates and have different vapour pressures. Zinc (or more properly zinc oxide) is detected in almost every crucible that has been used to melt copper alloys, even when the amount of zinc in the alloy is very low. On the other hand copper and tin are often detected at very low levels. The situation is further complicated by the possibility that the crucibles were used over a period of time to melt a range of different metals. It is striking therefore that zinc was detected at such low levels in three crucibles (SF8121, SF6672 and SF7360). In these three cases it is possible that a tin bronze was being melted rather than a brass or gunmetal.

Catalogue

256. Fragment of heavily vitrified clay, possibly a fragment of crucible. SF2215 context 3907.
257. Heavily vitrified fragment of crucible wall *c.* 2 mm thick. SF2804 context 3908.
258. Fragment of conical crucible base (cf. Tylecote 1986, fig. 50, 5, 9) in gritty purplish fabric. SF2945 context 3088.
259. Small fragment of crucible rim with cherry red vitrified surface, core fine-grained grey fabric. SF3488 context 4003.
260. Rim fragment with localised cherry red stained vitrification on upper surface in gritty purplish fabric. SF5733 context 5321.
261. Possible crucible fragment, perhaps a lug. Heavily vitrified. SF5798 context 3906.
262. Possible crucible fragment in fine grained grey fabric. SF5907 context 3908.
263. Rim fragment with localised cherry red stained vitrification on upper surface in gritty purplish fabric. SF6672 context 6121.
264. Large fragment of deep crucible with triangular mouth (e.g. Tylecote 1986, fig. 50, 9) in a fine grained purplish grey fabric with small (*c.* 0.5 mm) inclusions of charcoal and some red stained vitrification around the rim. SF7360 context 6279.
265. Large fragment of wall and rim from crucible with shallow, bowl shaped profile (e.g. Tylecote 1986, fig. 50, 2, 3, 4). Wall much thicker than other examples at *c.* 10 mm. Very fine grained, dark grey fabric, cherry red vitrification around rim. SF8110 context 5321.
266. Fragment of crucible rim similar to SF8110 (possibly same vessel) SF8120 context 5321.
267. Large fragment of crucible, possibly same vessel as SF8110 but with slightly more purple fabric. The inner surface is partly vitrified and retains small fragments of copper alloy. The rim is more intensely vitrified and is stained a dark cherry red colour. The outer surface is a pale buff colour and retains traces of the vessel's manufacture using fingers. SF8121 context 5321.

3. Mixed Slag and Vitrified Material. Thirty fragments were examined which appeared to be intimate mixtures of slag and vitrified material.

Conclusions

The range of industrial waste excavated at Irby suggests that a variety of metallurgical processes were being undertaken during the occupation of the site. Iron smithing seems to have formed the principal activity and most frequently occurring process; 123 definite fragments and a further 47 possible fragments of hearth bottom were identified. These quantities suggest either a single person working over a short period of time or that iron smithing was an intermittent activity taking place over a prolonged period of time (D. Dungworth, pers. comm.); unfortunately the stratigraphy does not allow these possibilities to be distinguished. Smithing took place in small bowl hearths, probably little more than shallow depressions scooped into the ground. The size of the slag cakes from this process indicates that the diameter of these hearths was a minimum of 40-50 mm and ranged up to at least 0.2 m. The industrial waste recovered from Trench XXII is much less fragmented than that from other trenches, indicating that metal working may have been concentrated in this part of the site. This is especially true of the hearth wall fragments and suggests that metallurgy may have been restricted to the southern part of the site. This suggestion is confirmed by the relatively low quantities of smithing waste (<5 g per 10 litre) recovered from sieved residues. Smithing was fuelled entirely by charcoal; coal does not appear to have been used (*pace* McDonnell 1991). Although no *in situ* hearth remains have been located, the industrial waste described above does allow some conclusions to be made. None of the hearths at Irby was designed to allow the removal of slag by tapping. The hearths were largely constructed of clay with crushed sandstone used as a filler. The form of some of the hearth wall fragments recovered indicates that the hearths were straight-walled. The fragments examined indicate that the walls were at least 30 mm thick though this should be treated as a minimum dimension as all of the pieces are extremely fragmentary.

The presence of crucible fragments on site, along with small fragments of lead and a piece of galena, suggest the working of other metals, principally lead casting, though copper working cannot be ruled out. Five mould fragments were found (see below, *Refractory Material*), four of which may be from the same mould. Although dated on the basis of its fabric to the mid Bronze Age, the object being cast could not be identified and the fragments were all found in late Roman contexts.

XRF analysis

A limited programme of XRF analysis was conducted on some samples of slag (details in site archive). The analyses were taken using the facilities of the Physics Department, University of Liverpool. The weathered surfaces of the samples were analysed in air. As a result, the effects of surface leaching on the analyses are uncertain; the analyses were restricted to elements heavier than aluminium. XRF analysis conducted in air is also of limited sensitivity (about 1%). A range of slag types were analysed (fragments of coarse and fine grained slag, hearth bottoms, furnace bottom) were present freshly broken surfaces were analysed.

All of the fragments analysed produced very strong peaks for iron; the minor peaks for antimony and lead are the result of background radiation. No calcium was detected; aluminium is too light to be detected by this method. Although the results of these analyses should be treated with a degree of caution for the reasons discussed above, a number of provisional conclusions can be made. First, the absence of other metals in significant quantities supports the view that these slags result from the working of iron. The absence of any detectable amounts of calcium is of interest as it indicates that the Irby slag is not fayalitic in composition and that lime was not used as a flux during the smelting/ smithing of iron at Irby.

The crucible fragments were analysed using EDXRF by D. Dungworth at the Ancient Monuments Laboratory. Copper, zinc, lead and tin were detected on all of them, confirming that they were used to melt copper alloys. Gold, silver and mercury were not detected.

SF	Context	Cu	Zn	Pb	Sn
2945	3008	D	W	W	W
6672	6121	W	D	D	S
7360	6279	S	D	D	S
8121	5321	W	D	W	S
8110	5321	S	S	W	W

Cu copper; Zn zinc; Pb lead; Sn tin
D - Detected, W - Weak, S - Strong

Table 4.22: Metals in crucibles detected by EDXRF

It is not possible to offer any firm suggestions about the composition of the alloys being melted in the crucibles for a number of different reasons. The different elements present in copper alloys oxidise at different rates and have different vapour pressures. Zinc (or more properly zinc oxide) is detected in almost every crucible that has been used to melt copper alloys, even when the amount of zinc in the alloy is very low. On the other hand copper and tin are often detected at very low levels. The situation is further complicated by the possibility that the crucibles were used over a period of time to melt a range of different metals. It is striking therefore that zinc was detected at such low levels in three crucibles (SF8121, 6672 and 7360). In these three cases it is possible that a tin bronze was being melted rather than a brass or gunmetal.

Context 5321 was a late Roman/early medieval layer sealed by a cobbled floor, context 6279 an unphased post-hole (estimated date 2nd to 4th century AD), context 6672 was the primary fill of a 3rd to 4th-century enclosure ditch, while context 3088 was a 2nd-3rd century AD layer of occupation debris. All appear to have been in secondary contexts.

Refractory Material

Elaine L. Morris

A total of five pieces (18 g) of refractory-type material was identified. These were examined by Dr Stuart Needham (British Museum) and his comments are included in the following report. The collection consists of four pieces of inner valve mould used in the production of prehistoric bronze working in some capacity. The fabrics of one mould fragment and the uncertain piece also were examined using petrological analysis to clarify the nature of the inclusions.

Fabrics

Two different fabrics were identified in this small group of refractory material. Fabric RFTY1 is a dense and finely textured fabric containing a sparse amount of both small quartz grains and igneous rock fragments. In contrast, fabric RFTY2 is a porous fabric containing an abundance of linear vesicles.

Petrological Report on the Refractory Material

David F. Williams

Fabric RFTY1; Thin Section ITS1, SF902, Context 649, Trench VI.
Soft, rough, sandy fabric with small sparse inclusions of a hard fine-textured dark coloured rock, mottled light buff outer surface and part core (Munsell 7.5YR 7/4) and very dark grey inner surface and part core (2.5Y N3/). Thin sectioning shows moderately frequent subangular quartz grains, generally below 0.50 mm in size, some shreds of mica and several fragments of a much weathered fine-grained igneous rock.

There seems at present no reason to suspect anything other than a fairly local origin for the Irby mould, the clay and/or temper deriving from the coulder clays of the district which contain a very wide range of much travelled igneous material (Wedd *et al.* 1923).

Fabric RFTY2; Thin Section ITS2, SF8195, Context 5341, Trench XXIX.
Soft, rough, very light weight extremely vesicular fabric, patch dark brown (10YR 5/3) to dark grey 7.5YR N/3) in colour. Thin sectioning confirms that the main component in the clay matrix is frequent elongate voids, representing organic material which was burnt

out during firing. In view of the high amount of organic material that must once have been present in the sherd, this was most probably deliberately added by the potter. Also present are some silt-sized quartz grains and a few clay pellets.

It is difficult to be certain of origins when dealing with such a common range of inclusions. One of the clays noted by Poole from Irby was described as fine and silty with no additional inclusions, possibly deriving from local marine deposits (see above, *Structural Daub and Fired Clay*). It is possible that this may have been used with the addition of organic material.

Forms and Functions

All of the pieces are very small and undiagnostic as to form; none displays evidence for the type of bronze object being made. Four of the pieces are extremely similar in fabric, firing conditions and thickness, and these may have derived from the same or possibly to valves from a mould. The significance of the fragments lies in the smoothed and unoxidised firing condition of the inner surfaces and the fabric. This fabric, RFTY1, is highly suitable for use as a refractory material, specifically as inner valve mould due to the presence of the fine and frequent temper which would have absorbed the thermal shock experienced during the use of the mould when receiving molten copper alloys. The unoxidised and smooth interior surface of the fragments indicates that this surface experienced a lack of oxygen during the heating process as would have been expected from a closed bivalve mould technique. The exterior surfaces are oxidised and unsmoothed.

The other piece is much thicker than those discussed above and has a very porous fabric which would have been less suitable for use as a prehistoric mould or crucible, but organic tempered fabrics were used during later periods to make moulds.

Discussion

The type of fabric used to make the four inner valve mould fragments found at Mill Hill Road, Irby is similar to the late Bronze Age moulds, crucibles and pottery recovered at the Breiddin hillfort, Powys where, also, a locally available medium grained, igneous rock (dolerite) had been identified in the fabrics (Howard 1991; Morris 1991; Musson 1991, 118-23; Tylecote and Biek 1991). The late Bronze Age moulds from Beeston Castle, Cheshire were quartz-tempered (Howard 1993) and unlike the pottery (Royle and Woodward 1993). Therefore with both quartz and igneous rock in the Mill Hill Road fabric, there is every reason to believe that these four pieces represent mid Bronze Age bronze working production at Irby using local clay resources for valve manufacture. The pieces are similar enough to each other in so many ways that there could be just one

or two valves represented, i.e. a single bronze-working event. The fifth fragment, which may have been used in bronze working or another industrial activity, is more likely to represent Roman activity due to the nature of the fabric if refractory, or could be simply fired clay of an undiagnostic function.

Catalogue of refractory type material

268. One piece, 2.4 g; fabric RFTY1; 6 mm thick; convex curvature; smoothed interior surface; unoxidised, dark grey interior and core; oxidised, orange exterior; SF56, Trench VIII, context 1003, Romano-British occupation deposit, Period V?

269. One piece, 1 g; fabric RFTY1; 6 mm thick; convex curvature; smoothed interior surface; unoxidised, dark grey interior and core; oxidised, orange exterior; SF407, Trench VI, context 629, Romano-British occupation deposit, Period V?

270. Two pieces, 4.3 g; fabric RFTY1; 6-9 mm thick; convex curvature; smoothed interior surface; unoxidised, dark grey interiors and cores; oxidised, orange exterior; SF902, Trench VI, context 649, Romano-British occupation deposit, Period V?

271. One piece, 6.1 g; fabric RFTY1; 10 mm thick; convex curvature; smoothed interior surface; unoxidised, dark grey interior and core; oxidised, orange exterior; SF3148, Trench XX, context 3307, unphased.

272. One piece, 4.1 g; fabric RFTY2; 9-11 mm thick; one flattened or cut edge similar to a rim on a convex curvature profile; smoothed interior surface; unoxidised, dark grey-black interior and core; oxidised, orange exterior; SF8195, Trench XXIX, context 5341, Romano-British occupation deposit, Period V?

Glass Objects and Vessels

H. E. M. Cool (report submitted 1998)

Personal Ornaments - Beads

The most interesting bead in this small assemblage is the large polychrome wave-decorated bead (no. 273; Plate XXI, Fig. 4.16). Large wave-decorated beads are not uncommon finds on Roman sites but most commonly they are made of deep blue glass with an opaque white wave pattern covering the whole depth of the bead (Guido 1978, 63, Group 5A). The Irby bead belongs to the category that Guido (1978, 64) gathered together to form her Group 5C, noting that they could not 'be regarded as other than a miscellaneous collection, each bead from which may be used for comparative purposes with others found in the future, so that one day classes may be distinguished amongst them'. No. 273 adds to this miscellany as I know of no other precisely similar bead. On the basis of the blue/green colour, one may hazard the suggestion that it was most likely to have been made during the later 1st to 3rd centuries as it would have been during this period that blue/green glass would have been most commonly available as cullet and could have been used by the bead makers.

The other glass beads are more common forms. The hexagonal green bead (no. 274) is an example of a form in use throughout the Roman period (Guido 1978, 96, fig. 37 no. 9), while long square-sectioned beads like no. 275 are most common during the late Roman period (Guido 1978, 96, fig. 37 no. 6). It is possible that the small globular bead (no. 276) is of Roman date, but such small globular beads have a very long life and are not intrinsically datable.

273. Annular bead. Blue/green translucent glass with translucent mid-blue decoration; strain-cracked. Slightly keeled D-sectioned. Two zig-zag trails now appearing as two series of isolated Vs. Exterior and interior of perforation heavily worn. Diameter 33 mm, perforation diameter 17 mm, thickness 12 mm. SF6603; Trench XIX context 3227, ?Roman occupation deposit. Plate XXI.

274. Long hexagonal bead. Opaque dark green. Length 5.5 mm, perforation diameter 2 mm, section 5 mm. SF1849; context 3616. Period IV (Roman?) occupation deposit.

275. Long square-sectioned bead. Translucent dark blue glass; fragment only. Present length 6 mm, thickness 3 mm. SF887; VI context 658; fill of Ditch 3, Period IV.

276. Globular bead. Opaque green glass. Length 3 mm, diameter 4 mm, perforation diameter 1 mm. SF1421; XIX context 3057, layer associated with Structure 19, Period VI.

Household items - Vessels

The only Roman vessel form that can be identified with any certainty is the blue/green prismatic bottle (Cool and Price 1995, 179) represented here by the body fragments nos 279-281. The form was very common during the later 1st to early to mid 3rd century, and it is not uncommon for it to be the only type of glass vessel recognised on rural sites occupied during that time.

A colourless vessel is represented by a body fragment from a Period IV context (no. 278). It probably comes from a piece of tableware of 2nd to 3rd-century date. A blue/green bowl or jar may be represented by the small rim fragment (no. 277) but the shade of blue/green glass

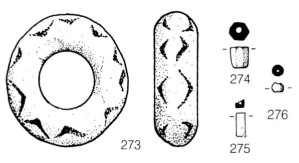

Fig. 4.16: 273-276. Glass beads. Scale 1:1

it is made of is not typical of Roman glass. This together with its discovery at the interface of the ploughsoil suggests it may be a relatively modern piece.

277. Jar or bowl rim? Blue/green glass. Out-turned rim with fire-rounded edge. Dimensions 15 x 10 mm, wall thickness 2 mm. SF310; VI context 623; ploughsoil interface.

278. Body fragment. Colourless glass. Dimensions 5 x 4 mm. SF10299; VIII context 1110; sample 2073; context 1110. Base of ploughsoil.

279. Prismatic bottle. Blue/green heavily strain-cracked fragment from flat side. SF8352; context 22; fill of Ditch 1 Period IV.

280. Prismatic bottle. Blue/green fragment from flat side. SF6685, XXXVI context 6215, unphased layer, Romano-British?

281. Prismatic bottle. Blue/green heavily strain-cracked chips from flat side. SF8550, XLII context 7014, unphased layer, Romano-British?

Roman Coins

Simon C. Bean

Discussion

The site yielded six Roman coins and a fragment of a probable seventh. Although this number is small compared to Roman sites elsewhere in Britain, Irby is one of the more productive sites in Merseyside. The Roman coins fall into four groups: the radiate of Tetricus, the *nummi* of Constantine, the Constantinopolis coin, and the irregular Falling Horseman coin.

The radiate, Constantinopolis and Falling Horseman coins belong to each of the three periods of highest coin loss on Roman British sites (e.g. Reece 1987, 19, 77, table 5.1, fig. 5.2; 1991). This increased loss should not be equated to increased economic activity. It is clear that in these periods coinage ceased to be a relatively high value scarce commodity and became a plentiful small change, leading to an increased likelihood of loss and non-recovery. The three *nummi* of Constantine form a neat group, all struck between AD 316-20. They seem over-represented and do not belong to a period of particularly high coin loss on other sites. One might suggest a relative influx of coinage to Irby at the time.

Plate XXI: 273. Glass bead

They were found sufficiently far apart to rule out the possibility of a disturbed hoard.

Most of the coins are little worn (although most have suffered post-depositional damage) suggesting that they were lost reasonably soon after issue. A few radiates are known from 4th-century contexts and hoards in Britain (Reece 1987, 21), but it seems unlikely that many persisted long after Diocletian's monetary reforms of AD 294 (enacted in Britain in AD 296 following the recovery of the province from Allectus). The *nummi* of Constantine were probably deposited within a decade of their issue, although they were clearly still regarded as currency in the mid 330s (e.g. Usk hoard D: Boon and Halsall 1982, 17-18). The smaller debased CONSTANTINOPOLIS and Falling Horseman coins may have survived longer amongst the wash of inferior, often irregular, later 4th-century small copper-alloy coinage.

Catalogue of Coins

282. Tetricus I. Radiate. Mint I or II. Cf. Cunetio 2617 (AD 271-274). Obv. Legend largely lost. Radiate and draped bust of Tetricus right. Rev. Legend largely lost. Salus standing left, feeding snake rising from altar from patera in right hand, holding rudder in left. Wt 1.50 g (edge damaged), die axis 0°; SF8255, context 5345, unphased occupation layer.
283. Constantine I, London mint. *Nummus*. RIC VII 89 (AD 316-17). Obv. IMP CONSTANTINVS P AVG Laureate and cuirassed bust left. Rev. SOLI INVIC-TO COMITI T|F/PLN Sol standing left, right hand raised and globe in left. Wt 2.38 g die axis 200°; SF6042, context 3150, unphased occupation layer.
284. Constantine I. Mint mark obscured. *Nummus*. Cf. RIC (London) VII 158 etc. (AD 318-20). Obv. ...]ONSTA[.... Bust with high crested helmet left, cuirassed, spear over right shoulder. Rev. [VICTORIAE]LAETAEPR [INCPERP] Two Victories standing holding ?shield over altar. Wt 1.41 g (chipped), die axis 0°; SF3997, context 1038, unphased occupation layer.
285. Constantine I, Trier mint. *Nummus*. RIC VII 266 (AD 320). Obv. ...]NST-[ANTI]NVS NC Bust of Constantine right wearing crested helmet and cuirass. Rev. VIR[...]-EXERCIT PTR Banner inscribed VOT/XX with seated captive either side. Wt 0.94 g (chipped), die axis 180°; SF7841, context 9560, unphased occupation layer.
286. House of Constantine. Trier mint. *Nummus* cf. RIC VIII 67 (AD 337-40). Obv. CONSTANTINOPOLIS Helmeted and cuirassed bust of Constantine left. Rev. TRS• Victory standing left with captive to left and shield to right. Wt 1.52 g, die axis 180°; SF7991, context 9603, F5, fill of medieval or later post-hole.
287. Irregular mint. After AD 353. Obv. Pearl diademed and draped bust right. Traces of legend around, ?letter A at base of diadem. Rev. Soldier spearing a barbarian, falling from horse. Traces of legend around. Wt 1.14 g, die axis 60°; SF5237, context 3055, Structure 19, Period VI.
288. Uncertain AE fragment, probably of post-radiate 3rd or 4th-century coinage. Wt 0.27 g; SF6406, context 3062, unphased occupation layer, probably related to S19.

The Metal Objects

H. E. M. Cool

Introduction

The following report catalogues all of the metalwork recovered during the excavations at Irby with the exception of the material from the ploughsoil and modern contexts. The material excluded consists of either undiagnostic fragments or objects that are obviously modern. The material catalogued here could all be of Roman date, with the exception of the probable La Tène II/III brooch, though it is only occasionally possible to suggest a closer date within the Roman period for individual items. The report was originally written in 1998 and remains essentially unchanged apart from the case of no. 306 whose identification has been revised in 2010.

The metalwork is catalogued according to likely function, and an overview of the assemblage is presented at the end of this section.

Personal Ornaments

The only metal items associated with dress and personal ornamentation identifiable with any certainty are the iron brooch (no. 289) and the hobnails (nos 290-293). Given the very small part of the brooch extant, a precise identification cannot be made but it clearly belongs in the La Tène II/III tradition. It is not possible to identify which of the many variants it belongs to. The bow is broken before it emerges from the chord and only the spring and pin are present. The discovery of no. 289 in the fill of a Period II Phase 3 post-hole linked with strong radiocarbon evidence indicates for an Iron Age date for the brooch. The discovery of the hobnails indicates that people wearing nailed shoes were present on the site during Phases III to IV. Originally such shoes were the preserve of soldiers, but by the later 3rd century they were widespread amongst the civilian population (Rhodes 1980, 113).

Two further personal ornaments may be represented by nos 294 and 295. These might both come from 4th-century light bangles (Cool 1993, 89). The edge nicks seen on no. 294 are reminiscent of those used to produce zig-zag decoration which is a common decorative scheme used on such bracelets. The resemblance could, however, be fortuitous and the 'decorative' scallops and nicks might be indicative of nothing more than rough working with the fragment possibly being some form of off-cut.

289. Brooch; La Tène II/III tradition. Iron. Spring of four turns with internal chord, and part of pin; bow missing. Length 31 mm. SF7302; XIX context 8227; Period II Phase P4, Structure 32.
290. Hobnail? Iron. Group of three corroded together. SF3617;

XXI context 3672; Period IV (Roman?) occupation deposit.

291. Hobnail. Iron. Complete with pyramidal head. Length 20 mm. SF5822; XXI context 3668; Structure 8; Period V.

292. Hobnail. Iron. Group of two corroded together. SF59; context 22; fill of Ditch 1, Period IV.

293. Hobnail? Iron. Head and short part of shank. Length 8 mm. SF50; context 608; fill of unphased ?Romano-British post-hole.

294. Bracelet? Copper alloy. Rectangular-sectioned hoop, widest to wrist; upper surface has scalloped upper surface caused by hammering; edges damaged and retain file marks and a few ?deliberate edge nicks. Diameter *c.* 40 mm, length 42 mm, section 4 x 2 mm. SF5658; context 5320, base of ploughsoil.

295. Bracelet. Copper alloy. Hoop damaged and now circular-sectioned; traces of vertical grooves over exterior; both ends broken. Diameter *c.* 45 mm, section 2 mm, length 43 mm. SF1417; context 3054; layer associated with Structure 18, Period VI.

Craft and Industry

The site has produced an interesting range of tools connected with craft and industry. The battered head of no. 296 suggests it was a smith's punch of the type designed to be held in a wire holder (Manning 1985, 9). The chisel-edged no. 297 may be a second example despite the head showing less obvious evidence of battering.

Carpentry is represented by several tools. A large part of a saw blade (no. 298) was recovered from the filling of a hollow in the natural. It has the typical parallel-sided blade seen on both hand and bow saws in antiquity (Manning 1985, 19). Where the terminal is preserved, these saws are usually assigned to one of the two types on the basis of the number of rivets that survive. The handle of a hand saw needs two rivets to stop the blade pivoting, whereas a bow saw blade can be held securely by a single rivet at either end. No. 298 has two rivets and could thus be a hand saw similar to one recovered from Battlesbury Camp, Wiltshire (Cunnington and Goddard 1934, 92 no. 7, pl. XXIVc). The direction of the wood grain, parallel to the blade edges would also seem most likely for the handle of a hand saw which would extend back from the blade. In a bow saw the handle joins the blade at an angle, and the grain might be expected to reflect this. The length of the blade preserved, however, strongly suggests that it came from a bow saw as it is difficult to see how a long, relatively narrow blade such as this could function efficiently as a hand saw.

Other carpentry tools include the two drill bits (nos 299 and 300) and a chisel (no. 301). No. 299 has the typical broken and twisted stem often seen on these drill bits. The stem is a point of weakness when the drill has jammed in the wood and the carpenter is attempting to remove it (Manning 1985, 27). The chisel is not a typical Roman form but is of the simpler form that Manning (1985, 24 nos B43-4) has suggested reflects an

earlier Iron Age date. No. 301 comes from a Period II/III context and is thus to be placed early in the Roman sequence at Irby, and perhaps reflects a continuation of native traditions into that period.

It is interesting to note that one of the lead spindle whorls (no. 302) came from a context of the same phase as it shows that alongside conservatism in some aspects of the material culture, the inhabitants were prepared to accept new forms of tools. The early Roman exploitation of the lead ores of the Mendips and north Wales for their silver content (Jones and Mattingly 1990, 184) would have greatly increased the amount of lead available for use. Though much of it would have been used in plumbing, its weight and ease of working made it an ideal medium for spindle whorls and it is clear that it was rapidly adopted for this use. Lead spindle whorls have been recovered from a Flavian context at Hayton, East Yorkshire (Johnson 1978, 82, no. 1, fig. 15.10) and in a late Flavian/Hadrianic context at Castleford, West Yorkshire (Mould 1998, 121, no. 2, fig. 43). The second lead spindle whorl from Irby (no. 303) could be of post-Roman date because it was recovered from a Period VI context and lead whorls continued to be used in the medieval period (Woodland 1990, 225, nos 192-6). The diameter of the perforation though suggests that it may well be Roman as it would have been appropriate for a spindle of that date, whereas medieval spindles tended to be thicker (Rogers 1997).

Leather working might be represented by no. 304. It is not one of the classic Roman awl shapes (Manning 1985, fig. 9), but it is definitely tapering to a sharp point and would have been ideal for piercing holes in leather. There are traces of minerally preserved leather on the handle and a leather covering would have provided a comfortable padding while it was in use. The possible needle fragment (no. 305) could have been used in either textile or leather working but as it lacks the upper end where the eye would have been, its identification as a needle is not secure.

The final tool (no. 306) was identified in 1998 when this report was originally written as the end of a modelling tool (Manning 1985, 31). Originally it was suggested that these were rare outside of London (*ibid*), but even by 1998 it was clear that an increasing number of them were being found elsewhere. Examples were noted on a variety of sites including small towns such as Baldock (Manning and Scott 1986, 150, no. 500 fig. 65), rural religious sites such as Nettleton (Wedlake 1982, 231, no. 24, fig. 101.77), military sites such as Carlisle (Padley 1991, 140, no. 371) and Kingsholm (Scott 1985, 36, no. 3, fig. 14), and other major urban centres such as Cirencester (Viner 1986, 112, no. 104, fig. 82) and Canterbury (Blockley *et al.* 1995, 1069, no. 684, fig. 463). Since the report was written it has been realised that they were not a multi-purpose tool but formed part of writing sets acting as a spatula to smooth the wax on

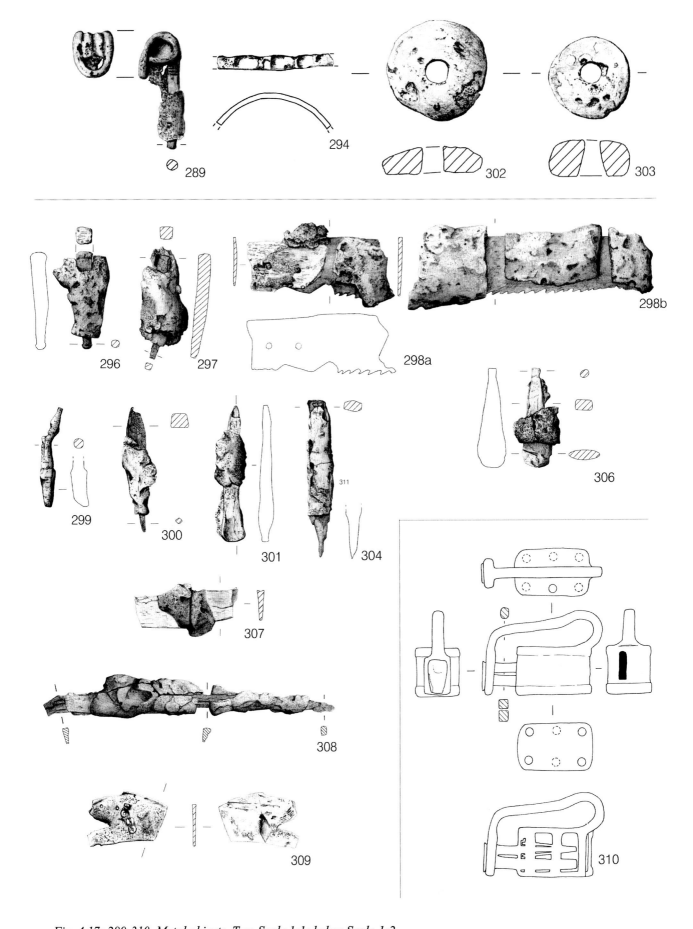

Fig. 4.17: 289-310. Metal objects. Top: Scale 1:1; below Scale 1:2

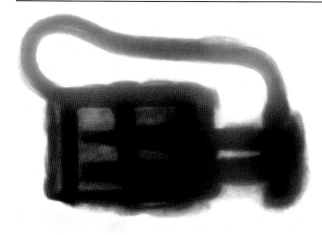

Plate XXII: 310 Iron padlock, X-ray

wax writing tablets (Crummy 2002). Table 4.26 has been adjusted to take this re-identification into account.

296. Punch? Square-sectioned bar tapering to burred square tip; head battered. Length 51 mm, maximum section 9 mm. SF8573; XLII context 7024; Romano-British occupation deposit.
297. Punch? Square-sectioned bar tapering to chisel edge. Slightly curved surface to head burred to one side. Length 56 mm, head section 7 x 6 mm. SF6199; XXI context 4660; Period IV, Structure 9.
298. Saw blade. Iron. Parallel-sided blade in 7 fragments retaining one terminal. Terminal has deliberate V-shaped notch separating toothed edge from area with handle and is damaged along lower edge and broken at back. Two rivets to secure handle remain; wooden handle now preserved as minerally preserved impressions with wood grain parallel to blade edge. Wood impressions stop in straight line above upper point of V-shaped notch. Raked toothed edge, teeth not set, worn and damaged in places. Width 30 mm, current length of blade 312 mm, 3 teeth per 10 mm. SF6273; XIX context 3183; Romano-British occupation deposit. (NB only terminal fragment and longest extant fragment of blade illustrated).
299. Drill bit. Square-sectioned broken and twisted stem; pyramidal head with broken tip. Length 53 mm, max. head section 9 x 8 mm. SF8017; XLI context 9626; Period IV, Structure 15.
300. Drill bit. Slender stem; pyramidal head with broken tip. Length 64 mm; maximum head width 10 mm. SF8560; XLII context 7015, Romano-British occupation deposit?
301. Chisel. Iron. Rectangular-sectioned bar tapering to point at one end and expanding to damaged blunt chisel end at other. Length 73 mm; maximum width 14 mm. SF7041; XIX context 8021; layer associated with Period II/III.
302. Spindle whorl. Lead alloy. Flat plano-convex whorl with central straight-sided perforation. Diameter 26 mm, diameter of perforation 6 mm, maximum thickness 7 mm, weight (cleaned) 25.77g. SF7819; XXXVI context 6187; layer associated with Period III/II.
303. Spindle whorl. Lead alloy. Off-centre perforation positioned towards thickest edge; perforation tapering. Diameter 21 mm, maximum diameter of perforation 7 mm, maximum thickness 9 mm. Weight (cleaned) 21.64 g. SF6591; XIX context 3234; Period VI, Structure 20.
304. Awl? Iron. Rectangular-sectioned bar; broken at one end and tapering with concave-side to point, other side of point damaged. Traces of ?mineralised leather on shank. Length 84 mm; section 12 x 6 mm. SF462; VIII context 1012;

Romano-British occupation deposit.
305. Needle? Iron. Narrow bar tapering to point at one end and broken at other. Length 40 mm. SF1520; context 3054; Period VI, Structure 18.
306. Wax spatula. Iron. Oval-sectioned broken shank expanding to triangular blade with slightly curved edge. Length 55 mm, shank section 5 x 4 mm, width of blade 17 mm. SF68; context 22; Fill of Ditch 1 Period IV.

Bladed tools

Two blade fragments were recovered (nos 307-308) but both are fragmentary and poorly preserved and neither can be identified with any certainty. No. 307 seems likely to have come from a knife. No. 308 does not retain the full cross-section of the blade but does show a ridge along the back. This suggests that the fragment may have come from a scythe as such a strengthening rim is characteristic on both the types of scythes in use in Roman Britain (Manning 1985, 49-50).

The fragment no. 309 has a triangular cross-section that would be appropriate to a blade and so has been catalogued in this section but there are problems with this identification. The curving row of bronze rivets is not a normal feature of Roman knife blades, nor would a knife be expected to have the deliberately formed V-shaped notch at one end. It is possible that the blade-like cross-section is fortuitous and that this is a decorative mount. The reverse of the fragment has the impression of wood preserved in the corrosion products and it may be that no. 309 was a box or chest fitting.

307. Blade? Iron. Fragment with back and (?) edge parallel, Fragment laminated but originally probably did have triangular section and edge. Length 56 mm, width 16 mm. SF5385; XXIX context 5310; Base of ploughsoil.
308. Blade? Iron. Back of blade with right-angled triangle section with ridge on one face close to back. Both ends and blade edge broken; one end square-sectioned. Now slightly twisted and extant surfaces (where cleaned) heavily pitted. Length 315 mm, width of back 9 mm. SF4019, VIII context 1038; Romano-British occupation deposit.
309. Blade? Iron and bronze. Fragment of iron blade with curved back and straight edge; both ends broken. Deliberate 'V'-shaped notch with bevelled edges closest to edge at widest end. Curving row of 6 bronze rivets in front of notch represented as powdery corrosion products. Three rivets nearest edge have large circular heads, other three are either smaller or now only represented by circular-sectioned shanks, the rectangular shank of a seventh rivet remains close to, and in front of, third large rivet. Extensive traces of mineralised wood on reverse. Length 40 mm, maximum width 26 mm. SF6924; XIX context 8069; Period IV Structure 9.

Fasteners and fittings

The most spectacular of the metal finds from Irby is the complete barb-spring padlock no. 310. This is an example of a Manning (1985, 96) Type 2 padlock with a looped hasp. In his discussion of the padlock cases and bolts of this type in the British Museum, Professor Manning quotes examples from the Hadrianic hoard at Brampton, the 4th-century hoard at Great Chesterford, Essex and a 3rd-century context at *Verulamium*. Thus the form was clearly current for much of the Roman period, but there are hints that it may have been most popular in Roman Britain during the late Roman period. Certainly where the distinctive lock bolts of this type have been found in dated contexts, they tend to be late Roman. Fourth-century examples may be noted at Barnsley Park, Gloucestershire (Webster and Smith 1982, 108, no. 41, fig. 26), Gadebridge Park, Herts (Manning 1974, 165, no. 381, fig. 70), Nettleton (Wedlake 1982, 228, no. 9, fig. 96.7) and Shakenoak (Brodribb *et al.* 1973, 118 no. 354, fig. 56). The bolt on no. 310 has two spines with the barbs at right angles to each other like the example from Rushall Down, Wiltshire (Cunnington and Goddard 1934, 237, no. 9, pl. LXXIX), and so the padlock would have needed a key with two holes like one from Barnsley Park, Glos. (Webster and Smith 1982, 109, no. 65, fig. 28).

Complete padlocks such as this are rare as they are too large for casual loss to be easy, and so it is not surprising that the best parallel for the Irby padlock came from the hoard at Great Chesterford (Neville 1856, 9, pl. 2 no. 21; Thompson 1994, illustration 81). The component parts consisting of the padlock case, the lock bolt and above all the distinctive keys are, however, quite common finds indicating a widespread concern for security. What they were securing cannot normally be identified, but it is worth noting that both the Sombernon-type and Bavay-type of late Roman slave shackles (Thompson 1994, 117-8, illustrations 76-82) were locked by padlocks of the Irby type.

The other items in this section are more miscellaneous. The cast copper alloy fragment no. 311 is too damaged for identification to be made other than to note it was clearly designed to have another component fitted into the slot. There are two studs (nos 312-313) and an iron plate that had been secured, perhaps to a box or chest, by a nail (no. 320). All of these could be of Roman date, but there is greater uncertainty over the date of the six copper-alloy nails and roves (nos 314-319). They were all found in Trench XXVIII and are so similar that it seems likely they were all originally part of the fittings of the same object. The condition of the metal is very good, which is unusual for the metalwork found securely stratified in Roman contexts on this site. Small functional nails such as this are not intrinsically datable, but the state of preservation suggests these are relatively modern. No. 314, however, was found in a Roman occupation context, so there is a slight possibility that they might all be of Roman date.

310. Barb-spring padlock. Iron; complete. Rectangular padlock case with rounded corners made from three sheets of iron; sheets forming top and bottom bending over at edges to enclose sheet forming sides and ends;

the whole held together by six bars visible on exterior as rivet heads and on interior in X-radiograph as three bars on each side. Upper sheet not curved over sides at key-hole end, and appears to be formed from beaten out end of curved, looped hasp as no evidence of a welded join between hasp and top of case can be detected on object or in X-radiograph. Bolt *in situ* with plug-shaped end lodged in loop of hasp and two spines entering case. X-radiograph suggests each spine has two barbs, that at top with barbs to top and bottom, while that at base with barbs to side. Large vertical key slot in casing at rear. Dimensions of casing 78 x 49 x 46 mm, length of hasp 125 mm, section of plug-end 37 x 22 mm. SF3995; context 1038; Romano-British occupation deposit (3rd-4th century AD?).

311. Binding? Copper alloy; much corroded and original surfaces generally missing. Curved block with D-section either side of central slot; slight channel around outer edge. Length 30 mm, depth 10 mm, thickness 9 mm. SF8034; 9560; context 954; occupation deposit Period II/III.

312. Stud. Copper alloy. Oval knob head with short tapering shank. Length 12mm, section 7 x 5 mm. SF1644; XIX 3060; context 568. Period VI, Structure 18.

313. Stud? Iron. Possible domed head with bent shank. Length *c.* 20 mm. SF6502; XXVII context 6408; cut feature associated with Structure 20, Phase VI.

314. Nail and rove. Copper alloy. Square-sectioned shank with expanded flat-topped head; shank bent to one side at tip and capped with slightly conical rove. Length 21 mm, head diameter 7 mm, rove diameter 11 mm. SF6368, context 6613; Romano-British occupation deposit.

No	SF no.	Context	Length	Head diameter	Rove diam
315	9548	6650	33	6	11
316	9548	6650	26	7	11
317	9548	6650	23	7	12
318	9548	6650	21	7	11
319	9104	6600	22	7	11

Table 4.23: 315-319.Copper-alloy nails and roves (descriptions as no. 314 above)

320. Nail and plate. Iron. Squared plate, now bent in two with one corner broken and missing. Short flat-headed nail perforating sheet in one corner. Length of plate 38 mm, length of nail 28 mm. SF98; context 22; Fill of Ditch 1, Period IV

Structural

The only structural finds that were recovered were iron nails. Those that are complete belong to the shorter end of the Roman nail range (Manning 1985, 134), though the size of the head of no. 333 suggests it came from a more substantial example.

321-365. Eight complete iron nails and 43 fragments from nails.

No.	SF	Per-iod	Struct-ure	Con-text	Comment	Length (where com-plete)
321	8183	II/III	Layer	9123	Shank fragment	-
322	6849	II/III	Layer	8021	Tip only	-
323	3545	II/III	Layer	3672	Shank fragment	-
324	7924	II/III	Layer	9560	Complete	50
325	8061	II/III	Layer	9596	Shank fragment	-
326	3233	II/III	Layer	3666	Head only	-
327	4208	IV	S7	1112	Tip missing	26
328	6496	IV	S9	3206	Head and shank fragment	-
329	7652		Layer	9012	Head and shank fragment	-
330	3526	V	S8	3718	Shank fragment	-
331	70	IV	D1	22	Complete	45
332	72B	IV	D1	22	Complete	82
333	34	IV	D1	22	Head and shank fragment	Head diam. 20mm
334	39	IV	D1	22	Shank fragment	-
335	65	IV	D1	22	Shank fragment	-
336	67	IV	D1	22	Shank fragment	-
337	71A	IV	D1	22	2 shank fragments	-
338	'in daub'	IV	D1	22	3 shank fragments	-
339	69	IV	D1	22	Shank fragment	-
340	1795	VI	S19?	3057	Shank fragment	-
341	10490	VI	S19?	3061	Shank fragment	-
342	5111	VI	S19	3055	Shank fragment	-
343	7740	-		9004	Tip missing	48
344	1472	-	-	1038	Shank	-
345	1473	-	-	1038	Head	-
346	3242	-	-	3307	Complete	51
347	2320	-	-	3307	Head and shank fragment	-
348	2981	-	-	3307	Shank fragment	-
349	876	-	-	1229	Shank fragment	-
350	6041	-	-	3150	Shank fragment	-
351	6079	-	-	3150	Tip only	-
352	6145	-	-	3150	Shank fragment	-
353	6150	-	-	3150	Tip missing	68
354	6786	-	-	8049	Complete	85
355	5884	-	-	3102	Shank	-
356	10310	-	-	3102	Head	-
357	4638	-	-	3101	Shank fragment	-
358	4669	-	-	3101	Shank fragment	-
359	4713	-	-	3765	Head and shank fragment	-
360	5517	-	-	4613	Head	-
361	2155	-	-	3907	Shank fragment	-
362	8234	-	-	5359	Shank fragment	-
363	5753	-	-	5321	Head and shank fragment	-
364	7009	-	-	6225	Shank fragment	-
365	8493	-	-	7200	Head	-

Table 4.24: Nos 321-365 Nails

Miscellaneous

Amongst the other miscellaneous items of metalwork only nos 366-368 call for any comment. No. 366 resembles one half of a drop hinge (Manning 1985, fig. 31, no. 2), though some bucket mounts also share this shape, see for example one from Gorhambury (Neal *et al.* 1990, 146, no. 545). The space within the loop though would be small for both these functions, and it might have had quite another purpose. A very similar item was recovered from Nettleton in a 3rd to 4th-century context (Wedlake 1982, 225, no. 14, fig. 96). No. 367 could also have come from a drop hinge or bucket mount. No. 368 is a classic example of the benefits of X-radiography of ironwork. As found it resembled an iron nail, but the X-radiograph revealed the complex spiral structure. It may have been the binding around a shaft, either to act as a ferrule or to prevent the shaft splitting because it had a tang inserted in it. It was clearly carefully made, and continued beyond the currently extant length.

366. Loop hinge or bucket mount. Iron. Rectangular-sectioned strap tapering to one end and bent over to form small closed loop; other end broken across perforation. Length 50 mm; strap section 16 x 6 mm. SF7949; XXXVI context 6189; occupation layer Period II/III.
367. Hinge or bucket mount? Iron. Rectangular sheet with square perforation towards one end. Length 40 mm, width 28 mm, thickness 5 mm, perforation diameter 7 mm. SF8744; XLII context 7043; Romano-British occupation deposit.

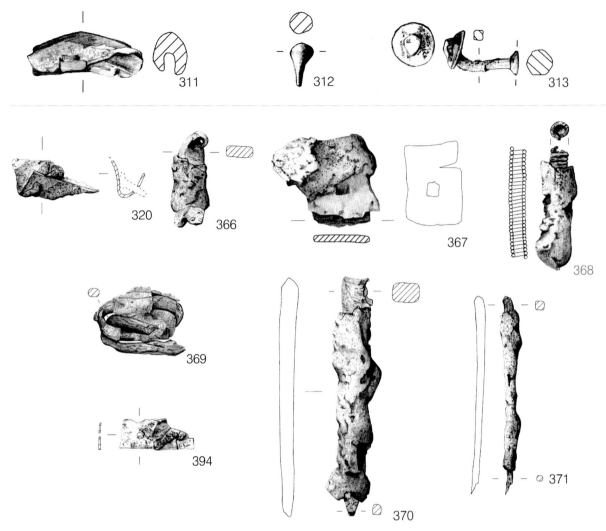

Fig. 4.18: 311-371. Metal objects. 311-313. Scale 1:1; 320-371. Scale 1:2

368. Spiral fitting. Iron. Hollow cylinder formed of thin iron rod made into spiral of 30 turns; both ends broken. Length 60 mm, diameter 9 mm, section of ?tube 2 mm. SF8463; XLIII context 7200; Romano-British occupation deposit

369. Chain. Iron. Two oval links. Length of link 49. SF9440; XXIX context 5310; Base of ploughsoil.

370. Spike. Iron. Rectangular-sectioned bar tapering to point; head damaged by corrosion but apparently ridged along long axis of section. Length 123 mm, max. section 14 x 10.5 mm. SF7635; XL context 9012; Romano-British occupation deposit.

371. Spike. Iron. Square-sectioned bar tapering to broken probably sharp point, broken head. Length 104 mm, max. section 4.5 mm. SF8771; XLII context 7043; Romano-British occupation deposit.

372. Spike or nail shank. Square section bar tapering to point; head broken. Length 75 mm, section 7.5 mm. SF4005; XXI context 3942. Unphased stakehole.

373. Bar. Copper alloy. 'D'-sectioned with both ends broken. Length 24 mm, section 5 x 3 mm. SF6251; context 3165; interface of occupation deposits with natural sands.

374. Block. Iron. Rectangular block tapering to one end; both ends broken. Length 83 mm, maximum section 43 x 23 mm. SF5840; XIX context 3096; Romano-British occupation deposit.

375. Sheet fragment, curved. Copper alloy. Dimensions 8 x 7 mm, thickness 1 mm. SF7944; context 9560; unphased

occupation deposit.

376. Sheet fragment. Copper alloy. Dimensions 12 x 11 mm, thickness 1.5 mm. SF7653; context 9012; occupation deposit.

377. Sheet fragment. Copper alloy. Dimensions 5 x 3 mm. SF8238; context 5345; occupation deposit associated with Structure 18, Phase VI.

378. Sheet fragment; folded. Lead alloy. Dimensions 39 x 21 mm. SF7947; LI context 9560; unphased occupation deposit.

379. Sheet offcut. Lead alloy. Run-off to one side and sharp edge to other where sheet has been removed. Dimensions Length 51 x 36 mm. SF6269; XIX context 3175; Post-hole associated with Structure 19, Phase VI.

380. Sheet offcut. Lead alloy. Dimensions 16 x 5 mm. SF9629; XXI context 5021; Modern.

381. Run-off fragment. Lead alloy. Length 15 mm. SF5441; XXI context 4612; Romano-British occupation deposit.

382. Run-off fragment. Lead alloy. Length 15 mm. SF258; context 1009; Romano-British occupation deposit.

383. Run-off fragment. Lead alloy. Length 34 mm. SF7824; XL context 9033; fill of oven? Feature 2, Period IV.

384. Run-off fragment. Lead alloy. Length 17 mm. SF3490; XXIII context 4003; Period VI Structure 18.

385. Run-off fragment. Lead alloy. Length 50 mm. SF3260; XIX context 3062; Romano-British occupation deposit

386. Block. Iron. Rectangular block tapering to one end;

both ends broken. Length 83 mm, maximum section 43 x 23 mm. SF5840; XIX context 3096; Romano-British occupation deposit.

387. Bar. Iron. Bent narrow square-sectioned rod tapering to one end; both ends broken. Length 97 mm, section 4 mm. SF6272; XIX context 3184; Romano-British occupation deposit.

388. Bar. Iron. Square-sectioned twisted rod. Length 14 mm., section 6 mm. SF7806; XXXVIII context 6674; occupation deposit.

389. Bar. Iron. Rectangular-sectioned; both ends broken. Length 26 mm; section 8 x 5 mm. SF5955; XIX context 3096; Romano-British occupation deposit.

390. Bar fragment. Iron. Length 40 mm. SF6784; XIX context 8020; Period II/III.

391. Bar fragment. Iron. Length 67 mm, SF454; VIII context 1009; Romano-British occupation deposit.

392. Wire fragment. Iron. Bent into loop at one end. Length 20 mm. SF10300; XIX context 3101; Romano-British occupation deposit.

393. Strip. Iron. Rectangular with one squared and one broken end; square perforation in squared end. Length 40 mm, section 15 x 1 mm. SF10853; context 22; Period IV, Ditch 1.

394. Strip. Iron. Rectangular; both ends broken. Length 29 mm; section 14 x 5 mm. SF1557; context 3307; Romano-British occupation deposit.

395. Strip fragment. Iron. Tapering to one end; both ends broken. Length 48 mm, section 10 x 3 mm. SF40; context 22; Period IV, Ditch 1.

396. Sheet fragment. Iron. One edge broken across perforation; all edges broken. Dimensions 29 x 18 mm, thickness 1.5 mm. SF85; context 22; Period IV, Ditch 1.

397. Sheet fragment. Iron. Length 35 mm. SF6487; XXXVI context 6204; Romano-British occupation deposit.

398. Sheet fragment. Iron. Length 25 mm, SF5696; XXIX context 5321; Later sealing Structure 18, Period VI.

399. Sheet, curved fragment. Iron. Length 50 mm. SF7753 XL context 9026; Fill of un-phased post-hole.

No	Metal	Period	Context	SF no
400	Copper alloy	IV	3781	5024
401	Copper alloy	IV	6121	7146
402	Copper alloy	-	3307	2019
403	Copper alloy	-	3096	5824
404	Copper alloy	-	3601	1418
405	Lead alloy	IV	3063	4527
406	Lead alloy	VI	4029	3498
407	Lead alloy	-	1085	4076
408	Lead alloy	-	3316	2485
409	Lead alloy	-	3102	5474
410	Lead alloy	-	3101	4792
411	Lead alloy	-	3101	9578
412	Lead alloy	-	5348	8206
413	Lead alloy	-	6468	7068
414	Iron	II/III	8020	7259
415	Iron	II/III	4659	5932
416	Iron	II/III	3676	4310
417	Iron	II/III	3677	3595
418	Iron	IV	1009	496

419	Iron	IV	1009	516
420	Iron	IV	1012	538
421	Iron	IV	3055	8270
422	Iron	IV	3055	9620
423	Iron	VI	3063	4251
424	Iron	-	3307	2315
425	Iron	-	3307	3001
426	Iron	-	3062	6407
427	Iron	-	3101	4754
428	Iron	-	3101	10302
429	Iron	-	3765	10301
430	Iron	-	6150	7067
431	Iron	-	9124	8176
432	Iron	-	7200	8495
433	Lead		3096	5909
434	Copper alloy		643	1029
435	Copper alloy		635	600
436	Copper alloy		634	615

Table 4.24: 400-436. Undiagnostic fragments of metal

Overview

The metalwork assemblage from Irby is not large, but it does have some interesting features that may contribute to an understanding of the site and this section will consider these. At the outset it is necessary to make clear that any absences from types from the assemblage are unlikely to be the result of poor survival. On some sites, acidic soil destroys metalwork and little survives in an identifiable state. This was the case at the Lousher's Lane excavations at Wilderspool (Hinchliffe and Williams 1992, 155), a fact that is particularly unfortunate as it would have been an ideal site to provide a comparative assemblage for the study of the Irby finds. The metalwork considered here is not always in good condition, the ironwork especially often proved to have little metal core remaining when investigative conservation was carried out (Ian Panter, archive report); but it did survive and it could be identified.

As will have been noted from the previous section, much of the metalwork is not intrinsically datable other than to the broad Roman period, and so the date of the assemblage has to be derived from the stratigraphy of the site. Only one item, the La Tène II/III brooch (no. 289), came from Period II; the rest is concentrated in Period IV to V contexts. This suggests that this is a 2nd- to 4th-century assemblage, though it is possible that very little metalwork was being used on the site by the mid to late 4th century given its paucity in Period V contexts.

For a 2nd- to 4th-century assemblage there are some curious omissions, the most obvious being the absence of brooches. The heyday of bow brooch wearing is the 1st to late 2nd-century period. The absence at Irby in the main Period IV-V occupation might reflect nothing more than the fact that the main activity on the site started after the late 2nd century. This, however, seems unlikely given the presence of significant quantities of 2nd-century pottery and the occurrence of prismatic glass bottles on the site. Alternately their absence could be another manifestation of the apparent lack of interest northern native populations outside of Roman nucleated settlements showed in bow brooches that Mackreth (1996, 7) has observed. Though it is always difficult to evaluate the importance of an absence from the archaeological record, a comparison to Wilderspool may be informative. This is a settlement in the same region and occupied at the same time. There are slight hints in the metalwork of a military presence (Hinchliffe and Williams 1992, 92, nos 8-11, fig. 49), but overall the main population would appear to have been civilian and native. The presence of bow brooches on both the Brewery site (Hinchliffe and Williams 1992, 90, nos 1-6, fig. 49) and at Lousher's Lane (Hinchliffe and Williams 1992, 155, no. 2, fig. 83) where metalwork was poorly preserved, suggests that bow brooches were in use by the native population of the region.

The absence of brooches is matched by a scarcity of other personal ornaments with the possible exception of the bracelets (nos 294 and 295), and the rarity of other copper-alloy items such as toilet equipment, the ubiquitous studs and tacks that must have decorated and fastened many objects. The iron assemblage also appears unusual. Again it may be usefully compared to that from the Brewery site at Wilderspool to illustrate this.

Jackson (1992, 72) describes the ironwork from Wilderspool as corresponding to 'the normal range of iron artefacts found on Romano-British sites – craftsmen's tools, agricultural and domestic equipment, structural and other fittings and, as usual, a large number of nails'. In his report the undiagnostic fragments are not catalogued. These would correspond to nos 386-399 and 414-432 here and so in the comparison that follows these have been excluded. On both sites iron nails dominate the ironwork assemblage forming 92% of the assemblage from Wilderspool and 70% of that from Irby. The remaining iron items are tabulated according to function in Table 4.26. The percentage figure has been included for ease of comparison and relates to the assemblage excluding nails.

The first thing that is noticeable from the table is that in the Irby assemblage fewer functions are represented. Admittedly Irby has a smaller assemblage but the absence of even a single example of the normal structural fittings such as wall hooks and joiner's dogs is striking. Taken with the smaller proportion of nails in the assemblage, this probably has implications for the building techniques used on the two sites. If one takes the use of nails and other iron structural fittings as an index of the adoption of Romanised building techniques

then at Irby there would appear to be a continuation of native traditions, as indeed is demonstrated by the building plans.

Function	Wilderspool	Irby
Weapons	1 (2%)	-
Transport	7 (16%)	-
Agricultural tools	2 (5%)	1 (5%)
Craftsmen's tools	4 (9%)	8 (36%)
Knives	7 (16%)	2 (9%)
Locks and keys	2 (5%)	1 (5%)
Cooking implements	1 (2%)	-
Writing equipment	1 (2%)	1 (5%)
Fittings	3 (7%)	2 (9%)
Structural fittings	6 (14%)	-
Miscellaneous	10 (23%)	7 (32%)
Total	44 (101%)	22 (101%)

Table 4.26: A comparison of the iron assemblages from the Brewery site, Wilderspool and Irby

A striking feature of the Irby assemblage, however, is the very high proportion of craft tools. As a category it swamps all of the others representing over one-third of the assemblage. Some of these may be native or non-typical Roman forms, for example the chisel (no. 301) and the awl (no. 304). Others like the saw (no. 298) and the drill bits (nos 299-300), however, are typical Roman forms and as has already been noted, the lead spindle whorl (no. 302 and possibly no. 303) represents the adoption of a Romanised artefact. If the identification of no. 306 as a wax spatula is correct then that indicates literacy in a Roman manner.

The story the metalwork assemblage appears to tell, therefore, is of a community that adopts some but not all of the trappings of Romanised life. Austerely they adopt the tools for work but reject new building techniques and the fripperies of Roman knick-knacks, though one or two women in the 4th century appear to have acquired the occasional bracelet. Against this background one has to wonder just what was being locked up at Irby with the handsome padlock (no. 310). It is possible to speculate that in this case it might indeed have fastened a slave shackle. An establishment populated with slaves might well be expected to have good tools but few other comforts, precisely the picture presented by the metalwork from the site.

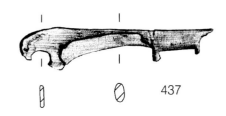

Fig. 4.19: 437. Medieval key

Medieval Metal Object

Robert Philpott

The only identifiable metal object of medieval date was recovered from the lower ploughsoil.

437. Copper-alloy key with shank of folded sheet metal, with two rudimentary wards, one damaged. The subrectangular bow is broken and has an oval hole. L 52 mm, W 12 mm, T 3 mm. SF284, context 1007.

Keys of sheet metal are not well known finds in Britain. However, there are twelve sheet-metal keys, probably for caskets, recorded from the Wirral shore at Meols, eroded during the 19th century from an abandoned medieval settlement (Egan 2007, 167, nos 2064-2075). Egan observes that these crude keys with shanks folded for strength are presumably makeshift replacements for lost or broken originals and are unlikely to have proved as durable as their cast originals.

The Amber

H. E. M. Cool

A small number of chips of tawny amber were recovered (no. 1). These seem most likely to have come from a bead. Though amber beads were in use in Roman Britain, most commonly in the 1st and 2nd centuries (Brewer 1986, 152), they were never common, and it is tempting to see them as luxury items. They became much more common in the post-Roman period and, given the Norse occupation on the site, it is likely that the bead was of that date (cf. for example Mainman and Rogers 2000, 2597).

438. Chips of amber with one weathered and other freshly broken surfaces. Weathered surface curved. Dimensions (largest fragment) 4 x 3 x 3 mm. SF692; VI 610.

Bone Objects

Robert Philpott

Bone is poorly preserved on the site, unless burnt (see Chapter 3, *The Animal Bone*), and the two objects recovered, neither of which is certainly earlier than the modern period, are very unlikely to reflect the true level of prehistoric, Romano-British or later use of bone. Of the two bone objects recovered, the first is likely to be modern, the second possibly so. Neither is illustrated.

439. Small fragment of sawn bone from cattle-sized long bone (S. Stallibrass pers. comm.). Burnt after deposition. L 24 mm, W 17 mm, T 4 mm. SF9505, context 3606, fill of modern garden feature.
440. A short length of the shaft of a bone ?pin of oval section. L 5 mm, W 3 x T 2 mm. SF4504, context 3062, unphased layer.

5: Irby in its Regional Setting

The Mesolithic Period 8500-4000 BC

R. W. Cowell

All but 14 of the 205 worked lithics from the excavations occur in disturbed contexts representing the presence of former prehistoric ground surfaces that have been reworked by later Romano-British and medieval activity. This means that the lithic assemblage cannot be combined with other sources of evidence to help understand the chronology and function of the structures on site. However, there is a body of data within the stone tool assemblage that does provide information of value to an understanding of the site's earlier history that is not forthcoming from the structural evidence, although the lack of stratigraphic control means that only the most general conclusions can be made about the nature of the earlier prehistoric occupation at Irby.

The more identifiable element within the assemblage is that relating to the Mesolithic period. There are indications, in the form of a small amount of North Welsh chert from the site that occupation at Irby may have commenced relatively early. Of the struck pieces of chert, 19 out of the 34 are from the same source as is used on two nearby early Mesolithic sites; at Greasby Copse *c.* 1 km to the north-east of Irby and Thurstaston Dungeon *c.* 1.5 km to the south-west of Irby, where this material was found almost exclusively (Cowell 1992). There are typological and raw material similarities with the chert assemblage from Rhuddlan, north Wales (Berridge 1994) which along with Trwyn Ddu, Anglesey (White 1978) provides the dating for the earliest sites in north Wales. Both sets of determinations place these sites towards the end of the period expected by analogy with stone tool assemblages of this type elsewhere. There are contextual uncertainties with these dates that may account for this to a large degree (David and Walker 2004, 302; Jacobi 1980). The only generally accepted date from Rhuddlan is a determination from a discrete pit layer bulked sample of 8739 ± 86 BP (BM-691) (8210 - 7580 cal BC (calibrations from David and Walker 2004, 302)). This is potentially several centuries later than the earliest dates for early Mesolithic sites in south Wales centred on a little before 8250 BC (a little before 9000 BP), which themselves are 300-500 years later than the earliest dates in England (David 2007, 63-70). The other less accepted determinations; from Rhuddlan of 8528 ± 73 BP (BM-822) (7680-7380 cal BC) and from Trwyn Ddu of 8590 ± 90 BP (HAR-1194) (7940-7480 cal BC) and 8460 ± 150 (Q1385) (7870-

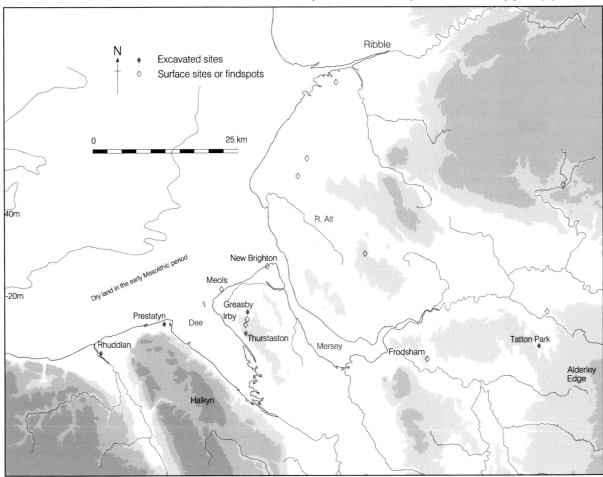

Fig. 5.1: Early Mesolithic sites in the Merseyside region

7080 cal BC) have mid points between *c.* 7600-7700 BC.

On the assumption, based on the wider prevailing pattern that early Mesolithic technologies in this region do not continue into the mid 8th millennium BC, then the expected approximate date for Greasby should be close to 8000 BC if not before. The Greasby assemblage, however, also contains a proportion of smaller oblique forms, in the same chert raw material as the larger types, which can occur in post-8000 BC Mesolithic assemblages. A particular example is from Prestatyn where dates of 8700 ± 100 BP (OxA-2268) and 8730 ± 90 BP (OxA- 2269) are associated with a stone tool assemblage with smaller simple oblique points found alongside a larger number of typologically late Mesolithic geometric scalene triangles (Bell 2007, Chapter 20). These dates calibrate within the range 8200-7540 BC (David and Walker 2004, 317) which puts the occurrence at Prestatyn of this type of technology amongst the earliest in Britain. However, at Greasby there is no late Mesolithic geometric triangle element, suggesting again that the use of this chert material on Wirral ought to date to a little after 8000 BC at the latest.

Longworth's work on the lithic raw materials from the Wirral sites suggests that the chert used in the stone tool-kits from these sites, which forms the

major part of the raw material used, originated in the carboniferous limestone hills of north Wales between Halkyn and Prestatyn (Longworth 2000). This particular association of obliquely blunted points and north Welsh chert is not found anywhere in the county, other than in this part of Wirral. At sites such as Rhuddlan, the same dark chert continued to be used into the late Mesolithic (Manley and Healey 1982). Although there are uncertain indications that this may be a feature of these two Wirral sites, as yet no later Mesolithic use of this type of chert has been convincingly identified in Merseyside generally. In fact the Wirral and north Welsh evidence is the most integrated in this part of the region for this early period with essentially a large gap in the distribution of sites between here and the Pennine foothills in Cheshire (Fig. 5.1).

The presence of north Welsh chert on Wirral suggests that regular movements across the Dee valley would have been a feature of the seasonal or annual cycle of mobile, local hunter-gatherers who brought lumps of chert back to the Wirral, where it was subsequently worked down for tools. With the present line of the coast being a feature of the late to post-Mesolithic period, the line of the early Mesolithic coast lay well to the west of the present north Wirral and west Lancashire lowlands (Fig 5.1). By *c.* 9000 BC *(c.* 9550 BP) sea level was at about the 20 fathom contour (-37 m OD) rising to about 10 fathoms (-18 m) by *c.* 7500 BC (*c.* 8500 BP) (Bell

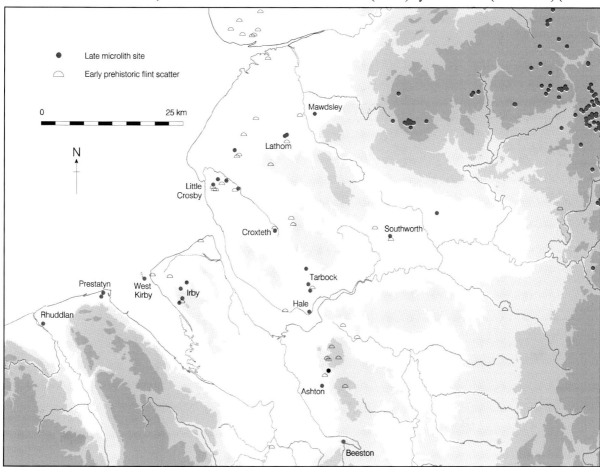

Fig. 5.2: Late Mesolithic sites in the Merseyside region

2007, 8). This former coastal plain is likely to have been the focus for much early activity in the area although the evidence has been buried by the subsequent rise in sea level in Liverpool Bay.

The contours of the buried early Holocene profile of the Dee estuary are not particularly well known in detail, other than that a portion of a rock cut profile lies at a depth of -18 m (Bell 2007, 5), so that palaeocoastal reconstruction has to be extremely general. However, with a generalised sea level lower than -18m OD before *c.* 7500 BC it is unlikely that the present lower Dee was tidal during the late 8th and 9th millennium BC (the most likely dates for the Wirral sites) other than perhaps through the possibility of a small proto-estuary somewhere around the present mouth later in that period. The likelihood is that the most direct movement into Wales from north Wirral, across the Dee valley, was less difficult at this time than later as sea level progressively rose to levels comparable to that of today by *c.* 6000 BC (Cowell and Gonzalez 2007).

The total flint assemblage from the Greasby site consists of *c.* 13000 pieces, while the less extensively excavated Thurstaston site has produced *c.* 4000 pieces. These assemblages include a wide range of tools, as well as large amounts of waste debris, suggesting that they were sites where a range of activities took place. This is also suggested by the presence of pits, at least one hearth and a possible pebbled surface at Greasby (Cowell 1992).

Irby is one of a number of other surface sites using this raw material type, which are located in a fairly restricted zone along the west-facing sandstone slopes of Wirral which today overlook the Dee estuary, but which would have been many kilometres inland in the early Mesolithic. This ridge lies between *c.* 70-80m OD, with the sites occurring in a narrow area, about five kilometres north-south, between Greasby and Thurstaston (Fig. 5.1). These sites are very different in assemblage composition, however, being represented by only small amounts of material spread over small areas, in contrast to the two main sites, which provided surface concentrations of finds of between 100-500 pieces over areas of *c.* 2500 m². The former would seem to represent different kinds of sites, perhaps associated with smaller task groups than were present at the larger locations at Greasby and Thurstaston.

Most of the lithic assemblage from Irby, however, is flint and most of this is local, with 87% of it confidently identified as being from the boulder clay, and much of the rest being miscellaneous types of flint that could well be from the same source. Natural nodules of this material have been recorded widely across the boulder clay areas of the county during fieldwalking (Cowell 1991a; Cowell and Innes 1994) and would have been available in stream banks and natural outcrops in prehistory. Fourteen pieces of flint from the site have

reasonable indications that they may be of beach origin.

The form of the typologically Mesolithic microlith element suggests a later Mesolithic date (*c.* 7800-4000 BC (Waddington 2007)) for the use of some of the flint raw material at Irby. Along with similar evidence from a number of other sites in Merseyside (Fig 5.2) this suggests that patterns of raw material procurement had altered during the Mesolithic. Flint was little used on the two excavated earlier Mesolithic Wirral sites and if raw material source is a valid way of distinguishing in general terms between the earlier and later part of the period on the Wirral, then the trend would be for most of the other likely Mesolithic elements at Irby to be later, rather than earlier.

The assemblage includes up to 27 (depending on the strength of the identification) implements, blades, cores and debitage that form the main potential late Mesolithic element, although not all are typologically distinctive enough to be sure that there may not be an early Neolithic element included, as the two periods share a number of characteristics in stone technology that can be difficult to distinguish without a range of contextual and radiocarbon associations. The potential for a Neolithic element seems less likely, however, as there are no typologically distinctive early Neolithic implements in the assemblage to suggest an accompanying body of less typologically distinctive waste material is present.

The more certain later Mesolithic pieces include five of the six pieces with microlithic retouch and two pieces of microlithic debitage, while potentially seven of the 11 blades, three of the six platform cores and two pieces of core waste may also be of this period. It is probable that some of the very small flint waste from the site, classed as of uncertain date, also belongs to the activity represented by the above. There are also a number of less chronologically specific tools in the assemblage that can be paralleled at coastal Mesolithic sites in Wales and south-west Scotland, although these can be found also on Bronze Age sites, for example, and so have an uncertain status.

In very general terms, some of the elements associated with this material would appear to fit with Myers's (1989) argument that by this phase of the Mesolithic, the previous large-scale patterns of raw material procurement for stone tools had broken down. Associated with changes in stone tool technology and in the structure of individual sites at this time, it appears that new economic and possibly social patterns of behaviour had developed, although the Irby site appears to have retained its importance into this period as an occasional, repeatedly used landscape location. These changes are probably linked to a number of significant environmental changes that had been taking place during the Mesolithic, culminating in a dramatically different environment at the end of the period compared with that at its beginning, so that by *c.* 5900 BC mixed oak woodland with alder, hazel and elm dominated a landscape that was much reduced by loss of land to sea-level rise (Innes and Tomlinson 1991; 2008).

The Mesolithic material occurs in most of the central trenches on the site. Unfortunately it is not possible to know how much horizontal displacement may have taken place due to the later activity, which makes it difficult to identify the minimum area covered by the Mesolithic activity. Although in absolute terms it is of small size, after the sites of Greasby and Thurstaston, this is the next largest group of Mesolithic material from the Wirral (Cowell 1992). It is impossible to interpret the nature of the Mesolithic occupation at the site from the lithic assemblage alone as, apart from the difficulty of distinguishing how many occupations it represents, it is also unclear how representative this collection is of the original assemblage. The cores, blades, flakes and probably some of the debitage result from the working down of cores and the production of blanks for tools. This may represent activity on a specialised site dedicated to the working of stone, or it may represent only part of a range of activities on a site that also included other 'domestic' functions. Each type of site would probably have had different characteristics in terms of its size, the length of time it was occupied, and the number and make-up of the social group responsible.

Irby though may represent one element in a chain of different types of activity sites spread across the landscape in the later Mesolithic. Other sites with assemblages of similar character, although lacking the microlithic component and thus potentially including some elements dating to the early Neolithic, have been located by fieldwalking within a few kilometres to the south along the sandstone ridge (Philpott and Cowell 1992) and on land flanking the coastal wetlands to the north-west (Cowell and Innes 1994, 25-70). They are also known from chance finds and excavations conducted in the early 20th century along the present north Wirral coast. Activity sites are found where isolated low cliffs of sandstone or boulder clay rise from the coastal plain at places such New Brighton, Red Rocks in Hoylake and Little Eye island near West Kirby (summarised in Cowell and Innes 1994), although more recent collection has identified a single later Mesolithic microlith from Little Eye along with the less chronologically specific struck flint (Cowell in prep. a).

The Bronze Age

R. W. Cowell

The Irby site has produced structural evidence with associated pottery, possible oven fragments, bronze-working, weaving and the farming of cereals that points to the discovery of a rare Bronze Age domestic

settlement in the region. This is only complemented by the recent discovery of a Bronze Age settlement at Oversley Farm, on the site of the second Manchester Airport runway (Garner 2007). Most evidence here, however, related to the early Bronze Age, prior to 1500 BC. The middle Bronze Age phase only consisted of two pits with a small assemblage of struck flint that could be residual.

Most settlements of the period between *c.* 1500-1000 BC are found in southern England. The earlier ones consist of moderately sized rectilinear enclosures associated with scatters of pits and rather fragmentary post-built buildings (Barrett *et al.* 1991). A little later in the period the chalklands of south England see farmsteads integrated into a system of fields, trackways, ponds and associated burial grounds (Drewett 1980). The south-west has a fewer number of long-lived but intermittently occupied farmsteads with associated fields (Nowakowski 1991) while in East Anglia, at Fengate, ditched field systems laid out on the edge of a wetland have occasional buildings dispersed amongst them (Pryor 1980).

These parts of southern England may not necessarily provide the best parallels for Irby, because of potential differences in environmental or social factors between the two but it does at least provide a framework against which the Irby evidence can be set. In fact, Irby has a number of features that are found commonly in those southern sites. Most middle Bronze Age houses are based on the creation of a repeated ordering of space within them. These include circular or oval double-ring post constructions and mainly south-easterly or southerly doorway aspects, which are differentiated and structurally embellished, often with special deposits in the post-holes or slots (Bruck 1999, 155; Parker Pearson 1996).

A complete suite of post-holes has probably not been recovered from the excavations for the structure at Irby, which makes the definitive structural interpretation less easy here. This has resulted in two alternative interpretations; of a large single roundhouse and two successive smaller structures overlapping on the same plot (Chapter 2, Structure 27), with an adjacent fragmentary, third structure (Structure 28). It therefore depends on which interpretation is preferred as to how closely the evidence from Irby parallels that of the main settlement types so far known from the middle Bronze Age of southern England.

Of the two alternatives, the first, the double-ring post building provides the closer comparison. Other than this significant structural trait, points of similarity include the entrance at Irby which faces south-west, and has indications of a potential porch, or at least an entrance that is specially marked, while the post-sockets include pottery and clay artefacts (Fig. 2.5). On balance

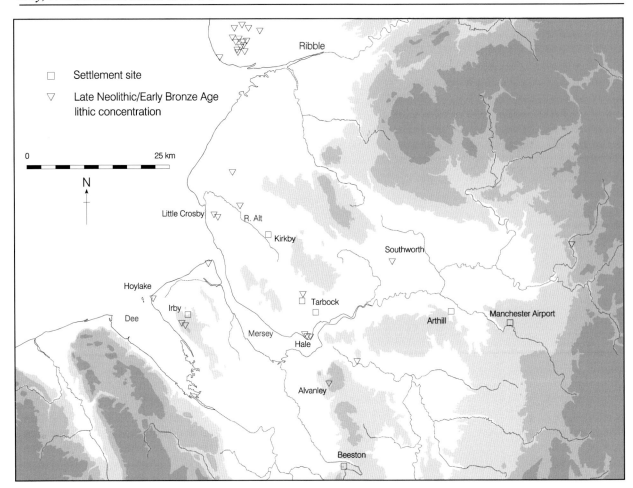

Fig. 5.3: Bronze Age sites in the Merseyside region

though a double-ring post building has been rejected by the excavator as being less likely than that two successive overlapping single-post circular structures are represented. The multiple structure option provides little comparison with existing middle Bronze Age structures, with only the potential deliberate deposition of pottery in the two post-holes of the possible south-westerly entrance to Structure 27B (cuts 7424, 8353) being noteworthy.

Both interpretations from Irby also include several points of departure from the existing body of comparative data. Many other Bronze Age houses display signs of symmetry in their alignments and equal spacing of posts either side of the main axis, suggestive of a degree of formality in their construction. This feature is hard to see in either of the Irby interpretations, with neither regular spacing of posts nor a symmetrical axis from doorway to rear wall being evident. The difficulties of recognition of features during the excavation process at Irby should be borne in mind, however. Secondly, the size of the Irby structures in both interpretations does not conform to those of houses further south. The double-ring post structure option produces the largest structure, at a little less than 15 m diameter, but even in the multiple construction alternative option both structures are around the 14 m diameter mark. Most southern downland houses, such

as at the enclosed settlement at Thorny Down, Wiltshire or the slightly later buildings at Black Patch, Sussex or Shearplace Hill, Dorset tend to be around 7 m to 9 m in diameter. The occasional floor area, such as that at Shearplace Hill, House A reaches a little over 10 m, although this interpretative size is contested elsewhere as being too large (Guilbert 1981, 304). Further north, the nearest middle Bronze Age house to that at Irby, lies at Glanfeinon, Powys which has two alternative interpretations for the floor area, of which the preferred option for the excavator is the larger one, measuring *c.* 10 m in diameter (Britnell *et al.* 1997). The postulated structures at Irby seem too large for the typical middle Bronze Age farming group found in southern England. One explanation may be that they potentially served a larger group than the family, perhaps in some communal way. The tight range of radiocarbon dates, the lack of pottery away from the structure and the general lack of flintwork potentially of this date suggest that the occupation may not have been long-lived. This also appears to be a feature of middle Bronze Age settlements in general. From a relatively large corpus of sites from southern England such settlements are interpreted as largely single phase occupations. Where rebuilding is evident, as at Black Patch and Itford Hill, Sussex or Thorny Down, Wiltshire, this involved a new layout of buildings on a different part of the site (Bruck 1999, 146). The general consensus is that such settlements might be occupied for periods ranging between a few decades to 50-100 years. On sociological grounds, based on a settlement being established at marriage and lasting until the head of household and spouse die, Bruck (1999, 149) suggests between 20-40 years. Children might then, if not before, set up a new settlement away from the former site.

A functional model of buildings based on size and artefactual associations has been proposed for middle Bronze Age settlements from southern England (Drewett 1980; Ellison 1981, 419-21). The general distinction is between major roundhouses and ancillary buildings. The former tend to be the larger structures, often with porches, and are associated with fineware pottery, for the consumption of food and drink, flint flakes, whetstones, evidence for spinning and weaving as well as potential fine objects made of bronze or various kinds of stone. Ancillary buildings are interpreted from the incidence of coarseware pottery, quernstones and flint scrapers. Sometimes pits in the house may suggest storage of foodstuffs. However, a number of buildings do not conform to this general model and tend to be associated with a mixture of artefacts redolent of the two types. This may be due to change in use of the building over the lifetime of the settlement (Bruck 1999, 151).

The finds included in the Irby house consist of locally made decorated and plain pottery, three struck flints of undiagnostic type, two spherical clay weights, potential oven clay, emmer wheat and naked barley. Although the assemblage is very small those elements present suggest it may have been more likely associated with the storage and possibly preparation of food. Some of the mould fragments (see above, *Refractory Material*) may be associated with this phase, being in a similar fabric to other Bronze Age examples. However, all were found in Romano-British contexts.

The evidence from Irby, therefore, suggests that a farmstead was occupied, possibly repeatedly, on up to three occasions, each time possibly for a limited time span, probably some time during the 14th century BC. It must have been associated with fields or plots for growing wheat and barley. Cropmarks in the field to the north may form part of a field system and trackway (Fig. 5.7) although they are of uncertain date with no grounds currently to associate this with the Bronze Age phase. Such evidence is unique for this period in the region. There is a small body of evidence from the more immediate area that has been recovered that may be of some relevance to a wider understanding of the Irby site (Fig. 5.3) (Cowell in press). There are problems of interpretation for much of this evidence, as it largely comes from small excavations and surface lithic material that is difficult to date tightly, which is not of the standard of the excavated evidence from Irby. However, when combined with palaeoenvironmental evidence it provides the basis of a working hypothesis for the wider

landscape and settlement pattern context either out of which a site such as Irby developed or, perhaps, given the imprecision of the dating evidence, operated within. The suggested pattern is one of mobility associated with temporary activity loci alongside places in the landscape that were either occupied for longer periods or perhaps reflect sites with more concentrated short term activity. The balance of the available evidence perhaps makes this pattern more relevant to the landscape east of the river Mersey and largely for the centuries prior to the period when the Irby site was in use. To the west, in Wirral, there is less evidence to know how relevant it is here.

More work is needed on other Wirral sites to test if the Irby site could be associated with the kind of mobile pattern that is suggested above by the evidence to the east of the Mersey and whether one element of land-use on the Wirral peninsula may have consisted of a series of short-term sedentary sites operating within a larger system based on shorter pulses of economic or social mobile activity, or whether more permanent fixed farmsteads provided the basic element of the settlement pattern at this time.

The Iron Age

Robert Philpott

The Iron Age occupation at Irby is difficult to characterise due to extensive later disturbance. Although structures are elusive, two curving post-hole alignments have been suggested as possible Iron Age buildings (S32, S33; discussed in Chapter 2) and amid the mass of unphased post-holes it is possible that other Iron Age structures remain unrecognised. That circular buildings would be expected in the Iron Age here is suggested by the fact that this the classic later prehistoric building type across the whole of Britain (Cunliffe 2005, *passim*). The form occurs from the Bronze Age, and at Irby in the mid Bronze Age (see above), throughout the Iron Age and continues in rural settlements well into the Roman period.

The site was linked into the wider local and regional economy. Finds of Cheshire Stony VCP containers indicate that the site was in receipt of salt from the Middlewich-Nantwich area, while a steatite decorated spindle whorl, dated on stylistic grounds to the 3rd century BC (see Chapter 4, *Steatite Spindle Whorl*), had very probably emanated from localised deposits in Anglesey 80 km to the west. A La Tène II/III brooch is too fragmentary to be closely datable. The VCP is not sufficiently diagnostic of date to assist with the chronological problems on the site, though its occurrence at a site where Iron Age occupation is attested by the two radiocarbon dates of 410-200 cal BC (OxA-8485-6; Table 2.1) argues for a mid Iron Age date. Palaeoenvironmental work has identified cereal grains, indicating consumption and probably arable cultivation, which radiocarbon dates place within a phase of settlement in the period 410-200 cal BC (2275 ± 40, OxA-8485; 2270 ± 40, OxA-8486). Despite the difficulties in interpreting the stratigraphic record for the Iron Age, the significance of the activity at Irby is enhanced by the scarcity of excavated Iron Age sites within the county, or indeed in the wider region of the lowland north west.

In a survey of Iron Age Britain as part of the English Heritage initiative on research agendas, north-west England including Cheshire and Lancashire was described as a 'black hole' in terms of current understanding of the subject (Haselgrove *et al.* 2001, 25). This recognises not only the difficulty of characterising the Iron Age society and culture of the region but also reflects a lack of study until recently to tackle the problem. In such areas 'any discovery of Iron Age material has an importance of a different magnitude from other parts of Britain' (Haselgrove *et al.* 2001, 24). However, a new burgeoning of interest in the Iron Age of the region is reflected in the variety of recent publications. Surveys have been published of the Iron Age evidence for the lowland north west in the excavation report for Brook House Farm, Halewood, Merseyside (Cowell and Philpott 2000), while others cover the historic counties of Lancashire (Haselgrove 1996) and Cheshire (Longley 1987; Matthews 1999; 2001). The increasing pace of the recognition and investigation of Iron Age sites can be measured through the appearance of recent site reports or interim statements. Keith Matthews has conveniently summarised the excavations of certain or putative Iron Age sites in Cheshire and beyond[1] (Matthews 2001). To these should now be added the Chester amphitheatre site which has produced Iron Age cultivation, probable settlement and finds of VCP (Anon 2006). Irby is one of the few Iron Age settlements apart from hillforts to be excavated within the borders of the historic county of Cheshire. Only Bruen Stapleford since then has seen substantial excavation on a settlement site (Fairburn 2002a), although a late prehistoric date has been claimed for Legh Oaks, High Legh (Nevell 2002). In cases such as Oldcastle near Malpas, possible Iron Age settlements proposed by Matthews have produced neither datable artefacts nor well defined structures.

Neighbouring areas, particularly to the north of the Mersey, have also begun to yield Iron Age sites. These include Great Woolden Hall, Salford (Nevell 1999a) and Brook House Farm, Halewood (Cowell and Philpott 2000, 27-66), while interim statements have appeared for both Dutton's Farm, Lathom, Lancashire (Cowell 2002; 2003; 2005a) and Mellor, Stockport (Mellor Archaeological Trust 2002; Redhead and Roberts 2003; Nevell and Redhead 2005). The final reports

should provide at a minimum some basic data on settlement and building forms, the use and source of durable material culture at the settlements, and at least a broad chronological framework, despite the notorious difficulties of the radiocarbon curve for the Iron Age. Although the sites are few in number, the geographical spread is wide and begins to hint at differences on a sub-regional level, as well as differences in function between sites. This is a theme addressed in a recent critical analysis of the excavated evidence for the lowland north west by Ron Cowell. His review attempts to address the growing tendency within the region to use the limited available data to erect hypotheses which they are incapable of supporting (Cowell 2005a). To the south of Cheshire, the Wroxeter Hinterland Project and Survey report sets out the Iron Age context for the growth of the Romano-British town and its surrounding countryside within Shropshire (Gaffney and White 2007). Despite the different nature of the site, Iron Age hillforts at Beeston Castle, Cheshire and The Breidden, Montgomeryshire provide some parallels in structural terms as well as in the problems posed by the stratification.

The Northern Cornovii

There is no direct evidence of the name of the tribe who inhabited the Wirral peninsula in the late Iron Age. However, most modern scholars place Wirral within the territory of the Cornovii in the Roman period, whose core was focused on the tribal capital, *Viroconium Cornoviorum*, at Wroxeter, Shropshire, probably replacing the Iron Age hillfort on the Wrekin (Webster 1975). The Cornovii had neither their own coinage nor it appears any distinctive metalwork or pottery – at least in the northern part of their territory – which enables an Iron Age cultural or material grouping to be recognised which might correspond to the tribe (Longley 1987, 103-14; Cunliffe 2005, 210). The boundaries of the tribe pose problems in identification which have been discussed by various authorities (Cunliffe 2005, 210; Webster 1975; Higham 1993, 30-3; White and Barker 1998, 32). The geographer Ptolemy, writing *c.* AD 140-150, called Chester a *polis* of the Cornovii, suggesting that Cornovian territory extended into Cheshire, and probably as far as the Mersey, in the late Iron Age (Petch 1987, 115), though this may be, as Carrington (2006) has pointed out, more a general indication of location than a technical description, since it is unlikely that Chester had any municipal status at the time. The Mersey is generally held to have formed their northern boundary with the Brigantes, a tribe based in the Pennines and its flanks, who had hegemony over a number of smaller tribal groups, some of whose names, such as the Carvetii and Tectoverdi, are documented in the North (Higham and Jones 1985; Rivet and Smith 1979, 470-2; Cunliffe 2005, 210-15). The identity of the tribal entity immediately to the north of the Mersey may be preserved in Ptolemy's record of the place-name

---

[1] However, details of some sites require revision, there being no Iron Age occupation at Kirkby Vicarage, for example (see Chapter 2 above; Adams 1995), while the discussion of Irby inevitably relies on outdated interpretations.

Portus Setantiorum, 'harbour of the Setantii' (Rivet and Smith 1979, 135, 456-7), probably located between the Ribble (*Belisama*) and the *Moricambe* estuary, probably on the Wyre in the vicinity of Fleetwood. Ptolemy gives the cognate name *Seteia* for the Mersey estuary, suggesting that the Setantii were a tribal group based in south-west Lancashire and the Fylde[2]. Others, however, prefer a more northerly location. Shotter, for example, suggests the port lies at an undiscovered site near the southern end of Windermere (1997, 114). The Flintshire coast was occupied by the Deceangli (Rivet and Smith 1979, 331).

Tribal identity was often forged through situations of conflict and opposition. Tribal allegiances and alliances could shift with time, fracturing into smaller entities or coalescing into larger ones. The late proto-history of Iron Age to Roman Britain illustrates the tendency of tribes to amalgamate and subsume others, or, as Tacitus observes, to break into rival warring factions which would unite on occasion to repel a common enemy. Thus the Cornovii, as they emerge from prehistory, may be a Roman adoption of a tribal identity for administrative convenience rather than necessarily representing a stable long-term entity from the pre-Roman period.

The origin of the tribal name of the Cornovii may be of direct relevance to the Wirral peninsula. In Britain, three tribes bore the name, located in Cornwall, Caithness, and Shropshire/Cheshire. The root of the name is the British *corn-* 'horn'. Although Anne Ross has suggested that the name referred to a cult or totemic name based on birds or animals, perhaps by extension indicating adherence to the horned god, Cernunnos (Ross 1974, 189; Webster 1975, 22; Longley 1987, 108), a more plausible alternative derives from the fact that in each case the tribes lived on 'horns' of land, or promontories (Thomas 1966, 86). Rivet and Smith suggest that in the case of the Cornovii of Shropshire and Cheshire this may refer to the Wirral peninsula, or possibly the vertical 'horn' of the Wrekin (1979, 325). Against this, in the case of Cornwall, it has been argued that such an interpretation was only meaningful to modern people familiar with looking at maps. However, the nature of the land as a promontory is immediately evident to anyone travelling along the coast by boat, or in the case of Wirral viewing the land from high ground either to east or west. In the case of both Wirral and Cornwall, the existence of a west coast maritime trade route around their shores in the Iron Age is well attested. In the case of the three distinct peoples who lived on the promontories, the name may have derived from outsiders, such as traders or neighbouring tribal groups, who were familiar with this distinctive aspect of their territories from a maritime perspective. As Rivet and

Smith have observed, 'in many cases a people does not need to name itself; a name is often given by outsiders, foreigners, and only taken to itself by a people at a later stage' (1979, 281). The name may have been adopted by those tribal members who recognised the nature of their territory through familiarity with its configuration from the shore (Philpott 2007b, 383-4).

For the Cornovii of Cheshire and Shropshire this coastal perspective is lent particular significance in the light of the harbour at Meols which operated from the mid Iron Age onwards. Far from being a geographically peripheral area of the territory, distant from the emerging core of the tribal area in the Wroxeter area of Shropshire, the name may have been bestowed by outsiders in the first instance on the northern element of the tribe, and possibly by the travellers and traders who were familiar with a long-lived port within its territory.

Regional Settlement Patterns in the Iron Age and Romano-British Period

Whatever the tribal affiliations of the population of Cheshire and Wirral, the settlement pattern in the county during the Iron Age is not yet well understood. Hillforts, being highly visible, and until recently virtually the only obvious indicators of Iron Age settlement in the county, have received most attention from archaeologists concerned with the late prehistoric period (Longley 1987, 105-14). These hilltop enclosures set on the sandstone ridge extending from the Mersey in the north to the Malpas-Peckforton ridge in the south have been interpreted as placed to exploit the plain on either side (Ellis 1993, 90). It is widely recognised that the term hillfort is a broad category covering a range of settlements which is far from homogenous. At the top of the settlement hierarchy, at least in terms of the area enclosed and the massiveness of their construction, are major sites such as Beeston Castle and Eddisbury where the substantial defences denote developed Iron Age hillforts. However, with the notable exception of Beeston (Ellis 1993), archaeological interventions have been limited in scope, or undertaken at a time when excavation standards and techniques were not as advanced as today. The quality of publication and interpretation of excavations such as those at Eddisbury leaves many questions open. The concentration of archaeological effort on one, albeit broad, class of site potentially gives a highly partial and distorted view of the settlement pattern and chronology.

A series of smaller but still substantial enclosures has been considered to form a second tier in the settlement hierarchy (Longley 1987, 105). These tend to lie in two principal topographical situations. Some, such as Oakmere and Peckforton, were built beside natural meres or pools, while others, such as Bradley, Kelsborrow, Helsby and Burton Point in Wirral, possessed substantial earthworks which were

---

[2] In view of the obscurity of the tribal name Setantii, the root of which is not found in Celtic languages, Andrew Breeze (2006) has recently suggested the emendation *Metantii,* meaning 'reapers, cutters down'. A similar change he applies also to Ptolemy's term *Seteia* to give *Meteia.*

supplemented by natural defensive positions on steep scarps or promontories. These sites have been viewed by some, such as Ellis (1993, 90), as defended early Iron Age sites, which may have been fairly short-lived and owed their existence and characteristics to the special circumstances, such as increased competition, of the early Iron Age. The chronology of these sites is not well established and is based in most cases either on very limited investigation of the sites or by analogy with other regions, but some have suggested the evidence points to the early abandonment of the Cheshire hillforts, like those of the southern Pennines in Lancashire which mostly date to the early 1st millennium BC (Haselgrove 1996, 67). The current evidence, albeit slight in quantity and chronologically imprecise, points to the Cheshire sites having been abandoned by the mid Iron Age (Matthews 1999, 176; 2001, 4-8; Nevell 1999b, 23).

Until the 1980s the hillforts and surviving earthwork enclosures were virtually the only evidence for Iron Age Cheshire (Longley 1987). A programme of aerial reconnaissance in Cheshire, West Lancashire and Merseyside since 1987 has revealed a small but widely dispersed series of ditched enclosures which are likely to represent a third, and somewhat broadly defined, class of site within the late prehistoric rural settlement pattern. There is a variety of forms and dimensions but the general class of enclosure appears to be a significant component of the late prehistoric and rural Romano-British settlement pattern (Nevell 1999a, fig 2.6; Collens 1994; Philpott 2000d, 182-6; 2008, 40-5, fig. 8; Matthews 2001). This receives confirmation at a regional level in the recent extensive survey of Roman rural settlement in England, which observes of the north west, 'enclosed settlements formed the overwhelming majority throughout the region', largely of small enclosures, in a dispersed settlement pattern (Taylor 2007, 43). In Cheshire few have been investigated by fieldwalking and fewer by excavation, so the chronology of the sites is poorly understood and any discussion is inevitably somewhat speculative. Amongst these is a form of which some examples, at least on morphological grounds, are likely to be Iron Age in date. The shared characteristics are the presence of double ditches and the curvilinear or irregular form of the enclosure. In Cheshire enclosures of this type are not common and have only been recognised so far in the major river valleys of the Weaver and the Dee (Philpott 2000, 183-4, fig. 8.3).

Potential confirmation of an Iron Age date for at least some enclosures of this type comes north of the Mersey. At two sites, Brook House Farm, Halewood and Great Woolden Hall, Salford, excavation has demonstrated an Iron Age origin for double-ditched curvilinear enclosures. The Iron Age site at Great Woolden Hall was built on a low promontory so required ditches for only part of its circuit (Nevell 1999a). At Brook House

Farm, Halewood the full circuit had been interrupted by a modern road but the internal features and ditches indicated an Iron Age date, which was confirmed by a sequence of radiocarbon dates (Cowell 2000b, table 3.10). On the eastern margin of the region, a large curvilinear enclosure at Mellor has two ditches, both with Iron Age material in the primary fills. The full extent of the outer ditch has not been determined but it appears to enclose a substantial area on the hilltop. The alignment of the two ditches suggests that they converge so were probably not in contemporary use, although the junction has not been examined to determine which is earlier. The inner, and more massive, ditch has produced radiocarbon dates of 830-190 cal BC (Beta-146416) from an interface between Iron Age and Romano-British fills. An internal palisade slot has been identified running parallel to the inner ditch. The deepest and most impressive section of the inner ditch lay on the scarp of the slope which, if combined with an internal bank, would have formed a substantial and imposing earthwork. A date from one roundhouse drainage gully came at Cal BC 520 to 380 (Beta-173892, 2σ) while a gully which cut through the earlier feature produced dates of 410-360 cal BC and 280 cal BC and 240 cal BC (Beta-17893, 2σ) (Noble and Thompson 2005, 28). The site was re-occupied in the Roman period, apparently after a gap, but still employing the partially infilled internal ditch (Redhead and Roberts 2003; Noble and Thompson 2005; Leary 2005).

A small number of single-ditched curvilinear enclosures is known. One example, recorded by aerial photography at Irby in Wirral only 1 km from the Mill Hill Road site, has three circular structures visible in the interior and produced two sherds of Iron Age VCP in fieldwalking, while another at Brimstage has possible structures visible in the interior. A probable enclosure at Burton, seen only as a partial circuit, may be another. A further example at Hale, north of the Mersey, has produced Roman pottery and metal finds in the vicinity. Although the presence of Roman pottery indicates occupation at that date, the absence of Iron Age finds in such a materially poor region cannot be taken as proof, without detailed investigation, that the site was not occupied at that time.

In the Mersey basin, alongside the relatively few large curvilinear enclosures, there is a considerable number of single-ditched square or subrectangular examples. Discrete enclosures of this type are known from sites such as Greasby (Wirral), Brereton (two adjacent sites), Norton and Halton, and north of Mersey, at Winwick and Arbury. Neat square enclosures at Ochre Brook in Tarbock and Southworth Hall (both north of the Mersey) have produced Romano-British material but nothing earlier in excavation (Philpott *et al.* 1993), though the majority have seen no fieldwork to test the full range of occupation.

A site such as Court Farm, Halewood (Adams and

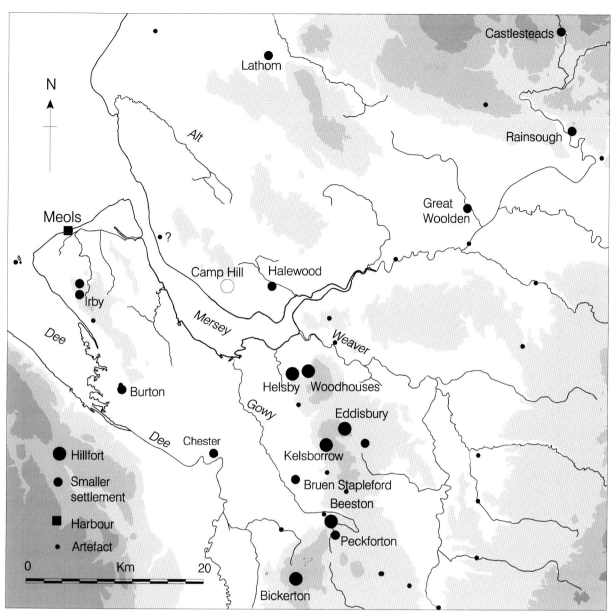

Fig. 5.4: Iron Age sites in the Merseyside region

Philpott in prep.) north of the Mersey represents an additional class of unenclosed settlement dated to the Roman period but not before. It resembles a hamlet or small village rather than a single farmstead but the absence of ditches makes such settlements difficult to locate through aerial reconnaissance. Within the Roman period, villas are virtually absent from northern Cornovian territory, with only one certain example at Eaton-by-Tarporley. Others have been claimed for Cheshire (e.g. Petch 1987, 213; Matthews 1994, fig. 8.3) but no convincing corroborative evidence has yet been published. This stands in contrast to the core of Cornovian territory in Shropshire where at least eight villas were recorded by 1975 and at least two more since (Webster 1975, 83; White and Barker 1998, 68-9).

Caution is required in assuming that all enclosure sites are later prehistoric or Romano-British in date. An example of a site at least partially enclosed by a re-cut ditch at Moreton, Wirral, produced a mid 10th-

century coin from the final fill (see below). A double-ditched square enclosure at Hermitage Green, Winwick, investigated in 2001, appeared to consist of two separate systems with the inner ditch probably predating the outer by several hundred years, but with late medieval or early post-medieval pottery in the secondary fills, suggesting a medieval or later date (Fletcher 2001). Thus a minority of the sites observed as cropmarks may belong to other periods than are usually thought.

While the Mill Hill Road site at Irby appears to have been double-ditched during the Romano-British phase, without full excavation the complete form in plan is uncertain, and the picture is complicated as it appears to have had a primary ditched enclosure to the east, to which was later appended a double-ditched enclosure to the west. The evidence suggests a Romano-British date and no clear evidence of an enclosure was found within the excavated area for the Iron Age phase. Further south, conjoined enclosures have been recognised in the Welsh

173

Marches, taking a variety of forms but sometimes appearing to represent a progressive development of agglomeration (Whimster 1989, 51). In the absence of excavation on most of these sites the sequence of development remains uncertain and at others excavation would no doubt reveal a more complex picture than is evident from the cropmarks alone.

There is sufficient evidence from neighbouring regions to urge great caution in using morphology as an indicator of chronology (Collens 1994). It is instructive to compare the emerging regional pattern with that of other regions where subrectangular enclosures are known to be of Iron Age origin. In the heartland of Cornovian territory in Shropshire, a number of regular quadrilateral single-ditched enclosures (mostly rectangular) have their origin in the Iron Age (Whimster 1989, 40; Stanford 1995; Hunn 2000, 142) and multi-period occupation has been recorded on enclosures of different types (White and van Leusen 1997, 136; Gaffney and White 2007). In north-eastern England, for example, many more Iron Age sites are known than in the north west, and the standard Iron Age enclosure form is subrectangular, with one or more circular buildings in the interior (Haselgrove 1984, 12-16; Willis 1999, 83, fig. 7.2). In the Tame and Trent valleys, Iron Age enclosures are often subrectangular in form (Smith 1977, 51-3, fig. 2). Whether the emerging pattern of enclosure form in the lowland north west represents a genuinely regional difference or simply reflects the inadequate size of the excavated sample is not yet known. It is conceivable that the developmental sequence of enclosure morphology within central and southern Cornovian territory of Shropshire could be somewhat different from that of the northern Cornovian lands. One of the many fruitful areas for future research is the question of regionality within the Iron Age and Romano-British periods to examine regional or sub-regional variation within enclosure forms. Many questions therefore remain over the chronology and function of different forms of enclosure, and without a programme of fieldwork to test a sizeable sample of the known enclosures any chronological typological scheme remains speculative.

Any discussion of enclosure form and size needs to take account of functional and cultural factors. The size of enclosures is often uncritically used as a crude index of relative status. From the large hilltop enclosures downwards, there is some variety in size and complexity of enclosures which on the face of it may indicate a limited degree of social differentiation between settlements in Cheshire or north of the Mersey. However, the extent of the area enclosed may depend on factors such as the number of buildings and size of the population to be housed, and how the interior space of the enclosure was used. Agricultural practices such as the number of cattle overwintering and whether cattle were kept outdoors or stalled under cover may have

an impact on the space required within an enclosure (Haselgrove 1984, 12). The presence of widely spaced ditches may denote space for corralling livestock, as at Brook House Farm, Halewood and at other newly discovered enclosures in Cheshire. Similarly, the extensive outer ditch at Mellor which encloses a substantial parcel of land on the hilltop has been interpreted as appropriate for corralling and managing livestock as well as surrounding arable land (Noble and Thompson 2005, 27-8). Until the interior of a sample of enclosed sites is examined in detail it will be unwise to use area alone as a basis for determining status. A further complication in working from uninvestigated enclosures is that it is far from certain that the settlements being compared are in fact contemporary, and chronological trends in enclosure size or form may be obscured by the lack of dated examples.

A further variable is that different forms of enclosure may also have developed in response to differences in function and site economy. Different forms may have been appropriate to different agricultural regimes. It has been suggested that isolated enclosures are likely to be curvilinear in form as this is the most efficient shape for enclosing space within the shortest circuit of ditch and bank. By contrast square or rectangular enclosures are better suited to arable regimes where the form of the enclosure fits into a pattern of arable fields whose broadly rectilinear shape is dictated by the action of the plough (Fowler 1983; Higham and Jones 1985, 78-9).

The siting of a farmstead such as Brook House Farm, Halewood on heavy clay soils, with little evidence of clearance or of cereal pollen in the vicinity of the enclosure, together with the broadly spaced ditches, argues for a strong pastoral component to the economy of the site, even if this could not be confirmed by the animal bone assemblage which was only preserved in waterlogged ditch deposits. The site also stands on the tidal inlet of the Ditton Brook, giving ready access by water to the Mersey estuary. In contrast, the settlement at Irby was situated with an eye to the exploitation of different soils and vegetation in the immediate vicinity, being on the junction between the light sandy soils, ideal for easy tillage (a landuse supported by the presence of Iron Age cereals), and the wetter and heavier soils overlying boulder clay, more suited to pasture.

Dutton's Farm, Lathom, West Lancashire (Cowell 2002; 2005a) offers an interesting parallel in certain respects to Irby. The Lathom site is on a patch of well drained land overlying windblown sand, now classified as Grade 1 arable. Neither Irby nor Lathom has produced certain evidence of an enclosing ditch in their Iron Age phases, although in both cases such a ditch could lie outside the excavated area. Although Lathom has not yet produced direct evidence of cereals in environmental sampling, it has produced a quern of prehistoric type, indicating the processing of cereals, as well as two four-post structures of a type usually interpreted as a granary (Cowell 2005a, 68-70). These two sites urge caution in assuming that all Iron Age rural sites in the region take the form of enclosures. Inevitably, as long as the principal method of detecting the sites is aerial reconnaissance or the recognition of surviving earthworks then enclosed sites will dominate the visible settlement pattern as only they show up under favourable conditions in this region. Much rarer will be the sites discovered through other means, such as newly discovered site at Bruen Stapleford, Cheshire (Fairburn 2002a) or Lathom which were found through pipeline monitoring, but only a much larger body of data on settlements will enable us to determine how far unenclosed sites formed a part of the settlement hierarchy during the Iron Age.

With the proviso over the possibility that enclosure ditches could have lain outside the excavated areas, Ron Cowell has suggested that these sites form a class of open settlement, located on relatively well drained land, which were situated primarily to take advantage of soils suitable for arable cultivation (Cowell 2005a, 75-6). Sites of this type, he argues, may represent a lower order of settlement type than the larger enclosures, which often have relatively massive earthworks and are situated to exploit land suitable for stock rearing rather than arable. These strands of evidence for arable and pastoral are unlikely to be mutually exclusive, with the mixed farming economy probable at both but the emphasis of the economic activity may be rather different. In the north west, the material culture does little to confirm or refute such a hypothesis since sites produce so few durable finds. However, if livestock and land represented major sources of wealth rather than more durable and archaeologically visible metalwork or pottery such pastoral centres may have represented concentrations of wealth.

Sub-regional differences may be beginning to emerge in the archaeological record. Cowell draws a distinction between the areas either side of the Mersey. He notes that though Cheshire has substantial hillforts at the top of the hierarchy, sites of this type appear to be absent north of the Mersey although substantial enclosures such as Brook House Farm or Portfield, Lancs. potentially parallel the second tier of 'defended' settlements in Cheshire. In southern Cornovian territory Martin Carver has emphasised the complexity of settlement hierarchy of Iron Age Shropshire. He characterised the settlement pattern within Iron Age Shropshire as consisting of a wide range of types, from simple enclosures, 'defended enclosures', hillfort-like enclosures in low-lying situations and hillforts, which together comprise 'a chronological, functional or social hierarchy of a most complex kind' (Carver 1991, 4).

One area of potential difference between the heartland of Cornovian territory and the northern area is the higher density of recorded enclosures in the core territory.

Up to 1994 no fewer than 187 enclosures have been recorded by aerial reconnaissance in the hinterland of Wroxeter, an area defined broadly as a rectangle 30 km east-west and 20 km north-south focused on the town (Jones 1994). A more recent study up to 1999 as part of the Wroxeter Hinterland Project produced a total of 324 enclosures from an area of 1200 km² (Gaffney and White 2007, 250-4). This represents a marked contrast with the current situation in Cheshire as a whole, including Wirral, where an area of roughly 2400 km² has roughly 70-80 recorded enclosures, only one-eighth of the Shropshire density. This is likely to be at least in part due to the intensity of aerial reconnaissance, which has been far greater in the core area of the Severn valley, as well as the presence of soils there which are in general more responsive to cropmark development. Whether the lower intensity of archaeological effort and the prevalence of clay soils and pasture in Cheshire, which tend not to produce good cropmarks, are sufficient to account for the difference is uncertain. There may genuinely have been a lower density of settlement in the northern Cornovian territory, or even settlement types without prominent enclosure ditches which would not lend themselves to identification through aerial reconnaissance.

While the lower site density in Cheshire as a whole may indeed represent the case in the Iron Age and Romano-British period, only further work will determine to what extent this is an accurate reflection of a historical reality. Nevertheless certain restricted areas of historical Cheshire do appear to show a greater density of sites or finds than has been detected elsewhere. As Domesday demonstrates for the late 11th century – the first time that a comprehensive record of settlements occurs for the county – there are significant differences in the density of population across the county. That these may have had their roots in long-enduring patterns of settlement is suggested by evidence such as the distribution map of Roman finds produced by Petch (1987, 186, fig. 30) which shows the eastern part of the county is noticeably thin in finds by comparison with the west and centre. Although aerial reconnaissance has proved the single most effective method of extensive survey to locate sites, it is largely dependent upon the presence of settlements enclosed by ditches, and thus automatically rules out open sites or those enclosed by palisades or other less deeply founded types of boundary. If sites are included that have been found by other means, such as metal-detecting or chance finds, then Wirral displays a significant scatter of Iron Age evidence within the county.

Iron Age Sites in Wirral

Within the last two decades a small but growing body of evidence has begun to emerge for Iron Age sites in Wirral apart from Mill Hill Road, Irby. Chief amongst these is Meols which stands in a class of its own as a

Plate XXIII: Oval enclosure at Telegraph Road, Irby, photographed in 1981

long-established mid and later Iron Age port (Matthews 1996; 1999; Philpott 2007a; 2007b), and the evidence is summarised below. As regards other sites, the evidence currently available falls into four overlapping categories; chance finds, fieldwalking, aerial reconnaissance and excavated evidence. Isolated sherds of prehistoric pottery have been recovered as chance finds and in fieldwalking. A few kilometres from Irby, at Hessle Drive, Heswall, a single sherd of possible late Bronze Age or Iron Age date was found probably in association with a stone-packed post-hole (D. Garner pers. comm.). It is likely that these structural remains represent settlement activity but this remains to be confirmed. A single late Bronze Age or Iron Age sherd was found in fieldwalking at Caldy and in the same field a curvilinear ditch cropmark has been noted in aerial reconnaissance. In one case the site takes the form of an oval enclosure, at Telegraph Road, Irby (Pl. XXIII), which has produced two sherds of Cheshire VCP and a possible late Bronze Age or Iron Age sherd. Roman pottery was recovered in systematic fieldwalking in the same field, although only one sherd came from the area of the enclosure, but a dense concentration of Roman metal finds nearby suggests that a Romano-British settlement lay about 400 m away. In the interior of the enclosure, the cropmarks of three circular features can be seen, which are almost certainly roundhouses of the usual late prehistoric type, spaced equidistantly within the interior, and therefore perhaps in contemporary use. A single-ditched curvilinear enclosure, of rather larger size, adjacent to a stream at Brimstage, is a prime candidate for another late prehistoric enclosure, but in the absence of fieldwork remains undated. An undated curvilinear feature observed as a cropmark at Burton, Wirral may be part of a further enclosure, while nearby a small earthwork demarcating a promontory at Burton Point in south-west Wirral has been interpreted as an Iron Age feature on morphological grounds (Longley 1987, 109, fig. 20; Crawford-Coupe 2005), although there is no

direct dating evidence for the site.

The material remains are in most cases not closely datable and sparse in quantity. However, when viewed in the context of the rarity of Iron Age material of any kind in the north west, it acquires considerable significance for determining settlement patterns and density. This is particularly true in the case of isolated pottery finds which are unlikely to have moved far from their place of discard. While the concentration of Iron Age material in the area of Irby, Thurstaston and Heswall in Wirral is in part a reflection of the intensity of fieldwork in this still-rural locality, it does suggest the presence of a number of settlements. However, it is not sufficient to allow a detailed analysis of the nature of settlement, its chronology and economy. In the context of the emerging settlement pattern around Irby, it is difficult to assess whether the apparent density of settlement is typical of the rest of the Wirral peninsula, or whether it is a particularly densely settled locality in the Iron Age. *A priori* it is unlikely that the density of population was consistent across the peninsula and one might anticipate a degree of selectivity in the choice of settlement sites, favouring particular topographical situations or soils. The lack of chronological control makes it impossible to determine whether there is settlement shift or conflation of more than 600 years of settlement. On the face of it, at least in those areas which have been intensively examined, it seems that this area of Wirral has a relatively dense Iron Age occupation by comparison with much of the remainder of historic Cheshire. The presence of a visible population, if sustained into the early stages of the Roman occupation of the region, might have some implications for the ability of the native farmers of the hinterland of the legionary garrison Chester to supply at least a proportion of the agricultural produce required at Chester from the AD 70s onwards.

The settlement distribution as it is currently understood may owe something to climatic and geological factors. Despite often being characterised as a county of heavy and poorly drained clay soils, there are within Cheshire numerous localised areas of well-drained land where light soils overlie sandstone outcrops or sand and gravel river terraces. These lighter soils readily lose their nutrients unless replenished by manuring but were more easily worked with an ard, a simple plough lacking a mould-board to turn the sod. Wirral and west Cheshire had some distinct advantages over regions further to the east or north during the period of deteriorating climatic conditions which form the backdrop to the Iron Age in England. As conditions worsened during the Iron Age with increased rainfall and a lower mean temperature, the attractions and benefits of some of the Cheshire sites will have become more obvious. Localised climatic effects may have proved significant factors in settlement location. Wirral and the Mersey estuary lie within the rain-shadow of north Wales, giving a markedly lower rainfall than areas to the north and east. In addition the large body of water surrounding the peninsula through the Irish Sea and the estuaries of the Dee and Mersey produces a noticeable coastal warming effect which results in longer growing seasons and more frost-free days even than localities as near as mid Cheshire.

The Irby site shows occupation in both the Iron Age and Roman period but the current excavation was not able to resolve the question of continuity from Iron Age to Romano-British. Whatever the situation for this specific period, the site is certainly an example of the repeated use of the same location for settlement at different times, a characteristic identified through excavation at a number of sites in the region, including Great Woolden Hall, Brook House Farm in Halewood, Brunt Boggart at Tarbock and Mellor. The degree of continuity of settlement location over long periods is striking. The nearby site at Telegraph Road in Irby (Pl. XXIII) may provide a model for shift of settlement focus. The consistency of the association suggests primary foci within the landscape were used repeatedly for settlement. This may have involved the continuous use of cleared arable land while the location of the associated settlement shifted periodically within defined estates or landholdings. The deliberate re-use of settlement sites might be intended to assert or reinforce ownership rights by incomers or by descendants of earlier inhabitants, where the significance of previous settlements was preserved through folk memory or through visible traces such as earthworks or vegetational differences. Intangible factors such as the association with ancestral settlements may have played a part in preserving the particular significance of a place, while functional factors associated with the availability of resources or favourable topography, which might include nearby water sources, the presence of well-drained soils, and the existence of arable land within established and maintained field systems, may all have had a role in the re-settlement of particular locations.

Meols

The most significant mid to late Iron Age site in the Wirral peninsula is Meols on the northern coast. It is one of the key sites in the north west at this time, not only in terms of the number of finds but also for their variety. The Iron Age finds range in date from the 5th or earlier 4th century BC to the early 1st century AD. The Iron Age evidence from Meols has been recently published in detail (Philpott 2007a; 2007b) so only a summary is given here.

The Meols assemblage points to long-range contacts in the late first millennium BC. Pre-Roman coins found since the 19th century included three 3rd-century BC Carthaginian drachms, two Armorican staters of the Coriosolites, dated 75-50 BC, and a Belgic gold coin of uncertain type (Hume 1863, 290; Watkin 1886, 284; Nicholson 1980, 24, no 36; Warhurst 1982, xxi, Pl.

I, nos 3 and 4; Laing and Laing 1983, 6-7; Matthews 1999; Bean 2007). These 'exotic' finds, recovered over a period of 150 years, are consistent with a pattern of a long-lived Atlantic trade route (Laing and Laing 1983; Longley 1987, 104; Cunliffe 2005, 465-84) which linked the Mediterranean via Brittany with a western coastal route in Britain. A group of four *asses* of Augustus found at Meols may form part of the late Iron Age trade during the early-mid 1st century AD, but is perhaps more likely to relate to early military activity in the pre-Flavian period.

Further support for the existence of pre-Roman trade around the west coast is found in a thin scatter of isolated finds along the route (Cunliffe 2005, 472-4; Boon 1977; 1988; Arnold and Davies 2001, 1; Philpott 2007b, 381-2). Such finds, along with the nature of Mediterranean contacts now emerging from Meols, go some way to supporting Matthews's argument (1999, 177) that the 5th-century BC Massiliote amphora said to have been dredged from the Dee is a genuine ancient loss.

The existence of continental contacts with southern Britain in the Iron Age is well established, and contact with the Iberian and Mediterranean world between the 5th and 2nd century BC is demonstrated through ancient texts as well as archaeological finds (Cunliffe 2002; 2005, 465-84). Lloyd and Jennifer Laing argued that the finds of Carthaginian coins indicated trade with the Mediterranean in the late 3rd century BC (Laing and Laing 1983). This receives some support from the distribution of pre-Roman Mediterranean coins elsewhere in the north west (Nevell 1994, 37; Philpott 2007b, 382) to which now can be added another find, a Syrian tetradrachm of Philip III (dated to after 64 BC), from Bidston, Wirral (PAS LVPL-217656). While it is conceivable that some of these coins are modern introductions collected as souvenirs by soldiers during service in the Mediterranean or by tourists and subsequently lost, the possibility remains that some are the physical residue of the attested ancient trade route filtering into the broader hinterland. Further possible indicators of traded goods, or of the late Iron Age exchange of technology, are two late Iron Age beads from Cheshire, although a post-conquest introduction of one from Linenhall Street, Chester is possible (Matthews and Vickers 2003; Matthews 2003). Until such finds occur in securely stratified contexts in the north west, any individual find will always be open to doubt, even if cumulatively the weight of material evidence does tend to point to some being ancient losses.

Higham (1993, 29) placed little emphasis on the significance of the 'very limited evidence' for direct contact with the classical world, questioning the location of the harbour at Meols as a landing place for a trade which was focused west of the Dee (1993, 29), and suggested that salt offered an alternative item of trade to minerals. This theme was developed more recently by Keith Matthews, who examined the nature of trade and trade routes at Meols (1996; 1999). He has argued that Meols like Hengistbury Head in Dorset was an emporium, a trading settlement with a good harbour which forms a point of contact between traders and the population in the hinterland. Barry Cunliffe saw Hengistbury as the point at which Armorican traders bringing exotic goods such as wine, glass, pottery and figs met local traders, who had brought a range of mineral products, livestock and manufactured goods from both the immediate hinterland and a wider procurement zone. Hengistbury was the place where the materials were assembled, modified and exchanged (Cunliffe 1987, 339-45). Local traders were responsible for redistribution of the imported goods into the hinterland. Cunliffe envisaged three zones, the immediate hinterland of the site, the broader zone of procurement which extended as far as western Cornwall, and a third, outer zone of no contact, which includes the rest of western and all of northern Britain. Matthews takes issue with the last zone (1996, 16-17), arguing that the north-western material has not been taken into account in the model of Atlantic coast trade routes and he challenges the view that the north was not involved in this trade. He suggests that the relatively local trade in Cheshire salt may have involved an international merchant class and cites a number of possible coastal sites in south-west England and Wales as candidates for a series of ports on the trade route towards Meols, while the network may extend further north, along the Cumbrian coast as far as Stevenston Sands in Strathclyde (Matthews 1999, 186).

The distribution of Cheshire stony VCP in the Iron Age points to one commodity which can plausibly be associated with Meols (Higham 1993; Matthews 1996; 1999), even if none has actually been found there. Not only has Meols, most unusually for the north west, produced a number of other finds of the appropriate period, but also its situation on the north Wirral coast places it strategically for the coastal distribution of salt, marked by its signature of VCP containers, around north Wales and into the Severn estuary (Morris 1985; Fig. 5.5).

It is unlikely that Meols was the destination of an international trade which is based solely on salt since the mineral can be obtained along the south coast of England much closer to the continent (Morris 2001, 398-410, figs 122, 123). It appears more probable that the distribution of salt along the Welsh coast travelled in a local and regional trade on the back of other goods, such as minerals, furs or slaves which would leave no trace at the port. Indeed, the list of exports from Britain given by the geographer Strabo (d. *c.* AD 21) includes such archaeologically invisible items as cattle, hides, slaves, grain, and dogs bred for hunting (*Geog.* IV.5.2). It is perhaps significant that during the medieval period the chief objects of trade from northern England were perishables such as leather, furs and fish (Laughton 1996, 69). The

mineral wealth of Clwyd, in particular lead, which was exploited by Roman entrepreneurs as early as the AD 70s, was considered by some to be the target of Mediterranean traders (e.g. Laing and Laing 1983; Longley 1987). Meols was seen as a depot analogous to the Isle of Wight for the trade in Cornish tin.

Meols may have functioned during the Iron Age as a port of trade, where manufacturing and conversion of raw materials such as leather, ores and so on took place, or it may have been a place from which cattle, slaves, fish, or furs drawn from the hinterland were exported. Meols may have been not only a port of call on a long-range west coast trade route for ships destined for ports further north, but also involved in local trade along the coast involving short journeys. Thus the exotic objects at Meols may have arrived directly from ships of Mediterranean or Gaulish origin or indirectly in the hands of intermediaries.

The character of the settlement which was the recipient, or entrepôt, of this long-range trade is uncertain. At least four circular buildings were observed during erosion of the dunes, in one case overlain by a medieval rectangular wooden structure (Cox 1895; Philpott 2007b, 386-7), and these may be Iron Age in date.

Meols with its long-range trading connections is clearly an exceptional site in the north west of England and was the most important port open to the Cornovii in the Iron Age. The presence of circular buildings may indicate a permanent settlement, although the chronology is far from certain. Although Matthews (1999, 187) has suggested that there may have been a small resident community of foreign merchants here, based on the presence of a small number of coins, it is far from certain that the volume and frequency of trade was sufficient to support such a community. The coastal trade was seasonal and may well have been organised around markets and fairs which were traditionally held at pre-arranged times generally on the borders of tribal lands in neutral territory. The port at Meols lay on the margin of Cornovian territory but within close sailing distance of two other tribal groupings, the Deceangli to the west across the Dee estuary and the Brigantes, or Setantii, across the Mersey and its location in a liminal zone may have been an important element in the significance of the port over long periods. Its marginal position within Cornovian territory, distant from the tribal heartland in Shropshire, gave it a degree of neutrality, and perhaps less rigid embedded and other social controls, the situation postulated for Redcliff, a port situated on the Humber on the boundary of two tribes (Willis 1996, 217). Such a status has been argued for Meols in the Viking period as an enclave remote from political interference and oversight, by contrast with the highly regulated situation in Chester (Griffiths 1992, 68; 2007, 402-4). If one of the roles of the port was the procurement of raw materials and conversion to manufactured items for exchange, then the zone of procurement may have embraced not only the metal deposits of northern Cheshire (Alderley Edge) but also those of north-east Wales. A coastal community which engaged in trade during the sailing season would probably have relied for the remainder of the year on an economy based on pastoral and agricultural activity, perhaps supplemented by exploiting the rich coastal resources of fish and molluscs.

Iron Age Material Culture and Trade

In terms of material culture, some progress has been made in recent years in characterising aspects of northern Cornovian society. Cheshire has begun to produce a trickle of metal finds of Iron Age date. The recording in 2009 through the Portable Antiquities Scheme of a new find of a La Tène III brooch from the Nantwich area serves to reinforce the scarcity of Iron Age metalwork (PAS LVPL-CD8AD8). This is thrown into stark relief by the total number of Iron Age finds recorded by the Portable Antiquities Scheme in Cheshire, Merseyside and Greater Manchester, up to October 2009, which stood at just 13 items, in comparison to 862 of Roman date (PAS database). The volume of material is limited and even major excavations on known sites have produced only small metalwork assemblages. At Beeston Castle, for example, Iron Age metal finds are not numerous, although the assemblage includes a set of fine copper-alloy fittings from a leather vessel, two bracelets, a horse harness link and a binding strip, as well as a small quantity of ironwork, including tools, a spearhead and a pin (Foster 1993; Stead 1993).

Elsewhere in Cheshire the small quantity of high-status metalwork is of a kind which may be associated with a warrior elite, such as horse fittings and weapons. Of certain Iron Age date is an enamelled scabbard chape of Piggott's Group II (Piggott 1950), probably of 2nd-century BC-early 1st-century AD date, found in Middlewich (Strickland 2001, 15, fig. 19). Cheshire has also produced a series of metal horse fittings, in the form of terrets and a harness mount. The terrets are long-lived types which span the late Iron Age to mid Roman period (Macgregor 1976, 48) and their discovery on some newly established Roman sites which lack late Iron Age occupation argues for a post-conquest date for at least some pieces. Thus, examples from Chester, Wilderspool and Stamford Bridge are likely to be Roman in date (Macgregor 1976, 38-48; Thompson 1965, fig. 20 no 24; Robinson and Lloyd-Morgan 1985).

Several ox-head mounts, fittings from wooden buckets, are now recorded in the county, and others are known from neighbouring areas (Hawkes 1951, 191-9). One from Crewe (Nevell 1999a, fig. 2.1) is late Iron Age in type, dating to the late 1st century BC or a little later (J. Foster pers. comm.), while others include two from

Nantwich (N. Herepath pers. comm.; Connelly and Power 2005, 34), and single examples from south Wirral and Brereton (Cheshire SMR 2502), which also indicate a native tradition of metalwork extending from the late Iron Age well into the Roman period. Macgregor has noted the northern emphasis of representations of bulls (1976, 153-4). Too much should not be read into one small group of metalwork, particularly in view of the uncertainty in dating of the finds, but the symbolism of the bull's head as a motif for such prestige metal items may reflect the importance of cattle not only in the rural economy as a source of meat, milk and leather but also in native society as an expression of wealth. Perhaps significantly, the only other type of native Iron Age form of metalwork which is commonly met with is the terret, an item of horse harness. Together these show the significance to their owners of the livestock of a pastoral economy.

Two very late Iron Age beads recorded from Cheshire have been mentioned above (Matthews and Vickers 2003; Matthews 2003). A report on the first of these notes that the method of manufacture, by blowing, was developed on the continent in the 1st century BC, indicating that the bead was either imported or represents the early importation of the new technology prior to the Roman conquest.

Other sites hint at differences in social status, with a greater emphasis on display and material wealth. Mellor appears to show high-status activity in the Iron Age, including metalworking represented by copper ore and crucibles, VCP from mid Cheshire, and pottery from the Peak District (Noble and Thompson 2005, 29). Irby receives Cheshire salt and at least one object in the form of the steatite spindle whorl which hints at regional trading contacts. Brook House Farm, Halewood also has VCP and evidence of metalworking though little sign of the metal products themselves (Cowell 2000b).

The scarcity of Iron Age metalwork is not confined to the northern Cornovii. The publication by Roger White of a small number of finds from the Wroxeter hinterland has recently emphasised the relative poverty of the relatively well-studied southern Cornovian territory in Shropshire. These include two La Tène I brooches and a small number of other finds, including one Celtic coin, which brings the total up to eight Dobunnic coins from Wroxeter or its immediate area, with two more further afield (Gaffney and White 2007, 143-5). The coins have been interpreted either as introductions by the early Roman army, the coins remaining in circulation in the early post-conquest years, or as the property of Dobunnic traders moving to the area in the wake of the army.

Pottery

The Iron Age in the north west of England has traditionally been viewed as aceramic, with the exception of the Cheshire Stony VCP salt containers (e.g. Morris 1985; Matthews 1994). Such a view was based on the restricted evidence of small and mostly early excavations in the hillforts. Given the fragility of many prehistoric pottery fabrics and their vulnerability to destruction through ploughing, the material rarely survives to be found in fieldwalking. That the region was not wholly aceramic was demonstrated by Nevell who published a small series of late prehistoric pottery vessels from the Mersey Basin (1994). His five vessel types were all from north of the Mersey, although a sherd of coarse gritty fabric, considered to be Iron Age but not published in detail, was found at Lousher's Lane, Wilderspool (Hinchliffe and Williams 1992, 100).

Other sites north of the Mersey can now be added to the distribution. Lathom has produced a small quantity of late prehistoric pottery in the gully of a roundhouse during excavations by the Liverpool Museum Field Archaeology Unit (Cowell 2002, 6; 2005a, 68). The curvilinear enclosure at Mellor has produced Iron Age pottery including the majority of a single handmade barrel-shaped vessel for which petrographic analysis suggested a source 15-20 km distant in the Castleton-Peak Forest area. Mellor also lay within the distribution network of Cheshire Stony VCP, and a small amount of other probable late prehistoric pottery is present (Cumberpatch *et al.* 2005, 35-43).

On current evidence it is less easy to identify a consistent tradition of pottery use south of the Mersey in Cheshire. Although, few Iron Age sites other than hillforts have been excavated, excavation is starting to show evidence for pottery use, albeit of a very limited nature and often dated to the early Iron Age. Pottery of this date is present at Eddisbury (Varley 1964, 90, fig. 38.3), and at Maiden Castle, Bickerton with its single sherd of a high-shouldered bucket-jar which has been attributed to the early Iron Age (Varley 1964, fig. 38.4; Longley 1987, 107). Beeston Castle has also produced early Iron Age pottery, including Wrekin fabric 2 from Shropshire, and there are hints of possible early Iron Age pottery at Irby. Single sherds of probable late Bronze Age or Iron Age pottery are recorded from two locations in Wirral, at Heswall and Caldy. A few sherds of handmade pottery from Mill Hill Road, Irby were thought by Jeremy Evans to be possibly late Iron Age or early Romano-British in date, though the lack of diagnostic criteria combined with their apparently residual status in later contexts makes this difficult to verify (see Chapter 4, *Roman Pottery*). Matthews has suggested that all the closely dated Iron Age pottery in Cheshire is from the early part of the period. If the hillforts had indeed gone out of use by the mid Iron Age, as has been claimed (e.g. Matthews 2000, 8), then the absence of later Iron Age pottery within them is something of a foregone conclusion. Nonetheless, dating evidence is sparse and we cannot yet see a consistent tradition of pottery use in the late Iron Age of the kind

which is evident in the north-east of England (Willis 1999, 83-90), or potentially in lowland north west, across the Mersey. In north-east England, pottery is found at many of the far larger sample of excavated Iron Age sites but it is restricted in quantity. There the small-scale use of vessels could be equated in some cases with as few as one vessel per decade for a whole site. Willis concludes that there was a 'social awareness of pottery … but not a habit of common/everyday use' (Willis 1999, 90). Pottery may have been confined to vessels for special activities or in particular specialised social or ceremonial contexts rather than for everyday use.

Salt

Most of the findspots of both coins and other metal items lie in southern Cheshire. In part this reflects the intensity of metal-detecting activity in that area but the finds tend to concentrate in the Nantwich to Middlewich area, precisely that part of south Cheshire which has been identified through petrographic analysis of Cheshire Stony VCP as the source of Iron Age salt production (Morris 1985). The area is rich in natural brine springs which flow to the surface and although there is no direct dated evidence of Iron Age salt production so far, an undated pit north-east of Crewe excavated in 1992 contained VCP, in close proximity to a Roman pit containing briquetage (Price 1994). Despite a lack of Iron Age production sites so far, the widespread distribution of salt in the middle and later Iron Age employing Cheshire Stony VCP containers indicates a substantial production (Morris 1985). In the Roman period salt-working can now be seen to have been a significant industry at Middlewich and Nantwich, as well as in rural locations (Penney and Shotter 1996, 363-5; 2001; Leah 2003; Burnham *et al.* 2003, 318), and the Iron Age origins of the industry are certain in general terms, if not precisely located thus far.

The organisation of salt production and distribution in the Iron Age in Cheshire is a matter for speculation. It has been suggested from the expanding distribution and from the massive quantity of standardised containers used for drying and transportation of salt at Droitwich that salt production was increasingly a specialised activity during the late Iron Age (Haselgrove 1989, 6). White and Barker (1998, 34-5) have argued that the organisation of a longer-range trade in salt demands strong control by the aristocracy over the production and distribution of the product. Such a view, they recognise, runs counter to the usual view of the Cornovii as a politically fragmented and decentralised tribe, based on the evidence of the large number of hillforts within the core Cornovian territory in Shropshire.

Others have argued that elite control over the production and distribution is not necessary. The level of technological expertise for salt production was relatively low, using coarse hand-made containers, simple hearths, water channels and plank-lined pits. Although a seasonal activity as it required solar heat for the initial evaporation, the level of technology and investment of labour were perhaps no more intensive than the household industry for pottery production. The product was probably made however for consumption outside the immediate household, perhaps by those with particular skills, suggesting to Morris that a household industry (using de Roche's terminology) might be appropriate (Morris 2001, 396-7). Morris has argued that, as the inland brine springs in Britain have produced no evidence of defensive structures or a high status cemetery which might denote the special status of the salt-producing community, there is no evidence of strict control of the resource (Morris 1996, 50-1). In Cheshire there are many potential sources of brine as saline springs occur over a wide area mostly where valleys cut across the wet rock head (Nevell 2005, fig. 6). Such an extensive range of localised brine sources may have been too widely dispersed for a strong measure of centralised or elite control to be easily exercised unless, as Morris points out, this was effected through means such as social taboo.

A possible model for the production and distribution of salt is offered by the case of prehistoric tin mining in Cornwall. Cunliffe suggests that mining of the ore was unlikely to be the work of full-time professionals but was probably a seasonal activity organised like a cottage-industry on a family or extended family basis. It could be combined with activities such as shepherding. The marketing required more complex organisation. Here Cunliffe suggests that markets would be held at certain fixed places at agreed times to which individual producers would take their wares and sell to traders from the continent who would arrive by sea for the markets, one of which is recorded by Diodorus Siculus as Ictis (Cunliffe 2005, 470-2; 2002, 76, 85-6). Such a model requires no elite control over production and distribution. The distribution is undertaken by the producers themselves, who bring the processed material to the market place in their carts, and negotiate directly with the continental merchants. Although there is no guarantee that the social system hinted at there is necessarily the same in the north west of England, the merit of the observation is that it is derived not from extrapolation from anthropological parallels but from contemporary observation of an analogous trade in minerals in Iron Age Britain.

Distribution of VCP

The distribution of VCP marks the trade in salt crystallised out and then transported in ceramic vessels rather than a trade in the vessels themselves. Morris distinguishes two distinct phases of distribution of the material, with a marked change from a 'core' distribution area of no further than 50 km in the early Iron Age, after about 500 BC, and an 'extended' pattern

in the later Iron Age where the material travels up to 140 km from source, indicating transportation both along the coast and then inland using riverine routes, as far as the Severn into the territory of the Dobunni in Herefordshire, Worcestershire and Gloucestershire (Morris 1985, 367-70, figs 10-12). Previous distribution maps of Cheshire Stony VCP show a significant southwards trend to the distribution with relatively few sites north of the source area. This is rapidly changing as further archaeological work increases the density of investigated sites in Cheshire itself and also sites in Greater Manchester and Merseyside (Fig. 5.5). The material is now recorded from Cheshire in formal excavations at Beeston Castle (Royle and Woodward 1993, 74), Bruen Stapleford (Morris 2002, 31-3), and probably at Wilderspool (Hinchliffe and Williams 1992, 100). There are reports of VCP amongst residual prehistoric material from Abbey Green, Chester and Handbridge on the Dee (Matthews 2001, 13), while reinterpretation of old finds suggests VCP was present at Eddisbury (Varley 1950). Fieldwalking has also produced VCP in the Weaver valley at Sutton Weaver (R. Cowell pers. comm.), and in fieldwalking at Telegraph Road, Irby (two sherds).

The settlement at Irby also lay within the distribution network of salt in VCP containers from mid Cheshire. Certainly the salt appears to have been distributed along the Weaver valley, probably the principal river routeway from the production zone in the Nantwich-Middlewich area to the Mersey. The same route was used to convey salt to Liverpool from Cheshire in the 17th century (Hyde 1971, 3). By such a route it reached at least two sites north of the Mersey, at Brook House Farm, Halewood (Cowell 2000b) and Great Woolden Hall, Salford (Nevell 1999a), probably making use of tributaries of the Mersey, the tidal reaches of the Ditton Brook, and the Glaze Brook respectively. It may be no coincidence that the earliest Iron Age finds from Meols date to the 5th century BC at the same time as the expansion of the salt trade occurs. Recent finds from the Iron Age enclosure at Mellor, on the Pennine fringe, about 35 km from Middlewich, extend the northward distribution of VCP still further, and demonstrate that, as in the medieval period, an overland long-distance distribution network for Cheshire salt complemented the riverine/estuarine routes.

The distribution was not constrained by tribal boundaries as we can reconstruct them at the time of the Roman conquest (Cunliffe 2005, 208-14). During the late Iron Age the distribution of VCP indicates that the trade in Cheshire salt crossed the Mersey, and appeared along the north Wales coast, as far as Anglesey and west Wales, and penetrated even as far as south Shropshire and into territory of the Dobunni in the lower Severn estuary (Fig. 5.5). The Severn estuary lay within the area which had received salt from the much closer Droitwich salt industry in Worcestershire during the middle Iron

Age (Morris 1996, 51). Recent finds have extended the range of Cheshire Stony VCP eastwards into the territory of the Corieltauvi as far as Leicestershire (Breedon-on-the-Hill and Normanton-le-Heath), Derbyshire (Aston upon Trent and Swarkestone Lowes), Nottinghamshire (Gamston), and Staffordshire (Fisherwick) through the Soar and Trent valleys (Elsdon 1994, 37-8; Knight 2002, 141; see Chapter 4, *Cheshire Salt Containers*). Knight notes that the Lincolnshire coastal salterns were closer than the Cheshire source, but points out that the distribution networks are unknown for the Lincolnshire salt and organic containers may have been used which do not survive. As the distribution of Cheshire salt into the lower Severn demonstrates, the distribution of this commodity did not depend solely on proximity to the source. There may have been social or political links which are now invisible which rendered these longer-range connections viable. Alternatively Cheshire salt may have qualities which were more prized than the material from closer to hand.

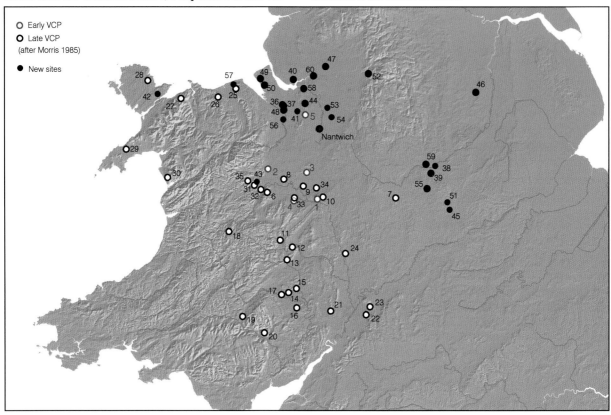

Fig. 5.5: Distribution of Cheshire Stony VCP (after Morris 1985, figs 9 and 10: sites 1-35, with additions)

1	The Wrekin	23	Danes' Camp, Conderton	43	Collfryn (Britnell 1989, 124-5)
2	Old Oswestry	24	Blackstone	44	Eddisbury (Varley 1950)
3	Bury Walls	25	Moel Hiraddug	45	Enderby Morris 1994, 385)
4	Sharpstones Hill - Site A	26	Dinorben	46	Gamston (Knight 1992, 87)
5	Beeston Castle	27	Braich-y-Ddinas	47	Great Woolden Hall (Nevell 1999a)
6	The Breidden	28	Pant-y-Saer	48	Handbridge (Matthews 2001, 13)
7	Fisherwick	29	Garn Boduan	49	Irby (this volume)
8	The Berth	30	Pen Dinas, Llanaber	50	Irby, Telegraph Road (R. Cowell unpublished)
9	Ebury Hill	31	Collfryn		
10	Castle Farm	32	Arddleen	51	Kirby Muxloe (Clay 2001, 11)
11	Burrow Hill	33	Sharpstones Hill-Site E	52	Mellor (Cumberpatch *et al.* 2005, 40-2)
12	Bromfield enclosure	34	Wall Camp, Kynnersley		
13	Croft Ambrey	35	Llywn Bryn-Dinas	53	Middlewich (Dodds 2005, 29-30)
14	Credenhill	36	Abbey Green, Chester (Matthews 2001, 13)	54	Moston (Price 1994, 4)
15	Sutton Walls			55	Normanton-le-Heath (Elsdon 1994)
16	Dinedor	37	Amphitheatre, Chester (Anon 2006)	56	Poulton (Nevell 2005, 11)
17	Kenchester enclosure	38	Aston upon Trent (Morris 1999)	57	Prestatyn (Blockley 1989, 166)
18	Cefn Carnedd	39	Breedon-on-the-Hill (Elsdon 1994, 38)	58	Sutton Weaver (R. Cowell unpublished)
19	Twyn Llechfaen				
20	Twyn-y-Gaer	40	Brook House Farm, Halewood (Cowell 2000b, 44-5)	59	Swarkestone Lowes (Elliott and Knight 1999)
21	Midsummer Hill				
22	Beckford II	41	Bruen Stapleford (Morris 2002, 31-3)	60	Wilderspool (Hinchliffe and Williams 1992, 100)
		42	Bryn Eryr (Longley 1998, 248)		

Amongst the Iron Age finds from Cheshire is a small number of British coins from two neighbouring tribes. A stater of the Dobunni, the tribe whose capital stood at Cirencester, Gloucestershire, was found at Knutsford (PAS LVPL80), while three coins of the Corieltauvi, located in the East Midlands, are recorded from findspots near Nantwich, Halton and Warmingham (Tindall 1993; Matthews 1999; Strickland 2001, 15, fig. 20). Although Higham dismisses the Corieltauvian coins as either losses from later collections or items brought by mercenaries returning home (Higham 1993, 27), this argument loses much of its force in the context of the discovery of VCP from half a dozen sites in the east Midlands (Fig. 5.5). For a society which did not use coinage, the Iron Age coin finds do not represent direct cash payment for goods but are best regarded as objects of value received through gift exchange. Morris considered that the mid-late Iron Age distribution of Cheshire salt resembled down-the-line distribution pattern, travelling over distances of more than 100 km (1996, 51, fig. 5.3a). The salt trade provides a mechanism for the flow of small quantities of durable metal objects into the production area, and demonstrates the wide network of trading and social contacts between communities in Cheshire and those in the east Midlands. The vast majority of these links have left no material trace.

Excavation shows that salt containers were reaching settlements north of the Mersey, such as Great Woolden Hall and Brook House Farm, Halewood (Nevell 1999a; Cowell 2000b, 44-5). Determining the north-western limit to the distribution is hampered by a dearth of excavated Iron Age sites beyond the Mersey. However, the absence of VCP from the late Iron Age site at Lathom, West Lancashire, which was occupied from the 2nd century BC into at least the early Roman period (Cowell 2002, 5; 2005a, 68-70), suggests the trading networks and social contacts between communities which effected the distribution of the material may not have extended beyond the watershed of the Mersey tributaries, at least during that period (R. Cowell pers. comm.). The extensive mosses of northern Merseyside and West Lancashire running from the coast towards Manchester have traditionally been viewed as a bar to communication and settlement, which 'effectively cut off the North-west to land access from the south and served equally as barrier and defence' (Howard-Davis *et al.* 1988, 2). This sparsely populated belt of mossland formed a natural boundary zone between the settlements of the Mersey basin and those to the north, about which at present virtually nothing is known. The Mersey basin may have been seen as a naturally defined territory in the same way as the Ellesmere moraine has been seen as a natural boundary not only to the historic county of Cheshire but also between what might be termed core Cornovian territory and that of the 'northern Cornovii' (e.g. Matthews 2001, 3). In the latter case the topographical 'barrier', essentially a major watershed,

was far less marked, but already appears to have formed a cultural divide in the Bronze Age.

A further consideration is that communities further north in the Ribble basin may have had alternative sources of salt through the evaporation of sea water, a technique which was practised widely in southern and eastern England in the Iron Age (Cunliffe 2005, 509-13). Thus far there are no records of late prehistoric saltings from the north-west coastline, although salt was evaporated from sea-brine on the Lancashire coast in the 16th century and an early 13th-century reference to a salt pit at North Meols indicates the potential for exploitation of this source at an earlier period (Camden 1695, 794; Lewis 2002, 12).

The significance of salt for the occupants of the Iron Age farmstead is difficult to reconstruct. One of its chief purposes is to preserve meat, for which it has a long ancestry, but preserving hides and making cheese are other uses, the latter enabling storage of a milk surplus (Morris 2001). However, Reynolds calculated that for salting meat, over 20 kg of salt would be required for a cubic metre of meat (1979, 78). While undoubtedly a valued commodity, salt was not essential for preserving meat or fish, as either can be smoked or wind-dried. The small numbers of vessels recovered from sites such as Irby suggest it was a prestigious commodity with restricted use rather than one in regular use as a routine preservative for large quantities of meat. It is of course conceivable that the low level of VCP found at sites such as Irby reflects only one source of salt, while salt made at coastal salterns could have been transported in organic containers of wood or leather, leaving no trace in the settlements.

Other Finds

Other Iron Age finds provide occasional hints of trading patterns or social contacts within Cheshire. The pottery at Beeston includes nine sherds of Wrekin Fabric 2, indicating no more than one or two vessels transported from mid Shropshire to mid Cheshire (Royle and Woodward 1993, 73). Coin finds are discussed above, and may form part of the network of communications and trade which was based on distribution of salt. The steatite spindle whorl (SF2931) from Irby is an unusual object with its striking decoration, originating in Anglesey. The soft nature of the raw material makes it ideal for skilled craftwork in the production of highly detailed decoration. The presence of this item at Irby indicates contact between communities here and in Anglesey. It is conceivable that the object had been passed 'down the line' in a sequence of gift exchanges and furthermore it is possible that the object passed through the port of Meols on its way to Irby, following the coastal trade route. This may well represent a rare piece of evidence for the distribution of prestige imports into the hinterland of Meols.

The extent to which the Mersey acted as a tribal boundary delimiting social networks of communities on either side, or alternatively formed corridor of trade and contact between those communities and others in the interior of Cheshire or further north along coast of Lancashire, and to north Wales is a subject for further research. Certainly the salt distribution indicates movement around the Welsh coast, though a lack of excavated sites to the north inhibits further consideration of the pattern in that direction.

Social Organisation in the Iron Age

The type of society to which the occupants of the settlement at Irby belonged is poorly understood at present. The recognition that marked regional differences existed in the way Iron Age societies were organised means that each region needs to be considered in its own right (Haselgrove *et al.* 2001, 23). The north west has been usually characterised as having an undeveloped social structure at the time of the Roman occupation (however, for a different view, see Matthews 2001, 30-5). Elsewhere the socio-economic structure of native Iron Age groups was often used and modified by Roman authorities. This part of the Cornovian territory may have lacked a cohesive tribal hierarchy of the kind which elsewhere was used by the Roman authorities to shape the provinces' administrative structure.

The lowland north west as a whole has produced little sign of the accumulation of luxury items such as horse gear or weapons which in areas of southern England point to a marked social differentiation between an elite and the lower orders within a stratified society. On the face of it, the social system as far as it can be reconstructed through the imperfect evidence of artefacts, air reconnaissance and excavation does not seem to point to the emergence of a highly stratified society. There is no evidence of the major nucleated settlements in northern Cornovian territory in the later Iron Age which correspond to those in other areas, such as the territory of the Corieltauvi. Clearly wealth can be accumulated in other ways than coin or metalwork and archaeologically visible goods. A society based on a restricted and relatively shallow social hierarchy, with loose adherence by individual local households to a chieftain-based group, membership being defined on the basis of kinship, may have held wealth in perishable and archaeologically invisible forms, including land and livestock such as horses or cattle, while prestige and social standing may be derived from social relations such as clientship and patronage, through birth or individual ability such as martial prowess. However, as Gaffney and White (2007, 279-81) point out, the fact that the tribe did not build oppida like the southern English tribes, preferred organic vessels over ceramic ones, and did not mint coins is not a reason to consider them undeveloped, backward or inferior. 'It is hardly right to judge the success or failure of Cornovian

society on the basis of the presence or absence of objects that may have held little or no social value for them' (Gaffney and White 2007, 280). However, the limited quantity of metal artefacts of late Iron Age type in the north west may provide some evidence of the emergence into archaeological visibility of a local elite class amongst the northern Cornovii of Cheshire. One group is significantly based within the salt-producing area, but a few finds from Wirral hint at access amongst local communities in the hinterland to exotic material imported through the port at Meols, although the return for such trade was not monetary. Gaffney and White note a similar pattern amongst the central Cornovian region of Shropshire. Although what they term 'the material correlates of Cornovian value' may be largely invisible archaeologically, there is a small number of metal finds which are not of low quality or status and they emanate from lowland sites, rather than hillforts (2007, 279-81) which hints at a degree of preferential access to status goods. In terms of settlements, a class of site, the multiple-ditched enclosure, such as the excavated site at Collfryn, may occupy a superior position within regional settlement hierarchy. Furthermore, they argue that the rapid development of the town of *Viroconium Cornoviorum* after the Roman conquest indicates the existence of a stratified society.

Insights from more widely researched regions may provide an analogy which we can test against the growing evidence as a basis of social organisation in the north west. Perhaps the most appropriate model is that proposed by Colin Haselgrove for late Iron Age society in the north-east of England, which he characterised as a generalised competitive 'tribal system'. Such societies are made up of a series of units at ascending levels of inclusion (Haselgrove 1984, 20-21; 1989, 16). The smallest unit in this social formation is the household or local domestic-group. These were linked together in a series of clans, 'relatively small-scale corporate groups, each headed by an elite, but retaining a strong emphasis on the communal control of resources within the collective territory'. These smaller units were bound together in wider culturally differentiated groups, linked by common descent and clientship ties, which correspond with the tribal entities recorded in the late 1st century AD. Competition for rank was played out at the level of the basic household group, both within and between clans, wealth and power being accumulated through gift exchange and marriage alliances. One of the fundamental characteristics of such a society was the instability and transience of the largest corporate grouping, the tribe. Common action was limited to spheres such as territory, ancestry or shared ritual, and then only in the face of outside pressure. Although heads of households may have risen to the fore as leaders of the larger group at times of threat through personal prestige, prowess or the forging of alliances, any long-term coercive power was severely weakened by the fragile and transient nature of their authority. Such societies were characterised by a lack of permanent centralised authority (Haselgrove 1984, 21).

The characteristics of this social system in the archaeological record are in a lack of obvious absolute ranking in terms of a settlement hierarchy, or of a developed degree of political centralisation. The failure of the north-east north of the Humber and Trent, as well as the north west, to take on innovations found further south-east, such as coin use, suggests fundamental differences in the nature of the society. In such a system the basic unit of society is therefore the extended household which in archaeological terms correlates with the discrete farmstead enclosure.

The origins of this kind of social system derive from a steadily growing population within a thinly populated region, where daughter settlements grow up to form clans linked by common ancestry. Over several generations these subsidiary settlements themselves become independent groups which begin in time to compete with their founding settlements. Within this hierarchical model, the tribal unit emerges as an over-arching group which regulates and arbitrates between the component clans over the use of unclaimed land and other resources (Haselgrove 1984, 21).

Richard Hingley has sought to identify the processes involved in social formations in the use of resources within the landscape. Within sparsely inhabited land-scapes with widely separated enclosed settlements, the isolated local group, the extended household, would be the most important unit of society, able to control and exploit territory independently of one another. Of less significance would be their membership at a higher level of a loose kinship-based group. Where settlements were more densely concentrated with common boundaries, the need to regulate and control access to resources be-tween local groups would lead to a more prominent role for larger-scale groups (cited in Haselgrove 1984, 21). Such a model has interesting implications for the nature of society in Cheshire where what appears to have been a generally low level of Iron Age population is far more likely to result in a society where the local group was the principal unit over much of the region. Indeed the Irby area is one of the very few in Cheshire, the Dee valley potentially being another, where our current knowledge of finds and site distribution suggests that the density of settlement might have been sufficiently high to lead to competition over resources and land.

Keith Matthews has discussed the nature of social organisation within Iron Age Cheshire (Matthews 2001, 30-5). He reaches conclusions which radically depart from the generally perceived low level of population and shallow social hierarchy of social organisation. In a discussion of the 'elite dominance model' he considers that an economic elite emerged during the early and middle Iron Age, basing its wealth and power on the

development and organisation of the long-distance exchange of salt and other products, and with direct continental contacts. This interpretation sees a close relationship between the smaller lowland promontory enclosures such as Peckforton or Oakmere and their neighbouring hillforts. The smaller enclosures may represent the residence of the developing elite while the larger hillforts contained their own larger populations. From this, he suggests that the middle Iron Age saw the localised chiefdoms developing into a more complex system. Increasingly large settlements required a stronger political authority than before and the emergent rulers based their power largely on economic control. The inherent instability of chiefdoms, he argues, makes it unlikely that what he considers to be the long-term social stability of the north west can be explained in terms of chiefdoms. The stability manifested itself in resistance to the incursion of Roman cultural practices and 'retained its coherence for more than a millennium' (Matthews 2001, 34). Instead he argues that this stability can only be explained in terms of social formation moving from chiefdom to a more complex state system. This would be some centuries before the process was complete in the south east. Furthermore, following the model of Kosse (Matthews 2001, 26, table 1), such a state system would consist of a hierarchy containing no fewer than five tiers, with a maximum population in the largest settlement of more than 2500, and a regional network for the next rung down of about 1500 km², corresponding to much of modern Cheshire.

However, such 'long-term stability' is not defined, and is appears to be largely based on the absence of durable material finds throughout the period. It might be countered that the strength and durability of the social structure within the northern Cornovian territory is determined by the low-level household group rather than at the unstable and fissile tribal elite level. Any stability may be explained as much by continuity in terms of settlement location and stability of land units and ownership at the lowest level of society. Long-term continuity in terms of settlement location and economic activity occurred through lack of major pressure on the landscape and an absence of serious competition for resources during the Iron Age and Romano-British period rather than through the development of a complex state system.

The Late Iron Age to Romano-British Transition

One of the research aims of the Irby excavation was to recover evidence to determine the continuity or otherwise of occupation from the late Iron Age to the Roman period. To demonstrate continuity would require either a series of datable artefacts or a closely dated stratigraphic sequence which spanned the end of the Iron Age into the early Romano-British period, essentially the period of the early to late 1st century AD.

The evidence from Brook House Farm, Halewood is instructive in that the presence of a small quantity of late 1st-century samian on a later prehistoric site may argue for a continuous occupation into the early Roman period from the late Iron Age but the possibility of a hiatus in occupation has also been postulated on the basis of a stand-still phase in the filling of the main enclosure ditch and the radiocarbon dates (Cowell 2000b, 62-3). If there was a break in occupation we cannot assess how long it lasted, but we can be confident that by the early years of the 2nd century, if not the last decades of the 1st, the site was once more in occupation and in receipt of manufactured items. The virtual absence of other Roman pottery from that site may argue for a relatively short phase of occupation during the Roman period or one which saw little Roman pottery in use. At Lathom, West Lancashire, continuity from late Iron Age to Romano-British has been demonstrated from a sequence of at least three overlapping circular buildings. The earliest yielded a radiocarbon date of the mid 4th-1st century BC (345-1 cal BC; Beta-153894; 2100 ± 40BP), while the latest contains several sherds of Romano-British pottery. The sequence of structures suggests a series of buildings spanning the 2nd or 1st century BC to at least the late 1st century AD (Cowell 2002).

At Irby, as discussed in Chapter 2, neither the stratigraphic sequence nor the artefact assemblage are sufficiently clear to enable a transitional period to be distinguished in the archaeological record. Radiocarbon dating of selected features from the earlier phases of occupation by chance concentrated on a phase of mid Bronze Age occupation and whilst pointing to the presence of mid Iron Age activity did little to enable it to be recognised across the site. No late Iron Age artefacts at Irby can be identified on either typological or stylistic grounds. The presence of VCP could represent the occupation of the site through an otherwise aceramic occupation phase in the later Iron Age. This is the position at Bryn Eryr, Gwynedd where the only ceramic material in the Iron Age is VCP (Longley *et al.* 1998, 192).

The physical relationship shows a degree of overlap between the distribution of Iron Age VCP and the main Romano-British structural phases at Irby (Fig. 2.12). It is likely that during the Romano-British period the focus of occupation shifted southwards and westward across the site, while the initial enclosure phase, represented by a palisade, appears to be in the eastern part of the site. It has been suggested that the absence of well defined and recognisable later 1st-century Romano-British features may indicate that the focus of settlement at that time lay outside the principal excavated area, perhaps within the eastern palisaded enclosure.

For the later part of the transitional period, following the permanent Roman occupation of the area, the material evidence from Irby becomes stronger, although once again not entirely free of uncertainty over the precise chronology. The pottery includes some South Gaulish samian, dated no more precisely than to the period AD 70-110 (see Chapter 4, *The Samian*) and a little coarse pottery which may be as early as the late 1st century (see Chapter 4, *Roman Pottery*). However, much of the samian is very fragmentary and shows evidence of repair, and this could be curated material buried long after its manufacture. While this might indicate that the site was already occupied at some stage during the last third of the 1st century or very early 2nd century AD, it does not enable us to determine exactly when occupation began. It may have been during that 40-year period or at an earlier date with the durable artefactual material, other than odd pieces, virtually absent from the site before the AD 70s. In any case, the rate at which Roman material culture was adopted on rural settlements is unclear, and may have varied depending upon individual attitudes to, and relationships with, the occupying military administration on the part of the native population but some time-lag might be anticipated. The evidence from Welsh site such as Bryn Eryr and Collfryn, points to differing rates of acculturation and adoption of Roman material culture. At the latter, pottery use did not become common until the end of the 2nd century (Britnell 1989, 119), a considerably longer time-lag than at Irby, although the quantity of datable pottery seems to increase in the later Roman period. The finds assemblage could be taken to represent the gradual acculturation of the native occupants of the Irby site during the last three decades of the 1st century AD.

The material evidence is thus insufficiently clear to enable us to distinguish between the two main possibilities: that the settlement continued in occupation from the late Iron Age through to the early Romano-British period without a break, or that occupation ended in the mid Iron Age and the site was re-occupied during the late 1st century AD. In terms of rural settlements from the region with their notorious poverty of durable, archaeologically visible artefacts this comes as little surprise, and indeed the presence of at least one datable mid Iron Age find, the steatite spindle whorl, is highly unusual. The finds evidence could indeed be interpreted as continuous late Iron Age occupation through to the Romano-British period with the cultural material only becoming present in significant quantities after the permanent Roman occupation of the area by the AD 70s, with the foundation of the legionary fortress at Chester.

The Roman Period

Robert Philpott

The Historical Context

The Cornovii are usually considered to be one of the tribes who yielded to the emperor Claudius soon after the Roman invasion of AD 43. However, Roman military interventions from the AD 40s onwards were likely to have involved Cheshire and the area to the north of the Mersey. The region certainly saw Roman military activity by Ostorius Scapula against the Deceangli of north Wales in AD 48, when disturbances amongst the Brigantes led to abandonment of the campaign in order to rescue Cartimandua. In AD 60 the Roman army under Suetonius Paullinus moved against Anglesey and the presence of intervening hostile ground has led to suggestions that Chester was the base for the attack, perhaps supported by the existing harbour at Meols where pre-Flavian coins and other items have been found, including a military belt-buckle (Philpott 2007c; 2007d). A pre-fortress auxiliary fort at Chester has been postulated by several authorities, either in the early Flavian period by Cerialis (Petch 1987, 135-6) or, following Shotter's re-examination of the coin evidence, in the mid Neronian period (Shotter 1998, 39-44; 2000b). The region also will have seen Roman soldiers on campaign against the Brigantes, attested by Tacitus probably in the AD 50s under Didius Gallus and again under Vettius Bolanus in AD 69, while the instability of the Brigantes under Cartimandua may have led to other interventions (Shotter 1997, 7-27). Probably by the early 60s, lead extraction had begun under official control at Halkyn (Petch 1987, 118, 135; Higham 1993, 38).

The beginning of permanent Roman occupation of north west England is marked by the foundation of the legionary fortress at Chester, *c.* AD 74. Forts associated with the permanent installation of garrisons can be seen in the early AD 70s further north than Cheshire. Ribchester on the river Ribble in Lancashire has a short-lived initial phase of construction of the fort and defences dated probably to AD 72 (Buxton and Howard-Davis 2000), while Carlisle has occupation showing felling of timber in the winter of AD 71-2 (Caruana 1992, 103).

Military control of northern Cornovian territory was secured through a series of forts, including Northwich with Flavian activity, at Harbutts Field, Middlewich, probably in the early 70s though not closely dated (Strickland 2001, 25), and another, further to the east at Manchester, probably constructed *c.* AD 78 (Redhead 2005, 56-7). The Cheshire forts do not appear to have remained in occupation beyond the mid 2nd century.

In the late 1st century a series of nucleated settlements such as Middlewich, Northwich and Wilderspool developed and engaged in the industrial production of salt, metalwork (iron and non-ferrous), glass, pottery and other commodities requiring hearths (Fig. 5.6; Burnham *et al.* 2003, 318). The establishment of an industrial centre at the important Mersey crossing at Wilderspool, may have been preceded by a fort on the opposite, north, bank though no unequivocal evidence has yet come to light for this (cf. Strickland 1995, 25). Increasingly, excavations show that the bulk of activity

falls within the period AD 90 to the early 3rd century but with a lower level of activity to the early 4th century. At Middlewich there is a strong decline in coin-loss after *c.* 260 (Shotter 2000c, 106), somewhat later than the decline at Wilderspool, Walton-le-Dale and Holt (Shotter 2000a; Rogers and Garner 2007). Excavations at Kingsley Fields, Nantwich show the inhabitants were involved in salt-working and from the 3rd century also cattle processing, involving tanning and leather working (Connelly and Power 2005, 38-9).

North of the Mersey, Wigan and Walton-le-Dale, which are both accessible by water, probably served as industrial centres, or storage depots for military supplies produced within the region, representing manufacturing for the military rather than run by the army (e.g. Shotter 1997, 81; Burnham 2006, 399). In the case of Wigan, its location on a coalfield is without doubt significant, while a possible Roman pottery waster hints at industrial production there (Clark 1991, 16, no 31). The results of the 2005 excavations on Millgate, which includes a bath-house and associated structure, will shed further light on its role (Redhead 2005, 59, fig. 5.19).

Jeremy Evans has argued that the sites along the Roman King Street – Middlewich, Wilderspool, Wigan and Walton-le-Dale – are not small towns in the conventional sense but are manufacturing centres. They have little in the way of buildings for habitation, but mostly have large sheds, often open-ended. The pottery supply shows high levels of samian, especially decorated forms, and of amphorae, a characteristic of military sites. Some types are most common at sites on or near the west coast, indicating a coastal supply route. Though not directly military itself, their pottery 'supply is being drawn from the same mechanism that is supplying military units in the region' (Evans forthcoming b). However, the finds and animal bone assemblages are of poor quality and there is an absence of living accommodation despite the presence of large aisled halls which has suggested a servile dimension to the population there (Evans forthcoming b). These settlements appear to have developed under military supervision in order to exploit the raw materials to produce manufactured goods intended largely for military consumption in the frontier zone to the north.

Romano-British Settlement in Wirral

Set within this broad geographical context, rural settlement remains relatively under-researched and often elusive. The most significant Roman site in Wirral was the port at Meols (discussed in detail in Philpott 2007c), and in view of its proximity, only 6 km to the north-west, with a more immediate economic impact on the farmstead at Irby. The port continued in operation from the late Iron Age through the early Roman period, as demonstrated by coins of Claudius AD 41-54 (3) and Nero AD 54-68 (5) (Watkin 1886, 282), two Aucissa

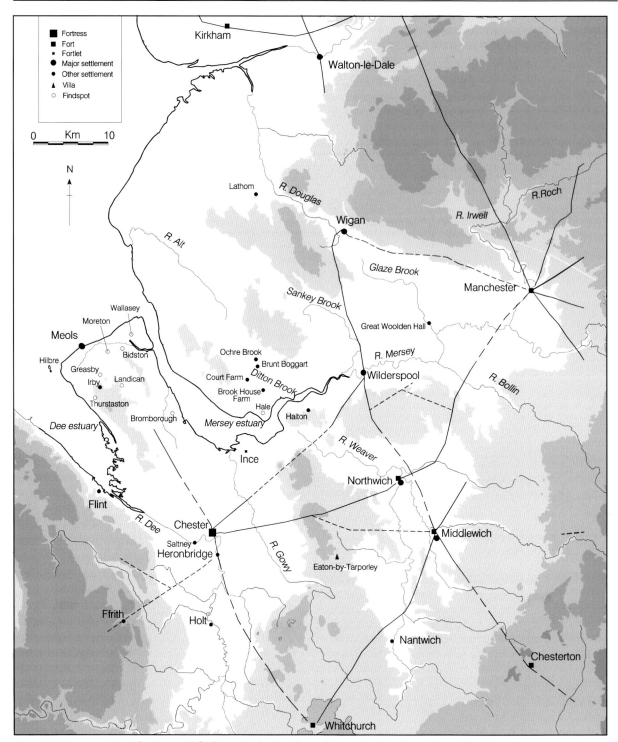

Fig. 5.6: Romano-British sites and findspots in lowland north west England mentioned in the text

brooches, and other pre-Flavian finds through to the late Roman period, the coin list ending with Magnus Maximus (383-388), although finds continue into the post-Roman period (Hume 1863; Bu'Lock 1960; Petch 1987, 195; Philpott 2007b). During the Roman period Meols is likely to have acted not only as a transshipment port for Chester but also as the local market for the rural settlements of northern Wirral such as Irby. Certainly such commodities as black-burnished ware, which were imported from Dorset by the coastal route, find their way into rural communities in some quantity. Jeremy Evans has suggested that the high proportion of BB1 in the Irby assemblage resulted from the proximity of the port of Meols (J. Evans pers. comm.).

In recent years western Wirral has produced a series of known or suspected Romano-British occupation sites, through aerial photography, fieldwalking or metal detecting. Within Irby township itself, near Harrocks Wood, *c.* 1.4 km from the Mill Hill Road site, a scatter of Romano-British oxidised ware has been located by fieldwalking (J. Whalley pers. comm.). This type of pottery suggests occupation during the 2nd or 3rd century AD but the site has not been further investigated. Further afield, on the township boundary between Irby and Thurstaston, a strong cluster of metal-detector finds, including brooches and seven coins, indicates the location of at least one further site, with late 1st to at least late 3rd-century occupation, while a thin spread of pottery and metal finds in adjacent fields may be a halo effect from this core, or may be associated with an oval enclosure observed as a cropmark site in the 1980s which lies close to the main metal-detector concentration. Fieldwalking in the immediate environs of the enclosure has produced Roman pottery, including a Hartshill-Mancetter mortarium rim, although within the enclosure itself only one Roman sherd but three prehistoric sherds were recovered. This may be a single settlement that shifted location during the late prehistoric or Romano-British period, or two distinct neighbouring sites. Potentially a significant factor in the location of the settlement was the nearby spring on the township boundary known in the medieval period as Londymere Well (Beazley 1924, 12). Clearance of the well in 1981-2 produced prehistoric flintwork as well as medieval finds, though nothing specifically Romano-British (Merseyside HER).

Evidence of Romano-British sites within a 5 km radius of Mill Hill Road include a subrectangular enclosure subdivided by a cross-ditch identified as a cropmark in Greasby, in a field which has produced Roman pottery in fieldwalking, while 3 km away a faint curvilinear enclosure is recorded at Landican, a place with an early British place-name (Thacker 1987, 240; Dodgson 1972), where once again fieldwalking in 1990 has revealed Roman oxidised ware; a 2nd-century coin had earlier been found close by. Small clusters of finds in West Kirby, Barnston, Raby, Newton and Heswall suggest further settlements existed there, while small quantities of Roman pottery and coins at both Moreton and Bidston, and a sherd excavated at Overchurch, in Upton township – all recovered from sites of later date – extend the distribution of probable settlement sites.

The western bias of the findspots within the Wirral peninsula has much more to do with modern urban de-velopment than the Romano-British settlement pattern. Chance finds point to several probable settlement sites, including coin finds from Bromborough and Lower Bebington and an amphora-like vessel from Kingsland Road, Tranmere (Petch 1987, 230; Philpott 1991), but the inability to carry out fieldwork over much of eastern Wirral makes it impossible now to redress the balance.

A little further away from Irby, the sandstone ridge in rural south-west Wirral has produced several concentrations of finds. Three discrete groups of brooches and other finds have been recorded in south Wirral, while an undated curvilinear cropmark, possibly an enclosure, has been recorded at another location in Burton. Current evidence suggests a fairly extensive network of small rural sites across the landscape of Wirral, with an apparent preference for the well-drained sandstone ridges. The aerial reconnaissance evidence indicates that enclosures are present but it is too early to

suggest they form the major settlement type.

The mid-Wirral Roman road, whose alignment is secure from the north gate at Chester only as far as Willaston-Raby (Jermy 1960; Margary 1967, 299-300; Petch 1987, 219), probably had the port at Meols as its destination. In the current imperfect state of knowledge, the road cannot be shown to have had a significant impact on the settlement pattern, although the distribution of known settlements is, inevitably, heavily biased to the less developed western part of Wirral. The location of settlements may have depended more on human factors such as the location of pre-existing landholdings of pre-Roman origin, as well as natural or environmental constraints such as topography, drainage, soil type and water resources than the ease of communication offered by the road. In any event, the proximity of some sites to the coast suggests the inhabitants took advantage of an alternative, and in many ways more convenient, source of transport for heavy goods or livestock using the twin estuaries of the Dee and Mersey from which access inland via those river systems and lesser rivers such as the Weaver. One potentially bulky commodity for which water transport would have been appropriate was coal from the outcrop at Neston, in south Wirral, which was used at the Mill Hill Road site.

The Romano-British site at Irby

The Romano-British settlement at Irby consisted of a palisaded enclosure of two phases, replaced by a ditched enclosure on the same general alignment, which was then enlarged to the west by the addition of a further enclosure, possibly with two contemporary ditches, and with a gateway. The full extent of the settlement was not precisely established in any direction. However, there is slight circumstantial evidence to suggest that its western boundary lay close to the limit of excavation. The ground begins to fall away steeply at this point and this would the logical point for the settlement to stop. A watching brief at no. 95 Mill Hill Road, about 140 m to the south of the excavated area, found no evidence for archaeological deposits. The conjoined enclosures together measured at least 95 m east-west and over 65 m north-south.

Within the Roman period the broad outlines of the chronology of settlement at Irby are fairly well established. The Iron Age to Romano-British transition is discussed above. Within the Roman period, there is clear evidence of Roman occupation at Irby by the late 1st or early 2nd century. The bulk of the pottery dates to the 3rd-4th centuries, arguing perhaps for an intensification of occupation in the western enclosure during that time. The coins indicate activity until at least the mid 4th century which is extended further by the presence of later 4th-century pottery. The presence of a post-Roman aceramic and virtually findless occupation phase means that several structures constructed with curvilinear gullies contain only residual Roman pottery of dubious validity as dating evidence and, as discussed in Chapter 2 and below, these are almost certainly of post-Roman date.

Very little of the eastern enclosure was investigated but in the interior of the western enclosure was constructed at least one circular building (S1), probably of Roman date. A circular building nearby (S12) appears to have been one of a sequence of structures on the same spot. Only S12 and its successor after an interval (S13) could be clearly defined as they used continuous gullies in construction rather than post-holes. Other buildings probably of Roman date include a sub-rectangular structure (S14), and a possible similar building S17, though in these cases the dating evidence was not strong. A rectangular building (S9) constructed with wall-gullies contained a mid-late 4th-century sherd though the ends of this were lost amongst complex intercutting features so its overall length is uncertain. Another building (S29) represented by a foundation gully has two radiocarbon dates spanning the mid 3rd to end of 6th century, which combined with a mid 4th-century coin argue for a late Roman or later date. Numerous post-holes point to the existence of several other structures but neither the chronology nor the plan of these was at all clear. Two possible curvilinear post-built structures, S10 and S15, may also be Roman in date but could not be assigned a clearly defined place within the sequence.

Location, Landscape and Resources

Topographically the Mill Hill Road site at Irby lies on the top of a low sandstone north-south ridge onto which boulder clay laps to the east and west (see Chapter 1). Most of the site lay on well-drained sandstone, and was free-draining. Local water resources include Greasby Brook in the valley no more than 350 m to the west and a spring 500 m to the south. The same elevated, well-drained situation occurs in a number of Romano-British sites located either as artefact scatters or enclosures in Wirral.

Although the occupation site and the area to the north of it lie over sandstone, the eastern part of the enclosure ditch cut through boulder clay while the boulder clay also lapped up the hill slope to the west, resulting in a distinctive change in vegetation growth which is evident in air photographs. The site appears to have been deliberately chosen to take advantage of the varied soils of which no fewer than three distinct types are represented within 1 km of the site. At the site itself the soils belong to the Rivington Series, the humo-ferric podzols of the Delamere Series at Thurstaston Hill, and extensive clay loam stagnogley of the Clifton Series within a short distance to the north-west and east (Beard *et al.* 1987).

The differences in soil type and solid or drift geology would have had an impact on vegetation type, resources and land use within the immediate environs of the farm in the Roman period. The environmental evidence suggests that the settlement at Irby was engaged in mixed agriculture at that time. Animal bone, as usual for the lowland north west, rarely survives unless burnt so removing evidence of a potentially important component of the rural economy. Beyond the fact that the evidence of poorly preserved bone and teeth indicates the presence of cattle and probably sheep, little more can be said. Evidence for grain production and processing is rather more prolific. The presence of a number of querns suggests some processing of grain on the site though it does not necessarily mean it was grown locally, although the environmental evidence for processing is present at certain phases.

The use of the thin lighter sandy soils on the ridge itself as arable land during the Iron Age and Romano-British periods is suggested by the thin scatter of 10 sherds of Roman pottery found by fieldwalking in the modern field immediately to the north of the site which is likely to represent material dispersed from farm middens to manure arable land. The same field has produced clear cropmarks (Plate I). Some are of geological origin, consisting of an irregular lattice of fine lines, broadly co-axial, which probably represents fissuring of the upper surface of the sandstone bedrock, resulting from periglacial frost-penetration, of a kind observed during the excavation. Others represent early field divisions, probably of three phases (Fig. 5.7). There are two distinct sets of linear marks of human origin, which appear to represent different phases of enclosed fields. One set of parallel linear marks appears more regular, apparently respecting the existing boundaries, and represents subdivisions of the existing field. One north-south division of these survived late enough to be mapped in 1824 (CRO D1648). Another roughly parallel pair of ditches is presumably earlier as it does not appear on historic maps, but still appears to respect overall field boundaries. Further elements consist of a pair of ditches which runs towards the excavated site, widening as it approaches the settlement. While this could be further geological faulting, the lines are not as irregular as the geological features. Across the modern road, about 150 m to the north-east of the excavated site, there is also an irregular subrectangular enclosure of uncertain date or function. A final element is an amorphous oval in the north-east corner of the field caused by the jettisoning of a WW2 bomb by a German aircraft returning from an air-raid on Liverpool (J. H. Billington pers. comm.).

The environmental report (see Chapter 3, *Charred Plant Remains*) indicates the presence of a variety of plants favouring specific habitats which point to the land-use in and around the site. Although the site itself lies on free-draining sand and sandstone, analysis of weed seeds from Irby environmental samples suggests that the soils were mostly nutrient-enriched and heavy, with few plants characteristic of the acidic sandy soils present.

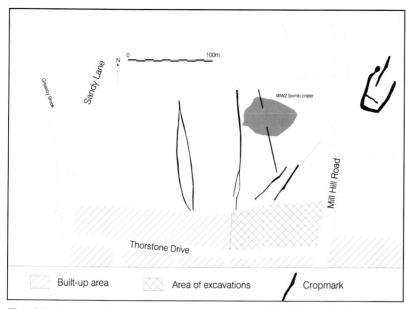

Fig. 5.7: Cropmarks in the vicinity of the site at Mill Hill Road, Irby

These suggest that the clay soils which lap up the lower slope of the ridge on both sides to west and east were used for crops rather than the thinner more acid soils of the upper sandstone ridge, although this could be a result of intensive manuring. There is also little sign of grassland taxa in the assemblage. In the post-medieval period, the field-name 'Smoores', of Norse origin, meaning 'butter pastures', does suggest, however, that the ridge and slopes were noted for the quality of the rich grass. There are few true wetland plants such as reeds and rushes but the presence of a stream in a little valley at the foot of the slope only 350 m to the west provides a suitable habitat for these plants.

The size of the agricultural unit which was farmed from Irby is unknown but broad parameters which have been suggested as appropriate for peasant holdings may give an indication of the order of magnitude of the potential estate. In Cumbria south of the Solway arable areas of 6-10 ha are indicated by blocks of enclosed fields attached to settlement enclosures, while individual site territories averaged 30-50 ha (Higham and Jones 1985, 72; Higham 1980, 44-6). From a theoretical perspective, Richard Reece has calculated that an appropriate size for a peasant holding worked by a single individual in the Roman period, as at Domesday, would be a unit of very roughly 50 acres (approx. 20 ha) based on physical constraints (Reece 1988, 3-5). Such a hypothetical unit at Irby, if arranged in a compact block, would equate to a square with sides of roughly 440 m, although in practice it is unlikely to have been such a neatly defined territory.

On an individual site basis, a useful concept in relation to the site at Irby is that of the 'catchment area' (Fowler 1983). This concerns the resources available to the farm, not only the arable land close to the site which itself need not have been held in a single block or grazing land beyond the arable, but also other resources such as

water, hay, timber, stone and clay potentially drawn from a wider area still, which could be viewed as a 'series of overlapping and differently shaped areas from within which the farm drew its resources'. The exploitation would have occurred through a complex series of movements, which as Fowler observes, were unlikely to be all met within a 2 km radius of the site. This introduces the important distinctions between land owned and rights of access to shared resources, as well as access to products from further afield such as salt and metalwork (Fowler 1983, 83). Although the precise boundaries of the holding are impossible now to recover, the environmental evidence for the local landuse mean that it is reasonable to expect that the estate extended as far as the stream in the valley, which would be required to water livestock, took in the spring to the north-east, and embraced the boulder clay soils in the lower valley slope to the west and downslope to the east, as well as northward along the sandstone ridge. The discovery of a 4th-century coin hoard from 330 m away in a field boundary could argue for the early origin of the hedge bank, although the precise position within the boundary is not recorded.

The presence on the site of heather and *Sieglingia* typical of heath margins suggests that not only did the extensive area of modern heathland which encircles the site to the south (Irby Heath in the post-medieval period), west and north of the site and extends to the thin humo-ferric podzols of Thurstaston Hill 1 km to the south-west was the most convenient source of heather for thatching and possibly also turves for building or fuel. The origins of the heath may lie in the Neolithic or Bronze Age where agricultural activity created openings in woodland which on acidifying soils were colonised by bracken or heather (Innes *et al.* 1999, 28).

Within a radius of two or three kilometres of the Mill Hill Road site one might envisage areas of heathland, perhaps grazed or exploited in common, stretches of woodland, an important economic resource which provided the coppiced hazel wood for construction of clay ovens and also hazelnuts, while immediately around the site the environmental and other evidence points to fruit trees, providing apples or pears, perhaps in an orchard, and arable fields producing cereals and peas and other crops not only on the light soils but also from the heavier clays. The damp boulder clay would naturally tend to support lush grass suitable for pasture or for hay-production. The density of sites, as currently understood, is not so great that there would appear to be great pressure on land, nor the imperative to define and partition the landscape extensively.

Examination of the environs of Romano-British rural settlements elsewhere has revealed the same tendency for a situation chosen to take advantage of a variety of soil types. The square enclosure at Southworth near Winwick lies on a rise close to the junction between sand and boulder clay (Philpott *et al.* 1993). A small oval enclosure at Legh Oaks Farm, High Legh, which produced 2nd-century sherds in the upper fill of the enclosure ditch, lay at the interface between the clay and Keuper Marl and sands and gravels (Nevell 1991, 18-9; Higham 1993, 56, fig. 2.6). A similar pattern can be seen in the north-east of England, where Thorpe Thewles, in common with many enclosures in that region, lay on the boundary between two soil types; in that case, between subsoils on clay and a sandier clay with some gravel (Heslop 1987, 113). In the Solway Plain, Cumbria, Bewley's detail analysis of the location of settlements with a view to the agricultural potential in a surrounding territory showed that many sites of Romano-British date, as well as those presumed – though with little supporting evidence – to be late prehistoric in date, were located with easy access to more than one soil type which would tend to have supported different vegetation and be suited to different landuse, whether grassland, arable cultivation or woodland. He argues, contrary to received views, that there the emphasis in the location of Romano-British settlements was on the availability of grassland rather than the lightest soils for arable cultivation, a pattern of exploitation derived from the late prehistoric period (Bewley 1994, 72-81). The Wroxeter Hinterland Project has identified a strong correlation between the location of enclosures and soil type. Within a 6 km radius of the Roman town, a large proportion of enclosure sites are located on land categories 3 and 4, characterised by relatively heavy soils, which are moisture-retentive and well suited to grassland, so more likely to have supported a pastoral than an arable regime (Gaffney and White 2007, 254-6). It is argued that they provided a wide range of products from leather, hides, bone, lard, wool and meat for the town. Further from the town, the enclosures are equally likely to occur on lighter, well-drained and easily workable soils, which may denote a mixed arable/pastoral economy.

The Organisation of Space in Enclosures

The settlement at Irby takes the form of an initial ditched enclosure to which a further enclosure was appended on the west. The area excavated within the eastern enclosure was too limited, and the degree of truncation too great, to produce more than a couple of post-holes. However, the quantity of deliberately dumped stone in the ditch fills of the eastern enclosure suggest that it also contained structures which were cleared when the ditch was infilled in the late 4th century; the associated pottery suggests domestic occupation there at least in the 3rd century, and some of the pottery consisted of large unabraded sherds.

Subdivision of the enclosure or the creation of a second adjacent enclosure is open to a range of interpretations. The apparent contemporaneous use of the two adjacent enclosures may indicate the subdivision of the site between social units into two nuclear families or two groups within an extended family, a subject discussed by Richard Hingley (1989, 59-64, 149-61). The growth of open area excavation provides increasing evidence for the subdivision and differential use of the interior of settlement enclosures. The total excavation of several sites in the north east makes them particularly suited to consideration in this way. Some appear to be divided into separate units each with distinct buildings, demarcated by internal boundaries. At Middle Gunnar Peak, Northumberland, a rectangular enclosure is divided into two distinct elements, which even have separate entrances (illustrated by Hingley 1989, fig. 26a). Hingley argues on the grounds of replication of domestic accommodation that many farms in Britain show evidence of being occupied by extended families. In some cases the single extended family may have consisted of a number of individual nuclear family groups, each forming an independent household (1989, 150). Hingley has suggested that the element which held the extended family together and prevented it from dissolving was land. He notes that in medieval Wales and early historic Ireland, land was controlled and owned by a three-generation family group descended from a common great-grandfather, and he suggests that a similar situation existed in Roman Britain, with joint control of land between adult brothers so 'the extended family in Roman Britain was derived from the joint ownership and/or control of farming land by the family group' (Hingley 1989, 151).

Although they have often been interpreted as separate family units or male/female zones, anthropological and ethnographic evidence warns against too simple a correlation of enclosure with family unit and also against the identification of the family unit as the same as modern society. The possibility of differential use has been raised and the north-eastern sites offer some potential for alternative explanations. Subdivision or enlargement may indicate different use of space for livestock rather than living accommodation or space for storage of agricultural produce. At Thorpe Thewles the subrectangular enclosure was divided internally into northern central and southern thirds; the central portion contained the main house with several ancillary structures, while the southern contained only one short-lived building, and this space immediately by the entrance was interpreted as being used for periodic livestock storage (Heslop 1987, 113). At the single-ditched Great Ayton Moor enclosure the northern half seems to have been used for livestock while the southern, separated from it by a ditch, contained the roundhouse. At an enclosed site near Hutton Rudby two widely spaced concentric ditches were interpreted as possibly contemporary, the inner containing the domestic space, the space between the ditches used as an animal pound (Heslop 1987, 114, fig. 62). A similar explanation as animal corrals has been suggested for widely spaced enclosure ditches at Collfryn, the concentric circle enclosures of Gwynedd (Cunliffe 2005, 302, 304-5), and closer to Irby, though Iron Age in date, at Brook House Farm, Halewood (Cowell 2000b).

Within the north west, the evidence is not as well defined since no enclosure has been fully excavated. However, enclosures have been observed in the region which may represent alternative methods of achieving a similar result. The subdivision of an enclosure can be seen from a cropmark less than 2 km from the Irby site. The subrectangular enclosure at Greasby, which measures 110 m by 70 m, has a clear internal cross ditch, which bisects the enclosure, dividing the interior into two roughly equal portions. Fieldwalking has produced a small quantity of Roman pottery from the field. In the Dee valley at Royton, Clwyd, a pair of adjacent enclosures linked at the corners by a short stretch of ditch may indicate the addition of an enclosure to increase the available space. An indication of what may be functional differences can be seen at Farndon in the Dee valley where two enclosures of rather different form apparently lie either side of a trackway. In the absence of excavation, the function and developmental sequence of these sites are uncertain but they potentially provide parallels for Irby in different means of enlarging the enclosed space.

One of the research aims at Irby was to determine the use of space on the site. Whilst we can observe the replacement of the palisaded enclosure by a ditched one, and can postulate the addition of the western enclosure onto an existing eastern ditched enclosure, there is little clear evidence of how these enclosures were used. Certainly during the Roman period the western enclosure contained a series of buildings, initially roundhouses, with some long-term stability in the location of structures, and there is considerable evidence of pottery use and discard as well as other activities such as food preparation using mortaria and cooking using jars over open fires. Grain processing may have taken place within S12 and an oven stood near or inside the same building. Other ovens were used and iron smithing practised, but none of these can be precisely located.

Enclosure entrances

The form of the entrance to the enclosure at Irby, though not fully exposed, appears to be represented by two large rock-cut post-holes, 2.7 m apart, with a second post-hole on the east side. A gully ran up at right angles to the eastern pair, stopping just beside them, and presumably forming a palisade line. This appears to be a simple gateway though a more complex structure may have lain outside the excavated area.

Enclosure entrances display a variety of forms and

complexity within the Iron Age and Romano-British period. Iron Age sites in south Wales include forms such as double-gates at either end of a corridor at Walesland Rath and a possible tower or fighting platform at Whitton but at the latter site Roman-period Phases II to IV (AD 55-115) saw a series of simple gates each with a substantial post-hole either side of the entrance and each associated with stone kerbs retaining the bank; the entrances were between 2 and 3 m wide (Wainwright 1971, 58-62, figs 9, 11, 12; Jarrett and Wrathmell 1981, 12-16). At their simplest, entrances may consist of a pair of post-holes, supporting a gate, which were set at the bank terminals. At the Romano-British farm at Silloth, Cumbria the entrance consisted of a pair of post-holes 2.6 m apart at either end of the shingle bank, set behind the enclosure ditch (Higham and Jones 1983, 59, fig. 10). At the Penrith site, the single entrance of an oval enclosure had a similar post-hole at each terminal of the internal bank, there just under 3.6 m wide, and substantial post-holes holding squared timbers as much as 0.3 m across, which were interpreted as supporting a gate or wattle barrier in the gap between them (Higham and Jones 1983, 50, fig. 5).

In north-east England, entrances at enclosures at Marden and Burradon in Northumberland had a palisade slot on either side of the entrance which held a fence to reduce the gap between the bank terminals, with a large post set in the end of the slot to support the gate. The Marden enclosure was not closely datable but probably Romano-British, while at Burradon a similar form of entrance was employed in both the early Iron Age enclosure and its 2nd-century AD Romano-British successor (Jobey 1962, 23-4; 1970, 56, 64-6, figs 3, 4). Simple post-pits at the terminals of palisade slots are also found in a succession of Iron Age entrances at Hengistbury Head, Dorset (Cunliffe 1987, 98, ill. 78).

Romano-British Structures

Within the Romano-British enclosure at Irby, two successive 'roundhouses' were identified with some certainty (S12, S13), although the later one is strictly speaking polygonal, comprising short straight sections (S13) of stone-packed gully rather than a strictly circular plan. The true circular building (S12) is formed in part of a curvilinear gully and for the rest as what were excavated as a series of overlapping post-holes but which probably formed a continuous gully, the cut of which was not visible as a single entity. A curvilinear gully (S1) is likely to represent a third Romano-British example, although not enough survives of the plan to demonstrate whether it was circular or oval. No clear evidence has merged for the position of the doorway in the Irby roundhouses.

The majority of buildings from civil contexts in the north west have been excavated in the industrial settlements, such as Wilderspool (May 1904; Hinchliffe and Williams 1992), Middlewich (summarised in Petch 1987, 202-8; Strickland 2001), or Walton-le-Dale (Esmonde Cleary 1998, 388). The main exceptions are the villa at Eaton-by-Tarporley (Petch 1987, 211, fig. 34), and rural buildings at Ochre Brook, at Brunt Boggart in Tarbock (Philpott 2000b) and Court Farm, Halewood (Adams and Philpott in prep.). At Birch Heath, Tarporley, Cheshire a small rural settlement was revealed in a pipeline (Fairburn 2002b) while at Poulton, Cheshire, the discovery of Roman tile, pottery and other finds has still not been accompanied by identifiable Roman period structures (Emery *et al.* 1996, 56).

The dominance of the roundhouse in the late Iron Age and into the Roman period in many areas of the country, including the north and south west, has been demonstrated by Jeremy Taylor's systematic survey of Roman rural settlement in England, reflecting the 'continuity of essentially Iron Age architectural forms' (2007, 31-4, fig. 4.7). He notes, however, in the north west and northern Marches the appearance of rectilinear buildings in the mid-late Roman period (2007, 31, fig. 4.8).

Within the lowland north west, there is a growing body of evidence (discussed above) for circular buildings in the few excavated Iron Age sites as well as in early Roman contexts (Table 5.2). The construction of circular buildings with a wall-gully packed with stones in the technique of construction used in S13 at Irby is found in an Iron Age context at the Breidden hillfort, in the Welsh Marches (Musson 1991, pl. 9C). A site of Iron Age or Romano-British date at near Bellister Castle, Northumberland (NAA 1997, 6-7, fig. 4 and pl. 1) had half of a circle of gully, 8.8 m in diameter, with stones measuring 0.2 to 0.7 m in diameter packing the gully. A smaller arc of a second structure also with some large rounded stones lay within the first and was interpreted as a second, earlier, house.

Roundhouses also occur in early phases of at least two of the Roman industrial settlements of the north west. A later 1st-century AD circular structure 8 m in diameter containing two adjacent hearth or furnace bases in the centre, perhaps for iron-smithing, was excavated near the river Ribble at Walton-le-Dale, Lancashire in the earliest phase of the industrial settlement (Esmonde Cleary 1998, 388). At Wilderspool a Phase 1 circular gully (2962) which appears to have surrounded a circular structure, lying within a rectilinear ditched enclosure (Hinchliffe and Williams 1992, 103, fig. 55), has the appearance of a simple rural farmstead enclosure. In the second phase, in the mid 2nd century, the expanding Romano-British settlement encroached on the site, and it was integrated into a series of contiguous ditched enclosures along a trackway. During Phase 2 a second roundhouse (2964) was constructed in a nearby enclosure (Hinchliffe and Williams 1992, 103, fig. 63).

Two further sites have produced roundhouses which

are visible only as cropmarks. At Telegraph Road, Irby three circular buildings can be seen spaced evenly within the interior of the oval enclosure (Pl. XXIII), while at Aughton, West Lancashire a central penannular structure, which had tentatively been interpreted as a henge from its two opposed entrances, is in fact more likely to be a house given its small size and deliberate positioning in the centre of an undated subrectangular enclosure.

At Irby, there was at least rectangular structure, a late Romano-British building (S9), though the foundation trenches are discontinuous, variable in surviving depth, and incomplete.

Polygonal buildings are paralleled elsewhere in England, though they occur mainly at Iron Age sites. An Iron Age polygonal structure at Little Waltham, Essex had a spacing of two posts and the intervening panel of 1.10 m (Structure C18: Drury 1978, 121). Roman examples are recorded in stone at Catsgore, Somerset and again at Little Waltham (Leech 1982, 27-9; Drury 1978, 118-24). A middle Iron Age enclosure at Wanlip, Leicestershire had a polygonal house, Structure 2, but the straight sections were longer than at Irby and there was a series of concentric post-holes on the exterior of the gully (Beamish 1998, 30-4).

Irby certainly displays the phenomenon of successive rebuilding of a circular structure on the same site, a pattern of social behaviour which is witnessed at many farmsteads in the Iron Age and Romano-British period. In the north west a succession of at least four, and possibly more, overlapping roundhouses has been excavated at Lathom, West Lancashire (Cowell 2002). The earliest in the sequence yielded a late Iron Age radiocarbon date of 345-1 cal BC (Beta-153894; 2100 ± 40BP), the latest one a Roman pottery sherd, suggesting continuous replacement through the late Iron Age to early Roman period. At Court Farm, Halewood more than one structure was rebuilt on the site of an earlier one (Adams and Philpott in prep.). A major practical consideration may have been the desire to avoid disrupting the layout of the enclosure interior by rebuilding in virtually the same spot. Some lateral displacement of the later building may have enabled retention of part of the floor area while making use of undisturbed ground for the new wall trench and possibly even allowing part of the superstructure such as the roof to be re-used in the later building. The successive rebuilding would allow continuity in the functioning of the farmstead with regard to structural elements which may leave little archaeological trace such as animal pens, fences or working areas, storage areas, or internal enclosure trackways. At the same time, the continued rebuilding on the same site may also have served to emphasise continuity of ownership and control of the settlement, retaining the integrity of the settlement and its layout. The lifespan of such buildings would depend on the degree of care in maintenance and the extent

Site	Diam	Construction	Date
Late Bronze Age			
Bruen Stapleford (Fairburn 2002a) S3	19 m	With narrow inner and wider outer ring gullies; One entrance gap of 1.0 wide to SE	One C14 date of 920-780 cal BC (2665 ± 45 BP; AA-49271) in inner gully. Late Bronze Age
Iron Age			
Lathom (Cowell 2003; 2005a): Roundhouse 1	10.3 m	Central post, gully and series of post-holes at *c.* 2 m intervals, and stakes for wall; prehistoric pottery in fill of gully; 2 entrances, E and W ; 2nd-1st century BC?	Radiocarbon date from gully (345-1 cal BC; Beta-153894; 2100 ± 40BP),
Lathom: Roundhouse 2	8.5 m	Internal firing of posts and external ring of stakes, some replacement of internal ring posts. One entrance, to SE.	
Lathom: Roundhouse 3	*c.* 7.6 m	Earlier than Roundhouse 4; heavily disturbed	
Lathom: Roundhouse 5		Possible roundhouse in sequence overlying Roundhouse 2	
Great Woolden Hall CS1 (Nevell 1999)		Outer post-trench 12.8 m diam, and inner ring of posts; short recut of wall to SE near entrance; latter faces SE, 1.8 m wide	C14 date: 65-15 BC (GrN 16849)
Great Woolden Hall CS2	*c.* 14.3 m	'Post-trench' with patches of charcoal, some surrounded by cobbles. Recut to trench on SE side. One entrance, to S; 'break' of 3.6 m in trench	C14 date: 120 BC- AD 80 (GrN 16850).
Bruen Stapleford (Fairburn 2002a) S4	each *c.*12 m	2 phase construction; Phase 1. Semicircular gully 9655; Phase 2. related small gullies with post-holes, one entrance	C14 date: 170 BC-60 cal AD (2035 ± 40BP; AA-49274)
Bruen Stapleford (Fairburn 2002a) S5		3 phases of gully with post-holes; Phase 1 *c.* 8 m diam; Phase 2 *c.* 8 m; Phase 3 uncertain	
Bruen Stapleford (Fairburn 2002a) S1	12.5 m diam	Single ring gully	C14 date: 390-160 cal BC (2195 ± 40 BP; AA-49277); VCP in pit cut by gully
Meols, Wirral (Potter 1890, 149; Cox 1895, 43-4; Griffiths *et al.* 2007, 21-3)		One with stone foundation; 2-3 others stake-built	Three-four roundhouses observed in coastal erosion; undated but possibly Iron Age
Romano-British			
Lathom: Roundhouse 4	*c.* 8.8 m	Late 1st-late 3rd century AD rebuild of earlier Roundhouse 3; heavily disturbed. Entrance to E	2 sherds of Romano-British pottery in fill
Walton-le-Dale, Lancashire (Esmonde Cleary 1998, 388)	8 m	Contained 2 adjacent hearths possibly for smithing	Romano-British Site Phase 1: late 1st century
Lousher's Lane, Wilderspool Structure 2962 (Hinchliffe and Williams 1992)	10.5 m	Circular gully, interpreted as open drain for building; short section of truncated shallow gully may be wall. One entrance to W, 2.3 m wide	Romano-British Site Phase 1 (cut by Phase 3 gully)
Lousher's Lane, Wilderspool Structure 2954 (1st phases)	8.5 m	Foundation gully; two opposed: entrances; that to NW 1.1 m wide, SE 1.8 m wide;	Romano-British Site Phase 2
Lousher's Lane, Wilderspool Structure 2954 (1st phases)	7.5 m	Foundation gully, rebuild of the above. One entrance to NW 1.1 m wide (as above)	Romano-British Site Phase 2
Irby S13	11.7 m	See Chapter 2 above	Polygonal structure
Irby S12	11 m	See Chapter 2 above	Circular structure
Irby S1	13-14 m?	See Chapter 2 above	Possible roundhouse
Birch Heath, Tarporley (Fairburn 2002b) S1	*c.* 7 m	Circular gully with butt ends, entrance to E *c.* 2.1 m wide	No direct dating evidence; Roman settlement
Birch Heath, Tarporley (Fairburn 2002b) S2	*c.* 6.5 m diam	'Circular' gully with butt ends, in fact subsquare; two lengths of narrow gully inside broader outer gully. Entrance to SE *c.* 1.7 m wide	C14 date: AD 70-350 (1825 ± 55 BP; AA-50088); 2nd century AD pottery

Table 5.2: Some Iron Age and Romano-British roundhouses in lowland north west England

to which damp could be excluded. The evidence of the modern reconstructions at Butser Ancient Farm, Hants and at Danish sites suggests a life of at least 50 years for wattle and daub thatched roundhouses; the reconstructed Pimperne House at Butser was in good order after 15 years, the outer wall proving difficult to demolish. The wattle work, once the daub had been removed, was found to be dry and strong and had not become embrittled in the way that exposed field fences routinely and rapidly deteriorate (Reynolds 1993; M. Nicolajsen pers. comm.).

Some rural sites display a sequence from roundhouses of prehistoric form though Romano-British date being superseded by rectilinear 'Romanised' buildings. The date of the shift varies considerably from region to region, and within a given region from site to site, farms in some regions adopting Roman house forms early after the conquest while elsewhere settlements continued with roundhouses into the 4th century. In the south and east of England the new house forms were in general adopted more quickly, but in conservative areas such as the north west the transition took far longer or never occurred at all. In North Cumbria where a number of rural settlements have been investigated the three dated examples of new rectilinear buildings were all 3rd or 4th century (Higham and Jones 1983, 65).

Few rectangular structures in Romano-British rural contexts can be cited from the immediate region but this may be a consequence of a dearth in excavated sites rather than a genuine scarcity of the type. The building at Ochre Brook, Tarbock within a rectilinear enclosure was tapering in plan, constructed of earth-fast posts with a probable internal partition (Philpott 2000c, 72-3, fig. 4.6). At Saltney, 3 km south-west of Chester, the remains of rough walls of sandstone rubble set in clay were associated with shallow ditches, interpreted as for drainage in the heavy boulder clay soil. Coins and pottery from the site indicate occupation from the end of the 1st or early 2nd to 4th century, while querns suggest cultivation of cereals (Newstead 1935; Thompson 1965, 16). Higham comments that the volume of roof tile from the site and its situation on the clay soils argues against it being a farmstead and he postulates a small nucleated settlement like that at Heronbridge nearby which he sees as having an industrial and market function (1993, 41-3).

Irby has produced a further possible Roman sub-square building (S14), although only two sides were visible. That this may form part of a rural building tradition in the region is suggested by a sub-square building of Romano-British date excavated in 2001 at Birch Heath, Tarporley, Cheshire (Fairburn 2002b, 62-4, fig. III.4). Structure 2 measured 6.7 m by 6.7 m externally and had been constructed with a narrow gully only 50 mm wide inside a wider gully 0.35 m wide. Although described as circular in the report, the structure clearly has flattened sides. At Whitton, South Glamorgan, there are parallels for sub-square buildings which may resemble that seen as a partial plan in Trench XXXVI (context 6175: Jarrett and Wrathmell 1981, fig. 37, nos 1 and 2).

At a Romano-British industrial settlement at Prestatyn in north Wales a series of rectangular buildings had been constructed with timber uprights set in post-holes (R4, R5 and R11). One of these, R5, has a clay floor and two hearths in the interior, while the same site also had a building, R7, measuring about 15 by 4 m constructed with a U-shaped trench within which were preserved a row of stakes, interpreted as wattles for a woven wall; some larger post-holes packed with stone were present on the wall line, and areas of clay flooring were present. A linear slot containing one post-hole was interpreted as holding a horizontal timber for a wall line (R8) (Blockley 1989).

The large nucleated settlement at Wilderspool has produced a variety of buildings including a range of rectangular or square structures. A simple rectangular post-built building (2961) is recorded from Lousher's Lane,

while another, 2963, consisted of two parallel gullies, and a stone footing forming one end wall. A row of post-holes parallel to the west side was seen as a possible veranda (Hinchliffe and Williams 1992, 103, 110, fig. 65). At the Brewery Site a rectangular timber building was found in Phase 1 with a continuous slot foundation into which posts had been set; it measured at least 12 m by 9 m (Hinchliffe and Williams 1992, 27, fig. 11).

For the Romano-British period at Irby the difficulties of excavation and lack of good chronological control make it uncertain precisely which buildings were in contemporary occupation. Coupled with the absence of useful functional evidence for most structures owing to the removal of almost all floors, it is difficult to determine what buildings were used for. The only exception is that the gully of S13 contained rubbish from a probable demolished clay oven and two fragments of quern, possibly derived from its predecessor, S12, on virtually the same spot.

The Romano-British Economy at Irby

The Finds Assemblage

Excavated finds assemblages can provide a wealth of fine-grained detail on a range of aspects, including the chronology of occupation and structural change, the activities practised, and the economic and social dimensions of a settlement and its inhabitants. Finds assemblages have frequently been used somewhat uncritically in the past as a measure of the status and wealth of a Romano-British settlement. Sites poor in durable artefacts were considered to be impoverished. However, this over-simplistic view can be positively misleading. Such characteristics cannot be determined from a single assemblage in isolation. First, the partial picture given by finds assemblages on dryland rural sites such as Irby is restricted to the durable and archaeologically visible objects such as those in metal, ceramic and stone, while the organic component, comprising all the items of bone, wood, and leather, is entirely absent. In a region where some sites have low levels of durable material culture this can present a highly misleading picture. Secondly, any given assemblage needs to be viewed against the wider level of use and discard of different artefact categories on contemporary sites within a regional context. A site which appears to be poor in artefacts set against a national perception of rural assemblages may be in fact relatively rich in finds within its region. A further problem with finds assemblages is that their composition and size are dependent upon a variety of other factors. Differential survival of the occupation deposits at a settlement will leave widely varying volumes of artefact-bearing deposits, so that sites where all occupation deposits are ploughed out leaving only the fills of negative features will contain far fewer artefacts than those with intact deeply stratified occupation deposits.

In addition, the variation in extent of excavation of the site will potentially leave some activities located outside the excavated area under-represented or absent from the archaeological record. The duration of occupation of a site will further affect the size and composition of the finds assemblage with patterns of use of certain classes of artefact fluctuating over time. Finally, the degree of integration into the Romano-British market economy of the occupants will have an impact on the volume of durable material available to be lost, broken or discarded. There is not therefore a straightforward relationship between the finds assemblage and status of individuals living there, nor does the finds assemblage give any like a complete picture of the range of activities practised on the site. Notwithstanding the problems of interpretation, the finds assemblage at Irby does provide at least a body of material against which other sites in the region can be compared. In addition the assemblage does provide valuable information on the level of acquisition of durable goods by the occupants, the movement of objects, and the extent to which rural sites were integrated into the market network.

The variation in levels of the use of different classes of material culture between regions is an important factor to be considered in assessments of status and wealth. The low level of coin and pottery use at rural Romano-British sites in the lowland north west has been discussed elsewhere, but it serves to illustrate the strong degree of variability between and within regions. Application of the method to rural sites in the north west has not yet been attempted but once a sufficient sample of rural assemblages has been excavated and published the comparison of sites of similar type may start to yield valuable evidence for understanding the relationship between sites on a local and regional level.

Pottery Supply and Economy

Pottery studies have highlighted differences between rural assemblages and those of urban or military origin, using functional analysis, notably through the work of Jeremy Evans on sites in the North, Midlands and other regions (1993; 2001). The Irby assemblage has very low proportions of some pottery forms, such as flagons, beakers and decorated samian, which are generally well represented in military sites (see Chapter 4, *Roman Pottery*). Levels of jars and mortaria at Irby are high, at 37.8% and 24.7% respectively. High jar totals, usually over 50%, with correspondingly low totals for dishes and bowls, are a characteristic of Romano-British rural sites in the North as opposed to urban or military groups (Evans 1993, 100). The relatively strong showing of mortaria has been noted as a consistent feature of military, urban and rural sites. The 'Roman' element at Irby, as opposed to vessels favoured on native rural sites, is slight, with few beakers, only one identifiable flagon, a few amphora sherds (23) and, somewhat unusually for a rural site, a small number of *tazze,* with

their distinctive frilled rims. The latter are used largely for burning incense or in purification rites and often occur, for example, at temple sites or as grave furniture in Romano-British burials (Philpott 1991, 193). They do occur within the region in small numbers in contexts which do not appear to be overtly religious or funerary, for example, at the *mansio* in Castle Street, Chester (Mason 1980, 38 no 52, 45 nos 99-100), or Pentre Farm, Flint (Webster 1989, 102, no 62) while the few examples from Wilderspool are in local fabrics (Hartley and Webster 1973, 87, no 59; Webster 1992, 71, 73, 77). The site at Irby lacks evidence of specialised 'cheese-presses', bowls with holes in the base and sides through which the whey was drained, which have been recorded at the industrial centre of Wilderspool and at the rural sites of Birch Heath, Tarporley and Mellor, where they presumably were used for dairy produce (Hinchliffe and Williams 1992, 132, no 462; Fairburn 2002b; Burnham *et al.* 2003, 318).

A small quantity of Flavian or early Trajanic samian is present at Irby though the quantity of diagnostic 2nd-century wares other than samian is not high. The black-burnished ware gives an indication of the volume of pottery in use over the period from AD 120 to about 350. Although in the north west the volume of BB1 in use in the 3rd century would be expected to be considerably greater than for the 2nd, nonetheless at Irby the 2nd-century level is very low in comparison with the 3rd-century material (J. Evans pers. comm.; Chapter 4, *Roman Pottery*). There are two principal alternative interpretations to account for this. First, the excavated part of the site saw a low level of activity during the 2nd century, with a great increase in activity or density of occupation in the 3rd and 4th centuries; or secondly, the level of activity remained broadly constant but the occupants were slow to adopt Roman pottery vessels for everyday use. The main exception appears to be the small quantity of South Gaulish samian which, though very abraded and undiagnostic of form, nonetheless can be dated more closely than the oxidised wares in a similar state. The presence of the South Gaulish samian should be seen in the context of the wider pattern of distribution on rural sites. There is an emerging pattern of an unexpectedly high number of South Gaulish samian vessels at rural sites in northern and upland Britain which arrives with the advance of the Roman army (Willis 1997). Samian appears at rural sites in Yorkshire and north-eastern England at the time of the conquest of northern Britain. In north Wales Evans has noted a high proportion of South Gaulish samian in the Flavian-Trajanic pottery at two rural sites (1998, 207). Willis has also detected amongst the South Gaulish samian a higher proportion of decorated wares than occurs at military or larger civil settlements (1997, 39-41). At Irby the material is too small and abraded to be assigned to form, other than one Drag. 18R, so this aspect cannot be assessed. Willis discerns in this a preference for the large decorated bowl forms where the decoration may have been of less importance to the consumer than the size and shape of the vessels. Evans postulates that the strong preference for large and expensive Drag. 37 bowls in the 2nd century at Bryn Eryr may result from its function as a communal drinking bowl (1998, 213-4). At Irby the range of 2nd-century forms is rather wider, most being cups or dishes more appropriate for table use, with a maximum of four Drag. 37 vessels (see Chapter 4, *The Samian*).

The location of Irby on the Wirral peninsula, only 6 km from Meols and 24 km from the legionary fortress at Chester, may account for the somewhat unusually large size and extended duration for a rural pottery assemblage in the region. The assemblage indicates access to the supplies of pottery through markets at Meols or Chester and indicates a production surplus to enable the occupants to acquire such manufactured items. The settlement also received products from Wilderspool and the Cheshire Plains, and possibly Holt, perhaps redistributed through the *canabae* of Chester as a major market during the early period. Overland distribution is most likely for material from Oxfordshire, Warwickshire and the Nene Valley, drawing on the same network as Chester and the other nucleated settlements. After the decline of the locally produced wares in the 3rd century, in the later Roman period Irby had access to the markets supplying the military sites. There is a strong showing of black-burnished ware from Dorset (33.6% by sherd count) and the relatively late date of the majority of the ceramics with the majority of the BB1 falling into the post-200 period (J. Evans pers. comm.). There is also material such as calcite-gritted ware in the later 4th century, which west of the Pennines occurs largely at military sites such as *Segontium* or Ribchester (Webster 1993, 254-5; Hird and Howard-Davis 2000, 192; Tyers 1996, 190), a distribution which indicates the operation of military supply contracts rather than free economic forces in view of the high transportation costs (cf. Evans 1989, 80). A result of the proximity to Meols may be the relatively large pottery assemblage by comparison to sites such as Brunt Boggart in the Mersey Basin or sites in Cheshire where pottery use was much lower level. The presence of the nearby market and port of Meols which remained active through the 4th century may account for continued supply to Irby, retaining the site's visibility in material terms by comparison to other rural sites in Cheshire.

The size of the pottery assemblage deserves consideration. The Irby pottery assemblage with 2592 fragments is large in comparison with those from rural sites in the neighbouring regions such as north Wales, West Yorkshire or Cumbria where rural sites have often produced only a handful of sherds (Evans 1998, 206-7; Evans forthcoming a). At the extreme end of the scale of material culture is a newly excavated site at Barker House Farm near Lancaster which produced structures dated to the Romano-British period by radiocarbon determina-tions but no datable Roman finds (Philpott 2006, 75).

Within the lowland north west only Court Farm, Halewood has produced such a high number of sherds, with a total of 3476 sherds (22.6 kg) (Adams and Philpott in prep.), while the Romano-British farmstead at Birch Heath, Tarporley produced 960 sherds (Dunn 2002, 77). This contrasts with considerably lower sherd counts from other sites; Enclosure A at Legh Oaks Farm, High Legh produced only seven Roman sherds, dated to the late 1st-2nd century AD (Nevell 2002, 124), a partially excavated rural site at Brunt Boggart Tarbock produced 108 sherds (Philpott 2000b), while in West Lancashire excavations up to 2005 at Dutton's Farm, Lathom produced about 95 sherds (Cowell forthcoming). The enclosure site at Halton Brow near Runcorn produced few sherds in trenching but including some amphora sherds, unusual at basic rural sites (Brown *et al.* 1975). This suggests that the Mersey basin has a higher degree of integration into the Roman market economy than other rural settlements outside the area. Court Farm, with its shorter duration of occupation but probably higher population than Irby appears to have seen particularly intensive use of pottery.

However, the sherd count by itself is not a sufficient indicator of pottery use, since it is dependent upon a range of factors. Amongst these are the duration of occupation at a given site, the total area excavated and the volume of Roman period deposits. In addition, the character of the deposits is also an important determinant of the survival of pottery, with surviving occupation deposits sealing features, provides a larger volume of potential ceramics than ploughed out or heavily truncated sites where the pottery has been released into ploughsoils and the ceramics have been degraded by unfavourable soil conditions. An unqualified comparison for example of the sherd count from the enclosure at Ochre Brook, Tarbock north of the Mersey, with the Irby site would conclude that the latter had higher use despite the fact that pottery appears to have been manufactured alongside tile at Ochre Brook. This ignores the much longer occupation at Irby, over 300 years by comparison with perhaps a century at Ochre Brook, and the fact that intact occupation deposits survived to a much greater depth at Irby, with truncation down to boulder clay of the most of the Romano-British deposits at Ochre Brook. At Court Farm sealed deposits contained the great majority of the pottery recovered in large-scale area excavation of the 2nd to 4th-century site, though the stratification overall was much more truncated (Philpott 2000).

A further factor is the destruction or severe abrasion of pottery in acid soils, a phenomenon which has been noted in Shropshire and Cheshire (Carver 1991, 6-8; Jones 1996, 30). Acid soils seem to soften many Roman pottery fabrics, which in turn renders them vulnerable to mechanical abrasion through ploughing. Personal observation indicates that the flaking and crumbling of the surface of pottery through exposure to frost in ploughsoil may be a major factor in the reduction of unglazed Romano-British sherds to amorphous lumps of fired clay. It is perhaps significant that sherds in sealed features, which are not subject to ploughing, often have an abraded and damaged upper surface while the lower is better preserved, supporting the view that frost is a major element.

Despite the range of factors which influence the preservation and recovery of pottery on rural sites, nonetheless a wide discrepancy has been observed between the size of assemblages which appear to reflect, however, imperfectly, the scale of pottery use at rural sites.

Two other aspects of ceramic use deserve consideration. Two vessels bear graffiti (see Chapter 4, *Roman Pottery*). One is a simple incised 'X' on the wall of a black-burnished jar. The other, on the wall of a grey-ware jar, consists of two surviving letters, probably 'LV[', before a break. The latter may be part of an owner's mark; the former may be a number or an illiterate mark of ownership, but either way conforming to the most common types of graffiti (Evans 1987, 201). Although these might indicate a literate population at Irby at some point, which is supported by the presence of a stylus, the marks could have been incised prior to arriving at the site. Although lacking any statistical validity by itself, it is worth noting that the presence of two graffiti out of a total of 2592 sherds is considerably above the expected rate on rural sites, which tend to have very low levels of graffiti. The two other sites noted by Evans, both in the south west, have less than one per 10,000 sherds (Evans 2001, 34, fig. 12). Evans concluded that marks of ownership indicated that pottery vessels, coarse as well as finewares, were regarded as items of intrinsic worth, not just for their contents (1987, 202).

To some extent this receives confirmation in the presence of a number of riveted pots. The use of riveting in a few samian vessels (which are scarce on the site as a whole) as well as in coarseware vessels represents a different attitude towards the vessels from that of modern consumer societies. If a vessel were still serviceable once it cracked, or broke, it was repaired rather than discarded. There is no certainty at Irby that proximity to the market or the ability to purchase or barter for a replacement was a major factor in the decision to repair a vessel. Lead rivets found as metal-detector finds from a rural site in south Wirral indicate some repair of vessels there too.

Other Finds

Within the ironwork from Irby, Hilary Cool has noted the absence of structural fittings such as joiner's dogs and wall hooks and has concluded that, together with a

lower level of nails than is evident at Wilderspool, for example, this has implications for the style of buildings; she suggests that new building techniques were rejected in favour of traditional methods. The currently available evidence suggests that native building traditions continued at Irby throughout the Roman occupation. The only counter to this argument is the single fragment of window glass which might suggest the presence of Roman-style buildings outside the excavated area. However, this single fragment by itself is not sufficient to indicate a building; it may instead be an introduced item similar to the odd roof tile fragment.

Personal ornaments on the site are not prolific. With the exception of a large glass bead probably dating to the earlier Roman period, there are relatively few items of personal ornament. Other than the Iron Age La Tène II/III example, there are no brooches from the site, although a Wirral-type brooch discovered by a metal-detectorist in a nearby field probably represents an outlier from the settlement (Philpott 1999a). There is some evidence of change in the artefact assemblage in the 4th century. Coin use becomes more common, and female personal ornaments begin to appear on the site. In both cases these may not indicate any special conditions or change at Irby since these movements were part of wider economic and social developments through the Roman period. The wider availability of copper-alloy bracelets in the late 3rd and 4th century has been remarked upon at other sites (e.g. Crummy 1983, 37; Barford and Hughes 1985, 151), where they represent a developing fashion. The absence of brooches may be related to the emphasis of occupation lying within the 3rd and 4th century, rather than the 2nd century when fibulae and plate brooches were at the height of their popularity. Aspects of personal decoration include the presence of chips of amber (context 610) which are most likely to have come from a bead, although the balance of probability is that these are related to Norse rather than Roman activity.

Textile production at Irby is indicated by a small number of spindle whorls, not only in the Iron Age (SF2931, a decorated steatite example), but also in the Roman period. The Romano-British whorls comprise one shaped from a wall sherd of an oxidised ware jar (SF20), two plain examples in lead (SF7819, context 6187; SF6591, context 3234), and a possible stone example (SF4267, context 3063). Although these may indirectly point to the presence of sheep through the spinning of wool, a seed of flax in one prehistoric context (7422) suggests that this may have been grown for its fibres, giving a possible alternative source of fibres for spinning. As flax does not need to be heated as part of the processing, it is unlikely to be charred. It may therefore be under-represented in the overall assemblage (see Chapter 3, *Charred Plant Remains*) and its role in the economy cannot be determined.

Exploitation of Local Resources

The finds assemblage for the Roman period at Irby demonstrates a keen awareness of local raw materials and resources on the part of the occupants. The use of local resources, coal, lead and iron involved the exchange of goods or at least contacts with people elsewhere in Wirral and further afield in north Wales. The lump of galena or lead ore which, though not analysed, probably came from the nearest source of lead in north Wales, 10 km away across the Dee estuary, suggesting the existence of social or commercial contacts. The site has produced several quern fragments. Most are flat rotary querns but there is one beehive quern and two saddle querns. Most, but not all, of the querns used the local sandstone, despite the close availability of the raw material. A saddle quern was shaped from a granite glacial erratic (SF8009, context 9614), but probably dates to the late prehistoric rather than Roman date. A fragment of a probable imported lava quern at Irby is paralleled by a small quantity of the same material, probably from a quern, at Ochre Brook, Tarbock (Philpott 2000, 85). That the local sandstone outcrops at Irby were used in historic times is evident from the discovery of an unfinished later millstone at Quarry Farm, Irby, only 500 m north of the site. However, the stone was apparently not suitable for the purposes of the medieval windmill which stood on Mill Hill. According to a rental of St Werburgh's dated 1431/2 millstones were to be taken from Little Christleton near Chester (cited in Chitty 1978b, 37-8). Irby quarry was certainly in operation by 1767 when the Woodchurch Churchwardens' Accounts record '77 loads of stone from Irby Hill' (Hewitt 1925, 9; Chitty 1978b, 38), and the Ordnance Survey maps show it was extensively quarried in the 19th century.

Numerous Roman contexts at Irby contain coal. Palynological analysis indicates the coal in the upper fill of Ditch 1 (context 22) was from Neston, south Wirral (see Chapter 4, *Analysis of Coal Samples*). There is a slight reservation in the dating as two medieval sherds, including a substantial jug base, from the same context – which contained largely Roman material – may indicate that a medieval feature was not recognised during excavation, or that there is localised contamination, which places some doubt over the Roman date of the coal. However, coal is present in a considerable number of secure Roman contexts, demonstrating its use even if not its precise source at that time. The small coal outcrop at Neston, which through geological faulting is restricted to a small locality in south-west Wirral, is documented as having been worked from the medieval period until 1928 (Hebblethwaite 1987, 7). Exploitation in the Roman period, however, would cause no surprise. Not only has a small amount of Roman material come from close to the outcrop but concentrations of Roman finds indicate the existence of several rural settlements in that part of Wirral. Furthermore, rural sites north of the Mersey, both at Ochre Brook, Tarbock and at Court Farm, Halewood, have produced coal in the Roman period. Analysis of the Court Farm material indicates a local source close by in Cronton. During the Roman period, coal is found in Britain on a wide variety of sites, from urban and military to rural settlements; there is no hint that the resource was closely controlled or supply restricted. The main use appears to have been for iron smithing though its use is attested in copper-alloy working, as at Heronbridge near Chester, domestic heating and more specialised functions such as in a cremation pyre in York (Dearne and Branigan 1995).

There is one unfinished armlet, probably in cannel coal or shale and a finished late Roman bracelet fragment. The north west has numerous deposits of cannel coal and shale, which occur widely in the Carboniferous Coal Measures in Merseyside, in eastern Cheshire and across the Dee in north Wales (Edwards and Trotter 1954; Hebblethwaite 1987, 5-7). This find appears to be a Roman-period loss though it could be a residual late prehistoric piece. The unfinished armlet may have been intended to be completed on site, though in the absence of other evidence it remains uncertain whether this was a minor local activity which happens to have left no other trace, or a one-off loss.

Metalworking and Other Industrial Activities

During the Roman period there is clear evidence for a range of industrial processes undertaken at the site. The presence of one fragment of possible refractory material which may have been used in bronze-working or another industrial process is 'more likely to represent Roman activity' than prehistoric (see Chapter 4, *Refractory Material*). Apart from the one probable Bronze Age mould, the other mould fragments are probably Romano-British in date. There is however no evidence for the type of object being manufactured. However, crucibles are also present, probably for copper-alloy working. Several deliberately worn or smoothed lumps of haematite may have been used for polishing metal objects.

Bronze-working is attested on other rural sites in association with Roman finds. North of the Mersey at Court Farm, Halewood, a Romano-British site produced crucibles for bronze-working, while at a site in south Wirral numerous fragments of melted copper alloy have been found in an area which has produced late 1st to 3rd-century Roman metalwork and pottery. There also is an unconfirmed report of a lead brooch, possibly a patron for casting, found at Thurstaston in a field which has produced a dozen or more Roman brooches. Further afield, Prestatyn in north-east Wales had Roman industrial production including bronze-working. The site produced a large number of mould fragments for the production of three-piece bridle bits, button-and-loop fasteners, dagger chapes and trumpet brooches

(Blockley and Day 1989, 183-92). At Heronbridge a bronze-working hearth was associated with a pit and an ash layer containing discarded moulds, crucibles charcoal and coal; the activity was dated to the period AD 90-130 (Hartley 1954).

Mackreth (1989, 87) discussed the organisation of bronze-working in the Roman period in the context of the industrial site at Prestatyn. He concludes that production of small items may have been in separate hands from the distributors, who may have travelled around a district; if production and distribution were in the same hands, production may have been seasonal, or the craftsman travelled from place to place with the tools of the trade and set up temporary workshops where the products were needed. The south-east has provided some evidence of itinerant workers. The presence of the small number of moulds and crucibles at rural sites such as Irby and Court Farm suggests that this specialised function was carried out by mobile craftsmen at the settlements. The type of objects manufactured at Irby cannot be determined, and the site itself has produced little in the way of copper-alloy objects which might represent the craftsman's output. That permanent workshops were also established in industrial centres is indicated by the excavated structures at Prestatyn and Wilderspool (Blockley 1989; Hinchliffe and Williams 1992). The two are not mutually exclusive. The itinerant craftsman may have served a largely rural population, while the industrial output from organised workshops such as Prestatyn and the Cheshire industrial centres may have been destined in part for a military market as well as for the inhabitants of the nucleated centres themselves. The presence of moulds for pony equipment and a chape for a dagger and sword at Prestatyn support the military connection. Non-ferrous metalworking across the Pennines in Yorkshire occurs at sites of all types and sizes, including villas and towns, though few native rural settlements have such activity. Justine Bayley has pointed out that, although metalworking predominates in military and urban sites, these are also the types of site that have seen most excavation, and rural settlements may well be under-represented (2002, 104). Carrington (2006) observes that the duplication of these industrial activities between town and country may indicate self-sufficiency on the part of those in the rural settlements and it may that the more entrepreneurial inhabitants were employing skills which were current in the industrial centres of the region, with a view to diversifying their economic base.

Many melted run-offs at Irby indicate that lead was being used on site, although with its low melting point and malleability it was a versatile and easily worked material, requiring neither specialist equipment nor knowledge. Lead was used at Irby for a variety of minor functions such as spindle whorls, plugs, riveting pottery, sheeting for various purposes and perhaps also for weights. The single lump of galena, mentioned above, is not native to the site, and it is probable that both the galena and the metallic lead derive from lead deposits in the Halkyn Mountain area of Flintshire across the Dee estuary in north Wales where lead mining was well established in the Roman period (Petch 1987, 227-8; O'Leary et al. 1989). The galena gives an important reminder that the Dee estuary provided access to the mineral resources, and social networks, of north Wales.

Much of the metalworking evidence at Irby comes from iron working. This is confined to iron-smithing, hammer-scale having been noted in environmental analysis, and there is no evidence of smelting. There is growing evidence that Irby as with other rural Romano-British sites in the region were engaged in smithing to manufacture and repair items such as agricultural and craft tools and to make such building materials as nails. Forging and smithing were specialist tasks and, as with copper-alloy working, may have been the preserve of itinerant smiths, as has been postulated for the East Midlands where iron slag has been found at many early Roman sites (Condron 1997).

Coin Use

Ultimately the source of coinage in the Dee-Mersey region was the Roman army, with its legionary headquarters at Chester. Through its well paid and dispersed troops and its purchasing power in acquiring supplies it will have introduced the local population to a coin-using economy (Davies 1983, 82). The garrisoning of the Cheshire forts was followed by the creation of a network of market and manufacturing or industrial settlements by the late 1st century such as Middlewich (Shotter 2000c; Strickland 2001), and Wilderspool (with a coin list of 210 pieces up to and including 1976 excavations: Shotter 1992, 152) and a little later at Northwich (Petch 1987). Together these created a flourishing cash economy during the late 1st to 3rd centuries, though the decline of the industrial centre at Wilderspool reduced coin use markedly there by the late 2nd century (Shotter 2000a, 93). The wider decline in the industrial settlements can perhaps be seen in the low level of coins in the period AD 259-275, at a time when many areas of Britain see a great expansion in coin use due to inflation resulting from debasement of the coinage.

The extent to which the use of coinage spread into the countryside is becoming clearer through the analyses of Shotter and Carrington combined with the growing record of the Portable Antiquities Scheme. These indicate the strong halo effect of coin loss around the Romanised centres but a lower density of coin finds in the countryside. The chief exceptions are a few rural locations in the countryside not associated with known farmsteads which could be meeting places such as shrines, or higher status occupation sites.

Coin loss depends on several factors (Reece 1987, 25-40, 71; Casey 1988, 40). The relative value of individual coins from the early empire until the 260s was high, and high value coins were more likely to be searched for when lost than low value ones. The high value of the coins meant they were of little use in small transactions. Large coins were more visible and would be more easily recovered than small ones. Losses were more likely to occur in a town where a greater volume of coinage changed hands and their loss less likely to be noticed than in a domestic context. The rate of loss of coins within rural farmsteads may perhaps be artificially low as an indicator of coin use in comparison with that of a public place such as a market place or town where buying and selling was actively carried out and a greater volume of coinage changed hands. The more often coins were handled the greater the likelihood of losses, particularly in crowded or busy places. Within the rural environment the opportunities for commercial transactions are likely to have been few and within a relatively controlled environment. The presence of very few coins on rural sites may under-represent the actual level of coin use due to the infrequency of manipulation of coinage. Coins may have been stored and treated more carefully with fewer casual losses than in public places such as towns and other major settlements (Casey 1988, 40). Paradoxically, most 'rural' coin loss, in the sense of coinage belonging to the occupants of rural settlements, may have occurred in towns or other markets.

Metal detecting at known rural sites has generally failed to produce any substantial groups of coins in the lowland north west, with coins often outnumbered at sites by brooches by a factor of at least one to two. Even making allowance for the difference in reporting levels and coverage of the ground by metal-detectorists, the results from the Portable Antiquities Scheme show that there are significant regional variations in the absolute volume of coin in circulation. The north west lags far behind the south and east of England in terms of volume of coins lost (Portable Antiquities Scheme 2003, tables 3, 5). Coin use was even lower in rural sites in northern Wales for instance until the introduction of base *antoniniani* of the Gallic emperors from AD 260, although even then some rural sites in Caernarvonshire and Merioneth were considered to have retained barter through the Roman period, though in a potentially significant parallel with Wirral, north-east Wales (Flintshire and Denbighshire) across the Dee was more closely integrated into a money economy by the early 4th century (Davies 1983).

The find lists and maps of Roman coins compiled by David Shotter (2000a) demonstrate differences across the region, with relatively low coin loss in south Lancashire by comparison with Cheshire. This pattern is supported by the excavated rural sites, none of which has produced more than a few coins. North of the Mersey, even though Tarbock produced a hoard

of 80 coins in the early 19th century (Watkin 1883, 237-8), no coins were found in excavations at either Ochre Brook or Burnt Boggart in the same township (Cowell and Philpott 2000), although more recent work near Ochre Brook has produced several metal-detector finds of 4th-century coins. Coins were also absent from excavated sites at Brook House Farm and Court Farm, both in Halewood (Cowell 2000b; Adams and Philpott forthcoming), Great Woolden Hall, (Nevell 1999b) and Southworth (Cowell in press). On occasion, apparently accidental losses occurred such as the small group of *denarii* found dispersed in a Romano-British trackway at Lathom, West Lancashire, in the early 2nd century perhaps through some circumstance such as a purse falling unnoticed into a muddy and deeply rutted trackway (Cowell 2002, 9).

There is a hint of a marginally higher level of coin use in rural sites south of the Mersey. In Cheshire the Eaton-by-Tarporley villa produced only seven coins in the 1980s excavations, all later than the mid 3rd century (Shotter 2000a, 87). A single unidentifiable Roman coin, an *as* or *dupondius,* was excavated at Birch Heath, Tarporley, while two coins of Vespasian, a posthumous issue of Faustina, a radiate of Claudius II and a 4th-century piece have been recovered from Mellor (Fairburn 2002b, 84; Shotter 2000a, 100; Mellor Archaeological Trust 2003). No coins were found at Beeston Castle though two brooches were recovered (Ellis 1993). There is no evidence of coin use on the site at Irby until the later 3rd century and from then on into the later 4th century a small trickle of coins is lost. A cluster of three within the period AD 316-320 does not appear to be a hoard as the findspots were dispersed across the site although the presence of these closely contemporary pieces could relate to a single transaction which introduced several coins of similar date to the site. In its relatively late adoption of coinage the site is not unusual, occurring at a time when the value of individual coins had declined (Reece 1987).

Shotter notes that the late 4th century is strongly represented in all three counties of the north west (2000a, 244). The coin list at Meols continues until Magnus Maximus (AD 383-388) and the influence of the port may be detectable in the number of later 4th-century coins from the surrounding area. These include late Roman coins in north Wirral, including one from Wallasey (a heavily worn double-*centenionalis* of Decentius with Chi-Rho reverse found in Central Park in 1989), a Valentinian II coin from Poulton-cum-Seacombe, and three others dated to Valentinian I, Valens, and either Valens or Gratian from close to the shore at Meols, while a coin of Gratian (367-75) is recorded from Barnston. That coins remained in use until the late 4th century at the Irby settlement is suggested by the small hoard from a nearby field which ends with one coin of 'Valens or Valentinian' perhaps dating it to the AD 364-78 (Merseyside HER).

The finds from individual sites reflect the vagaries of different settlement histories, and the quantities are too small to provide statistically valid samples to examine the pattern of rural coin use. To do this requires amalgamating all rural finds, as in Peter Carrington's study (2006), whilst acknowledging the pitfalls of using such a geographically dispersed dataset. From his analysis of rural coin finds from Cheshire, he noted 'a close and constant relationship between coin use in the countryside and that in the nucleated settlements'. Given the ultimate source of coinage was the military this is not in itself surprising. He argues that the casual coin losses in the countryside point to commercial transactions on the part of the rural population, whilst suggesting that cash, barter and traditional socially embedded transactions probably co-existed, with the relative importance dependent upon social level and context. Rural coin use mirrors that of the main nucleated settlements in the 4th century, and both show a marked decline after the period AD 294-324. The reduction in coin use is attributed by Carrington to the lower demand from a reduced military garrison for food and other products from the rural hinterland.

All of these factors suggest that, although the occupants of rural settlements used coins, their use was restricted to a limited range of types of transaction, such as payment of taxes, and in the late 1st century coins were relatively of such high value as to be carefully curated. Later on, the use of lower value coins indicates a move towards smaller-scale transactions. During the early empire in Britain rural coin loss was as a general rule lower than in the towns (Reece 1987). The occurrence of 46 recorded coin hoards in Cheshire (pre-1974 boundaries) supports the view that individuals were capable of accumulating monetary wealth in the countryside during the early empire as well as later. Shotter notes from a study of Roman coin finds in the north west that the creation of the *civitas* of the Cornovii presupposes the existence of rich people capable of carrying the burdens of such organisation. However, he points out that their identities are not known, and it is not known whether the hoards represented the resources of wealthy landholders or the savings of discharged soldiers, which, in the latter case, might therefore reflect the influence of the fortress at Chester (Shotter 2000a, 189). The distribution of hoards of the 1st and 2nd centuries concentrates in the vicinity of known military sites. Chester is a partial exception to this pattern with most of its hoards being deposited in the 3rd or 4th centuries. During this period the number of hoards increases in the countryside of the north west as a whole, with a tendency to cluster along river valleys or main roads. The distribution indicates their owners' access to better soil, resources and good communications which Shotter attributes to veteran settlement and the extension of the money economy into the rural communities. To some extent coin-loss becomes an index of increasing adoption of Roman values and material culture and also

of the effect of the creation of local markets stimulating local entrepreneurs to develop businesses based on agriculture and other products (Shotter 2000a, 190-1).

Local Rural Finds Assemblages

There are few other Romano-British assemblages in Wirral with which to compare the Mill Hill Road material. However, metal detecting in the last few years has brought to light two further sites in the peninsula which have produced a range of finds which provide at least some points of comparison. The first is a site in south Wirral, which has a very different emphasis from the Irby site. A single cup-headed pin hints at Iron Age occupation but otherwise the assemblage is Roman in date. Finds include a copper-alloy figurine of an eagle on a globe, a lead scale pan weight, a cosmetic spoon, and a copper-alloy stylus, while a fine native style ox-head bucket mount is closely paralleled by one from Dinorben, Denbighshire, probably of 3rd-century AD date. A substantial quantity of melted copper-alloy waste suggests bronze working on the site. There are reports of Roman silver coins from neighbouring fields, and seven Roman bronze coins have been reported. There is a narrow range of brooch types amongst the eleven now recorded. Most common are the Wirral-type brooches which it has been argued are a local form (Philpott 1999a; McIntosh 2009), but others are types found commonly in the lowland north west, a simple dolphin form, a more elaborate trumpet brooch with curvilinear inlaid design, and an enamelled plate brooch. The presence of more than 25 lead spindle whorls along with a considerable quantity of melted lead from the field suggests these items were manufactured there, but it may also indicate that a degree of specialisation in textile production as part of the site economy. The similar form of the facetted holes in the whorls perhaps suggests they were broadly contemporaneous. In that case the number of whorls may indicate greater volume of production rather than longer duration of operation. A small and largely unsystematic collection of surface pottery, with over 40 sherds, includes two samian sherds, a black-burnished rim sherd and a mortarium base, alongside much more numerous Cheshire Plains orange wares. Clearly the collection strategy from metal-detecting is different from that of an excavated site, filtering out, for example, the ironwork. Part of the difference in emphasis of the finds assemblage may result from a stronger representation of occupation during the late 1st to 2nd century, when the brooches were in use than at the Irby site, where occupation appears from BB1 to concentrate in the 3rd and 4th centuries.

Superficially the south Wirral assemblage has elements which appear more 'Roman' than native. The eagle on a globe was an attribute of Jupiter or of an emperor (Toynbee 1963, 150), although the Roman god Jupiter was sometimes in Britain identified with the Celtic thunder-god Taranis (Green 1982). The occupants had access to lead, probably from Flintshire immediately across the Dee estuary in north Wales. A find such as the stylus raises interesting, if ultimately unanswerable, questions about the identity of the user. Was it the property of the occupant of the farm, or of a visiting tax official or military officer? Styli from rural sites in the region are recorded at Irby (see no. 306) and at Ochre Brook, Tarbock, a site which produced evidence of tile manufacture for the 20th legion in the AD 160s (Philpott 2000c). The lead weights make little sense without commercial transactions to require them while the stylus suggests the need to keep accounts, record transactions at the site, or write correspondence.

Only 1 km away from the south Wirral site is another concentration of Roman finds, which comprise five brooches, a Roman coin (a Tetrican radiate copy, dated AD 270-80), and copper-alloy melted waste. Such a concentration is likely to indicate another rural settlement site, one which was also practising metalworking. Perhaps significantly another Roman bronze statuette of an eagle is recorded from nearby Shotwick (PAS website). The finds, including the latter eagle, have a more Romanised appearance than those from the Irby site. These south Wirral sites are unexcavated and there has thus been no opportunity to recover the full chronology of occupation span, to investigate buildings or to recover non-metal finds. However, there are hints in the distinctive Roman iconography of some finds, the stylus and hints of textile specialisation that these settlements, unlike Irby, lie within the zone of influence of the fortress at Chester, and possibly within the legionary *prata*.

Another Wirral site which has produced an important Roman artefact assemblage lies to the south of Irby. Metal-detecting in the 1970s and 1980s within three neighbouring fields produced a copper-alloy key, at least seven coins (a legionary *denarius* of Mark Antony, which may have circulated as late as the 230s/240s: Shotter 2000a, 10), early 3rd-century coins (a *sestertius* of Gordian III and a *denarius* of Severus Alexander) and a radiate copy of the late 3rd century AD, as well as over a dozen brooches, including an unconfirmed report of a lead brooch. Once again the recovery technique was not systematic and the proportion of the assemblage reported is uncertain. In addition, fieldwalking has produced a little Roman pottery from no fewer than five fields, including a Hartshill-Mancetter mortarium rim and Cheshire Plains sherds. Here the duration of visible occupation is rather more extended, perhaps from the late 1st through to at least the later 3rd century. Most unusually, there is artefactual evidence of activity into the post-Roman period with a 6th-century Anglo-Saxon small-long brooch from a nearby field (Philpott 2000a).

Without the secure knowledge that all finds from each site have been recorded, comparisons between sites need to be treated with caution. However, the differences between those elements of the finds assemblages which are directly comparable, the copper alloy and lead, for example, suggests that there are common elements. The two other Wirral sites have produced a number of brooches, in a restricted range of types, with a preference for the early 2nd-century Wirral type. These sites reinforce the conclusion reached on the evidence of the distribution of over 100 examples that this brooch type was manufactured in this part of the north west and may be a marker of social identity (Philpott 1999a; 2007d, 44; McIntosh 2009).

Unfavourable soil conditions cannot be the explanation for the lack of metal finds at Mill Hill Road as some copper-alloy items do survive there. Brooches are perhaps the second commonest artefact as metal-detector finds after coins on Roman sites in the lowland north west, and on some individual sites outnumber coins (Herepath 2004). The coastal site at Meols had produced about Roman 70 brooches and 120 coins by 1886 (Watkin 1886, 278, 282-3; Bean 2007). There is an emerging pattern in western Cheshire of certain rural sites producing significant quantities of brooches through metal detecting while other sites produce none. A number of potential factors may be in operation, including the chronology of occupation and differential preservation in various soils, although the social and economic status of the occupants must be a significant element. The chronology inevitably favours sites which were occupied in the later 1st to 2nd century when the use of fibulae was at its height. After the 2nd century, penannular forms became more common but they do not appear to be well represented on rural sites. By contrast, coin use did not become common in rural sites in the lowland north west until the later 3rd century. The absence of brooches from the Mill Hill Road site in Irby may be explained by the fact that the main period of intense occupation on the site fell within the later Roman period.

The concentrations of brooches may relate in part to manufacturing of these items, since at least two of the sites have produced metalworking waste. In general the finds are too damaged to be able to detect patterns of wear. On the other hand the concentrations may be related to the use, and loss, of brooches, especially if this were confined to, or preferred, by certain social groups. In this respect, brooches were not simply functional items but were worn as part of a suite of personal ornaments to construct and maintain identity. The wearing of particular brooch styles, such as the frequent occurrence in the region of Wirral brooches, has been interpreted as a means of expressing group or individual identity (Jundi and Hill 1998). It is perhaps significant that, with the exception of sites close to the estuary itself, brooches appear to be much less common north of across the Mersey in southern Brigantian (or Setantian?) territory than in northern Cornovian territory. This may be in part a creation of modern patterns of metal-detector use and finds reporting but it is also true of the small number of excavated sites (Cowell and Philpott 2000). The potential for expressions of preference in personal ornaments to enable us to identify regional or local identities is an aspect of artefact studies which requires further study. It remains to be seen whether the differential use of brooches and other potential markers across putative tribal boundaries will reinforce the distinctiveness of populations on either side or blur the boundaries.

The Rural Economy

The permanent Roman occupation of the north west with its sudden and rapid introduction of a large body of men into a series of newly created nucleated centres cannot have been achieved without a significant impact on the existing occupants, their landholdings and the resources of their estates. The hinterland of the fortress will have seen immediate large-scale demands for a wide range of raw materials and produce, such as timber for construction and fuel, leather for tents, shoes and equipment, stone, lead and lime for building work as well as grain and livestock for food. It has recently been estimated that the construction of the Flavian fortress would require over 31,000 tonnes of timber, the equivalent of felling several square kilometres of woodland (Mason 2002b, 89-91). Initially, food supplies were probably imported via the Dee estuary or overland, from Cornovian territory to the south and the establishment of a harbour at *Deva* was no doubt an early priority. It is likely that Meols continued to play an important role during the early stages of the fortress construction as a trans-shipment port on the west coast supply route. The relatively large amount of early coinage lost may indicate an enhanced role for Meols in the early stages of military supply, before the establishment of supply routes and development of local sources.

Although recent work in the region is beginning to identify late Iron Age settlements, on current evidence it is unlikely that the existing rural population would have been unable to meet the demands of the army, whether through requisition, taxation or purchase. However, fieldwork suggests that there was an expansion in the number of rural settlements in the early Roman period which may provide evidence that the population increased in the Roman period (Philpott 2000d, 187-91). A class of sub-square enclosures, represented by sites such as Ochre Brook or Southworth Hall, as well as the small 'hamlet'-like settlement at Court Farm Halewood, which all appear to lack pre-Roman material, may correlate to this development.

Such an expansion has been observed elsewhere in the North. The increase in the number of farmsteads in the Solway Plain in the hinterland of Hadrian's Wall has

been seen as a result of Roman conquest and occupation (Higham and Jones 1983), and was taken to indicate that the Solway region was a food-producing region for the Roman army (Jones and Walker 1983). However, in an analysis of the Solway Plain sites Bewley challenges the assumption that the majority of known Romano-British sites, mostly identified from aerial reconnaissance, in this low lying region were on the lightest soils most suited to arable farming and cereal production. The Romano-British sites were rather located with a view to availability of grassland, arguing for an economy based on animals rather than on arable and in particular cereal-based production. Though there are some areas of fields and field systems, he observes that their role within the total economy is as yet unproven. Acknowledging that the late prehistoric settlement pattern and economy in the region is poorly understood, he suggests the economic base was pastoral from the Bronze Age onwards, and he argues that the impact of the Roman occupation, whilst producing a quantitative change in the economy on the region's settlements, was not great in terms of stimulating production of cereals for military consumption (Bewley 1994, 72-81). Bewley's work represents an important caution against the uncritical acceptance of the impact of the Roman army which deserves further scrutiny in future research into the hinterland of the Roman military sites of Cheshire.

Within the context of Cheshire and the Mersey Basin, the location of at least some sites near the junction of different types of soils and geology suggests the exploitation of both light well-drained soils for arable cultivation as well as heavier soils for grassland. Such a mixed farming regime appears likely at Irby. The demands from the army for supplies, food and produce may have been met through a deliberate policy of settlement and colonisation of under-exploited land in the vicinity of the fortress to assist in securing the food supply.

The relationship between the rural farmsteads and the nucleated industrial settlements of the Cheshire and Lancashire plain has been little investigated so far. Some scholars have suggested that for the north of England 'it is difficult to escape the conclusion that tax burdens and other obligatory outgoings were the most pervasive forms of economic contact between the Romanised sections of the community ... and the farming community' (Higham 1991, 99). Similarly, Jeremy Evans argues that the evidence of pottery use and the volume of use of other material such as iron indicate a sharp division between the occupants of the farms on the one hand and the military and urban centres on the other, with the peasant farmers showing little interest in acquiring Roman material culture. There appears to be a distinction between sites in the Mersey-Dee basin which are relatively rich in such finds, and those further away in Cumbria, West Yorkshire or Lancashire where often assemblages are very small or in north Wales where assemblages of 250-500 sherds are usual (J. Evans forthcoming a). Evans states that the 'King Street sites did not have major commercial interactions with the local countryside, since Roman material culture does not arrive on rural sites in the region in any quantity at all'. Further, he suggests that the industrial sites were leased by *negotiatores* or civilian sub-contractors, perhaps with a largely servile workforce and supplying manufactured items to the military. There is no evidence in the hinterland of a market base sufficient to sustain the towns with an emphasis on industrial production.

Others, such as David Shotter, have argued that there is a close economic relationship between farms and these 'Roman' centres (Shotter 1997, 85). The *Vindolanda* tablets show that the procurement of supplies for military purposes on the northern frontier was achieved by various means, stimulating a 'flexible and sophisticated local economy' through cash purchase as well as requisition (Bowman 1994, 68). The wide variety of foodstuffs available there for the officer class included locally produced apples and eggs, beans and honey, but also included imported goods such as olives and wine. The military was no doubt active in the local market, probably stimulating demand and creating a local money economy. Bowman argues that references to cash purchases undermine the notion that the economy in the undeveloped frontier regions was dominated by primitive barter while military supplies were not solely acquired by an official system of requisition or compulsory purchase (1994, 68-70). As discussed above, rural sites in Cheshire in general, however, fail to show any great use of coinage until the late 3rd century. Although taxes would usually require to be paid in coin, this did not apparently have much of a role in stimulating coin use among the native population. It has been suggested that in this economically undeveloped region, where trade and exchange were not well developed amongst the native population, peasant farmers may have paid taxes in kind (Buxton and Shotter 1996, 77). The north west 'represents an anomalous area within the Province as it is within this area that the apparently conscious regime of 'Romanisation' can be seen most clearly to have failed' (Buxton and Shotter 1996, 83-4).

In two stimulating and detailed articles, Peter Carrington has examined the economic and administrative basis for the relationship between town or fortress and the countryside within Cheshire, and has modelled the supply requirements as well as the potential range of agricultural production and demand (Carrington 2006; 2008). His approach addresses the complexity of these relationships, recognising the different processes of social formation within the *canabae* of Chester and the countryside. and setting these in a chronological framework For Carrington, the relationship of town/ fortress and country should not be viewed not as binary opposites but rather as a gradation, where rural sites to

some extent participated in the monetary economy and at least up to the 3rd century consumed goods imported through the towns. After that the military demand on which the economy of the area was based declined and what he terms the 'network of connectivity' thinned out (Carrington 2006).

As a result, in Cheshire, the sharp decline in industrial settlements appears to have had an effect on the visibility of rural settlements by markedly reducing the flow of datable and durable material culture to the sites. Whether the economic decline of the industrial settlements results in the abandonment of the farms or whether the later Roman occupation phases on farms become virtually invisible through the decline in the availability of datable material culture remains to be determined through further research.

The degree of interaction between rural and industrial sites is obscured at present by the severe shortage of excavated Romano-British rural settlements within the lowland north west. A clearer but more subtle picture of the varying degree of contacts between farms in different parts of the region through time will emerge only with a far larger sample of substantial excavations.

The Social Context

During the Roman period, as before, the site at Irby may have formed one of a network of similar settlements bound to one another in some way by ties of kinship and allegiance. The ties of community may have fluctuated with time, with closer links between settlements based on marriage, and loosened or disrupted by disputes over land or resources, or disputes between personalities. Certain households or individuals would have enhanced the prestige of the family or individual by prowess or inheritance, enabling them to rise to local or wider dominance, and able through personal power to accumulate wealth through marriage, allegiance or ability to protect clients. How the personal prestige of prominent individuals was expressed in physical terms may have been through the creation of substantial earthworks, imposing elements within the landscape to the visitor. Pre-eminent households in local communities will have been those who commanded greatest resources and the retainers bound to them through gift exchange and other obligations.

During the Roman period the social organisation of the native rural population of the region will undoubtedly have been disrupted by the introduction of incoming settlers of varying origins. The impact of service in the Roman army with the settlement of veterans in the vicinity of the fortress is likely to have had an effect on the population density and social and geographical origins of the rural population. The Roman period introduced a new era of social mobility into what had previously been a conservative traditional society.

The inhabitants of rural sites in the Romano-British landscape of Cheshire will have had diverse origins, and the composition of the population will also have changed over time. Some will be the long-established ancestral farms of Iron Age antecedents. Others will be the farms of veterans on land granted by the military authorities, for which the rural findspot of the 'Malpas' diploma at Bickley is a strong contender. Some were probably the estates of officials (such as the Eaton-by-Tarporley villa), yet others will be the farms of incomers from neighbouring tribal areas or other areas of Britain. There is also the possibility of a deliberate policy of settlement in an underexploited landscape to increase the productive capacity within the hinterland of the military and then the industrial settlements. Such colonisation is attested in Lower Moesia (Poulter 1980; cited in Carrington 2006).

Some settlements may have been created as farms but in locations where they could also exploit mineral or natural resources, such as mining of coal, iron ore or stone, or raw materials through the production of manufactured items such as pottery. The location of production near markets may in some cases contrast with the source of some raw materials, in particular copper and iron, although some settlements such as Wilderspool and the Cheshire 'wich' towns had immediately local raw materials in the form of coal, clay and salt. The example of tile production for the 20th legion at Ochre Brook, Tarbock, north of the Mersey in a location which was inconvenient in terms of transportation, suggests that factors other than simple expediency may have dictated site location, and elements such as land ownership, perhaps under tribal control, or the presence of family estates may have played a part in determining precisely where settlements were positioned. It may also remind us that the landscape was not an empty one in which incomers could settle at will, even if the land was occupied and exploited at well under capacity.

The *Prata Legionis*

A complicating factor in Wirral may have been the creation of the *prata legionis*, which may well have introduced an alternative, military, source of authority determining for its own purposes the occupation and exploitation of territory. In the Roman period the legion, as a citizen body headed by a legionary commander, the *legatus*, could 'possess' a territory on behalf of the Roman People. This was wholly analogous to the status of land held by a chartered town or native *civitas,* both of which were regarded as a locally sovereign *respublica* (Mason 1988, 163). The term *prata* is used for the lands held by the legion, and in its original sense referred to pasture as opposed to arable, though not exclusively so. It originally referred to the extensive areas of grazing required by a legion for its animals. Mason considers that in addition to draught and baggage animals and

mounts for the cavalry *equites,* herds and flocks would be maintained by the legion for meat and other products. The livestock in total might run into some thousands of animals. In addition the *prata* might be expected to provide other raw materials and natural resources such as timber, clay and stone, as well as land set aside for large-scale manoeuvres and the construction of practice camps and siege works (Mason 1988, 164-5).

A change in the character of the *prata* occurred after the mid 1st century AD when legions tended to become permanently stationed in one place. The development of civilian extra-mural settlements, the *canabae*, was accompanied by a degree of autonomy by these civilian bodies, which took over 'full responsibility for the civil aspects of the administration of a legion's domains though ultimate control probably continued to reside with the legate' (Mason 1988, 165). Along with a change in status came the use of the term *territorium* rather than *prata.* Mason considers the change may reflect a division of the territory into a reserved military *territorium* and the civilian *prata*, the latter containing a growing number of civilian settlements.

Attempts to define the extent of legionary *prata* elsewhere in the empire have included plotting the distribution of buildings with legionary tile stamps in the hinterland. Though not without complications, this approach has met with some success on the continent where such structures are confined to well-defined zones around the fortress. The leasing of part of the legionary land to tenants, is as Mason points out, difficult to prove, but would be a strong probability in view of the advantage it would confer of securing a food supply close at hand. He suggests that in long-established fortresses part of the legionary land may have been leased in return for a proportion of the agricultural surplus (Mason 1988, 166-7). In the case of Chester, he argues that the *prata* lay to the north and east of the fortress, extending into Wirral and perhaps as far as a line between Neston and Ellesmere Port. The disadvantage of such an arrangement is that it would leave totally isolated the northern part of the peninsula under civilian administration so Mason concluded that the whole of Wirral might best be seen as part of the *prata* (Mason 1988, 180). Higham, on the other hand, suggests that the vitality of the beach settlement at Meols argues for exclusion from the *prata*, but that the quarries at Storeton should be within the boundaries. Whilst the association of the boundary of the later Viking enclave at Raby (Old Scandinavian *Ra-byr* 'boundary village') is attractive, its relevance to the Roman period remains entirely a matter of speculation (Higham 1993, 44).

There are various options for how the land might have been administered during the Roman period. The basis of land tenure would undoubtedly change as the land was originally commandeered from local owners (Higham 1993, 41). The land may have been leased by the *praefectus castrorum,* the camp commandant, to local people, allowing the native settlers to continue in occupation on their traditional farms. Wirral was one of the most densely occupied areas of Cheshire at Domesday and probably in the Iron Age and Roman periods too, as scatters of finds along the ridge particularly into south Wirral suggest. At Irby native tenants may conceivably have been descendants of the earlier occupants living on their ancestral lands. The contacts may have been largely restricted to the payment of rent and the extraction of taxes which were paid in coin or military requisitions. Farms within the *prata legionis* need not necessarily have had greater access to coinage than others outside the legionary land if their rent were paid in kind. Alternatively the farm may have remained within tribal lands in private ownership, perhaps as part of estates held either by the Cornovian elite, or by more localised landholding families under local chiefs as might be postulated for the Iron Age. The distribution of Roman finds in Wirral indicates a number of foci of activity in the western part of the peninsula, with older finds clustering in some parts of the eastern Wirral. The implication is that the peninsula contained a number (possibly running into dozens) of farmsteads during the Roman period. Their origin cannot be determined in the absence of excavation at known sites. Although there may have been an increase in the number and density of settlements during the Roman period, a situation which has been suggested elsewhere in the region (e.g. Tarbock area: Philpott 2000d), finds appear to indicate the late prehistoric origin of at least some sites (Mill Hill Road site; prehistoric pottery at the Telegraph Road, Irby site; and at Hessle Drive, Heswall, and at another site in south Wirral).

It is difficult to determine the impact on the economy or rural settlement pattern of inclusion in the legionary *prata.* If its functions were to secure the food supply and production of raw materials such as timber and leather for the legion, the impact on settlement patterns in the *prata* is also unknown. One might envisage official encouragement to outsiders to settlement within the area if the indigenous local population was too low to expand production of cereals and other produce required by the military thus producing an increase in the density of settlements.

It is worth considering therefore whether the site at Irby sheds any light on the extent of the *prata legionis*. This question may be approached at two different scales of investigation. On a broader landscape level it may be possible to determine differences in the distribution and nature of settlements within the *prata* from those outside, with the foundation of a significant number of new settlements within these legionary lands during the early occupation of the Roman fortress. The settlement of veterans might also be expected within the *prata legionis*. The identification of specialised production to meet legionary needs may be a further factor. In practice

such landscape study requires much more intensive fieldwork than has been possible so far, first of all to identify sites, followed by detailed site investigation to refine the chronology, structural component and economy of the settlements across the landscape. In the present state of knowledge where relatively little is known of the Roman countryside around Chester, there is insufficient information to test this approach.

On an individual site basis, the existence of an Iron Age phase at Irby, despite all the difficulties of identifying continuous occupation through the early Roman period, indicates that the farm was not founded *de novo* on a previously unoccupied site in the early Roman period, although the possibility that the site saw re-occupation of an abandoned farmstead as part of a policy of deliberate settlement cannot be ruled out. However, the presence of circular buildings in native style until perhaps the 4th century, followed by rectangular buildings at the end of the Roman period, argues for occupants continuing with traditional modes of building familiar from the Iron Age, whether descendants of the original Iron Age settlers or incomers from elsewhere in Britain, rather than those who identified strongly with Roman manners and architectural conventions. No strong influence was exerted on the inhabitants to adopt Romanised building styles, nor does it appear the occupants were inclined to do so. There is little evidence of Romanisation in the use of rectangular buildings until the late Roman period, nor is there any evidence from the ironwork that the occupants adopted Romanised building techniques. There is no evidence, nor should we expect it, of military involvement in house plans or construction methods. Jeremy Taylor in a recent discussion of rural settlement in Roman Britain has argued that changes in house type should not necessarily be viewed as Romanisation from the top down (Taylor 2001). Of far more concern to the Roman military commander would be to secure the supplies needed to maintain the garrison rather than to determine the style of the buildings in which the farmers, or tenants, who produced it lived or worked.

Another aspect which might allow the identification of connections between the occupants of the farmstead and the army is the finds assemblage. Recent approaches to the study of material culture have shown that a simplistic dichotomy between military and civilian assemblages fails to account for the complexities of 'military' sites with their civilian personnel (Allason-Jones 2001, 21-3; James 2001). There are no examples of weapons or armour, and these would not in any case be expected on a farm, and the ironwork assemblage is dominated by craft tools, with the addition of the possible slave-shackle padlock. A small number of items which are more common on military sites than rural may have filtered to the site through contacts with the fortress, although these need not necessarily be direct and could be mediated through third parties. In this category may be included the amphora fragments (23 sherds, or 0.89% by sherd count, representing no more than *c.* 10 vessels). They are far from exclusively military in destination, although it has been observed that Dressel 20 amphorae are most common on military sites, even though a sample of rural sites display low levels, of under 1% by sherd count (Evans 2001, 33, fig. 11). The odd ceramic roof-tile may also have been brought to the site, as small numbers of tiles are found at rural sites at Court Farm, Halewood (Adams and Philpott forthcoming) and Mellor (Mellor Archaeological Trust 2003, 11). A fragment of a lava quern, probably of German origin (SF8124), of a type which is common on military sites but is also found on occasion in rural contexts may have a similar source. A probable German lava quern fragment was found at Ochre Brook, Tarbock, where tiles were made for a short period by a civilian contractor for the 20th legion (Philpott 2000c, 85). They do occur occasionally at rural sites in areas such as north-eastern England where excavation has been more extensive (Buckley and Major 1998, 245). The scarcity of excavated sites in the lowland north west makes it impossible at present to assess how common these were on rural sites in this region. The presence of the long-lived legionary fortress at Chester provides a destination for imported querns and the possibility that some of these found their way through trade or exchange into the rural hinterland must be fairly high.

The finds assemblage in summary contains no objects of distinctively military type, nor any, apart from the lava quern, which are found occasionally on civil sites but are clearly military in origin. The presence of objects which are more often found on military than rural sites may indicate that the networks of supply or redistribution were not wholly military and some goods filtered out directly or indirectly into the countryside either through the marketplace or perhaps through personal or family contacts. At Irby any contact with the military is highly muted and all but invisible (or at least unidentifiable) in material terms.

A change in agricultural practice might provide evidence for specialised production for military consumption. In the case of Irby, Jacqui Huntley (Chapter 3) suggests that the plant remains continue with emmer and naked barley until the 4th century when there is a switch to bread wheat and oats. The agricultural regime remained essentially conservative and displays no sign of Romanisation. If the farm's occupants were resolutely conservative, and demonstrated no desire, or need, to conform to crop regimes suitable for the Roman army, then it suggests a degree of independence from centralised authority. Barley was used for animal feed and punishment rations in the Roman army but the presence of barley at other north-western military sites makes it possible that barley was adopted as part of the military, and civilian, diet in the region (Carrington 2006). In this case, it does not rule out the farm providing crops in kind for the military garrison, which may also have implications for the extent of the *prata legionis.*

At the Roman fort annexe at Ribchester, where the first evidence for cereal cultivation occurred in the latter part of Phase 2 (roughly AD 80-120), two main interpretations were proposed (Buxton and Howard-Davis 2000, 412). Either the garrison began to grow their own cereals to secure supplies in a relatively under-populated area, or it represented a change in the farming regime of local farmers, in response to the Roman presence. In the latter case the response may have been a voluntary act, to introduce a cash crop, or it may have been achieved through force or coercion, perhaps through taxation in kind. Here too the analysis of animal bone suggests the beef cattle in the fort originated in the locality or region (Buxton and Howard-Davis 2000, 418).

As to whether Irby, and this part of Wirral lay within the *prata legionis,* there is currently no evidence that it did so, according to the criteria suggested above. In order to address the question, the detailed examination of a far larger sample of Romano-British rural sites in the vicinity of Chester is required to determine patterns of artefact use, site chronologies, environmental evidence of crops and other economic indicators for activities practised at farms. Determining whether these patterns of economy and activity show significant variation between the sites close to Chester and those at some distance requires a range of sites of different overlapping periods in order to even out the idiosyncrasies of individual site histories. There is perhaps a hint of the impact of Chester on the rural hinterland in the south Wirral sites noted above, where Romanised finds assemblages appear to contrast with that from Irby. However, it may simply be that we are asking the wrong questions and the ultimate tenure of the land did not create visible differences in the material record which are amenable to examination through archaeological techniques.

The Early Medieval Period

Robert Philpott

Early Medieval Wirral and Cheshire

Although the early medieval historical background for the pre-1974 county of Cheshire has been discussed in detail by Thacker (1987, 238-47) and Higham (1993), the early post-Roman period in Wirral is obscure. Thacker suggests that the effect of the end of the formal Roman control in the early 5th century was felt only gradually in Cheshire and it is likely that late Roman administration survived in some form as the area remained in British control until the 7th century. Wirral and the lower Dee were linked with the kingdom of

Powys by the 7th century. The Britons of Powys were defeated by the Anglian kingdom of Northumbria at the Battle of Chester in AD 616, an event which appears to have an archaeological dimension through the discovery of skeletal remains at Heronbridge with radiocarbon determinations of the same era (Mason 2006, 520-1). The Northumbrian domination of Wirral and Cheshire lasted only briefly, before being ousted by Penda of Mercia in AD 633 and the Mercian influence was paramount from then on (Thacker 1987, 243-4).

Place-names suggest that west Cheshire, including Wirral, in the early post-Roman period retained a Christian British population, with Landican originally being the ecclesiastical centre for an area which became the extensive parish of Woodchurch. The place-name Landican consists of the Old Welsh *lann* for 'enclosure' with an Old Welsh personal name Tegan. Pensby within the same parish also has a British origin (Thacker 1987, 239-40). Other churches in Wirral have produced evidence for pre-conquest origins. Circular church yards (often taken to be pre-conquest in date, though the oval chapel yard at Moreton is probably post-conquest) are known at Wallasey, Overchurch and West Kirby, while the place-name Wallasey refers to the 'island of the Welsh' or British, at a time when the status of the Welsh was in decline with respect to the Anglo-Saxon population.

Within Cheshire as a whole, British place-names continue to show linguistic changes typical of Welsh until the 7th century, but not later. The rise of the Anglo-Saxon language in the late 6th and early 7th century to linguistic dominance has been characterised as 'gradual and relatively undramatic, involving no cataclysm and causing little disturbance of settlement pattern and religious sites'. Settlement locations may have been relatively fluid even if the territorial boundaries within which they shifted were more stable (Thacker 1987, 243).

The Norse Settlement in Wirral

The first recorded Viking involvement in Cheshire occurred in AD 893 when a Danish army organised an expedition from their base in Essex to besiege 'a deserted city in Wirral called Chester', as the *Anglo-Saxon Chronicle* calls it, and overwintered there before returning to the south-east. Cheshire, and Wirral more particularly, acquired greater prominence with the increasing importance of the strategic route linking the Viking kingdoms of Dublin and York. A decade later in AD 902, Vikings arrived from a different direction to settle. Early annals, notably the Irish *Three Fragments*, record the expulsion of a Norse leader Ingimund (Hingamund) from Dublin and recount his abortive attempts to settle in Anglesey by force, followed by the grant of lands 'near Chester' in Mercian territory by Æthelflæd, the wife of the Mercian lord.

F. T. Wainwright's compelling study of the narrative has led to its acceptance as rooted in historical events (Wainwright 1948, 161-5; Thacker 1987, 254-7; Fellows-Jensen 1985; Griffiths 1992, 67-9; 2007 Edmonds 2009).

Striking confirmation of the location of the Norse settlement comes from the place-names of Wirral. These consist of both habitative and topographical names, reflecting this phase of settlement either by Norse accompanied by Irishmen or by Vikings who had spent some time in Ireland (Dodgson 1972; Fellows-Jensen 1985, 17; Higham 1993, 107). The place-name of Irby explicitly records this episode of Viking settlement in the combination of the Norse elements *Íri* (Irishmen) and the suffix *-býr*, meaning 'farm of the Irish' (Dodgson 1972, 264). Gelling has suggested that the settlement may have been an infiltration of Norwegian farmers who occupied uncultivated land left by the English, and occupied new settlements which were named in their own language. According to this view, Ingimund might have been subsequently induced to attack Chester by existing 'Norsemen and Danes' who were local lords in existing ancient English villages near to Chester (Gelling 1992, 132-3). Several habitative names indicate Viking-period settlement in the neighbouring townships (Frankby, Thurstaston) rather than toponyms. Thurstaston, a neighbouring township to Irby, is an English *tūn* of a Scandinavian named Thorsteinn. Gelling observes that elsewhere the latter formation is taken to refer to an ancient English settlement taken over by an upper-class Scandinavian (1992, 133). The presence of the place-name Thingwall, ON *þingvǫllr*, 'meeting place of the assembly', indicates a measure of self government for the Norse community (Fellows-Jensen 1985, 168-9), probably located at Cross Hill. In the churchyard of St Bridget's, West Kirby, a Norse-period hogback stone was discovered, probably of 11th-century date. The form of the stone, with its bowed sides and shingled roof of convex ridge-back shape, clearly depicts a building. Although this may in part reflect artistic convention – so much so that Collingwood (1928, 18-21) claimed that the 'original meaning of the house-shape has been forgotten' – it is likely that it bore a close relation to recognisable contemporary building styles. Schmidt (1973) has argued that hogback tombstones reproduce elements of Viking buildings, probably long-houses, and adduces numerous examples of buildings of convex-sided plan, both from archaeological excavation and contemporary representations. Rahtz takes a similar line, arguing that the form of hog-backed tombstones and house-shaped caskets found in northern England is related to the building tradition of this type (1976, 88). Such a house would have been familiar to the occupants of the farmsteads within the Norse area of Wirral.

It is unlikely to be coincidence that Irby with its Irish association lies close to two other Irish place-names in

Wirral, both of which, like the excavated site at Irby, lie within Woodchurch parish. The first is Noctorum, from Old Irish *cnocc tírim* 'dry hill', which Fellows-Jensen argues must have been coined by Gaelic-speaking settlers, possibly from the Isle of Man, though the Wirral name occurs in Domesday over a century before the earliest Manx reference (1985, 373). The second is the township name Arrowe, which Dodgson derives from Middle Irish *áirge* (shieling) rather than its Scandinavian descendant *erg*, though the meaning is the same (Dodgson 1972, 262). Fellows-Jensen (1985, 61) offers a possible derivation from a British river-name *arg-* meaning 'white, bright'. Furthermore, she draws attention to the location of *ærgi* names in Cheshire and Lancashire, in that few are located in hilly areas where one might expect them to occur in a shieling-type economy (1985, 294-7). Pearsall notes that the generic *ærgi* names in Cumberland were used of shielings 'on residual sites in areas largely given over to arable use', as opposed to *sætr* names which occurred in traditionally pastoral areas. The small cluster of Irish names in this part of Wirral could conceivably denote a holding based on a permanently occupied farm at Irby with a seasonal shieling within neighbouring Arrowe, a township which even in the post-medieval period lacked a nucleated settlement. A further Wirral place-name, Liscard, which lies on the north-eastern corner of Wirral, has recently been re-assessed as a name of Irish rather than Welsh origin and is dated to close to the conventional division between Old and Middle Irish (Coates 1998).

Archaeological Evidence for Early Medieval Settlement

The relatively numerous fragments of evidence for British Christianity in Wirral by comparison with much of the rest of Cheshire are associated with sparse artefactual or settlement evidence. The early post-Roman period in artefactual terms in Wirral is dominated by Meols (Griffiths 2007). Meols has produced a pilgrim flask, from the shrine of St Menas near Alexandria in Egypt (Thompson 1956), two Byzantine coins have been recorded from nearby Leasowe (Philpott 1999b), while early sceattas and several penannular brooches probably dating to before the 7th century AD and two buckle plates indicate regionally based trade and activity (Bu'Lock 1960; Griffiths 2007). Two further Byzantine coins are known from north Wirral: a *decanummium* of Justinian I, minted in Carthage in AD 540/1, was found in Moreton not far from the excavated site on Hoylake Road (discussed in more detail below), while a *follis* of the same emperor was recovered from the shore at Seacombe in 2007 (PAS LVPL-874C64), and both may be ancient losses in the hinterland of the port. Fulford (1989) has discussed the trading connections between Britain and the Mediterranean, and has concluded that in the period *c.* AD 475 to *c.* 550 western Britain was on the periphery of a trade route originating from the

eastern Mediterranean. As in the Iron Age, tin was probably the commodity sought, but voyages need not have been numerous, perhaps numbering tens rather than hundreds per annum. Further corroboration of a Byzantine trade between the Mediterranean and western Britain comes from recent coin finds in Cornwall and Devon (PAS CORN-72D1D7; DEV-464726: PAS 2007, 69). Harris has suggested that Meols formed part of a Mediterranean trading network, possibly originating in Syria, and on account of its position would have been a prime stopping off point for ships making their way round the coast of western Britain as well as a point of departure for ships to Ireland. The later coins, including that of Maurice Tiberius, may have arrived through a Frankish merchant or possibly in the other direction to the east via a Mercian intermediary, being rather late for the direct Byzantine route, which may have ceased *c.* 550 (Harris 2003, 147-8, 153-4).

A hint of earlier Anglo-Saxon activity in the region is provided by a small-long brooch of 6th-century AD date found at the Telegraph Road site, Irby which has also demonstrated evidence of a shifting Iron Age and Romano-British settlement (Philpott 2000a). This highlights the potential for continuity of occupation of certain sites in the immediate vicinity of the Irby site within the Wirral landscape.

Early medieval artefacts of any kind, whether ceramic, metal or other material, are rare either as site or chance finds in the north west as a whole (Thacker 1987, 286-92; Philpott 1999b). In the north west region (Cheshire, Merseyside, Greater Manchester) only 25 finds of early medieval date had been reported up to October 2009, compared with 862 Roman finds (PAS database). The few finds recovered from Cheshire and Merseyside display a consistent pattern in that their findspots lie close to concentrations of Romano-British finds or to known Romano-British sites (e.g. Philpott 1999a). The scarcity of finds not only makes it difficult to locate sites in the first instance but it also means that it is very hard to assign excavated structures or features to this period with any confidence, unless supported by secure radiocarbon or stratigraphic evidence (Higham 1986, 242-3; Newman 2006, 91-3). Typically, the Irby site was discovered during the excavation of remains of other periods, and the dating is dependent upon the discovery of a single diagnostic artefact amongst a strong background of residual Roman material.

Structural evidence of this date is rare in a rural context in the north west of England. At Tatton, in north Cheshire two buildings were found which were thought to be broadly contemporaneous with a large enclosure defined principally by a shallow palisade trench (Higham 1999, 48-56; 2004a, 308-10). The first structure, Building C, was thought to be constructed before one of the palisades, and measured about 6 m long by 2.2-2.4 m wide internally; it was defined by two parallel construction trenches forming the long sides. An internal partition was marked by a cross trench but the ends were not detected. There were no associated artefacts and no radiocarbon determinations for the building. A second building (Building J) consisted of two near-parallel trenches set 4.6-6.5 m apart, and at least 24 m long, but with no clear evidence of end walls. It stood about 20 m from Building C. The eastern end wall was revealed only as shallow post-pits but like the long walls these may have stood in a shallow and truncated trench. Traces of burning on the subsoil inside suggested a former hearth position. The function of the house was considered likely to have been residential but given its great length it may also have housed livestock. Finds were extremely sparse, and included two fragments of gritstone rotary quern re-used in medieval contexts, and a few small pottery sherds initially thought to be Roman but probably in fact redeposited medieval sherds.

The dating of the Tatton structures and enclosure relied on radiocarbon dates and an absence of datable cultural material. A calibrated radiocarbon date of cal AD 130-610 (HAR-5715; 1660 ± 90BP) came from a cobbled floor adjacent to and contemporary with the building. Two dates from the construction trenches of Building J were calibrated at 390 cal BC – 250 cal AD (HAR-4496; 2030 ± 120BP), and 170 cal BC – 390 cal AD (HAR-5111; 1910 ± 110BP). A third sample was probably contaminated. The upper end range of the earlier dates overlapped with the date from the cobbled surface. As the samples from Building J were oak, and potentially a century or more old when felled for use as construction timber, Higham concluded that Building J should date to AD 300-600. The apparent absence of diagnostic Roman cultural material other than a bead at the mere some distance away was considered decisive in placing the occupation phase within the early post-Roman period.

One of the few excavated sites in the region with evidence of Anglo-Saxon structural remains was located at Hoylake Road, Moreton, less than 5 km north of Irby. The site was excavated in 1987-8 by the Archaeological Survey of Merseyside but remains unpublished. An enclosure ditch had been recut twice and within the enclosed area parts of three superimposed timber-built structures were found, the latest with a sunken floor on which was much burnt grain. Finds were extremely scarce but included a unique silver penny of Eadwig (AD 955-959) of Circumscription Cross type in the upper fill of the enclosure ditch. The coin was issued at a south-western mint, probably Exeter (Cook and Besly 1990, 229, Pl. 22, no 81), and provides an indication from the hinterland of the port at Meols that the west-coast trading route continued to operate in the mid 10th century. A possible contemporary find is a mudstone hone of a form consistent with a late Anglo-Saxon date, which has an undated parallel at Meols (Griffiths and Philpott 2007, 245-7, pl. 57, no 3328). Equally significantly, the site at Moreton also produced a couple

of sherds of Roman pottery and a mid 4th-century coin of *Gloria Exercitus* type, suggesting earlier activity close by, though no unequivocal Romano-British features were found within the excavated area.

A further site at Court Farm, Halewood, north of the Mersey, also has a significant Romano-British settlement, a hamlet rather than a single farm, which also has a series of later pits cut along the line of an earlier ditch. A wooden stake in a pit yielded a radiocarbon date of 680-980 cal AD (Beta-108098; 1210 ± 60BP) although a clear settlement component could not readily be identified here (Adams and Philpott in prep.). The pits appear to have cut through an earlier but still post-Roman ditch, which may have formed a palisaded enclosure, using the stakes which were discarded in the base. Apart from reinforcing a pattern where Romano-British sites remained in use or were re-occupied after an interval, it also suggests that the settlement (if it was such, rather than a livestock enclosure) may have been set within a ditched enclosure. In this respect the site may resemble that at Moreton, although in both cases the extent of the excavated ditches was limited.

One of the few sites to produce a good sequence of deposits of the Saxo-Norman period comes from an urban context, at Lower Bridge Street, Chester. The site has produced a series of cellared bow-sided buildings of 10th-century date (Mason 1985, 8-23; Ward *et al.* 1994). Here dating of the sequence was assisted by a small but critical pottery assemblage of fewer than 200 Saxo-Norman sherds, predominantly Chester ware, but the assemblage of non-ceramic finds was very limited (Rutter 1985, 40-55, 62).

Ecclesiastical sites have proved most consistent in yielding evidence of early medieval material. Several parish church sites have produced stone sculpture of the Anglo-Saxon and Anglo-Scandinavian periods (Bailey 2010). One of the earliest is the Anglo-Saxon runic inscription from Overchurch, probably from a tomb, and 9th century in date (Thacker 1987, 277). A series of later stone sculptures belongs to this period, either emanating from or related to an Anglo-Viking workshop associated with St John's at Chester, with examples from a number of early church sites such as Bromborough, Woodchurch and Neston (Thacker 1987, 279; Bailey and Whalley 2006). A recently discovered miniature hogback tombstone at Bidston in north Wirral, found immediately adjacent to the church, reinforces the ecclesiastical context of the sculptured stones but in this case demonstrates links with the workshop in Brompton, North Yorkshire (Bailey and Whalley 2006). The monastic cell dedicated to St Hildeburgh on Hilbre Island in the Dee estuary off the north-west coast of Wirral provides the general context for a late 11th-century grave slab, probably from a cemetery, a sandstone cross head found in 1852, and a bead of blue glass with yellow and green ornament found in 1865, probably of 7th-century date (Hume 1863, 162; Ecroyd Smith 1866, 210-11; Chitty and Warhurst 1977, 25, no. 14; Thacker 1987, 279).

The chief exception to the impoverished durable material culture for the Norse and Saxo-Norman periods is the beach market site at Meols which produced not only a large group of Hiberno-Norse ring-pins and a small amount of finds of other types, but also coins which span the late Saxon to Norman period (Hume 1863; Bu'Lock 1960; Griffiths 1992; 2007; Bean 2007). A small number of Viking finds provides material support to the historical and place-name evidence for Norse settlement and trade in Wirral. Three recent finds in south Wirral have begun to redress the balance away from the dominance of Meols at this period. A Viking silver ingot (Bean 2000) was found in a field which has produced evidence of metalworking in silver and copper alloy and the possibility of a Viking-period settlement site here is strong. Also in south Wirral a Carolingian denier of Charles the Bald, King of the West Franks, dated to AD 840-75 or 875-7 was found (Cowell and Philpott 1994, 11). Continental coins of this type were present in quantity in the Cuerdale hoard found in the river Ribble, deposited in *c*. AD 905-910. It has been suggested they were obtained in a Viking raid on Aquitaine in western France in AD 898 (Archibald 1992, 18-20). The latter may have been a casual loss from a Viking settler in the early 10th century. The third south Wirral find is a halfpenny of Anlaf Guthfrithsson of York (939-41) (Griffiths *et al.* 2007, 404). A little further afield, but relevant to the early 10th-century Norse settlement of Wirral and the political manoeuvres of that era is the Viking silver hoard of 21 bracelets of Hiberno-Norse type and an ingot, from Huxley, near Chester, probably buried *c*. 900-910 (Ager 2007; Graham-Campbell and Sheehan 2009).

Current evidence suggests the period from the end of the Roman period to AD 1200 was virtually aceramic in the lowland north west on rural sites (Davey 1991, 124). Within Cheshire the only consistent late Saxon-early Norman ceramic tradition is Chester or Stafford-type ware, which is part of an urban tradition of pottery use largely confined to late Saxon *burhs* or markets of the West Midlands and Cheshire, including Chester and Stafford from the early 10th century to mid 11th century (Rutter 1985; Ford 1995, 29-31; Ford 1999, 32-4). Apparently only limited quantities reached rural sites, but the overwhelmingly urban distribution may in part be a reflection of the difficulty of locating Saxo-Norman rural settlements and the scarcity of excavations on them. In recent years sherds have been reported from rural sites at Tatton and Cow Grange Worth, near Ellesmere Port in Cheshire, at Barton Blount in Derbyshire, and at other sites in Worcestershire and Herefordshire (Rutter 1985, 53-4). A small amount of early Stamford Ware is also known from the Chester

region (Davey and Rutter 1977, 18; Thacker 1987, 283). Given that post-Roman or Anglo-Saxon metalwork is in general rare in the region, apart from Chester (Thacker 1987, 286-8) and the wholly remarkable exception of the port at Meols (Hume 1863; Bu'Lock 1960; Chitty and Warhurst 1977; Griffiths 1992; 2007), the virtual absence of datable finds from the Saxo-Norman period at Irby is not surprising, and does not by itself rule out the possibility of an early medieval date for some of the activity on the site.

Early Medieval Structures at Irby

The evidence from Irby needs to be considered in the context of the archaeological and historical evidence for settlement within Wirral and further afield. Several strands of evidence point to occupation during the early medieval period at Irby, probably belonging to at least two phases.

The presence of calcite-gritted ware from north-eastern England indicates that the site remained in occupation at least until late in the 4th century. This ware is present only in small quantities at a few excavated sites in north-west England and north Wales. The 15 calcite-gritted sherds at Irby are heavily abraded and small, weighing on average no more than 3 g, suggesting they had suffered considerable trampling and disturbance after discard. By the early 5th century, datable cultural material such as pottery and coins cease to circulate so it is difficult to identify occupation beyond this date without either a tightly defined stratigraphic sequence or radiocarbon dates, but preferably with both. The abrasion of the Roman pottery could have been a result of the better attested re-occupation in the later medieval period rather than occurring through continued occupation immediately at the end of the Roman period.

The case for early medieval occupation from the stratigraphic sequence has been considered in some detail in Chapter 2. The sequence is not sufficiently securely stratified at Irby to postulate early post-Roman occupation on stratigraphic grounds alone although the radiocarbon dating certainly makes this a distinct possibility in the case of S29, which may be late Roman or early post-Roman in date. Two radiocarbon dates span the periods 230-440 cal AD and 350-600 cal AD, while a Roman coin dated 337-40 in the gully fill suggests a date not before the second half of the 4th century. In addition, several large post-holes within the main area of excavation cut through 4th-century deposits and may belong to this phase as may fragments of others such as Structure 29. However, these could not be related to any identifiable ground plan and contained no datable material. The small but significant assemblage of medieval pottery in the uppermost deposits, with a few sherds stratified in structural features, demonstrates the existence of a later medieval occupation phase, probably dating to the 13th-15th century (see below). The small

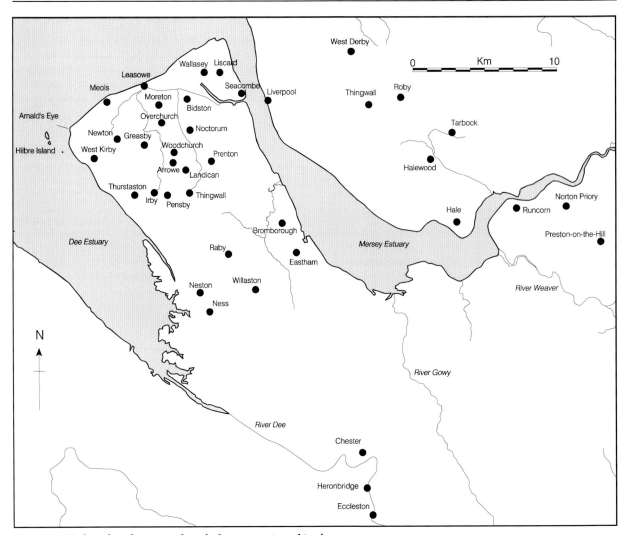

Fig. 5.8: Medieval and post-medieval places mentioned in the text

quantity may indicate that the main occupation phase of the site was over before pottery use became widespread in Wirral in the 13th century

A separate phase of building marked by curvilinear gullies falls between the late Roman/early post-Roman and the later medieval phases. The case is argued for three curvilinear or bow-sided structures marked by gullies (S3, S6 and S7) and a further possible example, which has a curved stone wall foundation (S16). No complete plan is preserved so the form is not certain but enough survives of one to identify the end of a building (S6), while a bow-sided wall and a probable straight end to the same building are present in S7 (see Chapter 2). Unfortunately the structures are not closely datable either stratigraphically or through associated artefacts. In an interim report it was considered that the bow-sided buildings at Irby were mid Roman in date (Philpott and Adams 1999) but detailed analysis of the stratigraphy and the evidence of finds suggests that these buildings post-date structures which themselves cut through deposits containing late 4th-century material while the position of two of the curvilinear structures required the Romano-British enclosure ditches to have been filled in. If the arguments proposed in Chapter 2 for the relative

chronology of these structures are accepted, then the bow-sided structures must be post-Roman in date. The revised stratigraphic sequence now suggests that they belong to the early medieval period with a *tpq* of the late 4th century, and a *taq* of the 13th century. The lack of datable finds and the truncation by ploughing of the later phases of the stratigraphy makes it difficult to date the later buildings at Irby with any degree of precision. This long stretch of time corresponds to a long aceramic period in the North-West which also saw a dearth of artefacts of metal or other durable materials. By analogy with structures from other sites they are likely to date to the Anglo-Scandinavian period, no earlier than the 10th century.

The only building which has produced diagnostic dating evidence of the early medieval period is a fragment of a possible rectangular building, S24, which contained a near-complete and unabraded spike lamp (SF 4888, context 5034), dated to the 10th-12th century. Such an object was used as a hanging lamp suspended in an iron ring. It was found in a small excavation trench away from the main area to the south so its relationship to the rest of the site is not well understood. However, its presence in the construction trench for a building

(S24) makes it important evidence for a Saxo-Norman building. The construction method of the rock-cut slot was unlike that of most features on the site in that it contained clay packing at the base. Too little was excavated to have any clear idea of the building plan but the fragment revealed consists of a T-shaped cut marking the junction of a cross wall with a main external wall. Other than indicating that the building appeared to be broadly rectilinear with a probable internal partition and was of substantial construction little more can be said.

The spike lamp is the only unequivocal artefactual evidence for a phase of activity which otherwise would have confidently been assigned to the Roman period on the basis of finds in the fill and surrounding deposits. In the absence of datable material of the 5th century or later, the swamping effect of the relatively prolific but residual Romano-British finds tends to obscure the possibility that occupation may have continued into the post-Roman period. Post-holes, pits and gullies will continue to contain Romano-British pottery and have nothing contemporary to contribute to the overall chronological sequence.

A further hint of early medieval activity on the site is given by fragments of amber, possibly from a bead. Amber beads are frequent finds in Anglo-Saxon cemeteries of the mid 6th to 7th centuries in southern and eastern England but they are rare in 'Celtic' areas where it was used as insets for jewellery from the late 7th to 9th centuries (Huggett 1988, 64-6; Campbell 1995). However, amber becomes much more common in Norse contexts in the form of beads and other objects. The discovery of the possible amber bead at Irby should perhaps rather be seen in the light of the Norse settlement in northern Wirral, to which the place-name Irby specifically refers. It is suggested that the evidence of 10th-12th century activity provides a more probable context for the occurrence of this item on a rural settlement.

It was with some initial reluctance on the part of one of the authors of this report that the bow-sided buildings were assigned to the early medieval period, in the virtual absence of any positive dating evidence. The difficulty of recognising post-Roman occupation in England is notorious. Simon Esmonde Cleary has expressed the problem of archaeological invisibility of this period. 'By the mid-5th century it is an artefact-poor archaeology of flimsy timber buildings and few burials' (2001, 91). The 'implosion of Romano-British material culture' leaves a woefully poor archaeological record in its wake, a product of the formation and ideology of the society which produced it. The scale of society diminishes rapidly, with socio-political units of small size, which have access to and control over fewer resources than large ones (Esmonde Cleary 2001). Higham has made a similar point specifically with regard to the north west, observing that 'the end of the artificial, Roman,

economy has deprived the archaeologist of diagnostic, artefactual evidence on all but a small minority of sites' (1986, 242). The subject of the techniques for dating sites, and artefacts, in this intractable period has more recently been discussed at length by Roger White (2007, 20-9).

A similar problem in dating post-Roman structures was encountered at the Baths Basilica site in the Roman city at Wroxeter, even though here a long structural sequence of several building phases which overlay the 4th-century deposits associated with the partially demolished basilica building could be assigned to the post-Roman period on stratigraphic grounds. The deposits were accompanied by large quantities of Roman residual material but virtually no contemporary finds. The only absolute dating evidence for the post-Roman sequence consisted of a single coin, a brooch and a pin along with a few sherds of pottery and several radiocarbon dates. The authors observe 'it has been particularly alarming to see how little reliance can be placed on conventional dating methods usually taken as standard in the Roman period' (Barker *et al.* 1997, 245, table 17).

Rural sites, if anything, are even harder than urban to date to this period. A rare early medieval rural site at Fremington, Cumbria was dominated by Romano-British finds, though sufficient later material was present to indicate a later date (Oliver *et al.* 1996). The palisaded enclosure with two buildings at Tatton in Cheshire was also difficult to date in the absence of associated artefacts, but a combination of radiocarbon dates and absence of Romano-British artefacts was used to place this in the post-Roman period (Higham 1999, 57).

In these circumstances, the dearth of identifiable material culture for a rural settlement such as Irby after the end of the Roman period is not surprising. Thus, there are two opposing views which might be suggested for the site. Either the site remained in occupation beyond the end of the Roman period, into the 5th century, producing as might be expected nothing in the way of archaeologically durable material culture; or the site ceased to be occupied by the conventional end of the Roman period and was not re-occupied until the late Saxon or Norman period. The radiocarbon dating is compatible with some post-Roman occupation but could also be interpreted as a wholly Romano-British occupation.

In previous interim statements (Philpott 1993; 2000b; Philpott and Adams 1999) the bow-sided buildings at Irby were discussed in relation to a probable bow-sided building of apparent Romano-British date at Brunt Boggart, Tarbock (Philpott 2000d, 198-200, fig. 8.4). The plans of better preserved examples at Wilderspool and Court Farm, Halewood show that structures of this type consisted of two conjoined arcs, like overlapping circles, with opposed entrances in the middle of the long sides. These were Romano-British, dated to within the 3rd-4th centuries AD. The Irby buildings on closer examination appear to be rather different in plan, at least as far as the incomplete plans allow any certainty, in that they appear more like bow-sided buildings with slightly convex or straight ends.

In general terms parallels for buildings of this kind – bow-sided – or subrectangular framed buildings tend to be characteristic of the early medieval period, although the search for comparative examples ranges over several cultural phases within the early medieval period in north-west England, from post-Roman, through Anglo-Saxon, to Norse, and finally Saxo-Norman. The problem is compounded by a virtual total lack of excavation of early medieval sites in the lowland north west combined with a dearth of excavated buildings from an 800-year aceramic period from the end of the Roman period through to the 13th century. This long period is very poorly represented in the archaeological record of the region, as is highlighted in the recent resource assessment for the Archaeological Research Framework for north west England (Newman R. 2006).

However, a small number of early post-Roman examples of bow-sided buildings can be found in western Britain. Wroxeter in Shropshire provides the largest sequence of buildings from the period of the early 5th century to *c.* 650-700 AD (Barker *et al.* 1997). These include the narrow bow-sided structure Building 1, in Phase Y2, which measured 12.7 m long by 1.8-3.0 m wide, and was divided by a cross passage served by opposed doors. The main posts either rested on or only slightly penetrated the ground surface. The walls were thought to be wattled between the posts, and the form of the house suggests a hipped roof. Phase Y1 had three sides of another bow-sided, Building 3, measuring 10.4 m long, this time with two internal partitions and possibly associated with a furnace, while a possible third bow-sided example, Building 2, was suggested by a stretch of curved wall (Barker *et al.* 1997, 127-8, 172).

Structures at Whithorn (Dumfries and Galloway) in Phase I dated to the period *c.* AD 500-730 have rounded corners and bowed sides, although in general these are rather smaller than the Irby structures. The reconstructed length of Phase I Building 1 at Whithorn is about 8.5 m by 5 m (Hill 1997, fig. 3.5). Four distinct types were recognised within the same general plan, with different types of construction for the walls and superstructure. The types consist of wicker buildings, stake-walled buildings, structures with a timber sill and timber-framed wattle buildings (Hill 1997, 70).

More convincing parallels are found in the Viking period. The classic Viking house plan across the Irish Sea and North Atlantic region shows a considerable degree of consistency and takes the form of a bow-sided or sub-rectangular structure, the long-house, with a byre at one end and a dwelling house at the other. The structures usually had sleeping benches along the walls and an elongated fireplace in the middle of the floor. The form occurs in stone (and turf) in upland areas and in timber, even on treeless islands such as the Faroe Islands, Shetland (e.g. Dahl 1970), or Iceland (Lucas 2003). Manx sites display greater variety in building plan, though the two Viking-age buildings at The Braaid are rectangular and bow-sided, replacing a circular native roundhouse (Wilson 2008, 95-9). At sites in the Western Isles, such as Cille Pheadair or Bornais in South Uist, excavation has revealed sequences of occupation involving repeated re-building of similar forms of bow-sided house after twenty or thirty years (Parker Pearson *et al.* 2004; Sharples 2004). This form of house has been considered a 'cultural emphasizer' and 'must have had an almost symbolic importance to the settlers', arising from a clear, strong concept of what a house and home signified to the mobile Scandinavian farmers who settled across the North Atlantic zone (Larsen and Stummann Hansen 2001, 116-7, fig. 3).

Excavations in the series of Irish coastal towns founded by the Norse have revealed details of urban buildings. Wallace has defined a series of seven Hiberno-Norse building types based on excavated examples. Most relevant in the context of Irby are the building forms from Dublin which is historically attested as the place of origin of the Norse settlers in Wirral. In Dublin the most common form, which had already appeared before AD 900, was Wallace's Hiberno-Norse Type 1, a rectangular, low-post and wattle walls, with rounded corners and a roof supported by two pairs of large posts or groups of posts placed in from the side and end-walls. A stone-kerbed hearth occupied the mid line of the house, and doorways were in the end walls. A long central strip was flanked by low revetted bench areas against the walls (Edwards 1996, 184-5, fig. 93c; Wallace 2001, 44-9).

This raises the difficult issue of ascribing a particular building form to an ethnic group. In 1985, Gillian Fellows-Jensen could write, 'as far as I am aware, no Anglian or Viking settlement sites have been excavated in the north-western counties that form the subject of the present study' [i.e. the pre-1974 counties of Cheshire, Lancashire, Cumberland and Westmorland, and Dumfriesshire] (1985, 399). Across the Pennines, the upland settlement of Ribblehead in North Yorkshire was occupied during the Viking period but Fellows-Jensen and King note that there is no way of determining from the objects found there whether the farm was first occupied by Viking settlers who were exploiting new land in the second half of the 9th century, or whether there had been Anglians there from the breakdown of Roman influence (Fellows-Jensen 1985, 399-400; King 2004). Upland rural farmsteads at Simy Folds, Co. Durham have characteristics such as stone benches, which are found in Norse houses elsewhere, and radiocarbon dates in the early medieval period but the identity of the inhabitants, whether Britons, Anglians or Scandinavians, cannot be determined for certain (Coggins 2004).

Julian Richards has discussed the problems of identifying Scandinavian settlements in the Danelaw from archaeological evidence. He notes that 'it remains true that there are very few excavated settlements of the period 800-1000' (2000, 295) and discusses the claimed identifications of Scandinavian buildings elsewhere in the British Isles, notably in Scotland and the Isle of Man. Three main characteristics have been ascribed to Scandinavian settlements. The first is particular building forms, notably the rectangular and in particular the bow-sided plan, with other details of construction; second is the arrival of new artefact types, while the final element is evidence of settlement disruption or dislocation. However, he notes that the attribution of Scandinavian ethnicity to particular building forms is far from unambiguous, while the other forms of evidence are equally open to a variety of interpretations. In England unequivocal Scandinavian settlement remains elusive. Three upland sites in the north of England, including the Ribblehead site mentioned above, have been claimed as possible examples, though the dating evidence is far from precise and, echoing Fellows-Jensen's conclusion, the supposed Viking finds are not distinctively Scandinavian.

In southern and eastern England the existence of bow-sided buildings is related to the presence of these structures in Jutland and their occurrence in late Anglo-Saxon England has been attributed to Viking influence (Rahtz 1976, 88; Richards 2000, 301). Rahtz (1976, 88) observed that 'even if the origins of the type are pre-Viking it seems likely that their introduction into England is related in some way to Scandinavian influence' on the grounds that all the known examples occurred either in Scandinavian areas, or in late contexts, and in the north or east.

In the absence of a definitive catalogue of buildings, Richards lists examples of bow-sided structures dating to the 9th to 11th centuries. He notes that some of the examples such as Cheddar, North Elmham and Goltho have a symmetrical bow-sided form with a tripartite internal structure. They are often substantial structures, up to 24 m long, but occur alongside rectangular buildings. In this case they may belong to the social elite, while smaller examples in places such as Chester, Thetford and St Neots may have been used by merchants (Richards 2000, 301).

Richards concludes that 'it is possible that the bow-sided houses were a symbol of Scandinavian power and culture, an assertion of identity, but it is notable that they are not direct copies of Scandinavian archetypes. Bow-sided structures in England are frequently smaller than their Danish counterparts', and unlike in their homeland they were not intended as agricultural buildings. He continues, 'if the bow-sided house was a Scandinavian cultural trait its infrequency in England is perhaps puzzling', but suggests that, like the hog-back tombstone, they represent another example of the creation of an Anglo-Scandinavian identity in particular circumstances (Richards 2000, 302).

The question of settlement disruption or dislocation is also not unique to Scandinavian settlements, but the period is increasingly seen as one where the development and reorganisation of settlements into nucleated villages occurred in the Danelaw. The rarity of Scandinavian objects from rural sites creates a further problem and in many cases definitive evidence of such material is lacking. However, with appropriate corroborative evidence such as place-names or territorial organisation, finds may indicate a Scandinavian presence on a site. As Richards observes, 'the problem is that in England Scandinavian culture rarely exists in an undiluted form. Unlike the situation in parts of Scotland or the Isle of Man, it is the creation of a new identity that we are dealing with here, not the imposition of a Scandinavian one' (Richards 2000, 302). Richards cites Cottam in East Yorkshire as a strong candidate for Anglo-Scandinavian settlement (Richards 1999). There are two main phases of occupation, with a series of regularly planned sub-rectangular enclosures, revealed through magnetometry, and the site has produced large numbers of Anglian and Anglo-Scandinavian metal artefacts, including a few of a distinctive Scandinavian type, along with Anglo-Saxon pottery sherds. Building evidence is less clear-cut due to truncation of the site, leaving only clusters of post-holes in defined areas. Plotting of finds indicates two foci, one predominantly with late 8th-century finds associated with a sub-rectangular ditched enclosure, the other to the north was associated with further ditched enclosures, but more significantly late 9th to 10th-century finds clustered in the latter area. Excavations revealed a Viking-age farmstead associated with the latter marked by a cluster of post-holes at the head of a ditched trackway. Most boundaries were shallow, in contrast to a substantial entrance with a massive external ditch, internal rubble bank perhaps topped by a palisade and a timber superstructure found in post-holes either side of the gate. The new settlement form was accompanied by new artefact types in a mixed Scandinavian and Anglian style, including a newly created type of copper-alloy bell (Richards 2000, 303-6).

The implications for Irby need to be considered in the light of the criteria proposed for identification of Scandinavian settlement. First, at Irby the building plans of the putative bow-sided or elliptical buildings are incomplete, although sufficient evidence survives of two to suggest plausibly they took this form. The end of one building (S6) and the curvilinear form and arguably the straight end of F7 appear to be bow-sided; they are not palisade gullies, as they have stone-packed post-holes set along their length. The buildings are not associated with datable early medieval artefacts but, as argued above, the associated Romano-British pottery is likely all to be residual. The presence of a possible enclosure ditch (Ditch 4), again without finds, and respecting the line of the infilled but probably still visible Romano-British enclosure ditches could be associated with the structures but once again the stratigraphy is not able to demonstrate, or refute, this.

Second is the evidence of new artefact types. Certainly the artefact assemblage at Irby does not demonstrate the adoption of new Scandinavian-style artefacts because the site lacks a significant artefact assemblage for the early medieval period. The spike lamp is Anglo-Saxon in its cultural affinities rather than Scandinavian but the date range is consistent with the Anglo-Scandinavian period in Wirral. Few finds have been recovered from the region as a whole for the early medieval period and the absence of finds associated with this phase of activity on the site, whilst distinctly unhelpful, is not surprising.

In terms of settlement dislocation, as far as can be determined from the poor chronological control, the site at Irby appears to have been disused either at the end of the Romano-British or in the early medieval period. The new phase of settlement represented by the bow-sided buildings cuts across long-infilled Romano-British ditches, though the existence of a little later medieval pottery in the upper fills of the ditches suggests that the former settlement was still evident on the ground. It seems likely that if the site remained unploughed the overgrown remains of abandoned buildings and enclosure ditches from the Romano-British settlement would still have been visible. The re-occupation of this particular site, if that is indeed what it is, in the Anglo-Scandinavian period may have been chosen for the same practical reasons which led to the original Iron Age and Romano-British settlements – the conjunction of a variety of soils, a free-draining site and water source nearby. However, the choice of location at an early settlement may represent a deliberate appropriation and statement of ownership of the land, superseding the previous, albeit perhaps abandoned, settlement within the landscape.

A further element of the argument comes from the historical evidence of place-names which for Irby is peculiarly strong and precisely rooted in historical events. As has been mentioned above, Irby township bears a Norse place-name, which refers explicitly to a settlement or farmstead (*'-býr'*) of Irishmen (*'Íri'*), or Vikings from Ireland. This event has a clear historical context in the settlement of Ingimund and his followers shortly after the expulsion of the Norse and Irish in AD 902 from Dublin. The field in which the site was situated was called the 'Smoores', a place-name derived from

the Old Norse word *smjor* 'butter pastures' (Dodgson 1972, 265), i.e. high quality pasture. Apart from indicating that at least part of the site, or its immediate vicinity, was used as pasture during the period when Norse was spoken, it hints too at the good quality of the land. However, we cannot be sure that the field-name was applied to the whole block of fields in their current configuration, nor is it certain that this would preclude a settlement existing on one part of the 'butter pastures'. The two Irish Gaelic township names, Noctorum and Arrowe, close to Irby and both within the same parish of Woodchurch were presumably bestowed by a group of Irish-speakers amongst the Norse settlers in a restricted area of the north Wirral peninsula.

The place-name allied to the historical accounts make the excavated site at Irby a strong candidate for Norse settlement of first-generation incomers, in the early 10th century AD, settling on what may have been an abandoned, but still visible, farmstead site. The parallels in outline with the Hiberno-Norse building forms which developed in Irish Viking towns, as well as more direct parallels in form with Viking rural buildings are consistent with this being a settlement of Irish Norse.

The argument for an Anglo-Scandinavian phase at Irby is thus to some extent circumstantial but there is activity of the relevant date, though otherwise the exiguous artefact assemblage neither confirms nor refutes the 10th-century reoccupation. Although not absolutely conclusive, the site is a strong candidate for an Anglo-Scandinavian settlement, of a type which has proved exceedingly elusive in north-west England.

Parish and Township Boundaries

The parochial organisation of Wirral before the 11th century is obscure, owing, as Higham observes, to the Scandinavian settlement, the subsequent reorganisation and a period of self-government to the north-west of Raby, and the relative wealth of the landowners (Higham 1993, 131-3; 1995, 6). He suggests that the name 'Wirral' was earlier applied to a larger district than the peninsula, since the *Anglo-Saxon Chronicle* for AD 893 refers to 'Chester, a deserted city in Wirral'. Wirral may have been the area directly dependent upon Chester before the Viking period and be equated with the *parochiae* of Chester's two minster churches, St John's and St Werburgh's. By Domesday, the Hundred of Willaston, probably meeting at Hadlow near Willaston, incorporated land on the outskirts of Chester, which was later transferred to Broxton Hundred. In Wirral Higham discerns traces of an early system of territorial organisation which pre-dated the Viking settlement. Eastern Wirral was dominated by the large parish of Bromborough, at whose heart in 1066 was the Earl's estate of Eastham, while to the west was another large parish of Neston. At each there is pre-conquest sculpture and this with the early dedications and extensive medieval parishes, indicate that both date back at least to the 10th century at the latest (Higham 1993, 132). In other Cheshire hundreds there is a consistent pattern where the hundreds are divided between two large and early parishes. In Wirral the picture is complicated by the presence of Landican, with its Welsh place-name and a priest recorded at Domesday. The later medieval parish of Woodchurch consisted of no fewer than ten townships. There is also a probable early church at Overchurch, the only church site with pre-Viking sculpture, but this later became no more than a manorial church, attached to St Werburgh's.

Somewhat unusually for Wirral, the township of Irby which contained 744 acres (301 hectares) is divided between two medieval parishes, Thurstaston to the south-west and Woodchurch to the north-east (Fig. 5.9). The Tithe Award map of 1849 (Pl. XXIV) shows much of the land attached to each parish lying within compact units within the township but some portions are fragmented and display a complex pattern of interlocking blocks belonging to the two parishes. This is particularly marked around Irby Hall and the nucleated village, where the hall and a small parcel of adjacent land lie in Thurstaston, virtually completely encircled by land in Woodchurch and sometimes with neighbouring small closes in different parishes. That the dispersal and inter-mixing of plots between the parishes had earlier been even more complex is indicated by an agreement dated 1796 between the Rectors of Woodchurch and Thurstaston for the exchange of 'intermixed tithe property … for the mutual convenience to themselves and the occupi-ers' (Cheshire RO EDP/P50/2/6-9). No other township in Wirral, with the exception of Newton-cum-Larton to the north, displays such a degree of intermixing of land between different parishes.

The churches at Woodchurch and Thurstaston, between whose parishes Irby was divided, were known to have been in existence at least by the late 11th and early 12th centuries respectively and that at Woodchurch was probably a considerably earlier foundation. Although the 'Wude church', or Woodchurch, is first mentioned by name in 1093, Domesday mentions a priest under the adjacent township of Landican, a place-name from the Old Welsh *lann*, 'enclosure' or 'churchyard', and the Old Welsh personal name Tegan, probably either an unknown saint or an early benefactor, a form of place-name dating to no later than the 7th century (Dodgson 1972, 267; Thacker 1987, 240). It is probable that the Landican was the ecclesiastical centre for the area which became the large parish of Woodchurch. Ormerod suggests that an area of land adjacent to the church, within the vill of Landican, was given the name Woodchurch after the Domesday survey was compiled. Woodchurch was subsequently applied to the parish as a whole, an area which embraced nine townships, and parts of two more including Irby (Ormerod 1882, 520-1). Confirmation of the pre-conquest date of

Woodchurch is provided by a fragment of a plain ring-head cross with grooved ring, dated to the early 10th century, which is built into the Norman fabric of the church (Bu'Lock 1972, 82).

The earliest reference to the church at Thurstaston is the grant of the church to the Abbey of St Werburgh by Matthew de Rodelent in *c.* 1125 (Tait 1920, 48; Burne 1962, 7). In 1724 the church was said to have stood in the courtyard of Thurstaston Hall. In fact the church was outside the immediate hall but closely adjacent. However, the reference to a 'chapel' in a quitclaim of William son of Matthew de Thurstaston suggests the church probably originated as a chapel to the hall (Raines 1845, 173; Tait 1920, 58). An earlier church building was demolished about 1820 and is said to have contained a 'Saxon door with zigzag mouldings' (Beazley 1924, 95-6). The parish is small and contained all of the township of Thurstaston and part of Irby. Tait has suggested that the parish of Thurstaston was carved out of that of West Kirby (Tait 1920, 58), itself a church of some antiquity which has produced an 11th-century hogback tombstone of Norse type (Collingwood 1928).

Although the modern parochial system crystallised between the 11th and end of the 13th century, Margaret Gelling has observed, 'the close relationship between Anglo-Saxon estates and lesser churches had the effect – most beneficial for historians – of confirming and fossilising the boundaries of land-units which were in most cases of considerable antiquity when the churches were built' (Gelling 1992, 183-5). There seems little doubt that at Irby the patchwork of land-units reflects an early division between different estates associated with the churches of Woodchurch and Thurstaston, prior to the grant of Irby to the Abbey of St Werburgh. By 1093 when this township was granted as the 'manor of Erby in Wirhalle' to the Abbey (Ormerod 1882, 510), the complex parish pattern must already have existed as it certainly would not have been created afterwards once the township was held as a single unit by the abbey. The subdivision must therefore pre-date 1093.

The pattern of parish fragmentation suggests that an in-tensively partitioned and complex pattern of ownership already existed by the late Saxon period when parish boundaries were beginning to harden. Within the town-ship of Irby at least two estates were held as unconsoli-dated, fragmented holdings. Such a situation reflects a long process of development, with partitions and subdi-visions, perhaps through the exchange, sale, inheritance and gift of different plots of land, in part through the effects of partible heritance which appears to have frag-mented the holdings into relatively minor sections. Higham observes that the proliferation of numerous small estates, as small as the township or fraction, in the late Saxon period may have resulted from the prolonged military crisis of the later 9th and 10th centuries, which required that the Mercian lords grant land to thegns as a

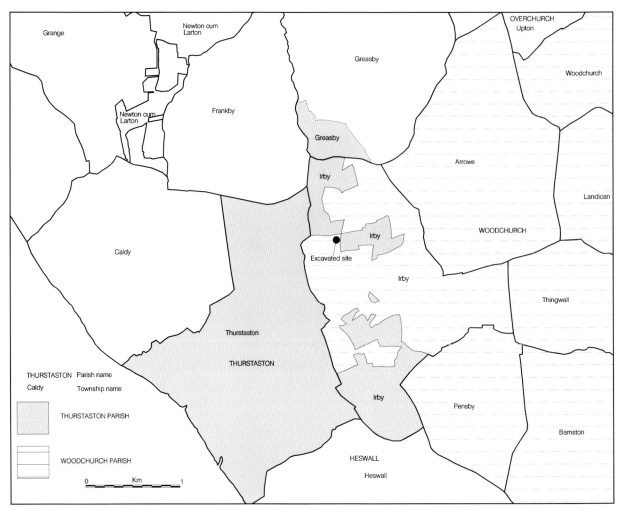

Fig. 5.9: Wirral townships and parishes in the Irby area

reward for military service. This led to the fragmentation of earlier land-units and the opportunity for new owners to rename their land (Higham 1993, 181). Furthermore it has been suggested that the buying and selling of small portions of land, a common phenomenon by the 10th century in England, was the result of Viking activity (Fellows-Jensen 1985, 343).

The place-name of Irby may allow us to glimpse an earlier stage in the development of the township and estate. As the Norse 'farmstead of the Irish', Irby is a strong candidate for the primary settlement of northern Wirral by a mixed group of Norse and Irish who were expelled from Dublin in AD 902. The fact that the farm or settlement took the name of the incomer indicates he had some pre-eminence in the local landholding, and the name of his settlement, which distinguished him by ethnic origin rather than by name, replaced any earlier place-name amongst the dominant Norse-speaking stratum of society in the Viking 'enclave' of north Wirral. The settlement evidence from the township of Irby makes it one of the best candidates known thus far in Wirral for continuous occupation from the Roman period and it is possible that it was not uninhabited in the early 10th century. If so, the Irishmen arriving in 902 on land granted by Æthelflæd 'near Chester' may have replaced a Saxon lord in tenurial terms and possibly

physically displaced him in practical terms. However, it remains a possibility, if somewhat speculative, that the complex landholding pattern which had developed in the centuries before being fossilised by the parish boundaries reflected a partition between different estates and individuals, conceivably between incomer and existing owner.

The parish boundary dividing Thurstaston and Woodchurch makes a slight change in direction beside the Romano-British settlement, apparently respecting the earlier alignment of the northern enclosure ditch. If the parish boundary was indeed determined by the late Saxon period, then it may have deviated slightly to avoid a deserted settlement which remained visible as a prominent earthwork or alternatively to include an existing settlement within one land unit rather than another.

Settlement Nucleation

A corollary of the fragmented parish structure in contrast with the unitary post-conquest ownership of the township is that within such a holding, a single open field system would be unlikely to develop. The unified ownership under the Abbey may have provided the opportunity both to lay out and organise a field system worked communally, and perhaps at the same time the

220

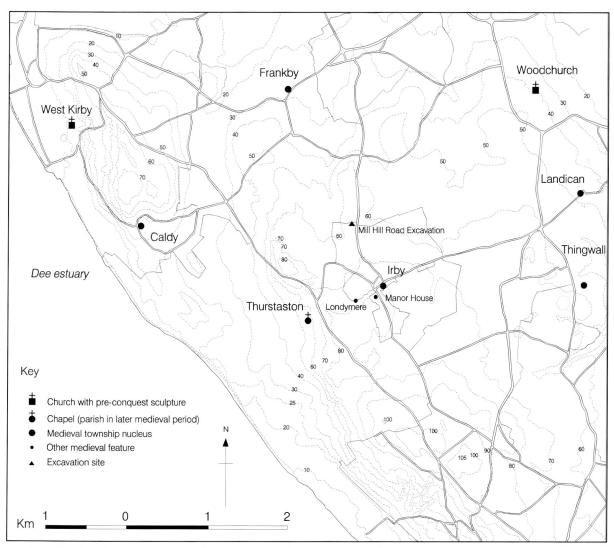

Fig. 5.10: Medieval churches and settlements in the Irby area mentioned in text

stimulus to nucleation of the village adjacent to the monastic manor site.

There has been much debate nationally over the date at which open fields were established. Elsewhere in England archaeological evidence for the tendency towards establishment of nucleation of settlements indicates that the process took place over an extended period. At Chalton in Hampshire the chalk downland saw some shift of settlement from early Saxon sites occupied in the 6th and 7th centuries on hill top sites but were abandoned for valley locations by the 9th century. In Northamptonshire the same process of abandoned farms in the middle Saxon period can be seen through deserted sites of scattered farms noted in fieldwalking at the same time as nucleated villages were established. In Yorkshire the re-planning of extensive landscapes has been attributed to the period following the extensive devastation of the harrying of the North in 1069-70. It is thought that the reapportionment of land on new and planned lines in the late 11th century took place on manors devastated by William the Conqueror (Steane 1985, 155).

Within the lowland north west the problem has not yet received much attention from archaeologists. At Domesday Wirral, along with the Dee valley, was one of the most densely populated areas of Cheshire, with the highest level of plough-teams and relatively wealthy for the county (Thacker 1987, 335). There is little mention of woodland in Wirral, with only one manor, Prenton, recorded as having woodland. Furthermore, as Higham observes, woodland names are notably scarce in Wirral, suggesting the area was not characterised by a wooded landscape at the period when the late Saxon phase of place-name formation occurred (1989, 24). Together these suggest that most of the land was cleared, and that surviving woodland was managed, by contrast with east Cheshire where recorded woodland is much more common (Thacker 1987, 332). The legal entity of Wirral forest, which embraced the whole hundred of Wirral, was probably created in the early 12th century. The term denoted the area where forest law prevailed, in order to protect the deer and boar rather than necessarily being densely or continuously wooded (Higham 2004b, 107-8). The numerous parishes in Wirral, including single township parishes such as Overchurch and Thurstaston, also point to a relatively dense population for the county. However, Higham has argued that the dispersed settlement pattern in medieval Cheshire resulted from a low population. However, Higham has suggested that within Cheshire the low population was inadequate to muster the plough-teams necessary to work communally organised field systems until perhaps as late as the 13th century (Higham 1987, 9). Until the 13th century 'it is unlikely that sufficient households were available on many manors for nucleation to be a viable option', and lords were unable to encourage nucleation without combining manors and their workforces (Higham 1987).

The rise in population led to an expansion onto marginal waste and woodland rather than establishing new farms alongside existing ones. The impetus was thus towards greater dispersal of settlement by occupation of newly cultivated land towards the edge of townships rather than towards nucleation. The local lords either broke new land themselves or extracted rents from tenants who did so. Higham further saw the main drive to nucleation coming from sites such as the rural estates in the hands of bishops which developed some of the characteristics of nucleated villages, such as Burton in Wirral and

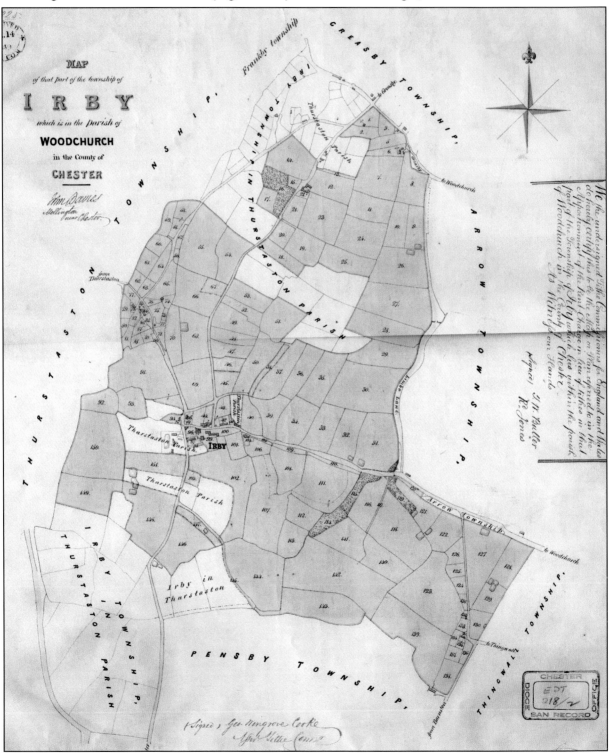

Plate XXIV: Tithe Award map of Irby, 1849 (Cheshire RO EDT 218/2), by permission of Cheshire Record Office

Tarvin. The main other class of site, apart from the salt wiches, were seigniorial boroughs established in the later 13th century. These, however, had little impact on the pattern of rural settlement.

In Irby itself the process of agricultural expansion can be seen in the progressive attitude of the abbots of Chester. Under Simon of Whitchurch the abbey had assarted 20 acres of land from heath and waste in Irby (Hewitt 1929, 13), while his successors continued to improve the land through marling; in 1347-48 the abbot was responsible for no fewer than 65 new marl pits in Irby and 35 in neighbouring Greasby (Hewitt 1929, 22).

The Later Medieval Settlement

Later Medieval Irby

In the medieval period, for the first time, the division of the landscape into identifiable territorial units can be recognised. Although Irby is not mentioned by name in Domesday at 1086, the manor was granted along with Greasby to the Benedictine abbot and convent of St Werburgh at Chester by Hugh Lupus in his charter of 1093 and remained in their possession until the dissolution in 1540. The manor house, Irby Hall, which is set within a moated enclosure, is considered to lie on the site of the abbey manor house (Mortimer 1847, 265-6; Ormerod 1882, 510).

The excavated site lay within a former field which in 1849 formed part of the estate of the Trustees of Bertie Entwhistle, held by James Stubbs (Tithe field no 54: Woodchurch parish, CRO EDT 218/2). In 1824 the same field, Smoores (measuring in area 5 a 2 r 28 p), was in the estate of Revd B. E. Johnson, which consisted of a rather scattered holding in Irby (CRO D1648), and was surrounded on all sides by land belonging to General Glegg. Johnson's estate is presumably the holding purchased by Revd Croxton Johnson, rector of Wilmslow, and formerly the property of the Balls of Irby, who descend from Thomas Ball of Irby and Boughton, second son of Thomas Ball of Tushingham, whose ancestors were settled there in 1316-17. The Irby estate was farmed by Thomas Ball jnr, under the abbot of St Werburgh in the reign of Henry VII. This and other property passed to the Revd T. Peters and Mr T. Evans. The other chief landowners, the Gleggs, acquired the manor and their estate in the mid 17th century (Ormerod 1882, 510-1).

By the post-medieval period the nucleated village can be seen to have developed close to the hall. The earliest map of Irby dates to as late as 1824 but reveals a cluster of houses and farms, some of which are likely to have been built in the 16th and 17th centuries, probably within plots of medieval origin lining the main street. Amongst these is the farm of William Ball which bears a datestone of 1613 (Irvine 1959, 32). Although the direct dating evidence for the existence of the nucleated settlement is relatively late in date, there is little doubt that the medieval village lay at the focus of the field system from an earlier period.

Medieval documents and post-medieval field-names such as 'Townfield' recorded in 1605 and several 'loons' field-names, such as the 'Sower Lands' in 1648 (Irvine 1959, 31; Dodgson 1972, 265), indicate that the township in the medieval period operated on the common field system, probably based on two open fields (Chitty 1978a, fig. 9). The intermixed nature of the holdings is illustrated by a grant of 1579 recording Thomas Young's holding which consisted of three butts in Gorsty Hey, six more in the Mill Field and seven in the Porto Field (CRO Acc 1386/3). The Tithe Award map of 1849 (Cheshire RO EDT 218/2; Pl. XXIV) shows the pattern of early open field boundaries fossilised in the later field pattern with a series of long reversed-S curving boundaries north-east of the village, while a fragment of the field system survives today south-east of the village as one of the best preserved areas of ridge and furrow cultivation in Wirral. A few early field-names are recorded, including the Mekonsuch, first noted in 1639, which was probably named after the nearby watercourse or 'sīc' in the valley and lay near the excavated site to the west. The fields are also referred to as Meckansedge or Mechansedge but by the Tithe Award of 1849 this has become Michansedge or Mickansedge (Dodgson 1972, 265).

The township boundary between Irby and Thurstaston was only finally settled in the early 14th century. A document of *c.* 1307-23 defines the boundary and refers to a well called Londymere which was walled round with large stones (*Chartulary of Chester Abbey* part ii, 387; Beazley 1924, 12). The location of the well has been identified on the township boundary west of Irby Hall. Division of the townships at the well indicates that it was an important water source, shared between the inhabitants of both townships. The well was still used by the people of Irby until the 19th century. Excavations in the early 1980s at the well revealed neat stone walling and produced some medieval pottery as well as prehistoric flint (Merseyside HER), reinforcing the identification of the well as the Londymere.

Medieval Buildings at Irby

Two of the Irby buildings (S18, S19) employed shallow stone foundations which presumably supported timber superstructures, as they are too narrow and insubstantial to support a stone foundation. S16 also had stone foundation walls, but has been tentatively assigned to the early medieval period (see Chapter 2). All appear to be the truncated and plough-damaged remains of dwarf foundation walls. The stones were not bonded with clay and in the absence of a cut appeared to be resting either in a very shallow trench or pressed into the ground surface. Without some form of bonding they would not have stood above the ground for any considerable height, the stones simply being rounded lumps rather than shaped blocks which might be built to some height as dry-stone walling. In one case, S19, it is probable that the long walls of the structure had slightly different forms of construction, with a dwarf wall on the northern side and a shallow foundation trench on the south.

The presence of a fragmentary and plough-damaged clay floor in the gap between the ends of two wall foundations in S18 is difficult to interpret. However, the limited excavation area means that only a small section of the wall was visible and from this it was impossible to reconstruct the plan of the building. The apparent curving form of the walls may be a result of some dispersal of stones by the plough, although the small area excavated bears a resemblance in plan to a fragment of an apsidal building. In all cases, the absence of durable roofing material of clay or stone indicates roofs thatched with organic material such as straw, reeds or turf. The long post-built structure S21 may represent a replacement or addition to S19.

There may be some chronological development in the change in construction method. In a discussion of vernacular building in England, Christopher Dyer (1986)has observed a widespread change from post-built structures to use of dwarf walls in the 13th century. If this transition were applicable to the north-west, and occurred at the same time as in the west Midlands, then it may be possible at Irby to see a change from post-built S21 and S24, latter in the Saxo-Norman period, to the dwarf wall construction of the S18 and S19.

Inevitably, the form of the medieval settlement at Irby is unclear as only part was excavated. There is more than one phase of activity and the settlement appears to have been rearranged during the medieval period. At least one building lay some distance to the south in Area XXV/XXVI in the Saxo-Norman period and the presence of one later medieval jug base of 13th-14th-century date in the upper fill of the main ditch (Ditch 1) suggests continued medieval activity into the 14th century.

Parallels for Later Medieval Buildings

Stuart Wrathmell concluded from a study of excavated medieval peasant buildings at Wharram Percy, North Yorkshire that the recorded vernacular tradition of the area was a valid starting point for a model to study the excavated evidence (Wrathmell 1989). However, few medieval peasant buildings have been excavated in Cheshire or more widely across the lowland north west. The absence of a tradition of archaeological investigation on rural sites in the region can be illustrated by the state of research into medieval settlements up to 1968. By that year Hurst was able to record 290 investigations of medieval buildings in

England but none of these lay in the historic counties of Cheshire or Lancashire (Hurst 1989). Subsequently, the majority of those excavated are moated sites and to date it remains the case that very little work has been undertaken on lesser medieval rural structures in Merseyside or Cheshire (summarised in Newman C. 2006, 119-25).

The excavation of the medieval settlement at Tatton in north Cheshire is a notable exception, involving large-scale area excavation of a peasant settlement (Higham 2000). The sequence of timber buildings appears to begin before 1200, and possibly as early as the 10th or 11th century, and continued to within a generation of 1400, with structures consistently employing earth-fast posts. A surviving timber indicates that at least one structure was in oak. A building in Phase 1 was rectilinear in plan and constructed of post-holes, 14.4 m along the ridge and 4.6 m wide at the centre, with all four walls bowing slightly outwards. An area of fired clay within the building was probably a hearth (Higham 2000, fig. V.9). The building was assigned to the period pre-1200 and possibly earlier by Higham on the grounds of the horizontal stratigraphy and the absence of pottery from component post-holes, pottery of 13th-14th-century date being ubiquitous in other contexts of the type. The presence of a single sherd of Chester ware and a clay loom-weight of mid to late Saxon type imply some activity at Tatton in or before the 11th century, which might best be accommodated by associated with this structure (Building F) (Higham 2000, 85-8). At Brunt Boggart, Tarbock, a probable peasant cottage was excavated, probably from associated pottery dated to the 13th or 14th century (Speakman 2000). Neither of the two proposed reconstructions was wholly satisfactory owing to the irregularity of the plans produced but it seems likely that it had the form of an elongated rectilinear structure constructed with earth-fast posts and a shallow gully (Philpott 2000b, 126-32).

The marginal hamlet of Fazakerley which was established probably by the 13th century on the edge of the open field of Walton, near Liverpool, was excavated in 1994-5 but remains unpublished. One building, M1265, was subrectangular in plan, measured 9.5 by 6.5 m, and had an entrance in the eastern end of the north-facing side, which gave access to the toft. Two layers of cobbling were noted in the entrance. There was little evidence of the superstructure, though clay walls and a possible padstone for a cruck were recorded. The hollowed floor was suggested to have resulted from cleaning out of a byre or barn. The structure was erected before 1150-1295 cal AD (810 ± 60 BP; Beta-88456) and finds from the layers over the cobbling indicated abandonment in the 14th or 15th century (Wright 1996, 42-3, 91-8).

At West Derby, close to the Norman motte and bailey castle site, a building was defined by a surviving clay floor, a probable hearth, a possible padstone and the line of an internal partition, representing a small structure at least 9.8 m long and between 3.8 and 4.2 m wide, probably of 13th century date (Philpott in prep.).

The medieval settlement at Meols is the chief source of comparative information on medieval buildings in Wirral (Griffiths *et al.* 2007, 19-21). Unfortunately no plans or photographs survive of the buildings and the structures are not closely datable. Nonetheless, the antiquarian accounts provide detailed information on structures which were eroding out of sand dunes along the north Wirral coast during the later 19th century. Three distinct types of medieval structure were observed. The first consisted of rough stone foundation, occasionally with tooling or dressing of blocks, into which upright timbers were set. The floors were of blue (estuarine or marine) clay laid on a deposit of sand which had been used to raise the level. The second consisted of clay walls of rectangular buildings, while the third were simple wattle constructions, lacking both clay floors and stone foundations, in which it was suggested animals were kept. They may have been pens rather than roofed buildings.

The north west so far lacks sufficient excavated data to confirm the applicability of the observation that during the 13th century some regions saw a major change in construction method. In place of the earth-fast timber posts, which had been used since prehistoric times, came new types of foundations using low dry-stone walls, clay walls or padstones to support the main upright timbers. Excavated peasant buildings of the 13th century in most cases conformed to the sizes of later medieval structures, measuring from 12-16 feet wide (3.7-4.9 m) and from 25 to 50 feet (7.6-15.2 m) in length. In addition, long-houses were more widely encountered prior to 1350 than after then, and these could exceed 60 feet (18.3 m) in length, housing animals and humans under one roof. However, there is regional variation both in the chronology and the techniques employed (Beresford and Hurst 1971, 93-5; Dyer 1986, 35-40). More recent studies including that by Gardiner (2004) indicate that the pattern of development is more complex than previously considered, with timbers placed on the ground or low stone footings in use from around AD 800.

The relevance of this for the site at Irby is difficult to determine as rural peasant buildings have seen little investigation in the north west. Following the broad sequence of the replacement of earth-fast posts by dwarf stone foundations, this might argue at Irby that S21, with its padstones and earth-fast timbers, predated S19, which uses a dwarf wall of at least theoretically later form. The padstones may have been inserted to support a timber post which had rotted in the ground (cf. Gardiner 2004, 348), a practice found in earlier structures but not confined to them. However, on stratigraphical grounds S21 appears to be the later. Building styles may have

remained conservative in the area, though far too little is known of the full range of peasant buildings in the medieval period to know how typical that was of the rest of the county.

A significant factor in the choice of construction materials is that the site at Irby lay directly over sandstone bedrock. The availability of the stone which appears in some cases to have come from clearance of the fields as the stone was rolled and rounded rather than freshly dug or quarried. The post-holes in many cases were packed with sandstone blocks, while the foundation walls in sandstone also require easy access to the raw material. The re-use of blocks removed from earlier buildings is also a distinct possibility. The clay floor of S18 was a thin layer of yellow boulder clay.

Surviving vernacular buildings from the West Midlands confirm that medieval peasant building construction was based on the unit of the bay, with dimensions of roughly 15 feet (4.6 m) square. The great majority of buildings in Worcestershire where the size is recorded were either of two or three bays; much rarer were buildings of one, five and six bays (Dyer 1986, 23-4). In the East Midlands, later medieval documents occasionally specify the size of a bay, usually between 14 and 16 feet (4.3-4.9 m), with a length usually of 30 or 40 feet (9.2 or 12.2 m) (Dyer 1986, 31). Considerable regional variety is met in the construction methods. Dyer notes that in the West Midlands cruck construction was common, usually on dwarf stone walls, whereas the East Midlands posts were either set in the ground or on padstones (Dyer 1986, 32).

Long-houses, which were a regional type not found all over England, were more common in the 13th century than after 1350. They might serve all the functions required in a peasant farmstead, with animal shelter, grain and other storage, and living accommodation all under a single roof. However, in many areas in the period 1200-1350 both documentary and excavated evidence shows that peasant farmsteads consisted of a variety of buildings. The farmhouse was a consistent component, but it was often accompanied by a corn barn or *grangia*. Other ancillary buildings included kilns, kitchens, oxhouses, stables and 'outhouses' (Dyer 1986, 34-5; Wrathmell 1989, 9).

Later Medieval Finds Assemblages

The finds assemblage from the medieval settlement at Irby is limited not only in quantity but also in scope. It consists almost entirely of pottery, in the form the most part of small, highly fragmented and abraded sherds. Metal finds of medieval date appear to be absent with the exception of a sheet metal key found in a lower ploughsoil layer (SF284). No intact occupation layers with exclusively medieval finds were recovered, and the deposits appear to have been trampled and disturbed, introducing a large amount of residual Romano-British material into the uppermost deposits. What may be small pockets of medieval deposits are present in the upper fills of the ditches where soil layers have developed over buried ditches and have then sunk down over time into the upper fills.

Other than Chester ware with its predominantly urban context, and a low level of imported material such as Stamford ware, the widespread use of ceramics in Cheshire does not begin again until the mid-late 12th century. The earliest securely stratified material occurs in early contexts of *c.* 1134-1200 at Norton Priory while late 12th century groups are present in Nantwich (Greene and Noake 1977, 54-7; Vaughan 2008). In Merseyside, West Derby castle moat has produced medieval pottery which probably dates to the first half of the 13th century as the castle was abandoned by *c.* 1250 (Davey 1991, 124), while at Norton Priory, green-glazed jugs with rouletted decoration became common in the first half of the 13th century (Greene and Noake 1977, 54-7; Vaughan 2008). The adoption of pottery by the 13th century by the occupants of a rural peasant holding is suggested by the excavation at Brunt Boggart in Tarbock. They were well able to afford a quantity of locally made ceramic vessels for food storage and preparation (Speakman 2000, 149). Other medieval rural sites in Cheshire such as Tatton, despite being 50 kilometres east of Irby, also show the widespread adoption of medieval pottery in the 13th century, with only a single sherd of Chester ware to indicate earlier pottery use (Higham 2000, 86).

Meols has produced an artefact assemblage which spans the early medieval through to post-medieval period, and provides an indication when pottery use becomes established in the region. Other than urban centres, where pottery use earlier than 1200 or so might be expected, Meols is perhaps the key place in Wirral where one might expect to see the introduction of pottery from other parts of Britain or beyond where its use was established, given its strong late Saxon and Norman coin list and its well developed trading connections. Although the coins suggest a rise in activity from the mid 10th century through the Norman period to the mid 14th century, the pottery assemblage of just over 70 sherds has no material earlier than the mid 13th century, with a significant group in the mid 13th-early 14th century, by analogy with material from Henrician castles of north Wales, and a small amount of later medieval material (Axworthy 2007).

The finds do little to illuminate questions of social status or activity in the medieval period. The only class of datable medieval artefact is pottery. The introduction of pottery within a rural domestic context where vessels were traditionally in a range of organic materials, wood, leather, horn or basketwork, appears to have been a fairly late development in the region, probably not before the 13th century in rural contexts.

In most circumstances organic materials do not survive. However attempts have been made in London, Winchester and elsewhere where organic preservation is better, to assess the relative frequency of wooden vessels against those of other materials. Wooden vessels are thought to have been fairly cheap and more numerous than those of pottery or metal in the 14th century, and cups, plates and dishes could be bought for six to the penny, whilst at an earlier date wood may have been even more prevalent (Egan 1997, 112; Dyer 1982, 39). The unusually favourable conditions of preservation at the nearby coastal site at Meols have yielded several medieval wooden vessels (Morris 2007), although the sample was not systematically recovered. Another possibility is that of a degree of conservatism in rural communities. The same pattern of a virtually aceramic period from the 5th to 12th century occurs in the Welsh Marches when pottery was very rarely used until the 12th century except in urban contexts (Gelling 1992, 179-80). Rural resistance has been observed to the adoption of pottery by the Welsh population around the town of Monmouth in south Wales until as late as the mid 13th century despite its ready availability from the late 11th (Courtney 1997, 101). There is a wealth of documentary references in account rolls from England to indicate that the cost of an earthenware dairy pot in the late 13th and early 14th century was between ½d and 1d, while drinking vessels sometimes seem to have been cheaper, perhaps owing to their smaller size (Courtney 1997, 103). Pottery vessels were considerably cheaper than metal vessels and in general are thought to have been low priced, made by artisans for the lower-class and local market (Dyer 1982, 37).

While the innovation of using pottery was initially led by urban, ecclesiastical and military populations, and took some time to filter down through the social strata being adopted only slowly by the rural population. However, the presence of a small quantity of 14th-15th pottery at Irby suggests that the apparent low volume in use cannot be wholly attributed to the medieval occupation occurring during a transitional phase when the use of pottery had not yet become commonplace. The quantity of pottery in use may be related not so much to chronology as to the function of the settlement and the status of its inhabitants. Pottery may have been available in the medieval markets but beyond the means of the peasant farmer. Another possibility is that the part of the settlement excavated might have consisted of agricultural outbuildings such as a barn rather than a dwelling house.

Other than the key mentioned above, no unmistakably medieval metalwork is present amongst the finds. Other excavated medieval rural sites in the lowland north west demonstrate a similar poverty of metalwork, so that sites at West Derby (14th century), Roby (probably 14th-15th century), Brunt Boggart in Tarbock (13th-14th century), and Fazakerley, where a toft was laid out in the late 12th or early 13th century (Wright 1996), also lack small metal artefacts. This presents a stark contrast with the enormous finds assemblage from the medieval village and port at Meols which has produced a vast range of material dating largely from the 13th-mid 14th century and derived from eroding coastal deposits, from a settlement engulfed by sand which was forced to move inland. A study of the medieval metal finds from Meols by Geoff Egan and Patrick Ottaway indicates a large amount of lead-tin items, of personal dress accessories, and a vast range of items such as craft and agricultural tools, eating utensils, riding equipment, as well as personal objects such as pilgrim tokens, and personal seals (Griffiths *et al.* 2007). It is probable that the great size of the Meols assemblage is in part due to one or more inundations by windblown sand which buried quantities of usable artefacts, removing them from circulation. The exceptional circumstances at Meols may represent the difference between an artefact assemblage lost or abandoned in use, and those on many sites of discarded, lost or broken, but not salvaged for recycling. The possibility that Meols was used as a transhipment port for materials and men during the campaigns of Edward I in north Wales represents a major potential source of coins, metal fittings and dress accessories beyond that of a rural hamlet. Irby almost completely lacks this dimension of social and economic life. Accident of survival is clearly a major factor in the absence of the lead-tin material from the sandstone soils at Irby but copper-alloy might be expected to survive rather better.

Abandonment of the Medieval Settlement

The abandonment of the settlement at Irby on artefactual grounds appears to have occurred at some time during the 14th or 15th century. The pottery of 16th- to 17th-century and later date from the site is derived from the ploughsoil where it may well be derived from manuring of arable fields rather than from the occupation directly on that spot, although some medieval sherds were probably incorporated in that deposit through reworking of the uppermost occupation deposits by the plough. The abandonment of the settlement at Mill Hill Road, Irby may have been part of the move away from dispersed discrete settlements towards the nucleation of the settlement.

Individual circumstances, now irretrievable, may lie behind the move, or the settlement may have simply shifted to a nearby location outside the excavated area. However, a further possibility is that the abandonment related instead to the nucleation of the settlement close to the site of the hall. As discussed above,by 1316-17 the Ball family was established in Irby and farmed land under the abbot of St Werburgh. By 1824 the Smoores field was held by a successor to the Balls, Revd Johnson. William Ball is recorded on a datestone of 1613 at Irby Farm in the centre of the nucleated village, demonstrating that the main farm for this estate had moved to the village at least by this date. There is no certainty that the Mill Hill Road site represented the residence of the Balls, or their predecessors, though the existence of several medieval buildings suggests that this is not impossible. It is conceivable that the abandonment of the site represents the transfer by the Balls to the main village nucleus, near to the manor. By contrast with the management of some other monastic estates in Wirral, such as those of Birkenhead Priory or Basingwerk Abbey, the manors of the Abbey of St Werburgh were based on nucleated villages such as Greasby, Irby and Eastham (Chitty 1978a, 16). The site of Irby Hall is identified as the manorial site granted by Hugh Lupus in 1093 to St Werburgh's, and the shift to the hall site by the new owners may mark a move to nucleation by the Abbey.

Post-Medieval Irby: The Site Evidence

The excavations have shed little light on post-medieval settlement in Irby, but the ploughsoil contained a quantity of post-medieval pottery, which presumably relates to the manuring practices of the local farm on arable land. Alongside local wares is a small quantity of imported pottery, consisting of North Devon gravel-tempered ware and south-western French polychrome Saintonge ware and Beauvais, of the 16th-17th century. The position of Irby on the Wirral peninsula gave the village's inhabitants access to the products of maritime trade and exchange via the west coast trade route to south-west England and the continent. The nearby anchorage at Redbank near Thurstaston on the west Wirral coast was frequently mentioned in the customs accounts from the mid 14th century onwards (Wilson 1969; Dodgson 1972, 281). The resurgence of trade with France in the second half of the 15th century becomes archaeologically visible through the rise in late Saintonge and Hispano-Moresque wares, followed in the 16th century by a move northwards of the principal sources which can be demonstrated at Chester through the arrival of vessels from Beauvais (Davey and Rutter 1977, 21). From 1301 until 1566 the customs accounts for the chamberlain of the exchequer of Chester detail the substantial quantities of wine imported from western France, especially from Gascony, and show an increase in the early 16th century in Spanish and to a lesser extent Portuguese wine (Wilson 1969). The ships frequently called at Brittany and the Cornish coast on the journey. The North Devon pottery industry was heavily directed towards export through the ports of Bideford and Barnstaple during the 17th century, not only to England and Wales but also across the Irish Sea to the Isle of Man, expanding by 1600 to Ireland and further afield to North America by 1635 (Grant 1993). Coastal trade from North Devon with Chester was frequent, in exchange for lead ore, while the Barnstaple port books indicate that trade with Liverpool began in the mid 17th century and increased later in that century.

A growing demand for Cheshire salt from the late 1670s onwards resulted in ships sailing for Liverpool and Chester with cargoes of saleable earthenware in the later 17th century (Grant 1983, 88, 93). Finds of 17th- or early 18th-century North Devon vessels have been recognised not only in excavated assemblages in Liverpool (Davey 1985, 84), Chester (Davey and Rutter 1977, 28) and Sefton Old Hall, Merseyside (Davey 1991, 136), but also in fieldwalking by the Liverpool Museum Field Archaeology Unit at Ness, close to the Dee estuary port.

The pottery assemblage from ploughsoil at the excavated site of Irby also includes a range of dark-glazed wares of types probably produced within the Merseyside region or in north Wales, at Buckley. The post-medieval material however, has not been subject to detailed analysis for this report, although the material has the potential to make a small but significant contribution to the understanding of ceramic use and trade in the coastal part of Cheshire.

References

Adams M. H. 1995 *An Early-Middle Bronze Age Settlement Site at St Chad's Vicarage, Kirkby, Merseyside,* Unpublished report, Liverpool Museum.

Adams M. 2009 *An Archaeological Watching Brief on Land Adjacent to Bromborough Court Moat, Pool Lane, Bromborough, Wirral. NGR SJ 344 840,* Unpublished NMLFAU Report.

Adams M. and Pevely S. 2006 *An Archaeological Excavation at Newton Hall, Cheshire Close, Newton-le-Willows, St Helens, Merseyside. Final Report,* Unpublished NMLFAU Report.

Adams M. H. and Philpott R. A. in prep. *Excavations on a Romano-British and Early Medieval Site at Court Farm, Halewood, Merseyside,* NML monograph, Liverpool.

Adams M. and Speakman J. I. 2001 *An Archaeological Excavation at Ince Manor and Monastery Cottages, Ince, Cheshire. NGR SJ 4495 7655,* Unpublished NMLFAU Report.

Addyman P. V. 1981 'Cruck buildings: the evidence from excavations' in Alcock N. W. *Cruck Construction. An introduction and catalogue,* CBA Research Report 42, London, 37-9.

Addyman P. V. and Priestley J. 1977 'Baile Hill York' *Archaeol J* 134, 115-56.

Ager B. 2007 'Huxley, Cheshire: Hoard of Viking silver bracelets (2004 T453)' in DCMS *Treasure Annual Report 2004,* DCMS, London, 62-3.

Ahmad C. and Adams M. 2004 *An Archaeological Evaluation at Scholes Hall, Eccleston, St Helens, Merseyside. Interim Report. NGR SJ 489 934,* Unpublished NMLFAU Report.

Allan J. P. 1984 *Medieval and Post-Medieval Finds from Exeter 1971-1980,* Exeter City Council and the University of Exeter.

Allason-Jones L. 2001 'Material culture and identity' in James S. and Millett M. (eds) *Britons and Romans: advancing an archaeological agenda,* CBA Research Report 125, London, 19-25.

Allason-Jones L. and Miket R. 1984 *The Catalogue of Small Finds from South Shields Roman Fort,* Soc Antiqs of Newcastle upon Tyne Monograph Ser 2, Newcastle.

Allen C. S. M. 2007 'The Early Bronze Age Pottery' in Garner D. J. *The Neolithic and Bronze Age Settlement at Oversley Farm, Styal, Cheshire. Excavations in advance of Manchester Airport's Second Runway, 1997-8,* BAR Brit Ser 435, Archaeopress, Oxford, 53-76.

Allen J. R. L. and Fulford M. G. 1996 'The Distribution of South-East Dorset Black Burnished Category 1 Pottery in South-West Britain' *Britannia* 27, 223-81.

Andersen S. T. 1979 'Identification of wild grass and cereal pollen' *Danmarks Geologiske Undersogelse Arbog 1978,* 69-92.

Anon 2006 'Iron Age farm beneath the amphitheatre?' *The Past Uncovered: Newsletter of Chester Archaeology* Oct 2006, 1-2.

Archibald I. G. and Archibald Z. H. 2005 'Treboeth – the burnt town: a preliminary investigation of early Christian to early Modern industrial activity in Handbridge, Chester' *J Chester Archaeol Soc* 80, 9-67.

Archibald M. M. 1992 'Dating Cuerdale: the Evidence of the Coins' in Graham-Campbell G. (ed.) *Viking Treasure from the North West: The Cuerdale Hoard in its Context,* Liverpool Museum Occasional Papers 5, NMGM, Liverpool.

Arnold C. J. and Davies J. L. 2001 *Roman and Early Medieval Wales,* Sutton Publishing, Stroud.

Axworthy J. 2007 'Pottery: Later medieval and post-medieval' in Griffiths D. W., Philpott R. A. and Egan G. *Meols: The Archaeology of the North Wirral Coast,* Oxford University School of Archaeology Monograph 68, Oxford, 251-63.

Bailey R. N. and Whalley J. 2006 'A Miniature Viking-Age hogback from the Wirral' *Antiq J* 86, 345-56.

Bailey R. N. 2010 *Corpus of Anglo-Saxon Stone Sculpture, IX: Cheshire and Lancashire,* Oxford.

Barfield L. H. 1991 'Hot Stones: Hot Food or Hot Baths?' in Hodder M. A. and Barfield L. H. (eds) *Burnt Mounds and Hot Stone Technology,* Sandwell Metropolitan Borough Council.

Barford P. M. and Hughes M. 1985 'Other Objects of Copper-Alloy' in Blockley K. *Marshfield: Ironmongers Piece Excavations 1982-3: An Iron Age and Romano-British Settlement in the South Cotswolds,* BAR Brit Ser 141, Oxford, 151-71.

Barker P., Haldon R. and Jenks W. E. 1991 'Excavations on Sharpstones Hill near Shrewsbury, 1965-71' *Trans Shropshire Archaeol Hist Soc* 68, 15-57.

Barker P., White R., Pretty K., Bird H. and Corbishley M. 1997 *The Baths Basilica Wroxeter: Excavations 1966-90,* English Heritage, London.

Barnatt J. 1994 'Excavations of a Bronze Age unenclosed cemetery, cairns, and field boundaries at Eagleston Flat, Curbar, Derbyshire 1984, 1989-90' *Proc Prehistoric Soc* 60, 287-370.

Barrett J. C., Bradley R. J. and Green M. 1991 *Landscape, Monuments and Society: the Prehistory of Cranborne Chase,* Cambridge University Press, Cambridge.

Bayley J. 2002 'Non-Ferrous Metalworking in Roman Yorkshire' in Wilson P. and Price J. (eds) *Aspects of Industry in Roman Yorkshire and the North,* Oxbow Books, Oxford, 101-8.

Beamish M. 1998 'A Middle Iron Age Site at Wanlip, Leicestershire' *Trans Leicestershire Archaeol Hist Soc* 72, 1-91.

Bean S. C. 2000 'Silver Ingot from Ness, Wirral' in Cavill P., Harding S. E. and Jesch J. *Wirral and its Viking Heritage,* English Place-Name Society, Nottingham, 17-18.

Bean S. C. 2007 'Coins and Tokens: pre-Roman to post-medieval' in Griffiths D. W., Philpott R. A. and Egan G. *Meols: The Archaeology of the North Wirral Coast,* Oxford University School of Archaeology Monograph 68, Oxford, 295-350.

Beard G. R., Thompson T. R. E. and Lea J. W. 1987 *Soils of the Liverpool District,* Memoirs of the Soil Survey of Great Britain, Harpenden.

Beazley F. C. 1924 'Thurstaston …an account of the Parish, Manor and Church', reprinted with additions from *Trans Hist Soc Lancashire and Cheshire* 75.

Bell M. 2007 *Prehistoric Coastal Communities: The Mesolithic in Western Britain,* CBA Research Report 149, Council for British Archaeology, York.

Beresford G. 1987 *Goltho: The development of an early medieval manor c. 850-1150,* English Heritage Archaeological Report 4, London.

Beresford M. W. and Hurst J. G. (eds) 1971 *Deserted Medieval Settlements,* London.

Berridge P. 1994 'The Lithics' in Quinnell H. and Blockley M. R. (eds) *Excavations at Rhuddlan, Clwyd 1969-73: Mesolithic to Medieval,* CBA Research Report 95, Council for British Archaeology, London, 95-114.

Bestwick J. D. and Cleland J. H. 1974 'Metal Working in the North-West' in Jones G. D. B. and Grealey S. *Roman Manchester,* Manchester Excavation Committee, Altrincham, 143-57.

Bewley R. H. 1994 *Prehistoric and Romano-British Settlement in the Solway Plain, Cumbria,* Oxbow Monograph 36, Oxford.

Blockley K. 1989 *Prestatyn 1984-5: An Iron Age Farmstead and Romano-British Industrial Settlement in North Wales,* BAR Brit Ser 210, Oxford.

Blockley K. 1990 'Excavations in the vicinity of Forden Gaer Roman Fort, Powys, 1987' *Montgomeryshire Collections* 78, 17-46.

Blockley K., Blockley M., Blockley P., Frere S. and Stow S. 1995 *Excavations in the Marlowe Car Park and surrounding areas,* The Archaeology of Canterbury V, Canterbury.

Blockley K. and Day M. 1989 'Moulds' in Blockley K. *Prestatyn 1984-5: An Iron Age Farmstead and Romano-British Industrial Settlement in North Wales,* BAR Brit Ser 210, Oxford, 183-92.

Boardman S. and Jones G. 1990 'Experiments on the effects of charring on cereal plant components' *J Archaeol Science* 17, 1-11.

Boon G. C. 1977 'Greco-Roman Anchor-stock from N Wales' *Antiquaries J* 57, 10-30.

Boon G. C. 1988 'British coins from Wales' in Robinson D. M. (ed.) *Biglis, Caldicot and Llandough. Three Late Iron Age and Romano-British Sites in South-east Wales. Excavations 1977-79,* Oxford, 92.

Boon G. C. and Hassall M. 1982 *Report on the Excavations at Usk 1965-1976. The Coins, Inscriptions and Graffiti,* University of Wales Press, Cardiff.

Bottema S. 1975 'The interpretation of pollen spectra from prehistoric settlements (with special attention to Liguliflorae)' *Palaeohistoria* 17, 17-35.

Bowman A. K. 1994 *Life and Letters on the Roman Frontier: Vindolanda and its People,* British Museum Press, London.

Breeze A. 2006 'Three Celtic Toponyms: *Setantii, Blencathra* and *Pen-y-Ghent' Northern History* 43 (I), 161-5.

Brewer R. J. 1986 'The beads and glass counters' in Zienkiewicz J. D. *The legionary fortress baths at Caerleon. Volume II. The finds,* Cardiff, 146-56.

Britnell W. J. 1989 'The Collfryn Hillslope Enclosure, Llansantffraid Deuddwr, Powys: Excavations 1980-82' *Proc Prehistoric Soc* 55, 89-134.

Britnell W. J., Silvester R. J., Gibson A. M., Caseldine A. E., Hunter K. L., Johnson S., Hamilton-Dyer S. and Vince A. 1997 'A Middle Bronze Age Round-house at Glanfeinion, Powys, near Llandinam, Powys' *Proc Prehistoric Soc* 63, 179-97.

Brodribb A. C. C., Hands A. R and Walker D. 1973 *Excavations at Shakenoak Farm, near Wilcote, Oxfordshire Part IV: Site C,* Oxford.

Bronk Ramsey C. 1995 'Radiocarbon calibration and analysis of stratigraphy' *Radiocarbon* 36, 425–30.

Bronk Ramsey C. and Hedges R. E. M. 1997 'Hybrid ion sources: radiocarbon measurements from microgram to milligram' *Nuclear Instruments and Methods in Physics Research B* 123, 539–45.

Brown A., Leaning J. B. and Little J. H. 1975 'Excavations at Halton Brow, Runcorn, 1967' *J Chester Archaeol Soc* 58, 85-9.

Brownbill J. 1928 *West Kirby and Hilbre,* Liverpool.

Bruck J. 1999 'Houses, Lifecycles and Deposition on Middle Bronze Age Settlements in Southern England' *Proc Prehistoric Soc* 65, 145-66.

Bruhn P. M. 1966 *The Roman Imperial Coinage. Vol. VII. Constantine and Licinius A.D. 313-337,* (edited by C. H. V. Sutherland and R. A. G. Carson) Spink and Son Ltd, London.

Buckley D. G. and Major H. 1990 'Quernstones' in Wrathmell S. and Nicholson A. *Dalton Parlours Iron Age Settlement and Roman Villa,* Yorkshire Archaeology 3, West Yorkshire Archaeology Service, Wakefield , 105-20.

Buckley D. G. and Major H. 1998 'The Quernstones' in Cool H. E. M. and Philo C. (eds) *Roman Castleford. Excavations 1974-85. Volume I: The Small Finds* Yorkshire Archaeology 4, West Yorkshire Archaeology Service, Wakefield, 241-7.

Bu'Lock J. D. 1960 'The Celtic, Saxon and Scandinavian Settlement at Meols in Wirral' *Trans Hist Soc Lancashire Cheshire* 112, 1-28.

Bu'Lock J. D. 1972 *Pre-Conquest Cheshire 383–1066,* Chester Community Council, Chester.

Burne R. V. H. 1962 *The Monks of Chester: The History of St Werburgh's Abbey,* SPCK, London.

Burnham B. C. 2006 'Roman Britain in 2005. 4. Northern counties' *Britannia* 37, 392-405.

Burnham B. C., Hunter F., Fitzpatrick A. P., Hassall M. W. C. and Tomlin R. S. O. 2003 'Roman Britain in 2002' *Britannia* 293-382.

Buxton K. and Howard-Davis C. 2000 *Bremetennacum. Excavations at Roman Ribchester 1980, 1989-1990,* Lancaster Imprints Series no 9, Lancaster University Archaeological Unit, Lancaster.

Buxton K. and Shotter D. C. A. 1996 'The Roman Period' in Newman R. (ed.) *The Archaeology of Lancashire,* Lancaster University Archaeological Unit, Lancaster, 75-91.

Camden W. 1695 *Britannia, newly translated into English,* London.

Campbell E. 1995 'Amber' p. 23, in Wilkinson P. F. 'Excavations at Hen Gastell, Briton Ferry, West Glamorgan, 1991-92' *Medieval Archaeology* 39, 1-50.

Carrington P. (ed.) 1994 *From Flints to Flower Pots: Current research in the Dee-Mersey region*, Archaeological Service Occasional Paper No. 2, Chester City Council.

Carrington P. 2006 'Towards a model of Roman society in Cheshire, First to third centuries AD' http://www. chesterarchaeolsoc.org.uk/R_cheshire_model.html

Carrington P. 2008 'Feeding the wolf in Cheshire: models and (a few) facts' in Thomas R. and Stallibrass S. (eds) *Feeding the Roman army: the archaeology of production and supply in north-west Europe*, Oxbow Books, Oxford.

Caruana I. D. 1992 'Carlisle: Excavation of a Section of the Annexe Ditch of the First Flavian Fort' *Britannia* 23, 45-110.

Carver M. O. H. 1991 'A Strategy for Lowland Shropshire' *Trans Shropshire Archaeol and Hist Soc* 67, 1-8.

Casey J. 1988 'The interpretation of Romano-British site finds' in Casey J. and Reece R. (eds) *Coins and the Archaeologist*, 2nd end, Seaby, London, 39-56.

Chadburn R. and Hill P. 1997 'Exotic, imported and transformed stones' in Hill P. *Whithorn and St Ninian: The Excavation of a Monastic Town 1984-91*, Sutton Publishing, Stroud, 468-74.

Chitty G. 1978a 'Wirral Rural Fringes Survey' *J Merseyside Archaeol Soc* 2, 1-25.

Chitty G. 1978b 'Irby Mill Excavations 1979' *J Merseyside Archaeol Soc* 2, 37-45.

Chitty G. and Warhurst M. 1977 'Ancient Meols: Finds from the Cheshire Shore in Merseyside County Museums' *J Merseyside Archaeol Soc* 1, 19-42.

Clapham A. R., Tutin T. G. and Warburg E. F. 1962 *Flora of the British Isles*, 2nd edn, Cambridge University Press, Cambridge.

Clark R. 1991 *Hallgate, Wigan: Excavation Report*, Unpublished report, Greater Manchester Archaeological Unit.

Clarke J. C. 1998 'Other Artefacts of Stone' in Cool H. E. M. and Philo C. (eds) *Roman Castleford. Excavations 1974-85. Volume I: The Small Finds*, Yorkshire Archaeology 4, West Yorkshire Archaeology Service, Wakefield, 253-65.

Clay P. 2001 'Leicestershire and Rutland in the First Millennium BC' *Trans Leicestershire Archaeol Hist Soc* 75, 1-19.

Close-Brooks J. 1972 'Two steatite lamps' *Proc Soc Antiquaries Scot* 104, 295-7.

Coates R. 1998 'Liscard and Irish Names in Northern Wirral' *J English Place-Name Soc* 30, 23-6.

Coggins D. 2004 'Simy Folds: Twenty Years On' in Hines J., Lane A. and Redknap M. (eds) *Land, Sea and Home*, Soc for Medieval Archaeol Monograph 20, Leeds, 325-34.

Coles J. M. 1971 'The Early Settlement of Scotland: Excavations at Morton, Fife' *Proc Prehistoric Society* 37, Part II, 284-366.

Collens J. 1994 'Recent discoveries from the air in Cheshire' in Carrington P. (ed.) *From Flints to Flower Pots: Current research in the Dee-Mersey region*, Archaeological Service Occasional Paper No. 2, Chester City Council, 19-25.

Collingwood W. G. 1928 'The Early Monuments of West Kirby' in Brownbill J. *West Kirby and Hilbre: A Parochial History*, Henry Young and Sons Ltd, Liverpool, 12-26.

Condron F. 1997 'Iron Production in Leicestershire, Rutland and Northamptonshire in Antiquity' *Trans Leicestershire Archaeol Hist Soc* 71, 1-20.

Connelly P. and Power D. 2005 'Salt Making in Roman Nantwich: Recent Discoveries at Kingsley Fields, Welsh Row' in Nevell M. and Fielding A. P. (eds) *Brine in Britannia: Recent Archaeological Work on the Roman Salt Industry in Cheshire*, Archaeology North West 7 (for 2004-5), 31-40.

Cook B. J. and Besly E. M. 1990 'Coin Register 1989' *British Numismatic J* 59 (for 1989), 221-33.

Cool H. E. M. 1993 'The copper alloy and silver gravegoods' in Farwell D. E. and Molleson T. I. *Poundbury Volume II The Cemeteries*, Dorset Natural History and Archaeological Society Monograph 11, 89-96.

Cool H. E. M. and Philo C. (eds) 1998 *Roman Castleford. Excavations 1974-85. Volume I: The Small Finds*, Yorkshire Archaeology 4, West Yorkshire Archaeology Service, Wakefield.

Cool H. E. M. and Price J. 1995 *Roman vessel glass from excavations in Colchester 1971-85*, Colchester Archaeological Report No 8, Colchester.

Coombs D. G. and Thompson F. H. 1979 'Excavation of the hillfort of Mam Tor, Derbyshire' *Derbyshire Archaeol J* 99, 7-51.

Cormack W. F. 1970 'A Mesolithic Site at Barsalloch, Wigtownshire' *Trans Dumfries Galloway Nat Hist Antiq Soc* 47, 63-80.

Cormack W. F. and Coles J. M. 1968 'A Mesolithic Site at Low Clone, Wigtownshire' *Trans Dumfries Galloway Nat Hist Antiq Soc* 45, 44-72.

Cornwall I. W. 1958 *Soils for the Archaeologist*, Phoenix House Ltd, London.

Courtney P. 1997 'Ceramics and the history of consumption: pitfalls and prospects' *Medieval Ceramics* 21, 95-108.

Cowell R. W. 1991a 'Prehistory of Merseyside' *J Merseyside Archaeol Soc* 7, 21-61.

Cowell R. W. 1991b 'Interim Report on the Survey of the Wetlands in Merseyside: 1990-91' *North West Wetlands Survey Annual Report 2*, Lancaster University, Lancaster, 13-20.

Cowell R. W. 1992 'Greasby, North Wirral. Excavations at an early Mesolithic site: Interim report' *Archaeology North West: Bulletin of CBA North West*, 4, 7-15

Cowell R. W. 2000a 'Ditton Brook' in Cowell R. W. and Philpott R. A. (eds) *Prehistoric, Roman and medieval excavations in the Lowlands of North West England: Excavations along the Line of the A5300 in Tarbock and Halewood, Merseyside*, NMGM, Liverpool, 7-26.

Cowell R. W. 2000b 'Brook House Farm, Halewood' in Cowell R. W. and Philpott R. A. *Prehistoric, Romano-British and Medieval Settlement in Lowland North West England: Archaeological excavations along the A5300 road corridor in Merseyside*, NMGM, Liverpool, 27-66.

Cowell R. W. 2000c 'The Early Prehistoric Period in Southern Merseyside' in Cowell R. W. and Philpott R. A. (eds) *Prehistoric, Roman and medieval excavations in the Lowlands of North West England: Excavations along the Line of the A5300 in Tarbock and Halewood, Merseyside,* NMGM, Liverpool, 165-8.

Cowell R. W. 2000d 'The Late Prehistoric Period in the North West' in Cowell R. W. and Philpott R. A. *Prehistoric, Romano-British and Medieval Settlement in Lowland North West England: Archaeological excavations along the A5300 road corridor in Merseyside,* NMGM, Liverpool, 169-74.

Cowell R. W. 2000e 'The Neolithic and Bronze Age in the lowlands of North West England' in Harding J. and Johnston R. (eds) *Northern Pasts: Interpretations of the Later Prehistory of Northern England and Southern Scotland,* BAR Brit Ser 302, Oxford, 111-30.

Cowell R. W. 2002 *Romano-British and Late Prehistoric Excavations at Duttons Farm, Lathom, West Lancashire: 2nd interim report: 1999-2001,* Unpublished report, Liverpool Museum.

Cowell R. W. 2003 *Prehistoric and Romano-British Excavations at Duttons Farm, Lathom, West Lancashire: Third interim report: 1999-2002,* Unpublished report, Liverpool Museum.

Cowell R. W. 2005a 'Late Prehistoric Lowland Settlement in North West England' in Nevell M. and Redhead N. (eds) *Mellor: Living on the Edge. A Regional Study of an Iron Age and Romano-British Upland Settlement,* University Manchester Archaeological Unit, Greater Manchester Archaeological Unit and Mellor Archaeological Trust, Manchester, 65-76.

Cowell R. W. 2005b 'Prehistoric Hunter-Gatherers on Alderley Edge' in Timberlake S. and Prag A. J. N. W. *The Archaeology of Alderley Edge* BAR Brit Ser 396, Oxford, 20-32.

Cowell R. W. in press 'Excavations at Southworth near Winwick, north Cheshire and the Neolithic and early Bronze Age background in the southern lowlands of the North West' *J Merseyside Archaeol Soc* 13.

Cowell R. W. in preparation a 'Excavations at two early Mesolithic sites on the Wirral, Merseyside'.

Cowell R. W. in preparation b 'Prehistoric Field Survey in the lowlands of North West England'.

Cowell R. W. and Gonzalez S. 2007 'Evolution of the north Wirral coast during the Holocene: 10,000 years ago to the present' in Griffiths D. W., Philpott R. A. and Egan G. *Meols: The Archaeology of the North Wirral Coast,* Oxford University School of Archaeology Monograph 68, Oxford, 355-61.

Cowell R. W. and Innes J. B. 1994 *The Wetlands of Merseyside,* North West Wetlands Survey 1, Lancaster Imprints 2, Lancaster.

Cowell R. W. and Philpott R. A. 1994 'Some Finds from Cheshire reported to Liverpool Museum' *Cheshire Past* 3, 10-1.

Cowell R. W. and Philpott R. A. 2000 *Prehistoric, Romano-British and Medieval Settlement in Lowland North West England: Archaeological excavations along the A5300 road corridor in Merseyside,* NMGM, Liverpool.

Cox E. W. 1895 'Traces of submerged lands on the coasts of Lancashire, Cheshire and North Wales' *Trans Hist Soc Lancashire Cheshire* 46 (n.s. 10, for 1894), 19-56.

Crawford-Coupe G. 2005 'The Archaeology of Burton Point' *J Chester Archaeol Soc* 80, 71-90.

Crummy N. 1983 *Colchester Archaeological Report 2: The Roman small finds from excavations in Colchester, 1971-9,* Colchester Archaeological Trust Ltd, Colchester.

Crummy N. 2002 'Wax spatula handle from Yorkshire' *Lucerna: Roman Finds Group Newsletter* 23, 6-8.

Cumberpatch C., Walster A., Ixer R. and Morris E. 2005 'Mellor: A Review of the Later Prehistoric Ceramics' in Nevell M. and Redhead N. (eds) *Mellor: Living on the Edge. A Regional Study of an Iron Age and Romano-British Upland Settlement,* Manchester Archaeological Monographs 1, Manchester, 35-43.

Cunliffe B. 1987 *Hengistbury Head Dorset. Vol. 1: The Prehistoric and Roman Settlement, 3500 BC –AD 500,* Oxford University Committee for Archaeology Monograph 13, Oxford.

Cunliffe B. 2002 *The Extraordinary Voyage of Pytheas the Greek,* Penguin Books, London.

Cunliffe B. 2005 *Iron Age Communities in Britain,* 4th edn, Routledge, London.

Cunliffe B. and Poole C. 1991 *Danebury: An Iron Age Hillfort in Hampshire. Vol. 4: The excavations 1979-1988: the site,* CBA Research Report 73, London.

Cunliffe B. W. and Poole C. 2000a *The Danebury Environs Programme. The Prehistory of a Wessex Landscape. Volume 2. The Sites – Part 2 Bury Hill, Upper Clatford, Hants, 1990,* English Heritage and OUCA Monograph 49, Oxford.

Cunliffe B. W. and Poole C. 2000b *The Danebury Environs Programme. The Prehistory of a Wessex Landscape. Volume 2. The Sites – Part 3 Suddern Farm, Middle Wallop, Hants, 1991 and 1996,* English Heritage and OUCA Monograph 49, Oxford.

Cunnington M. E. and Goddard E. H. 1934 *Catalogue of the antiquities of the Wiltshire Archaeological and Natural History Society at Devizes. Part II,* Devizes.

Curwen E. C. 1937 'Querns' *Antiquity* 11, 133-51.

Dahl S. 1970 'The Norse settlement of the Faroe Islands' *Medieval Archaeology* 14, 60-73.

Davey P. J. 1985 'North Devon Gravel Tempered Ware' in Davey P. J. and McNeil R. 'Excavations in South Castle Street, Liverpool 1976 and 1977' *J Merseyside Archaeol Soc* 4 (for 1980-1), 84.

Davey P. J. 1991 'The Post-Roman Pottery' *J Merseyside Archaeol Soc* 7 (for 1986-7), 121-42.

Davey P. J. and Rutter J. A. 1977 'A Note on Continental Imports in the North West 800-1700 A.D.' *Medieval Ceramics* 1, 17-30.

David A. 2007 *Palaeolithic and Mesolithic Settlement in Wales, with special reference to Dyfed,* BAR British Series 448, Archaeopress, Oxford.

David A. and Walker E. 2004 'Wales during the Mesolithic Period' in Saville A. (ed.) *Mesolithic Scotland and its*

Neighbours; The Early Holocene Prehistory of Scotland, its British and Irish context and some Northern Europe Perspectives, Society of Antiquaries of Scotland, Edinburgh, 299-337.

Davies J. 1983 'Coinage and Settlement in Roman Wales and the Marches: some observations' *Arch Cambrensis* 132, 78-94.

Dearne M. and Branigan K. 1995 'The Use of Coal in Roman Britain' *Antiq J* 75, 71-105.

De Roche C. D. 1997 'Studying Iron Age production' in Gwilt A. and Haselgrove C. (eds) *Reconstructing Iron Age Societies,* Oxbow Monograph 71, Oxford, 19-25.

Dickinson B., Hartley K., Hird L., Howard-Davis C. and Shotter D. 2000 'The Pottery' in Buxton K. and Howard-Davis C. *Bremetennacum. Excavations at Roman Ribchester 1980, 1989-1990,* Lancaster Imprints Series 9, Lancaster University Archaeological Unit, Lancaster, 155-226.

Dimbleby G. W. 1985 *The Palynology of Archaeological Sites,* Academic Press, London.

Dodds L. 2005 'Salt Making in Roman Middlewich: Part 2. Discovery and Rediscovery. Excavations along King Street, 2001-2' in Nevell M. and Fielding A. P. (eds) *Brine in Britannia: Recent Archaeological Work on the Roman Salt Industry in Cheshire,* Archaeology North West 7 (for 2004-5), 25-30.

Dodgson J. McN. 1972 *Place-Names of Cheshire. Part IV,* English Place-Name Society 47, Cambridge University Press, Cambridge.

Drewett P. 1980 'Black Patch and the Later Bronze Age in Sussex' in Barrett J. and Bradley R. (eds) *Settlement and Society in the British Later Bronze Age,* BAR 83, Oxford, 377-96.

Drury P. J. 1978 *Excavations at Little Waltham 1970-71,* CBA Research Report 26, Chelmsford Excavation Committee and CBA, London.

Dunn G. 2002 'The artefacts' in Fairbun N. 'Birch Heath, Tarporley: Excavation of a Rural Romano-British Settlement' *J Chester Archaeol Soc* 77, 75-87.

Dyer C. 1982 'The Social and Economic Changes of the Later Middle Ages, and the Pottery of the Period' *Medieval Ceramics* 6, 33-50.

Dyer C. 1986 'English peasant buildings in the later middle ages (1200–1500)' *Medieval Archaeology* 30, 19–45.

Ecroyd Smith H. 1866 'Notabilia of the Archaeology and Natural History of the Mersey District during Three Years, 1863-4-5' *Trans Hist Soc Lancashire Cheshire* 18 (n. s. 6, for 1865-66), 195-228.

Ecroyd Smith H. 1867 'The Archaeology of the Mersey District, 1866' *Trans Hist Soc Lancashire Cheshire* 19 (n.s 7), 169-88.

Ecroyd Smith H. 1872 'Archaeology in the Mersey District' *Trans Hist Soc Lancashire and Cheshire* 24 (n.s 12, for 1871-2), 131-51.

Edmonds F. 2009 'History and Names' in Graham-Campbell J. and Philpott R. (eds) *The Huxley Viking Hoard: Scandinavian Settlement in the North West,* National Museums Liverpool, 3-12.

Edwards N. 1996 *The Archaeology of Early Medieval Ireland,* B. T. Batsford, London.

Edwards W. and Trotter F. M. 1954 *British Regional Geology: The Pennines and Adjacent Areas,* 3rd edn, HMSO, London.

Egan G. 1997 'Medieval Vessels of Other Materials – A Non-Ceramic View from London' *Medieval Ceramics* 21, 109-14.

Egan G. 2007 'Later medieval non-ferrous metalwork and evidence for metal working: AD 1050-1100 to 1500-50' in Griffiths D. W., Philpott R. A. and Egan G. *Meols: The Archaeology of the North Wirral Coast,* Oxford University School of Archaeology Monograph 68, Oxford, 77-188.

Elliott L. and Knight D. 1999 'An Early Mesolithic Site and First Millennium BC Settlement and Pit Alignments at Swarkestone Lowes, Derbyshire' *Derbyshire Archaeol J* 119, 79-153.

Ellis P. (ed.) 1993 *Beeston Castle, Cheshire: a report on the excavations 1968-85 by Laurence Keen and Peter Hough,* English Heritage Archaeological Report 23, London.

Ellison A. 1981 'Towards a socio-economic model for the middle Bronze Age in southern England' in Hodder I., Isaac G. and Hammond N. (eds) *Pattern of the Past: studies in honour of David Clarke,* Cambridge University Press, Cambridge, 413-38.

Elsdon S. 1979 'Iron Age pottery', in Wheeler H. 'Excavations at Willington, Derbyshire, 1970-1972' *Derbyshire Archaeol J* 99, 162-78.

Elsdon S. M. 1991 'The Iron Age and Anglo-Saxon Pottery' in Sharman J. and Clay P. 'Leicester Lane, Enderby: An Archaeological Evaluation' *Trans Leicestershire Archaeol Hist Soc* 65, 10-12.

Elsdon S. M. 1992 'The Iron Age Pottery' in Clay P. 'An Iron Age Farmstead at Grove Farm, Enderby, Leicestershire' *Trans Leicestershire Archaeol Hist Soc* 66, 38-52.

Elsdon S. M. 1994 'Briquetage' in Thorpe R. and Sharman J. with Clay P. 'An Iron Age and Romano-British Enclosure System at Normanton le Heath, Leicestershire' *Trans Leicestershire Archaeol Hist Soc* 68, 37-8.

Emery M. M., Gibbins D. J. L. and Matthews K. J. 1996 *The Archaeology of an Ecclesiastical Landscape: Chapel House Farm, Poulton (Cheshire) 1995,* Chester City Council/ University of Liverpool.

Esmonde Cleary A. S. 1998 'Roman Britain in 1997: I. Sites explored: England' *Britannia* 29, 381-432.

Esmonde Cleary A. S. 2001 'The Roman to medieval transition' in James S. and Millett M. (eds) *Britons and Romans: advancing an archaeological agenda,* CBA Research Report 125, London, 90-7.

Evans D. H. 1979 'Gravel Tempered Ware: A Survey of Published Forms' *Medieval and Later Pottery in Wales* 2, 18-29.

Evans J. 1987 'Graffiti and the Evidence of Literacy and Pottery use in Roman Britain' *Archaeol J* 144, 191-204.

Evans J. 1989 'Crambeck; the development of a major northern pottery industry' in Wilson P. R. (ed.) *Crambeck Roman Pottery Industry,* Yorkshire Archaeol Soc, Leeds, 43-90.

Evans J. 1993 'Pottery function and finewares in the Roman North' *J Roman Pottery Studies* 6, 95-118.

Evans J. 1998 'The Roman Pottery' in Longley D., Johnstone N. and Evans J. 'Excavations on Two Farms of the Romano-British Period at Bryn Eryr and Bush Farm, Gwynedd' *Britannia* 29, 206-26.

Evans J. 2001 'Material approaches to the identification of different Romano-British site types' in James S. and Millett M. (eds) *Britons and Romans: advancing an archaeological agenda*, CBA Research Report 125, London, 26-35.

Evans J. forthcoming a ''Romanization', pottery and the rural economy in the North West' Unpublished paper from Aspects of Romanisation in the North West conference 1999.

Evans J. forthcoming b 'King Street and the Roman frontier in the North-West'.

Fairburn N. 2002a 'Brook House Farm, Bruen Stapleford: Excavation of a First Millennium BC Settlement' *J Chester Archaeol Soc* 77, 9-57.

Fairburn N. 2002b 'Birch Heath, Tarporley: Excavation of a Rural Romano-British Settlement' *J Chester Archaeol Soc* 77, 58-114.

Fellows-Jensen G. 1985 *Scandinavian Settlement Names in the North-West*, C. A. Reitzels Forlag, Copenhagen.

Fletcher M. 2001 *Parkside Colliery, Newton-le-Willows, Merseyside. Archaeological Evaluation: Land to South of St Oswald's Brook, Hermitage Green, Warrington, Cheshire*, Unpublished client report by Matrix Archaeology, August 2001.

Ford D. A. 1995 *Medieval Pottery in Staffordshire, AD 800-1600: A Review*, Staffordshire Archaeol Studies 7, City Museum and Art Gallery, Stoke-on-Trent.

Ford D. 1999 'A Late Saxon pottery industry in Staffordshire: a review' *Medieval Ceramics* 22-23 (for 1998-99), 11-36.

Foster J. 1990 'Other Bronze Age artefacts' in Bell M. *Brean Down Excavations 1983-1987*, English Heritage Archaeological Report 15, London, 158-75.

Foster J. 1993 'Iron Age copper alloy objects' in Ellis P. (ed.) *Beeston Castle, Cheshire: a report on the excavations 1968-85 by Laurence Keen and Peter Hough*, English Heritage Archaeol Report 23, London, 50-3.

Fowler P. J. 1983 *The Farming of Prehistoric Britain*, Cambridge University Press.

Fulford M. G. 1989 'Byzantium and Britain: a Mediterranean perspective on Post-Roman Mediterranean Imports in Western Britain and Ireland' *Medieval Archaeology* 33, 1-6.

Gaffney V. L. and White R. H. 2007 *Wroxeter, the Cornovii and the Urban Process: Final report on the work of the Wroxeter Hinterland Project and Wroxeter Hinterland Survey, 1994-1997, Vol. 1. Researching the hinterland*, J Roman Studies Supplementary Ser 68.

Gardiner M. 2004 'Timber Buildings without Earth-Fast Footings in Viking-Age Britain' in Hines J., Lane A. and Redknap M. (eds) *Land, Sea and Home, Settlement in the Viking Period*, Society for Medieval Archaeology Monograph 20, Maney, Leeds, 345-58.

Gardner W. and Savory H. N. 1964 *Dinorben: A Hill-fort occupied in Early Iron Age and Roman Times*, The National Museum of Wales, Cardiff.

Garner D. J. 2007 *The Neolithic and Bronze Age Settlement at Oversley Farm, Styal, Cheshire. Excavations in advance of Manchester Airport's Second Runway, 1997-8*, BAR Brit Ser 435, Archaeopress, Oxford.

Gelling M. 1992 *The West Midlands in the Early Middle Ages*, University of Leicester.

Gelling P. S. and Stanford S. C. 1965 'Dark Age Pottery or Iron Age Ovens?' *Trans Birmingham Warwickshire Archaeol Soc* 82, 77-91.

Gillam J. P. 1970 *Types of Roman Coarse Pottery Vessels in Northern Britain*, 3rd edn, Newcastle upon Tyne.

Gillespie R. 1991 'A Note on Geoffrey Keating's Description of Fulachta' in Hodder M. A. and Barfield L. H. (eds) *Burnt Mounds and Hot Stone Technology*, Sandwell Metropolitan Borough Council, 69-70.

Goldberg P. and Macphail R. I. 2006 *Practical and Theoretical Geoarchaeology*, Wiley Blackwell , Oxford.

Graham-Campbell J. and Sheehan J. 2009 'The Catalogue' in Graham-Campbell J. and Philpott R. (eds) *The Huxley Viking Hoard: Scandinavian Settlement in the North West*, National Museums Liverpool, 51-7.

Grant A. 1983 *North Devon Pottery: The Seventeenth Century*, University of Exeter.

Green M. J. 1982 'Tanarus, Taranis, and the Chester altar' *J Chester Archaeol Soc* 65, 37-44.

Greene J. P. and Noake B. 1977 'Norton Priory (NOR)' in Davey P. J. (ed.) *Medieval Pottery from Excavations in the North West*, Institute of Extension Studies, University of Liverpool, 54-9.

Griffiths D. 1992 'The Coastal Trading Ports of the Irish Sea' in Graham-Campbell J. (ed.) *Viking Treasure from the North West. The Cuerdale Hoard in its Context*, NMGM, Occasional Papers 5, Liverpool, 63-72.

Griffiths D. W. 2007 'The early medieval period' in Griffiths D. W., Philpott R. A. and Egan G. *Meols: The Archaeology of the North Wirral Coast*, Oxford University School of Archaeology Monograph 68, Oxford, 399-406.

Griffiths D. W. and Philpott R. A. 2007 'Other stone objects: later medieval and undated' in Griffiths D. W., Philpott R. A. and Egan G. *Meols: The Archaeology of the North Wirral Coast*, Oxford University School of Archaeology Monograph 68, Oxford, 244-7.

Griffiths D. W., Philpott R. A. and Egan G. (eds) 2007 *Meols: The Archaeology of the North Wirral Coast*, Oxford University School of Archaeology Monograph 68, Oxford.

Grimes W. F. 1930 'Holt, Denbighshire. The Works-Depôt of the Twentieth Legion at Castle Lyons' *Y Cymmrodor* 41.

Guido M. 1978 *The Glass Beads of the Prehistoric and Roman Periods in Britain and Ireland*, Report Research Committee Society of Antiquaries of London 35, London.

Guilbert G. C. 1981 'Double-ring Roundhouses, Probable and Possible, in Prehistoric Britain' *Proc Prehistoric Soc* 47, 299-317.

Guilbert G. C. 1982 'Prehistoric Artefacts from the 1960-7 Excavations' pp. 36-55, in Brassil K. S., Guilbert G. C., Livens R. G., Stead W. H. and Bevan-Evans M. 'Rescue Excavations at Moel Hiraddug between 1960 and 1980' *J Flintshire Historical Soc* 30 (for 1981-2), 13-88.

Hall D., Wells C. E. and Huckerby E. 1995 *The Wetlands of Greater Manchester,* North West Wetlands Survey 2, Lancaster University Archaeological Unit, Lancaster.

Hambleton E. and Stallibrass S. 2000 'Faunal remains' in Haselgrove C. and McCullagh R. (eds) *An Iron Age coastal community in East Lothian: The excavation of two later prehistoric enclosure complexes at Fishers Road, Port Seton, 1994-5,* AOC Archaeology Group and Historic Scotland, Edinburgh, 147-57.

Harding D. W. 1974 *The Iron Age in Lowland Britain,* Routledge and Kegan Paul, London.

Harding D. W., Blake I. M. and Reynolds P. J. 1993 *An Iron Age Settlement in Dorset - Excavation and Reconstruction,* Monograph Series 1, Department of Archaeology, University of Edinburgh.

Harris A. 2003 *Byzantium, Britain and The West: The Archaeology of Cultural Identity AD 400-650,* Tempus Publishing Ltd, Stroud.

Harris B. E. and Thacker A. T. (eds.) 1987 *A History of the County of Chester,* 1. Oxford University Press, University of London.

Hartley B. R. 1954 'Heronbridge Excavations: Bronze-Worker's Hearth' *J Chester N Wales Architect Archaeol Hist Soc* 41, 1-14.

Hartley K. F. and Webster P. V. 1973 'The Romano-British Pottery Kilns near Wilderspool' *Archaeol J* 130, 77-103.

Haselgrove C. 1984 'The Later Pre-Roman Iron Age between the Humber and the Tyne' in Wilson P. R., Jones R. F. J. and Evans D. M. (eds) *Settlement and Society in the Roman North,* School of Archaeological Sciences, University of Bradford and Roman Antiquities Section, Yorkshire Archaeol Soc, Leeds, 9-23.

Haselgrove C. 1989 'The Later Iron Age in Southern Britain and Beyond' in Todd M. (ed.) *Research on Roman Britain 1960-89,* Britannia Monograph 11, London, 1-18.

Haselgrove C. 1996 'The Iron Age' in Newman R. (ed.) *The Archaeology of Lancashire: Present State and Future Priorities,* Lancaster University Archaeology Unit, 61-73.

Haselgrove C., Armit I., Champion T., Creighton J., Gwilt A., Hill J. D., Hunter F. and Woodward A. 2001 *Understanding the British Iron Age: An Agenda for Action,* Trust for Wessex Archaeology Ltd, Salisbury.

Hawkes C. F. C. 1951 'Bronze-workers, Cauldrons, and Bucket-animals in Iron Age and Roman Britain' in Grimes W. F. (ed.) *Aspects of Archaeology in Britain and Abroad,* H. W. Edwards, London, 172-99.

Healey E. 1987 'Lithic Technology' in Smith C. A. and Lynch F. M. *Trefignath and Din Dryfol, The Excavation of Two Megalithic Tombs in Anglesey,* Cambrian Archaeological Monographs 3, 50-9.

Healey E. n.d. *Typological Guide to Prehistoric Lithics,* Undated Mss. Intended for Lithics Society Publication, Unpublished.

Hebblethwaite S. M. 1987 'Physique' in Harris B. E. and Thacker A. T. (eds) *A History of the County of Chester,* 1. Oxford University Press, University of London, 1-35.

Hedges R. E. M., Bronk C. R. and Housley R. A. 1989 'The Oxford Accelerator Mass Spectrometry facility: technical developments in routine dating' *Archaeometry* 31, 99–113.

Henson D. and Hurcombe L. 1993 'The non-flint lithic finds' in Ellis P. (ed.) *Beeston Castle, Cheshire: a report on the excavations 1968-85 by Laurence Keen and Peter Hough,* English Heritage Archaeol Report 23, London, 59-62.

Herepath N. 2004 'A survey of Roman brooches from Cheshire' *Lucerna (The Roman Finds Group Newsletter)* 27 (January 2004), 9–12.

Heslop D. H. 1987 *The Excavation of an Iron Age Settlement at Thorpe Thewles, Cleveland, 1980-1982,* CBA Research Report 65, London.

Hewitt W. 1925 'The Ancient Parishes of Wirral' *Birkenhead News* Dec. 1925.

Hewitt H. J. 1929 *Mediaeval Cheshire: An economic and social history of Cheshire in the reigns of the three Edwards,* Manchester University Press.

Higham M. 1995 'Scandinavian settlement in north-west England, with a special study of *Ireby* names' in Crawford B. E. (ed.) *Scandinavian Settlement in Northern Britain,* Leicester University Press, Leicester, 195-230.

Higham N. J. 1980 'Native Settlements West of the Pennines' in Branigan K. (ed.) *Rome and the Brigantes: The impact of Rome on Northern England,* Dept Prehistory and Archaeology, University of Sheffield, 41-7.

Higham N. J. 1986 *The Northern Counties to AD 1000,* Longman, London.

Higham N. J. 1987 'Patterns of Settlement in Medieval Cheshire: An Insight into Dispersed Settlement' *Medieval Settlement Research Group Annual Report* 2, 9-10.

Higham N. J. 1990 'Forest, Woodland and Settlement in medieval Cheshire: a Note' *Medieval Settlement Research Group Annual Report* 4, 24-5.

Higham N. J. 1991 'Soldiers and Settlement in Northern England' in Jones R. F. J. (ed.) *Roman Britain: Recent Trends,* J. R. Collis Publications, University of Sheffield, 93-101.

Higham N. J. 1993 *The Origins of Cheshire,* Manchester University Press.

Higham N. J. 1995 'Territorial organization in pre-Conquest Cheshire' in Scott T. and Starkey P. (eds) *The Middle Ages in the North-West,* Leopard's Head Press, Oxford, 1-14.

Higham N. J. 1999 'The Tatton Park Project, Part 1: Prehistoric to Sub-Roman' *J Chester Archaeol Soc* 74 (for 1996-7), 1-61.

Higham N. J. 2000 'The Tatton Park Project, Part 2: The Medieval Estates, Settlements and Halls' *J Chester Archaeol Soc* 75 (for 1998-9), 61-133.

Higham N. 2004a 'Viking-Age settlement in the North-Western Countryside: Lifting the Veil?' in Hines J., Lane A. and Redknap M. (eds) *Land, Sea and Home,* Soc for Medieval Archaeol Monograph 20, Leeds, 297-311.

Higham N. J. 2004b *A Frontier Landscape. The North West in the Middle Ages,* Windgather Press, Bollington.

Higham N. J. and Jones G. D. B. 1983 'The Excavation of Two Romano-British Farm Sites in North Cumbria' *Britannia* 14, 45-72.

Higham N. J. and Jones G. D. B. 1985 *The Carvetii,* Alan Sutton, Stroud.

Highley D. E. 1974 *Talc,* Mineral Resources Consultative Committee Mineral Dossier 10, HMSO, London.

Hill J. D. 1995 *Ritual and Rubbish in the Iron Age of Wessex,* BAR Brit Ser 242, Tempvs Reparatvm, Oxford.

Hill P. 1997 *Whithorn and St Ninian. The Excavation of a Monastic Town, 1984-91,* Sutton Publishing, Stroud.

Hillman G. 1981 'Reconstructing crop husbandry practices from charred remains of crops' in Mercer R. (ed.) *Farming Practice in British Prehistory*, Edinburgh University Press, Edinburgh, 123-62.

Hillman G. 1992 'Grain processing at 3rd century Wilderspool' in Hinchliffe J. and Williams J. H., *Roman Warrington: excavations at Wilderspool 1966-9 and 1976*, University of Manchester, Department of Archaeology, Manchester, 167-9.

Hillman G., Mason S., de Moulins D. and Nesbitt M. 1995 'Identification of archaeological remains of wheat: the 1992 London workshop' *Circaea* 12 (for 1996), 195-209.

Hinchliffe J. and Williams J. H. 1992 *Roman Warrington. Excavations at Wilderspool 1966-9 and 1976*, Brigantia Monograph No. 2, University of Manchester.

Hingley R. 1989 *Rural Settlement in Roman Britain,* B. A. Seaby, London.

Hird L. and Howard-Davis C. 2000 'Coarsewares' in Buxton K. and Howard-Davis C. *Bremetennacum. Excavations at Roman Ribchester 1980, 1989-1990,* Lancaster Imprints Series no 9, Lancaster University Archaeological Unit, Lancaster, 155-93.

Hodder M. A. and Barfield L. H. 1991 *Burnt Mounds and Hot Stone Technology,* Sandwell Metropolitan Borough Council.

Hodges R. 1991 *Wall-to-Wall History: The story of Roystone Grange,* Duckworth, London.

Howard H. 1991 'Refractory Ceramic Fabrics from the Breiddin Hillfort' in Musson C. *The Breiddin Hillfort, A Later Prehistoric Settlement in the Welsh Marches,* CBA Research Report 76, London microfiche supplement, 212-31.

Howard H. 1993 'The Metalworking Evidence' in Ellis P. (ed.) *Beeston Castle, Cheshire: a report on the excavations 1968-85 by Laurence Keen and Peter Hough,* English Heritage Archaeol Report 23, London, 54-6.

Howard-Davis C. 2000 'Other Artefacts' in Buxton K. and Howard-Davis C. *Bremetennacum. Excavations at Roman Ribchester 1980, 1989-1990,* Lancaster Imprints Series no 9, Lancaster University Archaeological Unit, Lancaster, 295-300.

Howard-Davis C,. Stocks C. and Innes J. B. 1988 *Peat and the Past. A Survey and Assessment of the Prehistory of the Lowland Wetlands of North-West England* English Heritage and Lancaster University, Lancaster.

Howe M. D., Perrin J. R. and Mackreth D. F. 1980 *Roman Pottery from the Nene Valley: a Guide,* Peterborough City Museums Occasional Paper 2.

Huggett J. W. 1988 'Imported Grave Goods and the Early Anglo-Saxon Economy' *Medieval Archaeology* 32, 63-96.

Hughes G. 1994 'Old Oswestry Hillfort: Excavations by W. J. Varley 1939-1940' *Archaeologia Cambrensis* 143, 46-91.

Hume A. 1863 *Ancient Meols: Some Account of the Antiquities near Dove Point on the Sea Coast of Cheshire,* J. Russell Smith, London.

Hunn J. R. 2000 'Hay Farm, Eardington, Shropshire: Excavation of an Iron Age and Romano-British Enclosure' in Zeepvat R. J. (ed.) *Three Iron Age and Romano-British Rural Settlements on English Gravels,* BAR Brit Ser 312, Oxford, 123-44.

Huntley J. P. 1996 'Irby, The Wirral. An assessment of the environmental samples' *Durham Environmental Archaeology Report,* 27/96.

Huntley J. P. 2000a 'The charred and waterlogged plant remains' in Haselgrove C. and McCullagh R. (eds) *An Iron Age coastal community in East Lothian: The excavation of two later prehistoric enclosure complexes at Fishers Road, Port Seton, 1994-5,* AOC Archaeology Group and Historic Scotland, Edinburgh, 157-70.

Huntley J. P. 2000b 'Plant Remains' in Buxton K. and Howard-Davis C. *Bremetennacum. Excavations at Roman Ribchester 1980, 1989-1990,* Lancaster Imprints Series no 9, Lancaster University Archaeological Unit, Lancaster, 349-59.

Huntley J. P., Huntley B. and Birks H. J. B. 1981 'PHYTOPAK: a suite of computer programs designed for the handling and analysing of phytosociological data' *Vegetatio* 45, 85-95.

Huntley J. P. and Stallibrass S. 1995 *Plant and Vertebrate Remains from Archaeological Sites in Northern England: data reviews and future directions,* Architectural and Archaeological Society of Durham and Northumberland Research Report 4, Durham.

Hurst J. G. 1989 'Gazetteer of Excavations at Medieval House and Village Sites (to 1968)' in Beresford M. and Hurst J. G. (eds) *Deserted Medieval Villages,* Allan Sutton Publishing, Gloucester, 145-68.

Hurst J. G., Neal D. S., and van Beuningen H. J. E. 1986 *Pottery Produced and Traded in North-West Europe,* Rotterdam Papers 6, Rotterdam.

Hyde F. E. 1971 *Liverpool and the Mersey: An Economic History of a Port 1700-1900,* David and Charles, Newton Abbot.

Innes J. B. and Tomlinson P. R. unpubl. *Studies in the Environmental History of Merseyside,* Merseyside County Museums, Liverpool.

Innes J. B. and Tomlinson P. R. 1991 'Environmental Archaeology in Merseyside' *J Merseyside Archaeol Soc* 7, 1-20.

Innes J. B. and Tomlinson P. R. 2008 'A palaeoenvironmental overview of the Merseyside area' *J Merseyside Archaeol Soc* 12, 7-26.

Innes J. B., Tooley M.J. and Lageard J. G. A. 1999 'Vegetational Changes before the Norman Conquest' in Greenwood E. F. (ed.) *Ecology and Landscape Development: A History of the Mersey Basin,* Liverpool University Press/ NMGM, Liverpool, 21-31.

Irvine W. F. 1959 'Footpath dispute at Irby in 1605' *Cheshire Sheaf* 51, 31.

Jackson R. P. J. 1992 'The Iron Objects' in Hinchliffe J. and Williams J. H. *Roman Warrington. Excavations at Wilderspool 1966-9 and 1976,* Brigantia Monograph No. 2, University of Manchester, 78-86.

Jacobi R. M. 1978 'Northern England in the 8th Millennium bc: an Essay' in Mellars P. (ed.) *The Early Postglacial Settlement of Northern Europe,* Duckworth, London, 243-94.

Jacobi R. M. 1980 'The Early Holocene Settlement of Wales', in Taylor A. J. (ed.), *Culture and Environment in Prehistoric Wales,* BAR 76, Oxford, 131-206.

James S. 2001 'Soldiers and civilians: identity and interaction in Roman Britain' in James S. and Millett M. (eds) *Britons and Romans: advancing an archaeological agenda,* CBA Research Report 125, London, 77-89.

Jarrett M. G. and Wrathmell S. 1981 *Whitton An Iron Age and Roman Farmstead in South Glamorgan,* University of Wales Press, Cardiff.

Jermy K. 1960 'Roman Roads in Wirral' *J Chester Archaeol Soc* 43, 1-13.

Jobey G. 1962 'An Iron Age Homestead at West Brandon, Durham' *Archaeologia Aeliana* 40 (4th series), 1-34.

Jobey G. 1970 'An Iron Age Settlement at Homestead at Burradon, Northumberland' *Archaeologia Aeliana* 48 (4th series), 51-95.

Johnson S. 1978 'Excavations at Hayton Roman fort, 1975' *Britannia* 9, 57-114.

Jones A. 1994 'The Landscape of the Wroxeter Hinterland: the cropmark evidence' in Ellis P. *et al.* 'Excavations in the Wroxeter hinterland 1988-1990: The archaeology of the Shrewsbury bypass' *Trans Shropshire Archaeol Hist Soc* 69, 100-8.

Jones A. 1996 'Roman pottery' in Emery M. M., Gibbins D. J. L. and Matthews K. J. *The Archaeology of an Ecclesiastical Landscape: Chapel House Farm, Poulton (Cheshire) 1995,* Chester City Council/University of Liverpool, 29-30.

Jones G. D. B. and Mattingly D. 1990 *An Atlas of Roman Britain,* Blackwell, Oxford.

Jones G. D. B. and Walker J. 1983 'Towards a minimalist view of Romano-British agricultural settlement in the North-West' in Chapman J. C. and Mytum H. C. (eds) *Settlement in North Britain 1000 BC to AD 1000,* BAR Brit Ser 118, Oxford, 185-205.

Jones G. E. M. 1984 'Interpretation of archaeological plant remains: Ethnographic models from Greece' in van Zeist W. and Casparie W. A. (eds) *Plants and Ancient Man,* Balkema, Rotterdam, 43-61.

Jones H. and Adams M. 2008 *An Archaeological Watching Brief on Land Adjacent to Bromborough Court Moat, Pool Lane, Bromborough, Wirral. NGR SJ 344 840,* Unpublished NML Field Archaeology Unit Report.

Jundi S. and Hill J. D. 1998 'Brooches and Identities in First Century AD Britain: more than meets the eye?' in Forcey C., Hawthorne J. and Witcher R. (eds) *TRAC 97: Proceedings of the Seventh Annual Theoretical Roman Archaeology Conference Nottingham 1997,* Oxbow Books, Oxford, 125-37.

Kelly R. S. 1982 'The excavation of a Medieval Farmstead at Cefn Graeanog, Clynnog, Gwynedd' *Bulletin Board Celtic Studies* 29, 859-908.

Kelly R. S. 1992 'The Excavation of a Burnt Mound at Graeanog, Clynnog, Gwynedd in 1983' *Archaeologia Cambrensis* 141, 74-96.

Kent J. P. C. 1981 *The Roman Imperial Coinage. Vol. VIII. The Family of Constantine I A.D. 337-364,* (edited by C. H. V. Sutherland and R. A. G. Carson) Spink and Son Ltd, London.

Keys L. and Pearce J. 1998 'Hanging lamps' in Egan G. *The Medieval Household: Daily Living c. 1150-c. 1450,* Museum of London, London.

King A. 2004 'Post-Roman Upland Architecture in the Craven Dales and the Dating Evidence' in Hines J., Lane A. and Redknap M. (eds) *Land, Sea and Home,* Soc for Medieval Archaeol Monograph 20, Leeds, 335-44.

Knight D. 1992 'Excavations of an Iron Age Settlement at Gamston, Nottinghamshire' *Trans Thoroton Soc* 96, 16-90.

Knight D. 2002 'A Regional Ceramic Sequence: Pottery of the First Millennium BC between the Humber and the Nene' in Woodward A. and Hill J. D. (eds) *Prehistoric Britain: The Ceramic Basis,* Oxbow Books, Oxford, 119-42.

Laing J. and Laing L. 1983 'A Mediterranean Trade with Wirral in the Iron Age' *Cheshire Archaeol Bull* 9, 6-8

Larsen A.-C. and Stummann Hansen S. 2001 'Viking Ireland and the Scandinavian Communities in the North Atlantic' in Larsen A.-C. (ed.) *The Vikings in Ireland,* The Viking Ship Museum, Roskilde, 115-26.

Laughton J. 1996 'The port of Chester in the later Middle Ages' in Carrington P. (ed.) *"Where Deva spreads her Wizard Stream": Trade and the Port of Chester,* Chester City Council, 66-71.

Leah M. 2003 'Roman Nantwich revealed' *Cheshire Archaeology News* 10, 1-2.

Leary R. 2005 'Mellor: The Romano-British Pottery 1998-2003' in Nevell M. and Redhead N. (eds) *Mellor: Living on the Edge. A Regional Study of an Iron Age and Romano-British Upland Settlement,* Manchester Archaeological Monographs 1, Manchester, 44-8.

Leech R. H. 1982 *Excavations at Catsgore 1970-1973: A Romano-British Village,* Western Archaeological Trust, Bristol.

Lewis J. 2002 'Sefton Rural Fringes' in Lewis J. and Cowell R. (eds) 'The Archaeology of a Changing landscape: The Last Thousand Years in Merseyside' *J Merseyside Archaeol Soc* 5-88.

Longley D. M. T. 1987 'Prehistory' in Harris B. E. and Thacker A. T. (eds) *A History of the County of Chester,* 1. Oxford University Press, University of London, 36-114.

Longley D. 1998 'Bryn Eryr: An Enclosed Settlement of the Iron Age on Anglesey' *Proc Prehistoric Soc* 64, 225-73.

Longley D., Johnstone N. and Evans J. 1998 'Excavations on two farms of the Romano-British period at Bryn Eryr and Bush Farm, Gwynedd' *Britannia* 29, 185-246.

Longworth C. 2000 'Flint and chert availability in Mesolithic Wirral' *J Merseyside Archaeol* 10, 1-17.

Lucas G. 2003 *Hofstaðir 2002. Interim report*, Fornleifastofnun Íslands, Reykjavík.

MacGregor M. 1976 *Early Celtic Art in North Britain*. 2 vols, Leicester University Press.

Mackreth D. F. 1989 'Brooches' in Blockley K. *Prestatyn 1984-5: An Iron Age Farmstead and Romano-British Industrial Settlement in North Wales*, BAR Brit Ser 210, Oxford, 87-99.

Mackreth D. 1996 'Colchesters in the North' *Roman Finds Group Newsletter* 11, 5-8.

Mainman A. J. and Rogers N. S. H. 2000 *Finds from Anglo-Scandinavian York*, Archaeology of York 17/14, York.

Manley J. and Healey E. 1982 'Excavations at Hendre, Rhuddlan, The Mesolithic Finds' *Archaeologia Cambrensis* 131, 18-48.

Manning W. H. 1974 'Objects of iron' in Neal D. S. *The Excavation of the Roman Villa in Gadebridge Park, Hemel Hempstead 1963-8*, Soc Antiqs Res Report 31, London, 157-87.

Manning W. H. 1985 *Catalogue of the Romano-British Iron Tools, Fittings and Weapons in the British Museum*, British Museum, London.

Manning W. H. and Scott I. R. 1986 'The Iron Objects' in Stead I. M. and Rigby V. *Baldock. The Excavation of a Roman and Pre-Roman Settlement, 1968-72*, Britannia Monograph 7, London, 145-62.

Margary I. D. 1967 *Roman Roads in Britain*, John Baker London.

Marsh G. 1981 'London's Samian Supply and its Relationship to the Development of the Gallic Samian Industry' in Anderson A. C. and Anderson A. S. (eds) *Roman Pottery Research in Britain and North-West Europe: Papers Presented to Graham Webster*, BAR International Series 123, I, 173-238.

Mason D. J. P. 1980 *Excavations at Chester: 11-15 Castle Street and Neighbouring Sites 1974-8. A Possible Roman Posting House (Mansio)*, Grosvenor Museum, Chester.

Mason D. J. P. 1983 'Eaton-by-Tarporley SJ 57176341: Excavations at the Roman Villa, 1982' *Cheshire Archaeol Bulletin* 9, 67-72.

Mason D. J. P. 1985 *Excavations at Chester. 26-42 Lower Bridge Street 1974-6. The Dark Age and Saxon Periods*, Grosvenor Museum, Chester City Council.

Mason D. J. P. 1988 ' "*Prata Legionis*" in Britain' *Britannia* 19, 163-89.

Mason D. J. P. 2002a 'The Foundation of the Legionary Fortress: Deva, the Flavians and Imperial Symbolism' in Carrington P. (ed.) *Deva Victrix: Roman Chester Re-assessed*, Chester Archaeological Society, Chester, 33-51.

Mason D. J. P. 2002b 'The Construction and Operation of a Legionary Fortress: Logistical and Engineering Aspects' in Carrington P. (ed.) *Deva Victrix: Roman Chester Re-assessed*, Chester Archaeological Society, Chester, 89-112.

Mason D. 2006 'AD 616, the Battle of Chester' *Current Archaeol* 202, 517-24.

Matthews K. J. 1993 'A futile occupation' in Barber J. (ed.) *Interpreting Stratigraphy-Edinburgh 1992*, AOC (Scotland) Ltd, Edinburgh.

Matthews K. 1994 'Archaeology without artefacts: The Iron Age and Sub-Roman Periods in Cheshire' in Carrington (ed.), *From Flints to Flower Pots: Current research in the Dee-Mersey region*, Archaeological Service Occasional Paper 2, Chester City Council, 51-62.

Matthews K. 1996 'Iron Age sea-borne trade in Liverpool Bay' in Carrington P. (ed.) *'Where Deva spreads her Wizard Stream': Trade and the Port of Chester*, Chester Archaeology Occasional Paper No. 3, Chester, 12–23.

Matthews K. J. 1999 'The Iron Age of North-west England and Irish Sea Trade' in Bevan B. (ed.) *Northern Exposure: interpretative devolution and the Iron Ages in Britain*, Leicester Archaeology Monographs 4, Leicester, 173-95.

Matthews K. J. 2001 'The Iron Age of North-west England: A socio-economic model' *J Chester Archaeol Soc* 76 (for 2000-1), 1-51.

Matthews K. 2003 'Lightning can strike twice!' *The Past Uncovered (Newsletter of Chester Archaeology)* October 2003, 3.

Matthews K. and Vickers T. 2003 'Iron Age bead from Tarporley rediscovered' *The Past Uncovered (Newsletter of Chester Archaeology)* June 2003, 3.

May J. 1996 *Dragonby. Report on Excavation at an Iron Age and Romano-British Settlement in North Lincolnshire* 2 vols, Oxbow Monograph 61, Oxbow Books, Oxford.

May T. 1904 *Warrington's Roman Remains*, Warrington.

McCarthy M. R. and Brooks C. M. 1988 *Medieval pottery in Britain, AD 900-1600*, Leicester University Press, Leicester.

McDonnell J. G. 1991 'Irby Industrial Waste', Unpublished assessment report.

McIntosh F. 2009 'Wirral Brooch; a regional variant of Roman bow brooch' *Lucerna* 38 (July 2009), 3-5.

Megaw R. and Megaw V. 1989 *Celtic Art*, Thames and Hudson, London.

Mellor Archaeological Trust 2002 *The Hillfort at Mellor: Update on 2001 excavation*, Mellor Archaeological Trust, Mellor.

Mellor Archaeological Trust 2003 *The Hillfort at Mellor: Excavations 1998-2002*, Mellor Archaeological Trust, Mellor.

Mellor Archaeological Trust 2006 *The Medieval Period*, www.mellorarchaeology.org.uk.

Middleton R. 1993 'Landscape Archaeology in the North West and the definition of surface lithic scatter sites' in Middleton R. (ed.), *North West Wetland Survey Annual Report 1993*, Lancaster, 1-8.

Middleton R., Wells C. E. and Huckerby E. 1995 *The Wetlands of North Lancashire* North West Wetlands Survey 3, Lancaster Imprints 4, Lancaster.

Miles T. J. and Saunders A. D. 1970 'King Charles Castle, Tresco, Scilly' *Post-Medieval Archaeology* 4, 1-30

Mook W. G. and van der Plicht J. 1999 'Reporting ^{14}C activities and concentrations' *Radiocarbon* 41, 227-39.

Moore P. D. and Webb J. A. 1978 *An Illustrated Guide to Pollen Analysis,* Hodder and Stoughton, London.

Morris C. 2007 'Wooden objects: later medieval and post-medieval' in Griffiths D. W., Philpott R. A. and Egan G. Meols*: The Archaeology of the North Wirral Coast,* Oxford University School of Archaeology Monograph 68, Oxford, 241-3.

Morris E. L. 1981 'Petrological Report on the Beaker and Iron Age Ceramics from Midsummer Hill' in Stanford S. C. *Midsummer Hill,* Privately Printed, Hereford, 151-5.

Morris E. L. 1984 'Petrological Report for the Ceramic Material from the Wrekin' in Stanford S. C. 'The Wrekin Hillfort Excavations 1973' *Archaeol J* 141, 76-80.

Morris E. L. 1985 'Prehistoric Salt Distributions: Two Case Studies from Western Britain' *Bulletin of the Board of Celtic Studies* 32, 336-79.

Morris E. L. 1991 'Later Prehistoric Pottery Fabrics from the Breiddin Hillfort' in Musson C. R. *The Breiddin Hillfort, A Later Prehistoric Settlement in the Welsh Marches,* CBA Research Report 76, London, microfiche supplement, 196-204.

Morris E. L. 1994 'Production and Distribution of Pottery and Salt in Iron Age Britain: A Review' *Proc Prehistoric Soc* 60, 371-93.

Morris E. L. 1996 'Iron Age Artefact Production and Exchange' in Champion T. C. and Collis J. R. (eds) *The Iron Age in Britain and Ireland: Recent Trends,* J. R. Collis Publications, Dept of Archaeology and Prehistory, University of Sheffield, 41-65.

Morris E. L. 1999 'Other ceramic materials' in Hughes G. (ed.) 'The Excavation of an Iron Age Cropmarked Site at Foxcovert Farm, Aston-on-Trent' *Derbyshire Archaeol J* 119, 176-88.

Morris E. L. 2001 'Salt Production and Distribution' in Lane T. and Morris E. L. (eds) *A Millennium of Saltmaking: Prehistoric and Romano-British Salt Production in the Fenland,* Lincolnshire Archaeology and Heritage Reports Series 4, Heritage Lincolnshire, Sleaford, 389-404.

Morris E. L. 2002 'The VCP' in Fairburn N. 'Brook House Farm, Bruen Stapleford: Excavation of a First Millennium BC Settlement' *J Chester Archaeol Soc* 77, 31-3.

Mortimer W. W. 1847 *The History of the Hundred of Wirral,* Whittaker and Co., London.

Mould Q. 1998 'The lead-alloy artefacts' in Cool H. E. M. and Philo C. (eds.) *Roman Castleford Excavations 1974-85. Volume I: the small finds,* Yorkshire Archaeology 4, Wakefield, 121-8.

Musson C. R. 1991 *The Breiddin Hillfort, A Later Prehistoric Settlement in the Welsh Marches,* CBA Research Report 76, London.

Myers A. 1989 'Reliable and maintainable technological strategies in the Mesolithic of mainland Britain' in Torrence R. (ed.) *Time, Energy and Stone Tools,* Cambridge University Press, 78-91.

NAA 1997 *A69 Haltwhistle Bypass: Archaeological Watching brief on Behalf of A69 Haltwhistle Construction JV,* Unpublished client report, Northern Archaeological Associates, Barnard Castle.

Neal D. S., Wardle A. and Hunn J. 1990. *Excavation of the Iron Age, Roman and medieval settlement at Gorhambury, St. Albans,* English Heritage Archaeological Report 14, London.

Needham S. 1996 'The Study of Occupation Refuse and Deposits' in Needham S. and Spence T. *Refuse and Disposal at Area 16 East, Runnymede. Runnymede Bridge Research Excavations,* Volume 2. British Museum Press, London.

Nevell M. 1989 'Great Woolden Hall Farm. Excavations on a Late Prehistoric/Romano-British Native Site' *Greater Manchester Archaeol J* 3, 35-44.

Nevell M. 1991 'A Field Survey of High Legh Parish. Part One, Prehistoric and Roman Evidence' *Archaeology North-West* 2, 16-9.

Nevell M. 1994 'Late Prehistoric Pottery types from the Mersey Basin' in Carrington P. (ed.) *From Flints to Flower Pots: Current research in the Dee-Mersey region,* Archaeological Service Occasional Paper 2, Chester City Council 1994, 33-41.

Nevell M. D. 1999a 'Great Woolden Hall Farm. A model for the material culture of Iron Age and Romano-British rural settlement in North West England?' in Nevell M. D. (ed.) *Living on the Edge of Empire, Methodology, Models and Marginality. Late-Prehistoric and Romano-British Rural Settlement in North West England,* CBA North West 3 (No 13, for 1998), Manchester, 48-63.

Nevell M. D. 1999b 'Iron Age and Romano-British Rural Settlement in North West England: theory, marginality and settlement' in Nevell M. D. (ed.) *Living on the Edge of Empire, Methodology, Models and Marginality. Late-Prehistoric and Romano-British Rural Settlement in North West England,* CBA North West 3 (No 13, for 1998), Manchester, 14-26.

Nevell M. 2002 'Legh Oaks Farm, High Legh: The Value of Sample Excavation on Two Sites of the Late Prehistoric and Roman Periods' *J Chester Archaeol Soc* 77, 115-29.

Nevell M. 2005 'Salt Making in Cheshire; The Iron Age Background' in Nevell M. and Fielding A. P. (eds) *Brine in Britannia: Recent Archaeological Work on the Roman Salt Industry in Cheshire,* Archaeology North West 7 (for 2004-5), 9-14.

Nevell M. and Fielding A. P. 2005 (eds) *Brine in Britannia: Recent Archaeological Work on the Roman Salt Industry in Cheshire,* Archaeology North West 7 (for 2004-5).

Nevell M. and Redhead N. (eds) 2005 *Mellor: Living on the Edge. A Regional Study of an Iron Age and Romano-British Upland Settlement,* Manchester Archaeological Monographs 1, University Manchester Archaeological Unit, Greater Manchester Archaeological Unit and Mellor Archaeological Trust, Manchester.

Neville R. C. 1856 'Description of a remarkable deposit of Roman antiquities of iron, discovered at Great Chesterford, Essex, in 1854' *Archaeol J* 13, 1-13.

Newman C. 2006 'The Medieval Period Resource Assessment' in Brennand M (ed.) *The Archaeology of North West England, An Archaeological Research Framework for North West*

England: Volume 1 Resource Assessment, Archaeology North West 8, 115-44.

Newman R. 2006 'The Early Medieval Period Resource Assessment' in Brennand M (ed.) *The Archaeology of North West England, An Archaeological Research Framework for North West England: Volume 1 Resource Assessment,* Archaeology North West 8, 91-114.

Newstead R. 1927 'Excavations at Hilbre, 1926' *Trans Hist Soc Lancashire Cheshire* 78, 136-42.

Newstead R. 1935 'Roman Chester: the Extra-Mural Settlement at Saltney' *Annals Archaeology Anthropology (University of Liverpool)* 22, 3-18.

Newstead R. and Droop J. P. 1937 'A Roman Camp at Halton, Cheshire' *Annals Archaeology Anthropology (University of Liverpool)* 24, 165-8.

Nicholson S. M. 1980 *Catalogue of the Prehistoric Metalwork in Merseyside County Museums,* Merseyside County Museums and University of Liverpool, Liverpool.

Noble P. and Thompson A. 2005 'The Mellor Excavations 1998 to 2004' in Nevell M. and Redhead N. (eds) *Mellor: Living on the Edge. A Regional Study of an Iron Age and Romano-British Upland Settlement,* Manchester Archaeological Monographs 1, Manchester, 17-34.

Norman C. 1977 'A Flint Assemblage from Constantine Island, North Cornwall' *Cornish Archaeology* 16, 3-9.

Nowakowski J. 1991 'Trethellan Farm, Newquay: the excavation of a lowland Bronze Age settlement and Iron Age cemetery' *Cornish Archaeology* 30, 5-242.

Ó Ríordáin B. 1971 'Excavations at High Street and Winetavern Street, Dublin' *Medieval Archaeology* 15, 73-85.

O'Leary T. J., Blockley K. and Musson C. 1989 *Pentre Farm, Flint 1976-81: An official building in the Roman lead mining district,* BAR Brit Ser 207, Oxford.

Oliver T., Howard-Davis C. and Newman R. 1996 'A Post-Roman Settlement at Fremington, near Brougham' in Lambert J., Hair N., Howard-Davis C., Newman R. and Oliver T. *Transect through Time: The Archaeological Landscape of the Shell North Western Ethylene Pipeline,* Lancaster Imprints, Lancaster, 127-69.

Ormerod G. 1882 *History of the County Palatine and City of Chester,* (revised 2nd edn, ed. T, Helsby), 3 vols, Routledge, London.

Ottaway P. and Rogers N. 2002 *Craft, Industry and Everyday Life: Finds from Medieval York,* The Archaeology of York: The Small Finds 17/15, CBA, York.

Padley T. G. 1991 'The Metalwork, glass and stone objects from Castle St., Carlisle, Carlisle: Excavations 1981-2' Fascicule 2 of McCarthy M. *Roman Waterlogged remains at Castle St,* Cumberland and Westmorland Antiquarian and Archaeological Soc Research Series 5.

Parker Pearson M. 1996 'Food, Fertility and Front Doors in the First Millennium BC' in Champion T. C. and Collis J. R. (eds) *The Iron Age in Britain and Ireland: Recent Trends,* J. R. Collis Publications, University Sheffield, 117-32.

Parker Pearson M., Smith H., Mulville J. and Brennand M 2004 'Cille Pheadair: the Life and Times of a Norse-Period Farmstead c. 1000-1300' in Hines J., Lane A. and Redknap

M. (eds) *Land, Sea and Home,* Soc for Medieval Archaeol Monograph 20, Leeds, 235-54.

Peacock D. P. S. 1980 'The Roman millstone trade: a petrological sketch' *World Archaeology* 12, 43-53.

Penney S. and Shotter D. C. A. 1996 'An Inscribed Roman Salt-pan from Shavington, Cheshire' *Britannia* 27, 360-5.

Penney S. and Shotter D. C. A. 2001 'Further Inscribed Roman Salt Pans from Shavington, Cheshire' *J Chester Archaeol Soc* 76 (for 2000-1), 53-61.

Petch D. F. 1987 'The Roman Period' in Harris B. E. and Thacker A. T. (eds) *A History of the County of Chester,* 1. Oxford University Press, University of London, 115-236.

Philpott R. A. 1991 'Merseyside in the Roman Period' *J Merseyside ArchaeolSoc* 7 (for 1986-87), 61-74.

Philpott R. A. 1993 'A Romano-British Farmstead at Irby, Wirral, and its Place in the Landscape' *Archaeology North-West* 5, 19-25.

Philpott R. A. 1994 'The Implications of Irby' in Carrington P. (ed.) *From Flints to Flower Pots, Current Research in the Dee-Mersey Region,* Chester, 26-32.

Philpott R. A. 1999a 'A Romano-British Brooch Type from North West England' *Britannia* 30, 274-86.

Philpott R. A. 1999b 'Three Byzantine Coins found near the North Wirral Coast in Merseyside' *Trans Historic Soc Lancashire and Cheshire* 148, 197-202.

Philpott R. A. 2000a 'Recent Anglo-Saxon Finds from Merseyside and Cheshire and their archaeological significance' *Medieval Archaeology* 43, 194-202.

Philpott R. A. 2000b 'Brunt Boggart' in Cowell R. W. and Philpott R. A. (eds) *Prehistoric, Roman and medieval excavations in the Lowlands of North West England: Excavations along the Line of the A5300 in Tarbock and Halewood, Merseyside,* NMGM, Liverpool, 117-64.

Philpott R. A. 2000c 'Ochre Brook, Tarbock' in Cowell R. W. and Philpott R. A. (eds) *Prehistoric, Roman and medieval excavations in the Lowlands of North West England: Excavations along the Line of the A5300 in Tarbock and Halewood, Merseyside,* NMGM, Liverpool, 67-116.

Philpott R. A. 2000d 'The Romano-British Sites in their Regional Context' in Cowell R. W. and Philpott R. A. (eds) *Prehistoric, Roman and medieval excavations in the Lowlands of North West England: Excavations along the Line of the A5300 in Tarbock and Halewood, Merseyside,* NMGM, Liverpool, 175-204.

Philpott R. A. 2006 'The Romano-British Period Resource Assessment' in Brennand M (ed.) *The Archaeology of North West England, An Archaeological Research Framework for North West England: Volume 1 Resource Assessment,* Archaeology North West 8, 59-90.

Philpott R. A. 2007a 'Later prehistoric material: *c.* 500 BC to AD 1-50' in Griffiths D. W., Philpott R. A. and Egan G. *Meols: The Archaeology of the North Wirral Coast,* Oxford University School of Archaeology Monograph 68, Oxford, 36-9.

Philpott R. A. 2007b 'The Iron Age' in Griffiths D. W., Philpott R. A. and Egan G. *Meols: The Archaeology of the North Wirral Coast,* Oxford University School of Archaeology Monograph 68, Oxford, 379-87.

Philpott R. A. 2007c 'The Roman period' in Griffiths D. W., Philpott R. A. and Egan G. *Meols: The Archaeology of the North Wirral Coast,* Oxford University School of Archaeology Monograph 68, Oxford, 387-99.

Philpott R. A. 2007d 'Roman material: AD 1-50 to 400-450' in Griffiths D. W., Philpott R. A. and Egan G. *Meols: The Archaeology of the North Wirral Coast,* Oxford University School of Archaeology Monograph 68, Oxford, 39-58.

Philpott R. A. 2008 'Roman Merseyside: Twenty five years on' *J Merseyside Archaeol Soc* 12, 27-60.

Philpott R. A. in preparation 'Excavations on a Medieval Site at Meadow Lane, West Derby, 1989'.

Philpott R. A. and Adams M. H. 1999 'Excavations at an Iron Age and Romano-British Settlement at Irby, Wirral, 1987-96: An Interim Statement' in Nevell M. D. (ed.) *Living on the Edge of Empire, Methodology, Models and Marginality. Late-Prehistoric and Romano-British Rural Settlement in North West England,* CBA North West 3 (No 13, for 1998), Manchester, 64-73.

Philpott R. A. and Cowell R. W. 1992 *An Archaeological Assessment of Land East of Telegraph Road, Irby,* Unpublished report, Liverpool Museum.

Philpott R. A., Simmons P. and Cowell R. W. 1993 *An Archaeological Evaluation at Southworth Hall Farm, Croft, Cheshire, February 1993,* Unpublished report, Liverpool Museum.

Piggott S. 1950 'Swords and scabbards of the British Early Iron Age' *Proc Prehistoric Soc* 16, 1-28.

Piggott S. 1970 *Early Celtic Art,* Catalogue of exhibition in Royal Scottish Museum, Edinburgh University Press.

Poole C. 1984 'Objects of baked clay' in Cunliffe B. *Danebury: an Iron Age hillfort in Hampshire Volume 2,* CBA Research Report 52, 398-407.

Poole C. 1987 'Loomweights of baked clay' in Cunliffe B. *Hengistbury Head, Dorset. Volume 1,* OUCA Monograph No 13, 165-7.

Poole C. 1991 'Objects of baked clay' in Cunliffe B. and Poole C. *Danebury: an Iron Age hillfort in Hampshire. Volume 5,* CBA Research Report 73, 377.

Poole C. 1995 'Study 14: Loomweights versus oven bricks' in Cunliffe B. *Danebury: an Iron Age hillfort in Hampshire. Volume 6. A hillfort community in perspective,* CBA Research Report 102, 285-6.

Poole C. 1997 'Irby, Wirral, Site 30 Daub and Fired Clay Assessment' in Philpott R.A. and Adams M. *Excavation of an Iron Age and Romano-British Rural Settlement in Irby, Wirral, Merseyside. Assessment Report and Updated Project Design,* Unpublished, NMGM, Liverpool.

Poole C. 2000a 'Structural daub and clay' in Cunliffe B. and Poole C. *The Danebury Environs Programme The Prehistory of a Wessex Landscape Volume 2 - Part 1 Woolbury and Stockbridge Down, Stockbridge, Hants 1989,* EH and OUCA Monograph 49, 60-1.

Poole C. 2000b 'Structural daub' in Cunliffe B. and Poole C. *The Danebury Environs Programme The Prehistory of a Wessex Landscape Volume 2 - Part 2 Bury Hill, Upper Clatford, Hants 1990,* EH and OUCA Monograph 49, 60-2.

Poole C. 2000c 'Structural oven daub' in Cunliffe B. and Poole C. *The Danebury Environs Programme The Prehistory of a Wessex Landscape Volume 2 - Part 3 Suddern Farm, Middle Wallop, Hants 1991 and 1996,* EH and OUCA Monograph 49, 128-42.

Poole C. 2000d 'Structural daub and baked clay' in Cunliffe B. and Poole C. *The Danebury Environs Programme The Prehistory of a Wessex Landscape Volume 2 - parts 6 Houghton Down, Stockbridge, Hants, 1994,* English Heritage and OUCA Monograph 49, 115-19.

Poole C. unpubl. 'The Fired Clay from Thistleton, Cambridgeshire' Unpublished report for English Heritage.

Portable Antiquities Scheme 2003 *Portable Antiquities Scheme Annual Report 2001/02-2002/03,* Resource, London.

Portable Antiquities Scheme 2005 *Portable Antiquities Scheme Annual Report 2004/05,* Museums and Libraries Association, London.

Portable Antiquities Scheme 2006 *Portable Antiquities Scheme Annual Report 2005/06,* Museums and Libraries Association, London.

Portable Antiquities Scheme 2007 *Portable Antiquities Scheme Annual Report 2006,* Department of Culture, Media and Sport/ Museums and Libraries Association, London.

Potter C. 1890 'Antiquities of the Meols Shore' *Trans Hist Soc Lancashire Cheshire* 40 (for 1888), 143-52.

Poulter A. G. 1980 'Rural communities (*vici* and *komai*) and their role in the organisation of the limes of Moesia Inferior' in Hanson W. S. and Keppie L. J. F. (eds) *Roman Frontier studies 1979: papers presented to the 12th international congress of Roman frontier studies,* BAR Int Ser S71, Oxford, 729-44.

Price J. 1994 'The Discovery of an Early Saltworking Site near Crewe' *Cheshire Archaeology* 3, 4-5.

Pryor F. 1980 *Excavation at Fengate, Peterborough, England: The Third Report,* Northants Arch Soc Monograph 1, Arch Monograph ROM 6, Canada.

Raftery B. 1983 *A Catalogue of Irish Iron Age Antiquities,* Marburg.

Rahtz P. 1976 'Buildings and rural settlement' in Wilson D. M. (ed.) *The Archaeology of Anglo-Saxon England,* Cambridge University Press, 49-98.

Raines F. R. 1845 *Notitia Cestriensis by Gastrell,* Chetham Soc 8.

Redhead N. 2005 'Mellor: Its Local and Wider Archaeological Significance' in Nevell M. and Redhead N. (eds) 2005 *Mellor: Living on the Edge. A Regional Study of an Iron Age and Romano-British Upland Settlement,* Manchester Archaeological Monographs 1, Manchester, 49-64.

Redhead N. and Roberts J. 2003 'Mellor: a new Iron Age hillfort' *Current Archaeology* 16 no 9 (issue 189), 400-3.

Reece R. 1987 *Coinage in Roman Britain,* B. A. Seaby Ltd, London.

Reece R. 1988 *My Roman Britain,* Cotswold Studies, Cirencester.

Reece R. 1991 *Roman Coins From 140 Sites in Britain,* Oxbow Books, Oxford.

Rees H. 1986 'Ceramic Salt Working Debris from Droitwich' *Trans Worcestershire Archaeol Soc* 10 (3rd series), 47-54.

Reynolds P. J. 1979 *Iron-Age Farm: The Butser Experiment*, British Museum Publications Ltd, London.

Reynolds P. J. 1993 'Experimental Reconstruction' in Harding D. W., Blake I. M. and Reynolds P. J. (eds) *An Iron Age Settlement in Dorset, excavation and reconstruction*, University of Edinburgh Department of Archaeology Monograph Series 1, Edinburgh.

Rhodes M. 1980 'The leather footwear' in Jones D. M. (ed.), *Excavations at Billingsgate Buildings 'Triangle', Lower Thames Street, London, 1974*, London and Middlesex Archaeol Soc Special Paper 4, London, 99-128.

Richards J. D. 1999 'Cottam: an Anglo-Scandinavian Settlement on the Yorkshire Wolds' *Archaeol J* 156, 1-111.

Richards J. D. 2000 ' Identifying Anglo-Scandinavian Settlements' in Hadley D. M. and Richards J. D. (eds) *Cultures in Contact: Scandinavian Settlement in England in the Ninth and Tenth Centuries* Brepols Publishers n.v., Turnhout, Belgium, 295-310.

Richmond I. A. 1961 'Roman Timber Building' in Jope E. M. (ed.) *Studies in Building History*, Odhams Press Ltd, London, 15-26.

Rivet A. L. F. and Smith C. 1979 *The Place-Names of Roman Britain*, B. T. Batsford, London.

Robinson D. J. and Lloyd-Morgan G. 1985 'Stamford Bridge' *Cheshire Archaeol Bulletin* 10 (for 1984-5), 95.

Rogers G. B. 1974 'Poteries Sigillées de la Gaule Centrale, I: Les Motifs Non Figurés' *Gallia Suppl.* 28, Paris.

Rogers I. and Garner D. 2007 *Wilderspool and Holditch. Roman 'Boom-Towns on the 'Road North'*, BAR Brit Ser 449, Archaeopress, Oxford.

Rogers P. W. 1997 *Textile production at 16-22 Coppergate*, The Archaeology of York 17/11, York.

Ross A. 1974 *Pagan Celtic Britain*, Sphere Books Ltd, London.

Royle C. and Woodward A. 1993 'The Prehistoric Pottery' in Ellis P. (ed.) *Beeston Castle, Cheshire: a report on the excavations 1968-85 by Laurence Keen and Peter Hough*, English Heritage Archaeol Report 23, London, 33-78.

Rutter J. A. 1977 'Upper Northgate Street Hoard Pot' in Davey P.J. 1977 *Medieval Pottery from Excavations in the North-West*, University of Liverpool, 22-3.

Rutter J. A. A. 1985 'The Pottery' in Mason D. J. P. *Excavations at Chester: 26-42 Lower Bridge Street 1974-6. The Dark Age and Saxon Periods*, Grosvenor Museum Archaeological Excavation and Survey Reports 3, Grosvenor Museum, Chester, 40-55.

Sanders J. 1973 'Late Roman shell-gritted ware in Southern Britain', B.A. dissertation, Institute of Archaeology, University of London.

Savory H. N. 1971 *Excavations at Dinorben, 1965-9*, National Museum of Wales, Cardiff.

Schmidt H. 1973 'The Trelleborg House Reconsidered' *Medieval Archaeology* 17, 52-77.

Scott I. R. 1985 'Ironwork' in Hurst H. R. *Kingsholm*, Gloucester Archaeological Report 1, Cambridge, 36-40.

Seager Smith R. and Davies S. M. 1993 *Black Burnished Ware Type Series. The Roman Pottery from excavations at Greyhound Yard, Dorchester, Dorset*, Dorset Natural History and Archaeological Society Monograph Series 12, 1993.

Sharples N. 2004 'A Find of Ringerike Art from Bornais in the Outer Hebrides' in Hines J., Lane A. and Redknap M. (eds) *Land, Sea and Home*, Soc for Medieval Archaeol Monograph 20, Leeds, 255-72.

Shotter D. C. A. 1992 'The Roman Coins' in Hinchliffe J. and Williams J. H. *Roman Warrington. Excavations at Wilderspool 1966-9 and 1976*, Brigantia Monograph 2, University of Manchester, 152-4.

Shotter D. C. A. 1997 *Romans and Britons in North-West England*, 2nd revised edn, Centre for North-West Regional Studies, University of Lancaster.

Shotter D. C. A. 1998 'Chester: the Evidence of Roman Coin Loss' *J Chester Archaeol Soc* 75 (for 1998-9), 33-50.

Shotter D. C. A. 2000a *Roman Coins from North-West England: Second Supplement*, Centre for North-West Regional Studies, Lancaster.

Shotter D. C. A. 2000b 'Chester: The Evidence of Roman Coin Loss' *J Chester Archaeol Soc* 75 (for 1998-9), 33-50

Shotter D. C. A. 2000c 'Middlewich: The Evidence of Roman Coin Loss' *J Chester Archaeol Soc* 75 (for 1998-9), 51-60.

Smith C. 1977 'The Valleys of the Tame and Middle Trent – their Populations and Ecology during the Late First Millennium B.C.' in Collis J. (ed.) *The Iron Age in Britain – a review*, Department of Prehistory and Archaeology, University of Sheffield, 51-61.

Smith C. (ed.) 1979 *Fisherwick: the Reconstruction of an Iron Age Landscape*, BAR Brit Ser 61, Oxford.

Speakman J. 2000 'Medieval Pottery' in Cowell R.W. and Philpott R.A. *Prehistoric, Romano-British and Medieval Settlement in Lowland North West England: Archaeological excavations along the A5300 road corridor in Merseyside*, NMGM, Liverpool, 140-54.

Spikins P. 1999 *Mesolithic Northern England: Environment, population and settlement*, BAR Brit Ser 283, Oxford.

Stallibrass S. 1995 'Review of the vertebrate remains' in Huntley J. P. and Stallibrass S. *Plant and vertebrate remains from archaeological sites in northern England: data reviews and future directions*, Architectural and Archaeological Society of Durham and Northumberland Research Report 4, Durham, 84-198.

Stanford S. C. 1974 *Croft Ambrey*, Adams and Sons, Hereford.

Stanford S. C. 1981 *Midsummer Hill: an Iron Age hillfort on the Malverns*, published by the author, Leominster.

Stanford S. C. 1982 'Bromfield, Shropshire – Neolithic, Beaker and Bronze Age sites, 1966-79' *Proc Prehistoric Soc* 48, 279-320.

Stanford S. C. 1984 'The Wrekin Hillfort Excavations 1973' *Archaeol J* 141, 61-90.

Stanford S. C. 1995 'A Cornovian Farm and Saxon Cemetery at Bromfield, Shropshire' *Trans Shropshire Archaeol Hist Soc* 70, 95-141.

Stead I. M. 1993 'Iron objects' in Ellis P. (ed.) *Beeston Castle, Cheshire: a report on the excavations 1968-85 by Laurence Keen and Peter Hough,* English Heritage Archaeological Report 23, London, 53-4.

Steane J. M. 1985 *The Archaeology of Medieval England and Wales*, University of Georgia Press, Athens.

Strickland T. 1995 *The Romans at Wilderspool; The story of the first industrial development on the Mersey,* Greenalls Group PLC, Warrington.

Strickland T. 2001 *Roman Middlewich: A Story of Roman and Briton in Mid-Cheshire,* The Roman Middlewich Project, Middlewich.

Stuiver M. and Polach H. A. 1977 'Reporting of ^{14}C data' *Radiocarbon* 19, 355–63.

Stuiver M. and Reimer P. J. 1986 'A computer program for radiocarbon age calculation' *Radiocarbon* 28, 1022–30.

Stuiver M., Reimer P. J., Bard E., Beck J. W., Burr G. S., Hughen K. A., Kromer B., McCormac F. G., van der Plicht J. and Spurk M. 1998 'INTCAL98 radiocarbon age calibration, 24,000–0 cal BP' *Radiocarbon* 40, 1041–84.

Tait J. (ed.) 1920 *The Chartulary or Register of the Abbey of St Werburgh, Chester*, Chetham Soc ns 79.

Taylor J. 2001 'Rural society in Roman Britain' in James S. and Millett M. (eds) *Britons and Romans: advancing an archaeological agenda,* CBA Research Report 125, London, 46-59.

Taylor J. 2007 *An Atlas of Roman Rural Settlement in England,* CBA Research Report 151, York.

Thacker A. T. 1987 'Anglo-Saxon Cheshire' in Harris B. E. and Thacker A. T. (eds) *A History of the County of Chester,* 1. Oxford University Press, University of London, 237-92.

Thomas A. C. 1966 'The character and origins of Roman Dumnonia' in Thomas A. C. (ed.) *Rural Settlement in Roman Britain,* CBA Research Report 7, London, 74-98.

Thompson F. H. 1956 'Pilgrim's flask from Meols' *J Chester Archaeol Soc* 45, 48-9.

Thompson F. H. 1965 *Roman Cheshire*, Cheshire Community Council, Chester.

Thompson H. 1994 'Iron Age and Roman slave-shackles' *Archaeol J* 150 (for 1993), 57-168.

Thorpe R., Sharman J. and Clay P. 1994 'An Iron Age and Romano-British Enclosure System at Normanton le Heath, Leicestershire' *Trans Leicestershire Archaeol Hist Soc* 68, 1-63.

Tindall A. 1993 'An Iron Age Coin from near Nantwich' *Cheshire Past* 2, 5.

Toynbee J. M. C. 1963 *Art in Roman Britain*, 2nd edn, Phaidon Press, London.

Tutin T. G., Heywood V. H., Burges N. A., Moore D. M., Valentine D. H., Walters S. M. and Webb D. A. 1964-80 *Flora Europaea*, vols 1-5, Cambridge University Press, Cambridge.

Tyers P. A. 1996 *Roman Pottery in Britain*, B. T. Batsford Ltd, London.

Tylecote R. F. 1986 *The Prehistory of Metallurgy in the British Isles,* The Institute of Metals, London.

Tylecote R. F. and Biek L. 1991 'The metalworking' in Musson C. R. *The Breiddin Hillfort, A Later Prehistoric Settlement in the Welsh Marches,* CBA Research Report 76, London, 147-9.

University A. S. D. 2008 *East and West Brunton, Newcastle plant macrofossil and pollen analysis.* Report 1794.

van der Veen M. 1992 *Crop husbandry regimes: an archaeobotanical study of farming in northern England 1000 BC - AD 500,* J. R. Collis publications, Department of Archaeology and Prehistory, Sheffield.

Varley W. J. 1950 'Excavations of the Castle Ditch, Eddisbury, 1935-38' *Trans Hist Soc Lancashire Cheshire* 102, 1-68.

Varley W. J. 1964 *Cheshire Before the Romans,* A history of Cheshire 1, Cheshire Community Council, Chester.

Vaughan J. 2008 'The Medieval Pottery' in Brown F. and Howard-Davis C. *Norton Priory: Monastery to Museum. Excavations 1970-87,* Oxford Archaeology North, Lancaster, 333-44.

Viner L. 1986 'Objects of iron' in McWhirr A. *Houses in Roman Cirencester,* Cirencester Excavations III, Cirencester, 111-4.

Waddington C. 2007 *Mesolithic Settlement in the North Sea Basin; a Case Study from Howick, North-East England,* Oxbow Books, Oxford.

Wainwright F. T. 1948 'Ingimund's Invasion' *English Historical Review* 63, 145-69, reprinted in Wainwright F. T. 1975 *Scandinavian England* (ed. Finberg H.), Chichester, 131-61.

Wainwright G. J. 1967 *Coygan Camp: A Prehistoric, Romano-British and Dark Age settlement in Carmarthenshire,* Cambrian Archaeol Association, Cardiff.

Wainwright G. J. 1971 'The Excavation of a fortified Settlement at Walesland, Rath, Pembrokeshire' *Britannia* 2, 48-108.

Walker J., Blainey L. and Wild F. C. 1986 'The Ceramic Finds' in Bryant S., Morris M. and Walker J. S. F. *Roman Manchester: A Frontier Settlement,* Greater Manchester Archaeological Unit, 85-130.

Wallace P. F. 2001 'Ireland's Viking Towns' in Larsen A.-C. (ed.) *The Vikings in Ireland,* The Viking Ship Museum, Roskilde, 37-50.

Ward G. K. and Wilson S. R. 1978 'Procedures for comparing and combining radiocarbon age determinations: a critique' *Archaeometry* 20, 19–31.

Ward M. 1989 'The Samian Ware' in Blockley K. *Prestatyn 1984-5, An Iron-Age Farmstead and Romano-British Industrial Settlement in North-Wales,* BAR Brit Ser 210, Oxford, 139-54.

Ward M. 1993 'A Summary of the Samian Ware from Excavations at Piercebridge' *J Roman Pottery Stud* 6, 15-22.

Ward S. W. 1994 *Excavations at Chester: Saxon Occupation within the Roman Fortress. Sites excavated 1971-1981*, Chester City Council.

Warhurst M. 1982 *Sylloge of Coins of the British Isles: Volume 29. Merseyside County Museums*, British Academy, London.

Watkin W. T. 1883 *Roman Lancashire* (reprinted 1969), SR Publishers Ltd, Wakefield.

Watkin W. T. 1886 *Roman Cheshire* (reprinted 1974, with introduction by D. F. Petch), EP Publishing Ltd, Wakefield.

Webster G. 1975 *The Cornovii*, Duckworth, London.

Webster G. and Smith L. 1982 'The Excavation of a Romano-British Rural Settlement at Barnsley Park: Part II' *Transactions Bristol Gloucestershire Archaeol Soc* 100, 65-189.

Webster P. V. 1968 'The Coarse Pottery' in Jones G. D. B. and Webster P. V. 'Mediolanum: Excavations at Whitchurch, 1965-6' *Archaeol J* 125, 222-43.

Webster P. V. 1971 'Coarse Pottery from the 1968-70 Excavations' in Jones G. D. B. 'Excavations at Northwich' *Archaeol J* 128, 66-73.

Webster P. V. 1973 'The Roman-British Pottery Kilns near Wilderspool' *Archaeol J* 130, 77-103.

Webster P. V. 1974 'The Coarse Pottery' in Jones G. D. B. and Grealey S. *Roman Manchester,* Manchester Excavation Committee, Altrincham, 89-118.

Webster P. V. 1976 'Severn Valley Ware: A Preliminary Study' *Trans Bristol Gloucestershire Archaeol Soc* 94, 18-46.

Webster P. V. 1982 'Romano-British coarse pottery in North West England - an introduction' *Lancashire Archaeology J* 2, 13-31.

Webster P. V. 1988 'The Coarse Pottery' in Jones G. D. B. and Shotter D.C.A. *Roman Lancaster,* Brigantia Monograph 1, University of Manchester, 103-45.

Webster P. V. 1989 'The pottery' in O'Leary T. J., Blockley K. and Musson C. *Pentre Farm, Flint 1976-81: An official building in the Roman lead mining district*, BAR Brit Ser 207, Oxford, 94-123.

Webster P. V. 1991 'Pottery supply to the Roman North-West' *J Roman Pottery Studies* 4, 11-18.

Webster P. V. 1992 'The Coarse Pottery' in Hinchliffe J. and Williams J. H. *Roman Warrington. Excavations at Wilderspool 1966-9 and 1976*, Brigantia Monograph 2, University of Manchester, 42-77.

Webster P. V. 1993 'Coarse Pottery' in Casey P. J. and Davies J. L. *Excavations at Segontium (Caernarfon) Roman Fort, 1975-1979*, CBA Research Report 90, London, 250-309.

Wedd C., Smith B., Simmons W. and Wray D. 1923 *Geology of Liverpool*, Memoirs of the Geological Survey, London.

Wedlake W. J. 1982 *The excavation of the shrine of Apollo at Nettleton, Wiltshire, 1956-1971*, Reports of the Research Committee of the Antiquaries of London, London.

Welfare A. T. 1985 'The Milling-Stones' in Bidwell P. T. *The Roman Fort of Vindolanda*, HBMC Archaeological Report 1, London, 154-64.

Wenban-Smith F. F. 2007 'The Early Bronze Age Lithics', in Garner D. *The Neolithic and Bronze Age Settlement at*

Oversley Farm, Styal, Cheshire Excavations in advance of Manchester Airport's Second Runway, BAR Brit Ser 435, Archaeopress, Oxford, 76-94.

Wheeler H. 1979 'Excavation at Willington, Derbyshire, 1970-1972' *Derbyshire Archaeol J* 99, 58-220.

Wheeler R. E. M. 1925 *Prehistoric and Roman Wales*, Clarendon Press, Oxford.

Whimster R. 1989 *The Emerging Past: Air Photography and the Buried Landscape*, RCHME, London.

White R. B. 1978 'Excavations at Trwyn Du, Anglesey 1974' *Archaeologia Cambrensis* 127, 16-39.

White R. H. and Barker P. A. 1998 *Wroxeter: Life and Death of a Roman City*, Tempus Publishing Ltd, Stroud.

White R. H. 2007 *Britannia Prima. Britain's Last Roman Province*, Tempus Publishing, Stroud.

White R. H. and van Leusen P. M. 1997 'Aspects of Romanization in the Wroxeter Hinterland' in Meadows K., Lemke C. and Heron J. (eds) *TRAC 96: Proceedings of the Sixth Annual Theoretical Roman Archaeology Conference*, Oxbow Books, Oxford, 133-43.

Willis S. 1996 'The Romanization of pottery assemblages in the East and North-East of England during the first century A.D.: A comparative analysis' *Britannia* 27, 179-222.

Willis S. 1997 'Samian: Beyond Dating' in Meadows K., Lemke C. and Heron J. (eds) *TRAC 96: Proceedings of the Sixth Annual Theoretical Roman Archaeology Conference*, Oxbow Books, Oxford, 38-54.

Willis S. 1999 'Without and Within: aspects of culture and community in the Iron Age of north-eastern England' in Bevan B. (ed.) *Northern Exposure: interpretative devolution and the Iron Ages in Britain*, Leicester Archaeology Monographs 4, University of Leicester, 81-110.

Wilson D. M. 2008 *The Vikings in the Isle of Man*, Aarhus University Press, Aarhus.

Wilson K. P. (ed.) 1969 *Chester Customs Accounts, 1301-1566*, Rec Soc Lancashire Cheshire 111.

Woodiwiss S. 1992 *Iron Age and Roman Salt Production and the Medieval Town of Droitwich*, CBA Research Report 81, London.

Woodland M. 1990 'Spindle whorls' in Biddle M. *Object and Economy in Medieval Winchester*, Winchester Studies 7.ii, Oxford, 216-25.

Woodward A. and Marsden P. forthcoming 'The Prehistoric Pottery from Eye Kettleby, Leicestershire' (for University of Leicester Archaeological Services).

Wrathmell S. 1989 *Domestic Settlement 2: Medieval Peasant Farmsteads*, York University Archaeological Publications No 8, York.

Wrathmell S. and Nicholson A. 1990 *Dalton Parlours: Iron Age Settlement and Roman Villa*, West Yorkshire Archaeology Service, Wakefield.

Wright J. 1996 *Higher Lane, Fazakerley, Merseyside: Final report of evaluation and excavation*, Unpublished report Lancaster University Archaeological Unit (in MSMR).

Young C. J. 1977 *The Roman Pottery Industry of the Oxford Region*, BAR 43, Oxford.

Abbreviations

AOD	Above Ordnance Datum
BAR	British Archaeological Reports
CBA	Council for British Archaeology
CRO	Cheshire Record Office, Chester
Dr.	Dragendorff
EDXRF	Energy-dispersive X-ray fluorescence
LRO	Lancashire Record Office, Preston
Mersey-side HER	Merseyside Historic Environment Record (formerly Sites and Monuments Record), Liverpool
NAA	Northern Archaeological Associates, Durham
NMGM	National Museums and Galleries on Merseyside (to 2003)
NML	National Museums Liverpool (from 2003)
NGR	National Grid Reference
OD	Ordnance Datum
PAS	Portable Antiquities Scheme
PRO	Public Record Office
RCHME	Royal Commission on the Historical Monuments of England
RIC	*The Roman Imperial Coinage,* series edited by C. H. V. Sutherland and R. A. G. Carson
SF	Specially-recorded find
taq	*Terminus ante quem*
tpq	*Terminus post quem*
US	Unstratified
VCP	Very Coarse Pottery (briquetage)
XRF	X-ray fluorescence

Glossary of Lithic Technology Terms

Bipolar technique: the pebble is set directly on a stone 'anvil' and its top edge hit directly by a hammerstone, often without a flaked surface having been prepared to take the blow for detaching the removal.

Blade: a regular, generally straight-sided flake that has a length:breadth ratio greater than 2:1.

Chip: a small, generally flat, waste piece, sometimes with flake characteristics, less than 10 mm in length.

Chunk: an irregular piece of waste or shatter from the knapping process.

Core: the remnants of natural pebbles or other lumps of lithic raw material from which a series of removals has been made.

Core rejuvenation flake: a flake resulting from the modification of core platforms during the knapping process to maintain the predictability of the shape and size of the removals.

Cortex: the natural, outer, granular surface of flint pebbles.

Debitage: all the chips and shatter that come from opening up the original nodule, shaping the core, or retouching blanks or implements. It is material that is generally discarded during the knapping process, much of it being quite small.

Direct percussion: a method of knapping where the stone is struck directly with a hammer (stone (hard), or e.g. bone or antler (soft)) in order to detach or retouch a piece. *Indirect* percussion involves hitting an intermediary object (a punch) with the hammer.

Flake: a removal with a more irregular shape than a blade, can be wider than long, whose minimum length is 15mm.

Implement: a blank, either a removal or piece of waste, with further edge retouch. Sometimes this modifies the blank in a way that produces a standard formal shape that is common to prehistoric technologies nationally. Other times the retouch may be limited and informal without reference to chronological or culturally defined parameters.

Microburin: the waste products of the manufacture of microliths

Microlith: a small distinctively shaped implement on a blade or bladelet, datable to the Mesolithic period, generally thought to represent projectile points.

Platform: the generally level end or side edge of a core, generally produced by flaking, which is used as the surface from which to detach removals.

Primary removal: a flake or blade removed from the core with its dorsal surface formed by the cortex of the pebble.

Removal: either blades or flakes detached from the parent core. At the outset of the knapping process they have the purpose of shaping the original nodule. Later in the sequence more controlled removals are made from the core, which can form the blanks for further retouch into implements.

Reduction sequence: the process by which a pebble or lump of flint or chert is worked down, producing distinctive products at each stage of the sequence.

Residual: applied to artefacts that are not in their original context, having been transported into contexts that formed at a later date through erosion, the cutting of pits and ditches etc., which will generally contain later artefacts also. The earlier material cannot be used, therefore, to suggest a date for the context into which they have become incorporated.

Secondary removal: a removal with both inner and external, cortical, parts of the pebble on its dorsal side.

Small flake: a piece with flake characteristics but between 10-15 mm in length.

Standard reduction technique: used here as a non-bipolar method, using direct or indirect hand-held percussion methods.

Technology: here, all the features associated with the method of working the stone e.g. hand-held or bipolar knapping, hard or soft hammer etc from the distinctive traits left on waste, removal and implement categories.

Tertiary removal: blade or flake detached from the core after all the outer cortex has been removed from the parent nodule.

Typology: here, the ordering into groups of common, repeated shapes and traits associated with the by-products of working stone tools that can help define chronological parameters for particular styles.

Appendix 1: Tables of Environmental Samples

This appendix provides detailed tables of the environmental samples referred to in Chapter 3.

Period II

Trench number	36	36	36	36	37	37	43	37	36	36	44	44	19	19	19	19
Context number (Fill)	6298	6300	6304	6321	6466	6488	7275	6490	6330	6332	7422	7423	8135	8171	8173	8175
Context Number (Cut)	6324	6334	6306	6325	6472	6489	7274	6491	6331	6333	7424	7426	8137	8197	8189	8186
Sample number	2743	2751	2539	2746	2276	2348	2881	2350	2763	2752	2891	2892	2307	2369	2370	2367
Volume processed (litres)	11	11	6	9	8	17	10	16	10	12	17	12	19	35	17	5
Feature/Structure									S27	S27	S27	S27	S27	S27	S27	S27
Assessed only	1	1														
Avena grain - oats																
Cerealia undiff.	2	2		2	6		1	1	1		6	13	132	194	3	
Hordeum hulled - barley				1				1		1	15	11	1	11	1	
Hordeum indet.			2								9	23	6	74	1	
Hordeum naked				9							266	47	36	111	2	
Triticum aestivum grain										1						1
Triticum dicoccon			1	1							102	49	143	283	16	
Triticum sp(p). grain					2										1	
Carex (trigonous) - sedges											1					
Chenopodium album - fat hen																
Fallopia convolvulus - black bindweed					3						1					
Galium aparine - cleavers											1	1				
Gramineae <2mm - small grasses						1					1					
Hyoscyamus niger - henbane											2					
Polygonum aviculare											1					
Polygonum lapth./persicaria											1					
Polygonum periscaria											1					
Polygonaceae undiff.																
Rumex obtusifolius-type																
Sieglingia decumbens											1		1			
Hordeum 6-row rachis internode											4					
Hordeum basal internode											1					
Hordeum rachis internode											11			3		
Secale rachis internode											1					
Triticum brittle rachis internode											1					
Triticum dicoccon glume base											69	7	50	117		6
Triticum dicoccon spikelet - complete											1					
Triticum dicoccon spikelet fork											22	3	13	34		
Triticum glume								1					2		1	
Triticum spelta glume											4					4
Corylus avellana nut frag. - hazel			2					1			13	3		6		
Linum usitatissimum - flax											1					
Malus/Pyrus - apple/pear											8		1			
Legume <4mm											1					
Total seeds/10 litres	2	2	4	3	20	3	1	4	1	2	545	157	385	833	25	11

Appendix Table 1

248

Period II continued

Trench number	36	19	19	19	19	19	19	19	19	36	36	41	Total
Context number (Fill)	8351	8215	8221	8223	8225	8227	8229	8236	8240	8354	8367	9764	
Context Number (Cut)	8353	8217	8222	8224	8226	8228	8230	8224	8226	8355	8368	9772	
Sample number	2686	2398	2403	2414	2412	2407	2411	2415	2413	2694	2724	2785	
Volume processed (litres)	14	7	12	10	2	10	7	7	9	8	4	10	
Feature/Structure	S27	S28?		S27 or S28	S28	S32 or S28	S32 or S28	C14 date	S28	S27?		S33	
Assessed only													
Avena grain - oats	1												1
Cerealia undiff.	2	1				3					1		370
Hordeum hulled - barley		1	4	50	25	3		7	40	1	3	3	179
Hordeum indet.	2				140							4	261
Hordeum naked				999	100			309	278			3	2160
Triticum aestivum grain													2
Triticum dicoccon			3	645	350			297	296				2186
Triticum sp(p). grain	2		3			5				1		1	15
Carex (trigonous) - sedges													1
Chenopodium album - fat hen					5								5
Fallopia convolvulus - black bindweed	1				5				2				12
Galium aparine - cleavers	1								12			1	16
Gramineae <2mm - small grasses												1	3
Hyoscyamus niger - henbane													2
Polygonum aviculare			1										2
Polygonum lapth./persicaria												1	2
Polygonum periscaria													1
Polygonaceae undiff.					5								5
Rumex obtusifolius-type	1												1
Sieglingia decumbens													2
Hordeum 6-row rachis internode												19	23
Hordeum basal internode				4								1	6
Hordeum rachis internode				24	10							23	71
Secale rachis internode													1
Triticum brittle rachis internode												2	3
Triticum dicoccon glume base		1	1	464	140			79	61		8	15	1018
Triticum dicoccon spikelet - complete													1
Triticum dicoccon spikelet fork				130	30		1	36	4			3	276
Triticum glume													4
Triticum spelta glume				8	10				1	1			28
Corylus avellana nut frag. - hazel					5	1			1				32
Linum usitatissimum - flax													1
Malus/Pyrus - apple/pear				16				11					36
Legume <4mm									7				8
Total seeds/10 litres	10	3	12	2340	825	12	1	739	702	4	11	77	6734

Appendix Table 1 continued

Period IV

Trench number (Roman numerals)	19	36	36	36	36	36	36	21	36	19	41	36	36
Context number (fill)	8083	6145	8320	6149	6130	6174	6177	3765	6155	8110	9609	6138	6167
Context number (cut)	8154	8305	8327	6153	6139	6175	6178	3769	6139	8103	9572	6139	6172
#samples amalgamated					5								
Sample number	2314	2532	2582	2268		2449	2458	2075	2316	2258	2692	2217	2441
Volume processed (litres)	8	9	7	17	122	11	3	8	18	8	9	25	34
Feature/Structure	F1	S12	S12	S13	S13	S14	S14		F9	S13	S13	F9	S14
Assessed only										1	1		
Avena grain - oats					6				2			24	1
Cerealia undiff.		3			28		10		9			62	2
cf. Secale cereale					1								
Hordeum hulled - barley	1	1	3		17	1		1				41	1
Hordeum indet.				1	4				8	1	1		1
Hordeum naked				1	1								
Secale cereale grain					1								
Triticum aestivum grain					13				1			18	
Triticum dicoccon			1	1									1
Triticum (hexaploid)					3								1
Triticum sp(p). grain		1		1	1		7		6			26	1
Triticum spelta					1								
Anthemis cotula - stinking mayweed													1
Bromus sp(p). grain					1				1				
Carex (lenticular) - sedges					1								
Carex (trigonous) - sedges		1			1								
Chenopodium album - fat hen					1								1
Eleocharis palustris - spike rush													
Fallopia convolvulus - black bindweed	1				2								1
Galium aparine - cleavers									1				
Gramineae <2mm - small grasses						1							1
Ilex - holly													
Plantago lanceolata - ribwort plantain					1								
Polygonum aviculare					1								
Polygonum lapathifolium					1								
Polygonum lapth./persicaria					2								
Polygonum periscaria	1				5								1
Polygonaceae undiff.													1
Raphanus raphanistrum pod frag.					3				1			6	
Rumex acetosella													
Rumex obtusifolius-type					1	1							1
Sieglingia decumbens		1			3								
Veronica hederifolia					1								
Avena awn					1								1
Hordeum 6-row rachis internode													
Triticum aestivum rachis node					1								
Triticum brittle rachis internode					1	1	3						1
Triticum dicoccon glume base		1				2	7						1
Triticum dicoccon spikelet fork													1
Triticum glume			1			1							3
Triticum spelta glume					1								2
Pisum sativum - pea					1								
Brassica sp(p).	3												
Corylus avellana nut frag. - hazel					1								
Legume <4mm					2								
Total seeds/10 litres	6	8	5	4	108	7	27	1	29	1	1	177	24

Appendix Table 2

Period IV continued

Trench number (Roman numerals)	19	19	19	19	40	40	Total
Context number (fill)	8011	8039	8040	8124	9107	9033	
Context number (cut)	8012	8041	8041	8012	9116	9096	
#samples amalgamated							
Sample number	2277	2297	2298	2279	2706	2685	
Volume processed (litres)	15	3	21	3	8	19	
Feature/Structure	S9	S9	S9	S9	S9	F2	
Assessed only							
Avena grain - oats							33
Cerealia undiff.				7			121
cf. Secale cereale							1
Hordeum hulled - barley	1		1				68
Hordeum indet.		10	1				27
Hordeum naked			11				13
Secale cereale grain							1
Triticum aestivum grain							32
Triticum dicoccon		3			1		7
Triticum (hexaploid)							4
Triticum sp(p). grain	1		19			1	64
Triticum spelta		3					4
Anthemis cotula - stinking mayweed							1
Bromus sp(p). grain	1					3	6
Carex (lenticular) - sedges							1
Carex (trigonous) - sedges							2
Chenopodium album - fat hen							2
Eleocharis palustris - spike rush						1	1
Fallopia convolvulus - black bindweed							4
Galium aparine - cleavers							1
Gramineae <2mm - small grasses							2
Ilex - holly							0
Plantago lanceolata - ribwort plantain							1
Polygonum aviculare							1
Polygonum lapathifolium							1
Polygonum lapth./persicaria							2
Polygonum periscaria							7
Polygonaceae undiff.	1						2
Raphanus raphanistrum pod frag.							10
Rumex acetosella							0
Rumex obtusifolius-type							3
Sieglingia decumbens							4
Veronica hederifolia							1
Avena awn							2
Hordeum 6-row rachis internode							0
Triticum aestivum rachis node							1
Triticum brittle rachis internode	1					3	10
Triticum dicoccon glume base		3	1				15
Triticum dicoccon spikelet fork			1				2
Triticum glume	1					5	11
Triticum spelta glume						6	9
Pisum sativum - pea							1
Brassica sp(p).							3
Corylus avellana nut frag. - hazel							1
Legume <4mm							2
Total seeds/10 litres	6	19	34	7	1	19	484

Appendix Table 2 continued

251

Period V

Trench number	31	41	41	21	19	Totals
Context number (fill)	3715	9567	9603	3668	1086	
Context number (cut)	3724	9579	9579	3684	1087	
#samples amalgamated						
Sample number	2006	2697	2677	2005	1035	
Volume processed (litres)	20	8	24	11	8	
Feature/Structure	F3 pit	S29	S29	S8	S7	
Assessed only			C14 date			
Avena grain - oats	17					17
Avena awn						0
Cerealia undiff.	18		1	1		20
Hordeum hulled - barley	5		1	1		7
Hordeum indet.	18			2		20
Hordeum naked						0
Secale cereale grain	5					5
cf. Secale cereale				2		2
Triticum aestivum grain	12					12
Triticum dicoccon						0
Triticum (hexaploid)	5					5
Triticum cf. spelta						0
Triticum spelta						0
Triticum sp(p). grain				3		3
Anthemis cotula - stinking mayweed	1					1
Bromus sp(p). grain	3	1				4
Carex (trigonous) - sedges						0
Chenopodium album - fat hen						0
Eleocharis palustris-spike rush						
Fallopia convolvulus - black bindweed	2					2
Galium aparine - cleavers						0
Hyoscyamus niger - henbane						0
Polygonum aviculare	1					1
Polygonum lapath./persicaria	44					44
Polygonum periscaria	1					1
Rumex acetosella						0
Sambucus nigra						0
Sieglingia decumbens	2					2
Culm nodes - cereal straw						0
Hordeum basal internode						0
Hordeum rachis internode						0
Triticum aestivum rachis node						0
Triticum brittle rachis internode	1					1
Triticum dicoccon glume base						0
Triticum dicoccon spikelet fork					1	1
Triticum glume						0
Triticum spelta glume			1			1
Triticum spelta spikelet fork						0
Triticum spikelet fork						0
Brassica sp(p).	1					1
Raphanus raphanistrum pod frag.	5					5
Rumex obtusifolius-type	1					1
Ilex- holly	1					1
Corylus avellana nut frag. - hazel		1		2		0
Gramineae <2mm - small grasses	2					
Legume <4mm	1					0
Total seeds/10 litres	146	2	3	11	19	157

Appendix Table 3

Period VI

Trench number	37	37	42	44	40	40	19	19	19	19	21	21	43	43	43	48
Context number (fill)	6408	6440	7026	7409	9037	9067	3087	3090	3231	3237	3639	3694	7212	7215	7219	7231
Context number (cut)	6435	6435	7022	7408	7022	9039	3093	3084	3233	3239	3693	3656	7213	7213	7213	7213
#samples amalgamated	2													2		
Sample number		2394	2840	2820	2639	2648	1046	1055	2135	2137	1091	1092	2812		2234	2828
Volume processed (litres)	61	18	10	42	10	7	12	10	9	6	16	7	13	56	16	10
Feature/Structure	S21?	S21?					C14 date	S21			S21	S21	F6	F6	F6	F6
Assessed only										1						
Avena grain - oats	1				1									1		
Cerealia undiff.	2		1					3				1	1	1		
Hordeum hulled - barley	2			1					1					1	1	
Hordeum naked				1												
Hordeum indet.	2			1										1		
Triticum aestivum grain																
Triticum (hexaploid)																17
Triticum dicoccon				1										1		
Triticum cf. spelta					1											
Triticum spelta						3										
Triticum sp(p). grain	2				4	2	2							2		
Bromus sp(p). grain	1				6	14		2						1		4
Carex (trigonous) - sedges														1		
Chenopodium album - fat hen				1												
Fallopia convolvulus - black bindweed	1													1		
Galium aparine - cleavers																5
Hyoscyamus niger - henbane												4				
Polygonum lapath./persicaria	1						1									
Polygonum periscaria	1			1										1		
Rumex acetosella																
Sambucus nigra														1		
Sieglingia decumbens					2	1								1		
Culm nodes - cereal straw				1												
Hordeum basal internode																
Hordeum rachis internode														1		
Triticum aestivum rachis node																
Triticum brittle rachis internode					1									1		
Triticum dicoccon glume base						1								1		
Triticum dicoccon spikelet fork				1										1		
Triticum glume					2	11		2								
Triticum spelta glume	1				1	6		4	1	2		1		1		
Triticum spelta spikelet fork														1		
Triticum spikelet fork																
Corylus avellana nut frag. - hazel		1		1										1		3
Rosa thorn										2						
Legume <4mm	1						1	1						1		
Totals	15	1	1	13	16	36	4	12	2	4	1	5	1	21	1	29

Appendix Table 4

Period VI continued

Trench number	43	29	29	29	29	48	43	Totals
Context number (fill)	7244	5348	5335	5323	5324	7232	7233	
Context number (cut)	7215	5350	5337	5333	Layer	7213	7213	
#samples amalgamated							3	
Sample number	2849	2787	2771	2759	2762	2826		
Volume processed (litres)	32	8	12	10	12	10	22	
Feature/Structure	F6	S20	S20	S20	S18 layer	F6	F6	
Assessed only								
Avena grain - oats	1						1	5
Cerealia undiff.	1	1				2	4	17
Hordeum hulled - barley	1					1	5	13
Hordeum naked								1
Hordeum indet.		1						5
Triticum aestivum grain							2	2
Triticum (hexaploid)								17
Triticum dicoccon		1	1					4
Triticum cf. spelta								1
Triticum spelta						1		4
Triticum sp(p). grain	8					2	3	25
Bromus sp(p). grain	4					3	3	38
Carex (trigonous) - sedges	2		1					4
Chenopodium album - fat hen							1	2
Fallopia convolvulus - black bindweed						1		3
Galium aparine - cleavers								5
Hyoscyamus niger - henbane								4
Polygonum lapath./ persicaria							2	4
Polygonum periscaria	2					2		7
Rumex acetosella					1			1
Sambucus nigra	1			1		2		5
Sieglingia decumbens	3		1				1	9
Culm nodes - cereal straw								1
Hordeum basal internode	1							1
Hordeum rachis internode							1	2
Triticum aestivum rachis node							1	1
Triticum brittle rachis internode	1	1	1					5
Triticum dicoccon glume base								2
Triticum dicoccon spikelet fork								2
Triticum glume								15
Triticum spelta glume	3		1			2		23
Triticum spelta spikelet fork						1		2
Triticum spikelet fork			2					2
Corylus avellana nut frag. - hazel								6
Rosa thorn								2
Legume <4mm	1						1	6
Totals	29	4	7		1	17	25	246

Appendix Table 4 continued

Index

Illustrations are denoted by page numbers in *italics*.